Social
Competence
of Young
Children

Social Competence of Young Children

Risk, Disability, & Intervention

edited by

WILLIAM H. BROWN, PH.D.

Department of Educational Studies
University of South Carolina
Columbia, South Carolina

SAMUEL L. ODOM, PH.D.

Frank Porter Graham Child Development Institute
University of North Carolina at Chapel Hill
Chapel Hill, North Carolina

and

SCOTT R. McCONNELL, PH.D.

Center for Early Education and Development
and Department of Educational Psychology
University of Minnesota
Minneapolis, Minnesota

·P A U L·H·
BROOKES
PUBLISHING CO.®

Baltimore • London • Sydney

Paul H. Brookes Publishing Co.
Post Office Box 10624
Baltimore, Maryland 21285-0624

www.brookespublishing.com

Typeset by Spearhead Global, Inc., Bear, Delaware.
Manufactured in the United States of America by
George H. Buchanan Printing, Bridgeport, New Jersey.

Individuals described in this book are composites, pseudonyms, or fictional accounts. Individuals' names have been changed and identifying details have been altered when necessary to protect their confidentiality.

Library of Congress Cataloging-in-Publication Data

Social competence of young children : risk, disability, & intervention / edited by William
H. Brown, Samuel L. Odom, Scott R. McConnell.
   p. cm.
  ISBN-13: 978-1-55766-923-0 (pbk.)
  ISBN-10: 1-55766-923-6
  1. Socialization.   2. Children with social disabilities—Education.
3. Social skills in children.   4 Children with disabilities.   I. Brown, William H., Ph. D.
II. Odom, Samuel L.   III. McConnell, Scott R.   IV. Title.
LC192.4.S618 2008
303.3′24—dc22   2007036935

British Library Cataloguing in Publication data are available from the British Library.

Contents

About the Editors

William H. Brown, Ph.D., Professor, Department of Educational Studies, University of South Carolina, Columbia, South Carolina 29208

Dr. William H. ("Bill") Brown earned his master's degree in education in 1974 from the University of Tennessee at Chattanooga and a doctorate in special education and mental retardation studies in 1985 from Vanderbilt University. He joined the faculty at the University of South Carolina (USC) in 1995, and, in addition to his work in the Department of Educational Studies in the College of Education, he is a member of the USC Research Consortium on Children and Families. Previously, he held positions in Nashville as Research Assistant Professor at Vanderbilt University (1987–1995), Assistant Director of the John F. Kennedy Center for Research in Human Development (1988–1995), and Director of the Susan Gray School for Children (1982–1993).

Dr. Brown has written multiple articles and chapters about programs for young children and their families and served as co-editor of *Inclusion of Preschool Children with Developmental Delays in Early Childhood Programs* (with Maureen Conroy; Southern Early Childhood Association, 1997). He also serves as the editor of the *Journal of Early Intervention* and is an editorial board member for *Topics in Early Childhood Special Education, Assessment for Effective Intervention,* the *Journal of Early Intervention,* and *Early Childhood Research Quarterly.*

Throughout his career, Dr. Brown has held professional positions as a preschool teacher, service coordinator with families of young children with developmental delays, director of a large early intervention program for children with and without disabilities, teacher educator, researcher, and child advocate. In 1993, he was awarded the Professional of the Year Award by the Tennessee Association for Retarded Citizens (The Arc of Tennessee). In 2002, he received the Partner in Education Award for the Child Development Programs in Richland School District Two in Columbia, South Carolina, and he was awarded the 2006 College of Education Research Award at USC.

Dr. Brown's professional interests include research related to young children's social competence, preschool inclusion, and young children's physical activity in preschools and the community, as well as personnel preparation in early childhood and early childhood special education.

Samuel L. Odom, Ph.D., Director, Frank Porter Graham (FPG) Child Development Institute, and Professor of Education, The University of North Carolina at Chapel Hill, Chapel Hill, North Carolina 27599

Prior to his work at The University of North Carolina at Chapel Hill, Dr. Samuel L. ("Sam") Odom previously served in faculty positions at Indiana University and

Peabody College/Vanderbilt University. Dr. Odom received a master's degree in special education in 1976 and an educational specialist degree in educational psychology from the University of Tennessee at Knoxville in 1979. He earned his doctorate in 1982 in education and human development from the University of Washington.

Throughout his career, Dr. Odom has held positions as a preschool teacher, student teaching supervisor, program coordinator, teacher educator, and researcher. He has written many articles and chapters about programs for young children and their families and has served as the co-editor of five books on early childhood special education, including the first edition of this book (*Social Competence of Young Children with Disabilities: Issues and Strategies for Intervention*; Paul H. Brookes Publishing Co., 1992) with Drs. Scott R. McConnell and Mary A. McEvoy. Dr. Odom is an associate editor for *Exceptional Children* and is on the editorial board of *Journal of Early Intervention, Topics in Early Childhood Special Education, Journal of Autism and Developmental Disabilities*, and *Early Childhood Research Quarterly*. He received the Special Education Outstanding Research Award from the American Educational Research Association Special Education Special Interest Group in 1999, the Merle Karnes Contribution to the Field Award from the Division for Early Childhood of the Council for Exceptional Children (CEC) in 2001, and the Outstanding Special Education Research Award from CEC in 2007.

Dr. Odom's research interests include interventions and teaching approaches that promote social competence of young children, effective intervention approaches for children with autism, and early childhood curricula that promote children's school success.

Scott R. McConnell, Ph.D., Director of Community Engagement, Center for Early Education and Development, and Professor, Department of Educational Psychology, University of Minnesota, Minneapolis, Minnesota 55455

Dr. McConnell joined the faculty of the University of Minnesota in 1986 after serving as a research associate and assistant professor of child psychiatry at the University of Pittsburgh from 1982 to 1986. While at the University of Minnesota, Dr. McConnell also has served as Director of the Institute on Community Integration (a University Affiliated Program in Developmental Disabilities) from 1991 to 1997 and as Director of the Center for Early Education and Development from 1999 to 2005. Dr. McConnell received a master's degree (1980) and a doctoral degree (1982) in educational psychology at the University of Oregon.

Throughout his career, Dr. McConnell has held positions as a classroom teacher, trainer of school psychologists and early childhood educators, academic administrator, and researcher. He has authored peer-reviewed articles and chapters on assessment, intervention, and research with young children (particularly in the areas of social interaction, early intervention, and early language and literacy development), and he co-edited the first edition of this book (*Social Competence of Young Children with Disabilities: Issues and Strategies for Intervention*; Paul H. Brookes Publishing Co., 1992) with Drs. Samuel L. Odom and Mary A. McEvoy. Dr. McConnell serves on the editorial boards of *Journal of Early Intervention, Topics in Early Childhood Special Education*, and *Focus on Autism and Other Developmental Disorders*, and he has served as guest associate editor, associate editor, or guest reviewer for other journals in special education and early childhood education.

Dr. McConnell's professional interests include research on assessment of developmental progress for preschool and early elementary children, early intervention for children with disabilities and other risk factors, and integration of services at local and state levels.

Contributors

Judah B. Axe, M.A.
Doctoral Student
The Ohio State University
PAES Building, Room A315
305 West 17th Avenue
Columbus, Ohio 43210

Alison E. Baroody, B.S.
Department of Child Development and
   Family Studies
Purdue University
101 Gates Road
West Lafayette, Indiana 47907

Edward H. Bovey II, M.A.
Positive Early Learning Experiences Center
University of Colorado at Denver and
   Health Sciences Center
1380 Lawrence Street, Suite 650
Denver, Colorado 80204

Virginia Buysse, Ph.D.
Senior Scientist
FPG Child Development Institute
The University of North Carolina at
   Chapel Hill
Campus Box 8180, 105 Smith Level Road
Chapel Hill, North Carolina 27599

Maureen A. Conroy, Ph.D.
Professor
Virginia Commonwealth University
1015 West Main Street
Richmond, Virginia 23284

Karen E. Diamond, Ph.D.
Professor
Department of Child Development and
   Family Studies
Purdue University
101 Gates Road
West Lafayette, Indiana 47907

Erik Drasgow, Ph.D.
Associate Professor
Department of Educational Studies
College of Education
235-I Wardlaw Hall
820 Main Street
University of South Carolina
Columbia, South Carolina 29208

Paddy C. Favazza, Ed.D.
Senior Research Associate
Center for Social Development and
   Education
University of Massachusetts–Boston
1000 Morrissey Boulevard
Boston, Massachusetts 02125

Barbara Davis Goldman, Ph.D.
Research Scientist
FPG Child Development Institute
Research Associate Professor
Department of Psychology
The University of North Carolina at
   Chapel Hill
Campus Box 8180, 105 Smith Level
   Road
Chapel Hill, North Carolina 27599

Howard Goldstein, Ph.D.
Donald M. Baer Professor
Department of Communication
   Disorders
107 Regional Rehab Center
The Florida State University
Department of Communication
   Disorders
Tallahassee, Florida 32306

James W. Halle, Ph.D.
Professor
Department of Special Education
University of Illinois at Urbana-Champaign
1310 South Sixth Street
Champaign, Illinois 61820

Marci J. Hanson, Ph.D.
Professor
Department of Special Education
San Francisco State University
1600 Holloway Avenue
San Francisco, California 94132

Robin L. Hojnoski, Ph.D.
Assistant Professor
Department of Education and Human
   Services
Lehigh University
27 Memorial Drive West
Bethlehem, Pennsylvania 18015

Heidi Hollingsworth, Ph.D.
Instructor and Co-Program Coordinator,
    B-K Graduate Programs
School of Education
The University of North Carolina at
    Chapel Hill
Chapel Hill, North Carolina 27599

Soo-Young Hong, M.S.
Graduate Student
Department of Child Development and
    Family Studies
Purdue University
CDFS Building, 101 Gates Road
West Lafayette, Indiana 47907

Sunhwa Jung, Ph.D.
Senior Research Associate
Oakstone Academy
2655 Oakstone Drive
Columbus, Ohio 43231

Lisa L. Knoche, Ph.D.
Research Assistant Professor
Nebraska Center for Research on Children,
    Youth, Families and Schools
University of Nebraska–Lincoln
238 Teachers College Hall
Lincoln, Nebraska 68588

K. Alisa Lowrey, Ph.D.
Assistant Professor
Department of Educational Studies
University of South Carolina
235-E Wardlaw Hall
820 Main Street
Columbia, South Carolina 29208

Christine A. Marvin, Ph.D.
Associate Professor
Special Education and Communication
    Disorders
University of Nebraska–Lincoln
202 Barkley Memorial Center
Lincoln, Nebraska 68583

Jeanette A. McCollum, Ph.D.
Professor Emeritus
University of Illinois at Urbana-Champaign
51 Gerty Drive
Children's Research Center, Room 61
Champaign, Illinois 61820

Hedda Meadan, Ph.D.
Assistant Professor
Department of Special Education
Illinois State University
Campus Post Office Box 5910
Normal, Illinois 61790

Kristen N. Missall, Ph.D.
Assistant Professor
Department of Educational and Counseling
    Psychology
University of Kentucky
235 Dickey Hall
Lexington, Kentucky 40506

Melissa L. Olive, Ph.D.
Assistant Professor
Department of Special Education
The University of Texas at Austin
1 University Station D5300
Austin, Texas 78712

Michaelene M. Ostrosky, Ph.D.
Professor
Department of Special Education
University of Illinois at Urbana-Champaign
276C Education Building
1310 South 6th Street MC 708
Champaign, Illinois 61820

Jeanna M. Rathel, M.Ed.
Clinical Instructor
Department of Educational Studies
University of South Carolina
Wardlaw College of Education
Columbia, South Carolina 29208

M. Jamila Reid, Ph.D.
Research Associate
University of Washington
1107 Northeast 45th West
Suite 305
Seattle, Washington 98195

Diane M. Sainato, Ph.D.
Associate Professor
Special Education Section
School of Physical Activity and
    Educational Services
The Ohio State University
365 Arps Hall, 1945 North High Street
Columbus, Ohio 43210

Mary D. Salmon, Ph.D.
REACH Autism Program Manager
Columbus Public Schools
1469 East Main Street
Columbus, Ohio 43205

Naomi Schneider, M.S.
Doctoral Candidate
Department of Communication Disorders
The Florida State University
107 Regional Rehab Center
Tallahassee, Florida 32306

Ilene S. Schwartz, Ph.D.
Professor and Chair
Area of Special Education
University of Washington
Post Office Box 357925
Seattle, Washington 98195

Susan M. Sheridan, Ph.D.
Willa Cather Professor and Professor of
    Educational Psychology
Department of School Psychology
University of Nebraska–Lincoln
216 Mabel Lee Hall
Lincoln, Nebraska 68588

Gary N. Siperstein, Ph.D.
Professor, Director
Center for Social Development and
    Education
University of Massachusetts–Boston
100 Morrissey Boulevard
Boston, Massachusetts 02125

Tanya SooHoo, M.A.
Doctoral Candidate
Department of Special Education
San Francisco State University
1600 Holloway Avenue
San Francisco, California 94132

Phillip S. Strain, Ph.D.
Professor of Educational Psychology and
    Psychiatry
University of Colorado at Denver Health
    and Sciences Center
1380 Lawrence Street, Suite 650
Denver, Colorado 80204

Yasemin Turan, Ph.D.
Assistant Professor
San Diego State University
5500 Campanile Drive, NE 72
San Diego, California 92182

**Carolyn Webster-Stratton, Ph.D., M.S.N,
    M.P.H.**
Professor
Family and Child Nursing
University of Washington
1411 8th Avenue West
Seattle, Washington 98119

Tracey West, M.Ed.
Research Associate
FPG Child Development Institute
The University of North Carolina at
    Chapel Hill
105 Smith Level Road
Campus Box 8180
Chapel Hill, North Carolina 27599

Preface

Anthropologists have long asserted that our sociability (i.e., the tendency to interact with others) has been a fundamental attribute of our humanity (cf. Tattersall, 2002). Moreover, historically, educators have viewed children's emerging social competence as an especially important dimension of human development and, when indicated, an aspect of development that may be influenced positively by well-targeted and effective interventions (e.g., Brown, Odom, & Conroy, 2001; Guralnick & Neville, 1997; McConnell, Missall, Silberglitt, & McEvoy, 2002; McEvoy, Odom, & McConnell, 1992; and chapters in this volume). Indeed, we might reasonably argue that the expansion of early childhood education in general (cf. Meisels & Shonkoff, 2000), and early childhood special education in particular (cf. Safford & Safford, 1996), has been associated with the idea that promoting young children's social competence is directly related to their preparation for school and later life.

In 1992, Samuel L. Odom, Scott R. McConnell, and Mary A. McEvoy edited a book titled *Social Competence of Young Children with Disabilities: Issues and Strategies for Intervention*, which was intended "... to provide a summary of both current knowledge about the social competence of young children with disabilities and intervention practices to promote social competence" (p. ix). Across the years, many friends and colleagues have inquired about "updating" the initial volume and this is the result. The 15 chapters are organized in two sections: 1) Nature and Development of Young Children's Emerging Peer-Related Social Competence; and 2) Strategies and Tactics for Peer-Related Social Competence Assessment and Intervention, which is then concluded by a thoughtful and provocative reflective chapter by Gary N. Siperstein and Paddy C. Favazza.

We are delighted with two aspects of this second edition. First, we purposely solicited and thankfully secured the assistance of an outstanding group of authors who are either established or emerging scholars and who have a wealth of knowledge about young children's social competence, particularly interventions based on the best available evidence to support social development. Second, in addition to chapters covering a variety of developmental difficulties and disabilities (e.g., developmental delays, communication and language disorders), we expanded the breadth of the volume's contents by adding several new chapters. The authors in these new chapters summarize and discuss the literature on 1) cultural and linguistic influences, 2) friendships in early childhood, 3) interventions in general early childhood classrooms, 4) a social-emotional curriculum for children at risk for school failure, 5) interventions for children with challenging behaviors, 6) interventions for children with autism spectrum disorders, 7) interventions for children with severe disabilities, and 8) family-based interventions. We sincerely hope that our and our co-authors' efforts will be informative and useful to others who are interested in young children's social competence.

REFERENCES

Brown, W.H., Odom, S.L., & Conroy, M.A. (2001). An intervention hierarchy for promoting preschool children's peer interactions in natural environments. *Topics in Early Childhood Special Education, 21,* 90–134.

Guralnick, M.J., & Neville, B. (1997). Designing early intervention programs to promote children's social competence. In M.J. Guralnick (Ed.), *The effectiveness of early intervention* (pp. 579–610). Baltimore: Paul H. Brookes Publishing Co.

McConnell, S.R., Missall, K.N., Silberglitt, B., & McEvoy, M.A. (2002). Promoting social development in preschool classrooms. In M.R. Shinn, H.M. Walker, & G. Stoner (Eds.), *Interventions for academic and behavior problems II: Preventive and remedial approaches* (pp. 501–536). Bethesda, MD: National Association of School Psychologists.

McEvoy, M.A., Odom, S.L., & McConnell, S.R. (1992). Peer social competence intervention for young children with disabilities. In S.L. Odom, S.R. McConnell, & M.A. McEvoy, (Eds.), *Social competence of young children with disabilities: Issues and strategies for intervention* (pp. 113–134). Baltimore: Paul H. Brookes Publishing Co.

Meisels, S.J., & Shonkoff, J.P. (2000). Early childhood intervention: A continuing evolution. In J.P. Shonkoff & S.J. Meisels (Eds.), *Handbook of early childhood intervention* (pp. 3–31). Cambridge, UK: Cambridge University Press.

Odom, S.L., McConnell, S.R., & McEvoy, M.A. (Eds.). (1992). *Social competence of young children with disabilities: Issues and strategies for intervention.* Baltimore: Paul H. Brookes Publishing Co.

Safford, P.L., & Safford, E.J. (1996). *A history of childhood & disability.* New York: Teachers College Press.

Tattersall, I. (2002). *Monkey in the mirror: Essays on the science of what makes us human.* San Diego, CA: Harcourt, Inc.

Acknowledgments

At first glance, the writing and publishing of an edited volume appears relatively straightforward. Nevertheless, bringing a well-crafted, contemporary edited book to fruition is an arduous endeavor and requires the contributions of a number of people. As editors, we want to gratefully acknowledge the efforts and support of the following individuals. First, we are thankful to Heather Shrestha, Editorial Director, and Laurel Craven, Acquisitions Editor, of Paul H. Brookes Publishing Co., for their guidance, recommendations, and support as we reflected on and developed the prospectus for this revised volume. Second, anyone who has participated in the writing or editing of a book knows that the "heart and soul" of an edited volume is the time, energy, and expertise authors devote to writing their contributed chapters. We are deeply indebted to the many authors who diligently developed, wrote, and then refined their chapters. Third, the efforts of writers, even excellent writers, benefit greatly from the tedious, albeit necessary, work of high-quality and meticulous editing. We are very appreciative of the technical editing of Leslie Eckard, Senior Production Editor. Her patience and charm during the final editing greatly improved the individual chapters and the edited volume. Finally, social support is a necessary but often unseen ingredient in our incredibly busy lives. We want to acknowledge our family members Carson Mosso, Douglas and Will Odom, and Nora and Reid McConnell-Johnson. They make our efforts worthwhile and bring us much joy.

To Mary A. McEvoy
(1953–2002)
Researcher, advocate, and friend to many

Mary served as an editor of the first edition of this book (*Social Competence of Young Children with Disabilities: Issues and Strategies for Intervention;* Paul H. Brookes Publishing Co., 1992) and was a long-time friend and colleague to all three of us. She was an enthusiastic contributor to and consumer of research on social competence of young children with and without disabilities, and she was a remarkably socially competent individual herself! Mary's life and career continue to represent to us what Nicholas Hobbs called a "*caring and competent professional.*" Her work, her energy, her humor, and her commitment are evident in our lives and in the work presented in this book.

—*W.H. Brown, S.L. Odom, and S.R. McConnell*

Nature and Development of Young Children's Emerging Peer-Related Social Competence

CHAPTER 1

Social Competence of Young Children

Conceptualization, Assessment, and Influences

SAMUEL L. ODOM, SCOTT R. MCCONNELL,
AND WILLIAM H. BROWN

If you can read this first sentence, you are a social being. Not only have you learned to decode a complicated symbol system and extract meaning from it, you understand that another human has written it to communicate meaning. Although reading this text lacks the dynamics of interactions in which most socially competent humans engage, it still is a social transaction in that it entails a meeting of minds and the interchange of behaviors (i.e., the authors' writing and your reading). We humans have been successful as a species in part because of our social nature. Interdependence, reciprocity, and responsivity characterize our actions in a social world of work, play, family, and community. For most, social attraction to and interest in others appears early in infancy and continues throughout life, and it sets the stage for individuals, young and old, to engage competently in social interaction with other humans in this world and even across species (e.g., interactions with pets).

Our social abilities unfold over the early years of life, and in fact a major developmental achievement is to acquire skills, beginning in early childhood, that will allow us to be effective and appropriate in our interactions with others. This natural course of early learning and development sets the stage for social adjustment later in life, and when limitations or challenges to social development occur early in life, they may have life-long implications.

The purposes of this chapter are to examine the concept of social competence for young children and describe factors that affect its expression and development. The chapter begins with a brief definition of social competence and a description of the conceptual organization for this chapter. The importance of social competence for young children is emphasized by its association with longitudinal outcomes in elementary school, high school, and on into adulthood. Assessment "operationalizes" the social competence construct in that it specifies methods for measuring social actions, skills, and abilities of children. In a section on assessment, we describe different approaches to assessing features of children's social performance (e.g., observation, sociometrics) and an approach to pooling information across methods and social agents in a child's environment. A child's social competence is associated with and influenced by other characteristics of the child and elements of the world in which he or she lives. Borrowing a conceptualization from Whitehurst and Lonigan (1997), we call these "inside-out" and "outside-in" variables (See Figure 1.1). In two later sections of this chapter, we will describe the association of both types of influences on the development of children's social competence. The chapter concludes with future implications for research and development.

SOCIAL COMPETENCE: A BRIEF DESCRIPTION

Peer-related social competence of young children is the focus of this book. Although for most children, competence in social interaction extends across social partners such as family members and peers (Guralnick, Neville, Hammond, & Connor, 2007), the forms of interactions with peers differ from adult–child interactions (Russell, Pettit, & Mize, 1998). Social competence is displayed in the interactions that occur between an individual child and members of his or her peer group. In such interactions, at least two dimensions of competence are important. The social behaviors a child uses must be effective in achieving his or her social goals and the selection of behaviors must be appropriate for the context (Wright, 1980).

Social goals are the desired outcomes that children have when they direct a behavior toward another peer (Renshaw & Asher, 1983). Examples of such social goals for young children could be attention, assistance, information seeking or providing, pretend play, comfort, support, and even aggression (Brown & Odom, 1996). Numerous researchers have noted that children use behavioral strategies to accomplish the necessary tasks within an interaction that lead to their achieving their social goal (Brown, Odom, & Holcombe, 1996; Erdley & Asher, 1999; Guralnick, 1999). Social competence may be represented in the success with which young children select and use behavioral strategies that are effective in achieving the goal.

Success in achieving a goal, however, is only half the story. The second dimension of social competence is the use of behavioral strategies that are appropriate for the social context (Rose-Krasnor, 1985). Social appropriateness is defined by the norms of the peer group or classroom, age of the child, sex of the child, and culture (Chang, 2004). For example, a child might have a goal of getting one of the two toys that is in a peer's possession. One behavioral strategy might be to grab one of the toys and run (object aggression); another would be to offer to trade a toy that he or she has for one the second child has (share/trade). In both examples, the child achieves his or her social goal of obtaining the toy from the other child. In most social contexts, however, the first strategy is inappropriate and the latter is more appropriate. Selection of behavioral strategies or even social goals that are appropriate for the contexts reflects competence.

Social competence, as generally conceptualized, operates on a continuum. Highly competent young children select appropriate and effective behavioral strategies, are well-accepted in their peer group, and have reciprocated friendships as early as 3–4 years of age (Vaughn, Colvin, Azria, Caya, & Krzysik, 2001). At the other end of the continuum, children who lack competence tend to be aggressive

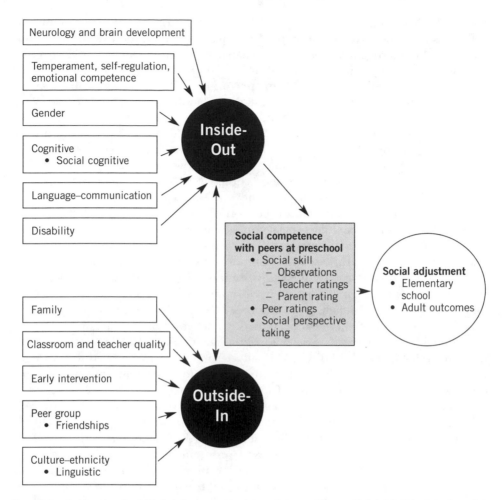

Figure 1.1.   Inside-out and outside-in influences on social competence. (*Source:* Whitehurst, G.J., & Lonigan, C.J. [1997]. Child development and emergent literacy. *Child Development, 69,* 848–872.)

and disruptive or they are socially withdrawn and isolated. These socially inappropriate patterns of behavior are described as "externalizing" or "internalizing," respectively. Children with a high degree of externalizing or internalizing behavior are often rejected or ignored by their peer group. Certainly other factors affect peer social acceptance and rejection, such as sex of the social partner, race, appearance, and some types of disabilities, but usually the competence with which children use effective and appropriate social behavioral strategies is a major determinant of peer relationships (Ladd, 2005). For that reason, peer social relationships are often used as a "marker variable" (i.e., broad indicator) of social competence (Odom, Zercher, Li, Marquart, Sandall, & Brown, 2006).

Assessment of Social Competence in Young Children

Although effectiveness and appropriateness of children's social behavior are central features of children's social competence, we have argued that the assessment of social competence should employ a more multidimensional and pragmatic approach (McConnell & Odom, 1999; Odom & McConnell, 1985; Odom et al., 1999). As such, we have offered a performance-based definition of social compe-tence as "the interpersonal social performance of children with other children or adults as judged by significant social agents in the child's environment" (from Odom & McConnell, 1985, p. 9). This performance-based conceptualization has direct relevance for selection and evaluation of different methods for assessing social competence in young children. Individual component measures of social behavior are essential and important. An assessment that draws information from only one source or informant is not likely to present a full and complete descrip-tion of the social competence of young children, however. Rather, a full and com-plete assessment of social competence should be based on a multicomponent model that draws information from all needed sources, with the assumption that information from these different sources contributes both shared and unique vari-ance to descriptions of a child's social competence.

This performance-based model calls for a multivariate approach to assessment and description; again, this assessment model must support inclusion and analysis of individual components and the collective information that can be drawn across these components. Previous work on performance-based approaches to social com-petence (Hops, 1983; McFall, 1982; Odom & McConnell, 1985) provides a basis for this model. Practically, these earlier efforts call for a set of measures that describe both individual behavior and social impact, evaluating individual measures for evi-dence of reliability and validity, and finally, testing empirical procedures for com-bining these different sources of information into a smaller, conceptually and empirically sound set of measures of social competence.

Several authors have followed such a performance-based approach. McConnell and Odom (1999) conducted one empirical test of a multi-measure, performance-based approach in their study of 173 preschoolers with disabilities and 49 preschoolers without disabilities. Assessments included direct observation measures of child social behavior (i.e., social initiations, responses, and time in interaction), a summative observer rating scale, teacher ratings on a standardized scale, and peer ratings from classmates. Principal components analysis extracted four factors, with social behavior (both direct observation and summative rat-ings) and social impact (teacher ratings, but not peer sociometric) loading on the first and most robust principal component. Two of four resulting multivariate meas-ures of social competence from this analysis demonstrated discriminant validity in describing the social competence of children with and without disabilities.

For children with specific language impairments, McCabe and Marshall (2006) employed a multi-methods assessment of social competence that consisted of a direct observation measure, teacher ratings, and parent ratings. Although chil-dren's performance was assessed in different settings and from different perspec-tives, they did find significant association across settings (e.g., direct observation in class, parent ratings of behavior at home), indicating shared variance across measures. With elementary-aged school children in Finland, Junttila, Voeten, Kaukiainen, and Vauras (2006) collected rating scale information from parents, teachers, peers, and children themselves (i.e., self-ratings) on children's social com-petence, finding significant but low agreement on both prosocial and negative dimensions of social competence. They proposed that the low correlations among informants indicated that each was contributing unique information for their multi-method assessment of social competence.

A multi-methods assessment requires reliable measurement of social perform-ance from different sources and perspectives. These classes of measures of social behavior include 1) *direct observational assessment* of child social behavior in natura-listic play and interaction settings, 2) *teacher and parent rating* of child behavior, and 3) *social problem solving* by individual children. In addition, information is sometimes provided by peers through *sociometric assessment* completed by classmates or other children and *friendship* measures. A brief review of assessment technologies in each of these areas is provided next.

Observational Assessment

For a variety of reasons, direct observation of children's behavior has a long and storied role in assessment of social competence among preschool children. In part, this history reflects a theoretical bias; much of the research on children's social behavior, social interaction, social skills, and social competence has been con-ducted by developmental and behavioral psychologists, and each discipline has a long tradition of *in situ* observation of specific behaviors (Sackett, 1977). There is also a good measure of face validity to the use of observational methods for describ-ing social behaviors and competence; by definition, the events of interest occur in social interactional settings, with attendant requirements for unobtrusive, natura-listic, and dynamic assessment procedures. Observational methods fit well here.

Interestingly, relatively little formal scholarship has been devoted to observa-tional assessment of social behavior in young children. A search of online refer-ences in education and psychology yielded only 35 identified references, some dating back to the 1970s and earlier, that considered psychometric analysis of obser-vational measures of social competence. In recent years, two reviews (Bierman, 2004; Brown, Odom, & Holcombe, 1996) have summarized and detailed next steps in observational assessment of social behavior and competence for young children.

The Brown and colleagues' (1996) review of observational methods described ways in which contemporary observational assessment of social competence builds on traditions from applied behavior analysis, pragmatics language research, and developmental psychology. Brown and colleagues go on to describe an observa-tional system, the System for Observation of Children's Social Interactions (SOCSI) that assesses three aspects of naturalistic social interactions. First, SOCSI calls for recording behavioral strategies employed by young children (e.g., calling, com-menting, object aggression, share/trade) and the success or nonsuccess of these strategies. Second, SOCSI records each child's social goals (as judged by a nonpar-ticipant observer) as associated with each behavioral strategy. These goals, akin to the "functions" typical of functional analysis (i.e., outcomes or intended outcomes), describe the broader direction and structure of a child's observed social behavior. Third, SOCSI provides a method for recording how successful the behaviors are in achieving the intended outcomes in the observed interactions.

Several individual studies have explored the possible utility of observational measures that could be used across settings and investigations (Bronson, 1994; Farmer-Dougan & Kaszuba, 1999). These measures represent initial efforts but, like the SOCSI, have not demonstrated wide application in research or practice. Simi-larly, efforts have been directed to development and validation of observational measures of social interaction for progress monitoring (Carta, Greenwood, Luze, Cline, & Kuntz, 2004; Silberglitt, 2004). These measures, developed specifically for wide-scale dissemination, may be particularly promising for bringing more consistency to assessment of social interaction and observed social behaviors among infants, toddlers, and preschool children.

Alternatively, a number of researchers have employed observational measures that appear similar at the level of labels and definitions of social behavior (although direct comparability is an empirical question). Considering formats reviewed by Brown and colleagues (1996) and Bierman (2004), a strong case can be made for including more narrowly defined social behaviors, including social initiations and responses to initiations as well as a summative measure of time in social interaction, as elements of an observational measure contributing to assessment of social competence (see Odom & Ogawa, 1992, for an earlier review).

Teacher and Parent Ratings of Child Behavior

Education and psychology have long made use of ratings of child social behavior by adults (e.g., parents, teachers) who have frequent opportunities to observe a child's behavior. Although form and function of rating scales vary widely, and although there is ongoing analysis of the relations between parent and teacher ratings (Bierman, 2004; Fagan & Fantuzzo, 1999; Manz, Fantuzzo, & McDermott, 1999), some instruments have been developed and used specifically for describing children's social performance. These tools offer a means to describe larger, more situationally diverse samples of individual child behavior, and as such extend the possible reach of assessment conducted by observational means.

More tools are available that capture teachers' or child care providers' ratings for purposes of assessing the peer social performance of preschool children. The Social Skills Rating System or SSRS (Gresham & Elliott, 1990) was originally developed to assess both prosocial and problem behaviors of elementary-age children. After its original development, a preschool version was developed and validated. Although items were not developed reflecting the developmentally distinct elements of preschool social interaction, and while the normative sample for preschoolers was relatively small, the SSRS is widely used and produces scaled scores that are well-suited to gathering teacher—and in some instances parent—ratings of child social behavior (Fagan & Fantuzzo, 1999; Manz, Fantuzzo, & McDermott, 1999).

More recently, the Ages & Stages Questionnaires®: Social-Emotional (ASQ:SE) (Squires, Bricker, & Twombly, 2002) has become available. The ASQ:SE was developed as part of a comprehensive screening system. The ASQ:SE can be completed by either parents or child care providers and teachers, with separate item sets for children in eight age groups from 6 to 60 months of age. The ASQ:SE has been rigorously researched with a norm sample of more than 3,000 children. Although intended primarily as a developmental screener, the ASQ:SE can be used as an important part of a more comprehensive assessment that includes parent or paraprofessional ratings of child social behavior.

Several more instruments also provide assessment of social behavior through parent or teacher rating, generally as part of a larger developmental or adaptive behavior appraisal. The Battelle Developmental Inventory (BDI Newborg, Stock, Wnek, Guidubaldi, & Svinicki, 1984/1988) is a developmental assessment commonly used in preschool programs for determining special education eligibility and program progress. One part of the BDI, the Personal–Social Domain assessment, is commonly completed by parent or teacher report on a series of developmentally sequenced items. Normative scale scores can be derived. A variety of measures intended to screen for or assess the presence of problem behaviors (including the Child Behavior Checklist [CBCL; Achenbach & Rescorla, 2000], the Devereux Early Childhood Assessment [Devereux Foundation, 1998], and the Early Screening Profile [Walker, Severson, & Feil, 1995]) are also available, but these tools have a primary focus on assessment of problem behaviors. Although such assessment might be a component of social competence assessment, evidence clearly indicates that *social competence* and *problem behavior* are not necessarily on the same continuum, and may need to be assessed separately.

Finally, several scales are emerging from research both on children's social competence and early school adjustment that may have utility in future applications of a multi-measure model of social competence assessment. Ladd and colleagues (e.g., Ladd, 1990; Ladd & Coleman, 1997; Ladd, Kochenderfer, & Coleman, 1996) have conceptualized social competence as a central part of early school adjustment and have included measures of social behavior in their research-based Teacher Rating Scale of School Adjustment (Birch & Ladd, 1997). Missall (2002) created the Scale of Early School Adjustment (adapted from Walker & McConnell, 1995), an 18-item Likert-type scale that attempts to assess teacher ratings of both social competence and children's competence at meeting the behavioral demands of early schooling. These emerging scales offer researchers and practitioners reliable and important measures of dimensions of social competence that appear particularly relevant for children in the transition between preschool and kindergarten or elementary programs.

Social Problem Solving

Social problem solving has received attention in social competence development, intervention, and assessment for a number of years (Spivak & Shure, 1974). In short, social problem solving reflects a child's skill and capacity to monitor and assess ongoing social situations, to generate multiple possible responses in those situations, and to select and monitor one or more of these possible responses in ways that maximize social relations and impact. (These ideas are similar to, but predate, more comprehensive social cognitive models of children's social relations; see Crick & Dodge, 1994.)

Direct assessment of social problem solving among young children is relatively rare due to logistical and conceptual challenges associated with demands of data collection. Nonetheless, some have argued that direct assessment of social problem-solving skills is not only possible but also central to a complete assessment of children's social functioning (Rubin & Krasnor, 1986), and the field has made several efforts to expand practical approaches to this assessment challenge.

Carolyn Webster-Stratton and her colleagues have developed this approach to assessment as part of ongoing evaluation and research of the *Incredible Years Parents, Teachers, and Children's Training Series* curriculum (http://www.incredibleyears.com; see also Webster-Stratton & Lindsay, 1999). Building on earlier work by Spivak and Shure (1974) and Rubin and Krasnor (1986), Webster-Stratton and colleagues developed the WALLY game, an interactive "fantasy" task designed to assess qualitative and quantitative dimensions of children's social problem solving. In the WALLY game, a child is presented with 12 colored pictures, each illustrating a hypothetical problem situation addressing object acquisition or friendship. The child is asked by the examiner to solve the problem depicted in each picture, with encouragement to offer as many possible responses as possible. Each child's response is scored into one of 16 positive strategies (e.g., *admit to causing an accident, apologizing*) or 17 negative ones (e.g., *take all materials for oneself*). These coded responses are then summarized into two scores, a "total positive strategies" score and a ratio of positive to negative strategies. In Webster-Stratton and Lindsay's (1999) analysis, earlier evidence of internal sensitivity, treatment sensitivity, and construct validity was extended with evidence of moderate correlations with observed child social behavior and negative correlations with rates of negative inter-actions with parents and parent problem behavior scores on the CBCL. In addition, in Webster-Stratton and Lindsay's (1999) extended analysis, readers can discern ways in which the WALLY game particularly, and social problem-solving assessment more generally, can enter into a multidimensional description of the social com-petence of preschool-aged children.

Sociometric Assessment

Sociometric assessment is another hallmark of social competence assessment, with a long history of research and application in helping to describe children's social development (Hartup, 1983; McConnell & Odom, 1986). Sociometric assessments are those in which children offer evaluations of social relationships with or social characteristics dimensions of their peers; with young children, these ratings are often facilitated by photographs of individual children to be rated.

The specific rating dimensions of sociometric assessments vary widely, from general friendship and social preference evaluations (e.g., "*How much do you like to play with [one child]?*" or "*Who is your best friend in this group?*") to requests to identify specific behavioral characteristics. In social competence assessment of young chil-dren, two sociometric approaches dominate. *Peer ratings* are collected to assess social relationships. In peer ratings (e.g., McConnell & Odom, 1999), one child is asked to evaluate all other children in a group (e.g., a preschool classroom) on a *common* dimension (e.g., *play partner preference*). Peer ratings produce responses from every child about every child, and provide a single score that can be scaled across children. In contrast, test administrators collect *peer nominations* by having an individual child select a set number of children from a given group (e.g., a preschool classroom) based on a certain criterion (Dodge, 1983). Peer nominations produce scores vary-ing from zero to a varying maximum. In addition, peer nominations—particularly those that compare social preferences with non-preferences (positive and negative nominations)—can be used to form children into distinct sociometric groups (e.g., accepted, rejected, neglected; Carlson, Lahey, & Neeper, 1984).

The research literature on sociometric assessment is deep, wide, and long-lasting, yielding myriad answers to many practical questions. In general, some evidence suggests that, among preschool children, peer nomination techniques are more reliable (Olson & Lifgren, 1988), but there are distinctions possible with sub-group analyses that require peer nominations (Dodge, 1983; Dodge, Coie, Pettit, & Price, 1990). As noted later in this chapter, the choice between peer nominations and peer ratings when selecting and using sociometric assessment in research may be influenced by the particular emphasis—summative effects versus more detailed analysis of inside-out or outside-in components of social competence. Practitioners may be more directly influenced by pragmatic issues, including logistical factors in collecting and analyzing data and selecting measures that demonstrate the most robust relations with other indices of social competence. For this latter group, peer nomination strategies may be best suited.

Friendship Measures

Identification and assessment of friends and friendships is a special case of socio-metric assessment; here, researchers are interested in reciprocal choices between two or more children. Consider peer nominations, as just described; when completing these measures, many children will often identify a particular individual in a class as very popular (i.e., will select that child as one of three "best friends" in a peer nomination assessment). But these frequently nominated children will have a smaller number of *reciprocal* choices—children that select them as "best friends" and that they, in turn, nominate similarly. The same situation can occur with children who are less frequently nominated, too; the salient fact is that two or more children each identify the other(s) as their friend or preferred playmate.

Friendships, as indexed by reciprocal choices, are associated with positive social outcomes for preschool children generally (Vaughn et al., 2001; Walden, Lemerise, & Smith, 1999) and for young children with disabilities specifically (Buysse, 1993; Buysse, Goldman, & Skinner, 2002). Buysse (1991) developed the Early Childhood Friendship Survey to standardize and simplify identification and assessment of friendships. The survey consists of open- and closed-ended questions in three sections. First, the survey queries respondents (either parents or teachers) about a child's dyadic friendships. The second section presents items assessing uni-lateral "friendships" in which the child being rated makes initiations to another child, but with little reciprocation. The third section asks raters to describe unilat-eral friendships in which the rated child receives social initiations from another child, but rarely reciprocates. The scale has been used with success in several stud-ies (e.g., Bauminger & Shulman, 2003; Buysse, 1993), and appears to simplify the identification and assessment of friendship status in groups of children. Given con-ceptual/theoretical (Berndt, 2004; Ladd, 2005) and empirical (Ladd, 1990; Buysse et al., Chapter 4) evidence of the contributions of friendships to both description and development of social competence, future multi-measure assessments of social competence might profitably include this tool.

Combining Measures in a Multi-Measure Model

Although logistical, statistical, and psychometric issues are beyond the scope of this chapter, later sections describe factors to consider in assembling a multi-measure "suite" of indicators for multivariate assessment of social competence. Selection and combination of measures should reflect conceptual and logistical coherence (Campbell & Fiske, 1959) as well as a close connection to research or practice ques-tions of greatest interest. Future research should replicate and extend existing demonstrations of multivariate assessment of social competence and continue development of a format that is practical for use in community settings.

IMPORTANCE OF SOCIAL COMPETENCE
WITH PEERS: LONGITUDINAL IMPLICATIONS

Social competence with peers is such an important issue in early development because of its longitudinal association with outcomes later in life. A number of early studies of social competence and peer relationships suggested an association between early peer-related social competence problems (i.e., reflected in problem behavior and or social rejection) and problems of social adjustment in adolescents and adults (Cowan, Pederson, Babajian, Izzo, & Trost, 1973; Roff, 1961; Ullman, 1957). Although methodologically flawed (Parker & Asher, 1987), the early studies did raise the concern about the persistence and long-term effects of early social competence deficits. Ladd (2005) noted that a second generation of studies began observing this longitudinal relationship more precisely, addressing questions about whether long-term effects resulted from children-specific deficits (see "inside-out" variables in later sections) or peer group and other external problems (see "outside-in" variables in later sections). For example, Herbert-Myers, Guttentag, Swank, Smith, and Landry (2006) found a strong association between a child's language, mother–child play, and impulsiveness at age 3 and peer social competence at age 8. In a short-term longitudinal study, Pihlakoski and colleagues (2004) found a positive relationship between a child's externalizing behavior at 3 years of age and parents' use of social services (e.g., mental health services) in early elementary school. Ladd and colleagues documented in a number of studies on the association between peer relationships and friendship during the preschool and kindergarten years and children's social and academic adjustment to elementary school (e.g., Ladd et al., 1996; Ladd & Price, 1987). With older children as participants, Rubin, Chen, McDougall, Bowker, and McKinnon (1995) documented associations between social withdrawal at age 7 and loneliness at age 14.

A shift in the literature marks what Ladd (2005) identified as third-generation longitudinal research on peer social competence and social relationships. In addition to documenting longitudinal associations, researchers are now asking questions about variables that mediate or moderate (i.e., influence) the relationship between early social competence and later outcome. Most of this research, to date, has been conducted with elementary-age children, although implications may apply to preschool. In their 10-year longitudinal study, Risi, Gerhardstein, and Kistner (2003) found a positive relationship between peer social preference and graduation rates, but the ethnicity and general socioeconomic level of the children attending the school were moderators. That is, the relationship was strong for Caucasian children from middle-income families and weak for African-American children from low-income families. In their longitudinal study of children with internalizing and externalizing behavior in the first 6 years of school, Henricsson and Rydell (2006) reported that the associations between early social relationships with peers and later academic achievement and social relationships was affected by (moderated by) the teachers' relationships with the students and the students' social competence. Sex of the child may also be a moderator. In a short-term study in which children were observed at the beginning and end of a preschool year, Fabes, Shepard, Guthrie, and Martin (1997) found that arousability measured at the beginning of the year predicted social adjustment and behavior problems at the end of the year for boys but not for girls, and even the relationship for the boys was mediated by the sex of the play partner with whom they spent the most time (i.e., arousable boys in girl partner groups had better adjustment and fewer play partners). We will discuss further the influence of a child's sex in the subsequent section.

For preschool children with disabilities, there is limited research on longitudinal relationships of early social competence and outcomes later in life, although the pattern observed in children without disabilities may well apply for children with disabilities. In one of the few studies conducted, Sigman and Ruskin (1999) followed children with autism, Down syndrome, and developmental delay from their toddler and preschool years to ages 10–13. Children with autism were the least social of the three groups at the early point in development, although social deficits were continuous across time for the Down syndrome group also. Early nonverbal communication and play skills were positively associated with later initiation of play behaviors for children with Down syndrome and peer engagement for the children with autism.

EFFECTS ON YOUNG CHILDREN'S SOCIAL COMPETENCE: INSIDE-OUT AND OUTSIDE-IN FACTORS

In their discussion of developmental factors that affect emergent literacy, White-hurst and Lonigan (1998) provided a conceptual analysis that distinguishes between those processes that operate "inside" a momentary task and are associated with competence, versus those processes that are larger than or "outside" a particular task and also are associated with competence. In particular, Whitehurst and Lonigan (1998) proposed that as young readers encounter text, there are features of reading that help children decode the material in front of them (e.g., phonemic awareness) and external processes, such as contextual units and knowledge of the context, that help them make sense of the materials they are engaging. They called these *inside-out* and *outside-in* skills, respectively. We have borrowed and stretched (but hopefully not distorted) Whitehurst and Lonigan's conceptualization to describe variables or factors that are associated with and may well affect young children's social competence with peers. As seen in Figure 1.1, there are features or characteristics of a child that are associated with social competence, and we categorize these as "inside-out influences." Similarly, influences external to children affect their expression and development of social competence, and we describe these as *outside-in factors*. Although portrayed simplistically in this diagram, the relationship among these variables is undoubtedly quite complex. Certainly, a dynamic relationship exists for the inside-out variables, and a reciprocal relationship must exist between the inside-out and outside-in variables. As noted previously, the third-generation research on children's social competence is beginning to untangle relationships among these features (Ladd, 2005).

Inside-Out Influences on Young Children's Social Competence

Inside-out influences are characteristics, skills, and abilities of a child that are associated with his or her social performance. Some are immutable, like the child's sex, neurology, or some types of disabilities (e.g., Down syndrome). Others may well be affected by children's experiences and other elements of the child's environment (e.g., cognitive and language skills may be affected by quality of child care, which may then contribute to more positive social competence).

Neurology and Brain Development

Over the first years of life, children's brains mature in ways that allow them to acquire language and use it in social contexts (Kagan & Herschkowitz, 2004). Advances in neuroscience are allowing us to understand the relationship between early social behavior and brain activity, and to see where differences in brain activity are reflected in children's social behavior. In a series of studies, Fox and colleagues observed 4-year-old children in social situations and tasks and also assessed brain activity using an electroencephalogram (EEG; Fox et al., 1995; Henderson, Fox, & Rubin, 2001). They found that more socially competent children had greater EEG activity in the left frontal lobe, whereas children who were more withdrawn in social situations had greater right frontal lobe activity. They believe that such activity may be associated with children's temperaments, which in turn is related to children's social behavior. In their study of infants, Mundy, Card, and Fox (2000) reported that left frontal lobe activity was associated with an infant's tendency to initiate joint attention, a precursor of social and language development. For children with autism, Dawson, Klinger, Panagiotides, Lewy, and Castelloe (1995) found less left frontal lobe activation in social tasks as compared with children without disabilities who were matched in terms of mental age. Similarly, for children with high-functioning autism, Sutton and colleagues (2005) documented greater left frontal lobe asymmetry (i.e., more activity in the left than right lobe) for individuals with fewer social impairments and greater right lobe asymmetry for children with greater social impairments. As neuroscience and measurement technology advances, greater understanding of brain-behavior relationships and its relevance for children's social competence will unfold.

Temperament, Self-Regulation, and Emotional Competence

Although having somewhat different definitions, temperament, emotional regulation, and emotional competence are related in that they reflect a generalized style of responding, controlling, and understanding emotions in social (and nonsocial) situations. Temperament includes such characteristics as intensity of a child's response, reactivity to social situations, emotion features of the response (e.g., anger, joy, fear), and sociability (e.g., preference for being with others) (Goldsmith et al., 1987; Kagan, 1994). In a longitudinal study, Rimm-Kaufman and Kagan (2005) found that infant temperament characteristics (inhibited and uninhibited styles of responding) in evidence as early as 4 months were associated with children's later adjustment in kindergarten. For preschool-age children, Diener and Kim (2004) noted that children rated higher on risk factors associated with temperament (e.g., who were more highly reactive) were rated by teachers as having lower prosocial and higher externalizing behaviors. When examining the sociability of preschool children, Coplan, Prakash, O'Neil, and Armer (2004) identified two types of social withdrawal for children with low sociability: one based on social fear and anxiety and another based on social disinterest.

The ability to control or regulate emotions and behavior in social settings is a key temperamental characteristic associated with social competence of young children. Fantuzzo and colleagues (Fantuzzo, Sekino, & Cohen, 2004; Mendez, Fantuzzo, & Cicchetti, 2002) found a strong relationship between both temperament and emotion regulation and peer play competence of African-American children from the inner city. With a group of preschoolers from middle-income families, Blair, Denham, Kochanoff, and Whipple (2004) documented that children's ability to cope with emotional situations in an active, adaptive manner rather than in a passive manner was associated with the development of prosocial behaviors.

Furthermore, Denham and colleagues (2001) proposed that emotional competence is an essential feature of the development of young children's social competence with peers. In their research with 3- and 4-year-old children, Denham and colleagues (2003) found a significant association between emotional competence (i.e., emotional expressiveness, regulation, and knowledge) and social competence, measured both during the preschool year and kindergarten year. In a study of preschool children's peer play, Lindsey and Colwell (2003) determined that emotion regulation and emotional understanding were the key features related to the competence with which children played with peers.

Gender Differences

Regardless of whether young girls and boys are different in their social competence because of inherent sex differences or because societal expectations shape children's behavior, differences do exist and may be seen as early as the toddler years. Baillargeon and colleagues (2007) discerned gender differences in problem behavior as early as 17 months of age (more problem behaviors detected the earlier the age) and noted the stability of such behavior problems up through 29 months. In preschool, a general finding is that girls engage in more prosocial behavior in the preschool years (Eisenberg et al., 1997), and Vaughn and Azria (2000) found, in their sample of African American preschoolers, that girls had more reciprocated friendships than did boys. Styles of interaction in peer play groups differ also; for example, Waas and Graczyk (1999) observed that boys were more negative toward peers who exhibited internalizing behaviors, whereas girls responded more negatively to externalizing behavior. When examining aggression directed toward peers, Ostrove and Keating (2004) documented that boys engaged in more verbal and physical aggression and girls engaged in more relational aggression (e.g., rejecting behavior). In her study of Theory of Mind (ToM) in preschool children, Walker (2005) found that girls were much more successful socially than boys.

Peer acceptance in preschool appears to predict acceptance in kindergarten, but Keane and Calkins (2004) reported that aggressive behavior in kindergarten mediated this relationship for boys and both sneaky behavior (a negative influence) and sharing (a positive influence) mediated the relationship for girls. Clearly, by preschool-age, differences in social performance exist for boys and girls, and on some dimensions, girls exhibit relatively more mature forms of social behavior.

Cognitive Skills

Developmental skills certainly affect the competence of children's social performance, and a number of skills, abilities, and capacities may be grouped under the cognitive skills area. Attention to task is one skill that relates to children's ability to interact with others, in that one must be able to maintain attention to an ongoing interaction to be a participant. In their study of preschool children, Bennett-Murphy, Laurie-Rose, Brinkman, and McNamara (2007) found that performance on a vigilance task (which measured attention) was associated with social and reciprocal play. The specific direction of children's attention as well as maintenance of attention is an important cognitive/perceptual skill. For children with autism, a gaze-tracking technology has been developed to track the locations of a child's gaze and understand to what features of a task or social situation a child is attending.

Klin, Jones, Schultz, Volkmar, and Cohen (2002) determined that adolescents with autism tended to not look at the eyes of their social partner but looked more at the mouth, body, or away, and that gaze at the face was associated with other measures of social competence. Although not applied yet with preschool children, such assessment technology holds promise for some young children with disabilities because it does not rely on verbal responses.

Joint attention to an activity, task, or visual display is another ability that emerges early in life and may be related to the development of social competence. Joint attention is the ability to pay attention to an event, object, or activity with a social partner such as a parent or peer. For infants who are typically developing, it emerges between 12–18 months of age. Van Hecke and colleagues (2007) found that initiating joint attention and responding to joint attention at 12 months of age were associated with children's social competence and externalizing behavior when the children were 30 months of age. Others (Carpenter & Tomasello, 2000) have noted the strong association between joint attention in infancy and later communication and social development. Deficits in joint attention are particularly problematic for children with autism; in their longitudinal study, Dawson and colleagues (2004) found that preschoolers with autism engaged in substantially less joint attention than peers who were developmentally matched.

Implicit in the discussions and measurement of joint attention is that the focal child understands that she and the social partner are attending to the same thing. Such awareness of the presence, capacity, and actions of the social partner is sometimes called *social cognition, social perspective taking,* or *ToM*. All of these concepts presume that in early childhood, children develop the awareness that other social partners have perspectives and cognitions similar to themselves, and children may use such knowledge to engage in socially competent behavior. ToM tasks have been used most frequently with elementary-age and older children. In two studies, however, Watson, Nixon, and Capage (1999) have found a positive association between preschool children's performance on a ToM task (False Beliefs) and their social skills with peers, as rated by their teacher.

Overall cognitive ability may also have an influence on social competence. Certainly, as children grow older and cognitive skills mature, they use those enhanced capacities in the interactions with peers. This expression may be seen in the maturation and increased frequency of sociodramatic play. Crick and Dodge (1994) proposed a social information processing model of social competence that is based on cognitive abilities, and Mayeux and Cillessen (2003) have used this conceptual framework to document the association of social problem-solving skills with other measures of social competence for children in kindergarten and first grade. Diamond (2002) noted that cognitive and problem-solving skills were likely to have a major influence on the social competence of young children with disabilities, and Odom and colleagues (2006) found that on a measure of general development, preschool children with disabilities who were socially accepted by peers in inclusive settings had higher scores than did children with disabilities who were socially rejected. In their intervention work to promote social competence with preschool children with development delays, Guralnick, Connor, Neville, and Hammond (2006) found that the children who benefited most from the intervention were children with lower cognitive capacities. It was possible that children with lower cognitive skills might also have had the lowest social performance, were most in need of the intervention, and had skills deficits that matched the skills being taught by the intervention.

Communication and Language Skills

Communication is a key element in social interaction among peers, and to some extent, social communication and social competence is inextricable (Prutting, 1982). The association of communication skills and language development on social competence is well documented in the literature. In their study of young children who had been born preterm or full-term, Herbert-Myers and colleagues (2006) determined that social connectedness, compliance, and noncompliance with peer requests were strongly associated with language skills when children were 3 and 8 years of age. Language and play skills at 3 years were associated with peer competence at 8 years. For African-American preschool children enrolled in Head Start, Mendez and colleagues (2002) reported that children's language abilities were related to their competence in playing with peers in the classrooms. When studying social relationships of preschool children with disabilities in inclusive settings, Odom and colleagues (2006) found that communication was a theme related to both social acceptance (i.e., competent communication) and social rejection (i.e., when communication was poor). Finally, it appears that for children with speech and language impairment, problems with peer-related social competence exist (Guralnick, Connor, Hammond, Gottman, & Kinnish, 1996; Hart, Fujiki, Brinton, & Hart, 2004; Marton, Abramoff, & Rosenzweig, 2005), which may imply that language and communication skills are one of the more important inside-out skills.

Disability

A disability is an inside-out influence that is quite broad in characteristics and impairment. At the outset, it is important to specify that some preschool children with identifiable disabilities are quite socially competent. In their study of peer social relationships in inclusive settings, Odom and colleagues (2006) found that approximately 28% of their sample was well accepted in the classroom, suggesting quite adequate social competence. Many young children with disabilities, however, have social competence problems. Using a performance-based, multi-method assessment of social competence described previously, McConnell and Odom (1999) reported a significant difference in peer-related social competence for preschool-age children with developmental delays and same-age peers without developmental delays. Reviewing his long history of research, Guralnick (1999) noted the concern about social competence for children in his studies (primarily children with mild developmental delays) and for social integration when children are in inclusive settings. In subsequent chapters in the second section of this book, authors will review social competence concerns for children having different disabilities, so literature related to this is not covered here.

Outside-In Influences on Young Children's Social Competence

Peer social competence is also affected by experiences emanating from outside a child. Following an ecological systems perspective proposed by Bronfenbrenner (1979), one can conceptualize these influences as being proximal (or close) to the child, such as family or classroom environments, or distal (or more distant) from the child's immediate environment, such as culture. In this section, outside-in influences are organized in a proximal to distal order extending from family influences to classroom influences to cultural influences.

Family Influences

Because many outside-in influences (e.g., culture) are mediated by the family context and family members' relationships, it is difficult to separate family influence from some other influences, and a discussion of the inter-relationship of these outside-in influences appears in a later section. Family influences can be sorted into specific characteristics of the mother and mother–child interaction, the broader influence of family members or family as a unit, and the home environment in which the family lives.

In their review of the literature on family influences, McCollum and Ostrosky (Chapter 2) propose that the influences follow three pathways. First, family interactions and relationships may have implicit links to social competence. A primary example of the family relationship influence is the initial attachment relationships, most often occurring between the child and mother. Evidence has been found indicating that the quality of attachment is associated with the quality of social relationships that a child establishes with peers (Liebermann, Doyle, & Markiewicz, 1999). In their meta-analysis, Schneider, Atkinson and Tardif (2001) found modest effects sizes for the association of attachment to peer relationships in early childhood, with effect sizes being larger for middle childhood and adolescent peer relationships.

Second, family members may directly teach or promote peer interaction. Sometimes this occurs in the normal course of family life. For example, Downey and Condron (2004) reported that young children benefited socially from the presence of siblings in the home, with the assumption being that children learn some social interaction skills from interactions with their siblings. Parents may also be directly involved in interventions. In an intervention study, Mize and Pettit (1997) taught mothers to coach their children about appropriate responses to social situations, which resulted in positive changes in their children's peer social acceptance in the classroom. In their chapter, Sheridan, Knoche, and Marvin (Chapter 14) describe a range of intervention programs that involve parents directly in promoting the socially competent behavior of their children.

Third, family members may promote children's peer-related social competence by providing opportunities for children to experience peer interactions. For African-American children attending Head Start programs, Fantuzzo and McWayne (2002) found a positive relationship between children's home-based play with peers and their prosocial behavior in a Head Start classroom. In their research with mothers of children with mild cognitive delays, Guralnick, Neville, Connor, and Hammond (2003) reported that parents' arrangement of playdates was one of several family influences (the others were socialization strategies, social support, and parent stress) associated with peer social competence.

In addition to direct family influences, the stability of the home environment and resources available in the home environment affect children's development of peer-related social competence. With preschool children's problem behavior, Hoglund and Leadbetter (2004) found that multiple home moves were associated with ratings of problem behavior, although this relationship was mediated by variables in the classroom. Koblinsky, Gordon, and Anderson (2000) noted the difference in levels of peer-related social competence for children who were homeless and children having a secure home setting. More broadly, socioeconomic level of the family appears to affect children social competence with peers (Vaughn, Vollenweider, Bost, Azria-Evans, & Snider, 2003), although these relationships are certainly mediated by other influences such as quality of the preschool classroom environment (Brophy-Herb, Lee, Nievar, & Stollak, 2007).

Classroom and Teacher Influences

Some young children spend a substantial portion of their early childhood years in child care and preschool classroom settings. In these settings the quality of the physical environment and the quality of the interactions and relationship with the teacher may influence the development of a child's peer-related social competence. In Chapter 5, Sainato, Jung, Salmon, and Axe describe the influences of toys and play materials, structure of the activity, and spatial arrangement on social behavior of young children. To determine the effect of toys on the social behavior of young children with disabilities, Kim and colleagues (2003) conducted a meta-analysis that revealed that social toys had a substantial effect on children's social participation. Similarly, the structure (e.g., clarity of theme, role definition) of play activities appears to promote interaction among peers (DeKlyen & Odom, 1989), as does the size of space accorded play activities (Brown, Fox, & Brady, 1987; Chapter 5, this volume). In studies of more general child care quality and child outcomes, researchers have found a positive and longitudinal relationship between the quality of the early childhood classroom environments and measures of social and communication skills (Peisner-Feinberg et al., 2001) and general competence (Maxwell, 2007). In addition, general early childhood curricula, when well organized and well implemented, are a primary context for promoting prosocial behavior and social competence of young children (Diamond, Hong, & Baroody, Chapter 8, this volume).

A primary feature of a classroom setting is the teacher's style of interaction with children, the relationship that is established between teacher and children, and the social climate that exists in the classroom (Hamre & Pianta, 2006). In a longitudinal study of child care, Howes (2000) found that children's competence with peers in second grade was associated with the social-emotional climate of their preschool and quality of the child–teacher relationship. In their analysis of preschool children's classroom environments, Brophy-Herb and colleagues (2007) documented a direct relationship between both teacher behavior and classroom social climate and children's social competence with peers. They noted that classroom climate, particularly, mediated the relationship between teacher behavior and preschooler's social competence.

Early Intervention

For young children with identified disabilities and other unidentified children with social problem behavior, specific intervention approaches have been developed to promote social competence. Brown, Odom, and Conroy (2001) proposed that such interventions exist on a continuum of intensity, which was defined as the amount of teacher training and time required for their successful implementation. The second section of this book contains chapters that describe these approaches in detail, so little further information will be provided here. Such interventions do, however, represent important outside-in influences.

Peer-Group Influences

In addition to classroom social climate created by the teacher, the characteristics and nature of the peer group in early childhood classrooms has a major influence on the development of peer-related social competence. In their study of preschool children noted previously, Brophy-Herb and colleagues (2007) reported that children experiencing higher stress exhibited lower levels of peer social competence when in classes with other children with lower levels of social competence, suggesting that peer group competence was a factor for these at-risk children. With first-grade children, Hoglund and Leadbetter (2004) observed that higher levels of prosocial behavior among peers in classrooms and lower levels of victimization promoted children's social competence.

A particularly important example of peer group influence occurs for children with disabilities and inclusive settings. Preschool inclusion is based, in part, on the assumption that the presence of socially sophisticated peers without disabilities will provide more opportunities for children to acquire social competence skills through observation and interaction with peers than might occur in segregated special education preschools involving only other children with disabilities (Guralnick, 2001; Odom, 2000). In the meta-analysis mentioned earlier, Kim and colleagues (2003) found a positive affect of inclusive peer groups on the social behavior of young children with disabilities. Rafferty, Piscitelli, and Boettcher (2003) examined the effect of inclusive settings on the language and social competence of children with disabilities in inclusive and noninclusive preschools and determined that children with severe disabilities had significantly higher social performance in inclusive classrooms, although differences did not occur for children with milder developmental delays. In their study of inclusive preschools, Wolfberg and colleagues (1999) analyzed interaction patterns among children and found that peer group cultures exist within classrooms and that those peer influences were both supportive and unsupportive of classmates with disabilities. Sainato and colleagues (Chapter 5) summarize the literature on the range of variables associated with peer-group composition (i.e., group size, familiarity, gender, and ratio) and social performances of young children.

Friendships

Among peers, friendships are a special type of relationship that are often reflected in a mutual attraction between two children, mutual selection for social engagement in play activities, and mutual identification of the other child as a friend (i.e., reciprocal friends). Buysse, Goldman, West, and Hollingsworth (Chapter 4) provide a comprehensive review of the definitions and literature on friendships of young children. In their study of children in Head Start, Vaughn and colleagues (2001) found that reciprocal friendships increased across years, that they consist more often of same-gender participants, and that children who had reciprocal friendships were more likely to have higher levels of social competence. Other researchers, studying wider ranges of preschool children, report similar associations between friendships and social competence (Lindsey, 2002; Sebanc, 2003). In their study of social acceptance and rejection of preschool children with disabilities in inclusive settings, Odom and colleagues (2006) reported that one primary theme related to social acceptance was friendships, and that children who were socially rejected tended to have fewer friends (i.e., as identified by teachers and parents) than did children who were accepted. This finding is consistent with Berndt's (2004) suggestion that children's friendships may promote children's success in the social world.

For children with disabilities, there is conflicting information about the occurrence and development of friendships. In their observational and longitudinal work, Guralnick and colleagues (1996) have noted that children with mild developmental delays, as compared with children without disabilities and children with communication disorders, rarely develop friendships, and the difficulties in establishing reciprocal friendships extend at least into the early elementary years (Guralnick, Neville, Hammond, & Conner, 2007). In contrast, Buysse and colleagues (2002) found that parents and teachers report that preschool children with disabilities do have "special friendships" (i.e., reciprocal friendships).

These substantially different conclusions about friendships of preschool children with disabilities may well be a function of the methods used to assess friendship (e.g., observational and laboratory versus teacher and parent report of community relationships). Also, it does appear that even when reciprocal friendships exist or are emerging for preschool children with disabilities, they may sometimes differ in quality from those of same-age peers without disabilities (Freeman & Kasari, 2002). Such differences may not be critical in the formation of peer-related social competence because it appears that just the availability of a friend may foster prosocial interaction and perhaps protect against social rejection in inclusive settings.

Culture

We may define culture as a set of shared values that govern attitudes and behavior. Culture can be reflected by values of ethnic groups (e.g., the Asian or African-American culture), socioeconomic groups (e.g., middle-class, working-class, low income), or even peer cultures that exist in classrooms. Moreover, features of culture, such as ethnic identity and practices, are translated through other cultural microsystems, such as families and peer groups. In Chapter 3, Hanson and SooHoo have provided a detailed review of cultural issues that affect children's social competence. A direct example of ethnic cultural differences may be seen in an observational study of parenting styles by Chinese and American parents of preschools, conducted by Jose, Huntsinger, Huntsinger, and Liaw (2000), which found that Chinese parents were more directive with their children than mainstream American parents, but they showed similar warmth in their interaction with their preschool children. Cohen, Hsueh, Zhou, Hancock, and Floyd (2006) noted the important role that respect among peers plays in the development of social relationships and social competence for Chinese children. Socioeconomic differences were examined in a study by Vaughn and colleagues (2003), in which they observed peer interactions of children in Head Start and community preschools. They noted more negative social initiation in Head Start programs, suggesting different peer group norms in classrooms. They also found, however, a positive relationship between negative behavior with peers and social competence, which led them to suggest that negative interactions may play a role in social competence in some contexts.

These data, as well as other research (Chen, Chang, & He, 2003), suggest that norms for behavior are often established by peers and often at the classroom level. Such norms set the standard for appropriateness of peer behavior, which was noted previously as one criterion for social competence. It is also important to note that at times, these norms set by cultural or microcultural groups may conflict with the values of adults or mainstream culture. As Bronfenbrenner reminds us, children operate in different microsystems that may have different behavioral requirements and expectations. So, to extend our notion of social competence, perhaps an added dimension of competence is that children "learn the rules" for effective and social behaviors in multiple social contexts from both peers and adults. This feature makes social competence an extremely difficult ability for some children with disabilities, particularly autism spectrum disorders, which are partially defined by social difficulties.

Relationship of Inside-Out and Outside-In Variables and Implications for Future Research and Practice

Many aspects of young children's lives, as seen in the previous sections, influence the development of social competence. Although for the sake of clarity, inside-out and outside-in influences were identified separately, there would certainly be reciprocal influences across variables. For example, the cognitive functioning level or communication skills of a child (an inside-out variable) would undoubtedly affect family influences (e.g., stress), classroom influences (e.g., inclusive or special education classroom), and intervention influences (e.g., the choice of a peer-mediated or teacher directed intervention). The associations among such influences present a challenge for scientists interested in understanding the developmental processes, acquisition of social competence, and the efficacy of intervention programs, as well as for practitioners, who must develop effective intervention programs for young children who are having social competence difficulties. Yet, with challenges come opportunities.

A primary challenge for scientists, as noted, has been the measurement of social competence. As proposed in this chapter, a multi-method assessment of social competence may provide a robust assessment, yet most of the studies reviewed in the previous sections on inside-out and outside-in influences have employed single or limited outcome measures. In fact, questions may exist about whether intervention effects for children would be strong enough to be measured by composite assessment measures. Alternatively, it is possible that interventions might have differential effects across settings and informants, in which case individual assessments may be more sensitive to the effects of different types of interventions. In their study of the social competence of children with disabilities in multiple settings, Guralnick and colleagues (2007) observed that the children's social performance was similar in laboratory play group with peers and interactions on several tasks with their mothers, suggesting a consistency in their social competence across social partners and tasks. In their examination of different social competence interventions, Odom and colleagues (1999) found that different interventions did affect different child outcome variables. The match between assessment of social competence, characteristics of the child (inside-out variables), and characteristics of the setting or environment (i.e., outside-in variables) is an important direction for future research. Similarly, the determination of how the range of influences noted in this chapter affect or interact with the effects of specific intervention approaches, like those described in subsequent chapters, is an important next step in intervention research.

With the complexity noted previously, practitioners might be overwhelmed with the task of selecting an intervention or set of interventions for children in their classrooms. The information about complexity, however, presents the opportunity for us to become wiser practitioners. The developmental literature leads us to observe the different ways children show their competence in interaction with peers, which we may observe by adopting a culturally sensitive lens (Hanson & SooHoo, Chapter 3) or understanding the different social expectations we might have for children with different characteristics (e.g., for boys and girls). Similarly, it reminds us that some children having social competence problems may display them in different ways, for example, through physical or relational aggression or social withdrawal and isolations. For the last 30 years, there has been a fairly active literature on interventions to promote young children's social competence, and much of the current literature is summarized in subsequent chapters. Selecting wisely the intervention approach to be used in the classroom or community and with a specific child, collecting child performance data on the child's response to the intervention, and moving up the continuum of intensity when the child does not respond is an important plan of action (Brown, Odom, McConnell, & Rathel, this volume). Such a strategy fits well with the current evidence-based approach to early intervention and early childhood education (Buysse & Wesley, 2006).

REFERENCES

Achenbach, T., & Rescorla, L. (2000). *Child behavior checklist for ages 1.5–5.* Burlington, VT: Achenbach System of Empirically Based Assessment.

Baillargeon, R.H., Normand, C.L., Seguin, J.R., Zoccolillo, M., Japel, C., Perusse, D., et al. (2007). The evolution of problem and social competence behaviors during toddlerhood: A prospective population-based cohort survey. *Infant Mental Health Journal, 28,* 12–38.

Bauminger, N., & Shulman, C. (2003). The development and maintenance of friendship in high-functioning children with autism: Maternal perceptions. *Autism, 7,* 81–97.

Bennett-Murphy, L.M., Laurie-Rose, C., Brinkman, T.M., & McNamara, K.A. (2007). Sustained attention and social competence in typically developing preschool-aged children. *Early Child Development & Care, 77,* 133–149.

Berndt, T.J. (2004). Children's friendships: Shifts over a half-century in perspectives of their development and their effects. *Journal of Developmental Psychology, 50,* 206–223.

Bierman, K.L. (2004). *Peer rejection: Developmental processes and intervention strategies.* New York: Guilford Press.

Birch, S.H., & Ladd, G.W. (1997). The teacher–child relationship and children's early school adjustment. *Journal of School Psychology, 35*(1), 61–79.

Blair, K.A., Denham, S.A., Kochanoff, A., & Whipple, B. (2004). Playing it cool: Temperament, emotion regulation, and social behavior in preschoolers. *Journal of School Psychology, 42,* 419–443.

Bronfenbrenner, U. (1979). Contexts of child rearing: Problems and prospects. *American Psychologist, 34,* 844–850.

Bronson, M.B. (1994). The usefulness of an observational measure of young children's social and mastery behaviors in early childhood classrooms. *Early Childhood Research Quarterly, 9,* 19–43.

Brophy-Herb, H.E., Lee, R.E., Nievar, M., & Stollak, G. (2007). Preschoolers' social competence: Relations to family characteristics, teacher behaviors and classroom climate. *Journal of Applied Developmental Psychology, 28,* 134–148.

Brown, W.H., Fox, J.J., & Brady, M.P. (1987). Effects of spatial density on 3- and 4-year-old children's socially directed behavior during freeplay: An investigation of a setting factor. *Education and Treatment of Children, 10,* 247–258.

Brown, W.H., Odom, S.L., & Conroy, M.A. (2001). An intervention hierarchy for promoting preschool children's peer interactions in natural environments. *Topics in Early Childhood Special Education, 21,* 90–134.

Brown, W.H., Odom, S.L., & Holcombe, A. (1996). Observational assessment of young children's social behavior with peers. *Early Childhood Research Quarterly, 11,* 19–40.

Buysse, V. (1991). *Early Childhood Friendship Survey for Parents and Caregivers.* Chapel Hill, NC: University of North Carolina, Frank Porter Graham Child Development Center.

Buysse, V. (1993). Friendships of preschoolers with disabilities in community-based child care settings. *Journal of Early Intervention, 17,* 380–395.

Buysse, V., Goldman, B.D., & Skinner, M.L. (2002). Setting effects on friendship formation among young children with and without disabilities. *Exceptional Children, 8,* 503–517.

Buysse, V., & Wesley, P.W. (2006). *Evidence-based practice in the early childhood field.* Washington, DC: ZERO TO THREE Press.

Campbell, D., & Fiske, D. (1959). Convergent and discriminant validation by the multitrait-multimethod matrix. *Psychological Bulletin, 56,* 2, 81–105.

Carlson, C.L., Lahey, B., & Neeper, R. (1984). Peer assessment of the social behavior of accepted, rejected, and neglected children. *Journal of Abnormal Child Psychology, 12*(2), 187–198.

Carpenter, M., & Tomasello, M. (2000). Joint attention, cultural learning, and language acquisition: Implications for children with autism. In A.M. Wetherby & B.M. Prizant (Eds.), *Autism spectrum disorders: A transactional developmental perspective* (pp. 31–54). Baltimore: Paul H. Brookes Publishing Co.

Carta, J.J., Greenwood, C.R., Luze, G.J., Cline, G., & Kuntz, S. (2004). Developing a general outcome measure of growth in social skills for infants and toddlers. *Journal of Early Intervention, 26,* 91–114.

Chang, L. (2004). The role of classroom norms in contextualizing the relations of children's social behaviors to peer acceptance. *Developmental Psychology, 40,* 691–702.

Chen, X., Chang, L., & He, Y. (2003). The peer group as a context: Mediating and moderating effects on relations between academic achievement and social functioning in Chinese children. *Child Development, 74,* 710–727.

Cohen, R., Hsueh, Y., Zhou, Z., Hancock, M. H., & Floyd, R. (2006). Respect, liking, and peer social competence in China and the United States. *New Directions for Child & Adolescent Development, 114,* 53–65.

Coplan, R.J., Prakash, K., O'Neil, K., & Armer, M. (2004). Do you "want" to play? Distinguishing between conflicted shyness and social disinterest in early childhood. *Developmental Psychology, 40,* 244–258.

Cowan, E.L., Pederson, A., Babijian, H., Izzo, L., & Trost, M.A. (1973). Long-term follow-up of early detected vulnerable children. *Journal of Consulting and Clinical Psychology, 41,* 438–446.

Crick, N.R., & Dodge, K.A. (1994). Social information-processing mechanisms in reactive and proactive aggression. *Child Development, 67,* 993–1002.

Dawson, G., Klinger, L.G., Panagiotides, H., Lewy, A., & Castelloe, P. (1995). Subgroups of autistic children based on social behavior display distinct patterns of brain activity. *Journal of Abnormal Child Psychology, 23,* 569–583.

Dawson, G., Toth, K., Abbott, R., Osterling, J., Munson, J., Estes, A., et al. (2004). Early social attention impairments in autism: Social orienting, joint attention, and attention to distress. *Developmental Psychology, 40,* 271–283.

DeKlyen, M., & Odom, S.L. (1989). Activity structure and social interactions with peers in developmentally integrated play groups. *Journal of Early Intervention, 13,* 342–352.

Denham, S.A., Blair, K.A., DeMulder, E., Levitas, J., & Sawyer, K. (2003). Preschool emotional competence: Pathway to social competence? *Child Development, 74,* 238–256.

Denham, S., Mason, T., Caverly, S., Schmidt, M., Hackney, R., Caswell, C., et al. (2001). Preschoolers at play: Co-socialisers of emotional and social competence. *International Journal of Behavioral Development, 25,* 290–301.

Devereux Foundation. (1998). *Devereux early childhood assessment program.* Lewisville, NC: Kaplan Companies.

Diamond, K.E. (2002). The development of social competence in children with disabilities. In P. Smith & C. Hart (Eds.), *Blackwell handbook of childhood social development* (pp. 570–587). Malden, MA: Blackwell Publishing.

Diener, M.L., & Kim, D-Y. (2004). Maternal and child predictors of preschool children's social competence. *Journal of Applied Developmental Psychology, 25,* 3–22.

Dodge, K.A. (1983). Behavioral antecedents of peer social status. *Child Development, 54,* 1386–1399.

Dodge, K.A., Coie, J.D., Pettit, G.S., & Price, J.M. (1990). Peer status and aggression in boys' groups: Developmental and contextual analyses. *Child Development, 61,* 1289–1309.

Downey, D.B., & Condron, D.J. (2004). Playing well with others in kindergarten: The benefit of siblings at home. *Journal of Marriage and Family, 66,* 333–350.

Eisenberg, N., Fabes, R.A., Shepard, S.A., Murphy, B.C., Guthrie, I.K., Jones, S., et al. (1997). Contemporaneous and longitudinal prediction of children's social functioning from regulation and emotionality. *Child Development, 68,* 642–664.

Erdley, C., & Asher, S.R. (1999). A social goals perspective on children's social competence. *Journal of Emotional & Behavioral Disorders, 7,* 156–167.

Fabes, R.A., Shepard, S.A., Guthrie, I.K., & Martin, C.L. (1997). Roles of temperamental arousal and gender-segregated play in young children's social adjustment. *Developmental Psychology, 33,* 693–702.

Fagan, J., & Fantuzzo, J.W. (1999). Multirater congruence on the social skills rating system: Mother, father, and teacher assessments of urban head start children's social competencies. *Early Childhood Research Quarterly, 14*(2), 229–242.

Fantuzzo, J., & McWayne, C. (2002). The relationship between peer-play interactions in the family context and dimensions of school readiness for low-income preschool children. *Journal of Educational Psychology, 94,* 79–87.

Fantuzzo, J., Sekino, Y., & Cohen, H.L. (2004). An examination of the contributions of interactive peer play to salient classroom competencies for urban Head Start children. *Psychology in the Schools, 41,* 323–336.

Farmer-Dougan, V., & Kaszuba, T. (1999). Reliability and validity of play-based observations: Relationship between the play behaviour observation system and standardised measures of cognitive and social skills. *Educational Psychology, 19,* 429–440.

Fox, N.A., Rubin, K.H., Calkins, S.D., Marshall, T.R., Coplan, R.J., Porges, S.W., Long, J.M., & Stewart, S. (1995). Frontal activation asymmetry and social competence at four years of age. *Child Development, 66,* 1770–1784.

Freeman, S.F., & Kasari, C. (2002). Characteristics and qualities of the play dates of children with Down syndrome: Emerging or true friendships? *American Journal on Mental Retardation, 107,* 16–31.

Goldsmith, H.H., Buss, A.H., Plomin, R., Rothbart, M.K., Thomas, A., Chess, S., et al. (1987). Roundtable: What is temperament? Four approaches. *Child Development, 58,* 505–529.

Gresham, F.M., & Elliott, S.N. (1990). *Social skills rating system: Preschool level.* Circle Pines, MN: American Guidance Service.

Guralnick, M.J. (1999). Family and child influences on the peer-related social competence of young children with developmental delays. *Mental Retardation and Developmental Disabilities Research Reviews, 5,* 21–29.

Guralnick, M.J. (2001). *Early childhood inclusion: Focus on change.* Baltimore: Paul H. Brookes Publishing Co.

Guralnick, M.J., Connor, R.T., Hammond, M., Gottman, J.M., & Kinnish, K. (1996). Immediate effects of mainstreamed settings on the social interactions and social integration of preschool children. *American Journal on Mental Retardation, 100*(4), 359–377.

Guralnick, M.J., Conner, R.T., Neville, B., & Hammond, M.A. (2006). Promoting the peer-related social development of young children with mild developmental delays: effectiveness of a comprehensive intervention. *American Journal on Mental Retardation, 111,* 336–356.

Guralnick, M.J., Neville, B., Conner, R.T., & Hammond, M.A. (2003). Family factors associated with the peer social competence of young children with mild delays. *American Journal on Mental Retardation, 108,* 272–287.

Guralnick, M.J., Neville, B., Hammond, M.A., & Connor, R.T. (2007). The friendships of young children with developmental delays: A longitudinal analysis. *Journal of Applied Developmental Psychology, 28,* 64–79.

Hamre, B.K., & Pianta, R.C. (2006). Student-teacher relationships. In G. Bear, G. & K. M. Minke (Eds.), *Children's needs III: Development, prevention, and intervention* (p. 1106). Washington, D.C.: National Association of School Psychologists.

Hart, K.I., Fujiki, M., Brinton, B., & Hart, C.H. (2004). The relationship between social behavior and severity of language impairment. *Journal of Speech, Language, and Hearing Research, 47,* 647.

Hartup, W.W. (1983). Peer relations. In M. Hetherington (Ed.), *Handbook of child psychology* (Vol. IV, pp. 104–196). New York: Wiley.

Henderson, H.A., Fox, N., & Rubin, K.H. (2001). Temperamental contributions to social behavior: The moderating roles of frontal EEG asymmetry and gender. *Journal of the American Academy of Child and Adolescent Psychiatry, 40,* 68–74.

Henricsson, L., & Rydell, A.-M. (2006). Children with behaviour problems: The influence of social competence and social relations on problem stability, school achievement and peer acceptance across the first six years of school. *Infant & Child Development, 15,* 347–366.

Herbert-Myers, H., Guttentag, C.L., Swank, P.R., Smith, K.E., & Landry, S.H. (2006). The importance of language, social, and behavioral skills across early and later childhood as predictors of social competence with peers. *Applied Developmental Science, 10,* 174–187.

Hoglund, W.L., & Leadbetter, B.J. (2004). The effects of family, school, and classroom ecologies in changes in children's social competence and emotional and behavioral problems in the first grade. *Developmental Psychology, 40,* 533–544.

Hops, H. (1983). Children's social competence and skill: Current research practices and future directions. *Behavior Therapy, 14,* 3–18.

Howes, C. (2000). Social-emotional classroom climate in child care, child-teacher relationships and children's second grade peer relations. *Social Development, 9,* 191–204.

Jose, P., Huntsinger, C., Huntsinger, P., & Liaw, F. (2000). Parental values and practices relevant to young children's social development in Taiwan and the United States. *Journal of Cross-Cultural Psychology, 31,* 677.

Junttila, N., Voeten, M., Kaukiainen, A., & Vauras, M. (2006). Multisource assessment of children's social competence. *Educational and Psychological Measurement, 66*(5), 874–895.

Kagan, J. (1994). On the nature of emotion. Monographs of the Society for Research in *Child Development, 59*(2–3), 7–24.

Kagan, J., & Herschkowitz, N. (2005). *A young mind in a growing brain.* Mahwah, NJ: Lawrence Erlbaum Associates.

Keane, S.P., & Calkins, S.D. (2004). Predicting kindergarten peer social status from toddler and preschool problem behavior. *Journal of Abnormal Child Psychology, 32,* 409.

Kim, A-H., Vaughn, S., Elbaum, B., Hughes, M.T., Sloan, C.V.M., & Sridhar, D. (2003). Effects of toys or group composition for children with disabilities: A synthesis. *Journal of Early Intervention, 25,* 189–205.

Klin, A., Jones, W., Schultz, R., Volkmar, F., & Cohen, D. (2002). Visual fixation patterns during viewing of naturalistic social situations as predictors of social competence in individuals with autism. *Archives of General Psychiatry, 59,* 809–816.

Koblinsky, S., Gordon, A., & Anderson, E. (2000). Changes in the social skills and behavior problems of homeless and housed children during the preschool year. *Early Education and Development, 11,* 321.

Ladd, G.W. (1990). Having friends, keeping friends, making friends, and being liked by peers in the classroom: Predictors of children's early school adjustment? *Child Development, 61,* 1081–1100.

Ladd, G.W. (2005). *Children's peer relations and social competence: A century of progress.* New Haven, CT: Yale University Press.

Ladd, G.W., & Coleman, C.C. (1997). Children's classroom peer relationships and early school attitudes: Concurrent and longitudinal associations. *Early Education and Development, 8*(1), 51–66.

Ladd, G.W., Kochenderfer, B.J., & Coleman, C. (1996). Friendship quality as a predictor of young children's early school adjustment. *Child Development, 67,* 1103–1118.

Ladd, G.W., & Price, J.M. (1987). Predicting children's social and school adjustment following the transition from preschool to kindergarten. *Child Development, 58,* 1168–1189.

Liebermann, M., Doyle, M.B., & Markiewicz, D. (1999). Developmental patterns in security of attachment to mother and father in late childhood and early adolescence: Associations with peer relations. *Child Development, 70,* 202–213.

Lindsey, E.W. (2002). Preschool children's friendships and peer acceptance: Links to social competence. *Child Study Journal, 32,* 145–156.

Lindsey, E.W., & Colwell, M.J. (2003). Preschoolers' emotional competence: Links to pretend and physical play. *Child Study Journal, 33,* 39–52.

Manz, P.H., Fantuzzo, J.W., & McDermott, P.A. (1999). The parent version of the preschool *Social Skills Rating Scale:* An analysis of its use with low-income, ethnic minority children. *School Psychology Review, 28*(3), 493–504.

Marton, K., Abramoff, B., & Rosenzweig, S. (2005). Social cognition and language in children with specific language impairment. *Journal of Communication Disorders, 38,* 143–162.

Maxwell, L.E. (2007). Competency in child care settings: The role of the physical environment. *Environment and Behavior, 39,* 229–245.

Mayeux, L., & Cillessen, A.H.N. (2003). Development of social problem solving in early childhood: Stability, change, and associations with social competence. *The Journal of Genetic Psychology, 164,* 153–174.

McCabe, P.C., & Marshall, D.J., (2006). Measuring the social competence of preschool children with specific language impairment: Correspondence among informant ratings and behavioral observations. *Topics in Early Childhood Special Education, 26*(4), 234–236.

McConnell, S.R., & Odom, S.L. (1986). Sociometrics: Peer-Referenced Measures and the Assessment of Social Competence. In P.S. Strain, M.J. Guralnick, & H.M. Walker (Eds.), *Children's social behavior: Development, assessment, and modification* (pp. 215–284). San Diego: Academic Press.

McConnell, S.R., & Odom, S.L. (1999). A multi-measure performance-based assessment of social competence in young children with disabilities. *Topics in Early Childhood Special Education, 19*(2), 67–74.

McFall, R.M. (1982). A review and reformulation of the concept of social skills. *Behavioral Assessment, 4,* 1–33.

Mendez, J.L., Fantuzzo, J., & Cicchetti, D. (2002). Profiles of social competence among low-income African-American preschool children. *Child Development, 73,* 1085–1100.

Missall, K.N. (2002). Reconceptualizing school adjustment: A search for intervening variables. *Dissertation Abstracts International, 63*(5-A), 1712.

Mize, J., & Pettit, G.S. (1997). Mothers' social coaching, mother–child relationship style, and children's peer competence: Is the medium the message? *Child Development, 68,* 291–311.

Mundy, P., Card, J., & Fox, N. (2000). EEG correlates of the development of infant joint attention skills. *Developmental Psychobiology, 36,* 325–338.

Newborg, J., Stock, J.R., & Wnek, L., Guidubaldi, J., & Svinicki, J. (1984/1988). *Battelle Developmental Inventory.* Allen, TX: DLM.

Odom, S.L. (2000). Preschool inclusion: What we know and where we go from here. *Topics in Early Childhood Special Education, 20,* 20–27.

Odom, S.L., & McConnell, S.R. (1985). A performance-based conceptualization of social competence of handicapped preschool children: Implications for assessment. *Topics in Early Childhood Special Education, 4*(4), 1–19.

Odom, S.L., McConnell, S.R., McEvoy, M.A., Peterson, C., Ostrosky, M., Chandler, L.K., Spicuzza, R.J., Skellenger, A., Creighton, M., & Favazza, P.C. (1999). Relative effects of interventions for supporting the social competence of young children with disabilities. *Topics in Early Childhood Special Education, 19,* 75–91.

Odom, S.L., & Ogawa, I. (1992). Direct observation of young children's social interaction with peers: A review of methodology. *Behavioral Assessment, 14,* 407–441.

Odom, S.L., Zercher, C., Li, S., Marquart, J.M., Sandall, S., & Brown, W.H. (2006). Social acceptance and rejection of preschool children with disabilities: A mixed-method analysis. *Journal of Educational Psychology, 98,* 807–823.

Olson, S.L., & Lifgren, K. (1988). Concurrent and longitudinal correlates of preschool peer sociometrics: Comparing rating scale and nomination measures. *Journal of Applied Developmental Psychology, 9,* 409–420.

Ostrove, J.M., & Keating, C.F. (2004). Gender differences in preschool aggression during free play and structured interactions: An observational study. *Social Development, 13,* 255–277.

Parker, J.G., & Asher, S.R. (1987). Peer relations and later personal adjustment: Are low-accepted children "at risk"? *Psychological Bulletin, 102,* 357–389.

Peisner-Feinberg, E.S., Burchinal, M.R., Clifford, R.M., Howes, C., Kagan, S.L., & Yazejian, N. (2001). The relation of preschool child-care quality to children's cognitive and social developmental trajectories through second grade. *Child Development, 72,* 1534–1553.

Pihlakoski, L., Aromaa, M., Sourander, A., Rautava, P., Helenius, H., & Sillanpaa, M. (2004). Use of and need for professional help for emotional and behavioral problems among preadolescents: A prospective cohort study of 3- to 12-year-old children. *Journal of the American Academy of Child and Adolescent Psychiatry, 43,* 974.

Prutting, C.A. (1982). Pragmatics as social competence. *Journal of Speech and Hearing Disorders, 47,* 123–134.

Rafferty, Y., Piscitelli, V., & Boettcher, C. (2003). The impact of inclusion on language development and social competence among preschoolers with disabilities. *Exceptional Children, 69,* 467–479.

Renshaw, P.D., & Asher, S.R. (1983). Children's goals and strategies for social interaction. *Merrill-Palmer Quarterly, 29,* 353–374.

Rimm-Kaufman, S.E., & Kagan, J. (2005). Infant predictors of kindergarten behavior: The contribution of inhibited and uninhibited temperament types. *Behavioral Disorders, 30,* 331–347.

Risi, S., Gerhardstein, R., & Kistner, J. (2003). Children's classroom peer relationships and subsequent educational outcomes. *Journal of Clinical Child & Adolescent Psychology, 32,* 351–361.

Roff, M. (1961). Childhood social interaction and young adult bad conduct. *Journal of Abnormal Social Psychology, 63,* 333–337.

Rose-Krasnor, L.R. (1985). Observational assessment of social problem solving. In B. Schneider, K Rubin, & J. Ledingham (Eds.), *Children's peer relations: Issues in assessment and intervention* (pp. 57–74). New York: Springer-Verlag.

Rubin, K.H., Chen, X.Y., McDougall, P., Bowker, A., & McKinnon, J. (1995). The Waterloo longitudinal project: Predicting internalizing and externalizing problems in adolescence. *Development and Psychopathology, 7,* 751–764.

Rubin, K.H., & Krasnor, L.R. (1986). Social-cognitive and social behavioral perspectives on problem solving. In M.L. Perlmutter (Ed.), *Cognitive perspectives on children's social and behavioral development: The Minnesota Symposium on Child Psychology* (Vol. 18, pp. 1–68). Mahwah, NJ: Lawrence Erlbaum Associates.

Russell, A., Pettit, G.S., & Mize, J. (1998, September). Horizontal qualities in parent–child relationships: Parallels with and possible consequences for children's peer relationships. *Developmental Review, 18*(3), 313–352.

Sackett, G.P. (Ed.). (1977). *Observing behavior, Vol. 1: Theory and applications in mental retardation.* Baltimore: University Park Press.

Schneider, B.H., Atkinson, L., & Tardif, C. (2001). Child–parent attachment and children's peer relations: A quantitative review. *Developmental Psychology, 37,* 86–100.

Sebanc, A.M. (2003). The friendship features of preschool children: links with prosocial behavior and aggression. *Social Development, 12,* 249–268.

Sigman, M., & Ruskin, E. (1999). Continuity and change in the social competence of children with autism, down syndrome, and developmental delays. *Monographs of the Society for Research in Child Development, 64,* (No.1, Serial no. 256).

Silberglitt, B. (2004). Beyond situational specificity and other hypothetical constructs: A practical approach to general outcome measurement of preschool social skill development. *Dissertation Abstracts International, 64*(10–A), 3595.

Spivak, G., & Shure, M.B. (1974). *Social adjustment of young children: A cognitive approach to solving real-life problems.* San Francisco: Jossey-Bass.

Squires, J., Bricker, D., & Twombly, E. (with Yockelson, S., Davis, M.S., & Kim, Y.). (2002). *Ages & Stages Questionnaires®: Social-Emotional (ASQ:SE): A parent-completed, child-monitoring system for social-emotional behaviors.* Baltimore: Paul H. Brookes Publishing Co.

Sutton, S.K., Burnette, C.P., Mundy, P., Meyer, J., Vaughn, A., Sanders, C., et al. (2005). Resting cortical brain activity and social behavior in higher functioning children with autism. *Journal of Child Psychology and Psychiatry, 46,* 211–222.

Ullman, C.A. (1957). Teachers, peers, and tests as predictions of adjustment. *Journal of Educational Psychology, 48,* 257–267.

Van Hecke, A.V., Mundy, P.C., Acra, C.F., Block, J.J., Delgado, C.E.F., Parlade, M.V., Meyer, J.A., Neal, A.R., & Pomares, Y.B. (2007). Infant joint attention, temperament, and social competence in preschool children. *Child Development, 78,* 53–69.

Vaughn, B.E., & Azria, M.R. (2000). Friendship and social competence in a sample of pre-school children attending Head Start. *Developmental Psychology, 36,* 326–338.

Vaughn, B.E., Colvin, T.N., Azria, M.R., Caya, L., & Krzysik, L. (2001). Dyadic analyses of friendship in a sample of preschool-age children attending Head Start: Correspondence between measures and implications for social competence. *Child Development, 72*(3), 862–878.

Vaughn, B.E., Vollenweider, M., Bost, K.K., Azria-Evans, M.R., & Snider, J.B. (2003). Negative interactions and social competence for preschool children in two samples: Reconsidering the interpretation of aggressive behavior for young children. *Merrill-Palmer Quarterly, 49,* 245–278.

Waas, G.A., & Graczyk, P.A. (1999). Child behaviors leading to peer rejection: A view from the peer group. *Child Study Journal, 29,* 291–306.

Walden, T., Lemerise, E., & Smith, M.C. (1999). Friendship and popularity in preschool classrooms. *Early Education and Development, 10,* 351–371.

Walker, H.M., & McConnell, S.R. (1995). *Walker-McConnell Scale of Social Competence and School Adjustment: Elementary version.* San Diego, CA: Singular.

Walker, H.M., Severson, H.H., & Feil, E. (1995). *Early screening project.* Longmont, CO: Sopris West.

Walker, S. (2005). Gender differences in the relationship between young children's peer-related social competence and individual differences in theory of mind. *Journal of Genetic Psychology, 166,* 297–312.

Watson, A.C., Nixon, C.L., & Capage, L. (1999). Social interaction skills and theory of mind in young children. *Developmental Psychology, 35,* 386–391.

Webster-Stratton, C., & Lindsay, D.W. (1999). Social competence and conduct problems in young children: Issues in assessment. *Journal of Clinical Child Psychology, 28*(1), 25–43.

Whitehurst, G.J., & Lonigan, C.J. (1998). Child development and emergent literacy. *Child Development, 69,* 848–872.

Wright, M. (1980). Measuring the social competence of preschool children. *Canadian Journal of Behavioral Science, 12,* 17–32.

Wolfberg, P., Zercher, P., Lieber, J., Capell, K., Matias, S., Hanson, M., & Odom, S.L. (1999). "Can I play with you?" Peer culture in inclusive preschool programs. *Journal of the Association for Persons with Severe Disabilities, 24,* 69–84.

CHAPTER 2

Family Roles in Young Children's Emerging Peer-Related Social Competence

JEANETTE A. MCCOLLUM AND MICHAELENE M. OSTROSKY

Social and emotional components of peer competence are inseparable from one another and from the contexts in which they occur (Saarni, 1999). Social components include skills such as the accurate interpretation of social situations and appropriate reactions to situations, whereas emotional components include children's internalized expectations about other people and about themselves as well as their affective stance toward social interaction (Halberstadt, Denham, & Dunsmore, 2001; Hubbard & Coie, 1994).

Understanding the sources of individual differences in social and emotional abilities is important. Social and emotional components develop through interactions and relationships with others. Given the importance of social competence to short- and long-term development in children with and without disabilities, it is critical to explore the origins of individual differences in peer interaction. The family, in which the earliest interactions and relationships occur, is a reasonable starting point for this exploration (Mills & Rubin, 1993).

SETTING THE CONTEXT FOR UNDERSTANDING FAMILY–PEER LINKAGES

The purpose of this chapter is to explore linkages between two arenas of social competence, family and peer, with a focus on linkages between one particular subsystem within the family (parent–child) and a child's relationships with peers. It is important to emphasize, however, that parent–child relationships are embedded within many different kinds of contexts that influence their characteristics but are seldom included as a part of the research on family–peer linkages. These include family system factors such as emotional climate and marital satisfaction, as well as individual characteristics of family members such as gender, age, and psychological well-being. Many family contexts may also be directly influenced by having a child with a disability (Guralnick, 2005). Parents' ideas and beliefs about children and parenting, including ideas that reflect cultural background, also influence what parents do with their children (Harkness & Super, 1995; Schneider, Smith, Poisson, & Kwan, 2000).

Children's development provides another important context for understanding parent–child and child–peer relationships. Expectations for social competence as well as linkages between family and peer would be expected to differ depending on children's ages and developmental abilities. Depending on the particular disability and/or its severity, children may have strengths and deficits or delays that are directly related to social interaction (e.g., visual or hearing impairment) or central to development of emotional understanding and social competence (e.g., cognition, communication). Disabilities also may influence important contributors to social competence such as attention regulation (Dawson et al., 2004; Kasari, Freeman, Mundy, & Sigman, 1995), emotion recognition (Kasari, Freeman, & Hughes, 2001), and use of words to express internal states (Beeghly & Cicchetti, 1997). Linkages between parent–child relationships and children's competence with their peers are embedded within both family and developmental contexts for all children.

How Research on Family–Peer Linkages Has Evolved

Although family and peer systems have each been important arenas of research for many years, it was only in the mid- to late 1980s that they began to be studied as integrated relational systems, or "interconnected spheres of influence" (Ladd, 1992a). The late 1980s and 1990s saw a flurry of activity in the study of family–peer linkages. As described by Parke and O'Neil (2000), early research on family–peer linkages was primarily descriptive, addressing the question of whether different aspects of social competence could be predicted by different aspects of parenting. This work established multiple direct linkages between the parent–child and the child–peer systems.

The primary focus of research on family–peer linkages then shifted to processes that might account for these direct linkages. Researchers hypothesized possible mediators based on theory as well as on studies of child characteristics that were predicted by both parent–child interactions and relationships and by differences in social competence. Researchers became interested in studying these variables as potential mediating processes that might account for all or most of the variance in family–peer linkages, with many studies using a series of statistical analyses recommended by Baron and Kenny (1986). Increasing attention also was given to variables (e.g., gender, age) that might moderate direct linkages between family relational predictors and children's social competence. Although little similar research has been conducted with children with disabilities to determine whether and under what conditions these same linkages apply, friendship development is a critical social and quality-of-life issue for children with disabilities. Parents want their children to develop friendships and are concerned that a lack of friendships may negatively influence the quality of their children's lives (Strully & Strully, 1996). Much can be learned from the larger literature on family–peer linkages in general, as well as from the smaller body of literature on children with disabilities, with respect to understanding the origins of individual differences in social competence.

Parameters of this Review

A useful distinction has been made in the literature between influences of the implicit, unintentional family environment and those of the more explicit, intentional family environment as each relates to peer competence. To capture this distinction, several reviews of this literature have used three "pathways" as an organizing framework (e.g., O'Neil & Parke, 2000; Parke & O'Neil, 1997, 1999a, 1999b). These pathways include 1) family interactions and relationships (with implicit links to social competence), 2) family supervision of peer interaction and direct teaching of peer interaction skills (with explicit links to social competence), and 3) family-provided opportunities for experiencing peer interactions. These three pathways are used as an organizer for this chapter, although many studies contain variables that fit in more than one. For each pathway, normative child development research is described, followed by related research with children with disabilities.

This chapter is not intended as a research synthesis. Rather, the purpose is to provide an overview and a sampling of approaches and findings based on our reading of this wide-ranging literature and to consider how this research has been or could be applied to children with disabilities. In our reading, we focused on work conducted from a normative child development perspective, excluding a parallel body of work on clinical populations. Most studies reviewed were conducted with young children, with the majority of the children falling between the ages of 3 and 6 years. To select studies to read, we began with existing reviews of this literature (Ladd, 1992a; Ladd, 1992b; Ladd, Le Sieur, & Profilet, 1993; Ladd & Pettit, 2002; Ladd, Profilet, & Hart, 1992; O'Neil & Parke, 2000; Parke, Burks, Carson, & Cassidy, 1992; Parke, Burks, Carson, Neville, & Boyum, 1994; Parke et al., 2004; Parke & O'Neil, 1997, 1999a, 1999b; Pettit & Mize, 1993). We used these reviews to identify active lines of research and then searched for more recently published articles and chapters. We also conducted hand searches, beginning in 1995, of the most common research journals in which the articles identified had appeared, as well as in the most common journals in early childhood special education (*Journal of Early Intervention, Topics in Early Childhood Special Education*). Finally, we searched Psych–Info (http://www.apa.org/psycinfo/) using combinations of the terms *family, parent, peer, interaction, attachment,* and *disability.* Almost all of the studies identified were quasi-experimental, using either correlational or cross-sectional designs, leaving open questions of direction of effects between parent behavior and child characteristics and outcomes as well as questions about the potential influences of other variables that were not measured or controlled in these studies.

Other studies on family–peer linkages exist and are relevant, but were not included due to space limitations. The studies selected are not necessarily the most current; instead, they were chosen to illustrate a range of research approaches and findings, thereby providing a broader base for thinking about application to children with disabilities.

PATHWAY 1: PARENT–CHILD INTERACTIONS AND RELATIONSHIPS

Pathway 1 relates to the *implicit* family environment. That is, family members are unlikely to think of their interactions with their child in relation to how these may influence the child's competence with peers (Ladd & Pettit, 2002). Interactions are part of everyday family life, and linkages to relationships with peers occur through the influences of these interactions on how the child approaches and engages in interactions with peers. Most of the literature on family–peer linkages fits within this pathway. In addition, most of the research under Pathway 1 has been conducted from one of two broad research perspectives: attachment or parenting style (de Koeyer, 2001; Ladd & Pettit, 2002).

The major variables studied in Pathway 1 are summarized in Table 2.1. The first column in the table shows the primary attachment and parenting style variables that have been of interest as predictors of social competence, whereas the last column illustrates the most common social competence outcome variables studied. In constructing this last column and in our review, we used a conservative definition of social competence based on the accomplishment of social goals such as having friends and engaging in effective interactions with others rather than defining social competence in terms of social skills development, as recommended by Hubbard and Coie (1994). Many of the attachment and parenting style variables in the first column have been shown to predict directly to one or more variables in the last column. The center column contains components of social competence such as

Table 2.1.   Pathway 1: Family relationship predictors of young children's social competence with peers

Relationship features of predictive variables	Potential mediators	Social competence with peers outcome variables
Attachment relationship	**Representations of relationships**	**Relationships**
Availability	Emotional representations	Popularity, peer status, social acceptance
Warmth	Emotional experience of self and others	Number and quality of friendships
Sensitivity	Expectations for relationships	
Responsiveness	Balance of connectedness and autonomy	**Components of social competence**
Developmental support		Frequency of interaction
Parenting style	**Emotional processes**	Prosocial abilities (positiveness, cooperativeness, helpfulness)
Emotional and affective quality	Regulating emotions	School adjustment
Warmth	Understanding emotion	
Expressiveness	Regulating affective expression	
Response to distress	Empathy	
Response to negativity and conflict	**Cognitive processes**	
Discussion of emotion	Cognitive representations	
Interactional synchrony	Attributions	
Responsiveness and connectedness	Beliefs	
Horizontal structure	Idea of "relationship"	
Approach to discipline	Social goals and strategies	
	Initiating, responding, maintaining	
	Solving problems	
	Resolving conflicts	
	Play scripts and skills	
	Sharing affect and understanding	
	Sharing event scripts	
	Coordinating action	
	Balancing turns and roles	

social skills and core psychological processes that have been studied as mediating or intermediate variables that are predicted by one or more variables in column one and/or predict one or more social competence outcomes in column three. Many of these also have been studied as mediators that account for linkages between family and peer variables. We have used the larger categories in the first column as an organizing framework for Pathway 1, recognizing that many of these variables occur together (Gottman, Fainsilber-Katz, & Hooven, 1997).

Parent–Child Attachment and Social Competence with Peers

Attachment theory posits that children develop emotional and cognitive resources to support relationships with peers within their early relationships with significant others. Emotional and cognitive understandings (i.e., representations, working models) of self and others are thought to contribute to children's expectations about interactions and relationships, both in particular relationships and in relationships in general (Crockenberg & Leerkes, 2000; Mills & Rubin, 1993).

The most common measures of parent–child attachment are the Strange Situation (Ainsworth & Wittig, 1969), typically used in studies of children ranging from approximately 12–24 months old, and the Attachment Q-Set (Waters & Deane, 1985), used thereafter. The Strange Situation is a standardized observational procedure in which children are placed in one of several attachment classifications (e.g., secure, insecure) based on observation of their behavior with their primary caregiver and a stranger, with a focus on reunion with the caregiver after a brief period of absence. The Attachment Q-Set is a Q-sort procedure in which the caregiver (or other adult familiar with the child) reviews a series of written statements and then places them into categories (e.g., *like/unlike my child*) indicating the extent to which they are characteristic of the child. Profiles are then compared with that of a securely attached child, yielding a continuous measure of attachment security.

Many studies have shown linkages between attachment security and different kinds of peer competence outcomes using both longitudinal and concurrent designs. In general, children who are more securely attached to their primary caregivers have more positive interactions with their peers in early childhood and are more likely to have friends (de Koeyer, 2001).

A large-scale, multi-measure, longitudinal study from infancy to adolescence illustrates the general findings from this research (Sroufe, Egeland, & Carlson, 1999). A basic premise of the study was that peer competence has its roots in patterns of interaction and regulation in the parent–child relationship, specifically in the motivational, attitudinal, emotional, and relational outcomes of this relationship. This study confirmed predictions of linkages between early attachment and later peer relationships at multiple points (i.e., preschool, middle childhood, and adolescence). Results for preschoolers indicated that children who were ranked highest in social competence by teachers were those with secure attachment histories, based on Strange Situation classifications at 12 and 18 months. Behavioral observations (e.g., involvement in positive play, frequency of agonistic encounters, expressions of positive and negative emotions) confirmed these rankings. In addition, longitudinal data indicated stability of individual differences in peer ratings to adolescence. Other longitudinal studies have shown similar relationships between attachment security and overall social competence as measured by peer nominations (e.g., Cohn, 1990) and parent and teacher ratings (e.g., Bohlin, Hagekull, &

Anderson, 2005). Longitudinal linkages also have been made to the quality of friendships with peers (Youngblade, Park, & Belsky, 1993).

Similar results have been found when attachment and social competence are measured at the same point in time. Most of these studies have been with preschoolers, using the Attachment Q-Set as the measure of attachment. In a study by DeMulder, Denham, Schmidt, and Mitchell (2000), observers completed a Q-Set on children after multiple observations during home visits. Security of attachment was negatively related to level of stress in the home (measured via a parent questionnaire) and positively related to attachment to teachers (also using the Q-Set) and peer competence outcomes that included anger–aggression (as rated by teachers) and popularity with peers (using a peer sociometric procedure). Overall, children who were less securely attached to their mothers showed more anger and aggression in preschool. Boys (but not girls) who were more securely attached to their mothers were also more attached to their teachers and were more popular with their peers. These researchers also found that higher levels of family stress were inversely related to social competence, but only for boys. Child gender as a moderator of attachment–peer linkages has been reported in other studies as well (e.g., Cohn, 1990; de Koeyer, 2001).

Other individual differences (in particular, psychological characteristics) may also make unique contributions to different aspects of peer competence. Using a concurrent design, Szewczyk-Sokolowski, Bost, and Wainwright (2005) found that, whereas attachment security (as measured by the Attachment Q-Set) and temperament (i.e., behavioral inhibition measured by maternal ratings) made unique contributions to children's peer acceptance, peer rejection (based on a peer sociometric procedure) was more strongly predicted by temperament. Bohlin and colleagues (2005) found that the effects of early attachment and children's behavioral inhibition together predicted social competence with peers more strongly than did either variable alone, such that children who were more securely attached and who were less inhibited were better accepted by peers. Out-of-home care also added to this prediction, with evidence that peers were more accepting of children who had more nonparental care. Some studies also indicate that stronger linkages are present when measures of attachment security are combined with other parent–child predictors. For example, in a short-term longitudinal study of children from 18–24 months of age, Fagot (1997) found unique contributions for attachment and for observed parent–child interaction (discussed in the next section) to the quality of responses that children received from their peers.

One hypothesized mediator in attachment theory of the link between attachment and peer competence is the *internal working model*, in other words, what children come to expect from social relationships through their experience with an attachment figure. Few researchers have studied working models as mediators. de Koeyer (2001) used a doll story completion task to measure children's experiences of the parent–child relationship and of the self. Results showed that although shared positive emotion, viewed as a major component of the attachment relationship, was positively related to peer acceptance in the classroom, this direct relationship no longer held when children's subjective experience of the parent–child relationship was examined as a mediator. de Koeyer thus found support for working models as mediators. However, contrary to prediction, subjective experience of self as measured in this study did not mediate this linkage. In two separate studies, Verschueren, Marcoen, and Schoefs (1996) found that 1) greater attachment security predicted children's internal model of the self, and 2) the quality of the internal model was positively related to peer competence. These studies, however, did not directly address the link between attachment and social competence with peers with the internal model as a mediator. Mediators outside of the realm of representations also have been identified in attachment studies, including *false belief* (ability to take another's perspective) (McElwain & Volling, 2004), a variable that would be hypothesized as a mediator by social learning theory.

Parent gender as well as child gender may moderate linkages between attachment and peer competence; moreover, parent and child gender may interact, such that links between attachment security and social competence may differ between, for example, father–girl pairs and mother–boy pairs (e.g., Verschueren & Marcoen, 1999). Attachment relationships with mothers and fathers may provide different types of social and emotional experiences that support different aspects of later peer relationships in boys and girls (Parke et al., 2004).

A review of 63 studies (Schneider, Atkinson, & Tardif, 2001) revealed that although the overall effect size for studies of attachment–peer competence linkages was significantly different from zero, it was in the small to moderate range (.20). Similar effect sizes were, however, apparent in almost all of the studies. The authors concluded that security of attachment may be only one influence on children's competence with peers.

Parenting Style and Social Competence with Peers

The second research tradition on linkages between early parent–child relationships and later peer competence has been referred to collectively as *parenting style* (e.g., Darling & Steinberg, 1993). Early work on parenting style used the broad dimensions of authoritative and authoritarian styles described by Baumrind (1973). Most studies of family–peer linkages have used somewhat more specific dimensions of style (such as supportive parenting), or even more specific aspects of parenting such as those in the first column of Table 2.1. The assumption underlying this literature is that parenting style, through everyday parent–child interactions, influences a child's ability to understand and interpret affective cues, regulate emotions, and learn appropriate interaction skills, any or all of which may contribute to the child's competence with peers (Parke et al., 1994). In social learning theory, on which much of this literature is based, the primary mechanisms through which characteristics of parent–child relationships are transferred to peer relationships are thought to be through children's learning (based on observation, experience, and reinforcement) of interactional approaches, scripts, and understandings that are then applied to interactions and relationships with peers.

In Table 2.1, parent characteristics and behaviors are grouped into three clusters that represent the primary types of style variables studied as predictors, and that are used to organize this discussion of the linkages between parenting style and peer competence: emotional and affective quality, interactional synchrony, and approach to discipline. Style variables have been measured in many different ways including coding of observations or transcripts, self-ratings, and Q-sorts.

Emotional and Affective Quality

Substantial literature links various aspects of parents' expression of emotion and warmth to children's peer relationships. As shown in Table 2.1, studies of emotional and affective quality can be loosely grouped into studies related to warmth, expressiveness, response to distress, response to negativity and conflict, and discussion of emotion.

Warmth   Studies of the emotions that parents express during parent–child interactions represent the largest group of studies within the work on family–peer linkages. Warmth or similar constructs such as being positive have been found to predict directly to a variety of child outcome measures including sociometric status (Putallaz, 1987), children's behavior with peers (Carson & Parke, 1996), social acceptance (Isley, O'Neil, & Parke, 1996), and broad composite measures of social competence (Isley, O'Neil, Catfelter, & Parke, 1999). In one of the first studies to link maternal warmth to children's relationships with peers, Putallaz found that maternal warmth toward children differed based on sociometric classifications obtained from peers, with more warmth being associated with higher peer ratings. Children with different sociometric classifications differed during lab-based inter-actions with a peer and with their mothers. Children tended to match the affective styles of their mothers (e.g., to be agreeable and positive or controlling and nega-tive), and to use these same styles with their peers.

Mediated linkages also have been found, with mediators representing both emotional and cognitive components. Isley and colleagues (1999) found that chil-dren's expressed affect (measured during physical play with parents) mediated the relationship between parental positive affect (measured using rating scales during physical play) and children's social competence (measured via sociometrics and teacher ratings). Direct relations also were found in which popular children, who expressed more positive affect with their parents during play, also expressed more positive affect with their peers. Relations to peer competence also were more direct (not mediated) for parents' expression of negative affect. Isley and colleagues inter-preted this to mean that expression of negative affect may represent a more gener-ally negative parent–child relationship. Moderator effects for both parent and child gender were found such that both mediated and direct linkages were stronger in parent–child dyads of the same gender. These results replicated gender effects reported in an earlier study (Isley et al., 1996) in which parental affect and control predicted children's classroom acceptance; in that study, the most powerful pre-dictor of acceptance was fathers' positive affect, particularly for boys. Children's empathy also has been found to mediate between parental warmth and peer com-petence (Zhou et al., 2002).

Expressiveness   Researchers also have emphasized *emotional intensity*, or a gen-eral tendency to express emotions (Eisenberg et al., 2001). Several studies indicate that highly expressive families have children who are also highly expressive and who are socially competent with their peers (Boyum & Parke, 1995; Cassidy, Parke, Butkovsky, & Braungart, 1992). Boyum and Parke studied the relationship between family emotional expressiveness (i.e., frequency of exposure to affective displays), measured through videotaped observations at home, and children's sociometric rat-ings by peers and teacher ratings at school. Parents also completed questionnaires about their own expressiveness. Videotapes were coded for frequency and type of affect between different pairs of dyads (e.g., child–parent, parent–parent). Positive linkages were found between family expressiveness and peer competence; in addi-tion, intensity of fathers' positive expressiveness was the best predictor of higher sociometric ratings for boys, whereas intensity of mothers' positive expressiveness was the best predictor for girls. Eisenberg and colleagues also found relationships to child competence and differential effects for positive and negative emotion. In this study, the relations between mothers' expressed emotion and children's externalizing behavior and social competence were mediated by children's self-regulation (as measured during a puzzle task and from parent and teacher reports).

Response to Distress   Parents' styles of responding to children's distress, another variable related to emotional and affective quality, also have been linked to peer competence outcomes. Roberts and Strayer (1987) found that children whose parents responded to distress with situationally appropriate actions viewed their parents' actions as pragmatic; in addition, children who viewed their parents' responses as pragmatic were rated as more competent by their teachers, based on a Q-sort procedure. Observations of greater parental encouragement of expression of emotion during home visits, as well as self-reports of fathers' encouragement of emotional expression, also were related to higher child competence ratings. Parental warmth and response to distress, measured as separate constructs, were related; however, each was independently predictive of different aspects of social competence.

In a study of 6- to 8-year-old children (Davidov & Grusec, 2006), affect regulation was explored as a mediator between parental response to distress and warmth as predictors (based on observations during free play and data gathered via a warmth scale and coded essays) and peer competence (peer acceptance as perceived by child; teacher report of peer acceptance). Affect regulation was measured by observing children's reactions to simulated pain expressed by an adult researcher and via a child interview using vignettes of peer distress. Differential effects were found for response to distress and for warmth. Higher rates of responding to distress by both mothers and fathers predicted better regulation of negative affect. Mothers' responses to distress also predicted more empathic and prosocial responding by children (based on teacher report), whereas maternal warmth was positively related to better regulation of positive affect. In boys, warmth also predicted greater peer acceptance. Regulation of positive affect mediated between warmth and boys' peer acceptance, whereas regulation of negative affect mediated between mothers' response to distress and boys' and girls' empathic responding with peers. In both of these studies (Davidov & Grusec; Roberts & Strayer, 1987), effects were moderated by child and parent gender. In the latter study, age and temperament were also explored as moderators, although neither changed the relationships among predictors, mediators, and outcomes.

Response to Negative Emotion and Conflict   Parents' positive responses to conflict and to children's negative emotions may also be important in helping children learn effective behaviors. Conversely, parents' negative or harsh responses to children's negative emotions may teach children to suppress negative emotions, which may in turn influence children's ability to regulate their affect in ways that are appropriate to a situation (Fabes, Leonard, Kupanoff, & Martin, 2001). Carson and Parke (1996) used a physical play paradigm in the laboratory to study the relationship between mothers' and fathers' responses to their children's negative affect and teacher ratings of the same children's peer competence. Videotapes were coded on a second-by-second basis to study sequences of negative affect within the interaction. Fathers who were more likely to respond negatively to their children's negative affect displays had children who shared less, were more verbally aggressive with other children, and avoided other children in the classroom. Children who were more likely to respond negatively to their fathers' negative affect also were rated as being more physically aggressive with their peers. Mothers' responses were unrelated to peer competence.

Using naturalistic observations of family disputes in the homes of children who were 33 months old and then again of children's management of conflicts with a friend when these children were 72 months old, Herrera and Dunn (1997) found that maternal and sibling argument styles affected the children's ability to manage conflicts with peers. When a mother's arguments were related to her own needs, strategies with peers were negatively affected; when a mother's or a sibling's arguments considered the child's needs, strategies with peers were positively affected. Modeling a constructive argument style, rather than an absence of argument or nonresponsive argument style, may support children in learning skills for managing peer conflict.

Discussion of Emotion Closely related to response to negative emotion and conflict is a small body of research indicating that the extent to which parents openly discuss their children's emotions may promote young children's competence with peers. Many of parents' daily conversations with their children are about emotions (Dunn, Bretherton, & Munn, 1987), including discussion of emotions within the context of talking about peers (Laird, Pettit, Mize, Brown, & Lindsey, 1994). Children who hear and engage in more *emotion talk* with parents tend to use more emotion talk and understand emotions better than do children who do not hear and engage in emotion talk (Laible, 2004; Taumoepeau & Ruffman, 2006). They also tend to be better able to regulate their own emotions (Dunn & Brown, 1994; Dunn & Munn, 1985), and to be better at affective perspective-taking (Dunn, Brown, & Bearsall, 1991). No studies were found that directly tested linkages between everyday parent–child emotion talk and peer competence. However, young children who talk about feelings with other children also demonstrate more cooperative behavior with peers (Brown, Donelan-McCall, & Dunn, 1996). Children's understanding of emotions and the ability to describe appropriate causes of emotions have been linked to greater peer acceptance as well (Cassidy et al., 1992; Denham et al., 2003; Denham, Zoller, & Couchoud, 1994).

Interactional Synchrony

Research on *interactional synchrony*, the next cluster of variables in Table 2.1, emphasizes the dyadic nature of parent–child interaction rather than the characteristics of individual partners. Harrist and Waugh regard synchrony as dyadic interaction that is "mutually regulated, reciprocal, and harmonious" (2002, p. 557). Sensitivity and contingent responsiveness to a child's cues are thought to be critical to establishing synchrony, whereas directiveness and control are believed to disrupt dyadic synchrony. Some studies have found dyadic variables to be more powerful predictors of peer competence than interactive characteristics of the parent alone (e.g., de Koeyer, 2001). Two perspectives on dyadic predictors are explored below.

Responsiveness and Connectedness Harrist, Pettit, Dodge, and Bates (1994) used three dyadic states, based on observed engagement, affect, and connectedness, to describe the relationship between parent–child interaction and teacher-rated competence in kindergartners. These states included positive synchrony (interaction episodes were extended, non-negative, and connected), negative synchrony (episodes were extended, reciprocal interactions with negative tone), and nonsynchrony (episodes were low in connectedness and contingent social exchanges). A parent measure of children's aggression was obtained prior to kindergarten and was used to select a range of children based on high, medium, and low scores. Two home observations were then conducted, with written narratives made of all social interactions involving the child. These narratives were rated using the dyadic states noted above. Social competence was measured later in kindergarten using sociometric ratings by peers, observations of children, and teacher questionnaires. Dyadic style was found to be related to social competence variables for 11 of 18 comparisons. Higher teacher-rated competence was predicted by high levels of positive synchrony and lower levels of nonsynchrony. Peer-rated competence, however, was not related to mother–child synchrony.

In a set of two studies, Mize and Pettit (1997) defined dyadic synchrony as a combination of contingent responsiveness, warmth, and joint pleasure in the interaction. Parents' coaching strategies (Pathway 2, described next) also were included as a predictor. In Study 1, dyadic style and coaching contributed uniquely to teacher ratings of peer acceptance. In addition, there was a relationship between the two measures such that when the parent–child relationship was less responsive, coaching contributed to lower levels of boys' aggression with peers (i.e., under certain conditions, coaching partially moderated the effects of dyadic style). When dyadic synchrony was high, few gender differences were found. In Study 2, which included a more diverse sample of dyads, only style accounted for a significant portion of the variance in peer acceptance. The researchers concluded that style may be a stronger predictor for boys, whereas coaching may be stronger for girls. Overall, these studies demonstrated the predictive value of dyadic style but also found moderating effects for gender and for dyadic style.

Horizontal Structure   One feature of interaction that can only be studied with the dyad as a unit is the balance between parent and child. In the previous sections, several studies were cited that illustrated the influence of horizontality with respect to linkages between matching of positive or negative emotion and social competence with peers (e.g., Carson & Parke, 1996). Other studies have examined horizontality from the perspective of control or directiveness (e.g., Isley et al., 1996). A number of researchers have noted that parent–child play may be an ideal context for examining family–peer linkages because it elicits horizontal qualities, and over time, should support the child in taking on horizontal roles in peer play (e.g., Barth & Parke, 1993; MacDonald & Parke, 1984; Russell, Pettit, & Mize, 1998). Children also may learn roles and scripts for particular kinds of play (e.g., pretend and physical play) that they are likely to engage in with peers. Parent–child play, particularly physical play with the father, may provide an important context in which children learn to regulate their emotions (Parke et al., 2004).

Lindsey and Mize (2000) used pretend play and physical play settings to examine the role of emotion knowledge and self-efficacy (sense of own ability) as potential mediators of the relationship between mutual dyadic variables and peer competence. The dyadic measure used was mutual compliance or responsiveness (the extent to which parent and child responded to one another's initiations). Interactions in both play settings were observed in a laboratory. Mutual responsiveness in both situations was positively associated with social competence, as was emotion knowledge. In both settings, dyadic measures predicted children's social competence even after controlling for individual parent and child behavior, although results were stronger in pretend play than in physical play. Neither emotion knowledge nor self-efficacy was found to mediate the relationship between mutual responsiveness and peer competence. However, effects were moderated by parent gender, such that greater mother–child responsiveness in both pretend and physical play was associated with higher ratings of social competence by teachers, whereas father–child responsiveness predicted higher ratings of social competence only for physical play, and was linked to peer sociometric scores.

Approach to Discipline

In a review of the literature linking discipline and social competence, Ladd and Pettit (2002) noted that much of the more recent information comes from larger interactional studies in which some aspect of discipline (e.g., harsh control) is included as one variable, making it difficult to separate disciplinary style from other aspects of the parent–child relationship or to isolate the child outcomes that are affected. In general, however, more authoritative, inductive, and supportive approaches to discipline have been related to children's prosocial behavior and vice versa. Parents' disciplinary goals and strategies may directly model or reward specific behavioral patterns which, when learned, become part of children's behavioral style with peers (Rubin & Burgess, 2002; Sigel & McGillicuddy-DeLisi, 2002). Discipline also may affect children's peer competence more indirectly through the same cognitive and emotional processes discussed above and shown in the center column of Table 2.1.

An early study by Pettit, Dodge, and Brown (1988) included harshness of discipline as a predictor and children's social problem solving as a potential mediator of peer competence. Results showed that the effects of harsh discipline and exposure to aggressive models on children's social competence were mediated by children's social problem-solving skills. Bates, Pettit, Dodge, and Ridge (1998) found that restrictive parenting was positively related to externalizing behavior only under some conditions, and hypothesized that control may predict to poor outcomes only when that control is negative, as would be the case in harsh parenting. Children at 5 years of age with resistant temperaments who experienced restrictive control had higher ratings of externalizing at 7–11 years than did children with resistant temperaments who experienced less restrictive control; thus, in this study, temperament moderated the relationship between restrictive control and externalizing behavior. Child and parent gender also have been found to moderate linkages between disciplinary style and social competence (Casas et al., 2006; Crockenberg & Lourie, 1996). Children's expectations about the effects of using power-assertive methods for resolving conflict with peers are another potential moderator of this linkage (Hart, Ladd, & Burleson, 1990).

Ladd and Pettit concluded that the associations between discipline and social competence have been "limited in scope and not particularly strong" (2002, p. 277). Nevertheless, findings have been consistent across many studies; the harsher the parenting, the more likely it is that children are aggressive or externalizing in social situations, although with less harsh control, this effect may be moderated by child temperament and gender or by parent gender.

Pathway 1 Linkages in Children with Disabilities

Preschoolers with a broad range of disabilities have been reported to be less socially competent than their peers who are typically developing, and they have been found to have fewer friends (e.g., Freeman & Kasari, 1998; Guralnick, Hammond, Connor, & Neville, 2006; McConnell, 2002). The research reported previously indicates that individual differences among children in levels of social competence and in the quantity and quality of friendships are at least partially predicted by family interactions and relationships. However, virtually no normative research has been conducted that directly seeks to establish linkages between parent–child relationship variables in children with established disabilities and children's social competence with peers.

Research on linkages has important implications for considering influences on the social competence of children with disabilities because it places social competence within a developmental framework. In addition, it points toward the types of research that need to be conducted and toward hypotheses that need to be explored. The presence of a disability has been found to influence the characteristics of both attachment (e.g., Atkinson et al., 1999) and parent–child interaction (e.g., McCollum & Bair, 1994). Particular disabilities (with Down syndrome and autism being the most studied) may also directly influence core (potentially mediating) processes (e.g., Bieberich & Morgan, 1998; Kasari & Sigman, 1996; Sigman & Ruskin, 1999). Based on the literature above, however, it is also likely that parent–child relationships and interactions are related to social competence with peers, and to mediating processes, in ways that go beyond the direct influence of the disability.

Based on linkages that have been established among the variables in Table 2.1, the primary reasons for also exploring these linkages in children with disabilities are the following: 1) individual differences in parent–child interaction and relationship variables have been found to predict to individual differences in at least some of these processes/mediators, and 2) some of the latter have been found to predict to social competence outcomes with peers. A study by Siller and Sigman (2002) with children with autism illustrates the first linkage. In this study, parents who demonstrated high synchronization with their children during play interactions had children who demonstrated higher levels of joint attention and language. Results from intervention studies also show this relationship. A study by Mahoney and Perales (2003) demonstrated positive changes in children's attention, cooperation, initiation, joint attention, and affect following intervention to encourage parents' responsive interaction; as shown in Table 2.1, each of these is also a potential mediator of children's social competence with peers. Changes also were found in standardized measures of social-emotional functioning (as rated by mothers). It should be noted that most intervention studies of this type measure change in children only within the context of parent–child interaction; rarely are changes studied in other contexts or with standardized measures.

Travis, Sigman, and Ruskin (2001) provided an example of the second linkage between intermediate processes/skills and social competence with peers. They found that in children with autism, higher levels of initiating joint attention and of empathy were related to higher levels of engagement with peers on the playground as well as to more prosocial behavior during a laboratory task. Intervention studies also can be used to demonstrate this second linkage, from intermediate process/skill to social competence. For example, after an intervention to increase social-emotional understanding and social-interpersonal problem solving, high-functioning children with autism (ages 8–17 years old) not only provided more relevant solutions to social situations and more examples of complex emotions but they also received higher social skills scores from teachers. There is certainly reason to believe that a focus on similar potential mediators in young children, and within the family context, would also be related to changes in social competence.

Thus, although searching for family–peer linkages in children with disabilities may be difficult because of direct influences of the disability on both parent–child relationships and on core psychological processes, research indicates that it is important to do so in order to understand the origins of social competence in children with disabilities. Interventions can then be designed with these origins in mind.

PATHWAY 2: PARENT AS SUPERVISOR AND ADVISOR

Pathway 1 addressed different aspects of the largely unintended influence of parent–child interaction and relationships on children's competence with their peers. In Pathway 2, based on many fewer studies, parents intentionally, directly, and explicitly seek to influence their children's peer interactions by supervising and advising the child's interactions.

Lollis, Ross, and Tate (1992) described two broad types of roles that parents take during their children's interactions and play with their peers. The first of these is *interactive intervention*, in which the parent participates in peer play as a play partner, helping the flow of the interaction by establishing turn taking, maintaining children's interest in their peers or in play, prompting specific behaviors, and/or preventing conflicts or disruptions. Several studies indicate that interactive intervention may be related to children's competence with peers. Bhavnagri and Parke (1985, 1991) studied various aspects of children's interactions with unfamiliar peers given particular kinds of parental interventions. Results of the initial studies indicated that children achieved higher levels of social competence during times when mothers were more involved; however, the effect was temporary, with the level of social competence returning to baseline when mothers did not participate. These researchers also found greater gains in competence with younger as compared with older children (Bhavnagri, 1987; Bhavnagri & Parke, 1991). Younger children also benefited more from parent intervention strategies related to initiating and turn taking, and older children benefited more from assistance with maintaining play. These effects were replicated with both mothers and fathers as partners (Bhavnagri, 1987; Bhavnagri & Parke, 1991).

In *directive intervention*, the parent is an observer/director rather than an active participant (Lollis et al., 1992). Finnie and Russell (1988) selected two groups of children based on teachers' rating of differences in social status and then paired them for play with two unfamiliar children of average status. Mothers of children from high- and low-status groups were asked to give as much or as little assistance as they thought necessary to help their children join in the play. Three sets of maternal behaviors were coded: helping the child gain entry, facilitating or maintaining interaction, and dealing with conflict. Strategies that appeared to support interactive play included encouraging cooperation, participating in the activity, and validating children's interactions and play. Less skillful strategies included disrupting ongoing interaction, redirecting children to a new activity, and power assertive discipline. Mothers of more popular children used more of what the authors called *skillful strategies,* and vice versa. To investigate whether differences between groups might reflect mothers' ideas about appropriate strategies, mothers were asked about the advice they would give their children about peer interaction in hypothetical situations. Mothers of children with high social status talked more about positive, direct strategies, whereas mothers of children considered low status talked more about avoidance and vague or unspecific strategies.

In addition to participating in or supervising peer play, parents also may serve as advisors or consultants through conversations about peer interaction that occur outside of that context (i.e., "decontextualized" interventions, Lollis et al., 1992). For example, parents may engage children in conversations about how to manage conflicts, or they may help children think about how they could have resolved previous conflicts. A number of researchers have observed parent–child dyads talking about videotaped vignettes of peer dilemmas to obtain information on how parents might counsel their children about peers. Mize and Pettit (1997) asked mothers to use "prompted coaching" (i.e., using the vignettes to coach their children on what they should do in this situation) to help their children interpret and determine an appropriate response to videotaped dilemmas. Coaching of social behaviors also was observed in an unstructured situation during laboratory visits and sociometric measures were obtained in the children's classrooms. Relationship style also was rated. Both coaching (extent to which parent framed events in a nonhostile manner and endorsed friendly, outgoing strategies) and relationship style (synchrony and warmth) were positively associated with peer acceptance; however, only coaching children to use positive strategies was a significant predictor of lower teacher ratings of aggression. However, both relationship style and child gender moderated the correlation between coaching and aggression; positive coaching more strongly predicted lower levels of aggression when the relationship style was less responsive. However, this moderation occurred only in boys, not in girls.

The different contexts in which parents interact with or serve as coaches or advisors may give their children different kinds of peer-relevant skills. Pettit, Brown, Mize, and Lindsey (1998) compared parental behavior in three different interactive settings (parent–child play, involvement in child–peer play, and decontextualized social coaching) in relation to children's peer competence. Parents' behavior in the various settings predicted differently with regard to preschoolers' social competence; specific relationships between context and competence also varied depending on the gender of parent and child and in relation to particular outcomes. The authors concluded that dyadic play involvement and coaching may present different opportunities for socializing, and that these may function differently depending on the gender of the child and parent.

Pathway 2 Linkages in Children with Disabilities

The developmental literature described previously indicates that the quality of children's interactions with peers, an important step toward friendship, may be related to roles that parents take as supervisors, coaches, and advisors. Few studies have directly addressed these roles in families of children with disabilities. In one study of peer networks among boys with developmental delays and communication disorders as well as among boys without disabilities, Guralnick (1997) found that mothers primarily used indirect strategies such as monitoring, although mothers of the boys with developmental delays monitored more frequently than did mothers of boys who had communication disorders or who were typically developing. This finding was replicated in a later study that included both boys and girls (Guralnick, Connor, Neville, & Hammond, 2002). In this study, watching and checking on play occurred significantly more often for children with developmental delays than for children with communication disorders or children without disabilities.

It is possible, then, that mothers of children with certain types of delays may feel less comfortable leaving their children alone with peers. Similar to parents in the Pathway 2 studies reported previously, interviews with mothers of children with disabilities (Geisthardt, Brotherson, & Cook, 2002) indicated that their supervision of peer interactions was primarily indirect, with intervention occurring mainly when there was a disagreement. Parents also reported increased safety concerns when their children were invited to play at someone else's home, feeling safe to leave them only if they knew that others were willing to provide extra supervision. Perhaps due to the broader nature of the questions asked, these parents did not talk about specific strategies they might use to support their children's peer play.

Guralnick, Neville, Connor, and Hammond (2003) studied the strategies that mothers of young children with mild, primarily cognitive delays reported that they would use during their children's peer interactions. Strategies were quantified as to the amount of control exerted on the interaction, with the latter being rated on a 5-point scale from *nondirective* to *directive*, based on coding transcripts of interviews with mothers. Because response variability was limited for two of the social tasks to which mothers were asked to respond (i.e., making friends and being accepted into a new group), only responses related to the social task of sharing were used to measure control. Similar to the studies reviewed previously, degree of control predicted peer competence, with high control predicting lower competence. Interestingly, two of the scale points (3 and 4) appear to have been defined in terms reflective of increased scaffolding, which might be expected to support social competence in some children with disabilities (McCollum & Bair, 1994). In the same study, degree of child risk, indexed by cognitive and language development, was negatively related to children's social competence with peers. Because the analysis predicted only in one direction (from parent control to child competence), it is possible that higher control reflected parental responses to lower child competence. This interpretation is consistent with research on parent–child interaction indicating that directiveness by the parent may be an adaptive response to the child's need for support in accomplishing social or cognitive goals of interaction (Marfo, Dedrick, & Barbour, 1998; McCollum & Bair, 1994).

Given the social skills difficulties that many children with disabilities may have, indirect supervision may not be the most effective way for parents to support their children's peer interactions. Drawing on the literature described, it may be that parents who assume more interactive roles in their children's play enable children to enact and learn higher level playing and social skills. As noted by Guralnick (1999), the child–child interaction context is much less predictable and more complex than the parent–child context, and peers are much less likely to adapt to the idiosyncrasies of children with disabilities. More direct parental support may provide the conditions necessary to enable children to negotiate these complexities while practicing higher level peer skills. Guidance for parent support strategies is available from the literature reviewed previously, in other words, those strategies used by parents of socially competent children (e.g., Mize, Pettit, & Brown, 1995). In addition, the literature contains many examples of naturalistic strategies that have been used to support peer interactions (e.g., Kohler, Anthony, Steighner, & Hoyson, 2001). Parents could find these strategies useful as they support their children's peer interactions at home and in the community.

Parents' beliefs about how children develop, as well as about the modifiability of their own children's development, may influence the extent to which they supervise and coach their children during peer interaction (Mize et al., 1995). For example, Booth (1999) found that mothers of children with disabilities were likely to attribute their children's social competence to traits or dispositions related to their child's disability. Although other attributions also may influence parents' beliefs, attributions related to specific disabilities add another layer of complexity that may be based at least partially on a lack of knowledge about the modifiability of peer social skills. Unless parents believe that they can influence their child's peer relationships, and unless they have knowledge of strategies to use, their motivation to do so will be limited (Guralnick, 1999).

PATHWAY 3: PARENTS AS PROVIDERS OF SOCIAL OPPORTUNITIES

Many studies indicate that children gain important benefits from interactions with other children outside of the family (Ladd & Pettit, 2002). Pathway 3 refers to ways in which parents directly or indirectly provide their children with opportunities for peer interaction. Whereas characteristics of neighborhoods and other community settings in which children and families live and participate influence play and friendship patterns among children, parents also make purposeful choices that provide their children with access to peers. For example, when families consider where to live, they may consider the number of children who live in the neighborhood and factors such as availability of parks where children are likely to gather. Moreover, although parents may put their children in preschool for many reasons, they may view the socialization opportunities provided by preschool as beneficial to their children. Parents' own social networks also create opportunities for children to meet peers. Cochran and Niego (1995) found a 30%–44% overlap in 6-year-old children's and their mothers' social networks. The social networks of parents of slightly older children may influence both the number (Uhlendorff, 2000) and the quality (Simpkins & Parke, 2001) of children's friendships.

Parents also directly facilitate children's opportunities to interact with peers by increasing access to specific playmates (Ladd et al., 1992). Although there have been relatively few studies of the ways in which parents directly help children bridge the world of family and the world of peers, two studies by Ladd and colleagues illustrate the relationship between parents' initiation of peer contacts and preschoolers' peer competence. Ladd and Golter (1988) studied children's peer competence in relation to parents' efforts at initiating peer contacts. A telephone interview procedure was used to collect descriptive information about peer contacts occurring over several days; for each peer contact, information was collected on who initiated the contact and the location and duration of play. Data on the proportion of contacts initiated by children and parents were then derived. Measures of peer relationships included social behavior (classroom observations) as well as peer status (a nomination procedure) and likeability (peer ratings), collected both in preschool and later in kindergarten. Teacher perceptions of social competence and maladjustment also were collected using standardized measures. About half of the parents in the sample indicated that they initiated play contacts for their preschoolers, although the number of initiations varied widely. Parents who were "high initiators" had children with a larger number of playmates and more frequent play experience. No differences were found between groups for broad measures of social competence or for maladjustment. However, sons (but not daughters) of parents who were high initiators were better liked and less rejected than children of parents who were low initiators. Initiating and type of monitoring, although not highly correlated, both predicted to social competence, particularly to social status.

In a replication by Ladd and Hart (1992), comparisons of parent versus child initiations indicated that children who initiated more of their own peer contacts outside of school were better liked by peers and demonstrated less anxious behavior in school; in boys, however, parent initiation also was related to greater peer acceptance. The degree to which parents involved children in the process of arranging their own informal peer contacts was also positively related to how often children initiated their own contacts.

Pathway 3 Linkages in Children with Disabilities

Parents are very interested in their children's peer friendships, and believe it is important to guide their children in developing friends (Geisthardt et al., 2002). Like other parents, parents of children with disabilities also determine many of the circumstances under which their young children come in contact with other children (Stoneman, 1993).

A qualitative study of preschool children's peer communities outside of the school context found that children's contacts with others in their communities occurred through multiple social networks including neighborhoods, extended family, and family friends (Beckman et al., 1998). A sense of community and interconnections across contexts were found to influence the quality of social networks for families of children with and without disabilities. All families also reported using deliberate strategies to promote their children's interactions with peers, depending on the interests of their children and the resources available. Families also reported the same kinds of barriers to peer interaction including neighborhood safety, limited resources, and family schedules. Despite these many similarities, families of children with disabilities reported both additional strategies and challenges. For example, special events (e.g., basketball games) were used as a way to entice another child's participation in a joint activity, and families reported making physical adaptations to play spaces to accommodate their children's disabilities. Special challenges also were reported. For example, early intervention programs located outside of the neighborhood limited interconnections among potential sources of friends across home and school as well as maximizing time spent in transit and loss of time for play. Challenges related to children's disabilities (e.g., behavioral problems) were mentioned as a barrier to participating in some community and neighborhood settings. In a study of boys with developmental delays and a matched group of boys with communication disorders, Guralnick (1997) found more limited peer networks for both groups as compared with a matched group of boys without disabilities. As in the study by Geisthardt and colleagues (2002), linkages across school and community settings were less frequent in these groups, such that boys with disabilities had fewer peers who were in both settings. Thus, children with disabilities may require greater assistance from family members to connect with peers and establish friendships outside of the school context (Turnbull, Pereira, & Blue-Banning, 1999).

In their study of friendships of children ages 3–10 in their homes and neighborhoods, Geisthardt and colleagues (2002) conducted interviews and home observations to develop themes that appeared to characterize families' experiences. Parents reported that children with disabilities spent less time with peers than did their younger or older siblings, as well as less time than other children their age; those spending the most time with peers had primarily physical as compared with cognitive disabilities. Many parents reported a variety of ways to increase peer opportunities, although some parents did not report efforts to enhance their own child's peer relationships (with several appearing to accept their child's lack of friends as inevitable). Strategies reported were similar to those of children without disabilities such as choosing neighborhoods with many children, getting to know neighbors, involving the child in community groups, inviting other children to parties, and arranging play dates with classmates. Parents also reported advocating to have their children placed in neighborhood schools so that they would have access to the same children at home as at school. Several parents in this study also discussed the importance of cousins as playmates for their children. As noted by Turnbull and colleagues (1999), siblings' friends also create opportunities for contact with peers when they are invited over for playdates.

Guralnick and colleagues (2002) interviewed mothers about their efforts to arrange play opportunities for their young children (both boys and girls) with developmental delays, with communication disorders, and without disabilities. Differences were found among the three groups with respect to the frequency with which children played with peers, with children who were typically developing having the most frequent contact and children with developmental delays the least. Mothers of children who were typically developing arranged play situations more often than either of the other two groups, although most children in each group had invited peers to their homes within the past month. In a subsequent study, Guralnick and colleagues (2003) examined linkages between arranging efforts and peer competence for children with developmental delays; unlike the studies by Ladd and colleagues reviewed above, no statistically significant relationships were found between parents' efforts to arrange peer contact and children's social competence. Only child risk, parent stress, and parent control (described under Pathway 2) predicted children's competence with peers, all negatively. Further studies are needed to determine whether, how, and why children's disability may moderate this linkage.

Overall, these studies indicate that although children with disabilities may have less extended social networks, their families care about their networks and spend time trying to provide them with social opportunities. Given that social roles and social rules must be learned in context and play themes practiced repeatedly so they can be expanded to incorporate an ever-increasing set of cognitive and social variations, limited experience with peers almost certainly affects social competence.

DISCUSSION AND IMPLICATIONS

This chapter provides an overview of research related to three potential pathways through which families directly and indirectly influence their children's relationships with peers: parent–child relationships, supervising and coaching interactions with peers, and providing opportunities to interact with peers. By far the majority of work on linkages between family and peer relational systems has been conducted within the first pathway of indirect influences. Across all pathways the majority of research has been conducted with children who do not have disabilities. The results indicate that family interactions and relationships influence children's social competence in many ways. Furthermore, some portion of the family–peer linkage likely occurs through mediating processes in the child that are influenced by these interactions and relationships, although specific processes that consistently emerge as mediators have been difficult to isolate (Mize, Pettit, & Meece, 2000).

Each of the pathways offers a potentially fruitful avenue for future research directed toward understanding the origins of peer relationships in children with disabilities as well as for developing useful interventions. Nevertheless, this literature suffers from a number of methodological and conceptual limitations. Methodologically, much of this research has been either correlational or cross-sectional, although efforts have been made in some studies to rule out alternative hypotheses related to interpreting the direction of effects, primarily through the use of longitudinal designs. Interactions are by nature bi-directional, with each partner influencing the other (Patterson & Fisher, 2002). Not only do parents interact differently with children of different genders or age but also they adapt to individual differences in children's interactive styles. Studies have shown that at least some of these differences in parental interaction reflect adaptations that benefit children's learning and development (Landry, Garner, Pirie, & Swank, 1994; McCollum & Bair, 1994). Only one study was found in which experimentally induced changes in parent–child interaction were linked to changes in children's peer competence (LaFreniere & Capuano, 1997). Thus, whereas at a broad level the literature points toward parental influences on the child, additional research is needed to understand how this process works at the individual child level and how a disability may moderate these relationships.

A second methodological issue is that the way in which variables have been conceptualized, defined, and measured has not been consistent across studies. As described by Pettit and Mize (1993), this research has been characterized by a myopic focus on single socialization strategies. Although the research presents a cohesive picture of linkages, specific linkages and how they fit within a more general picture of parent–child interactions and relationships need further study. Finally, very little research has been conducted with children with disabilities. Research within Pathway 1 may be particularly difficult because of the influence of the child's disability on characteristics of parent–child interaction as well as on core developmental processes that may mediate family–peer linkages.

Several conceptual issues also arise with respect to interpreting this research both in general and in relation to young children with disabilities. First, congruent with our concern for the lack of common measures across studies, it is difficult to separate out specific aspects of parent–child relationships or interactions that account for the linkages. Instead, it is likely that many of the predictor variables are related to one another; clusters of behaviors, rather than individual behaviors, may be better predictors. This was illustrated in some of the studies reviewed in which attachment and interaction variables each added unique contributions to predictions of social competence

Second, parental beliefs may be an important part of these clusters. Parents may have a meta-emotion philosophy about their own and their children's emotions that provides a guide to how they think about goals for social competence and how their own behaviors and children's characteristics relate to these outcomes

(Gottman, Fainsilber-Katz, & Hooven, 1996, 1997). Beliefs, including those related to culture (Harkness & Super, 1995), remain a relatively unexplored part of the parent–child relational system as it applies to the development of peer competence.

Third, no one mediator has been found to account for all or even most of the linkages between family and peer interactions and relationships. Rather, multiple cognitive, emotional, and social skill mediators appear to be involved (O'Neil & Parke, 2000; Parke et al., 1992). Like the attachment and style variables, these are likely to occur in clusters; thus, no one mediator appears to be the only or even primary key to explaining family–peer linkages as defined by Baron and Kenny (1986), although some variables have consistently been found to explain at least part of the variance. Fourth, a number of variables have been found that moderate linkages, such that what predicts family–peer linkages has been demonstrated to vary depending on child and/or parent gender, child age, and psychological characteristics (primarily temperament) in the child. Although these effects have not been found in all studies, they have been demonstrated in enough studies to indicate that processes that link family relationships and children's social competence may differ depending on particular characteristics of parent and/or child. Differences in linkages based on gender in particular have been found in many studies. These studies indicate that boys and girls may have different types of relationships with their mothers and fathers and that different types of interactions may provide opportunities for developing different skills, cognitive processes, or emotional tendencies that carry over to peer interactions. Much additional research is needed in this area, since the form of the interactions found for parent and child gender have varied among studies in terms of variables studied and measures used (Russell & Saebel, 1997).

Other potentially important moderators that remain to be studied include variables that directly influence either parent–child interactions (e.g., maternal education) or children's cognitive or emotional development (e.g., developmental abilities). Physiological variables that affect self-regulation (Shonkoff & Phillips, 2000) also are likely to moderate linkages. Whereas many of these potential moderators have been studied in relation to parent–child interaction (e.g., level of emotional arousal, Eisenberg, Cumberland, & Spinrad, 1998; theory of mind, Symons, 2004) or in relation to social competence (e.g., emotional arousal, Calkins, Gill, Johnson, & Smith, 1999), they have not been studied extensively in relation to linkages between the two. Many of these same variables also may be influenced by the presence of a disability. Thus, characteristics or severity of a disability may act as a moderator of the linkages between family and peer relationships, such that the processes linking family interactions with children's social competence may differ, for example, in children with less versus more severe disabilities or in children with different types of disabilities.

Another limitation in the research highlighted in this chapter is the almost exclusive focus on mother–child relationships. As demonstrated by Parke and colleagues (2004), fathers also provide important, unique contributions to children's development of social competence. It is likely that other adult caregivers influence young children's social competence as well (Howes, Matheson, & Hamilton, 1994). Siblings also play a unique role in the development of children's emotional and social understanding, skills, and characteristics (Dunn, 1999); whereas parents adapt their behavior to those of the child in order to scaffold the child's participation, siblings who are close in age interact on a more horizontal level, eliciting and providing an opportunity for the child to practice and learn many of the same skills that are needed in peer interactions (e.g., sharing, negotiating conflict) (Youngblade & Dunn, 1995). Relationships with siblings may be an important arena for developing social and emotional understanding in general and in relation to other children in particular. Qualitative aspects of sibling relationships may be particularly important for developing social skills, emotional understanding, perspective taking, or conflict resolution (Dunn, 1999). As discussed under Pathway 3, siblings of children with disabilities also may provide important access to peer opportunities. The role of siblings in relation to all pathways deserves a great deal of additional attention.

While mindful of the limitations of this research, we turn our attention to implications that can be drawn for practice. Much intervention research has been conducted with young children with disabilities with the aim of teaching skills for peer interaction. The three pathways offer a somewhat different perspective on supporting children's peer interactions by placing these interactions within a developmental context and by highlighting developmental origins within family relationships. By doing so, the pathways provide guidance not only for intervention but also for promotion and prevention. Pathway 3 is the most straightforward; in order to develop social competence with peers, children need interactions and relationships with peers in many different kinds of contexts, both short-term and long-term. As noted earlier, these opportunities may be more difficult to orchestrate for children with disabilities. But parents can be assisted in thinking about and taking advantage of potential opportunities for peer interaction within their own families, friendship groups, and neighborhood networks, as well as within the community. Some opportunities may need to be created through mechanisms such as playgroups and playdates. Given these opportunities, Pathway 2 then provides guidance for strategies that parents could use to support their children's interactions with peers. For example, parents may want to learn strategies for supervising and supporting their children's peer interactions, based on observation and entry as a coach and/or play partner. Depending on the age or abilities of the child, strategies discussed above under interactive, directive, and decontextualized supervision may be relevant.

With respect to Pathway 1, although thinking about intervening in parent–child interactions and relationships as a way of influencing children's social competence with peers may be new, interventions that focus on parent–child attachment and on parenting style have received considerable attention (e.g., Mahoney & Perales, 2003). Recognizing that experimental studies are lacking to link changes in parent–child interaction to changes in social competence with peers, the models used in these interventions can nevertheless provide guidance for intervention efforts related to Pathway 1. Characteristics and qualities of parent–child interaction can be changed with intervention (McCollum & Hemmeter, 1997). Most of these studies have addressed changes in various aspects of parental sensitivity, an important aspect of parenting style. A meta-analysis of 70 studies (Bakermans-Kranenburg, van IJzendoorn, & Juffer, 2003) indicated that the most successful interventions were those that had a clear behavioral focus and included a moderate number of intervention sessions. A re-analysis of these same studies by Dunst and Kassow (2004) yielded similar results, with additional value found when videotapes were used for modeling sensitivity during parent–child interactions or for providing feedback to parents.

Some parent–child interaction intervention studies have included measures of child change. Of interest with respect to family–peer linkages is that some child change variables are similar to those included as mediators or core processes in Table 2.1. For example, Schertz and Odom (2004) noted that parent–child interaction interventions may be useful for addressing specific social deficits (i.e., joint attention) in children with autism. Similar arguments could be advanced for deficits that might be specific to children with other disabilities as well, such as emotion regulation (Kasari et al., 2001) and emotion recognition (Kasari et al., 1995) in children with Down syndrome. Whereas the question remains as to whether changes in these intermediate processes based on parent–child interaction interventions would then yield subsequent changes in children's social competence, the evidence that intervention into parent–child interaction can change at least some core processes clearly supports the development of "as if" interventions that use our best current child development information as a guide. Although most interaction intervention studies have addressed characteristics such as sensitivity and responsiveness, other variables included as predictors in Pathway 1 research also offer direction for practitioners. For example, talking about children's emotions within the context of everyday routines, reading stories about peer relations, and telling family stories may be important ways of promoting children's emotional and social competence. Although not reviewed in this chapter, many researcher- or teacher-implemented interventions have focused on changing children's understanding of emotion or social interaction skills, with subsequent measures of children's interactions with peers (e.g., Kohler et al., 2001). Similar strategies may be beneficial to parents, with an increased emphasis on documenting changes in peer-related social competence.

For all pathways, it is important to remember that parent–child interactions and relationships are influenced by many factors. Interventions that address interactions and relationships cannot be separated from these contexts but rather, should occur as one part of an overall program of prevention, promotion, and intervention that takes into account contextual variables such as family characteristics (e.g., parental education, financial resources, social supports, culture) and family patterns of interaction (Guralnick, 2005). Interventions that support families may, through their influence on parent–child relationships and interactions, also influence peer-related social competence.

Since the flurry of studies on family–peer linkages in the late 1980s and 1990s, during which time the focus on linkages was a clearly defined area of research, the search for linkages has moved toward more complex, multifaceted studies that are largely integrated into other areas of psychological research. However, much more can still be learned about the processes that explain these linkages. In the complex search for family–peer linkages, the next arena may well be experimental studies directed toward intervening into various aspects of family interactions and relationships, with subsequent measurement of children's interactions with peers. Research on young children with disabilities could play an important role in this effort.

REFERENCES

Ainsworth, M.D.S., & Wittig, B.A. (1969). Attachment and exploratory behavior of one-year-olds in a strange situation. In B.M. Foss (Ed.), *Determinants of infant behavior IV* (pp. 111–136). London: Methuen.

Atkinson, L., Chisholm, V.C., Scott, B., Goldberg, S., Vaughn, B.E., Blackwell, J., et al. (1999). Maternal sensitivity, child functional level, and attachment in Down syndrome. In J.I. Vondra & D. Barnett (Eds.), *Monographs of the Society for Research in Child Development, 64*, 45–66.

Bakermans-Kranenburg, M.J., van IJzendoorn, M.H., & Juffer, F. (2003). Less is more: Meta-analysis of sensitivity and attachment interventions in early childhood. *Psychological Bulletin, 129*, 194–215.

Baron, R.B., & Kenny, D.A. (1986). The moderator–mediator variable distinction in social psychological research: Conceptual, strategic, and statistical considerations. *Journal of Personality and Social Psychology, 51,* 1173–1182.

Barth, J.M., & Parke, R.D. (1993). Parent–child relationship influences on children's transition to school. *Merrill-Palmer Quarterly, 39,* 173–195.

Bates, J.E., Pettit, G.S., Dodge, K.A., & Ridge, B. (1998). Interaction of temperamental resistance to control and restrictive parenting in the development of externalizing behavior. *Developmental Psychology, 34,* 982–995.

Baumrind, D. (1973). The development of instrumental competence through socialization. In A.D. Pick (Ed.), *Minnesota symposium on child psychology, Vol. 7* (pp. 3–46). Minneapolis: University of Minnesota Press.

Beckman, P.J., Barnwell, D., Horn, E. Hanson, M.J., Gutierrez, S., & Lieber, J. (1998). Communities, families, and inclusion. *Early Childhood Research Quarterly, 13,* 125–150.

Beeghly, J., & Cicchetti, D. (1997). Talking about self and other: Emergence of an internal state lexicon in young children with Down syndrome. *Development and Psychopathology, 9,* 729–748.

Bhavnagri, N. (1987). *Parents as facilitators of preschool children's peer relationships.* Unpublished doctoral dissertation, University of Illinois, Urbana–Champaign.

Bhavnagri, N., & Parke, R.D. (1985, April). *Parents as facilitators of preschool peer interaction.* Paper presented at the Biennial Meeting of the Society for Research in Child Development. Toronto, Canada.

Bhavnagri, N.P., & Parke, R.D. (1991). Parents as direct facilitators of children's peer relationships: Effects of age of child and sex of parent. *Journal of Social and Personal Relationships, 8,* 423–440.

Bieberich, A.A., & Morgan, S.B. (1998). Affective expression in children with autism or Down syndrome. *Journal of Autism & Developmental Disorders, 28,* 333–338.

Bohlin, G., Hagekull, B., & Anderson, K. (2005). Behavioral inhibition as a precursor of peer social competence in early school age: The interplay with attachment and nonparental care. *Merrill-Palmer Quarterly, 51,* 1–19.

Booth, C.L. (1999). Beliefs about social skills among mothers of preschoolers with special needs. *Early Education & Development, 10,* 455–474.

Boyum, L.A., & Parke, R.D. (1995). The role of family emotional expressiveness in the development of children's social competence. *Journal of Marriage and the Family, 57,* 593–608.

Brown, J.R., Donelan-McCall, N., & Dunn, J. (1996). Why talk about mental states? Significance of children's conversations with friends, siblings, and mothers. *Child Development, 67,* 836–849.

Calkins, S.D., Gill, K.L., Johnson, M.C., & Smith C.L. (1999). Emotional reactivity and emotion regulation strategies as predictors of social behavior with peers during toddlerhood. *Social Development, 8,* 310–334.

Carson, J.L., & Parke, R.D. (1996). Reciprocal negative affect in parent–child interactions and children's peer competency. *Child Development, 67,* 2217–2226.

Casas, J.F., Weigel, S.M., Crick, N.R., Ostrov, J.M., Woods, K.E., Yeh, E.A.J., et al. (2006). Early parenting and children's relational and physical aggression in the preschool and home contexts. *Applied Developmental Psychology, 27,* 209–227.

Cassidy, J., Parke, R.D., Butkovsky, L., & Braungart, J. (1992). Family–peer connections: The roles of emotional expressiveness within the family and children's understanding of emotions. *Child Development, 63,* 603–618.

Cochran, M., & Niego, S. (1995). Parenting and social networks. In M.H. Bornstein (Ed.), *Handbook of parenting: Vol. 3, Status and social conditions of parenting* (pp. 393–418). Mahwah, NJ: Lawrence Erlbaum Associates.

Cohn, D.A. (1990). Child–mother attachment of six-year-olds and social competence at school. *Child Development, 61,* 152–162.

Crockenberg, S., & Leerkes, E. (2000). Infant social and emotional development in family context. In C.H. Zeanah (Ed.), *Handbook of infant mental health* (pp. 60–90). New York: Guilford Press.

Crockenberg, S., & Lourie, A. (1996). Parents' conflict strategies with children and children's conflict strategies with peers. *Merrill-Palmer Quarterly, 42,* 495–518.

Darling, N., & Steinberg, L. (1993). Parenting style as context: An integrative model. *Psychological Bulletin, 113,* 487–496.

Davidov, M., & Grusec, J.E. (2006). Untangling the links of parental responsiveness to distress and warmth to child outcomes. *Child Development, 77,* 44–58.

Dawson, G., Toth, K., Abbott, R., Osterling, J., Munson, J., Estes, A., et al. (2004). Early social attention impairments in autism: Social orienting, joint attention, and attention to distress. *Developmental Psychology, 40,* 271–283.

de Koeyer, I. (2001). *Peer acceptance, parent–child fantasy play interactions, and subjective experience of the self-in-relation: A study of 4- to 5-year-old children.* Veenendaal, The Netherlands: Universal.

DeMulder, E.K., Denham, S., Schmidt, M., & Mitchell, J. (2000). Q–sort assessment of attachment security during the preschool years: Links from school to home. *Developmental Psychology, 36,* 274–282.

Denham, S.A., Blair, K.A., DeMulder, E., Levitas, J., Sawyer, K., Auerbach-Major, S., et al. (2003). Preschool emotional competence: Pathway to social competence. *Child Development, 74,* 238–256.

Denham, S.A., Zoller, D., & Couchoud, E.A. (1994). Socialization of preschoolers' emotion understanding. *Developmental Psychology, 30,* 928–936.

Dunn, J. (1999). Siblings, friends, and the development of social understanding. In W.A. Collins & B. Laursen (Eds.), *Minnesota symposia on child psychology, Vol. 30, Relationships as developmental contexts* (pp. 263–279). Mahwah, NJ: Lawrence Erlbaum Associates.

Dunn, J., Bretherton, I., & Munn, P. (1987). Conversations about feeling states between mothers and their young children. *Developmental Psychology, 23,* 132–139.

Dunn, J., & Brown, J. (1994). Affect expression in the family, children's understanding of emotions and their interactions with others. *Merrill-Palmer Quarterly, 40,* 120–137.

Dunn, J., Brown, J., & Bearsall, L. (1991). Family talk about feeling states and children's later understanding of others' emotions. *Developmental Psychology, 27,* 448–455.

Dunn, J., & Munn, P. (1985). Becoming a family member: Family conflict and the development of social understanding in the second year. *Child Development, 56,* 480–492.

Dunst, C.J., & Kassow, D.Z. (2004). Characteristics of interventions promoting parental sensitivity to child behavior. *Bridges Practice–Based Research Syntheses, 3(3),* 1–17. Retrieved August 15, 2005, from http://www.evidencebasedpractices.org/bridges/bridges_vol3_no3.pdf.

Eisenberg, N., Cumberland, A., & Spinrad, R.L. (1998). Parental socialization of emotion. *Psychological Inquiry, 9,* 241–273.

Eisenberg, N., Gershoff, E.T., Fabes, R.A., Shepard, S.A., Cumberland, A.J., Losoya, S.H., et al. (2001). Mothers' emotional expressivity and children's behavior problems and social competence: Mediation through children's regulation. *Developmental Psychology, 37,* 475–490.

Fabes, R.A., Leonard, S.A., Kupanoff, K., & Martin, C.L. (2001). Parental coping with children's negative emotions: Relations with children's emotional and social responding. *Child Development, 72,* 907–920.

Fagot, B. (1997). Attachment, parenting, and peer interactions of toddler children. *Developmental Psychology, 33,* 489–499.

Finnie, V., & Russell, A. (1988). Preschool children's social status and their mothers' behavior and knowledge in the supervisory role. *Developmental Psychology, 24,* 789–801.

Freeman, S.F.N., & Kasari, C. (1998). Friendships in children with developmental disabilities. *Early Education and Development, 9,* 341–355.

Geisthardt, C.L., Brotherson, M.J., & Cook, C.C. (2002). Friendships of children with disabilities in the home environment. *Education and Training in Mental Retardation and Developmental Disabilities, 37(3),* 235–252.

Gottman, J.M., Fainsilber-Katz, L., & Hooven, C. (1996). Parental meta–emotion philosophy and the emotional life of families: Theoretical models and preliminary data. *Journal of Family Psychology, 10,* 243–268.

Gottman, J.M., Fainsilber-Katz, L., & Hooven, C. (1997). *Meta–emotion: How families communicate emotionally.* Mahwah, NJ: Lawrence Erlbaum Associates.

Guralnick, M.J. (1997). Peer social networks of young boys with developmental delays. *American Journal on Mental Retardation, 101,* 595–612.

Guralnick, M.J. (1999). Family and child influences on the peer–related social competence of young children with developmental delays. *Mental Retardation and Developmental Disabilities Research Review, 5,* 21–29.

Guralnick, M.J. (2005). Early intervention for children with intellectual disabilities: Current knowledge and future prospects. *Journal of Applied Research in Intellectual Disabilities, 18,* 313–324.

Guralnick, M.J., Connor, R.T., Neville, B., & Hammond, M.A. (2002). Mothers' perspectives of the peer-related social development of young children with developmental delays and communication disorders. *Early Education and Development, 13,* 59–80.

Guralnick, M.J., Hammond, M.A., Connor, R.T., & Neville, B. (2006). Stability, change, and correlates of peer relationships of young children with mild developmental delays. *Child Development, 77,* 312–324.

Guralnick, M.J., Neville, B., Connor, R.T., & Hammond, M.A. (2003). Family factors associated with the peer social competence of young children with mild delays. *American Journal on Mental Retardation, 108,* 272–287.

Halberstadt, A.G., Denham, S.A., & Dunsmore, J.C. (2001). Affective social competence. *Social Development, 10,* 79–119.

Harkness, S., & Super, C. (1995). Culture and parenting. In M.H. Bornstein (Ed.), *Handbook of parenting, Volume 2: Biology and ecology of parenting* (pp. 211–234). Mahwah, NJ: Lawrence Erlbaum Associates.

Harrist, A.W., Pettit, G.S., Dodge, K.A., & Bates, J.E. (1994). Dyadic synchrony in mother–child interaction: Relation with children's subsequent kindergarten adjustment. *Family Relations, 43,* 417–424.

Harrist, A.W., & Waugh, R.M. (2002). Dyadic synchrony: Its structure and function in children's development. *Developmental Review, 22,* 555–592.

Hart, C.H., Ladd, G.W., & Burleson, B.R. (1990). Children's expectations of the outcomes of social strategies: Relations with sociometric status and maternal disciplinary styles. *Child Development, 61,* 127–137.

Herrera, C., & Dunn, J. (1997). Early experiences with family conflict: Implications for arguments with a close friend. *Developmental Psychology, 33,* 869–881.

Howes, C., Matheson, C., & Hamilton, C.E. (1994). Maternal, teachers, and child care history correlates of children's relationships with peers. *Child Development, 65,* 264–273.

Hubbard, J.A., & Coie, J.D. (1994). Emotional correlates of social competence in children's peer relationships. *Merrill–Palmer Quarterly, 50,* 1–20.

Isley, S., O'Neil, R., Catfelder, D., & Parke, R.D. (1999). Parent and child expressed affect and children's social competence: Modeling direct and indirect pathways. *Developmental Psychology, 35,* 547–560.

Isley, S., O'Neil, R., & Parke, R.D. (1996). The relation of parental affect and control behaviors to children's classroom acceptance: A concurrent and predictive analysis. *Early Education and Development, 7,* 7–23.

Kasari, C., Freeman, S.F.N., & Hughes, M.A. (2001). Emotion recognition by children with Down syndrome. *American Journal on Mental Retardation, 106,* 59–72.

Kasari, C., Freeman, S., Mundy, P., & Sigman, M.D. (1995). Attention regulation by children with Down syndrome: Coordinated joint attention and social referencing looks. *American Journal on Mental Retardation, 100,* 128–136.

Kasari, C., & Sigman, M. (1996). Expression and understanding of emotion in atypical development: Autism and Down syndrome. In M. Lewis & M.W. Sullivan (Eds.), *Emotional development in atypical children* (pp. 109–120). Mahwah, NJ: Lawrence Erlbaum Associates.

Kohler, F.W., Anthony, L.J., Steighner, S.A., & Hoyson, M. (2001). Teaching social interaction skills in the integrated preschool: An examination of naturalistic tactics. *Topics in Early Childhood Special Education, 21,* 93–103.

Ladd, G.W. (1992a). Commentary: Play, parenting, and peer partners: Keys to understanding children's social development? *Early Education and Development, 3*(4), 401–406.

Ladd, G.W. (1992b). Themes and theories: Perspectives on processes in family–peer relationships. In R.D. Parke, & G.W. Ladd (Eds.), *Family–peer relationships: Modes of linkage* (pp. 3–34). Mahwah, NJ: Lawrence Erlbaum Associates.

Ladd, G.W., & Golter, B.S. (1988). Parents' management of preschoolers' peer relations: Is it related to children's social competence? *Developmental Psychology, 24,* 109–117.

Ladd, G.W., & Hart, C.H. (1992). Creating informal play opportunities: Are parents' and preschoolers' initiations related to children's competence with peers? *Developmental Psychology, 28,* 1179–1187.

Ladd, G.W., Le Sieur, K.D., & Profilet, S.M. (1993). Direct parental influences on young children's peer relations. In S. Duck (Ed.), *Learning about relationships, Vol. 2* (pp. 152–183). Newbury Park, CA: Sage Publications.

Ladd, G.W., & Pettit, G.S. (2002). Parenting and the development of children's peer relationships. In M. Bornstein (Ed.), *Handbook of parenting, Volume 5: Practical issues in parenting* (pp. 269–309). Mahwah, NJ: Lawrence Erlbaum Associates.

Ladd, G.W., Profilet, S.M., & Hart, C.G. (1992). Parents' management of children's peer relations: Facilitating and supervising children's activities in the peer culture. In R.D. Parke & G.W. Ladd (Eds.), *Family–peer relationships: Modes of linkage* (pp. 215–253). Mahwah, NJ: Lawrence Erlbaum Associates.

LaFreniere, P.J., & Capuano, F. (1997). Preventive intervention as means of clarifying direction of effects in socialization: Anxious–withdrawn preschoolers case. *Development and Psychopathology, 9,* 551–564.

Laible, D.J. (2004). Mother–child discourse surrounding a child's past behavior at 30 months: Links to emotional understanding and early conscience development at 36 months. *Merrill-Palmer Quarterly, 50,* 159–180.

Laird, R.D., Pettit, G.S., Mize, J., Brown, E.G., & Lindsey, E. (1994). Mother–child conversations about peers: Contributions to competence. *Family Relations, 43,* 425–432.

Landry, S.H., Garner, P.W., Pirie, D., & Swank, P.R. (1994). Effects of social context and mothers' requesting strategies on Down syndrome children's social responsiveness. *Developmental Psychology, 30,* 293–302.

Lindsey, E.W., & Mize, J. (2000). Parent–child physical play and pretense play: Links to children's social competence. *Merrill-Palmer Quarterly, 46,* 565–591.

Lollis, S.P., Ross, H.S., & Tate, E. (1992). Parents' regulation of children's peer interactions: Direct influences. In R.D. Parke & G.W. Ladd (Eds.), *Family–peer relationships: Modes of linkage* (pp. 255–281). Mahwah, NJ: Lawrence Erlbaum Associates.

MacDonald, K., & Parke, R.D. (1984). Bridging the gap: Parent–child play interaction and peer interactive competence. *Child Development, 55,* 1265–1277.

Mahoney, G., & Perales, F. (2003). Using relationship–focused intervention to enhance the social–emotional functioning of young children with autism spectrum disorders. *Topics in Early Childhood Special Education, 23,* 77–89.

Marfo, K., Dedrick, C.F., & Barbour, N. (1998). Mother–child interactions and the development of children with mental retardation. In J.A. Burack, R.M. Hodapp, & E. Zigler (Eds.), *Handbook of mental retardation and development* (pp. 637–668). Cambridge, NY: University Press.

McCollum, J.A., & Bair, H. (1994). Research in parent–child interaction: Guidance to developmentally appropriate practice for young children with disabilities. In B.L. Mallory & R.S. New (Eds.), *Diversity and developmentally appropriate practices: Challenges for early childhood education* (pp. 84–106). New York: Teachers College Press.

McCollum, J.A., & Hemmeter, M.L. (1997). Parent–child interaction intervention when children have disabilities. In M.J. Guralnick (Ed.), *The effectiveness of early intervention* (pp. 549–576). Baltimore: Paul H. Brookes Publishing Co.

McConnell, S. (2002). Interventions to facilitate social interaction for young children with autism: Review of available research and recommendations for educational intervention and future research. *Journal of Autism and Developmental Disorders, 32,* 351–372.

McElwain, N.L., & Volling, B.L. (2004). Attachment security and parental sensitivity during infancy: Associations with friendship quality and false–belief understanding at age 4. *Journal of Social and Personal Relationships, 21,* 639–667.

Mills, R.S.L., & Rubin, K.H. (1993). Parental ideas as influences on children's social competence. In S. Duck (Ed.), *Learning about relationships: Vol. 2, Understanding relationships processes series* (pp. 98–117). Thousand Oaks, CA: Sage Publications.

Mize, J., & Pettit, G.S. (1997). Mothers' social coaching, mother–child relationship style, and children's peer competence: Is the medium the message? *Child Development, 68,* 312–332.

Mize, J., Pettit, G.S., & Brown, E. G. (1995). Mothers' supervision of their children's peer play: Relations with beliefs, perceptions, and knowledge. *Developmental Psychology, 31,* 311–321.

Mize, J., Pettit, G., & Meece, D. (2000). Explaining the link between parenting behavior and children's peer competence: A critical examination of the "mediating process" hypothesis. In K.A. Kerns, J.M. Conteras & A.M. Neals-Barnett (Eds.), *Family and peers: Linking two social worlds* (pp. 137–168). Westport, CT: Praeger Publishers.

O'Neil, R., & Parke, R.D. (2000). Family–peer relationships: The role of emotion regulation, cognitive understanding, and attentional processes as mediating processes. In K.A. Kerns, J.M. Conteras, & A.M. Neal–Barnett (Eds.), *Family and peers: Linking two social worlds* (pp.195–205). Westport, CT: Praeger Publishers.

Parke, R.D., Burks, V.M., Carson, J.L., & Cassidy, J. (1992). Family contributions to peer relationships among young children. In R.D. Parke & G. Ladd (Eds.), *Family–peer relationships: Modes of linkage* (pp. 107–134). Mahwah, NJ: Lawrence Erlbaum Associates.

Parke, R.D., Burks, V.M., Carson, J.L., Neville, B., & Boyum, L.A. (1994). Family–peer relationships: A tripartite model. In R.D. Parke, & S.G. Kellam (Eds.), *Exploring family relationships with other social contexts* (pp. 115–145). Mahwah, NJ: Lawrence Erlbaum Associates.

Parke, R.D., Dennis, J., Flyr, M.L., Morris, K.L., Killian, C., McDowell, D.J., et al. (2004). Fathering and children's peer relationships. In M.E. Lamb (Ed.), *The role of the father in child development* (4th ed., pp. 307–339). New York: Wiley.

Parke, R.D., & O'Neil, R. (1997). The influence of significant others on learning about relationships. In S. Duck (Ed.), *Handbook of personal relationship: Theory, research, and interventions* (2nd ed., pp. 29–60). New York: Wiley.

Parke, R.D., & O'Neil, R. (1999a). The influence of significant others on learning about relationships: From family to friends. In R. Mills, & S. Duck (Eds.), *The developmental psychology of personal relationships* (pp. 15–48). New York: Wiley.

Parke, R.D., & O'Neil, R. (1999b). Social relationships across contexts: Family–peer linkages. In W.A. Collins, & B. Laursen (Eds.), *Relationships as developmental contexts: The Minnesota symposia on child psychology, Vol. 30* (pp. 211–239). Mahwah, NJ: Lawrence Erlbaum Associates.

Parke, R.D., & O'Neil, R. (2000). The influence of significant others on learning about relationships: From family to friends. In R. Mills, & S. Duck (Eds.), *The developmental psychology of personal relationships* (pp. 15–47). New York: Wiley.

Patterson, G.R., & Fisher, P.A. (2002). Recent developments in our understanding of parenting: Bidirectional effects, causal models, and the search for parsimony. In M.H. Bornstein (Ed.). *Handbook of parenting. Vol. 1, Children and parenting* (pp. 59–88). Mahwah, NJ: Lawrence Erlbaum Associates.

Pettit, G.S., Brown, E.G., Mize, J., & Lindsey, E. (1998). Mothers' and fathers' socializing behaviors in three contexts: Links with children's peer competence. *Merrill-Palmer Quarterly, 44,* 173–193.

Pettit, G.S., Dodge, K.A., & Brown, M.M. (1988). Early family experience, social problem solving patterns, and children's social competence. *Child Development, 59,* 107–120.

Pettit, G.S., & Mize, J. (1993). Substance and style: Understanding the ways in which parents teach children about social relationships. In S. Duck (Ed.), *Learning about relationships Vol. 2, Understanding relationships processes series* (pp. 118–151). Thousand Oaks, CA: Sage Publications.

Putallaz, M. (1987). Maternal behavior and children's sociometric status. *Child Development, 58,* 324–340.

Roberts, W., & Strayer, J. (1987). Parents' responses to the emotional distress of their children: Relations with children's competence. *Developmental Psychology, 23,* 415–422.

Rubin, K.H., & Burgess, K.B. (2002). Parents of aggressive and withdrawn children. In M.H. Bornstein (Ed.), *Handbook of parenting. Vol. 1, Children and parenting* (pp. 383–418). Mahwah, NJ: Lawrence Erlbaum Associates.

Russell, A., & Saebel, J. (1997). Mother–son, mother–daughter, father–son, and father–daughter: Are they distinct relationships? *Developmental Review, 17,* 111–147.

Russell, A., Pettit, G., & Mize, J. (1998). Horizontal qualities in parent–child relationships: Parallels with and possible consequences for children's peer relationships. *Developmental Review, 18,* 313–352.

Saarni, C. (1999). *The development of emotional competence.* New York: Guilford Press.

Schertz, H.H., & Odom, S.L. (2004). Joint attention and early intervention with autism: A conceptual framework and promising approaches. *Journal of Early Intervention, 27,* 42–54.

Schneider, B.H., Atkinson, L., & Tardif, C. (2001). Child–parent attachment and children's peer relations: A quantitative review. *Developmental Psychology, 37,* 86–100.

Schneider, B.H., Smith, A., Poisson, S., & Kwan, A.B. (2000). Connecting children's peer relations with the surrounding cultural context. In R. Mills & S. Duck (Eds.), *The developmental psychology of personal relationships* (pp. 175–198). New York: Wiley.

Shonkoff, J.P., & Phillips, D.A. (Eds.). (2000). *From neurons to neighborhoods: The science of early childhood development.* Washington, DC: National Academies Press.

Sigel, I.E., & McGillicuddy-De Lisi, A.V. (2002). Parent beliefs are cognitions: The dynamic belief systems model. In M.H. Bornstein (Ed.), *Handbook of parenting: Being and becoming a parent, Vol. 3* (pp. 485–508). Mahwah, NJ: Lawrence Erlbaum Associates.

Sigman, M., & Ruskin, E. (1999). Continuity and change in the social competence of children with autism, Down syndrome, and developmental delays. *Monographs of the Society for Research in Child Development, 64,* 1–114.

Siller, M., & Sigman, M. (2002). The behaviors of parents of children with autism predict the subsequent development of their children's communication. *Journal of Autism and Developmental Disorders, 32,* 77–89.

Simpkins, S., & Parke, R.D. (2001). The relations between parental friendships and children's friendships: Self-report and observational analyses. *Child Development, 72,* 569–582.

Sroufe, L.A., Egeland, B., & Carlson, E.A. (1999). One social world: The integrated development of parent–child and peer relationships. In W.A. Collins, & B. Laursen (Eds.), *Minnesota symposia on child psychology, Vol. 30, Relationships as developmental contexts* (pp. 241–261). Mahwah, NJ: Lawrence Erlbaum Associates.

Stoneman, Z. (1993). Attitudes toward young children with disabilities: Cognition, affect, and behavioral intent. In C. Peck, S.L. Odom, & D. Bricker (Eds.), *Integrating young children with disabilities in community programs: From research to implementation* (pp. 223–248). Baltimore: Paul H. Brookes Publishing Co.

Strully, J., & Strully, C. (1996). Friendships as an educational goal: What we have learned and where we are headed. In S. Stainback & W. Stainback (Eds.), *Inclusion: A guide for educators* (pp. 141–169). Baltimore: Paul H. Brookes Publishing Co.

Symons, D.K. (2004). Mental state discourse, theory of mind, and the internalization of self–other understanding. *Developmental Review, 24,* 159–188.

Szewczyk-Sokolowski, M., Bost, K.K., & Wainwright, A.B. (2005). Attachment, temperament, and preschool children's peer acceptance. *Social Development, 14,* 379–397.

Taumoepeau, M., & Ruffman, T. (2006). Mother and infant talk about mental states relates to desire language and emotion understanding. *Child Development, 77,* 465–481.

Travis, L., Sigman, M., & Ruskin, E. (2001). Links between social understanding and social behavior in verbally able children with autism. *Journal of Autism and Developmental Disorders, 31,* 119–130.

Turnbull, A.P., Pereira, L., & Blue-Banning, M.J. (1999). Parents' facilitation of friendships between their children with a disability and friends without a disability. *Journal of the Association for Persons with Severe Handicaps, 24,* 85–99.

Uhlendorff, H. (2000). Parents' and children's friendship networks. *Journal of Family Issues, 21,* 191–204.

Verschueren, K., & Marcoen, A. (1999). Representation of self and socioemotional competence in kindergartners: Differential and combined effects of attachment to mother and to father. *Child Development, 70,* 183–201.

Verschueren, K., Marcoen, A., & Schoefs, V. (1996). The internal working model of the self, attachment, and competence in five-year-olds. *Child Development, 67,* 2493–2511.

Waters, E., & Deane, K.E. (1985). Defining and assessing individual differences in attachment relationships: Q–methodology and the organization of behavior in infancy and early childhood. *Monographs of the Society for Research in Child Development, 50,* 41–65.

Youngblade, L.M., & Dunn, J. (1995). Individual differences in young children's pretend play with mother and sibling: Links to relationships and understanding of other people's feelings and beliefs. *Child Development, 66,* 1472–1492.

Youngblade, L.M., Park, K.A., & Belsky, J. (1993). Measurement of young children's close friendship: A comparison of two independent assessment systems and their associations with attachment security. *International Journal of Behavioral Development, 16,* 563–587.

Zhou, Q., Eisenberg, N., Losoya, S.H., Fabes, R.A., Reiser, M., Guthrie, I.K., et al. (2002). The relations of parental warmth and positive expressiveness to children's empathy-related responding and social functioning: A longitudinal study. *Child Development, 73,* 893–915.

CHAPTER 3

Cultural Influences on Young Children's Social Competence

MARCI J. HANSON AND TANYA SOOHOO

ARIKI IS TYPICALLY ATTENTIVE AND engaged in activities during story and small group time. He appears to enjoy playing with his peers. Teacher Charlie is worried about him, however, because Ariki rarely makes eye contact with him. He is thinking of referring Ariki for testing. Could he have social-emotional difficulties?

Basimah appears timid with adults in preschool. She refuses to sit on Teacher Charlie's lap during story time even though the other children love to gather around him for this prized activity. She will not even allow him to help her put her coat on to go outside to play. The teachers wonder about her home environment and ponder why she is so mistrusting of adults, particularly males.

Tyrell is one of the most active 4-year-olds on the playground. He is always running, playing, climbing, and grabbing the bikes and he is the last to put away toys and line up to return to the classroom. He seems to interact mostly with the adults in the preschool and often gets very aggressive with his peers. The teachers have mentioned this to his mother, who just laughs and says, "Yes, he can be naughty. He's all boy!" Tyrell's mother sees no problem with his behavior at school; however, the teachers are trying to figure out a plan to make her understand that he is at risk for social-emotional competence problems.

These young children have been "flagged" by the teacher as potentially at risk for social-emotional difficulties; however, although their teachers do not realize it, all three children are incredibly socially competent. Even at a very young age, they have learned the social rules of their families and neighborhoods. Ariki's family is from the Pacific Islands, and he has been well taught that it is impolite for children to stare or look directly into the eyes of an adult. Basimah's parents are concerned about their daughter's preschool experience because, in their Arab culture, it is not acceptable for males to touch females who are not their own children. They are thinking of pulling her out of the program even though they do not know of another that they can afford. They are torn about their options because they want Basimah to learn English and succeed later when she goes to public school. It is hard for them to understand why other families in their neighborhood who also come from similar Arab backgrounds are not more concerned about their children's schooling. Finally, Tyrell's mother believes that her son is developing right on target. She became a single parent following her husband's tragic heart attack. Tyrell is also cared for by his large extended family, which includes his grandmother, three aunts, and two uncles. Tyrell's mother is relieved that her son has so many caring adults in his life and that he can "hold his own" in their tough neighborhood and with other children. Many children in their neighborhood have grown up to join gangs, and she wants Tyrell to be able to protect himself while getting the education that he needs to succeed in school. She hopes that he will not be like so many of the gang members and unemployed youth in their community.

Service providers in today's world are fortunate to have the opportunity to work with children and families from a wide range of backgrounds in terms of ethnicity, race, languages spoken, beliefs, socioeconomic status, and cultural values. Although the population of children and their families are diverse and varied, educational expectations and cultural mores as defined through preschool behavior checklists and curricula do not always reflect this breadth. Rather, they are often aimed at the "majority culture" view of what constitutes "appropriate" behavior rather than a more culturally respectful and sensitive view of the diversity represented by the children and families receiving services.

The purpose of this chapter is to examine the influence of culture on the values and practices that families and professionals have about young children. These influences are often extremely subtle. Neither family members nor professionals may be aware of cultural influences in making judgments about children's behavior, educational goals, and parental and caregiver rearing styles.

DIVERSITY OF AMERICA'S CHILDREN

The population of the United States continues to become increasingly diverse. Diversity is most often used in reference to racial or ethnic differences only; however, it is evident across many other child and family dimensions such as family structures and membership, language, religious or spiritual practices, ability levels, socioeconomic levels, education, and social opportunity.

Whereas race is often used to describe populations, our broader understanding of the human genome and genetics reveals that it is not biologically meaningful (Olson, 2001; Smith & Sapp, 1996) in that *within*-group differences are as significant as *across*-group differences. However, race and ethnicity are socially relevant in terms of how families define themselves and how personnel working in service delivery systems interact with them.

Racial and ethnic diversity is particularly evident when examining demographic trends for America's children. Most often, higher birth rates and greater population increases are found in families from non–Anglo-European backgrounds. Demographic estimates revealed that in 2003, 60% of U.S. children were from White non-Hispanic backgrounds, 16% were Black–alone, and 4% were Asian–alone (ChildStats, 2005). In particular, the proportion of Hispanic/Latino children has increased faster than other demographic groups, shifting from 9% of the child population in 1980 to 19% of the child population in 2003. It is projected that by 2020, nearly one in five children in the United States will be of Hispanic/Latino heritage (ChildStats, 2005). In 2003, approximately 27% of the more than 900,000 preschoolers served by Head Start nationally spoke a language other than English at home, and more than 140 languages were represented in Head Start programs.

By far, Spanish was spoken the most (by 217,217 children), and East Asian languages were a distant second (by 11,437 children) (Italiano-Thomas, 2003). These population trends are particularly evident in certain states. For instance, in California, the 2006 student K–12 school population ethnic designation was 46.8% Hispanic, 31.3% White non-Hispanic, 8.1% Asian, 8.0% Black non-Hispanic, 2.6% Filipino, 0.8% American Indian, and 0.6% Pacific Islander. More than 40% of California's students (2.5 million) spoke a language other than English at home, and more than 25% were English language learners. The most recent projection is for increasing cultural, linguistic, and ethnic diversity in the state's school population (California State Department of Education, 2006).

These child demographic trends underscore the cultural and linguistic diversity of the overall U.S. population. It is evident that preschool-age children come from many different cultural and ethnic backgrounds (Lynch & Hanson, 2004). Cultural and linguistic diversity in our country's citizenry has produced both new challenges and opportunities for service delivery systems, particularly special education and early childhood education. These service issues include the need for personnel preparation in the development of cross-cultural competence, the development of curricula and materials that reflect *all* of America's children, the provision of supports and services for families from diverse backgrounds and perspectives, and the provision of language supports through translation and interpretation services, to name only a few (Bredekamp & Copple, 1997; Garcia & Malkin, 1993; Garcia & McLaughlin, 1995; Harry, 1992a, 1992b; Kagan & Garcia; 1991; Lynch & Hanson, 1993, 2004; Tabors, 1997).

CULTURAL IDENTITY: INFLUENCES ON CHILDREARING AND EDUCATION GOALS

Whereas the concept of *culture* is central to defining an individual's perspective and behavior, at the same time, it almost defies description or definition. It has been likened to a "second skin" or a subtle and often unconscious way of relating and behaving. To Hanson (2004), it is the "framework that guides and bounds life practices." Anderson and Fenichel described it as "a set of tendencies of possibilities from which to choose" (1998, p. 8). Attempts at definition are essential, however, as we endeavor to describe children's and families' actions and values in terms of cultural differences and similarities. These perspectives are best conceptualized as "tendencies" and "guidelines" rather than rigid or prescribed sets of behavior for individual groups. Indeed, assumptions that are based on cultural labels or stereotypes can result in generalizations that are often inaccurate and may well be harmful (Hanson, 2004). In fact, cultural identity is best considered through the perspective of a *continuum* of possible beliefs and practices whereby some families identify with some of those dimensions strongly and others, less so (Lynch, 2004). Just as some family members may elect to use traditional or native ways, others may choose actions that are "acculturated" with the new or dominant cultural group in which they reside (Hanson, 2004). Individuals' and families' beliefs, values, and practices also evolve or change over time so that their positions or preferences at one point may differ at other occasions or in other contexts. The discussion that follows will explore some of the potential ways in which children and families may differ in terms of goals for child development and the priorities and approaches for services.

Family Perspectives

The importance of considering a family's cultural identity in developing effective working partnerships has been described frequently in the literature (e.g., Hanson & Lynch, in press; Hanson, Lynch, & Wayman, 1990). Several dimensions, however, will be examined in this discussion as they relate to the provision of services for young children with disabilities, specifically, families' beliefs about the role of children and childrearing and their notions about disability and its causation and treatment.

Childrearing

Personal beliefs about what constitutes desirable and undesirable child behaviors as well as the best parenting methods are as varied as the families who implement them. Throughout history and across groups, these notions have shifted. In some periods and places, individuals have considered children to be burdens, whereas for individuals in other times and locations, children have been considered economic necessities as laborers (Safford & Safford, 1996). For other individuals still, children have been seen as precious gifts from God. Regardless, it is safe to assume that service providers will encounter families whose views of children and childrearing will differ, even radically, from their own.

One dimension along which families may differ is their view of the importance of dependent or independent behavior. For some groups, close physical proximity to the parent, particularly the mother, is valued, not only for the early years but also for a considerable period of time thereafter, and it may be common to see children nursing long after they are capable of feeding on their own. Other families may expect more autonomous child behaviors at an early age such as independent feeding, early toilet training, and independent play. Thus, different families will emphasize different developmental progressions. It is not uncommon to observe families moving from very child-focused interactions aimed at child gratification and nurturance in the child's early years to increasingly greater expectations of child independence, although the ages at which these shifts occur may vary. Children may be held and nurtured throughout the families' activities in the early years but then be required to separate from parents and other family members gradually and to play with other children or entertain themselves as they get older. Some children may even be assigned family responsibilities or chores at a relatively young age.

Some families will revel in their children's antics and domination of the families' attention and place children on "center stage," whereas for other families, "children are to be seen, not heard." These differences in childrearing goals and practices can be observed across cultural and ethnic groups as well as in different regions and socioeconomic groups.

Disability and Intervention/Treatment

Like perspectives of childrearing, notions regarding disability and risk conditions also can vary greatly across cultural and ethnic groups. For some groups, a disability is viewed as a random act that was not expected and for which families do not assume responsibility. Typically, these families will be amenable to seeking services with the expectation that interventions can ameliorate or remediate the condition. This perspective is in sharp contrast to families who may believe that the condition was a result of some transgression by the mother or father or even an ancestor. Other families may view the disability as caused by a ghost, demon, or evil spirit and for them, native healers will be sought to dispel these spirits. Still other families may view the disability as bad luck or misfortune and choose to accept this fate by living in accordance with the demands of the situation.

The type and degree of the family's experience in the new or dominant culture (such as the mainstream U.S. culture) and the degree to which the family chooses acculturation will influence their understanding of the views and intervention approaches in the dominant culture. Thus, family views of the causation of developmental delays may be highly variable depending on the family's history, ethnicity, immigration experiences, experiences with the new culture, and their degree of support and information about service systems that might be new and foreign to them. Likewise, their interpretation of the disability or condition will determine how they choose to respond. Family members who consider a disability to be shaming or stigmatizing may choose to avoid services and interactions with the public or service system at large. Others may choose native or traditional healers and supports and practices such as shamans or the use of herbs and amulets. Yet others may be comfortable seeking western health services and pursuing educational options such as special education. Families' openness to participate in services such as early childhood education and special education will be strongly influenced by the views and traditions that they carry with respect to the roles of children and family members as well as their views about disabilities and interventions.

The Role of Culture in Determining Goals and Expectations for Children

Children develop their social competence over time through interactions within their families, communities, and their larger social network. Bronfenbrenner and colleagues' ecological systems framework provides a model for understanding this integral relation between the developing child and the environment and for examining the interactions among ecological contexts (e.g., Bronfenbrenner, 1979; Bronfenbrenner & Morris, 1998). This framework describes a child's development as situated within a set of interacting structures or systems embedded or nested within one another. The structures/systems are referred to as the *microsystem, mesosystem, exosystem,* and *macrosystem*. The microsystem is "a pattern of activities, roles, and interpersonal relations experienced by the developing person in a given setting with particular physical and material characteristics" (Bronfenbrenner, 1979, p. 22). For the young child, the family and the child care center would be primary microsystems. The interrelationships among the child's microsystems constitute mesosystem issues. An example of this relationship for a young child and his or her family may be the connection between the home and preschool or child care center. Whereas mesosystems affect a child directly, the structures at the exosystem level (e.g., the family's social network, parents' employment, and policies of child care and education programs) affect a child indirectly. The macrosystem is made up of structures that organize the lower order systems; societal and cultural beliefs and values pertaining to childrearing practices or the definition of social competence are examples of these structures. This ecological systems framework elucidates how cultural mores, values, and practices can exert a strong influence on expectations for human behavior as well as on the opportunities that children have for acquiring socially relevant information.

Social competence is a term that has been defined in various ways by modern researchers. The lack of consensus on a given definition is a reflection of the numerous perspectives of theorists who study social competence (Dodge, Pettit, McClaskey, & Brown, 1986). The following are examples of working definitions: "the ability of young children to successfully and appropriately select and carry out their interpersonal goals" (Guralnick, 1990, p. 4); "behavior that reflects successful social functioning with peers" (Howes, 1988, p. 1); and "the possession and use of the ability to integrate thinking, feeling, and behavior to achieve social tasks and outcomes valued in the host setting and culture" (Topping, Bremner, & Holmes, 2000, p. 32). Rubin (1998) noted that social competence cannot be evaluated without appreciating individuals' beliefs about the goals of social interaction and interpretation of positive relationships with others. Given that one method of operationally defining social competence is through specific behaviors and behavior is seen by some as culturally based (Cartledge & Loe, 2001), then social competence might be analyzed best by investigators through an ecological lens that carefully considers the many environments and factors that influence children and families as well as the interactions among those variables. Because the goals of social interaction vary from culture to culture, judgments about the social competence of children will vary depending on the cultural contexts in which children are being examined. Thus, young children's behavior ought to be viewed within their families' cultural context (Cartledge & Loe, 2001), and any meaning attached to children's behavior and the goals of socialization should take into account cultural differences to enable a rich and comprehensive understanding of children's social competence (Harkness & Super, 1996).

DIVERSE VIEWS OF SOCIAL COMPETENCE

Children's behavior is shaped by structures from all levels of their ecological systems. Most children are raised in their families, and the families' cultural values govern how parents raise them. As mentioned earlier in the chapter, families living in the United States come from many different cultural and ethnic backgrounds that vary from one another in their beliefs and expectations about how children develop. Each family has their own personal set of ideals and values that they wish to inculcate in their children. For example, families transmit how they want their children to socialize with others and they deem which social behaviors are appropriate and valued and which are not. The brief discussion that follows provides some examples of how families view social competence for their children according to their cultural lens (Feng & Cartledge, 1996; Hanson, Lynch, & Wayman, 1990; Lynch & Hanson, 2004; Olaniran & Williams, 1995; Rivera & Rogers-Adkinson, 1997). It is important to remember that these familial practices are to be viewed as on a cultural continuum, described earlier in this chapter. Some families or family members may identify quite strongly with one end of the continuum, whereas others may place less stress on a given perspective or cultural practice.

Individualistic versus Collectivistic Perspective

One overarching cultural perspective is the family's emphasis on the role of the individual versus the social group or collective experience. Some families tend to value individuality highly and they may promote children's speaking out, following their own childhood desires, and learning to be as independent as possible—often even at an early age. An important goal may be encouraging children to become self-sufficient and autonomous individuals. As touched on earlier in the chapter, families who encourage independence may have young children sleep in their own beds, toilet train early, and dress themselves at an earlier age than families who value collectivism. Families with an individualistic perspective will probably teach children to develop their own opinions and to voice their ideas. Although children raised in these families may respect authority, they are taught to not trust authority unquestioningly. These children are expected to be inquisitive. Children from a culture that is seen as individualistic might also be viewed as having a competitive nature. Tyrell, described in the beginning of this chapter, shows his independence at school, and his mother is proud that "he can hold his own." Tyrell's independence sometimes leads to behaviors that are misinterpreted as defiance and as lacking respect toward adults and his peers.

At the other end of the cultural continuum, however, many families tend to be collectivistic in their perspectives. These families place great value on the interdependence between parents and children and other family members. Children from these families may identify themselves as one part of an interdependent and extended family. For example, parents might co-sleep or carry their children for a longer period of time even after their infants and toddlers are ambulatory. Children from such families are often encouraged to respect adults and to display "proper demeanor" at all times. Children learn to feel an obligation toward their family; moreover, they honor and may actively interact with extended kin. Hierarchical roles among family members may govern most family interactions. Some families teach their children to avoid confrontation and conflict with authority figures as well as with peers. In addition, the young children may be more comfortable in a cooperative setting because competition is not considered appropriate or as highly valued as it is in individualistic families.

Verbal and Nonverbal Communication

The manner in which family members model communication for their children also is influenced by the family's cultural background. Some families come from cultures considered *high context* and others from cultures that are considered *low context*. On the one hand, cultures that are high context rely less on verbal communication and more on nonverbal cues and messages (e.g., body movement, facial expressions) and on understanding through shared history and experience. In these families and communities, what is left unsaid may be more important than what is said. Cultures of low context, on the other hand, tend to communicate using direct and precise wording and may be less likely to notice gestures, moods, or environmental cues in the communication context. Thus, cultures differ in the ways in which information is transmitted either through words or through the context of the situation. These differences can lead to misunderstandings in communication if these differences are not acknowledged and understood.

Another practice that varies among families is the expression of emotion. For instance, some families teach their children to restrain feelings, especially those of anger and frustration. These children may be more guarded with personal feelings when compared with other children whose families emphasize outward expression of affect and emotions. Some children are expected to speak with adults only if authority figures initiate the conversation or to wait their turn to speak until after adults are finished talking. For other children, it is acceptable for them to engage in simultaneous talk with another person, even an adult. Whereas some children are expected to listen to an adult's message (i.e., one way communication), others are assertive and persistent about getting their own point across. These differences in communication style present interactional challenges in that one's propensity for communicating in a particular way may lead someone with a different style to misinterpret the behavior as rude, uninterested, or uninvolved.

Physical Interaction

The ways in which children interact with others may differ depending on their cultural background, particularly with respect to personal space and physical contact. Proximity between two adult conversationalists will vary due to culture, with individuals from some cultures having a preference for closer personal space, whereas others favor greater physical space when interacting. Eye contact is another feature of conversations that may be dependent on what is accepted cultural social behavior. Some cultures teach their children to avoid eye contact when talking or listening to authority figures or adults; more specifically, making eye contact with someone in authority is often viewed as disrespectful. Ariki, the first child from the opening chapter vignettes, may come from a culture that values this practice. If he were born into another culture that encouraged eye contact, his teacher may not have suspected him of having social-emotional difficulties. Other cultures view eye contact as being respectful because it is interpreted as showing that the person is actively involved in the conversation.

Another practice that may differ from culture to culture pertains to physical contact. Whereas individuals from some cultures view hugs or a pat on the head as endearing, others view it as inappropriate, especially if it is between non–family members. On the one hand, young children from cultures that show affection through physical contact may enjoy sitting in teachers' laps during story times; on the other hand, children from cultures that do not share this practice may feel uncomfortable in the similar non-familial situations. Basimah, also described at the beginning of the chapter, is an example of a child from a family whose cultural group tends to exhibit less physical contact with others outside her family and for which strict gender roles and practices are readily apparent.

These examples are but a few of the communication and interactional style differences that may be dictated by one's culture. Cultural clashes based on misunderstood and misinterpreted social behavior may occur if interaction partners are unaware of the meaning of others' behavior.

CULTURAL INFLUENCES ON PARENT–INFANT INTERACTION IN FAMILIES OF CHILDREN WITH DISABILITIES

From birth, children enter into a world that is filled with many opportunities to socialize. McCollum and McBride (1997) described the importance of the infant–toddler years and the natural and daily interactions of primary caregivers and children. These early interactions hold importance for children's development of emotional, communicative, social, and cognitive competence (Adamson, 1995; Bridges & Grolnick, 1995; Ratner & Bruner, 1978). Most child development research on early socialization, parenting, and parent–infant interaction has been based on studies of western Anglo-European individuals (Greenfield & Suzuki, 1998). Gaining information from families of children with disabilities, especially those from different cultures, is needed to understand and develop more culturally sensitive interventions regarding children's social competence. It is essential to consider and understand the families' cultural backgrounds during the process of helping children develop social competence (e.g., assessments, general curricula, specific intervention plans) because it is likely that the ways in which family members interact with their children may vary with their backgrounds. The ideals that parents have for how they want their children to gain socialization skills likely depend on their cultural beliefs and values. Chen and McCollum (2001), for instance, interviewed mothers of children with Down syndrome and found that the mothers' perception of their parent–child interactions reflected their cultural views. The results showed that mothers saw their interactions as contributing to their children's social competence and that the ways in which they interacted with their children were congruent with traditional cultural notions that were common to the mothers' collectivistic backgrounds. Not only may parents of children with disabilities have different perceptions regarding their children when compared with parents of children who are typically developing (e.g., Marfo & Kysela, 1988) but also their styles of interaction may also be strongly influenced by their cultural perspectives. Unfortunately, high-quality research in this area is scarce and the need is great for more research to better understand similarities and differences in the social values and perceptions of parent–child interactions among children with disabilities from various cultures (Chen & McCollum, 2001).

CULTURAL INFLUENCES IN EDUCATIONAL SETTINGS FOR YOUNG CHILDREN

Given that cultural influences greatly affect the goals and expectations that families have for young children's development, cultural variables also affect the experiences of young children in early education settings. One research project, the Early Childhood Research Institute on Inclusion (ECRII) (Odom, 2002), examined some of these influences with respect to children's relationships and family–program interactions. The goals of this national longitudinal project were to describe barriers to and facilitators of preschool inclusion and to identify strategies for enhancing inclusion opportunities for young children. The ECRII findings, thus, added to our understanding of the influence of cultural expectations in early education settings.

Children's Relationships in Inclusive Preschool Settings

One aspect of classroom climate is the distinct culture created by the children themselves, which is often referred to as *peer culture*. Corsaro (1985) identified three dimensions that characterized this peer culture; these included the children's sense of collective identity, the continual construction and renewal by children, and particular processes (i.e., interpretative procedures, fantasy play, discourse forms) and content (e.g., behavioral routines, values and concerns). One aspect of peer culture studied by the ECRII research project was children's *acceptance into and membership in peer interactions* (Hanson et al., 1998; Hanson & Zercher, 2001). The researchers found that children who were more socially and linguistically competent used more conventional verbal and nonverbal social cues and behaviors to initiate or enter into peer activities, such as asking, watching, and showing materials. Children with more significant delays, on the other hand, often resorted to more unconventional bids or strategies such as hitting or grabbing or an intrusive affectionate display such as a hug. These observations suggest that having a match in language, ability levels, and interests allowed children to interact more fruitfully with one another.

Another dimension examined was that of children *discovering common ground* for interaction. An example can be found in the following interaction among 4-year-old girls:

> One girl says to the other, "Tu es la Mama" (You are the mother). Analuna protests, "No, es mia—soy la Mama" (No, it's mine—I'm the mother). Analuna goes to the rolling bathtub and picks up a baby doll: "Tu mi bebe, tu mi bebe" (You my baby, you my baby). The other girls take roles alongside her (Hanson et al., 1998, p. 192).

When children were able to share "scripts" such as this one, they played more readily with one another. When children had different routines, either because of language differences or differences in their abilities to understand the theme or interact using conventions, they were often excluded from the play.

The interaction of culture, language, and disability functioned both as a barrier to inclusion and also as a facilitator (Hanson, Gutierrez, Morgan, Brennan, & Zercher, 1997). Instances were noted in the ECRII studies in which children who did not share the majority language of the classroom were isolated as a subgroup. However, in classrooms in which teachers bolstered or supported children's interactions, children were able to overcome these potential barriers and join together in activities.

Family and Program Personnel Interactions

Culture plays a significant and direct role not only with children's interactions with family members, peers, and caregivers in their primary environments—home and classrooms (termed *microsystems* in Bronfenbrenner's ecological framework)—but also on the interactions between members of those primary settings, or at the mesosystem level (Bronfenbrenner, 1979). Families' experiences and interactions with one another and with school personnel, too, were shaped in part by cultural and linguistic factors. Families' cultural values, for instance, played a role in their philosophy of preschool education (Hanson, 2002). Some families, based on their cultural values, stressed the major purposes of preschool to be teaching children manners, cleanliness, and how to follow teachers' directions. Other families emphasized the importance of their children's creativity and social interactions. At times a mismatch existed between the families' expectations of preschool and the curricular models or approaches promulgated by personnel in the school; these ecological disconnects may create tensions between members of children's mesosystems.

Language and socioeconomic differences also influenced parent–parent interactions in the schools. Many preschool programs for young children are publicly funded primarily for children from low socioeconomic groups. Children with disabilities are often enrolled in these programs, even if their family's socioeconomic status is considerably higher, in an effort to provide inclusive educational settings for them. At times parents' social networks were hampered by the cultural divides, as demonstrated in this quote by a single mother of a child with a disability:

> "They're usually married families. The Spanish speaking—well I know the women stay home. Take care of the kids. And the man works. Where I have to go to work, go to school, take care of him, and I don't get any help" (Hanson et al., 1998, p. 201).

Culture and language played the most significant role in parents' access to information, thus shaping their choices and decision making. The ECRII studies reported that professional opinions and options exerted the most powerful force over family decisions and choices (Hanson et al., 2000; Hanson et al., 2001; Hanson et al., 1998). Families differed in their degree of comfort with this situation. Some families, due to their cultural background and values, felt comfortable deferring almost exclusively to professional opinion, whereas other families felt left out of the process and stood up and questioned whether their legal rights were being supported. In addition, parents' abilities to advocate on behalf of their children were influenced by their cultural/linguistic background. Families from non–English-speaking backgrounds and cultures that were the most different from that of the majority culture were considerably hampered in their efforts to receive information and supports.

The philosophy of the school system or preschool personnel also shaped the experience for children and families (Hanson, 2002). In programs in which diversity was cherished and in which inclusion was seen as being a goal for ALL children, teachers were more likely to make adaptations or adjustments to accommodate the range of children and family characteristics (Hanson et al., 1998). In many classes teachers made extraordinary efforts to respect children's and families' values and preferences. One such example was the protocol for birthday parties in a particular classroom. On the day of a birthday party, Gisela, a youngster whose family is of the Jehovah's Witness faith and does not celebrate birthdays, was provided with a highly prized alternative activity during the birthday celebration in the classroom in lieu of attending the class party.

As this discussion has emphasized, culture and language variables interact with other child and family characteristics in every setting to influence the experiences that children will have. Teachers and other personnel who are savvy and aware of these influences can provide a more culturally sensitive and supportive environment for children and families.

IMPLICATIONS FOR SERVICE DELIVERY

Many early childhood leaders have championed the need for culturally responsive services in early childhood settings (Anderson & Fenichel, 1989; Barrera, 2000; Bredekamp & Copple, 1997; Lynch & Hanson 2004; Okagaki & Diamond, 2000). Teachers and other service providers can take important steps to ensure that their services are being delivered in a fashion that better supports young children and their families who come from socioeconomically, culturally, ethnically, and linguistically diverse backgrounds.

Supporting Children and Families from Various Backgrounds

Differences among individuals' backgrounds may be so subtle that they might be easily overlooked. Teachers may wish to initiate systematic strategies for learning about the preferences and individual characteristics of children and their families. These may include questions about how children typically spend the day, what they like to eat, with whom they like to play and so on. The *Introducing Me!* book in the *Me, Too!* series may provide a useful structure for gathering this type of information (Hanson & Beckman, 2001). Interviewing family members when children enroll in a program is an essential step to learning about the families' goals and preferences for their children, as well as about activities with which they are comfortable.

Demonstrating interest and respect for diversity demands that classroom activities and materials be reflective of the many backgrounds of the children in the community so that different languages, foods, books, and other activities and practices are featured and honored. However, this recommendation extends far beyond days that are set aside for holidays (e.g., Cinco de Mayo) or days in which children bring special "native" foods or wear "native" costumes. Rather, respect for these differences ought to include knowledge of different styles of communication (as well as languages) and different values, beliefs, and practices.

Becoming Culturally Competent

The journey to cultural competence is a lifelong one of knowledge building and exploration. This journey is a process, not an end product. Practitioners can enhance their skills in cultural competence through several steps, however (Lynch & Hanson, 2004). First and perhaps foremost is the process of *self-awareness*. Service providers should become aware of their own beliefs and values, biases, and preferences. This process begins with *examining one's own background and heritage* and becoming cognizant of customs, styles of interacting, beliefs, and actions that may have roots in one's family background. When individuals become aware of these factors, they can examine them and determine which are universal and which are pertinent to their own personal view of the world.

The second step involves *gathering information about other cultural and sociocultural perspectives*. One can gather this information by exploring new communities, meeting and talking with members from other groups, visiting neighborhoods and participating in celebrations, sampling foods from other cultures, reading books, watching films, traveling, taking classes, and learning a new language. Each of these strategies opens up new sources of knowledge and experience and can support the development and respect, knowledge, and appreciation for other cultural practices.

The next step is *applying the knowledge to practice*. Hand in hand with family members and "cultural guides" within communities, practitioners can infuse their programs and practices with new ideas and ways of interacting. These experiences may help stem the burnout that is all too common in educational settings and enhance the growth and learning opportunities of staff members.

Assessment and Selection of Child Goals

Establishing a true partnership with children's families will help ensure that assessment and goal development for children are more appropriate. Certainly children and their families who come from non–English-speaking backgrounds will be better supported by the use of interpreters and perhaps even "cultural guides," individuals who are knowledgeable about both the family's native culture and the dominant culture of the community or classroom. As the opening vignettes of this chapter illustrate, the behavior of individual children can be evaluated and interpreted quite differently based on whether the practitioner has knowledge of children and families' backgrounds and their language and culture. Many contemporary behavior checklists that are used in early childhood programs were developed with samples from the dominant culture, Anglo-European children. Moreover, the content of these early childhood assessments are heavily weighted toward and reflect the goals of the dominant culture. Whether or not a child self-feeds or is toilet trained at a particular age will be greatly influenced by the family's priorities rather than a developmental or maturational imperative.

Family's social and educational priorities extend to critical behaviors in the realm of social competence. Where, when, and how children make eye contact, touch, initiate, speak, as well as other critical social behaviors, are largely governed by socialization from children's families and communities. Thus, differences from normative social behavior may represent cultural influences rather than a developmental delay or deviance. Practitioners ought to proceed cautiously in making assumptions about the meaning of particular child and family behaviors.

Valuing Diversity and Avoiding Cultural Conflict

Service providers will be well-advised to become knowledgeable about the possible perceptions and cultural values of groups with whom they work. Moreover, effective personnel should be respectful of and open to working with community guides and cultural and spiritual leaders who may be outside of their comfort zone of traditional service practitioners. Many service providers may experience some traditional practices of families as bizarre and inappropriate. Nevertheless, the more that they are able to learn about families' views and culture, the more they will be able to forge an effective, collaborative working relationship and forgo unneeded and unproductive cultural clashes.

To explore the potential for cultural clashes and contemplate the difficulties inherent in working with families whose views may differ radically from mainstream services, the interested reader is referred to the book, *When the Spirit Catches You and You Fall Down* (Fadiman, 1997). This poignant true story follows an immigrant Hmong family in central California and describes their struggle to understand their child's significant disability and the services recommended to them. It also portrays the struggles of health care and social service providers who attempted to serve the child and the family. Although this story is more dramatic than most that service practitioners will encounter, teachers and other professionals undoubtedly will, from time to time, experience discomfort and confusion in their interactions with families who social perspectives and practices differ from their own. Entering these especially critical parent–professional interactions with open hearts and open minds is essential to establishing respectful and effective partnerships with families.

CONCLUSION

Professionals who have the privilege of working with young children and their families are given opportunities to meet individuals who come from a wide range of backgrounds that differ in many respects: socioeconomically, ethnically, racially, culturally, linguistically, and spiritually, as well as in terms of educational and social opportunities. With this privilege comes the obligation to meet children and families at least halfway and learn about their values and beliefs, concerns and priorities, and their preferred life practices. This requires professional and personal effort but it also provides an opportunity for renewal and growth with each new challenge and ensures the provision of more effective services.

REFERENCES

Adamson, L.B. (1995). *Communication development during infancy.* Madison, WI: Brown & Benchmark.

Anderson, P.P., & Fenichel, E.S. (1989). *Serving culturally diverse families of infants and toddlers with disabilities.* Washington, DC: National Center for Clinical Infant Programs.

Barrera, I. (2000). Honoring differences: Essential features of appropriate ECSE services for young children from diverse sociocultural environments. *Young Exceptional Children, 3*(4), 17–24.

Bredekamp, S., & Copple, C. (1997). *Developmentally appropriate practice in early childhood programs* (Rev. ed.). Washington, DC: National Association for the Education of Young Children (NAEYC).

Bridges, L.J., & Grolnick, W.S. (1995). The development of emotional self-regulation in infancy and early childhood. In N. Eisenberg (Ed.), *Review of personality and social psychology: Vol. 15. Social development* (pp. 185–211). Thousand Oaks, CA: Sage Publications.

Bronfenbrenner, U. (1979). *The ecology of human development.* Cambridge, MA: Harvard University Press.

Bronfenbrenner, U., & Morris, P.A. (1998). The ecology of developmental processes. In W. Damon (Series Ed.) & R.M. Lerner (Vol. Ed.), *Handbook of child psychology: Vol. 1: Theory* (5th ed., pp. 993–1028). New York: Wiley.

California State Department of Education. (2006). *California school statistics.* Retrieved February 27, 2006, from http://www.cde.ca.gov/ds/sd/cb/index.asp

Chen, J., & McCollum, J.A. (2001). Taiwanese mothers' perceptions of parent–infant interaction with children with Down syndrome. *Journal of Early Intervention, 24,* 252–265.

ChildStats. (2005). *America's children: Key national indicators of well-being 2005.* Retrieved February 18, 2006, from http://www.childstats.gov/americaschildren/index.asp.

Cartledge, G., & Loe, S.A. (2001). Cultural diversity and social skill instruction. *Exceptionality, 9,* 33–46.

Corsaro, W.A. (1985). *Friendship and peer culture in the early years.* Stamford, CT: Ablex.

Dodge, K.A., Pettit, G.S., McClaskey, C.L., & Brown, M.M. (1986). Social competence in children. *Monographs of the Society for Research in Child Development, 51*(2, Serial No. 213).

Fadiman, A. (1997). *The spirit catches you and you fall down: A Hmong child, her American doctors, and the collision of two cultures.* New York: Farrar, Straus, & Giroux.

Feng, H., & Cartledge, G. (1996). Social skill assessment of inner city Asian, African, and European American students. *School Psychology Review, 25,* 227–238.

Garcia, E.E., & McLaughlin, B. (with Spodek, B. & Saracho, O.). (Eds.) (1995). *Meeting the challenge of linguistic and cultural diversity in early childhood education: Yearbook in early childhood education* (Vol. 6). New York: Teachers College Press.

Garcia, S.B., & Malkin, D.H. (1993). Toward defining programs and services for culturally and linguistically diverse learners in special education. *Teaching Exceptional Children, 26,* 51–58.

Greenfield, P.M., & Suzuki, L.K. (1998). Culture and human development: Implications for parenting, education, pediatrics, and mental health. In W. Damon (Series Ed.) & R.M. Lerner (Vol. Ed.), *Handbook of child psychology: Vol. 1,: Theory* (5th ed., pp. 1059–1109). New York: Wiley.

Guralnick, M.J. (1990). Social competence and early intervention. *Journal of Early Intervention, 14,* 3–14.

Hanson, M.J. (2002). Cultural and linguistic diversity. In S.L. Odom (Ed.), *Widening the circle: Including children with disabilities in preschool programs* (pp. 137–153). New York: Teachers College Press.

Hanson, M.J. (2004). Ethnic, cultural, and language diversity in service settings. In E.W. Lynch & M.J. Hanson (Eds.), *Developing cross-cultural competence: A guide for working with children and their families* (3rd ed., pp. 3–18). Baltimore: Paul H. Brookes Publishing Co.

Hanson, M.J., & Beckman, P. (2001). *Introducing me!* In M.J. Hanson, P. Beckman (Eds.), *Me, Too!:* Vol. 1. Baltimore: Paul H. Brookes Publishing Co.

Hanson, M.J., Beckman, P.J., Horn, E., Marquart, J., Sandall, S., Greig, D., & Brennan, E. (2000). Entering preschool: Family and professional experiences in this transition process. *Journal of Early Intervention, 23,* 279–293.

Hanson, M.J., Gutierrez, S., Morgan, M., Brennan, E.L., & Zercher, C. (1997). Language, culture and disability: Interacting influences on preschool inclusion. *Topics in Early Childhood Special Education, 17*(3), 307–336.

Hanson, M.J., Horn, E., Sandall, S., Beckman, P.J., Morgan, M., Marquart, J., Barnwell, D., & Chou, H.Y. (2001). After preschool inclusion: Children's educational pathways over the early school years. *Exceptional Children, 68,* 65–83.

Hanson, M.J., & Lynch, E.W. (in press). Working with families from diverse backgrounds. In R. McWilliam (Ed.), *Working with families of young children with disabilities.* New York: Guilford Press.

Hanson, M.J., Lynch, E.W., & Wayman, K.I. (1990). Honoring the cultural diversity of families when gathering data. *Topics in Early Childhood Special Education, 10,* 112–131.

Hanson, M.J., Wolfberg, P., Zercher, C., Morgan, M., Gutierrez, S., Barnwell, D., & Beckman, P.J. (1998). The culture of inclusion: Recognizing diversity at multiple levels. *Early Childhood Research Quarterly, 13*(1), 185–209.

Hanson, M.J., & Zercher, C. (2001). The impact of cultural and linguistic diversity in inclusive preschool environments. In M.J. Guralnick (Ed.), *Early childhood inclusion: Focus on change* (pp. 413–431). Baltimore: Paul H. Brookes Publishing Co.

Harkness, S., & Super, C.M. (Eds.). (1996). *Parents' cultural belief systems: Their origins, expressions, and consequences.* New York: Guilford Press.

Harry, B. (1992a). *Cultural diversity, families, and the special education system: Communication and empowerment.* New York: Teachers College Press.

Harry, B. (1992b). Developing cultural awareness: The first step in values clarification for early interventionists. *Topics in Early Childhood Special Education, 12,* 333–350.

Howes, C. (1988). Peer interaction of young children. *Monographs of the Society for Research in Child Development, 53*(1, Serial No. 217).

Italiano-Thomas, G. (2003, July). The national reporting system and English language learners. *Head Start Bulletin, 76,* 18–19.

Kagan, S., & Garcia, E. (1991). Education of culturally and linguistically diverse preschoolers: Moving the agenda. *Early Childhood Research Quarterly, 6,* 427–443.

Lynch, E.W. (2004). Developing cross-cultural competence. In M.J. Hanson & E.W. Lynch (Eds.). *Developing cross-cultural competence: A guide for working with children and their families* (3rd ed., pp. 41–75). Baltimore: Paul H. Brookes Publishing Co.

Lynch, E.W., & Hanson, M.J. (1993). Changing demographics: Implications for training in early intervention. *Infants and Young Children, 6,* 50–55.

Lynch, E.W., & Hanson, M.J. (2004). *Developing cross-cultural competence: A guide for working with young children and their families (3rd ed.).* Baltimore: Paul H. Brookes Publishing Co.

Marfo, K., & Kysela, G.M. (1988) Frequency and sequential patterns in mothers' interactions with mentally handicapped and nonhandicapped children. In K. Marfo (Ed.), *Parent–child interaction and developmental disabilities* (pp. 64–89). Westport, CT: Praeger.

McCollum, J.A., & McBride, S.L. (1997). Ratings of parent–infant interaction: Raising questions of cultural validity. *Topics in Early Childhood Special Education, 17,* 494–520.

Odom, S.L. (Ed.). (2002). *Widening the circle: Including children with disabilities in preschool programs.* New York: Teachers College Press.

Okagaki, L., & Diamond, K.E. (2000). Responding to cultural and linguistic difference in the beliefs and practices of families of young children. *Young Children, 55*(3), 74–80.

Olaniran, B.A., & Williams, D.E. (1995). Communication distortion: An intercultural lesson from the visa application process. *Communication Quarterly, 43,* 225–240.

Olson, S. (2001, April). The genetic archaeology of race. *The Atlantic Monthly,* 69–80.

Ratner, N., & Bruner, J. (1978). Games, social exchange and the acquisition of language. *Journal of Child Language, 5,* 391–401.

Rivera, B.D., & Rogers-Adkinson, D. (1997). Culturally sensitive interventions: Social skills training with children and parents from culturally and linguistically diverse backgrounds. *Intervention in School & Clinic, 33,* 1053–4512.

Rubin, K.H. (1998). Social and emotional development from a cultural perspective. *Developmental Psychology, 34,* 611–615.

Safford, P.L., & Safford, E.J. (1996). *A history of childhood & disability.* New York: Teachers College Press.

Smith, E., & Sapp, W. (Eds.). (1996). *Plain talk about the Human Genome Project: A Tuskegee University conference on its promise and perils . . . and matters of race.* Tuskegee, AL: Tuskegee University Publications Office.

Tabors, P.O. (1997). *One child, two languages: A guide for preschool educators of children learning English as a second language.* Baltimore: Paul H. Brookes Publishing Co..

Topping, K., Bremner, W., & Holmes, E. (2000). Social competence: The social construction of the concept. In R. Bar-On & J.D.A. Parker (Eds.), *The handbook of emotional intelligence: Theory, development, assessment, and application at home, school, and in the workplace* (pp. 28–39). San Francisco: Jossey-Bass.

CHAPTER 4

Friendships in Early Childhood

Implications for Early Education and Intervention

Virginia Buysse, Barbara Davis Goldman,
Tracey West, and Heidi Hollingsworth

The ability to form meaningful relationships with others is one of the key determinants of the quality of life. Friendship, a particular type of social relationship, represents a culmination of interest and interaction with peers that is consolidated into a complex, enduring, and reciprocal relationship with a preferred social partner (Hay, Payne, & Chadwick, 2004). Bukowski, Newcomb, and Hartup (1996) observed that the word *friend* generally appears in a child's vocabulary by age 4, but they noted that friendships can emerge at a much earlier age. Mutually regulated friendships have been identified among toddlers and as occurring as early as infancy (e.g., Goldman & Buysse, 2007; Howes, 1996; Rubin, 1980; Vandell & Mueller, 1980).

Although early childhood professionals generally attest to the importance of friendship in the lives of young children, particularly with respect to promoting social adjustment and well-being, they may be less attuned to the powerful force that friendship exerts on other aspects of development, such as cognition and language, and to the adult's role in fostering these early friendships. It can be argued that children's earliest friendships are important in their own right. Young children encounter peers in group settings at an increasingly early age and need to develop strategies for relating to their peers effectively. But the more persuasive educational rationale for fostering positive peer relations is based on a growing body of empirical evidence indicating that having friends may support children's early learning and their adjustment to kindergarten—critical factors in promoting the transition to kindergarten and early school success (Bukowski & Sandberg, 1999; Costin & Jones, 1992; Gresham & Reschly, 1987; Ladd, 1990).

Other research evidence suggests that, compared with acquaintanceship, friendship may uniquely contribute to a child's development and adaptation in key domains that include cooperation and conflict management, expressed emotion, task orientation, self-awareness, and self-esteem, as well as to provide emotional and cognitive resources (Newcomb & Bagwell, 1996). Ladd and Kochenderfer (1996) observed two functions of friendship with demonstrated empirical validity during early childhood: as a context for skill development and as a source of emotional support and security (i.e., friends as a source of support in the transition to kindergarten, friends as attachment figures). Further support for the developmental significance of early friendships can be found in research showing that children who do not form friendships in early childhood are at risk for poor social outcomes and maladjustment when they get older (Parker, Rubin, Price, & DeRosier, 1995).

This chapter contains a review of research about friendships in early childhood, with a particular focus on the implications of this knowledge for professionals who work in early education programs (e.g., child care centers, child care homes, Head Start, prekindergarten, kindergartens, and the early elementary grades). We begin by offering a definition of friendship and by differentiating friendship from other forms of peer relations. Then, we examine several methods of identifying peer acceptance and friendship that have been used in research, noting the need for additional approaches that are both practical and relevant for early education settings. Next, we present a developmental framework to identify the forms or features of friendship across developmental stages, and we discuss the ways in which individual differences and disability may moderate this developmental trajectory. Finally, we consider the contributions of parents and teachers to friendship development and the implications of current understandings of friendship for early education and intervention, particularly with respect to the critical role of the teacher in identifying and nurturing children's developing friendships in the early childhood classroom.

DEFINING FRIENDSHIP IN EARLY CHILDHOOD

In their descriptions of peer relations, researchers have not reached consensus on a single conceptual framework but, rather, have developed constructs that focus on different dimensions of children's social behaviors with peers (see for example, Newcomb & Bagwell, 1995; Rubin, Bukowski, & Parker, 1998). Some researchers have conceptualized peer relations in terms of typologies of social acceptance, relying on children's perceptions of their peers to create categories such as *popular, rejected, neglected,* or *controversial* (Coie, Dodge, & Coppotelli, 1982). Others have focused on the types of social relationships that children form in terms of familiarity, directionality, or the quality of these relationships (e.g., acquaintances, unilateral relationships, just friends, good friends, best friends; Guralnick & Groom, 1988). Still others have turned their attention to the levels of social structure within peer groups (e.g., social interactions, social relationships, social networks or cliques) and the functions that children's friendships serve (e.g., companionship, intimacy and affection, instrumental assistance, emotional support, social comparison; Hartup, 1996; Parker et al., 1995).

Distinguishing Friendship from Other
Peer Relations: Defining Characteristics

To understand how early educators can support children's developing friendships, it is essential to begin with a shared understanding of friendship and to differentiate friendship from other forms of peer relations in early childhood. Within early education settings, it is possible to define peer relations at two levels: 1) friendships with individual peers, and 2) the peer group in which the relation between the individual and the group is defined in terms of the individual's status within the group (i.e., peer acceptance or social acceptance; Ladd & Kochenderfer, 1996). Asher, Parker, and Walker (1996) stressed the importance of distinguishing between friendship and peer acceptance. *Friendship* can be defined as a positive, reciprocal relationship between two children. *Peer acceptance* refers to an index of a child's social status among his or her peers in terms of whether children are accepted, rejected, or ignored. Researchers have coined the term *controversial* to refer to children whose social status is mixed. Children with controversial peer status are accepted by some peers and rejected or ignored by others. Ladd and Coleman (1993) noted that measures of friendship and peer acceptance are only moderately correlated. It is possible for a child who is not widely accepted by his or her peers to have at least one close friend.

In addition to distinguishing friendship from peer acceptance, friendship can be differentiated from other forms of social relationships with peers in the following ways:

1. *Friendships are dyadic in nature.* This "two-ness" characterizes and permeates all of the shared activities in which the two friends engage.

2. *In a friendship, each child must consider the other to be a friend.* The relationship must be reciprocal or bi-directional. This means that even within a peer group consisting of multiple friendship pairs, it is possible to identify a distinct friendship between any two of the children.

3. *Friendships of young children are closely tied to mutual liking and attachment.* When asked why someone is considered to be a friend, young children frequently respond, "Because I like him (or her)." At the same time, not all young children explicitly proclaim their affection and liking for a friend (particularly when they are very young), but often friendships can be inferred from children's play interactions with their social partners. Children form an attachment with a friend that is unique from the attachments they form with parents and other family members. Friendship attachments carry with them an expectation that friends spend more time together than do nonfriends (Bukowski, Newcomb, & Hartup, 1996).

4. *Friendships are voluntary.* Young children do not choose their siblings and other family members, but they are allowed to choose the peers they want as friends. The voluntary nature of friendship and children's developing understanding of what it means to have a friend may explain why many prekindergartners (i.e., 3- to 5-year-olds) find it necessary to declare their friendships and to make decisions on the basis of this friendship status (e.g., "Taletha is [is not] invited to my birthday party"). In their efforts to create a caring community in which every child experiences a sense of belonging, early educators sometimes inadvertently communicate in ways that do not recognize that children's friendships are voluntary. For example, a teacher may say, "We're all friends in this classroom." In this example, the teacher is using the term *friend* to promote notions of good citizenship and to create a positive classroom climate. It is also important for teachers to support children's developing understanding of what it means to have a special relationship with a close friend ("I noticed that you and your friend Ennis enjoyed reading books together in the quiet corner today.").

5. *Friendship includes the defining features of proximity and shared activities.* This addresses what children who are friends do when they are together. During

early childhood, children who are friends enjoy spending time together and being near each other. But friendship almost always entails more than just proximity. Young children who are friends often develop shared activities, routines, and rituals, and their interactions may be noticeably coordinated and reciprocal (Howes, 1996) and often involve pretend play (Howes, 1996; Howes, Matheson, & Wu, 1992). Friendships are built on common activities or objects such as toys—shared themes around which children can relate and that persist over time (Ladd, 1988).

6. *Friendships of young children are characterized by enjoyment and positive affect.* Although conflicts may arise among friends, interactions between friends more often convey mutual enjoyment with each other's company.

Identifying Friendship in Early Childhood

Bukowski and colleagues (1996) observed that identifying children's friendships relies on three sources: 1) what children tell us about these relations, 2) what parents and teachers report, and 3) what trained observers see with regard to children's social behaviors. Ideally, a convergent assessment approach whereby information from all three sources is obtained would be used to document children's friendships. However, this is unlikely to occur with very young children or children with delayed language skills because their capacity for describing peer relations is limited. In addition to these three sources, Bukowski and colleagues suggested that it is important to document the following types of information about children's friendships: the number of friends, the nature of children's friendships, and the patterns of social exchanges between friends. Different approaches have been developed for assessing peer acceptance and friendship in early childhood (Brown, Odom, & Buysse, 2002), and these are described next.

Assessing Peer Acceptance

Peer acceptance generally is assessed through two different sociometric techniques, peer nominations and peer ratings. The nomination approach, primarily used with school-age and older prekindergartners, requires individual children to name the children that they like or do not like in their class (or alternatively, children that they do or do not like to play with). Positive and negative nominations are scored for each child and standardized within classrooms and gender to generate an index of peer acceptance that can be categorized as *accepted, rejected, ignored,* and so forth. Sociometric peer ratings represent a variation of the nomination technique whereby children rate classmates on a Likert-type scale according to how much they like them (or would like to play with them) from 1 (*not at all*) to 5 (*a lot*). The peer rating technique has been shown to be reliable with preschoolers who are typically developing (Asher, Singleton, Tinsley, & Hymel, 1979), particularly when children are first taught to sort pictures of foods and toys by preference to determine if they understand the task (Odom et al., 1999).

Odom and his colleagues used peer ratings in conjunction with other methods to identify prekindergarten children with disabilities who were socially accepted or rejected (Odom, Zercher, Li, Shouming, Marquart, Sandall, & Brown, 2006). They found that approximately one-third of the children with disabilities (22 of 80) were socially rejected by their peers as compared with only one child who was typically developing who was rejected—a finding that was consistent with previous research. Using a peer rating technique adapted from Parker, Sprague, Flannery, Niess, and Zumwait (1991), a related study found that, although prekindergartners with disabilities received lower ratings than their peers who were typically developing, the reasons cited for selecting or rejecting their peers with disabilities were essentially the same as those given for children without disabilities (Buysse, Nabors, Skinner, & Keyes, 1997). Children who were typically developing chose peers as playmates, irrespective of ability status, because they liked them, considered them friends, or enjoyed the same toys and activities together. Conversely, children (both those with disabilities and those who were typically developing) who exhibited aggressive behaviors or personal characteristics that were problematic in other ways were not selected as preferred playmates, nor were they regarded as friends. These findings were consistent with the social rejection themes identified by Odom and his colleagues (2006) on the basis of case summaries.

Ten children ranging in age from 52 to 69 months were the focus of an exploration of how children with significant disabilities experienced peer culture in the context of inclusive preschool environments (Wolfberg et al., 1999). The age equivalent scores for these children ranged from 22 months to 46 months, with a mean of 33 months. Three children's levels of functioning could not be assessed, and overall developmental scores for seven of the children for whom assessment data were available were low. Four of the ten children with significant disabilities were well liked and viewed as highly desirable playmates on the basis of sociometric ratings, whereas six were among the least likely to be chosen as playmates. Consistent with their developmental levels, the attempts of the children with disabilities to join their social world were often similar to those of very young children, namely watching, following, touching, imitating peers, and playfully grabbing their toys. But they also shared their food and asked to play with the other children, and several children talked about their friends. Interaction themes within the inclusive preschool setting included expressing the desire to participate and experiencing both acceptance and rejection by their peers.

Assessing Friendship

The assessment of friendships generally involves asking children to name their friends using sociometric nominations, observing children's social interactions with peers, and asking parents and teachers to report children's friendships with peers. Sociometric nominations are difficult to administer to children who are very young or who have developmental disabilities. In addition, because children are permitted only a limited number of choices in selecting friends, this method has been criticized for either restricting the number of friendships a child can report or, in some cases, encouraging overestimates. Also, researchers have noted that verification of the reciprocity of children's choices frequently is lacking (Parker et al., 1995). A fundamental problem with observational methods for assessing friendships has been the lack of agreement about a behavioral criterion for determining friendship status. Moreover, observational methods have yielded extremely low rates of mutual friendships among preschool children with disabilities (Guralnick, Gottman, & Hammond, 1996). Friendships identified through questionnaires and interviews with parents and teachers are easy to administer, but these methods rely on perceived friendships. The Playmates and Friends Questionnaire for Teachers–Revised (Goldman & Buysse, 2005) is an example of a teacher-report measure that can be used to document the number and nature of children's relationships with peers in inclusive early childhood programs, and there is evidence of the validity of teachers' reported friendships using this questionnaire (Buysse, Goldman, & Skinner, 2002; available at http://www.fpg.unc.edu/~publicationsoffice/pdfs/ playmates_friends_rev.pdf).

To date, methods of assessing peer acceptance and friendships have been used primarily in research. In practice, parents and teachers generally rely on an implied definition of friendship. For example, parents and teachers may notice that two children show an interest in being near each other, spending time together, sharing common activities and play themes, and displaying affection for one another. Additional research is needed to translate peer acceptance and friendship assessment approaches designed for research purposes into practical and relevant methods for parents and educators to use at home and in early education settings. In the meantime, adults can observe children's social relations with peers and pay careful attention to individual children who may need additional support in learning how to get along with others and make friends.

FEATURES OF FRIENDSHIP ACROSS DEVELOPMENTAL STAGES

Friendships in early childhood are manifested differently at various developmental stages. Consequently, it is important for early educators to recognize that the signs of friendship in infants and toddlers are different from those of prekindergartners and older children. Understanding the normative aspects of friendship can assist early educators in forming realistic expectations for children at various developmental levels, identifying the precursors of emerging friendships, anticipating subsequent friendship goals and tasks, and making adjustments for children who have developmental delays or individual differences in how they relate to their friends. Following are brief descriptions of the primary forms and features of friendship for each developmental stage.

Infants and Toddlers

Friendships among infants and toddlers are characterized by social behaviors that reflect interest in peers such as looking, smiling, touching, and vocalizing; mutual looking, smiling, touching, and laughing; showing a desire to be near a preferred social partner (e.g., requesting to see or play with a friend); initiating and responding more with a preferred partner than with other children; and repeating specific play sequences or activities with a friend that have been shared in the past.

Older Toddlers

Older toddlers may have one or more friendships. These friendships are typically characterized by the children displaying mutual positive affect; playing games with a friend that involve imitative, complementary, or reciprocal roles (e.g., run–chase, hide and seek, throw and catch); engaging in collaborative pretend or fantasy play; having conversations with a friend; engaging in coordinated social play with objects;

creating private time with a friend by separating from the larger group or excluding other children who try to join in the play; and displaying prosocial behaviors (e.g., supporting or protecting a friend).

Prekindergartners (3- to 5-year-olds)

Prekindergartners are likely to have at least one friend and are more likely than younger children to have stable friendships. Their friendships are characterized by naming one's friends when asked; giving reasons for selecting someone as a friend; differentiating between best friends versus just friends; disclosing private information and feelings to a friend; using strategies to resolve conflicts with friends; engaging in conversations to share information, coordinate joint activities, and create a sense of two-ness through "we-talk" ("We're making a tunnel together, right?"); forming alliances with friends against others (occasionally); exhibiting more elaborate and frequent pretend or fantasy play with friends than at younger ages; requesting to play with friends outside of school; and excluding others from the activities that friends share together.

Children in the Early Elementary Grades

In the early elementary grades, it is common for children to spend a significant amount of time with their friends and to seek proximity to them (e.g., sitting next to each other during lunch, playing together on the playground). Friendships during this stage are characterized by communicating, showing affection, and sharing jokes and other activities with friends; turning to friends as an important source of instrumental and emotional support; disclosing private information and feelings to a friend with an expectation that confidentiality will be maintained; and having fewer cross-sex and cross-race friendships than at younger ages.

DEVELOPMENTAL PROCESSES AND SKILLS THAT UNDERLIE PEER RELATIONS AND FRIENDSHIP

Early educators need to recognize the wide variability that exists with respect to the timing and nature of friendship formation among individual children. Stable individual differences in how young children relate to their peers may emerge as early as infancy or the toddler years, according to some researchers. For example, precursors to problems with shyness or aggression in the first years of life have been shown to be related to these traits in prekindergarten, and toddlers who engaged in complex play with peers were reported to be more prosocial during prekindergarten and less likely to be aggressive or withdrawn when they were 9 years old (Hay et al., 2004; Howes & Phillipsen, 1998).

Several researchers have suggested that the ability to form and maintain friendships rests on specific cognitive, language, and self-regulatory skills that are needed to engage a social partner and sustain interactions (Asher et al., 1996; Gottman, 1983; Hay et al., 2004). Hay and her colleagues identified six primary developmental processes that underlie harmonious interactions with peers among infants and toddlers and serve as the foundation for making and maintaining friendships later on. These include 1) *joint attention* (i.e., the ability to coordinate attention with another); 2) *emotion regulation* (i.e., the ability to regulate one's emotions, particularly negative emotions); 3) *inhibitory control* (i.e., learning to inhibit impulses by relying on communicative gestures and words); 4) *imitation* (i.e., matching the behaviors of a social partner to promote complementary and reciprocal relations); 5) *causal understanding* (i.e., understanding a partner's status as an active and intentional agent); and 6) *language* (i.e., the ability to communicate one's desires and aims through language rather than resorting to physical aggression).

Hay and colleagues (2004) proposed that problems in key relationship processes such as emotion regulation or social understanding may be related to later problems with peers such as shyness or aggression. For example, delays in developing joint attention and theory of mind that are characteristic of children with autism spectrum disorder (ASD) help to explain why these children have difficulty relating positively to their peers. Therefore, attempts to influence children's peer-related social competence may need to begin earlier than initially thought. According to Hay and colleagues, during prekindergarten and early elementary school, when children spend substantially more time in group settings, social skills and group relations consolidate as children develop new ways of relating to peers. Playmate preferences, friendships, and social networks emerge as children learn how to relate to peers in groups. Social structures that include friendship, peer acceptance and rejection, dominance hierarchies, and gender segregation are supported by different types of social interactions. The types of social interaction skills that support these social preferences and groupings and foster friendships include the ability to engage in conversation, cooperate with others, act prosocially (e.g., being helpful, sympathetic, or kind), resolve conflicts, and participate in pretend play.

FEATURES OF FRIENDSHIPS

Ladd's (1988) review of friendship development in early childhood examined features of friendship for infants and toddlers, prekindergartners (i.e., children 3–5 years of age), and early grade-school children across three dimensions: 1) onset and stability of friendship (e.g., "When do children develop friendships and how long do they last?"), 2) the structure and composition of friendship (e.g., "Who do children choose as friends and how many do they have?"), and 3) friendship dynamics (e.g., "How do children behave with their friends?"). In the following section, Ladd's framework is used to summarize key conclusions from his and other published literature reviews on the nature of children's early peer relationships and friendships (see, for example, Ladd, 1988; Ladd, 2005; Ladd & Coleman, 1993; Ladd, Herald, & Andrews, 2006; Parker et al., 1995; Price & Ladd, 1986).

Onset and Stability of Friendship

Some evidence suggests that mutually regulated friendships exist among some infants (Bukowski et al, 1996; Goldman & Buysse, 2007; Howes, 1996; Ladd et al., 2006; Rubin, 1980; Vandell & Mueller, 1980); however, this is not the norm for most young children. Howes noted that most children with exposure to specific peers on a routine basis form differentiated relationships with peers (e.g., selecting particular peers, interacting with some peers in ways that are distinct from interactions with other peers) by the end of the first year. She also observed that, given regular opportunities to play together, toddlers between the ages of 12–18 months are capable of developing specific relationships with peers.

Determining the onset of friendship among infants and toddlers is compli-cated by the fact that methods for identifying friendships were developed for older children, and researchers who use methods that rely on trained observers apply dif-ferent behavioral criteria to determine friendship status (i.e., the proportion of time spent interacting positively with a peer). Because many young children lack the ability to communicate their friendship preferences, parents and teachers must rely on behavioral indicators to infer that a friendship exists. For example, adults can infer that a special friendship exists when young children demonstrate a pref-erence to spend time together and show that they enjoy playing together. Although friendships among very young children are generally less stable than those of older children, the duration of the friendship may be dependent on the extent to which there are opportunities for regular play interactions, something which is largely outside of the control of very young children.

Compared with infants and toddlers, preschoolers develop more stable play partners and have more friends and early grade-school children have more com-plex relationships and enduring friendships than do preschoolers. Precise esti-mates of the length of friendships at each developmental stage are not available, but, in general, the friendships of older children last longer than those of younger children until about the fourth grade, when friendship stability appears to reach a threshold (Berndt, as cited in Ladd, 1988). At least one study found that many friendships formed in prekindergarten were maintained throughout the transition to kindergarten and the entire kindergarten year (Ladd, 1990).

Structure and Composition of Friendship

Researchers also have examined the number of friends that children have at various developmental levels and the nature of these friendships. Determining a normative number of friendships is difficult because individual children vary widely in this regard. Ladd (1988, 2005) estimated that 75% of prekindergart-ners have at least one reciprocal friendship, whereas grade-school children generally identify several best friends, but these nominations are not always recip-rocated. Ladd also noted that current estimates suggest that 6%–10% of older chil-dren have no reported friends. Children tend to establish friendships with children who share similar characteristics or traits, but it is unclear whether similarity is a precursor to friendship or if friendship leads to similarity between friends (Bukowski et. al, 1996). Ladd observed that cross-race friendships are more com-mon during early childhood and decline as children get older, and that girls make fewer friends, but differentiate between friends and acquaintances more clearly than do boys.

Friendship Dynamics

Much of what is known about the dynamics of friendship relations has been acquired by examining the behavior that occurs between friends and nonfriends. Among infants, toddlers, and prekindergartners, signs of early friendship often begin with preferences for particular playmates and progress to play interactions with common themes and shared activities that persist over time. The play that occurs between friends versus less-familiar peers in this age group involves higher rates of social initiations, more elaborated interactions, and more positive affect

(Ladd, 1988). Grade-school friends generally spend more time together as they grow older. For all age groups, the interactions and play between friends is more connected, responsive, positive, and harmonious than the play between less-familiar peers.

FRIENDSHIPS OF YOUNG CHILDREN WITH DISABILITIES

Compared with the body of literature that exists on early childhood friendship patterns of children who are typically developing, the study of friendships in young children with disabilities has received relatively little attention. This section reviews what is currently known about friendship patterns among children with disabilities who are enrolled in early education programs.

Number of Friends

Findings regarding the number of friendships of children with disabilities who have friends are somewhat equivocal. For example, there is wide variability in the reporting of the number of children with disabilities who have mutual friendships. Buysse (1993) found that 55% of the children in her study had at least one mutual friendship based on teacher reports, whereas Field (1984) found that 43% of prekindergartners with developmental delays formed "close friendships," and Guralnick and Groom (1988) found that only 7.5% of children with developmental delays in this age group formed "reciprocal" friendships with peers. A more recent study (Buysse, Goldman, & Skinner, 2002) found that teachers in specialized early childhood programs (in which the majority of children had disabilities) reported a statistically significant difference in the number of friendships, with an average of 1.4 friends for children with disabilities and 2.0 friends for their peers who were typically developing. In contrast, teachers in child care programs in which the majority of children were typically developing reported an average of 1.6 friends for children with disabilities and 1.7 friends for their peers who were typically developing, with the difference not being statistically significant.

A recent qualitative study that used extensive observations and independent teacher reports identified six friendship pairs among four children with disabilities enrolled in Head Start classrooms (Dietrich, 2005). Each of the four children had at least one friendship with a child who was typically developing; one child with cerebral palsy had three friendships, two with children who were typically developing. In a related study, Wolfberg and colleagues (1999) reported that three of 10 children with severe disabilities enrolled in an inclusive preschool setting had mutual friendships, and one friendship was with a child who was typically developing.

The discrepancy in previous findings could be attributed to a variety of factors, including differences in the way in which friendship was defined and measured and differences in the characteristics of the study participants. The research is consistent in one finding: young children with disabilities generally form fewer reciprocal friendships than do children who are typically developing (Buysse et al., 1997; Guralnick et al., 1996). Other researchers have shown that prekindergartners who are typically developing show marked preferences for playing and forming friendships with similar peers who are typically developing (Guralnick et al., 1996; Hestenes & Carroll, 2000).

Social Behaviors of Children with Disabilities Who Have Friends

Findings also are mixed regarding the social behaviors of children with disabilities who have friends versus those who do not. Prekindergartners with developmental delays in early studies conducted by Guralnick and Groom (1988) and Strain (1984) apparently did not experience the same developmental advantages from friendships that children who are typically developing did. Unlike their counterparts who are typically developing, children with disabilities acted similarly in the presence of friends and nonfriends (Guralnick & Groom), and they seldom responded to the initiations of their friends (Strain). In contrast, other researchers have noted parallels between the friendships of children who are typically developing and those of children with disabilities (Field, 1984; Howes, 1983, 1984), observing that both groups of children who had friends were more verbal, more assertive, more extroverted, and displayed more affect (both positive and negative). A more recent study found that prekindergartners with disabilities who had at least one friend had more observed positive social behaviors during center time than did those with no friends, and that children with disabilities who had multiple friends exhibited the highest number of social behaviors (Goldman, Buysse, Skinner, & Edgerton, 2005). A related study concluded that, for some prekindergarten children with disabilities, having a friend may have functioned as a mediator of social acceptance (Odom et al., 2006).

The Dietrich (2005) study found that all six of the friendships she identified included mutual interest in being near each other, having fun and playing together, and showing affection. Sharing was a central component in five of the friendships and helping (e.g., protecting, offering comfort) was an additional focus in four of them. As an indication of the strong interest in each other as manifested by these friends, the children repeatedly sought to be with each other throughout the day (e.g., at center time, during free play outside, in teacher-directed groups). Similarly, Wolfberg and colleagues (1999) described the friendships of preschool children with severe disabilities as positive, mutual relationships that had no observable differences from those of other preschoolers. These friendships sometimes included one of the pair making adaptations for his or her social partner, such as bending down to be at eye level when talking with a friend in a wheelchair or sitting behind a friend at circle time to provide physical support.

Again, it is possible that the discrepancy in findings across these studies can be attributed to differences in child characteristics, the target behaviors, and the methods and measures used to document them. Future research is needed to address questions about the number and nature of friendships in young children with and without disabilities in ways that allow comparisons with extant data.

Child Characteristics and Setting Variables Related to Friendships in Children with Disabilities

Some researchers have assessed how specific child characteristics or aspects of the social ecology influence friendship formation and maintenance among young children with disabilities. For example, some evidence suggests that factors such as the nature and severity of a child's disability, the child's developmental level, and specific behavior characteristics (e.g., temperament, goal-directedness, attention span, frustration level, responsiveness, activity level) are associated with friendship status in young children with disabilities (Buysse, 1993).

Several studies have assessed the effects of early childhood settings on friendship status among children with and without disabilities. Guralnick and colleagues (1996) examined friendship formation among unfamiliar peers as a function of mainstreaming (typically referred to as *inclusion*, in which classes have a combined population of children who are typically developing and children who have disabilities) and specialized playgroups (i.e., groupings of children with similar developmental status). The study found fewer mutual friendships among children with developmental delays, compared with both children who are typically developing and children with communication disorders. The study did not detect a setting effect on friendship formation for either children who were typically developing or children with communication disorders. However, this effect could not be assessed for children with developmental delays because friendship formation occurred too infrequently among this group. In contrast, Buysse and colleagues (2002) found an effect for classroom setting for friendship status among prekindergartners with disabilities. In this study, in addition to obtaining significant differences between the number of friendships among children who are typically developing and children with disabilities in specialized settings, Buysse and colleagues found that children with disabilities had access to more available playmates, formed more friendships, and were more likely to have a friend who was typically developing if they were enrolled in child care versus specialized settings. The authors speculated that having access to many different playmates in child care settings may serve as a precursor to establishing friendships for children with disabilities because the availability of competent play partners promotes children's developing interest in their peers and affords them many opportunities to practice more advanced play skills that are the foundation for friendship formation. At the same time, the findings from Odom and his colleagues (2006) remind us that, although young children with disabilities may benefit from inclusive placements, there is also the risk for peer rejection for some children.

CONTRIBUTIONS OF PARENTS AND TEACHERS TO EARLY FRIENDSHIPS

It is important for early educators to understand adult influences on young children's social development and the potential for adults to foster early friendships. Research on parent and teacher influence on friendships in particular is scarce. However, there is relevant research describing parent and teacher influence on social competence or peer relations in general.

Parent Influence on Children's Friendships

Research focused on parent beliefs and practices regarding children's friendships suggests that many parents of children with and without disabilities place high value on friendships for their prekindergartners for the current and future functions that friendships serve (e.g., as a context for development of social skills) (Rhodes, 2002). According to Rhodes, parents believe that common interests and time spent together in the same early childhood setting lead to formation of friendships, whereas common interests and affection are among the reasons that friendships endure. Rhodes' investigation found that parents use the following practices to support their children's friendships: providing opportunities for interactions, social coaching, participating as an interactive partner, reading books on the topic of friendship, and acting as a social model. Parents of children with disabilities, in particular, expressed the desire for their children to have friends and believed that parental strategies were necessary in order to make that happen.

Rubin and Sloman (1984) identified five modes of parental influence on children's friendships. First, parents set the stage for friendships by choosing a neighborhood, school or child care, and their own preference for social associations. Second, parents arrange social contacts such as playdates for children. Third, parents coach children by providing advice about how friendships are established and maintained. Fourth, parents provide models of social relationships with respect to the social behaviors and strategies they use. Fifth, parents influence children's friendships by providing a home base in which secure parent–child relationships facilitate children's readiness for peer relationships.

Parke and colleagues (2002) described their Tripartite Model of family contributions to children's social development as including 1) parent–child relationships and interactions; 2) parental advising, consulting, and instructing; and 3) parental management and supervision. With regard to the first component, the authors explained that the quality of parent–child attachment is related to the quality of children's peer relationships, and these researchers found that warm, sensitive styles of interaction (rather than controlling, intrusive styles) were related to positive social outcomes. In the second component, parents provide direct instruction on how to initiate and maintain social relationships. In the third component, parents influence children's peer relations through monitoring, establishing play rules, arranging social contacts, and developing and maintaining their own social networks. According to Ladd and colleagues (Ladd & Pettit, 2002; Ladd, Profilet, & Hart, 1992), parents manage children's peer relations by creating formal and informal opportunities for peer contact (childcare, preschool, community activities, playgroups, and choice of neighborhood) and by supervising their play interactions.

Several studies suggest that parents play an important role in facilitating children's early peer relationships, particularly through arrangement of peer contacts for their children and supervision of children's interactions. Parents of children with and without disabilities value their child's peer relationships and play an active role in arranging and supervising play experiences between their child and other children in the community (Guralnick, 1997). However, additional evidence suggests that although active supervision may be more beneficial for young children, indirect supervision may be sufficient for older children (Bhavnagri & Parke, 1991; Ladd & Golter, 1988).

Teacher Influence on Children's Friendships

Several studies have investigated teacher beliefs regarding children's peer relationships (see Fang, 1996). Results of a qualitative study involving classroom observation and interviews with kindergarten children and teachers suggested that friendships between children who are typically developing and children considered to be at risk were affected by classroom activities and environment, which were themselves affected by teacher beliefs (Pruitt, Hollums, & Wandry, 1996). For example, more friendships between children who are typically developing and those considered at risk were maintained in a play-oriented versus a school-oriented classroom.

A study conducted by Kowalski, Pretti-Frontczak, and Johnson (2001) investigated the beliefs of 470 teachers in Head Start, public prekindergarten, and preschool special education classrooms. Teachers in all three groups rated social-emotional skills and abilities as more important than language and literacy or early math skills and abilities, and the higher the teacher's level of education, the higher the teacher rated social-emotional skills and abilities.

Kemple, Hysmith, and David (1996) investigated the beliefs of 22 preschool and kindergarten teachers regarding the promotion of peer social competence. Although teachers believed social and emotional goals to be important for young children, the data also revealed that teachers believed they had only a moderate amount of influence on children's peer social competence and did not perceive exerting that influence to be easy, a finding that is consistent with other research (Sparkman, 2003). Moreover, helping children make friends was the specific area in which teachers reported having the lowest influence, with the child's inherent nature reported by teachers as having the greatest influence.

Teachers' practices for fostering early friendships have also been investigated. Sparkman (2003) found that early childhood teachers reported using several friendship practices. These included placing a maximum on the number of children allowed to play in certain areas; using friendship stories, puppets, and role-play activities; modeling, demonstrating, and prompting of social skills and play skills to promote friendships; and allowing special friends to make the transition to the same classroom so that they could remain together.

Buysse, Goldman, and Skinner (2003) found that teachers generally employed strategies that did not interfere with children's friendship formation. In general, across all groups of children, teachers reported that they were more likely to use passive strategies such as allowing children to select their own friends and play together on their own than they were to use active strategies such as providing special toys or materials, arranging for two children to be together, or interpreting for a child with communication disorders. However, teachers were more likely to use active strategies to promote friendships if the friendship dyad included a child with a disability or two children with disabilities than if both members were children who were typically developing. Moreover, teachers rarely communicated with children's parents about their friendships at school.

IMPLICATIONS FOR EARLY EDUCATION AND INTERVENTION

In recent years, scholars and policy makers alike have emphasized the importance of focusing on both social-emotional competence and academics in promoting the development of young children and preparing them to succeed when they enter kindergarten (Child Mental Health Foundations and Agencies Network, 2001; Fenichel, 2001; Knitzer, 2002; National Research Council, 2000; Raver, 2002). Mounting evidence has shown that a child's ability to get along with peers and establish friendships in early childhood supports development and predicts later adjustment. This suggests that there is a need for empirically validated practices that have been shown to foster young children's developing friendships. However, the field lacks research-based interventions and practical guidance in this area. An evidence-based practice framework would capitalize on the field's collective wisdom and values (Buysse & Wesley, 2006) and address the need for specific practices in areas in which the research evidence is insufficient or nonexistent. With this in mind, some of the promising practices for fostering friendships in early childhood that are based on current empirical knowledge, theoretical frameworks, and recommended practices for supporting children's social development in general (Odom et al., 1999) are described, but with some adjustments or additional suggestions to address the particular goal of encouraging reciprocal social relationships between two children (i.e., friendships). Earlier attempts to provide guidance to classroom teachers about ways to foster friendships have focused primarily on helping children use social skills such as prosocial behaviors to promote positive peer relations (e.g., sharing, helping, comforting) rather than on the types of activities and opportunities that foster reciprocal friendships between two children. It is important to note that all of the promising practices described to support early friendships require validation through scientific research before we can label them as research-based.

APPLYING AN INTERVENTION HIERARCHY: FROM CLASSROOMWIDE STRATEGIES TO FOCUSED INTERVENTIONS FOR INDIVIDUAL CHILDREN

A review of the literature regarding ways in which educators can support children's social development suggests that practices based on applying an intervention hierarchy may hold the most promise. There is growing support in the early childhood field for instructional supports based on the systematic use of increasingly intense interventions (see, for example, Coleman, Buysse, & Neitzel, 2006; Fox, Dunlap, Hemmeter, Joseph, & Strain, 2003; Sandall & Schwartz, 2002). A conceptual framework proposed by Brown, Odom, and Conroy (2001) directly addresses children's social goals and organizes teaching strategies according to the level of intensity. In this hierarchy, classroomwide interventions form the base of the triangle. The next level consists of naturalistic interventions, then social integration activities, and, finally, explicit social skills training. Brown and his colleagues recommend starting with the least intensive interventions and progressing through the hierarchy only as necessary to meet the needs of the child. In the next section, a modified version of the Brown and colleagues's intervention hierarchy is used to describe promising practices for supporting friendship formation and maintenance at two levels: classroomwide interventions and more focused interventions for children who require additional supports to form friendships.

Classroomwide Interventions

Classroomwide interventions create a climate conducive to belonging and acceptance of individual differences, and lay the foundation for positive peer relations and friendships. Examples of such practices for very young children include reading stories about friendship and providing opportunities for children to choose activities that interest them, the time to pursue these activities, and the freedom to engage in interactions with preferred playmates who share the same interests.

Other classroomwide practices that are likely to encourage dyadic peer interaction, sustain existing friendships, and support the development of new friendships include strategies such as arranging the classroom environment to include small, cozy spaces just big enough for two and providing playground equipment that requires two to function. Providing multiple toys or sets of toys makes it easy for young children to do the same thing together and reduces potential conflicts. Allowing a friendship pair some interpersonal privacy, especially if the friendship is just emerging, gives children an opportunity to concentrate on their developing relationship with fewer distractions. Although this might mean that they need to exclude other children on occasion, educators can handle this in a way that is both protective of the emerging friendship and supportive of peers who want to join in the play (e.g., "They're playing together now; you can play with them later"). Once friendships are established, the pair can often figure out ways to be together even when they are part of a larger group (e.g., sitting next to each other at circle time). Allowing vigorous, noisy, or silly play at least occasionally supports one of the key functions of friendship—having fun together. Shared positive affect, often the result of noisy, silly, or vigorous play, can be the glue that bonds children together. Consequently, it may be necessary to permit children to engage in this form of play under certain conditions, especially for friendships that are just beginning.

Teachers also need strategies for ensuring that the school environment is conducive for positive peer relations and friendships between older children. Teachers can support friendships for older children by increasing acceptance of individual differences and promoting cooperative school environments through activities such as obtaining training in conflict resolution; inviting speakers from diverse culture, linguistic, or ability groups; and offering school citizenship and Key Club groups (Janney & Snell, 2006).

Focused Interventions

Focused interventions can be embedded to assist a child who is shy or has developmental delays to be near a friend or preferred social partner and to engage in shared activities. For example, the teacher can arrange for highly interesting activities to take place near a child with mobility problems, thereby enticing a preferred playmate or friend to join the activity. Early educators can view themselves as "matchmakers" for children who show a glimmer of interest in a peer, but who lack the specific skills to make a social bid or to enter the play of another. They can do this by setting up situations and activities that require the pair to coordinate their interactions or take turns (e.g., throwing and catching a ball, pouring liquid into a container held by a partner). Educators also can join children in their play, providing subtle support as needed in the context of their shared activities, and then sitting back to simply observe or even leave when things are proceeding well. Playing an active role may be particularly important in helping to initiate play interactions, but it is equally important to recognize when children can maintain social exchanges without adult involvement. To foster friendship formation among young children with communication delays, teachers may need to interpret or speak for those children. Finally, teachers can create ways of sharing information about children's friendships with their families to encourage friendship development outside of school.

Curricular and instructional adaptations are available for educators to offer additional friendship supports to elementary school students. Strategies such as peer tutoring, classwide tutoring, cooperative learning groups, buddy systems, social skills instruction, peer networking, and peer problem solving (see Janney & Snell, 2006, for a comprehensive description of these instructional strategies) can provide the social supports necessary to assist in developing appropriate friendships.

CONCLUSIONS AND FUTURE RESEARCH

This chapter discussed friendships in early childhood. In addition to offering a definition of friendship, methods for identifying peer acceptance and friendship were described along with features of friendship across developmental stages. Key influences on friendship formation were identified and promising practices to address the critical role of the classroom teacher in fostering children's earliest friendships were presented. Although more should be done to ensure that every early educator is familiar with the current knowledge base, there also is much that remains to be discovered about friendship through future research.

Additional longitudinal research is needed to reveal specific competencies and problems in the earliest years of life that predict friendship outcomes in children at later stages of development. Current knowledge suggests that it is possible to recognize the beginnings of friendship in infants and toddlers who show clear dyadic preferences and the desire to spend time with particular peers. Less understood is how individual differences in the peer relations of very young children are related to problems that emerge later on in establishing relationships with peers. Tracking children's developmental trajectories over time would provide additional information about how interaction and interest in peers during infancy is linked to the consolidation of skills needed to establish friendships during prekindergarten and the early elementary grades.

Future research also should focus on factors associated with friendship formation within the context of inclusive early childhood classrooms. In particular, there is a need to examine more closely friendship dyads consisting of a child who is typically developing and a child with disabilities—a unique friendship that occurs primarily as a result of inclusive policies and practices. Without additional information, we cannot say precisely how these friendships develop and are maintained over time, nor can we identify the specific strategies teachers should employ to encourage and support these friendships.

For all young children, there is a need for better documentation of within-group variation and individual differences in how children relate to their friends at different developmental levels (Bukowski et al., 1996). Previous studies have focused almost exclusively on comparisons of the social behaviors between friends and nonfriends; however, this approach may not capture all of the ways in which young children negotiate friendships with a preferred social partner within the broader context of peer group composition and structure. Those working with and caring for young children need a better understanding of what having a friend means to young children, who children choose as their friends and why, the stability and quality of children's friendships, how friendship affects development and academic learning, and how cultural and linguistic diversity and gender differences influence all of these factors.

Finally, as mentioned previously, much still needs to be learned about how to promote friendships among young children enrolled in early education programs and how this research knowledge might translate into practical guidance for early educators. A promising approach may be to build on earlier efforts aimed at assisting teachers in using an intervention hierarchy. A systematic use of increasingly intense interventions would begin with a classroom learning environment that provides a firm foundation for positive peer relations, then progress to more focused interventions for individual children who exhibit problems that may require additional supports. There is a need to develop and validate specific friendship interventions that are linked to practical assessment approaches for monitoring children's progress in finding playmates and making friends, particularly for children with diverse learning characteristics and abilities. All of these future directions will help to ensure that young children are given ample opportunities and the supports they need to develop positive peer relations and reciprocal friendships as part of a successful early school experience.

REFERENCES

Asher, S.R., Parker, J.G., & Walker, D.L. (1996). Distinguishing friendship from acceptance: Implications for intervention and assessment. In W.M. Bukowski, A.F. Newcomb, & W.W. Hartup (Eds.), *The company they keep: Friendship in childhood and adolescence.* (pp. 366–405). New York: Cambridge University Press.

Asher, S.R., Singleton, L.C., Tinsley, B.R., & Hymel, S. (1979). A reliable sociometric measure for preschool children. *Developmental Psychology, 15*(4), 443–444.

Bhavnagri, N.P., & Parke, R.D. (1991). Parents as direct facilitators of children's peer relationships: Effects of age of child and sex of parent. *Journal of Social and Personal Relationships, 8*, 423–440.

Brown, W.H., Odom, S.L., & Buysse, V. (2002). Assessment of preschool children's peer–related social competence. *Assessment for Effective Intervention, 27*(4), 61–71.

Brown, W.H., Odom, S.L., & Conroy, M.A. (2001). An intervention hierarchy for promoting young children's peer interactions in natural environments. *Topics in Early Childhood Special Education, 21*, 162–175.

Bukowski, W.M., Newcomb, A.F., & Hartup, W.W. (1996). Friendship and its significance in childhood and adolescence: Introduction and comment. In W.M. Bukowski, A.F. Newcomb, & W.W. Hartup (Eds.), *The company they keep: Friendship in childhood and adolescence.* (pp. 66–86). New York: Cambridge University Press.

Bukowski, W.M., & Sandberg, D. (1999). Peer relationships and quality of life. *Acta Paediatrica Supplements, 428*, 108–109.

Buysse, V. (1993). Friendships of preschoolers with disabilities in community–based child care settings. *Journal of Early Intervention, 17*, 380–395.

Buysse, V., Goldman, B.D., & Skinner, M. (2002). Setting effects on friendship formation among young children with and without disabilities. *Exceptional Children, 68*(4), 503–517.

Buysse, V., Goldman, B.D., & Skinner, M. (2003). Friendship formation in inclusive early childhood classrooms: What is the teacher's role? *Early Childhood Research Quarterly, 18*, 485–501.

Buysse, V., Nabors, L., Skinner, D., & Keyes, L. (1997). Playmate preferences and perceptions of individual differences among typically developing preschoolers. *Early Child Development and Care, 131*, 1–18.

Buysse, V., & Wesley, P.W. (Eds.). (2006). *Evidence-based practice in the early childhood field.* Washington, DC: ZERO TO THREE Press.

Child Mental Health Foundations and Agencies Network. (2001). *A good beginning: Sending America's children to school with the social and emotional competence they need to succeed.* Chapel Hill: University of North Carolina, FPG Child Development Institute.

Coie, J.D., Dodge, K.A., & Coppotelli, H. (1982). Dimensions and types of social status: A cross–age perspective. *Developmental Psychology, 18*, 557–570.

Coleman, M.R., Buysse, V., & Neitzel, J. (2006). *Recognition and response: An early intervening system for young children at risk for learning disabilities: Full report.* Chapel Hill: The University of North Carolina, FPG Child Development Institute.

Costin, S.E., & Jones, D.C. (1992). Friendship as a facilitator of emotional responsiveness and prosocial interventions among young children. *Developmental Psychology, 28,* 941–947.

Dietrich, S.L. (2005). A look at friendships between preschool-aged children with and without disabilities in two inclusive classrooms. *Journal of Early Childhood Research, 3,* 193–215.

Fang, Z. (1996). A review of research on teacher beliefs and practices. *Educational Research, 38*(1), 47–65.

Field, T. (1984). Play behaviors of handicapped children who have friends. In T. Field, J.L. Roopnarine, & M. Segal (Eds.), *Friendships in normal and handicapped children* (pp. 153–162). Norwood, NJ: Ablex Publishing.

Fenichel, E. (2001). Mothers, babies and depression: Questions and answers. *Zero to Three, 22*(1), 48–50.

Fox, L., Dunlap, G., Hemmeter, M.L., Joseph, G.E., & Strain, P.S. (2003). The teaching pyramid: A model for supporting social competence and preventing challenging behavior in young children. *Young Children, 58,* 48–52.

Goldman, B.D., & Buysse, V. (2005). *Playmates & friends questionnaire for teachers: Revised.* Chapel Hill: The University of North Carolina, FPG Child Development Institute.

Goldman, B.D., & Buysse, V. (2007). Friendships in very young children. In O.N. Saracho & B. Spodek, (Eds.), *Contemporary perspectives on socialization and social development in early childhood education,* (pp. 165–192). Greenwich, CT: Information Age Publishing.

Goldman, B.D., Buysse, V., Skinner, M., & Edgerton, D. (2005, April). *The differential impact of friendships vs. friends on peer interactions in preschool children with and without disabilities.* Poster presented at the Society for Research in Child Development Conference. Atlanta, GA.

Gottman, J.M. (1983). How children become friends. *Monographs of the Society for Research in Child Development. 48*(3), Serial No. 201.

Gresham, F.M., & Reschly, D.J. (1987). Dimensions of social competence: Method factors in the assessment of adaptive behavior, social skills, and peer acceptance. *Journal of School Psychology, 25,* 367–381.

Guralnick, M.J. (1997). Peer social networks of young boys with developmental delays. *American Journal on Mental Retardation, 101,* 595–612.

Guralnick, M.J., Gottman, J.M., & Hammond, M.A. (1996). Effects of social setting on the friendship formation of young children differing in developmental status. *Journal of Applied Developmental Psychology, 17,* 625–651.

Guralnick, M., & Groom, J.M. (1988). Friendships of preschool children in mainstreamed playgroups. *Developmental Psychology, 24*(4), 595–604.

Hartup, W.W. (1996). The company they keep: Friendships and their developmental significance. *Child Development, 67,* 1–13.

Hay, D.F., Payne, A., & Chadwick, A. (2004). Peer relations in childhood. *Journal of Child Psychology and Psychiatry, 45*(1), 84–108.

Hestenes, L.L. & Carroll, D.E. (2000). The play interactions of young children with and without disabilities: Individual and environmental influences. *Early Childhood Research Quarterly, 15*(2), 229–246.

Howes, C. (1983). Patterns of friendship. *Child Development, 54,* 1041–1053.

Howes, C. (1984). Social interactions and patterns of friendships in normal and emotionally disturbed children. In T. Field, J.J. Roopnarine, & M. Segal (Eds.), *Friendships in normal and handicapped children* (pp. 163–185). Norwood, NJ: Ablex Publishing.

Howes, C. (1996). The earliest friendships. In W.M. Bukowski, A.F. Newcomb, & W.W. Hartup (Eds.), *The company they keep: Friendship in childhood and adolescence* (pp. 66–86). New York: Cambridge University Press.

Howes, C., Matheson, C., & Wu, F. (1992). Friendship and social pretend play: Illustrative study #6. In C. Howes, O. Unger, & C.C. Matheson (Eds.), *The collaborative construction of pretend: Social pretend play functions.* Albany: State University of New York Press.

Howes, C. & Phillipsen, L.C. (1998). Continuity in children's relationships with peers. *Social Development, 1,* 230–242.

Janney, R., & Snell, M.E. (2006). *Social relationships and peer support* (2nd ed.). Baltimore: Paul H. Brookes Publishing Co.

Kemple, K.M., Hysmith, C., & David, G.M. (1996). Early childhood teachers' beliefs about promoting peer competence. *Early Child Development and Care, 120,* 145–163.

Knitzer, J. (2002). Implications for policy and practice. In *Set for success: Building a strong foundation for school readiness based on social–emotional development of young children.* The Kauffman Early Education Exchange, (Vol. 1, No. 2, pp. 1–5). Kansas City, MO.

Kowalski, K., Pretti–Frontczak, K., & Johnson, L. (2001). Preschool teachers' beliefs concerning the importance of various developmental skills and abilities [Electronic version]. *Journal of Research in Childhood Education, 16,* 5–14.

Ladd, G.W. (1988). Friendship patterns and peer status during early and middle childhood. *Developmental and Behavioral Pediatrics, 9*(4), 229–238.

Ladd, G.W. (1990). Having friends, keeping friends, making friends and being liked by peers in the classroom: Predictors of children's early school adjustment? *Child Development, 61,* 1081–1100.

Ladd, G.W. (2005). *Children's peer relations and social competence: A century of progress.* New Haven: Yale University Press.

Ladd, G.W., & Coleman, C.C. (1993). Young children's peer relationships: Forms, features, and functions. In B. Spodek (Ed.), *Handbook of research on the education of young children* (pp. 57–76). New York: MacMillan.

Ladd, G.W., & Golter, B.S. (1988). Parents' management of preschooler's peer relations: Is it related to children's social competence? *Developmental Psychology, 24*(1), 109–117.

Ladd, G.W., Herald, S.L., & Andrews, R.K. (2006). Young children's peer relationships and social competence. In B. Spodek & O.N. Saracho (Eds.), *Handbook of research on the education of young children* (pp. 23–54). Mahwah, NJ: Lawrence Erlbaum Associates.

Ladd, G.W., & Kochenderfer, B.J. (1996). Linkages between friendship and adjustment during early school transitions. In W.M. Bukowski, A.F. Newcomb, & W.W. Hartup (Eds.), *The company they keep: Friendship in childhood and adolescence* (pp. 322–345). New York: Cambridge University Press.

Ladd, G.W., & Pettit, G.S. (2002). Parenting and the development of children's peer relationships. In M.H. Bornstein (Ed.), *Handbook of Parenting* (2nd ed., pp. 269–309). Mahwah, NJ: Lawrence Erlbaum Associates.

Ladd, G.W., Profilet, S.M., & Hart, C.H. (1992). Parents' management of children's peer relations: Facilitating and supervising children's activities in the peer culture. In R.D. Parke & G.W. Ladd (Eds.), *Family–peer relationships: Modes of linkage* (pp. 215–253). Mahwah, NJ: Lawrence Erlbaum Associates.

National Research Council, (2000). *From neurons to neighborhoods: The science of early childhood development.* Committee on Integrating the Science of Early Childhood Development. In J. P. Shonkoff & D.A. Phillips (Eds.), Board on Children, Youth, and Families, Commission on Behavioral and Social Sciences and Education. Washington, DC: National Academy Press.

Newcomb, A.F., & Bagwell, C.L. (1995). The developmental significance of children's friendship relations. In W.M. Bukowski, A.F. Newcomb, & W.W. Hartup (Eds.), *The company they keep: Friendship in childhood and adolescence* (pp. 289–321). New York: Cambridge University Press.

Odom, S.L., McConnell, S.R., McEvoy, M.A., Peterson, C., Ostrosky, M., Chandler, L.K., Spicuzza, R.J., Skellenger, A., Creighton, M., & Favazza, P.C. (1999). Relative effects of interventions supporting the social competence of young children with disabilities. *Topics in Early Childhood Special Education, 19*(2), 75–91.

Odom, S.L., Zercher, C., Li, S., Shouming, L., Marquart, J.M., Sandall, S., & Brown, W.H. (2006). Social acceptance and rejection of preschool children with disabilities: A mixed-method analysis. *Journal of Educational Psychology, 98*(4), *807-823.*

Parke, R.D., Simpkins, S.D., McDowell, D.J., Kim, M., Killian, C., Dennis, J., et al. (2002). Relative contributions of families and peers to children's social development. In P.K. Smith & C.H. Hart (Eds.), *Blackwell handbook of childhood social development* (pp. 156–177). Malden, MA: Blackwell.

Parker, J.G., Rubin, K.H., Price, J.M., & DeRosier, M.E. (1995). Peer relations, child development, and adjustment: A developmental psychopathology perspective. In D. Cicchetti & D. Cohen (Eds.), *Developmental psychopathology: Vol. 2: Risk, disorder, and adaptation* (pp. 96–161). New York: Wiley.

Parker, R., Sprague, J., Flannery, K.B., Niess, J., & Zumwait, L. (1991). Measuring the social perceptions of persons with moderate and severe disabilities to construct social network maps. *Journal of Developmental and Physical Disabilities, 3*(1), 23–45.

Price, J.M., & Ladd, G.W. (1986). Assessment of children's friendships: Implications for social competence and social adjustment. In R.J. Prinz (Ed.), *Advances in behavioral assessment of children and families*, Vol. 2 (pp. 121–149). Greenwich CT: JAI Press.

Pruitt, P., Hollums, D., & Wandry, D. (1996). Classroom variables that appear to affect friendship development in young children who are at–risk. *B.C. Journal of Special Education, 20*, 78–96.

Raver, C.C. (2002). Emotions matter: Making the case for the role of young children's emotional development for early school readiness. *Social policy report: A publication for the Society for Research in Child Development, 16*(3), 3–19. Retrieved November 4, 2002, from http://www.srcd.org/spr.html.

Rhodes, H.G. (2002). Family practices and beliefs around the friendship socialization of preschool children. *Dissertation Abstracts International, 63*(03), 904A. (UMI No. 3047062).

Rubin, K.H., Bukowski, W., & Parker, J.G. (1998). Peer interactions, relationships, and groups. In W. Damon (Ed.), *Handbook of child psychology. Vol. 3, Social, emotional, and personality development* (5th ed, pp. 619–700). New York: Wiley.

Rubin, Z. (1980). *Children's friendships.* Cambridge, MA: Harvard University Press.

Rubin, Z., & Sloman, J. (1984). How parents influence their children's friendships. In M. Lewis (Ed.) *Beyond the dyad* (pp. 223–250). New York: Plenum Press.

Sandall, S., & Schwartz, I. (2002). *Building blocks for teaching preschoolers with special needs.* Baltimore: Paul H. Brookes Publishing Co.

Sparkman, K.L. (2003). *Promoting social and emotional competence in preschoolers with and without disabilities: What is the role of teachers' educational beliefs and practices?* Unpublished doctoral dissertation, University of North Carolina at Chapel Hill.

Strain, P.S. (1984). Social interactions of handicapped preschoolers in developmentally integrated and segregated settings: A study of generalization effects. In T. Field, J.L. Roopnarine, & M. Segal (Eds.), *Friendships in normal and handicapped children* (pp. 187–207). Norwood, NJ: Ablex Publishing.

Vandell, D.L., & Mueller, E.C. (1980). Peer play and friendships during the first two years. In H.C. Foot, A.J. Chapman, & J.R. Smith (Eds.), *Friendship and social relations in children.* New York: Wiley.

Wolfberg, P.J., Zercher, C., Lieber, J., Capell, K., Matias, S., Hanson, M., & Odom, S.L. (1999). "Can I play with you?" Peer culture in inclusive preschool programs. *The Journal of the Association for Persons with Severe Handicaps, 24*, 69–84.

CHAPTER 5

Classroom Influences on Young Children's Emerging Social Competence

DIANE M. SAINATO, SUNHWA JUNG,
MARY D. SALMON, AND JUDAH B. AXE

A child's first smile or first words are typically celebrated by observant parents. These early social attempts develop into an elaborate repertoire of verbal and physical gestures attenuated by development, experience, and culture. They are discrete behaviors that are observable, measurable, and influenced by the environment in which they occur. However, social interaction cannot be studied separately from environmental context. This foreground of observed social behavior of young children nests within a rich background of contextual and setting events that affect the behavior of young children (Bronfenbrenner, 1979; Davis & Fox, 1999).

The purpose of this chapter is to present the findings of selected studies on the impact of early childhood environments on the emerging social competence of young children with and without special needs. We first review studies exploring the influence of toys and materials, then we examine outcomes of studies of peer group composition and spatial variables and their relation to social outcomes. In addition, results of studies investigating the impact of classroom activities and activity structure on the social behavior of young children are reviewed. Future directions for the development of optimum early childhood settings are discussed.

TOYS AND MATERIALS

A thorough examination of environmental variables that positively influence play and social behaviors of young children should include exploration of the quality and quantity of toys and materials in early childhood settings. Toys and materials may be among the most readily manipulated facets of context (Burroughs & Murray, 1992). Play materials that are effective in eliciting and supporting social play provide teachers with an easily integrated, valuable, teaching tool in inclusive classrooms (Ivory & McCollum, 1999). The use of toys and materials to promote social interactions is also one of the most acceptable, feasible, and frequently employed interventions by preschool special educators (Odom, McConnell, & Chandler,

1993) and is consistent with developmentally appropriate practice (Carter & O'Gorham Hughes, 2001). Furthermore, the commitment to providing the earliest and most effective intervention in inclusive settings for young children with disabilities lends increased importance to understanding the environmental variables that facilitate children's social interactions and play with peers.

Toys and Social Value

Researchers have described the behavior of children with and without disabilities when playing with a variety of common toys and materials. Rankings of the social value or number of children playing together with a toy and the duration of use of play materials were evaluated in an early study of 10 preschool children who were typically developing (Hulson, 1930). Of the 18 materials evaluated, sand and hollow blocks were both highly preferred and socially interactive resources. A study by VanAlstyne (1932) assessed not only the social value and holding power of play materials but also their popularity and use by 112 children without disabilities ranging in age from 2½ to 5 years old who were attending seven nursery school classrooms. A social value index was determined for each material by analyzing the number of children playing together with a toy and by the sophistication of their subsequent play (i.e., level of social participation). Modeling clay, blocks, trucks, dolls, and dishes were among the items eliciting 30%–48% of children's observed social interactions. As important as the findings are, determination of the social value of toys and materials relies heavily on the judgment of the observer.

Toys and Level of Play

Evidence from observational studies of children's toy and material preferences conducted during the 1940s and 1950s is scarce; however, a renewed interest in the circumstances that predictably elicit children's social interactions and play is evident in the extant literature from 1970 to the present. In addition to examining the favorability of materials, investigators scrutinize the level of play (e.g., Rubin, 1977) as well as the social interactions of children with and without disabilities when interacting with toys (e.g., Stoneman, Cantrell, & Hoover–Dempsey, 1983). Rubin (1977) concluded that different types of materials not only supported different frequencies of interaction but also facilitated varying levels of social play. For example, parallel and solitary play were more likely when children used art materials, books, playdough, sand, and water. In contrast, house play (i.e., play with housekeeping items such as kitchen utensils and dishes) was associated with more cooperative play, eliciting 55% of the social interactions between the children. Similar findings emerged in a naturalistic study with both children who are typically developing and children with special needs in which blocks, housekeeping materials, and water play were associated with cooperative peer interactions (Stoneman et al., 1983).

Researchers across several studies have categorized toys and materials such as sand, blocks, and housekeeping items as materials that are likely to elicit higher levels of play and socially interactive behaviors (i.e., social toys) than other materials such as art materials and books (i.e., isolate toys) among preschool children with and without disabilities. In a recent study, Ivory and McCollum (1999) systematically provided social and isolate toys to evaluate the level of social play achieved by preschoolers with disabilities in an inclusive setting where participants were familiar with one another. Cooperative play was found to have occurred significantly more often with social toys than with isolate toys. Moreover, during the isolate-toy condition, parallel play was the most common level of play observed.

The link between play objects and subsequent social interactions or level of social play indicates that the kinds of toys and materials available within play settings influence the type of outcomes (e.g., Ivory & McCollum, 1999; Quilitch & Risley, 1973; Rettig, Kallam, & McCarthy-Salm, 1993). The presence of social toys (e.g. blocks, dress-up clothes, housekeeping materials, puppets) may create situations that serve as a "natural social scaffold" supporting higher levels of play for many children. Familiarity with peers and multiple experiences during more sophisticated levels of play may, in turn, increase the likelihood that important social behaviors will be incorporated into children's developmental repertoires. Hence, in a number of experimental and observational studies, the social value and levels of social interactions have been determined from children's observed social play, yet it is commonly acknowledged that a direct relationship between these two variables cannot be inferred (see, for example, Ivory & McCollum, 1999).

Toys and Infants

Toys have also been shown to play an important role in facilitating the social interactions of infants and toddlers with peers (e.g., Eckerman & Whatley, 1977; Jacobson, 1981; Rubenstein & Howe, 1976; Vandell, Wilson, & Buchanan, 1980). In an observational study of eight 1-year-olds, Rubenstein and Howe (1976) assessed the effects of the presence of peers in home environments on toddlers' interactions with their mothers and on the toddlers' play with their own toys. During the peer visits toddlers spent an average of 50% of their time directing social behavior to the peers. Of additional importance is the finding that in the presence of peers, the developmental level of play with objects was more sophisticated, and this difference appeared to be a function of interactions with peers.

In a later study 44 pairs of young children, infants (10–12 months), and toddlers (22–24 months) were observed in the presence of and absence of toys. Eckerman and Whatley (1977) noted that the presence of toys reduced the frequency of some social interactions with peers (e.g., smiling and laughing) of both age groups but provided novel opportunities for other peer interactions such as simultaneous manipulations of objects, social exchanges, and showing toys to each other. In a similar investigation, Vandall, Wilson, and Buchanan (1980) observed more peer interactions in an absence-of-toys condition, although the experimental condition had to be terminated earlier than the toy-present condition because infants were more likely to become distressed. In contrast, many infants appeared content to continue the toy-present conditions indefinitely. It is possible that the small, portable toys used in this investigation discouraged toddler–peer social interactions. Larger toys that could be shared may have fostered higher rates of peer interactions. The challenge to find appropriate large toys given the infants' emerging motor skills raises the possibility that toys may serve different functions during children's first and second years.

Social Communication

Research has shown that toys may affect the language discourse in play settings. Burroughs and Murray (1992) observed pragmatic behavior (i.e., social use of language) in preschool children during three play conditions, each involving different play material (playdough, farm set, and animal puppets). During play sessions, children's verbal utterances were recorded and categorized according to topic initiation, topic maintenance, topic extension, and topic extension–tangential. Burroughs and Murray found that all of the play materials were equally effective in eliciting conversation from preschool boys and girls, although gender differences in language discourse categories were apparent. For example, boys introduced more topics during play but girls remained on topic for longer periods. In addition, children initiated more topics while playing with puppets but maintained the topics of discussion for longer periods when playing with playdough.

O'Gorman Hughes and Carter (2002) examined the effects of social and isolate toys on the frequency of social interactions of two children with disabilities in an inclusive preschool. The investigators did not find consistent evidence for higher overall levels of interaction under either the social or the isolate toy conditions. Nevertheless, interactions, both verbal and gestural, were highest among children with disabilities in the isolate toy condition. However, interactions were highest among children with disabilities and their peers without disabilities when using social toys. O'Gorman Hughes and Carter's research suggests that the child's level of the social skills and characteristics of their play partners may serve as important a role as the actual toy type.

Social Stories

In addition to investigating types of toys that are likely to promote peer social interactions and higher levels of play, investigators have recently begun to explore the efficacy of other classroom materials for increasing the social competence of young children in inclusive settings. A material being employed in classrooms with increasing frequency is the Social Story (Gray, 1998). Social Stories are individualized short stories that may increase appropriate social interactions by teaching the relevant components of a given social situation. They focus on describing and explaining the cues in that situation as well as teaching appropriate responses.

Barry and Burlew (2004) studied two participants diagnosed with severe autism to assess the effects of Social Story instruction on students' abilities to make choices and to play appropriately during free play in a first-grade self-contained classroom. Participants were taught through repetition and opportunities for practice with corrective feedback. The stories were read daily to each participant. After hearing the story and looking at the illustrations, opportunities were created for the participants to practice the specific behaviors described in each story during center time. Following Social Story instruction, both students demonstrated gains in ability to make independent choices and to play appropriately during free-play.

Thiemann and Goldstein (2001) used Social Stories and other visual cues (e.g., picture cue cards) with video feedback to evaluate the effects of specific social skills in five children (between 6–12 years of age) with autism. Each student was grouped with two peers who were typically developing. Targeted skills included securing attention, initiating comments and requests, and making contingent responses. Following intervention, the children demonstrated improved rates of social behaviors compared with their baselines. Generalization of skills to new environments was noted for three of the children. Delano and Snell (2006) also evaluated the effects of social stories in three children with autism. Two of the boys were fully included in kindergarten classrooms, whereas the third child, age 9, attended a second-grade classroom. Improvements in social behaviors were sought without the use of additional simultaneous interventions (e.g., visual cues). Following implementation of the Social Story intervention, children demonstrated increases in the duration of their time spent socially engaged with a familiar peer and a novel peer in the intervention contexts. Increased use of targeted social skills (primarily contingent responding and initiating comments) was also noted for all of the children with autism. Evidence of generalization to the general education classrooms was noted for two of the three participants. Although research evaluating the effectiveness of Social Story interventions is relatively new, preliminary findings suggest that Social Stories may be an effective classroom intervention context for increasing children's prosocial behaviors. Moreover, as a positive behavioral support strategy, the use of Social Stories may decrease some children's challenging behaviors.

Other Considerations

Despite multiple educational opportunities in inclusive environments rich with age-appropriate toys and materials, young children with disabilities frequently do not achieve the maximum benefit of inclusion without specific instruction (see, for example, Guralnick, 2001; Rettig, 1994). For social interactions to occur, young children must possess the requisite social competence to enter and sustain their interactions (Hestenes & Carroll, 2000). Jacobson (1981) suggested that although all social interactions do not originate in object-centered contexts (e.g., toys present), object-centered play may promote the development of social interactions once children acquire the ability to employ joint attention with peers during toy play. With regard to young children with disabilities that limit or preclude opportunities to engage in object-centered play, understanding the link between early toy play and social-cognitive growth is an important area for continued research (see, for example, Sainato & Carta, 1992).

In addition to opportunities to engage in object-centered play, the ages of children (age is related to the complexity of play) and their developmental sophistication (e.g. joint attention skill independent of ability status) are other factors in better understanding peer interactions and the development of social competence. Consequently, additional research is warranted to examine variables including age, level of play, and existing social skills repertoires that may moderate or interact with different types of toys and materials.

GROUP COMPOSITION

Various aspects of group composition may affect the social behavior of preschool children. These social groupings include group size, familiarity of peers, age of peers, gender of peers, and the ratio of children with disabilities to children without disabilities.

Group Size

Researchers who examined the influence of the number of children in preschool classrooms on children's social behavior reported mixed results. Early studies on class size revealed limited influences on children's social behaviors. For example, Asher and Erickson (1979) found no difference in peer interactions or activity behaviors for children in child care center classrooms with either 8 or 16 children (with the teacher–child ratio held constant at 1:8). Similarly, Smith and Connolly (1986) suggested that the effects of group size were modest but that smaller group size (e.g., 10 children) predicted more cross-gender play, larger subgroups, and more fantasy play than did larger group size.

Recently, policy makers, parents, teachers, and others have argued for reduced class size to promote academic outcomes (e.g., Class Size Reduction Consortium, 2002). This movement has also led to the examination of smaller class sizes to address children's social behavior. For example, as part of the Early Childhood Longitudinal Study (ECLS) of the U.S. Department of Education, Finn and Pannozzo (2004) found that class size was not a statistically significant predictor of *individual* kindergarten children's approaches to learning or externalizing problem behaviors. The effect of class size on approaches to learning and externalizing problem behaviors with the *classroom* as the unit of analysis was significant, however. That is, children in classes (fewer than 20 students) were engaged in more appropriate behavior than children in larger classes. Similarly, researchers in the Early Childhood Research Network of the National Institute of Child Health and Human Development (2004) reported that first-grade students in classrooms of fewer than 20 students were rated by their teachers as having better social skills, less externalizing behavior, and closer teacher–student relationships than students in classrooms with 20 or more students. They noted, however, that the differences in their study were small and based solely on teacher reports. Finally, Kim (2001) examined the peer relationship formation and play behaviors of 70 preschoolers in classrooms of 20, 30, or 40 students and found that class size had differential effects on children's peer networks. Based on these studies, a consistently clear relationship between group size and children's social behaviors is not evident; nevertheless, one might conclude that smaller group size may have a small, albeit important, influence on improving some children's social behaviors.

Familiarity of Peers

The extent to which young children are familiar with their peers appears to be an influential variable on their social and play behavior. Doyle, Connolly, and Rivest (1980) found that peer familiarity was a variable that substantially predicted a range of social behaviors in 16 children enrolled in two childcare centers. Specifically, peer familiarity increased overall social interactions, the frequency of overtures to peers, and the complexity of toy play. Doyle and colleagues suggested that the complexity of toy play increased with well-known peers because children were more likely to imitate familiar peers, and this imitation increased the variety of toy play. In addition, Doyle and colleagues found that repeated exposure to familiar peers helped children learn to respond effectively to peers' social behavior. McCornack (1982) identified age as a variable influencing the effect of peer familiarity on play behavior. She found peer familiarity did not affect the play of younger (mean age 45 months) boys, but younger girls had more play behavior around familiar peers. Interestingly, older (mean age 58 months) boys generally had improved interactions with familiar peers and older girls were more socially involved with unfamiliar peers. McCornack suggested that because of the rapid growth in social sensitivity in girls between the ages of 4 and 6, they are more interested in developing new friendships. Harper and Huie (1985) found that for preschool children, familiarity of peers was especially influential during the first months of an academic year and was associated with less time spent in solitary play.

Age of Peers

Investigators have examined the extent to which the age of children's peers influences their social behavior. For example, Graziano, French, Brownell, and Hartup (1976) found first and third graders interacted more when building with blocks in same-age rather than mixed-age triads; however, the mixed-age triads improved the third graders' productivity with block building because they took on a "responsibility role" in the presence of the two first graders. A similar trend emerged in a study with 24 children (mean age 57 months) by Furman, Rahe, and Hartup (1979), who found that 24 children (mean age 57 months) who were socially withdrawn engaged in more social behaviors when interacting with younger rather than same-age peers. It was suggested that the children considered withdrawn had more success initiating and directing social interactions with the younger peers than with same-age peers.

The effects of age of peers have been shown to interact with gender of peers when influencing children's social behavior. For example, Langlois, Gottfried, Barnes, and Hendricks (1978) observed that 3-year-old boys talked less when paired with 5-year-old boys than with same-age peers, and 5-year-old boys also talked more when in same-age dyads. However, 3-year-old girls talked more with 5-year-old girls than with same-age peers, and the level of talking in 5-year-old girls was independent of the age of peers in the dyads.

Bailey, McWilliam, Ware, and Burchinal (1993) argued that much of the research on the influence of the age of peers on children's social behavior was limited in that the participants were not acquainted with each other and were not randomly assigned to conditions. They extended the research base by incorporating these two factors in a well-controlled experiment and found no statistically significant differences in the social behaviors of 32 children (ages 1–4) who were in same-age or mixed-age groups. Children with disabilities were included in the six-member groups and the investigators suggested that their inclusion might have contributed to the consistent findings between the two types of groups. Although results with respect to peers' ages have been mixed, it appears that the social behavior of children with social interaction difficulties may improve when they are paired with slightly younger peers.

Gender of Peers

In general, preschool children tend to play and interact socially with same-gender peers. For example, in a sample of 32 African American children, Langlois, Gottfried, and Seay (1973) found that 5-year-old boys and 3- and 5-year-old girls exhibited more social behaviors (e.g., talking, smiling, physical contact, and aggression) with same-gender peers; only the 3-year-old boys were more social with opposite-gender peers. According to Langlois and colleagues, interest in same-gender peers develops between ages 4 and 5, although this interest may develop before age 4 in girls. Serbin, Tonick, and Sternglanz (1977) also noted that preschool children tend to play in same-gender arrangements.

An important variable when considering the effects of children's gender on the social behavior of preschoolers is the quality of play as a function of peer gender. To address this, Fabes, Martin, and Hanish (2003) observed 203 children averaging 52 months in age over the course of 3 years. They found that the children spent most of their time playing with same-gender peers, rarely played with opposite-gender peers, and only approximately 25% of the participants played with mixed-gender peers (i.e., peers of both the same and opposite gender). In terms of the quality of play, boys tended to play in larger groups and engage in rough-and-tumble play, whereas girls spent more time playing in dyads and were generally calmer. Fabes and colleagues concluded that gender is "an organizing property of children's peer relationships" (2003, p. 931), and experiences in peer groups vary depending on the gender of the play partners.

Ratio of Students with and without Disabilities

Another group composition variable that may influence children's social interactions is the ratio of students with disabilities to students without disabilities. A series of studies evaluating the effects of different ratios on social interactions in preschool children revealed that, in terms of class composition, fewer children with disabilities (a greater degree of integration) predicted higher levels of social behavior. For example, Hauser-Cram, Bronson, and Upsur (1993) studied 153 preschool children with disabilities (e.g., Down syndrome, motor impairments, developmental delays) who attended early intervention classrooms. The Bronson Social and Task Skills Profiles (Bronson, 1985) was used to measure social behaviors. In addition, the children were observed in their classrooms engaging with peers, using strategies for organizing and maintaining interactions, sharing and turn taking, and influencing others verbally. Results of the assessments indicated that when cognitive performance was controlled statistically, more social behavior was observed in the children who were educated in classrooms with higher proportions of children without disabilities.

In a follow-up study, Bronson, Hauser-Cram, and Warfield (1997) used descriptive analyses to identify classroom predictors of favorable social outcomes in 5-year-old preschoolers with individualized education programs (IEPs). The Bronson Social and Task Skills Profiles was again employed to measure social behaviors along with direct observations of children's social initiations, organizations, maintenances, and responses during free play with peers. Bronson and colleagues found that children in classrooms with fewer than 50% with IEPs had significantly higher scores on their social assessments. In addition, students in classes with more than eight students performed better on their social assessments, as did children who were in classes with teacher–child ratios of 1:4 or lower. These results should be interpreted with caution because the design was correlational, not causal; random assignment to groups was not used; and students with higher cognitive performance were in classrooms with more children without disabilities. Nevertheless, these results provide limited evidence that students who are in classrooms with more children without disabilities and more adults will have favorable social contexts and outcomes.

In a related study, Buysse, Goldman, and Skinner (2002) evaluated the effects of two types of settings on friendship formation in young children with and without disabilities. Participants included 333 children ranging in age from 19–77 months who were in either inclusive specialized programs in which the majority of students had disabilities or inclusive child care centers in which the majority of children did not have disabilities. The researchers found that in inclusive specialized settings, students without disabilities had more friendships than did students with disabilities, but in the inclusive child care centers, the difference between the numbers of friends the children with and without disabilities had was not significant. In general, there were more available playmates for both groups of students in the inclusive child care settings because larger groups of children attended them. Buysse and colleagues also found that the severity of disability was not related to the number of children's reported friends. Another finding was that children with disabilities in the inclusive child care programs were more likely to have at least one friend than children with disabilities in the inclusive specialized programs. Furthermore, children with disabilities in inclusive child care programs were more likely to have friends without disabilities than children with disabilities in the inclusive specialized programs. Children without disabilities had the same number of friends in both inclusive settings. Buysse and colleagues (2002) noted that their data do not allow them to clearly determine an optimal ratio of children with disabilities to peers without disabilities, and they argued that the ratio was not as important as the number of social opportunities to form relationships. They also concluded that children with disabilities need a large pool of children without disabilities to interact with as playmates and to develop friendships.

Summary of Group Composition Variables

A number of group composition variables have the potential to influence the social behaviors of children in early education settings. Smaller group size appears to promote more social behavior, but this seems to be a relatively weak variable given that results have been mixed. Some researchers have reported that social behaviors are more enhanced around familiar peers than they are around unfamiliar peers, especially at the beginning of a school year and with older preschool children. Researchers' results examining the relationship of the ages of peers on children's social interactions have also been varied. Investigators have shown that children in same-age dyads are more social than are mixed-age pairs, sometimes older children were more social when grouped with younger children, sometimes gender influenced the effects of peers' ages, and sometimes the ages of peers had no influence. In terms of the influence of the gender of peers, children appear to be more social when they play with peers of the same gender, particularly after the age of 4. Finally, peer interactions and friendships for children with disabilities appear to occur more frequently when they are grouped with a higher proportion of peers without disabilities.

SPATIAL VARIABLES

The amount of physical space available to children in early childhood education settings is a variable that may affect children's social interactions (Driscoll & Carter, 2004). Although many of the studies examining the role of spatial density on social interactions are considered to be methodologically limited (see, for example, Davis & Fox, 1999), the major finding has been that within reason, the less space made available to children, the more likely their social interactions. For example, Smith and Connolly (1986) examined the influence of spatial density on social behavior in 3- and 4-year-old children in playgroup settings and found that spatial arrangements of 25, 50, or 75 square feet per child did not significantly influence children's social play or aggressive behaviors. However, the researchers determined that the amount of play equipment per child significantly affected preschoolers' social behaviors. For example, when there was more equipment per child, the children were more likely to play alone and in smaller groups. With less equipment per child, children were more likely to engage in unusual uses of toys, interactions with nontoy items (e.g., heating pipes), and solitary play. The children who had less equipment also engaged in more aggressive behavior. In a follow-up study comparing the effects of 15 square feet per child with 60 square feet per child, the latter predicted larger subgroups, more parallel play in subgroups of three or more children, more talking, less congregating around play activities (e.g., sandbox), more looking at books, more running, more rough-and-tumble play, and less aggression. The authors concluded that in more crowded conditions, socially cooperative play decreases and aggression increases.

Brown, Fox, and Brady (1987) compared the social behavior of 3- and 4-year-old children with and without disabilities in free play settings of either 19.3 square feet per child or 58 square feet per child and found that, as a group, child–child social interactions were higher in the more restricted setting. However, individual data for four children who were at risk for disabilities revealed that only three showed clear results in terms of increased social behavior in the smaller setting, and these results were modest. Furthermore, and contrary to other findings, negative behaviors such as aggression were less frequent in the smaller space, although an explicit behavior management system was in place during the study.

In a review of 12 studies published between 1972 and 1987, Driscoll and Carter (2004) evaluated the role of spatial density on social interactions in preschool children. Out of the 12 studies, 11 included children without disabilities as participants. The major finding from the review is that smaller space produces more social interactions in preschool children. However, Driscoll and Carter noted that the dearth of recent information as well as methodological limitations in the reviewed studies weakened any interpretations of the data. One of the issues plaguing the reviewed studies is an inconsistent use of the term *density*. Some of the different terms used, all having different meanings, are *social density, spatial density, equipment density,* and *crowding*. In addition, studies were conducted in different countries and analyzed peer groups and social behavior in different ways. Driscoll and Carter (2004) proposed further research using a small number of participants, studies that include adult–child interaction in addition to the spatial components, and more studies involving students with disabilities.

Davis and Fox (1999) reviewed 43 experimental and descriptive studies on the effects of environmental arrangements in classrooms on the engagement, social behaviors, and reduction in challenging behaviors of young children. Some of the reviewed environmental arrangements were seating arrangements, spatial proximity, spatial density, and inclusion variables. The authors attempted to determine the degree to which published studies were conducted in a way that allowed the environmental arrangements to be conceptualized as setting events (see, for example, Kantor, 1959). Setting events were defined as environmental variables that alter the effect of antecedents that evoke behavior or consequences that increase or suppress behavior. An example was given in which a student's academic behavior was reinforced with access to preferred music, a reasonable situation. However, if the music is placed near an extremely loud air conditioner (the setting event), it may lose any value as a reinforcer. Davis and Fox argued that researchers should carefully describe the antecedent and consequent events that directly surround instances of the outcomes of interest to better understand the role of the environmental arrangements on the levels of dependent variables. They reported that only a few of the reviewed articles included this specificity of information.

Another methodological issue reported by Davis and Fox was that only about a third of the reviewed studies included an assessment of the integrity of the implementation of the independent variable (i.e., environmental arrangement). This shortcoming weakens conclusions about the effectiveness of environmental arrangements on levels of behavior such as social interactions. It was also reported that much of the research on environmental arrangements has evaluated environmental packages as the independent variable, and researchers have not conducted component analyses of environmental arrangement manipulations. Because of the limited knowledge about the particular environmental arrangements that produce favored outcomes for students, teachers may be expending more effort than is necessary. Davis and Fox recommend more research on environmental arrangement of classrooms that considers their criticisms.

Summary of Spatial Density Studies

It appears that most examinations of spatial density have indicated that restricted space promotes social behaviors, although some exceptions have been reported. Another conclusion concerning the extant literature is the common methodological limitations, such as inconsistencies in terminology and measurement approaches. Nevertheless, some evidence indicates that spatial density may influence social and play behaviors in young children in early education environments.

CLASSROOM ACTIVITIES

A number of researchers have examined the influence of various classroom activities on the social interactions of young children with and without disabilities. Studies have been conducted across class activities as well as during free play activities.

Among studies comparing social interactions across class activities, Kohl and Beckman (1984) observed the social behaviors of 4- and 5-year-old children with disabilities and 3- and 4-year-old children without disabilities during four classroom activities (i.e., free play, fine motor activity, circle time, and snack time). Their results suggested that social interactions of children without disabilities occurred most often during free play (followed by snack time, circle time, and fine motor activity in order of frequency), whereas the social interactions of children with disabilities occurred most frequently during snack time and with decreasing frequency during free play, circle time, and fine motor activity (in that order). Even though children with disabilities interacted relatively often during free play, observations of children without disabilities indicated twice as many interactions occurring during this activity. No substantial difference was found between the social interactions of children with and without disabilities during circle time, snack time, and fine motor activity.

Odom, Peterson, McConnell, and Ostrosky (1990), in an ecobehavioral analysis of early childhood special education and early childhood education classrooms, observed 3- to 7-year-old children with disabilities and 3- to 6-year-old children without disabilities. Children with and without disabilities in both types of classrooms showed the highest rates of verbal social interactions during free play and clean-up activities, and the lowest rates of verbal social interactions during preacademic activities. Children with disabilities were least likely to talk with their peers during language programming, whereas children without disabilities interacted less during fine motor activities, class business, and story time. However, children with and without disabilities may exhibit engagement in different types of play. For example, in their study examining the ecology of inclusive early childhood programs, Kontos, Moore, and Giogretti (1998) stated that, on the one hand, children with disabilities (mean age of 4.4 years) were more likely to be involved in manipulatives, art, and books that required mostly fine motor skills and were completed with teacher supervision. On the other hand, peers without disabilities (mean age of 4.2 years) spent more time in dramatic play in which social and communicative skills were required.

In another study focusing on learning and activity centers, Brown and Bergen (2002) examined which specific classroom centers were more likely to facilitate play and social interactions between preschool children with and without disabilities. Brown and Bergen found that social interactions with peers occurred more frequently in water, computer, and house/dress-up activity centers in which adults were not consistently present. Parallel play occurred more frequently during art, creative expression, and woodworking. The social interactions of children with disabilities were observed to be brief and were most often not sustained. Teacher facilitation of peer interactions was not observed in any of the centers in their study.

In contrast, some studies have shown that although the social interactions of children with disabilities are not influenced by activity type, children without disabilities exhibit more social behavior during some activities (e.g., Burstein, 1986; Hamilton, 2005). For example, with regard to observations of children with disabilities (ages 2.8–6.0 years) and peers without disabilities (ages 2.1–5.3 years) in the same class, Burstein (1986) reported the social interactions of children with disabilities occurred at similar levels in all activity contexts (e.g., rug time, center time, and outdoor play) while they were interacting with adults. Hamilton (2005) observed preschoolers with Down syndrome and their peers without disabilities in a variety of play activities. Hamilton found that the type of activity did not affect the interactions of children with Down syndrome; however, children without disabilities demonstrated differing levels of social interactions during different activities. Specifically, children without disabilities interacted more with their peers during dramatic play and outdoor play and had lower rates of interactions during whole group activities such as music and story time.

Nabors, Willoughby, and Badawi (1999) examined the impact of the complexity of playground activities on social interactions of 3- to 5-year-old children with and without disabilities. They reported that children with disabilities were more likely to engage in cooperative play together during less complex or low-demand activities requiring motor skills (e.g., sliding, running) than during complex activities requiring higher levels of cognitive, social, and language skills.

Summary of Classroom Activities

Results from researchers' examinations of classroom activities have indicated that some specific activities are more likely to provide young children with more social opportunities for peer interactions (e.g., Kohl & Beckman, 1984; Odom et al., 1990). According to the nature of the activities, play activities may provide children with more occasions to interact with their peers than do preacademic activities, circle time, and other teacher-directed activities with preacademic classroom goals.

In contrast, some researchers have shown that the social interactions of children with disabilities are not influenced by activity type, whereas children without disabilities exhibit more peer interactions during some activities (e.g., Burstein, 1986; Hamilton, 2005). Unfortunately, few researchers reported well-specified details about the activities used in their studies. Although investigators may have reported using the same types of activities, these activities may have been created with a variety of structure, play materials, teacher presence or absence, and different group arrangements, and those factors may have influenced the children's social interactions. Other variables such as the teachers' roles may have greatly influenced the children's social interactions.

ACTIVITY STRUCTURE

Among studies examining the relationship between children's social interactions and activity structure, the term *structure* has been used in different ways. Some studies investigated teaching direction (or teacher involvement), whereas other studies examined the structuring of activities (e.g., organizing activities for facilitating social interactions). Therefore, the results and implications of these studies need to be taken cautiously.

Burstein (1986) investigated the effects of classroom variables on peer interactions while observing three settings such as rug time (e.g., music, story), center time (e.g., manipulatives, housekeeping, books), and outdoor play or recess. In Burstein's study, rug time was considered the most structured, followed by center time, with outdoor play considered the least structured activity. How one might evaluate the activity structure or teacher involvement to categorize these activities was not explicitly detailed. Burstein found that social interactions of preschool children with disabilities occurred most frequently during the less teacher-structured activities (e.g., highest levels during outdoor play, followed by center time, with the lowest levels during rug time). However, his results suggested that children with disabilities showed no differences in social interaction levels across the three activity settings while showing relatively low rates of peer interactions, and interacted mostly with adults.

In an earlier study, Shores, Hester, and Strain (1976) investigated the effects of teacher-structured activities on the social interactions of children 3 to 4 years of age with disabilities. Three types of free play settings were examined: 1) active teacher involvement, 2) no teacher involvement, and 3) teacher-structured free play. Shores and colleagues found that children had more social interactions when teachers structured free play (e.g., assigned roles to play but no further interaction after the prompt) rather than when they were in the other two play conditions. Children also interacted more when the teacher was not involved than when there was active teacher involvement in free play. In a second study, DeKlyen and Odom (1989) focused on the activity structure by organizing the activities that facilitated peer interactions. Children who were 3 to 6 years of age with disabilities and 3 to 4 years of age without disabilities were randomly assigned to two integrated and one special education classroom at the beginning of the study. In addition, teachers assigned children to one of three play activities and played with the same group throughout the study. With regard to the structure of the activities, the teachers' role included introducing play activities, establishing activity rules, assigning children's roles, and preparing and arranging play materials, rather than providing ongoing teacher directives. In the study, activity structure was rated by the degree to which teachers arranged the activities to facilitate peer interactions. As a result, children in both groups interacted more with their peers during the high-structure activities than during the low-structure activities; however, there was not a functional relationship between the frequency of teacher interaction and the activity structure.

In addition to the studies on the effects of the activity structure on peer interactions of young children, researchers have also shown that the type of teacher interactions or teacher involvement may affect peer interactions. In particular, in a number of studies, some teacher interactions are negatively related to children's peer interactions (see, for example, Chandler, Lubeck, & Fowler, 1992; DeKlyen & Odom, 1986; File, 1994; File & Kontos, 1993; Harper & McCluskey, 2003; Hundert, Mahoney, & Hopkins, 1993; Kontos & Wilcox-Herzog, 1997; McCormick, Noonan, & Heck, 1998; McWilliam & Bailey, 1995; Shores et al., 1976). That is, children may interact more with peers when the adults were not directly involved in activities; moreover, once children began to interact with adults, they were more likely to continue those interactions and not interact with their classmates (Harper & McCluskey, 2003). It was also reported that teachers have been more involved with children who are less socially competent or who are withdrawn (e.g., DeKlyen & Odom, 1986; Harper & McCluskey, 2003; Kontos & Wilcox-Herzog, 1997). In addition, when teachers have been directly involved with children, they often attend more to the cognitive aspects of the activities and to routine caregiving activities rather than focusing on facilitating peer interactions (e.g., Brown & Bergen, 2002; File, 1994; File & Kontos, 1993; Harper & McCluskey, 2003).

It has often been suggested that teacher involvement or teacher interactions may interfere with social interactions among children. Nevertheless, the types of teacher interactions or their roles within activities should be carefully considered in order to identify how they influence children's peer interactions (see, for example, File & Kontos, 1993; Harper & McCluskey, 2003; McCormick et al., 1998). It has been documented that social interactions of children with disabilities may be less likely without teachers' strategic interventions (Odom et al., 1993). High quality activity centers alone have been insufficient for consistently facilitating social interactions between children with and without disabilities (see, for example, Brown & Bergen, 2002). Therefore, the type of teacher involvement during classroom activities is a critical dimension in promoting children's social interactions. Indeed, File and Kontos (1993) suggested that the types of teacher involvement may be more important than the actual amount of their involvement in relation to the peer interactions of the children. For example, research has shown that when teachers were involved in children's play with a goal of enhanced cognitive play, children's social play decreased (File & Kontos, 1993). If the adults' roles are to promote children's peer interactions, when children's social interactions are unduly limited, teachers' strategic involvement (e.g., suggestions, judicious prompts) may be important in facilitating children's social behavior.

Researchers have examined other variables related to activity structure. For example, when children with and without disabilities engaged in classroom curriculum activities, especially large group preacademic activities, they demonstrate *less* peer engagement, but during small group activities preschoolers display *more* social engagement with their peers (McCormick et al., 1998). In addition, Bronson and colleagues (1997) noted that children who are in large classrooms with large proportions of children without disabilities and moderate teacher–child ratios, and who spend less than 50% of their time in one-to-one activities with adults, demonstrate better gains in social and task mastery skills.

Summary of Activity Structure

The results of the studies on activity structure have been somewhat unclear due to researchers' different definitions of "structure." In addition to the differences in basic terminology for activity structure across studies, other variables such as definitions of the dependent variables (peer interactions), group compositions, children's social and communication levels, and age differences of the participants may have affected individual study findings. Nevertheless, researchers' findings have indicated that activities that have higher structure with the clear purpose of facilitating social interactions may improve children's peer interactions. Moreover, the convergent information across a number of studies has indicated that when children with and without disabilities are involved in many teacher-directed activities, their social behaviors are less likely to provide children with disabilities the social opportunities to interact with peers, particularly if the goals of those teacher-directed activities are preacademic in nature (e.g., large group reading, one-to-one instruction). When teachers are directly and actively involved in many classroom activities, peer interactions occur less often than they do without adult involvement. Although the types of teacher involvement or interactions were not clearly described in most studies, some researchers reported that teachers provided more support for cognitive and caregiving activities than social interaction activities. Moreover, teachers' facilitation of peer interactions was not frequently observed during most classroom activities (see, for example, Brown & Bergen, 2002). Brown and Bergen (2002) also noted that many preschool activities are simply insufficient to consistently promote social interactions among children. Hence, teachers' roles when implementing and monitoring classroom activities are especially important for increasing and enhancing children's peer interactions, particularly when teachers focus on children's social interactions during routine preschool activities.

CONCLUSIONS

Early childhood classroom environments and the myriad of variables influencing the social behavior of young children in those environments set the stage for the development of young children's social competence. A review of the existing literature suggests that no single factor will be predictive of children's positive social outcomes. Whereas toys and materials may be particularly useful in eliciting desired social behaviors, other factors such as physical environments, activity demands, competence of peers, and the interactive behaviors of teachers may also be powerful influences on children's social behaviors and peer interactions. The finding that surfaced repeatedly in the literature regarding social competence and social behaviors of young children with disabilities was the potential for the positive influence of peers without disabilities in inclusive settings. Within inclusive settings, a range of environmental manipulations and interventions have produced positive social outcomes among children. Teachers of young children should be encouraged to establish inclusive classrooms employing toys and materials as well as social activities developed specifically for the promotion of social behavior. However, methodological issues concerning many of the studies reviewed continue to be problematic. For example, much of the research is descriptive in nature or focuses on only a few factors (e.g., impact of toys or spatial arrangements) without taking into account other relevant variables such as classroom characteristics and atmosphere, children's proximity, or behaviors of teachers and peers during important social activities (see, for example, Davis & Fox, 1999). The complex nature of classroom ecologies demands an examination of not only context but also setting events and the interplay among potent ecological and social factors in influencing children's optimal social development (Kontos, Burchinal, Howes, Wisseh, & Galinsky, 2002).

REFERENCES

Asher, K.N., & Erickson, M.T. (1979). Effects of varying child–teacher ratio and group size on day care children's and teachers' behavior. *American Journal of Orthopsychiatry, 49*, 518–521.

Bailey, D.B., McWilliam, R.A., Ware, W.B., & Burchinal, M.A. (1993). Social interactions of toddlers and preschoolers in same-age and mixed-age play groups. *Journal of Applied Developmental Psychology, 14*, 261–276.

Barry, L.M., & Burlew, S.B. (2004). Using social stories to teach choice and play skills to children with autism. *Focus on Autism and Other Developmental Disabilities, 19*, 45–51.

Bronfenbrenner, U. (1979). *The ecology of human development: Experiments by nature and design.* Cambridge, MA: Harvard University Press.

Bronson, M.B. (1985). *Manual for the Bronson Social and Task Skill Profile.* Chestnut Hill, MA: Boston College.

Bronson, M.B., Hauser-Cram, P., & Warfield, M.E. (1997). Classroom matters: Relations between the classroom environment and the social and mastery behavior of five-year-old children with disabilities. *Journal of Applied Developmental Psychology, 18*, 331–348.

Brown, M., & Bergen, D. (2002). Play and social interaction of children with disabilities at learning/activity centers in an inclusive preschool. *Journal of Research in Childhood Education, 17*, 26–37.

Brown, W.H., Fox, J.J., & Brady, M.P. (1987). Effects of spatial density on 3- and 4-year-old children's socially directed behavior during freeplay: An investigation of a setting factor. *Education and Treatment of Children, 10*, 247–258.

Burstein, N.D. (1986). The effect of classroom organization on mainstreamed preschool children. *Exceptional Children, 52*, 425–434.

Burroughs, E.I., & Murray, S.E. (1992). The influence of play material on discourse during play. *Journal of Childhood Communication Disorders, 14*, 119–128.

Buysse, V., Goldman, B.D., & Skinner, M.L. (2002). Setting effects on friendship formation among young children with and without disabilities. *Exceptional Children, 68*, 503–517.

Carter, M., & O'Gorman Hughes, C.A. (2001). Toys and materials as setting events on the social interaction of preschool children. *Australian Journal of Special Education, 25*, 49–66.

Chandler, L.K., Lubeck, R.C., & Fowler, S.A. (1992). Generalization and maintenance of preschool children's social skills: A critical review and analysis. *Journal of Applied Behavior Analysis, 25*, 415–428.

Class Size Reduction Research Consortium. (2002). *What we have learned about class size reduction in California.* Retrieved September 16, 2006, from http://www.classize.org/techreport/CSRYear4_final.pdf

Davis, C.A., & Fox, J. (1999). Evaluating environmental arrangement as setting events: Review and implications for measurement. *Journal of Behavioral Education, 9*, 77–96.

DeKlyen, M., & Odom, S.L. (1989). Activity structure and social interactions with peers in developmentally integrated play groups. *Journal of Early Intervention, 13*, 342–352.

Delano, M., & Snell, M.E. (2006). The effects of social stories on the social engagement of children with autism. *Journal of Positive Behavior Interventions, 8*, 29–42.

Doyle, A., Connolly, J., & Rivest, L. (1980). The effect of playmate familiarity on the social interactions of young children. *Child Development, 51*, 217–223.

Driscoll, C., & Carter, M. (2004). Spatial density as a setting event for the social interaction of preschool children. *International Journal of Disability, Development, and Education, 51*, 7–37.

Eckerman, C.O., & Whatley, J.L. (1977). Toys and social interaction between infant peers. *Child Development, 48*, 1645–1656.

Fabes, R.A., Martin, C.L., & Hanish, L.D. (2003). Young children's play qualities in same-, other-, and mixed-sex peer groups. *Child Development, 74*, 921–932.

File, N. (1994). Children's play, teacher–child interactions, and teacher beliefs in integrated early childhood programs. *Early Childhood Research Quarterly, 9*, 223–240.

File, N., & Kontos, S. (1993). The relationship of program quality to children's play in integrated early intervention settings. *Topics in Early Childhood Special Education, 13*, 1–18.

Finn, J.D., & Pannozzo, G.M. (2004). Classroom organization and student behavior in kindergarten. *Journal of Educational Research, 98*, 79–92.

Furman, W., Rahe, D.F., & Hartup, W.W. (1979). Rehabilitation of socially withdrawn preschool children through mixed-age and same-age socialization. *Child Development, 50*, 915–922.

Gray, C. (1998). Social stories and comic strip conversations with students with Asperger syndrome and high functioning autism. In: E. Schopler, G. Mesibov & L. Kunce (Eds.), *Asperger syndrome or high functioning autism?* (pp. 167–198). New York: Plenum Press.

Graziano, W., French, D., Brownell, C.A., & Hartup, W.W. (1976). Peer interaction in same- and mixed-age triads in relation to chronological age and incentive condition. *Child Development, 47*, 707–714.

Guralnick M.J. (2001). Social competence with peers and early childhood inclusion. In M.J. Guralnick (Ed.) *Early childhood inclusion: Focus on change* (pp. 293–306). Baltimore: Paul H. Brookes Publishing Co.

Hamilton, D. (2005). An ecobehavioural analysis of interactive engagement of children with developmental disabilities with their peers in inclusive preschools. *International Journal of Disability, Development, and Education, 52*, 121–137.

Harper, L.V., & Huie, K.S. (1985). The effects of prior group experience, age, and familiarity on the quality and organization of preschoolers' social relationships. *Child Development, 56*, 704–717.

Harper, L.V., & McCluskey, K.S. (2003). Teacher–child and child–child interactions in inclusive preschool settings: Do adults inhibit peer interactions? *Early Childhood Research Quarterly, 18*, 163–184.

Hauser-Cram, P., Bronson, M.B., & Upsur, C.C. (1993). The effects of the classroom environment on the social and mastery behavior of preschool children with disabilities. *Early Childhood Research Quarterly, 8*, 479–497.

Hestenes, L.L., & Carroll, D.E. (2000). The play interactions of young children with and without disabilities: Individual and environmental influences. *Early Childhood Research Quarterly, 15*, 229–246.

Hulson, E. (1930). An analysis of the free play of ten four-year-old children through consecutive observations. *Journal of Juvenile Research, 14*, 188–208.

Hundert, J., Mahoney, W.J., & Hopkins, B. (1993). The relationship between the peer interaction with disabilities in integrated preschools and resource and classroom teacher behaviors. *Topics in Early Childhood Special Education, 13*, 328–343.

Ivory, J.J., & McCollum, J.A. (1999). Effects of social and isolate toys on social play in an inclusive setting. *The Journal of Special Education, 32*, 238–243.

Jacobson, J.L. (1981). The role of inanimate objects in early peer interaction. *Child Development, 52*, 618–626.

Kantor, J.R. (1959). *Interbehavioral psychology*. Granville, OH: Principal Press.

Kim, Y.A. (2001). Peer relationships and play behaviors of children in three different sized classes over a four-month period. *Early Child Development and Care, 167*, 89–102.

Kohl, F.L., & Beckman, P.J. (1984). A comparison of handicapped and non handicapped preschoolers' interactions across classroom activities. *Journal of the Division for Early Childhood, 8*, 49–56.

Kontos, S., Burchinal, M., Howes, C., Wisseh, S., & Galinsky, E. (2002). An eco-behavioral approach to examining the contextual effects of early childhood classrooms. *Early Childhood Research Quarterly, 17*, 239–258.

Kontos, S., Moore, D., & Giogretti, K. (1998). The ecology of inclusion. *Topics in Early Childhood Special Education, 18*, 38–48.

Kontos, S., & Wilcox-Herzog, A. (1997). Influences on children's competence in early childhood classrooms. *Early Childhood Research Quarterly, 12*, 247–262.

Langlois, J.H., Gottfried, N.W., Barnes, B.M., & Hendricks, D.E. (1978). The effect of peer age on the social behavior of preschool children. *The Journal of Genetic Psychology, 132*, 11–19.

Langlois, J.H., Gottfried, N.W., & Seay, B. (1973). The influence of sex of peer on the social behavior of preschool children. *Developmental Psychology, 8,* 93–98.

McCormick, L., Noonan, M.J., & Heck, R. (1998). Variables affecting engagement in inclusive preschool classrooms. *Journal of Early Intervention, 21,* 160–176.

McCornack, B.L. (1982). Effects of peer familiarity on play behavior in preschool children. *The Journal of Genetic Psychology, 141,* 225–232.

McWilliam, R.A., & Bailey, D.B. (1995). Effects of classroom social structure and disability on engagement. *Topics in Early Childhood Special Education, 15,* 123–147.

Nabors, L., Willoughby, J., & Badawi, M. (1999). Relations among activities and cooperative playground interactions for preschool-age children with special needs. *Journal of Developmental and Physical Disabilities, 11,* 339–389.

National Institute of Child Health and Human Development. (2004). Does class size in first grade relate to children's academic and social performance or observed classroom processes? *Developmental Psychology, 40,* 651–664.

Odom, S.L., McConnell, S., & Chandler, L. (1993). Acceptability and feasibility of classroom-based social interaction intervention for young children with disabilities. *Exceptional Children, 60,* 226–236.

Odom, S.L., Peterson, C., McConnell, S., & Ostrosky, M. (1990). Echobehavioral analysis of early education/specialized classroom settings and peer social interaction. *Education and Treatment of Children, 13,* 316–330.

O'Gorman Hughes, C.A., & Carter, M. (2002). Toys and materials as setting events for the social interaction of preschool children with special needs. *Educational Psychology, 22,* 429–444.

Quilitch, H.R., & Risley, T.R. (1973). The effects of play materials on social play. *Journal of Applied Behavior Analysis, 6,* 573–578.

Rettig, M.A. (1994). Play behaviors of young children with autism: Characteristics and interventions. *Focus on Autistic Behavior, 9*(5), 1–7.

Rettig, M., Kallam, M., & McCarthy-Salm, K. (1993). The effect of social and isolate toys on the social interactions of preschool-aged children. *Education and Training in Mental Retardation, 28,* 252–256.

Rubin, K. (1977). The social and cognitive value of preschool toys and activities. *Canadian Journal of Behavioral Science, 9,* 382–385.

Rubenstein, J., & Howe, C. (1976). The effects of peers on toddler interaction with mother and toys. *Child Development, 47,* 597–605.

Sainato, D.M., & Carta, J.J. (1992). Classroom influences on the development of social competence in young children with disabilities. In S.L. Odom, S.R. McConnell, & M.A. McEvoy (Eds.), *Social competence of young children with disabilities: Issues and strategies for intervention* (pp. 93–109). Baltimore: Paul H. Brookes Publishing Co.

Serbin, L.A., Tonick, I.J., & Sternglanz, S.H. (1977). Shaping cooperative cross-sex play. *Child Development, 48,* 924–929.

Shores, R.E., Hester, P., & Strain, P.S. (1976). The effects of the amount and type of teacher–child interaction on child–child interaction during free play. *Psychology in the Schools, 13,* 171–175.

Smith, P.K., & Connolly, K.J. (1986). Experimental studies of the preschool environment: The Sheffield Project. *Advances in Early Education and Day Care, 4,* 27–66.

Strain, P.S., & Odom, S.L. (1986). Peer social initiations: Effective intervention for social skills development of exceptional children. *Exceptional Children, 52,* 543–551.

Stoneman, Z., Cantrell, M.L., & Hoover-Dempsey, K. (1983). The association between play materials and play behavior in a mainstreamed preschool: A naturalistic investigation. *Journal of Applied Developmental Psychology, 4,* 163–174.

Thiemann, K., & Goldstein, H. (2001). Social stories, written text cues, and video feedback: Effects on social communication of children with autism. *Journal of Applied Behavior Analysis, 24,* 425–446.

VanAlstyne, D. (1932). *Play behavior and choice of play materials of pre-school children.* Chicago: University of Chicago Press.

Vandell, D.L., Wilson, K.S., & Buchanan, N.R. (1980). Peer interaction in the first year of life: An examination of its structure, content, and sensitivity to toys. *Child Development, 51,* 481–488.

CHAPTER 6

The Critical Nature of Young Children's Emerging Peer-Related Social Competence for Transition to School

KRISTEN N. MISSALL AND ROBIN L. HOJNOSKI

The transition to kindergarten is an important time for children and their families on developmental and relational levels. Historically, the transition to kindergarten marked the inception of formal socialization and learning, and was viewed as a time for exploring the educational environment, learning to navigate social relationships with peers and teachers, and learning to follow the rules and routines of formal education (Seefeldt & Wasik, 2002). In more recent years, this perspective of transition has shifted to include an expanded focus on learning and pre-academics with increased attention to children's development and learning experiences prior to kindergarten (Graue, 1999; Ladd, 1996). Educators have begun to focus on readiness for school that includes the reciprocal and comprehensive influence of social and academic factors (McConnell & Missall, 2004; Meisels, 1999). As children develop and regularly engage in school settings, their school adjustment, or the extent to which they are meeting the academic and social demands of the educational environment, is considered to be critical (Ladd, Birch, & Buhs, 1999; McConnell et al., 1984; Missall, 2002). Because children's early schooling can be identified as the starting point of their trajectory toward later school success and adjustment, early school experiences and outcomes are particularly important. If successful transition to kindergarten is determined, in part, by the extent to which children competently engage socially *and* academically, then children need to enter kindergarten with well-developed social and academic skills presumably to be on track for school success.

Although the purpose of this chapter is to discuss important and specific elements of peer-related social competence as they relate to kindergarten preparedness and early school success, it is nearly impossible to focus on early school success without acknowledging the reciprocal influence of social and academic development and the connectedness of skill development in these domains over time. Thus, content is also devoted to aspects of social competence that are more directly related to

117

learning than to peer-related social competence. The goal of this chapter is to briefly review the importance of social competence, delineate theoretical and definitional issues specific to the transition to school, and discuss specific aspects of social competence and their relation to school adjustment and continued development.

WHY IS SOCIAL DEVELOPMENT "CRITICAL?"

From birth, humans are social beings; they want and need social interaction, and these early interactions set the stage for social development (Hartup, 1983; Chapter 1, this volume). Babies learn and apply fundamental social skills in their interactions with others that promote relationships and, in time, general competence. In the context of these relationships and interactions, children continue to develop behaviors and skills to adapt to and function in the daily environment. These behaviors and skills tend to create patterns of performance over time that influence an individual's interpersonal interactions and environmental adaptation throughout his or her life span. As early as infancy, the quality and reciprocity of social interactions have been associated with a number of later social and behavioral outcomes (Hartup, 1983; Putallaz & Heflin, 1990); the importance of ensuring early, healthy social development is clear. A child must develop competent social behaviors in order to ensure successful future development in educational and social arenas (Saunders & Green, 1993; Wentzel, 1991).

Competent social behaviors that develop early in life such as initiating and maintaining interactions, or self-regulatory behaviors such as attending and listening to others, are of increasing importance as children enter contexts outside of the home, specifically as children make the transition to formal schooling. These types of behaviors become more critical to school adjustment and particularly to social relationships with individuals and to group membership, or an individual's relation to the group (Schwartz, Garfinkle, & Davis, 2002). Although not explicitly academic in nature, these types of behaviors also affect early learning by facilitating engagement in the classroom or the extent to which a child appropriately interacts with the classroom environment (Ridley, McWilliam, & Oates, 2000; Rosenshine, 1981).

Social skills build and change over time as children grow physically and emotionally. For example, in considering the development of emotional regulation, the skill set of a toddler is vastly different from the skill set of a kindergartner. The developmental level of social regulation can significantly affect peer relationships as a child learns to interact with peers and negotiate social interaction. The significance of the impact increases as the distance between physical and emotional maturity increases. A toddler who collapses in tantrum because a peer refuses to share is seen as more socially appropriate than a kindergarten-aged child who responds similarly. A child who regularly engages in age-inappropriate social behavior is at risk for negatively affecting peer relationships (Ladd, Kochenderfer, & Coleman, 1997). This is important to recognize because early social patterns set the stage for later social patterns. For example, children who demonstrate early negative behavioral interactions with their caregivers are at risk for replicating these interaction patterns with other significant adults and peers as they enter school (Reid & Patterson, 1996). Furthermore, these negative interactions inhibit the development of preferred and prosocial skills and result in antisocial behavior patterns that tend to become more stable and resistant to intervention by 8 years of age (Walker, Colvin, & Ramsey, 1995).

Children who have maladaptive social and task-related behavioral patterns that are identifiable as early as preschool are likely to have difficulties across time in educational and social domains (Hinshaw, 1992; Ladd & Coleman, 1997; Masten et al., 1995). Early grade retention (Jimerson, Carlson, Rotert, Egeland, & Sroufe, 1997) as well as referral to special education (Walker & McConnell, 1995) is a risk for early elementary students viewed by their teachers as having poor social development. In addition, failure to establish positive relationships with peers before or during elementary school predicts problems during adolescence and adulthood (Moffit & Caspi, 2001; Parker & Asher, 1987). Retrospective and longitudinal studies of children with social and academic skill deficits indicate disproportionate representation in groups of juvenile offenders, high school dropouts, teenage pregnancy, and adults who report a high incidence of alcoholism, unemployment, divorce, dependence on public assistance, and referral for psychiatric treatment (McFadyen-Ketchum & Dodge, 1998; Parker & Asher, 1987). It is possible that as early as kindergarten, poor social development and negative school experiences may initiate a downward cycle for children in which outcomes such as academic difficulties, antisocial behavior, withdrawal from the school environment, and other negative sequelae become more likely (Ladd & Coleman, 1997; Masten & Coatsworth, 1995). Thus, ensuring that children develop skills that enable them to be socially competent across time and settings as they move into kindergarten is a critical element of facilitating continued successful, productive, and adaptive development.

SOCIAL DEVELOPMENT TERMINOLOGY AND DEFINITIONAL ISSUES

Although the consequences of poor social development are clear, the way in which social development is conceptualized and operationalized is less so, and there are a variety of theoretical models, definitional issues, and components of the construct. The study and explanation of social development is particularly difficult because of the linguistic struggle over defining related terminology, most notably *social competence*. There is no one, clear, accepted definition of the construct. Rather, there are theories and methods that articulate various pathways for the development and acquisition of social competence.[1]

Theoretical Models

One way to understand and describe social development and its behavioral or psychological manifestations is to use two conceptual frameworks identified by Mac-Corquodale and Meehl as "hypothetical constructs" and "intervening variables". As proposed by these authors, hypothetical constructs are "[abstract] processes or entities that are not directly observed or explicitly defined" (1948, p. 104) and require inference. Hypothetical constructs are not tangible, and their lack of definition can

---

[1]It is typically good practice to cite recently published literature under the assumption that newer theory and research encompasses and eclipses older work; however, this assumption does not always hold. The general area of school adjustment and social competence, in particular, has some highly valuable and relevant research from the 1970s and 1980s. Other related theoretical frameworks retain strong relevance as well. Throughout this chapter, cited literatures reflect what the authors feel are important and contemporary perspectives, regardless of publication date.

make them difficult to measure in an objective manner. Examples of hypothetical constructs include self-esteem, motivation, and adjustment. In contrast, intervening variables are discrete, observable, measurable, and operational events that are "strictly reducible to empirical terms" (MacCorquodale & Meehl, 1948, p. 101; e.g., time on-task, joint attention, hitting).

Consistent with this contrast between hypothetical constructs and intervening variables is the notion of "trait" and "molecular-behavioral" models (McFall, 1982). A trait model of social behavior posits social skillfulness as a hypothetical construct that refers to a "general, underlying personality characteristic that is reasonably stable over time and relatively consistent across situations" (McFall, 1982, p. 2). In this type of model, social skillfulness is not directly observable or measurable and can be represented by constructs such as attachment, temperament, and popularity. In the molecular model, social skillfulness is inextricably linked to social skills that "are construed in terms of very specific, observable units of behavior which are the building blocks of the individual's overall performance in each interpersonal situation" (McFall, 1982, p. 7; e.g., taking a turn, making a request, initiating play, sharing materials). As such, social skills are viewed as situation-specific even though social performance is likely to be consistent over time in situations that are similar (McFall, 1982). To summarize, hypothetical constructs or trait models appear to best provide descriptive information for broad conceptualization of social behavior, whereas intervening variables or molecular-behavioral models shift the focus to specific operationalized behaviors and skill-based performance.

Specific to social development, the two models may be used in complementary ways to better understand the complexity of behavior. For example, research on children's temperament describes young children's social behavior through dimensions of individual difference and environmental influences, using terminology to describe children's traits such as *difficult, easy,* and *slow-to-warm-up* (Chess & Thomas, 1986). Although temperament and specific social behaviors may exert reciprocal influence, the trait model places more importance on temperament mediated by patterns of caregiving (Chess & Thomas), whereas the molecular-behavioral model emphasizes the specific skills observed in social exchanges as an indicator of social competence (Howes, 1988; Odom & McConnell, 1985).

Social Competence in the Transition to School

Social competence in young children has been defined as an interaction between cognitive, social, and biological variables (Masten et al., 1995; Saunders & Green, 1993); an attribute that develops over time and reflects capacity to initiate, develop, and maintain satisfying relationships with others (Katz, 1987); a composite of adaptive behavior and social skills (Gresham & Elliott, 1987); and the frequency or rate of occurrence of various components of interaction and social behavior (McEvoy, Odom, & McConnell, 1992; Tremblay, Strain, Hendrickson, & Shores, 1981). Regardless of definitional specifics, social competence is an indisputably important element of child development that becomes a critical focus when children make the transition to school. Particularly as children enter kindergarten, adjustment to the demands of school becomes an increasingly important component of social competence. Along with knowing letters and numbers, children need to know how to share, follow rules, and play appropriately with peers and classroom materials.

These behaviors are not only valued but also often are the focus of evaluations of social development, or the degree to which children are socially competent (Meisels, 1999).

Increasing evidence suggests that young children's social competence can be differentiated into two different, but related, strains: learning-related social skills and peer-related social skills (Bronson, 1994; Cooper & Farran, 1988; McClelland & Morrison, 2003; McClelland, Morrison, & Holmes, 2000; McConnell et al., 1984; Missall, 2002; Walker & McConnell, 1995). In general, learning-related social skills include all of the social elements necessary to engage in academic tasks and successfully complete them, whereas peer-related social skills refer to the skills required for appropriate and competent interaction with others (both terms are discussed in greater detail later in this chapter). In order to successfully navigate the social school environment, children need both skill sets (Walker & McConnell, 1995).

Early School Adjustment

School plays an important role in helping children develop both academic and social skills. Indeed, the degree to which children develop competencies in these areas in their school environment is a good index of their early school adjustment. Early school adjustment has been defined as "the extent to which children are meeting the academic and behavioral, or social, demands of early schooling" from preschool through early elementary school (Missall, 2002, p. 15). Determining a child's adjustment to school requires in-depth understanding of their social development. However, "early school adjustment" and "social competence" are not synonymous. School adjustment has added dimensions of academic competence that are broader than self-regulatory social skills that help children to engage in and complete academic tasks successfully, as well as basic academic achievement skills. Factor analysis has shown strong relations between specific preacademic skills required for reading (e.g., early literacy skills of vocabulary, phonological awareness), social skill development, and teacher-rated school adjustment for both preschool-aged children and kindergartners (Missall, 2002). These findings indicate shared variance between measures of these constructs and suggest a common core or underlying construct (e.g., school adjustment; Missall, 2002).

Early school adjustment is also unique from school readiness. The term *school readiness* tends to refer to individual experiences and development prior to kindergarten (see Meisels, 1999), whereas early school adjustment spans the continuum of development from preschool through the first grades of formal schooling. Current literature about children's school success includes such popular areas as school readiness, school adjustment, dropout prevention, academic achievement, and social competence, yet given the breadth of these literatures, they in general rarely address children's social and academic states in a simultaneous manner across the transition into formal school. Thinking about school-related development in this manner is provocative.

Much of the research in school adjustment targets children in elementary school and focuses on school perceptions, school anxiety, school avoidance, and school performance (Ladd, 1990); school liking, loneliness, and perceived peer support (Ladd, Buhs, & Seid, 2000; Ladd & Coleman, 1997); temperament and peer preference (Taylor & Machida, 1994); social status (Ladd, Price, & Hart, 1988); peer relationships (Ladd, Kochenderfer, & Coleman, 1997); popularity (Buhs & Ladd, 2001); and teacher relationships (Demulder, Denham, Schmidt, & Mitchell, 2000; Pianta, Nimetz, & Bennett, 1997). Some research has specifically focused on children in kindergarten (Ladd, 1990; Ladd, Birch, & Buhs, 1999; Ladd, Buhs, & Seid, 2000), but studies examining the early school adjustment of children in preschool and into kindergarten are few (Ladd & Price, 1987; Missall, 2002). Furthermore, available research tends to provide descriptive information about psychological correlates of school adjustment (e.g., self-esteem, popularity, attachment) rather than work that lends to or suggests empirically based interventions. In other words, available information provides a framework for determining who might be at risk for school maladjustment, but does little to suggest how to ameliorate it. Given what is known about the early onset of risk and problem behaviors (Walker, Colvin, & Ramsey, 1995), as well as the importance of early academic development for facilitating school success (Geary, Hamson, & Hoard, 2000; Snow, Burn, & Griffin, 1998), this is an important area for further inquiry and exploration.

Conceptually, early school adjustment includes learning-related academic skills, peer- and adult-related social skills, and pure academic achievement skills. A preschool child's development in these areas, and their resulting early school adjustment, is affected by their early experiences in the home and with any formal or informal education prior to kindergarten, as well as by the environment of the school receiving the child in kindergarten. The school readiness literature has frequently debated the issue of whether children need to be ready for school or whether schools need to be ready for children (see Pianta & Cox, 1999). This interaction between what children bring to school and how schools respond to the unique needs of individual children who enter the school doors for the first time influences school adjustment tremendously (Ladd, Birch & Buhs, 1999; Pianta, Rimm-Kaufman, & Cox, 1999).

Although it can be argued that terminology and research related to preparation and success in early school are distinct, there is overlap and interaction. In short, children need academic and social competence to realize school success, and the related literatures address this in different ways. However, because in most schools, educators typically meet children for the first time on the first day of kindergarten, they often do not have the opportunity to identify children who would benefit from intervention prior to formal schooling, and their chances of influencing individual children's developmental trajectories are reduced. Yet, there is a direct link between early school adjustment and later school experiences.

A child's school adjustment in preschool can set the stage for later school experiences (Taylor & Machida, 1994). Therefore, it is important to identify children who have poor school adjustment during the primary years, if not before (i.e., in preschool or soon after kindergarten entrance) and intervene on their behalf (see Mize & Ladd, 1990). Educators are good candidates for monitoring children's adjustment because in addition to exerting academic influence they are aware of the classroom behavior of individual children, value socially competent behavior, and spend time teaching children how to behave and act responsibly (Walker & McConnell, 1995; Wentzel, 1991). In short, because teachers work so closely with children, they do a great deal to influence children's adjustment to school and they are also in a unique position to evaluate children's progress.

LEARNING-RELATED AND PEER-RELATED SOCIAL SKILLS

To evaluate and understand early school adjustment, three elements of behavior must be considered: 1) general skills, 2) dimensions of skills, and 3) relations between preschool and kindergarten skills. Moreover, a constellation of social and academic behaviors contribute to early school adjustment and predict school success. Here, they are discussed in part as learning-related social skills and peer-related social skills.

Learning-Related Social Skills

Learning-related social skills are behaviors that are essential for skill development and task completion or accomplishment, including listening, following directions (Agostin & Bain, 1997; Foulks & Morrow, 1989; McClelland, Morrison, & Holmes, 2000), appropriate group participation, on-task behavior, organization of work materials (McClelland & Morrison, 2003), assertiveness, initiative, an absence of disruptive and hostile-aggressive behaviors (Gresham, 1997; Harper, Guidubaldi, & Kehle, 1978); and negotiation skills (Piaget, 1926). Learning-related social skills may also include classroom behaviors that have an academic application but are at root social, including task-oriented conversation, compliance with teacher demands, self-regulation, and independence (Cobb, 1972; McKinney, Mason, Peterson, & Clifford, 1975; Reynolds, 1991).

Some research suggests the relationship between learning-related social skills and academic achievement is stronger than that between interpersonal skills and achievement. For example, in a sample of 650 kindergarten children, children who were rated low on learning-related social skills by their teacher in the fall and spring of kindergarten were more at risk for being identified with behavior problems when compared with children rated low on interpersonal skills (Cooper & Farran, 1988). Cooper and Speece (1988) found that low learning-related social skills were the most important predictors of special education referrals and school failure in first grade children.

Furthermore, evidence shows that learning-related social skills demonstrate social validity in terms of their importance to early school adjustment. A survey of kindergarten teachers, preschool teachers, and childcare providers indicated that behaviors such as listening to the teacher and complying with teacher demands were perceived by all three participant groups as critical to successful adjustment to kindergarten; social skills and positive interactions with peers were rated not as critical for academic survival as learning-related social skills (Foulks & Morrow, 1989). Also, in a national survey of more than 3,500 kindergarten teachers, almost half (46%) of respondents said that half or more of the children entering kindergarten had "difficulty following directions," but only 20% of teachers reported "problems with social skills" in half or more of the class entering kindergarten (Rimm-Kaufmann, Pianta, & Cox, 2000).

In addition to being predictors of early school achievement, learning-related social skills appear to be linked to continued school adjustment and success. In a study of 82 kindergartners drawn from a longitudinal sample of 540 children, hierarchical regressions indicated that the learning-related skills children had at the beginning of kindergarten accounted for unique variance in children's reading, mathematics, vocabulary, general information, and alphabet skills; learning-related social skills predicted academic skills beyond the influence of other important child, social, and family variables including IQ, amount of preschool experience, parent education level, and home literacy environment (McClelland et al., 2000). Moreover, learning-related social skills continued to be predictive of academic achievement at the end of second grade (McClelland et al., 2000). Finally, research suggests that learning-related social skills are measurable as early as preschool, and teacher ratings of these skills are stable over at least a 1-year period of time (McClelland & Morrison, 2003).

Taken together, the results of these studies are particularly worthy of consideration in the context of ensuring successful transition to formal schooling. Differentiation between learning-related social skills and interpersonal social skills is important to understanding the complex relationship of social competence to academic achievement and success. Although both types of skills contribute to a child's overall social competence, learning-related social skills contribute uniquely to school adjustment and thus, serve as an important target for intervention. Furthermore, the early emergence, individual variability, predictive value, and overall stability of children's learning-related social skills underscore the necessity of early efforts to ensure that children are developing behaviors for school success.

Improving Children's Learning-Related Social Skills

Research suggests that the amount of time a student is engaged with academic materials or activities in an organized fashion is the most crucial component of student achievement (Carnine, Silbert, & Kame'enui, 1990; Rosenshine, 1981). *Engagement,* or the time a child spends interacting with the classroom environment in an appropriate manner, conceptually includes behaviors representative of learning-related social skills, is recognized as a critical skill in early childhood, and has been used as an indicator of the quality of the classroom environment (McCormick, Noonan, & Heck, 1998; Ridley et al., 2000). Increasing engagement and decreasing disruptive behavior often are simultaneous and complementary goals of interventions for young children with and without disabilities (Barnett et al., 2002). Typically, interventions for learning-related social skills target specific behaviors such as active participation, task completion, and following directions.

Active participation and attendance in large-group activities are two learning-related skills that become increasingly important as children make the transition to kindergarten, where large group activities and instruction are more frequent (Chandler, 1996). Children with behavioral difficulties and children with disabilities often demonstrate less active participation and more off-task behavior in large group settings than their peers without disabilities (Sainato, Strain, & Lyon, 1987). Lack of involvement and attention increases the risk that children with disabilities will benefit less from instruction and encounter negative peer interactions, particularly if they exhibit higher levels of disruptive behavior while off-task. Thus, strategies to increase task-related behaviors and decrease disruptive behaviors are essential. Sainato and colleagues (1987) demonstrated the effectiveness of choral responding in decreasing levels of off-task behavior in three preschoolers with disabilities during a large-group activity. In a comparative evaluation of choral responding and response cards, results indicated increased active responding and on-task behavior as well as decreased inappropriate behavior for five preschool children with attentional problems (Godfrey, Grisham-Brown, Schuster, & Hemmeter,

2003). Although both choral responding and response cards resulted in improved behavior over conventional hand raising, response cards proved to be superior to choral responding, with anecdotal records indicating an increase for on-task behavior in children without attentional problems also. In addition, the teacher and the children selected response cards as the preferred strategy.

Although classroom-wide interventions may be effective in many cases, sometimes more child-specific interventions are necessary. Child-specific interventions may not only serve to enhance engagement but also to address specific problematic behaviors. For example, prompting, provision of choice, praise, and increased opportunities to respond were combined with environmental arrangements to address the challenging behaviors of two preschoolers in a community setting (Duda, Dunlap, Fox, Lentini, & Clarke, 2004). Interventions were found to be effective both at decreasing difficult behavior and in increasing engagement for both participants (Duda et al., 2004).

Engagement in large-group activities is an important skill for all children, and one that is likely to be essential in the transition to kindergarten. However, large-group activities may occur less frequently than self-directed play activities during the preschool years. Engagement in free play, then, may serve as a proxy for a child's general ability to engage appropriately and productively with instructional materials. Therefore, strategies to increase engagement in free play, although developmentally and contextually appropriate for preschoolers, may extend their impact to the more academic engagement necessary in kindergarten.

Environmental arrangements such as the size of the play environment, availability of materials, and adult presence, have been associated with variations in young children's play engagement (DeLong et al., 1994; Kontos, Burchinal, Howes, Wisseh, & Galinsky, 2002; Rettig, Kallam, & McCarthy-Salm, 1993). More directive interventions also have been explored as a means of increasing engagement in play. For example, a hierarchical intervention that combined picture cues with correspondence training procedures was explored as a means of increasing play engagement for four preschool children with disabilities (Bevill, Gast, Maguire, & Vail, 2001). The intervention package was found to be effective for all children, although varying levels of the intervention were required for each child to meet criterion for mastery.

In summation, learning-related social skills appear to be distinct from peer-related social skills, yet equally important in promoting a successful transition to formal schooling. Behaviors such as following directions, listening, active participation, and task completion can be viewed as indicators of engagement in the preschool classroom that facilitate school adjustment. Children who are equipped with such learning-related social skills are likely to benefit more from their early education experiences and have less difficulty responding to the task demands of formal schooling. Thus, these types of behaviors make ideal targets for intervention in the context of group activities or play, and research suggests that various strategies can be used effectively to increase children's engagement.

Peer-Related Social Skills

Increasing engagement in play and in other classroom activities likely involves interactions with peers and requires peer-related social skills to varying degrees. Peer-related social skills focus on behaviors related to interpersonal interactions and include initiation and maintenance of interactions, sharing, and demonstration of respect for other children (McClelland & Morrison, 2003). Even for young children, peer relationships are a significant component of school experiences and influence overall adjustment to school (Ladd, 1990; Ladd & Coleman, 1997). Similar to general social competence, peer social competence has been defined by a number of different indicators including friendships, peer social status, and specific social behaviors used in peer interactions (Odom, McConnell, & McEvoy, 1992; Phillipsen, Deptula, & Cohen, 1999).

Although the sheer number of friends that a child has does not necessarily correlate with school liking and adjustment (Ladd & Coleman, 1997), researchers suggest that children with extensive preschool experience who maintain friendships in the first 2 months of kindergarten are more likely to view school favorably and experience positive overall adjustment (Ladd, 1990). Moreover, kindergarten-age children who report low peer acceptance also report negative attitudes and general dislike toward school (Ladd & Coleman, 1997).

Clearly, social skills play a significant role in friendship and peer acceptance (Guralnick, 1992). Many of these skills are grounded in fundamental principles related to social interaction, that is, the initiation and response interchange required for engagement with others (Howes, Droege, & Phillipsen, 1992). Young children who engage in high rates of positive initiations tend to receive more positive initiations from peers and vice versa (McConnell et al., 1984), and children tend to maintain similar relationship patterns across kindergarten (Ladd, Kochenderfer, & Coleman, 1997). In one study that followed children who were making the transition from preschool to kindergarten, children who played cooperatively in preschool were seen as more sociable by kindergarten teachers and also became well-liked by their kindergarten classmates (Ladd & Price, 1987). In contrast, children who displayed aggressive behaviors and engaged in negative peer contacts in preschool were more likely to be seen as hostile-aggressive by kindergarten teachers and were more likely to be rejected by kindergarten peers (Ladd & Price, 1987).

In a more recent study across the kindergarten year, children who demonstrated prosocial skills early in kindergarten tended to develop a larger number of mutually selected friends and higher levels of acceptance among classmates, whereas those who exhibited more antisocial skills tended to develop fewer mutual friends, had lower levels of peer acceptance, and had more negative teacher–child relationships (Ladd, Birch, & Buhs, 1999). Furthermore, results from this same study showed that children with prosocial skills were more likely than their counterparts to engage in appropriate levels of classroom participation (e.g., independent and cooperative work styles) and experience higher levels of achievement.

Improving Children's Peer-Related Social Skills

Interventions to promote peer-related social skills have targeted social interaction in general as well as specific social behaviors that a child may use in play and peer interactions. In a study of preschoolers with autism in an integrated classroom setting, naturalistic teaching strategies such as inviting children to make choices, using comments and questions, inviting interaction with peers, and requiring expansions of verbalizations resulted in increases in general social interaction for the four participants across classroom activity areas (Kohler, Anthony, Steighner, & Hoyson, 2001).

Another instructional intervention targeting specific skills used puppets and scripts to teach the skills of greeting, initiating conversations, and maintaining conversations to a preschooler with visual impairments (Gronna, Serna, Kennedy, & Prater, 1999). These researchers observed a significant increase in the target behaviors following intervention and at 3 and 24 months post intervention. In addition, teacher ratings indicated a significant improvement in the preschooler's social behavior. At a group level, another study showed that social skill instruction and reinforcement of target skills was effective in increasing sharing and peer interaction behaviors in 38 preschoolers with developmental delays (Guglielmo & Tryon, 2001). In addition, intervention acceptability measures indicated that both teachers and children viewed the social skill intervention favorably.

Specific social skill instructional procedures also have been demonstrated to be effective for children without disabilities but with risk factors for social interaction difficulties due to excesses or deficits in social behavior. For example, prompting and contingent social praise were implemented to increase the use of play organizers, sharing, and assisting peers in four preschoolers with extreme social withdrawal. Results indicated an increase in the use of the targeted skills as well as in the duration of peer interactions during the intervention condition (Lindeman, Fox, & Redelheim, 1993).

Although child-specific interventions can be effective in increasing target behaviors, an examination of the differential effects of social skill interventions found that child-specific interventions had a negative impact on peer ratings over time (Odom et al., 1999). In the same study, peer-mediated interventions that utilized socially competent peers to engage children with risk factors in social interaction (Strain & Odom, 1986) positively affected peer interactions and increased teacher ratings of social competence without the negative effect on peer ratings. Furthermore, the effects of peer-mediated interventions appeared to generalize across time and setting.

Peer-mediated interventions have demonstrated success in increasing social interaction of young children with autism and other developmental disabilities (Goldstein, Kaczmarek, Pennington, & Shafer, 1992; Odom, Chandler, Ostrosky, McConnell, & Reaney, 1992). In one example, preschool children who were typically developing were taught to attend to, comment on, and acknowledge the social behavior of five classmates with autism during play sessions (Goldstein et al., 1992). An increase in frequency of total social behavior for the target children occurred when the peers used the facilitation strategies (Goldstein et al., 1992). In a similar investigation, preschool children who were typically developing were trained in strategies to initiate play with their classmates with disabilities, resulting in increases in peer initiations to the children with disabilities and increases in social interaction for the children with disabilities (Odom et al., 1992). Moreover, levels of social interaction were maintained as teacher and visual prompts to the peers were faded (Odom et al., 1992).

Social skill instruction also may be embedded in activities. For example, social skill training was delivered through a story and song format at the classroom level with children in Head Start who were at risk for emotional or behavioral disorders. Targeted skills included direction following, sharing, and problem solving. Children in the experimental group showed improvement on adaptive behavior, social interaction, and attention measures relative to the control group (Serna, Nielsen, Lambros, & Forness, 2000).

To summarize, although peer-related social skills may be measured in various ways (e.g., friendships, social status, observation of discrete skills), the ability to interact with peers in a meaningful and socially appropriate manner is an important developmental goal. The significance of successful peer interactions is further highlighted when the influence of such interactions on continued development, and ultimately, school adjustment is considered. For all children, but particularly children with disabilities, positive peer interactions may also facilitate development in other domains such as motor skills, language, and cognition (Guralnick, 1992). Furthermore, positive peer interactions increase the likelihood of, or set the stage for, additional and continued positive interactions which may serve as a protective factor when they transition to formal schooling (Ladd, 1990; Ladd, Kochenderfer, & Coleman, 1997; Ladd & Price, 1987). Interventions ranging from naturalistic prompting to activity-based instruction to explicit direct instruction have been demonstrated to be effective in increasing targeted social behaviors in both children with disabilities and children at risk for behavioral difficulties. Specific attention to peer interactions and intentional and strategic use of techniques to support positive peer-related social skills are likely to have both a short- and long-term impact on children's early educational experiences.

Adult–Child Relationships

Interventions that increase active participation in classroom activities, engagement in play, and specific social skills increase the likelihood that a child will have positive and satisfying interactions with both peers and adults in different environments. For young children making the transition to kindergarten, these relationships contribute significantly to the early school adjustment process.

Research has demonstrated that the higher the quality of the parent–child relationship and the firmer the sense of family relatedness, the better a child will be adjusted to school (Grolnick, Kurowski, & Gurland, 1999). Children who have a sense of closeness with their parents tend to experience higher levels of school adjustment with more friends, fewer conflicts, higher levels of peer acceptance, and frequent on-task behavior; and they are better in terms of following directions and overall classroom competency, as reported by teachers (Clark & Ladd, 2000; Pianta, Nimetz, & Bennett, 1997). Mothers who promote a warm and open relationship with their child will help their child to develop peer social skills, mutual friendships, good work habits, and independence in the classroom (Clark & Ladd, 2000; Pianta et al., 1997). Fathers have been shown to be particularly effective at teaching social lessons (e.g., emotional regulation, interaction skills) during hands-on, physical activities that transfer to a child's social behavior in the classroom (Lindsey, Mize, & Pettit, 1997; Pettit, Brown, Mize, & Lindsey, 1998). Also, parents who use proactive teaching strategies and calm discussion in disciplinary encounters tend to have children who are more socially and academically adjusted to school (Pettit, Bates, & Dodge, 1997). By modeling appropriate and nonaversive conflict resolution skills, parents may indirectly teach their children prosocial skills. Conversely, parents who engage in high rates of negative behaviors (e.g., criticism, harshness, hitting), low stimulation, and limited reinforcement of positive behavior tend to have children who engage in high rates of challenging behaviors and who have difficulties with peer interactions in preschool (Brotman, Gouley, O'Neal, & Klein, 2004).

In one longitudinal study, parents who were interested and involved in their child's peer activities starting in kindergarten had children who were best adjusted to school in kindergarten through sixth grade (Pettit et al., 1997). Parents who spend a great deal of time directly involved in their children's peer activities may have more opportunities to monitor their children's skill development and interaction style and have more opportunities for incidental teaching. Evidence also suggests that parents who engage in high levels of emotional talk, or talking to their children about emotional experiences and encouraging children to express their own emotions, have children with higher levels of peer competence (Gottman, Katz, & Hooven, 1996). Children with prosocial skills, then, appear to experience greater success in their relationships with peers. This success likely extends to children's relationships with teachers because research has shown that children with important social skills including self-regulation of emotions and independent work habits, as well as a lack of behavior problems, are more likely to establish appropriate relationships with their teachers (e.g., a relationship where a child is neither too distant nor too needy; Pianta et al., 1997).

Quality adult relationships also appear to have an effect on children's academic achievement. Children who have an appropriate and positive relationship with their teacher (as opposed to a dependent or "clingy" relationship) tend to have higher academic achievement as well as more mutual friendships and higher levels of peer acceptance (Clark & Ladd, 2000; DeMulder et al., 2000), and parental involvement at school is likely to increase child achievement in addition to social skill development (Marcon, 1999). In a study of the relation between parental involvement and social and academic competencies with 307 children and primary caregivers from low-income, ethnic minority families, results indicated positive relationships between supportive home environments and children's performance at school (McWayne, Hampton, Fantuzzo, Cohen, & Sekino, 2004). Specifically, children of highly involved parents who provided a rich home learning environment were observed to be cooperative, self-controlled, and engaged in home and school environments. They also had high levels of self-regulation in their peer play and higher levels of academic achievement and motivation (McWayne et al., 2004).

Parents and other caregivers serve as the first socialization agents of young children, and for several years, their influence is primary in their child's social development. The interactions parents have with their child as well as with other adults have a considerable impact on the social behaviors their child acquires and utilizes in negotiating relationships with others in different contexts. These experiences, in turn, affect early school adjustment by providing children with skills necessary for positive interactions with peers and adults that facilitate school success. Consequently, increasing parents' ability and motivation to initiate and sustain positive interactions and relationships with their children seems paramount to early intervention efforts aimed at school adjustment.

CONCLUSION

More than ever, specific attention is being paid to the early academic and social development of young children. Without a doubt, children need both social and academic skills to successfully transition to formal school and to continue to adapt successfully to their changing environments. Regardless of theoretical models, terminology issues, or specific focus, social competence is important to successful development across contexts. Lack of social competence has the potential for dele-terious consequences across social and academic arenas. Therefore, early efforts to ensure that children develop the necessary skills for effective and appropriate inter-actions are essential. Preschool learning environments and the transition to kinder-garten and formal schooling provide opportunities to enhance skill development and intervene when skill development is less than optimal.

Successful efforts likely need to focus on both learning-related social skills as well as peer-related social skills, as both have been demonstrated to be important to school adjustment and performance (Ladd, Birch, & Buhs, 1999; McClelland et al., 2000; McConnell et al., 1984; Missall, 2002). Differentiation between learning-related social skills and interpersonal social skills is important in understanding the complex relation of social competence to academic achievement and success (McClelland & Morrison, 2003; McClelland et al., 2000). Children need to know how to listen and follow directions, attend to and complete tasks, organize materi-als, and work independently (Agostin & Bain, 1997; Cobb, 1972; McClelland & Morrison, 2003; McKinney et al., 1975). Demonstration of these skills early on not only promotes a richer educational experience with its own benefits but also pre-dicts achievement in subsequent years (McClelland et al., 2000). As such, these skills should be modeled, explicitly instructed and reinforced, and targeted for intervention if they are lacking or limited. Similarly, children need peer-related social skills such as initiating interactions, negotiating, and maintaining those inter-actions to be able to develop friendships and be accepted by their peers (Howes et al., 1992; Ladd & Coleman, 1997). For young children, play offers an ideal context for the development of such skills, and environmental arrangements, peer-mediated interventions, and child-specific interventions can be used to increase successful peer interactions (Odom et al., 1999; Serna et al., 2000).

Finally, because the development of learning-related and peer-related social skills is embedded within the process of parental and teacher socialization patterns, it is critically important to ensure quality adult–child interactions that promote healthy social development (Gronick et al., 1999; McWayne et al., 2004; Pianta et al., 1997). Parents set the stage for healthy social development starting at birth through their relationship with their child as they begin to impart the behaviors used to sustain interactions. Their continued efforts at socialization have an impact on the child's subsequent peer and adult relationships as well as the child's adjust-ment and achievement as they make the transition into formal schooling.

As researchers consider future efforts in the related areas of social compe-tence, transition to school, school readiness, and school adjustment, important con-ceptual and empirical questions should be addressed. What is the relationship between school readiness and early school adjustment? Is one necessary for the other, or a prerequisite for the other? If school readiness is essential for school adjustment, how can school readiness be facilitated for all children so as to pro-mote school adjustment? What role does social competence play in both school readiness and school adjustment? Are there specific indicators of social compe-tence that serve as mediating or moderating variables when considering school readiness and school adjustment? A better conceptual understanding of these issues is likely to inform practitioner efforts to foster the development of social com-petence and promote a successful transition to school.

Furthermore, although some work has been done in the area of learning-related social skills as differentiated from peer-related social skills (McClelland &

Morrison, 2003; McClelland et al., 2000), added dimensions could be explored more extensively. For example, how do learning-related social skills and peer-related social skills each contribute uniquely to school readiness and early school adjustment? What contextual variables are related to the development of these skills, and are influencing variables different? A more in-depth understanding of the relationship between learning-related social skills and peer-related social skills could add an important dimension to a model of social competence.

Although the learning-related and peer-related social skills outlined in this chapter are important to promoting early school adjustment, not all children will develop these skills or related pre-skills or to the same degree prior to school entry. This raises issues about the implications of variable skill development on school adjustment. Does lack of skills necessarily mean children are not ready to start school or that they will not be well-adjusted or even successful once they are in school? Although historically, school readiness has been viewed as a within-child construct, this thinking is counter to best practice in terms of locus of the problem; a more transactional approach would shift some of the focus to the school's ability to support and nurture development of *all* children, not just those who meet a static standard of readiness (Carlton & Winsler, 1999).

This transactional perspective is based on the notion that it is precisely the types of experiences that children can have in school that will accelerate their development. Thus, rather than say a child is not ready for school, the receiving environment should be ready, or prepared to provide experiences that the child needs to develop abilities critical for school success. Similarly, the sending environment needs to be responsive to providing experiences and learning opportunities that will provide young children with the learning-related and social-related skills they need to start school. The transition to school could be facilitated through a comprehensive and coordinated plan that reflects the concerns and needs of the preschool, kindergarten, and home (Carlton & Winsler, 1999). At the least, parents and caregivers need information about important experiences that facilitate social development and early learning.

Although some emphasis has been placed on home–school collaboration across the transition to school in research, this is an area in need of more research (see Christenson, 1999). Furthermore, there is a need to know what specifically constitutes successful kindergarten transition (Lloyd, Steinberg, & Wilhelm-Chapin, 1999). Once this can be determined, progress toward successful transition can be monitored.

The early emergence, individual variability, predictive value, and overall stability of children's learning-related and peer-related social skills underscores the necessity of early efforts to ensure that children are developing behaviors necessary for school success, regardless of whether the sending environment is home or preschool. Careful attention should be given to simultaneously monitoring a child's early academic and social skills development. To accomplish this, researchers need to identify indicators of learning-related and peer-related social skills that can be reliably measured in preschool to facilitate timely intervention (Missall, 2002; Silberglitt, 2004). Such measures would assist with frequent monitoring of skill development that could inform intervention or instruction when children do not seem to be developing appropriate skills.

Future research should also attend to including a broader range of young children. Existing research on early learning and social interventions tends to focus on children with disabilities and other risk factors more heavily than children without identified disabilities or risks. Because all children need to start school with competent social and academic skills, it is important that research extend its inquiry to interventions and instruction for the general population of young children as well. Doing so will promote a more prevention-oriented approach to skill development before children start formal schooling.

The systemic use of positive behavior support (PBS) would reflect such an approach, and has potential applications in early education. The use of PBS systems may promote the development of both peer-related social skills and learning-related social skills during the preschool years (Stormont, Lewis, & Beckner, 2005). For example, at the universal level, emphasis may be placed on teaching and reinforcing following directions, being kind to others, and participating. There have been few empirical demonstrations of the use of such systems, however, and research would be necessary to determine contextual modifications as well as the effectiveness of this approach. At a more individual level, additional research is needed on how to best teach learning-related and peer-related social skills to young children. Often, a focus on early academic skills and behaviors in preschool classrooms is at odds with the child-directed, play-focused structure of many preschools (Hemmeter, 2000), which increases the importance of developing interventions that achieve goals in terms of skill development and that also have a good contextual fit with home and preschool environments.

It is not enough to merely raise awareness about the important elements of social competence and child development for school readiness and transition to school. Educators, researchers, and policy makers need to continue to push for facilitating and monitoring social- and learning-skill acquisition in preschool and very early elementary school, and intervening where necessary.

REFERENCES

Agostin, T.M., & Bain, S.K. (1997). Predicting early school success with developmental and social skills screeners. *Psychology in the Schools, 34*(3), 219–228.

Barnett, D.W., Hamler, K., Conway-Hensley, L., Maples, K., Murdoch, A., Nelson, K., Sand-Niehaus, J., & Siemoens, S. (2002). Preparing school psychologists for early intervention settings. In M.R. Shinn, H.M. Walker, & G. Stoner (Eds.), *Interventions for academic and behavioral problems II: Preventive and remedial approaches* (pp. 1021–1046). Bethesda, MD: National Association of School Psychologists.

Bevill, A.R., Gast, D.L., Maguire, A.M., & Vail, C.O. (2001). Increasing engagement of preschoolers with disabilities through correspondence training and picture cues. *Journal of Early Intervention, 24*(2), 129–145.

Bronson, M.B. (1994). The usefulness of an observational measure of young children's social and mastery behaviors in early childhood classrooms. *Early Childhood Research Quarterly, 9*, 19–43.

Brotman, L.M., Gouley, L., O'Neal, C., & Klein, R.G. (2004). Preschool-aged siblings of adjudicated youths: Multiple risk factors for conduct problems. *Early Education and Development, 15*, 387–406.

Buhs, E.S., & Ladd, G.W. (2001). Peer rejection as an antecedent of young children's school adjustment: An examination of mediating processes. *Developmental Psychology, 37*(4), 550–560.

Carlton, M.P., & Winsler, A. (1999). School readiness: The need for a paradigm shift. *School Psychology Review, 28*, 338–352.

Carnine, D.W., Silbert, J., & Kame'enui, E.J. (1990). *Direct instruction reading.* (2nd ed.). Columbus, OH: Charles E. Merrill.

Chandler, L.K. (1996). Strategies to promote physical, social, and academic integration in mainstream kindergarten programs. In G. Stoner, M.R. Shinn, & H.M. Walker (Eds.), *Interventions for achievement and behavior problems* (pp. 305–331). Bethesda, MD: National Association of School Psychologists.

Chess, S., & Thomas, A. (1986). *Temperament in clinical practice.* New York: Guilford Press.

Christenson, S.L. (1999). Families and schools: Rights, responsibilities, resources, and relationships. In R.C. Pianta & M.J. Cox (Eds.), *The transition to kindergarten* (pp. 143–177). Baltimore: Paul H. Brookes Publishing Co.

Clark, K.E., & Ladd, G.W. (2000). Connectedness and autonomy support in parent–child relationships: Links to children's socioemotional orientation and peer relationships. *Developmental Psychology, 36*(4), 485–498.

Cobb, J.A. (1972). Relationship of discrete classroom behavior to fourth-grade academic achievement. *Journal of Educational Psychology, 63,* 74–80.

Cooper, D.H., & Farran, D.C. (1988). Behavioral risk factors in kindergarten. *Early Childhood Research Quarterly, 3,* 1–19.

Cooper, D.H., & Speece, D.L. (1988). A novel methodology for the study of children at risk for school failure. *The Journal of Special Education, 22,* 186–198.

DeLong, A.J., Tegano, D.W., Moran, J.D., Brickey, J., Morrow, D., & Houser, T.L. (1994). Effects of spatial scale on cognitive play in preschool children. *Early Education and Development, 5*(3), 237–246.

DeMulder, E.K., Denham, S., Schmidt, M., & Mitchell, J. (2000). Q–Sort assessment of attachment security during the preschool years: Links for home to school. *Developmental Psychology, 36*(2), 274–282.

Duda, M.A., Dunlap, G., Fox, L., Lentini, R., & Clarke, S. (2004). An experimental evaluation of positive behavior support in a community preschool program. *Topics in Early Childhood Special Education, 24*(3), 143–155.

Foulks, B., & Morrow, R.D. (1989). Academic survival skills for the young child at risk for school failure. *Journal of Educational Research, 82*(3), 158–165.

Geary, D.C., Hamson, C.O., & Hoard, M.K. (2000). Numerical and arithmetical cognition: A longitudinal study of process and concept deficits in children with learning disability. *Journal of Experimental Child Psychology, 77*(3), 236–263.

Godfrey, S.A., Grisham-Brown, J., Schuster, J.W., & Hemmeter, M.L. (2003). The effects of three techniques on student participation with preschool children with attending problems. *Education and Treatment of Children, 26*(3), 255–272.

Goldstein, H., Kaczmarek, L., Pennington, R., & Schafer, K. (1992). Peer-mediated intervention: Attending to, commenting on, and acknowledging the behavior of preschoolers with autism. *Journal of Applied Behavior Analysis, 25,* 289–305.

Gottman, J.M., Katz, L.F., & Hooven, C. (1996). Parental meta-emotion philosophy and emotional life of families: Theoretical models and preliminary data. *Journal of Family Psychology, 10,* 243–268.

Graue, E. (1999). Diverse perspectives on kindergarten contexts and practices. In R.C. Pianta, & M.J. Cox (Eds.), *The transition to kindergarten* (pp. 109–142). Baltimore: Paul H. Brookes Publishing Co.

Gresham, F.M. (1997). Social skills. In G. Bear, K. Minke, & A. Thomas (Eds.) *Children's needs II: Development, problems and alternatives* (pp. 39–50). Bethesda, MD: National Association of School Psychologists.

Gresham, F.M., & Elliott, S.N. (1987). The relationship between adaptive behavior and social skills: Issues in definition and assessment. *Journal of Special Education, 21*(1), 167–181.

Grolnick, W.S., Kurowski, C.O., & Gurland, S.T. (1999). Family processes and the development of children's self-regulation. *Educational Psychologist, 34,* 3–14.

Gronna, S.S., Serna, L.A., Kennedy, C.H., & Prater, M.A. (1999). Promoting generalized social interactions using puppets and script training in an integrated preschool. *Behavior Modification, 23*(3), 419–440.

Guglielmo, H.M., & Tryon, G.S. (2001). Social skill training in an integrated preschool program. *School Psychology Quarterly, 16*(2), 158–175.

Guralnick, M.J. (1992). A hierarchical model for understanding children's peer-related social competence. In S.L. Odom, S.R. McConnell, & M.A. McEvoy (Eds.), *Social compe-*

tence of young children with disabilities: Issues and strategies for intervention (pp. 37–64). Baltimore: Paul H. Brookes Publishing Co.

Harper, G.F., Guidubaldi, J., & Kehle, T.J. (1978). Is academic achievement related to classroom behavior? *Elementary School Journal, 78*, 203–207.

Hartup, W.W. (1983). Peer relations. In E.M. Hetherington (Ed.), *Handbook of child psychology volume IV: Socialization, personality, and social development* (pp. 103–196). New York: Wiley.

Hemmeter, M.L. (2000). Classroom-based interventions: Evaluating the past and looking toward the future. *Topics in Early Childhood Special Education, 20*(1), 56–61.

Hinshaw, S.P. (1992). Externalizing behavior problems and academic underachievement in childhood and adolescence: Causal relationships and underlying mechanisms. *Psychological Bulletin, III*, 127–155.

Howes, C. (1988). Peer interactions of young children. *Monographs of the Society for Research in Child Development, 53*(1, Series No. 217).

Howes, C., Droege, K., & Phillipsen, L. (1992). Contribution of peers to socialization in early childhood. In M. Gettinger, S.N. Elliott, & T.R. Kratochwill (Eds.), *Preschool and early childhood treatment directions* (pp. 113–150). Mahwah, NJ: Lawrence Erlbaum Associates.

Jimerson, S., Carlson, E., Rotert, M., Egeland, B., & Sroufe, L.A. (1997). A prospective, longitudinal study of the correlates and consequences of early grade retention. *Journal of School Psychology, 35*(1), 3–25.

Katz, L.G. (1987). What should young children be doing? *American Educator: The Professional Journal of the American Federation of Teachers, 12*(2), 28–33, 44–45.

Kohler, F.W., Anthony, L.J., Steighner, S.A., & Hoyson, M. (2001). Teaching social interaction skills in the integrated preschool: An examination of naturalistic tactics. *Topics in Early Childhood Special Education, 21*(2), 93–103.

Kontos, S., Burchinal, M., Howes, C., Wisseh, S., & Galinsky, E. (2002). An ecobehavioral approach to examining the contextual effects of early childhood classrooms. *Early Childhood Research Quarterly, 17*(2), 239–258.

Ladd, G.W. (1990). Having friends, keeping friends, making friends, and being liked by peers in the classroom: Predictors of children's early school adjustment? *Child Development, 61*, 1081–1100.

Ladd, G.W. (1996). Shifting ecologies during the 5–7 year period: Predicting children's adjustment during the transition to grade school. In A. Sameroff & M. Haith (Eds.), *The five- to seven-year shift* (pp. 363–386). IL: University of Chicago Press.

Ladd, G.W., Birch, S.H., & Buhs, E. (1999). Children's social and scholastic lives in kindergarten: Related spheres of influence? *Child Development, 70*, 1373–1400.

Ladd, G.W., Buhs, E.S., & Seid, M. (2000). Children's initial sentiments about kindergarten: Is school liking an antecedent of early classroom participation and achievement? *Merrill–Palmer Quarterly, 46*(2), 255–279.

Ladd, G.W., & Coleman, C.C. (1997). Children's classroom peer relationships and early school attitudes: Concurrent and longitudinal associations. *Early Education and Development, 8*(1), 51–66.

Ladd, G.W., Kochenderfer, B.J., & Coleman, C.C. (1997). Classroom peer acceptance, friendship, and victimization: Distinct relational systems that contribute uniquely to children's school adjustment? *Child Development, 68*(6), 1181–1197.

Ladd, G.W., & Price, J.M. (1987). Predicting children's social and school adjustment following the transition from preschool to kindergarten. *Child Development, 58*, 1168–1189.

Ladd, G.W., Price, J.M., & Hart, C.H. (1988). Predicting preschoolers' peer status from their playground behaviors. *Child Development, 59*, 986–992.

Lindeman, D.P., Fox, J.J., & Redelheim, P.S. (1993). Increasing and maintaining withdrawn preschoolers' peer interactions: Effects of double prompting and booster session procedures. *Behavioral Disorders, 19*(1), 54–66.

Lindsey, E.W., Mize, J., & Pettit, G.S. (1997). Mutuality in parent–child play: Consequences for children's peer competence. *Journal of Social and Personal Relationships, 14*, 523–538.

Lloyd, J.W., Steinberg, D.R., & Wilhelm–Chapin, M.K. (1999). Research on the transition to kindergarten. In R.C. Pianta & M.J. Cox (Eds.), *The transition to kindergarten* (pp. 305–316). Baltimore: Paul H. Brookes Publishing Co.

MacCorquodale, K., & Meehl, P. (1948). On a distinction between hypothetical constructs and intervening variables. *Psychological Review, 55*, 95–107.

Marcon, R.A. (1999). Positive relationships between parent school involvement and public school inner–city preschoolers' development and academic performance. *School Psychology Review, 28*(3), 395–412.

Masten, A.S., & Coatsworth, J.D. (1995). Competence, resilience, and psychopathology. In D. Cicchetti & D.J. Cohen (Eds.), *Developmental psychopathology: Vol. 2. Risk, disorder, and adaptation* (pp. 715–752). New York: Wiley.

Masten, A.S., Coatsworth, J.D., Neemann, J., Gest, S.D., Tellegen, A., & Garmezy, N. (1995). The structure and coherence of competence from childhood through adolescence. *Child Development, 66,* 1635–1659.

McClelland, M.M., & Morrison, F.J. (2003). The emergence of learning–related social skills in preschool children. *Early Childhood Research Quarterly, 18,* 206–224.

McClelland, M.M., Morrison, F.J., & Holmes, D.L. (2000). Children at risk for early academic problems: The role of learning-related social skills. *Early Childhood Research Quarterly, 15*(3), 307–329.

McConnell, S.R., & Missall, K.N. (2004). Defining "school readiness." *NHSA Dialog: A Research-to-Practice Journal for the Early Intervention Field, 7*(1), 10–12.

McConnell, S.R., Strain, P.S., Kerr, M.M., Stagg, V., Lenkner, D.A., & Lambert, D.L. (1984). An empirical definition of elementary school adjustment: Selection of target behaviors for a comprehensive treatment program. *Behavior Modification, 8*(4), 451–473.

McCormick, L., Noonan, M.J., & Heck, R. (1998). Variables affecting engagement in inclusive preschool classrooms. *Journal of Early Intervention, 21,* 160–176.

McEvoy, M.A., Odom, S.L., & McConnell, S.R. (1992). Peer social competence intervention for young children with disabilities. In S.L. Odom, S.R. McConnell, & M.A. McEvoy (Eds.), *Social competence of young children with disabilities: Issues and strategies for intervention* (pp. 113–133). Baltimore: Paul H. Brookes Publishing Co.

McFall, R.M. (1982). A review and reformulation of the concept of social skills. *Behavioral Assessment, 4,* 1–33.

McFadyen-Ketchum, S.A., & Dodge, K.A. (1998). Problems in social relationships. In E.J. Mash & R.A. Barkley (Eds.), *Treatment of childhood disorders* (2nd ed., pp. 338–365). New York: Guilford Press.

McKinney, J.D., Mason, J., Peterson, K., & Clifford, M. (1975). Relationship between classroom behavior and academic achievement. *Journal of Educational Psychology, 67,* 198–203.

McWayne, C., Hampton, V., Fantuzzo, J., Cohen, H.L., & Sekino, Y. (2004). A multivariate examination of parent involvement and the social and academic competencies of urban kindergarten children. *Psychology in the Schools, 41*(3), 363–377.

Meisels, S. (1999). Assessing readiness. In R.C. Pianta & M.J. Cox (Eds.), *The transition to kindergarten* (pp. 39–66). Baltimore: Paul H. Brookes Publishing Co.

Missall, K.N. (2002). Reconceptualizing school adjustment: A search for intervening variables. *Dissertation Abstracts International, 63*(5–A), 1712.

Mize, J., & Ladd, G.W. (1990). A cognitive–social learning approach to social skill training with low-status preschool children. *Developmental Psychology, 26,* 388–397.

Moffit, T.E., & Caspi, A. (2001). Childhood predictors differentiate life-course persistent and adolescence-limited antisocial pathways among males and females. *Development and Psychopathology, 13,* 355–375.

Odom, S.L., Chandler, L.K., Ostrosky, M., McConnell, S.R., & Reaney, S. (1992). Fading teacher prompts from peer–initiation interventions for young children with disabilities. *Journal of Applied Behavior Analysis, 25,* 307–317.

Odom, S.L., & McConnell, S.R. (1985). A performance-based conceptualization of social competence of handicapped preschool children: Implications for assessment. *Topics in Early Childhood Special Education, 4*(4), 1–19.

Odom, S.L., McConnell, S.R., & McEvoy, M.A. (1992). Peer-related social competence and its significance for young children with disabilities. In S.L. Odom, S.R. McConnell, & M.A. McEvoy (Eds.), *Social competence of young children with disabilities: Issues and strategies for intervention* (pp. 3–36). Baltimore: Paul H. Brookes Publishing Co.

Odom, S.L., McConnell, S.R., McEvoy, M.A., Peterson, C., Ostrosky, M., Chandler, L.K., Spicuzza, R.J., Skellenger, A., Creighton, M., & Favazza, P.C. (1999). Relative effects of interventions supporting the social competence of young children with disabilities. *Topics in Early Childhood Special Education, 19*(2), 75–91.

Parker, J.G., & Asher, S.R. (1987). Peer relations and later personal adjustment: Are low-accepted children at risk? *Psychological Bulletin, 102*, 357–389.

Pettit, G.S., Bates, J.E., & Dodge, K.A. (1997). Supportive parenting, ecological context, and children's adjustment: A seven-year longitudinal study. *Child Development 68*(5), 908–923.

Pettit, G.S., Brown, E.G., Mize, J., & Lindsey, E. (1998). Mothers' and fathers' socializing behaviors in three contexts: Links with children's peer competence. *Merrill-Palmer Quarterly, 44*(2), 173–193.

Phillipsen, L.C., Deptula, D.P., & Cohen, R. (1999). Relating characteristics of children and their friends to relational and overt aggression. *Child Study Journal, 29*(4), 269–289.

Piaget, J. (1926). *The language and thought of the child.* London: Routledge & Kegan Paul.

Pianta, R.C., & Cox, M.J. (Eds.) (1999). *The transition to kindergarten.* Baltimore: Paul H. Brookes Publishing Co.

Pianta, R.C., Nimetz, S.L., & Bennett, E. (1997). Mother–child relationships, teacher–child relationships, and school outcomes in preschool and kindergarten. *Early Childhood Research Quarterly, 12*, 263–280.

Pianta, R.C., Rimm-Kaufman, S.E., & Cox, M.J. (1999). An ecological approach to kindergarten transition. In R.C. Pianta, & M.J. Cox (Eds.), *The transition to kindergarten* (pp. 3–12). Baltimore: Paul H. Brookes Publishing Co.

Putallaz, M., & Heflin, A.H. (1990). Parent–child interaction. In S.R. Asher & J.D. Coie (Eds.), *Peer rejection in childhood* (pp. 189–216). Cambridge, UK: Cambridge University Press.

Reid, J.B., & Patterson, G.R. (1996). Early prevention and intervention with conduct problems: A social and interactional model for the integration of research and practice. In G. Stoner, M.R. Shinn, & H.M. Walker (Eds.), *Interventions for achievement and behavior problems* (pp. 715–740). Bethesda, MD: National Association of School Psychologists.

Rettig, M., Kallam, M., & McCarthy–Salm, K. (1993). The effect of social and isolate toys on the social interactions of preschool-aged children. *Education and Training in Mental Retardation, 28*, 252–256.

Reynolds, A.J. (1991). Early schooling of children at risk. *American Educational Research Journal, 28*, 392–422.

Ridley, S.M., McWilliam, R.A., & Oates, C.S. (2000). Observed engagement as an indicator child care program quality. *Early Education and Development, 11*, 133–146.

Rimm-Kaufman, S.E., Pianta, R.C., & Cox, M.J. (2000). Teachers' judgments of problems in the transition to kindergarten. *Early Childhood Research Quarterly, 15*(2), 147–166.

Rosenshine, R.V. (1981). Academic engaged time, content covered, and direct instruction. *Journal of Education, 3*, 38–66.

Sainato, D.M., Strain, P.S., & Lyon, S.R. (1987). Increasing academic responding of handicapped preschool children during group instruction. *Journal of the Division of Early Childhood, 12*, 23–30.

Saunders, S.A., & Green V. (1993). Evaluating the social competence of young children: A review of the literature. *Early Child Development and Care, 87*, 39–46.

Schwartz, I.S., Garfinkle, A.N., & Davis, C. (2002). Arranging preschool environments to facilitate valued social and educational outcomes. In M.R. Shinn, H.M. Walker, & G. Stoner (Eds.), *Interventions for academic and behavior problems II: Preventive and remedial approaches* (pp. 455–468). Bethesda, MD: National Association of School Psychologists.

Seefeldt, C., & Wasik, B.A. (2002). Today's kindergarten: The past is present. In C. Seefeldt & B.A. Wasik (Eds.), *Kindergarten: Fours and fives go to school* (pp. 1–18). Upper Saddle River, NJ: Merrill Prentice Hall.

Serna, L., Nielsen, E., Lambros, K., & Forness, S. (2000). Primary prevention with children at risk for emotional or behavioral disorders: Data on a universal intervention for Head Start classrooms. *Behavioral Disorders, 26*(1), 70–84.

Silberglitt, B. (2004). Beyond situational specificity and other hypothetical constructs: A practical approach to general outcome measurement of preschool social skill development. *Dissertation Abstracts International, 64*(10–A), 3595.

Snow, C.E., Burns, M.S., & Griffin, P. (Eds.) (1998). *Preventing reading difficulties in young children.* Washington, DC: National Academies Press.

Stormont, M., Lewis, T.J., & Beckner, R. (2005). Positive behavior support systems; Applying key features in preschool settings. *Teaching Exceptional Children, 37*(6), 42–49.

Strain, P.S., & Odom, S.L. (1986). Peer social initiations: Effective intervention for social skills development of exceptional children. *Exceptional Children, 52*(6), 543–551.

Taylor, A.R., & Machida, S. (1994). The contribution of parent and peer support to Head Start children's early school adjustment. *Early Childhood Research Quarterly, 9*, 387–405.

Tremblay, A., Strain, P.S., Hendrickson, J.M., & Shores, R.E. (1981). Social interactions of normal preschool children. *Behavior Modification, 5*(2), 237–253.

Walker, H.M., Colvin, G., & Ramsey, E. (1995). *Antisocial behavior in school: Strategies and best practices.* Pacific Grove, CA: Brooks/Cole Thomson Learning.

Walker, H.M., & McConnell, S.R. (1995). *The Walker-McConnell Scale of Social Competence and School Adjustment–Elementary Version: A social skills rating scale for teachers.* Austin, TX: PRO-ED.

Wentzel, K.R. (1991). Social competence at school: Relation between social responsibility and academic achievement. *Review of Educational Research, 61*(1), 1–24.

Strategies and Tactics for Peer-Related Social Competence Assessment and Intervention

Peer Interaction Interventions for Preschool Children with Developmental Difficulties

WILLIAM H. BROWN, SAMUEL L. ODOM,
SCOTT R. MCCONNELL, AND JEANNA M. RATHEL

Contemporary thinkers have realized that as a species, our social and linguistic abilities have been a hallmark of our humanity (see Tattersall, 2002). Indeed, sociability, or the tendency to seek social relationships, has long been evident within the social interactions of infants and their adult caregivers as well as toddlers and their peers (Howes & James, 2002). Throughout early childhood, children's social interactions with adults and peers become more frequent; more sophisticated cognitively, linguistically, and socially; and longer in duration, with the ultimate outcome typically being the establishment of positive adult and peer relationships (see Hartup & Stevens, 1997; Rubin, Bukowski, & Parker, 1998). For the vast majority of young children, the development of their social competence has been uncomplicated and relatively straightforward. Most often, early positive parent–child relationships and the provision of a wide range of developmentally appropriate conditions including responsive adults and peers, frequent play opportunities, interesting materials, and meaningful activities have been sufficient to support young children's emerging social competence (e.g., Howes & James, 2002; Russell, Mize, & Bissaker, 2002). During early childhood, young children's social interactions provide the day-to-day contextual conditions and mechanisms for their acquisition of important and sophisticated developmental skills, especially emerging social, linguistic, and cognitive abilities (Brown & Conroy, 2001; Parke et al., 2002).

Despite the unremarkable course of social development for most young children, significant numbers of them are at risk for social interaction problems that

Preparation of this manuscript was supported in part by the U.S. Department of Education Office of Special Education Programs Grant #H325D010063A to the University of South Carolina. However, the content and opinions expressed herein do not necessarily reflect the position or policy of the University of South Carolina or the U.S. Department of Education, and no official endorsement should be inferred. Correspondence concerning this chapter should be addressed to William H. Brown, 820 Main Street, Department of Educational Studies, College of Education, University of South Carolina, Columbia, South Carolina 29208.

might influence the future development of their social competence (e.g., Brown, Odom, & Conroy, 2001; Diamond, 2002; Guralnick & Neville, 1997; Odom, McConnell, & McEvoy, 1992). In contrast with young children who have many positive social interactions and who establish affirmative adult and peer relationships, researchers have noted that children who have peer interaction difficulties (e.g., limited or negative social interactions, persistent aggressive behavior) and who fail to develop positive adult and child relationships are at elevated risk for social maladjustment in adolescence and adulthood (e.g., Newcomb & Bagwell, 1995; Parker & Asher, 1987; Rubin et al., 1998). Preschool children with a variety of developmental difficulties, including cognitive delays (e.g., Guralnick, Connor, Neville, & Hammond, 2006; Kopp, Baker, & Brown, 1992), early onset and persistent behavioral problems (e.g., Campbell, 2002; Webster-Stratton, & Reid, 2003), autism spectrum disorders (e.g., National Research Council, 2001; Rogers, 1998), histories of child maltreatment (e.g., Mueller & Silverman, 1989; Schatz, 2006), communication disorders (e.g., Guralnick, Connor, Hammond, Gottman, & Kinnish, 1996; Schneider & Goldstein, Chapter 11, this volume), and low-peer status (e.g., Ladd, Buhs, & Troop, 2002; Mize & Ladd, 1990) are at very high risk for peer interaction difficulties and the formation of poor peer relationships during childhood. Hence, the recognized importance of and interest in preschool children's peer-related social competence is based on two constant findings: 1) positive peer interactions are an important route for children's enhanced development; and 2) persistent peer interaction problems are a primary predictor of children's future social competence difficulties (Brown et al., 2001).

The critical role that young children's positive peer interactions play in the development of social competence has resulted in many early childhood and early childhood special educators advocating for the development and implementation of effective interventions to enhance children's social behavior (e.g., Bredekamp & Copple, 1997; Sandall, McLean, & Smith, 2000), particularly for preschoolers who are at risk for peer interaction and social competence difficulties (e.g., Brown et al., 2001; Diamond, 2002; Guralnick & Neville, 1997). For example, in a descriptive investigation of children with and without developmental delays in inclusive preschools, Brown, Odom, Li, and Zercher (1999) found significantly less social behavior among children with developmental delays relative to peers without disabilities in the same classrooms. Within the preschool social interaction literature, Brown and colleagues' results have been relatively well-replicated (see Diamond, 2002). In a related study of social status with the same sample of preschool children with and without disabilities, Odom and colleagues (in press) determined that approximately one third of the children with developmental delays were socially rejected by peers. Again, lower peer status for children with developmental problems, at least for slightly older children, is a common outcome in the social competence literature (see Hymel, Vaillancourt, McDougall, & Renshaw, 2002).

A number of social interaction interventions have been empirically validated, at least to some extent, with a variety of young children during the last four decades (see Brown & Conroy, 2001; Brown et al., 2001 for reviews). Evidenced-based social interaction intervention tactics have included the careful use of putative reinforcers, instructions, prompts, models, rehearsals, feedback mechanisms, discussions, or some combinations of those measures for improving peer interactions among young children (see Brown & Odom, 1994; Chandler, Lubeck, & Fowler, 1992). Likewise, several effective peer interaction intervention strategies have included environmental arrangements and teacher- and peer-mediated social interaction interventions or some combination of those approaches to enhance young children's interactions (see Brown et al., 2001; McEvoy, Odom, & McConnell, 1992). Despite the development and validation of peer interaction procedures, many educators have acknowledged a longstanding gap in the translation of research to practice with respect to the common employment of social interaction interventions (e.g., Brown & Conroy, 2001; McConnell, McEvoy, & Odom, 1992). Indeed, McConnell and colleagues (1992) argued that the ultimate influence of any intervention is dependent on both the *effectiveness* of the procedure and the *likelihood* that practitioners will implement the intervention.

Practitioners appear to highly value interventions that may improve children's social competence and believe that many children might benefit from those interventions. For example, in a survey of teachers in four states, Odom, McConnell, and Chandler (1994) found that preschool teachers reported that 74% of their preschool children needed to improve their social skills. More recently, West, Brown, Grego, and Johnson (in press) determined that 91% of survey respondents from the Division of Early Childhood (DEC) indicated that the young children they serve might benefit from interventions to enhance their peer interactions and social competence. Although the practitioners queried by Odom and colleagues (1994) and West and colleagues (in press) judged that a number of peer interaction intervention tactics were acceptable and feasible, and that they used several of the procedures at least to some extent in their classrooms, their reported use of those procedures was systematically lower than their perceptions of the acceptability and feasibility for the overwhelming majority of the individual intervention tactics.

Unfortunately, even with available validated social interaction interventions and the value that practitioners place on children's social competence, several researchers have reported that often teachers neither systematically use nor extensively employ peer interaction interventions (e.g., Brown et al., 2001; McConnell et al., 1992). Researchers have provided additional examples of the limited use of peer interaction interventions with preschoolers. For example, in their survey of recommended practices in early childhood special education, Odom, McLean, Johnson, and LaMontagne (1995) found that practitioners frequently used only 5 of 15 recommended strategies for promoting young children's social and emotional development. McConnell and colleagues (1992) used direct observation methods to determine whether preschool teachers used effective social interaction interventions. They reported that practitioners employed evidenced-based procedures at only a moderate to low level of implementation. Furthermore, they noted that the teachers were more likely to use less direct and global intervention approaches (e.g., environmental arrangements, discussions of children's social behavior) than they were to use individualized and well-targeted tactics (e.g., prompting peer interactions, reinforcing of social behavior) to promote children's peer-related social competence.

Finally, given that young children in special education programs are required to have individualized education programs (IEPs), Michnowicz, McConnell, Peterson, and Odom (1995) reviewed a sample of preschool children's IEPs. They determined that social goals were frequently not developed for children's individual plans. Consequently, based on the existing convergent evidence, Brown and Conroy (2001) concluded that although preschool teachers appear to value peer interaction interventions (e.g., Odom et al., 1994), they have been reluctant to use many existing evidenced-based social interaction interventions, particularly those that have incorporated explicit teaching tactics and strategies with multiple intervention components.

The purpose of our chapter is twofold. First, we present an intervention hierarchy, which has evolved conceptually since the mid-1990s, to assist practitioners in selecting effective peer interaction interventions for young children with social interaction problems. Within the discussion of the hierarchy, we selectively review evidenced-based and promising procedures for promoting preschool children's peer interactions and their positive peer relationships. Second, we discuss a deployment-focused model for research, development, and dissemination of evidence-based social interaction interventions for preschoolers (see Weisz, Jensen, & McLeod, 2004). Our presentation of information is meant to be applicable to children with and without developmental difficulties who might benefit from classroom-based peer interaction interventions.

AN INTERVENTION HIERARCHY TO PROMOTE PRESCHOOLERS' PEER INTERACTIONS

For more than a decade, we have addressed the research-to-practice gap related to the use of evidence-based peer interaction interventions with the strategic employment of an evolving conceptual framework for assisting practitioners in determining the types of interventions needed for young children in their preschools (e.g., Brown et al., 2001; Odom & Brown, 1993, see Figure 7.1). The intervention hierarchy consists of three levels (listed from bottom to top): 1) classroomwide interventions, 2) naturalistic peer interaction interventions, and 3) explicit social skills interventions. Our objective in developing the intervention hierarchy was to assist practitioners in thoughtfully planning peer interaction interventions that are well-matched to and effective in their early childhood programs (i.e., feasible for teachers and validated by researchers). The decision-making process is sequential in that we suggest that teachers employ the least-intrusive interventions first, requiring fewer changes in routines with fewer additional resources. Initially, we recommend that practitioners use three general classroomwide interventions, developmentally appropriate practice (DAP), inclusive early childhood education, and affective interventions to influence children's attitudes. When indicated, we suggest that teachers implement individualized peer interaction interventions. These individualized interventions may be from the naturalistic intervention level of the hierarchy such as *incidental teaching of social behavior* and *friendship activities* or the more intensive explicit social skills intervention level of the hierarchy such as *social integration activities* and *buddy skills training*. If a particular individualized intervention is not successful, we propose that practitioners proceed to another, more intensive intervention. The peer interaction intervention hierarchy is well matched to and compatible with both recommended practices (e.g., McEvoy & Odom, 1996; Sandall et al., 2000; Sandall, Hemmeter, Smith, & McLean, 2005) and naturalistic teaching strategies in early childhood special education (e.g., Pretti-Frontczak & Bricker, 2004; Rule, Losardo, Dinnebeil, Kaiser, & Rowland, 1998).

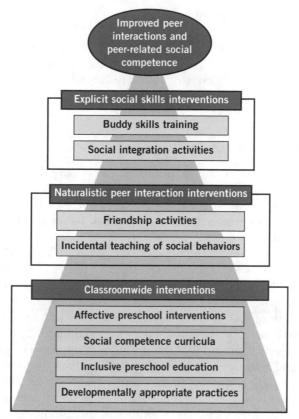

Figure 7.1. Hierarchy for promoting young children's peer interactions. From "An intervention hierarchy for promoting young children's peer interactions in natural environments" by W.H. Brown, S.L. Odom, and M.A. Conroy, 2001, *Topics in Early Childhood Special Education, 21,* 162–175. Copyright (2001) by PRO-ED, Inc. Reprinted with permission.

We argue that the decision-making process ought to be

"(a) *effective* (i.e., clearly improve children's peer interactions); (b) *efficient* (i.e., make meaningful use of children's and teachers' time); (c) *functional* (i.e., promote generalization and maintenance of social competencies needed in early childhood programs); and (d) *normalized* (i.e., the most natural intervention techniques possible)" (Brown & Conroy, 1997, p. 86).

At every level of our intervention hierarchy, we strongly suggest that practitioners carefully assess whether preschoolers' interactions have been changed for the better with increased positive peer interactions, more sophisticated social interactions, or emerging peer relationships. In particular, we advocate the use of direct observations in settings where children have opportunities to interact with peers as an essential assessment method to decide whether children's social interactions have been enhanced sufficiently (e.g., Brown, Odom, & Buysse, 2002; Odom, Schertz, Munson, & Brown, 2004). Following intervention, if systematic observations have not shown that preschoolers' peer interactions have improved, then teachers should select another, and possibly more intensive individualized intervention to be implemented (e.g., incidental teaching in addition to DAP). In subsequent subsections, we discuss each level of our intervention hierarchy in detail.

Classroomwide Interventions

Classroomwide peer interaction interventions are group-based approaches that may positively affect young children's peer interactions and peer relations within their respective classrooms. These strategies are viewed as universal interventions for preschool children, intended to be implemented with all children in a classroom setting (see Conroy & Brown, 2004).

Developmentally Appropriate Practices

Early childhood and early childhood special educators have disseminated relatively well-specified guidelines for high quality early childhood programs (e.g., Bredekamp & Copple, 1997; Sandall et al., 2000; Sandall et al., 2005). These guidelines have provided educators with a flexible framework for establishing DAP in preschools. For more than a decade, most early childhood special educators have acknowledged the fundamental importance of DAP as a foundation for providing individualized services for young children with and without disabilities (e.g., Cavallaro, Haney, & Cabello, 1993), and DAP has been adopted as a recommended practice in the field of early childhood special education (e.g., Sandall et al., 2000).

Our interpretation of DAP emphasizes the need for all early childhood practitioners to proactively promote children's peer interactions and peer relations. We, along with many others, contend that the presence of appropriate classroom materials and meaningful activities (e.g., Beckman & Kohl, 1984), well-planned learning centers (e.g., Petrakos & Howe, 1996), responsive teachers (e.g., McGee, Almeida, Sulzer-Azaroff, & Feldman, 1992), and socially responsive peers (e.g., Odom & Brown, 1993) are supportive contextual conditions for enhancing young children's preacademic and social engagement and their development. For example, developmentally appropriate environments have been arranged with multiple learning centers that promote most preschoolers' engagement with age-appropriate and meaningful materials and peers (e.g., sociodramatic play areas, block centers, emergent literacy centers) (e.g., Harms, Clifford, & Cryer, 1998).

Although we view DAP as an essential component of early childhood programs, the framework has not always been a sufficient contextual circumstance for promoting some young children's emerging peer interactions and peer relations (Brown et al., 1999). In some instances, individualized intervention is warranted. Individualized intervention does not necessarily mean that only a single child will be the focus of intervention, or that a child will be taught in a one-to-one teaching arrangement (see Brown & Conroy, 1997). Rather, individualized programming consists of reviewing individual children's assessment information and then planning and implementing interventions to support children's active engagement in developmentally enhancing activities. Hence, one, several, or even the whole class of children might participate in and benefit from individualized interventions employed to meet the needs of one or more classmates. This type of careful programming achieves the two foundational principles of DAP, that is, services should be *developmentally* and *individually* appropriate practices (Bredekamp & Copple, 1997).

Inclusive Preschool Education

Early childhood educators and early childhood special educators have recognized that inclusion of preschool children with and without developmental delays is a facet of DAP (e.g., Bredekamp & Copple, 1997; Sandall et al., 2000). Preschool inclusion has had legislative (e.g., Individuals with Disabilities Education Improvement Act of 2004 [PL 108–446]), empirical (e.g., Odom et al., 1996; Odom, Vitztum, et al., 2004), and professional support (e.g., Odom & McLean, 1996). Indeed, more than a decade ago, New and Mallory declared that an "ethic of inclusion" (1994, p. 1) has become apparent in the thinking of many early childhood education professionals.

A long-standing rationale for early childhood inclusion is to place young children with developmental delays in socially supportive and engaging preschool classrooms (Bricker, 1978). For preschoolers with developmental difficulties, the presence of peers without developmental delays is important in providing models of competent behavior and socially responsive playmates. Developmentally appropriate activities and the existing social circumstances established in many early childhood programs provide an especially suitable context for promoting and supporting preschoolers' peer interactions (see Odom & Brown, 1993). According to Ladd and Coleman (1993), two critical avenues for enhanced peer relations have been access (i.e., opportunities to socially interact with peers) and a robust history of positive peer interactions (i.e., frequent prosocial interactions with multiple familiar peers across sustained periods). Developmentally appropriate and inclusive preschools make available these two essential social paths for young children's emerging peer-related social competence. Unfortunately, extant information about inclusive preschools has shown that compared with peers without developmental delays, children with disabilities may be at risk for being socially excluded (e.g., Hestenes & Carroll, 2000; Odom et al., in press). However, given the possible social dynamics and clear potential for implementing well-targeted and individualized peer interaction interventions, a reasonable classroomwide strategy for practitioners who serve young children with and without developmental delays should be to establish DAP within inclusive preschools. Indeed, the combination of DAP and inclusion may well be an indispensable foundation for sustainable peer interaction intervention results for many young children with social interaction difficulties.

Social Competence Curricula

Well-specified curricula for preschool-age children that apply to the whole classroom have been developed and validated. The goal of these curricula is often to prevent the occurrence of problem behavior in young children by proactively developing social competence skills such as social problem solving, emotional literacy, emotion regulation, and the ability to make friends. Excellent examples of these curricula are the preschool classroom version of the *Incredible Years Parents, Teachers, and Children's Training Series* curriculum (http://www.incredibleyears.com; see also Webster-Stratton & Reid, 2003) and the *Promoting Alternative THinking Strategies (PATHS)* curriculum (Domitrovich, Cortes, & Greenberg, 2006).

Affective Preschool Interventions

Affective interventions foster children's affirmative attitudes about classmates who have developmental differences or disabilities (Brown et al., 2001). Affective approaches, which are comparable to disability awareness activities, are differentiated from other peer interaction strategies by an emphasis on altering young children's attitudes about peers with developmental delays. Since the late 1980s, early childhood educators have advocated affective approaches for facilitating the inclusion of preschool children with developmental delays (Derman-Sparks & Anti-bias Curriculum Task Force, 1989). Unfortunately, the guidelines for anti-bias strategies are unduly general, and the recommended practices have not been socially validated or empirically confirmed. With respect to young children with developmental delays, anti-bias guidelines have consisted of establishing inclusive classrooms and encouraging children with and without developmental delays to socially interact; promoting awareness of disabilities through materials in the classroom such as photographs, posters, and books; allowing children without developmental delays to learn about adaptive equipment and accessibility needs of peers with disabilities; inviting people with disabilities to make presentations to children and providing experiences that educate children about particular disabilities and related accessibility requirements; simulating social problems with children (with and without developmental delays) and solving the difficulty; and accurately challenging children's misconceptions about disabilities.

Favazza and Odom (1997) empirically validated a well-structured affective intervention for kindergarten-age children. Their classroomwide intervention package consists of reading storybooks related to disabilities with accompanying teacher-guided discussions about children with developmental delays. In addition to the storytime and discussion, planned integrated play activities with peers who have developmental delays are implemented. According to Favazza and Odom (1997), the multicomponent classroom intervention was successful in enhancing the kindergartners' perceptions of peers with developmental delays, as indicated by an assessment of children's attitudes about peers with disabilities. Favazza and Odom (1997) suggested that teachers who want to improve young children's attitudes about people with developmental differences should make available both indirect and direct positive classroom experiences related to individuals with disabilities. For example, it may be beneficial for teachers to read to children realistic stories about children with developmental delays that portray them in a positive manner and then conduct matter-of-fact classroom discussions about the characters and their circumstances. In addition, making disability awareness materials available widely within classrooms may increase familiarity and comfort with developmental differences. Finally, when using affective interventions, Favazza and Odom (1997) recommended direct experiences such as planning social and play activities with integrated ability groups to augment group book readings and discussions.

Even though Favazza and Odom (1997) employed their affective intervention with kindergartners, their approach is also applicable for preschoolers in early childhood programs. The incorporation of emergent literacy activities in early childhood activities has increased the use of books, print materials, and posters (Farran, Aydogan, Kang, & Lipsey, 2006). Teachers' employment of literacy materials that show peers with developmental delays in a positive manner appears to be a very appropriate method of enhancing literacy skills while improving children's attitudes about peers with developmental differences. Nevertheless, preschool children's understanding of classmates' different developmental abilities may not be sufficient to facilitate their social interactions with peers with developmental delays (e.g., Hestenes & Carroll, 2000). Favazza, Roe, Phillipsen, and Kumar (2000), and more recently, Han, Ostrosky, and Diamond (2006) delineated specific guidelines for teachers who are interested in using affective interventions with young children. If teachers implement DAP and inclusive early childhood services with accompanying affective intervention approaches to enhance preschoolers' attitudes about peers with developmental differences, and systematic classroom observations of children across time has determined that one or more children continue to have restricted peer interactions, then the use of individualized peer interaction interventions is warranted.

Naturalistic Peer Interaction Interventions

Naturalistic intervention strategies are implemented by practitioners within the context of routine classroom activities (Rule et al., 1998), incorporating instructional methods that are only as complex and as intrusive as necessary to improve children's engagement (Brown & Conroy, 1997). These strategies are characterized by systematic teaching that promotes skill acquisition and practice needed by young children with and without developmental delays to participate actively within preschool environments. Several similar naturalistic teaching approaches have been developed (e.g., activity-based intervention, embedded learning opportunities, pivotal response training). With respect to children's social behavior, we recommend two exemplary naturalistic strategies: incidental teaching of social behavior and friendship activities.

Incidental Teaching of Social Behavior

For more than three decades, educators have employed incidental teaching as an individualized and naturalistic intervention strategy for enhancing preschool children's development in early childhood settings (see Hancock & Kaiser, 2005). McGee and colleagues (1992) used incidental teaching techniques with young children with autism spectrum disorders in an inclusive preschool. They demonstrated that systematic use of incidental teaching within an inclusive classroom increased the quantity and quality of peer interactions for both children with and without disabilities.

Incidental teaching tactics can be distinguished from teacher-directed instruction because they are implemented within "...unstructured activities for brief periods of time and typically when children have shown an interest in or have been involved with materials, activities, or others" (Brown & Odom, 1995, p. 40). Brown, McEvoy, and Bishop (1991) found that routine activities in early childhood programs (e.g., learning centers, transitions, meals, outside play) provide excellent circumstances and opportunities for incidental teaching of social behavior. During incidental teaching of social behavior episodes, teachers promote children's peer interactions by employing adult models of social behavior or encouraging peers to demonstrate suitable social responses. Moreover, incidental teaching opportunities promote elaboration of young children's social behavior. For example, following a playground accident, a child might be encouraged to verbally convey empathy and concern for a peer who was hurt. Incidental teaching of social behavior might also serve as a naturalistic mechanism to provide young children with practice using social scripts (i.e., repeated everyday experiences in which individuals learn and practice culturally appropriate social behavior). Hence, incidental teaching of social behavior represents additional opportunities for preschoolers to acquire new social behaviors or to practice and elaborate on previously learned social responses during common daily activities. Brown and colleagues (Brown & Conroy, 1997; Brown et al., 1991) delineate specific guidelines for teachers who are interested in using incidental teaching of social behavior. As indicated by our hierarchy, if incidental teaching is inadequate for improving preschool children's peer interactions, then another naturalistic peer interaction intervention, friendship activities, or other individualized social interaction interventions such as social integration activities or "buddy skills training" may be needed to support children's social interactions.

Friendship Activities

Friendship activities, previously identified as "group affection activities" (McEvoy et al., 1988) and "group socialization procedures" (Brown, Ragland, & Fox, 1988), are another naturalistic peer interaction intervention for improving preschoolers' social interactions. Friendship activities are distinguished from other peer interaction interventions through purposeful altering of classroom activities to promote peer interactions by embedding social behaviors within common early childhood songs, games, and play activities (e.g., Brown & Conroy, 1997; Brown et al., 1988). For example, in the song "If You're Happy and You Know It," children pat their heads, stomp their feet, and jump up and down as instructed in the song. Alternatively, in the adapted friendship activity, children may pat a friend on the back, give a friend a high-five, or tickle a friend when they are "happy and they know it." In other activities, teachers may encourage preschoolers to make friendly statements, interact in affectionate ways, compliment a peer, smile, dance with one another, or share, all of which have a high probability of evoking positive peer social responding. These responses are embedded in such common activities as Simon Says; London Bridge; Musical Chairs; and Duck, Duck, Goose. Several investigators have demonstrated the effectiveness of friendship activities in improving both the frequency and duration of peer interactions in settings outside of the friendship activities (e.g., Brown et al., 1988; Frea, Craig-Unkefer, Odom, & Johnson, 1999; McEvoy et al., 1988).

Friendship activities have several distinct advantages. First, when teachers employ friendship activities, they transform their preschool activities into more supportive contexts for promoting young children's peer interactions. Second, practitioners encourage children's frequent rehearsal of important prosocial behaviors during a variety of activities with multiple peers. During friendship activities, the varied implementation of social skill interventions and practice within common classroom activities with familiar peers may promote generalization and maintenance of newly acquired or emerging social behavior to everyday common circumstances (i.e., ecologically valid situations) (see Brown & Odom, 1994). Finally, similar to affective interventions intended to alter children's attitudes concerning peers with developmental delays, friendship activities include teacher-guided discussions about the importance of positive interactions and friendships with classmates. These class conversations may assist in establishing and maintaining supportive classroom atmospheres for improved peer interactions and peer relations.

Analogous to incidental teaching of social behavior, friendship activities provide additional teaching and learning opportunities for children to acquire new social behavior or to elaborate or generalize previously acquired social responses during routine classroom activities (see Brown & Conroy, 1997). Because friendship activities are performed daily with groups of preschoolers for approximately 10 to 15 minutes, teacher planning time is necessary to organize and prepare the activities. With respect to teacher preparation, friendship activities are a slightly more intensive peer interaction intervention than is incidental teaching of social behavior. Nevertheless, as a pragmatic strategy, if incidental teaching is being employed with children in a classroom, it should be continued even after friendship activities are started (e.g., Brown et al., 2001). Because friendship activities are teacher planned and include judicious adult support for children's peer interactions, incidental teaching of social behavior episodes provide both additional social opportunities and an important "social bridge" that promotes generalization of children's peer interactions to less adult-directed and more child-initiated social circumstances. Both incidental teaching of social behavior and friendship activities are naturalistic peer interaction interventions that are easily incorporated into preschools. Brown and colleagues (Brown & Conroy, 1997; Brown, Ragland, & Bishop, 1989a) delineate specific guidelines for teachers who are interested in employing friendship activities.

Explicit Social Skills Interventions

For some preschoolers with peer interaction difficulties, naturalistic peer interaction interventions are not sufficient to promote their social interactions with peers. For these children, explicit individualized interventions that are more structured and intensive and that require more teacher planning, preparation, and guidance are necessary to improve peer interactions and peer relations. Explicit social skills interventions are characterized by relatively intensive training of well-specified social behaviors or strategies such as "stay, play, and talk with your buddy" (e.g., English, Goldstein, Shafer, & Kaczmarek, 1997). Some early childhood special educators directly train children with social interaction problems and their classmates without developmental delays in specific social behaviors, which include sharing, initiating socially, asking a peer to share, organizing play circumstances, agreeing, and assisting peers (e.g., Odom & McConnell, 1993). Two explicit social skills interventions, social integration activities and "buddy skills training," can be used to promote preschool children's peer interactions.

Social Integration Activities

Odom and colleagues have employed social integration activities as an explicit social skill intervention for enhancing preschool children's social interactions in early childhood settings (DeKlyen & Odom, 1989; Frea et al., 1999; Jenkins, Odom, & Speltz, 1989; Odom et al., 1988; Odom et al., 1999). The underlying principle for these activities is that teacher-planned and teacher-structured activities establish socially supportive circumstances for preschoolers who have peer interaction problems. Similar to friendship activities, within these socially supportive contexts, children with social interaction problems observe the competent play of peers, participate directly in social interactions with peers who have relatively sophisticated social interaction skills, and establish a history of positive peer interactions. The success of social integration activities is based on careful teacher planning and implementing of well-specified play activities that increase the likelihood of children participating in social interactions with classmates.

Social integration activities include four components (Odom et al., 1988): 1) selection of preschoolers with limited or negative social interactions and socially responsive peers to take part in teacher-structured play activities; 2) implementation of well-specified social activities in defined play centers for 5- to 15-minute time periods; 3) selection of play activities that make available many opportunities for positive play experiences and peer interaction; and 4) introduction of play themes and systematic encouragement of children's social participation (e.g., scaffolding play, social prompting) to promote social interactions among children. In regard to play themes, DeKlyen and Odom (1989) examined four types of play (i.e., functional play, constructive play, sociodramatic play, and games with rules) and found that sociodramatic play was the most supportive circumstance of the four peer interactions.

Teachers' responsibilities during social integration activities consist of careful planning, arranging, introducing, and ongoing monitoring of the activities with preschoolers. The introduction phase includes explicit suggestions to the children about how they might play with one another. For example, adults describe the play activity and themes as well as assign specific roles to children for participating in the social activity. Following organization and introduction of the play activity, teachers withdraw from direct participation in the playgroup and become monitors of preschoolers' play and peer interactions. If children fail to talk, share, play, or socially interact with peers for prolonged periods, the teachers suggest another play idea, comment on the play of the play partners, and when necessary, explicitly encourage children to socially interact with peers. Even though teachers explicitly provide information about children's play roles and themes and embed social prompts within social activities, teachers' direct participation is used judiciously and faded across time whenever possible.

Chandler (1998) delineated specific guidelines for teachers who are interested in using social integration activities within learning centers in preschools. For some preschool children with social interaction problems, however, more teacher-structured and more teacher-directed peer interaction interventions than friendship activities and social integration activities may be warranted. Hence, Chandler has recommended that teachers select those classroom centers and activities in which peer interactions are most likely (e.g., dramatic play areas, block centers), and that they group children who might benefit from peer interactions together while systematically encouraging them to socially interact with one another. If children's social interactions stop for prolonged periods of time, the teachers again encourage and support continued peer interactions. Chandler has called these procedures PALS centers.

Several investigators have demonstrated the effectiveness of social integration activities (e.g., DeKlyen & Odom, 1989; Frea et al., 1999; Jenkins et al., 1989; Odom et al., 1988; Odom et al., 1999). For example, Jenkins and colleagues (1989) randomly assigned children to social integration activities and a child-directed cognitive intervention. For preschoolers in social integration activities relative to the cognitive intervention, greater rates of peer interaction, higher language scores on standardized assessments, and better social competence ratings by teachers were found. In another study, Frea and colleagues (1999) investigated friendship activities and social integration activities and compared the peer interactions of two children involved in those social interaction interventions. They determined that one child responded more positively to social integration activities, whereas the other child was more socially interactive during friendship activities, leading to their hypothesis that preschoolers' individual differences may influence the differential results. In another intervention comparison study, Odom and his colleagues (1999) compared a social integration activities approach with three other social interaction interventions. Although the peer-mediated and teacher antecedent approaches

facilitated greater peer interaction, the social integration activities approach positively affected the social status of children with developmental delays. Odom and
his colleagues (1999) speculated that social integration activities might have a
greater potential for elevating children's social status than peer-mediated and
teacher antecedent social interaction interventions.

Buddy Skills Training

Another example of a contemporary explicit social skills intervention is buddy skills
training developed by English, Goldstein, and colleagues (e.g., English et al., 1997;
Goldstein, English, Shafer, & Kaczmarek, 1997). The underlying principle for
buddy skills training is that teachers train children with and without developmental delays in specific social behaviors and strategies to promote future peer interactions. English and colleagues (1997) employed peer strategy-use training sessions
to systematically teach socially competent peers a sequential set of social behaviors
that consisted of moving in proximity to children with peer interaction problems,
saying the peers' names, and maintaining proximity while talking and playing with
the peers. As mentioned previously, A simple mnemonic of "stay, play, and talk" with
your buddy was used in their training protocol, which also incorporated discussions, teacher models, guided practice and rehearsal, and independent practice
with coaching feedback. Teachers also functioned as "buddy coaches" and monitored children's play and social interaction after the training sessions. In addition,
reminders to "stay with your friend, play with your friend, and talk with your friend"
(English et al., 1997, p. 233) were included during intervention sessions across the
preschool day. After peer strategy-use training and practice sessions, dyadic training
was conducted with peers who were socially sophisticated and children with social
interaction difficulties during three routine preschool activities: learning centers,
snack, and large group.

English and colleagues (1997) and Goldstein and colleagues (1997) demonstrated that the buddy skills strategy-use training and dyadic training improved
social-communicative interactions (e.g., verbal requests, comments) of both children with and without social interaction problems. Although Goldstein and
colleagues (1997) were successful in achieving better sociometric status for the
preschoolers with peer interaction difficulties who participated in buddy skills training, the participants with developmental delays in the study by English and
colleagues (1997) did not improve their peer status. With respect to social validity
of the buddy skills training, teachers who were naïve to the procedures and who
viewed pre- and post-training videotapes rated the quality and quantity of
preschoolers' peer interactions as improved following the social skills intervention.

PRAGMATIC USE OF A PEER
INTERACTION INTERVENTION HIERARCHY

We, along with many others, contend that preschool children with developmental
delays would benefit from services in inclusive early childhood programs that
implement DAP guidelines. We also strongly believe it would be advantageous
for practitioners in those programs to adjust their classroom practices, and,
when needed, use a variety of peer interaction interventions to actively promote
children's social competence. Inherent in our hierarchy is the expectation that

teachers use interventions that are only as intensive as necessary to facilitate peer interactions, bearing in mind that individual differences (e.g., child characteristics, child interests) may affect intervention effectiveness (Frea et al., 1999). Moreover, the findings from Frea and colleagues (1999) remind us of the essential need to use direct observation methods to assess the effectiveness of peer interaction interventions (see Brown, Odom, & Buysse, 2002; Odom, Schertz, et al., 2004).

The peer interaction interventions delineated in the hierarchy are examples of evidence-based or promising practices that might assist practitioners in achieving better social outcomes for young children with and without peer interaction difficulties. Our hierarchy, which includes a continuum of interventions, provides practitioners with a practical decision-making process for supporting young children's peer interactions in early childhood programs. Indeed, we view it as a heuristic conceptual framework, to be used in a flexible manner, for improving preschoolers' peer-related social competence (see Brown et al., 2001). Our selective review of interventions is meant to be illustrative of the possible types of peer interaction interventions that are available and that are expected to be used prudently to enhance young children's social competence.

While implementing the classroomwide, naturalistic, and explicit social skills interventions (or similar empirically validated interventions), classroom observations will assist teachers in determining whether more intensive interventions are required to enhance particular children's peer interactions. Moreover, as practitioners encourage frequent and elaborate social interactions with peers, preschoolers' peer-related social competence might be improved greatly. In the end, children's enhanced peer interactions and improved peer-related social competence should begin to support the establishment of better peer relationships and friendships (see Richardson & Schwartz, 1998; Rubin et al., 1998). The usefulness of the hierarchy will be determined by its social validity (i.e., Do interventionists find it helpful and use it?) and its empirical validity (i.e., Does it improve interventionists' use of effective interventions and promote better peer interactions and peer relations?) (McConnell et al., 1992).

A DEPLOYMENT-FOCUSED MODEL FOR PRESCHOOLERS' PEER INTERACTION INTERVENTIONS

Although a variety of peer interaction interventions have been developed and evaluated to some extent, the research base for many of them is relatively limited. These interventions have been extremely promising; nevertheless, some have not achieved the level of confirmation required to be judged as evidence-based practices (see Odom et al., 2005). Moreover, limitations may be especially evident for the use of complex, multicomponent peer interaction interventions for teachers who want to use them during common circumstances within their classrooms.

Hence, we believe that additional research and development of "teacher-friendly" peer interaction interventions that can be readily employed during routine situations with typical resources are sorely needed (see Brown & Conroy, 2001). At the present time, contemporary "practitioner-friendly" interventions such as friendship activities (e.g., Brown et al., 1988; McEvoy et al., 1988), incidental teaching of social behavior (e.g., Brown et al., 1991), and PALS centers (e.g., Chandler, 1998), have a relatively restricted research base. For example, the empirical validation of friendship activities is presently limited to four published single-subject research designs with fewer than 15 preschoolers with a wide range of developmental needs. Friendship activities and many other peer interaction interventions need to be systematically replicated and further refined with more diverse populations of children and teachers within a greater variety of preschool circumstances. In particular, efficacy, effectiveness, and sustainability investigations are required to better judge both the generalizability and ecological validity of most extant peer interaction interventions. Moreover, careful examination of peer interaction interventions is very much needed given the recent designation of children's social competence as one of the three primary child outcomes for early childhood education (see Greenwood, Walker, & Bailey, 2005).

With respect to psychosocial treatments for children with behavioral and emotional disorders, Weisz and colleagues (2004) proposed a deployment-focused model to propagate evidence-based interventions. Weisz and colleagues (2004) were concerned with the gap between research and practice in the delivery of children's mental health services. They lamented the fact that multiple evidence-based interventions exist, at least with respect to efficacy, but that those treatments are rarely employed in everyday clinical practice outside of university affiliated research settings. Their model consists of three aims, which include:

> ". . . 1) producing treatments that can fit smoothly into everyday practice, working well with clinic-referred individuals treated in clinic settings by practicing clinicians; 2) generating evidence on treatment outcome in actual clinical practice, the kind of evidence clinicians need most in order to assess the likely utility of treatments for their settings; and 3) producing a body of evidence on the nature, necessary and sufficient components, boundary conditions (i.e., moderators), and change processes (i.e., mediators) associated with treatment impact that is externally valid and relevant to the treatment in genuine practice conditions." (Weisz et al., 2004, p. 11).

If one changes their language from *clinicians* to *teachers, clinic settings* to *classrooms,* and *treatments* to *interventions,* we believe that Weisz and colleagues' (2004) arguments and aims are especially applicable to early childhood education and are similar to but more precisely elaborated than Guralnick's (1997) argument for "second-generation research" in early intervention. Specifically, Guralnick (1997) asserted that a significant need exists to determine which interventions work with what populations of children and families and under which circumstances. Weisz and colleagues (2004) proposed a six-step, deployment-focused model for research: 1) Protocol/Manual, 2) Efficacy Test, 3) Field Cases, 4) Effectiveness I, 5) Effectiveness II, and 6) Staying Power). The purpose of the proposed model is to assist practitioners and researchers in systematically investigating and determining the efficacy and generalizability of interventions for children and families.

Step 1: Protocol/Manual

Weisz and colleagues (2004) advocated a protocol and manual step with the initial development, refinement, pilot test, and writing of a manual for any viable intervention protocols. Moreover, they recommended that intervention protocols be theoretically grounded and empirically validated for the children's particular behavioral needs (e.g., decreased aggressive behavior, improvement of children's peer interactions). They stated that authors of manuals should clearly delineate relevant intervention components as well as any needed accompanying intervention materials and conditions. Unfortunately, with respect to improvement of preschoolers' peer interactions and peer relations, many interventions remain at the level of general guidelines. Nevertheless, several theoretically grounded and empirically validated curricula with well-developed manuals have been disseminated (e.g., *The Integrated Preschool Curriculum: Procedures for Socially Integrating Handicapped and Nonhandicapped Children* [Odom et al., 1988]; *A Socialization Curriculum for Preschool Programs that Integrate Children with Handicaps* [Brown, Ragland, & Bishop, 1989b]; *Dina Dinosaur's Social, Emotional and Problem-Solving Curriculum* [Webster-Stratton, 1990]; *Play Time/Social Time* [Odom & McConnell, 1993]).

Step 2: Efficacy Test

Weisz and colleagues (2004) recommended a second step that consists of the initial efficacy testing of interventions. The goal of this second developmental phase is to begin to determine positive benefits of intervention protocols under optimal circumstances. Weisz and colleagues (2004) advocated the employment of experimental and control groups (i.e., between-group research designs) for these initial efficacy studies. Odom and colleagues (2005) argued to extend tests of efficacy to well-conducted single-subject studies, particularly those that systematically replicate previous investigations. The outcome of the efficacy phase is to establish whether an intervention is promising enough under relatively well-controlled conditions to warrant further evaluation in common circumstances in typical community settings.

Step 3: Field Cases

Weisz and colleagues (2004) proposed a third step with single-subject research designs for further pilot testing of interventions in community settings, albeit by practitioners who have a relationship with researchers and who know the intervention procedures well. Moreover, they recommended that the community settings be as representative as possible of the common community circumstances under which the interventions will be employed. The goal of this phase is to produce further efficacy and fidelity of intervention data while also obtaining critical information concerning the interventions "goodness of fit" with less than optimal circumstances. With respect to existing preschool children's peer interaction intervention efficacy studies, many, if not most, early childhood researchers have employed single-subject research designs and often with relatively close practitioner-researcher collaboration. Weisz and colleagues (2004) noted that this step of the investigative process is when researchers can begin to explore potential moderators such as age, developmental status, gender, and culture.

Step 4: Effectiveness I

Weisz and colleagues (2004) recommend a fourth step to serve as partial effectiveness tests. They argue for between-group designs with random assignment of participants (e.g., children, teachers, programs) to evaluate adapted intervention protocols from the previous three steps and to make comparisons with salient dimensions of typical community circumstances. A goal of the initial effectiveness phase is to determine in a systematic manner the extent to which previously developed and partially tested interventions work with the children in need of intervention, within community settings without additional resources and personnel, when implemented by practitioners in those settings, and when compared directly with "business as usual" in community programs. Another goal of the initial effectiveness step is to better determine the putative effectiveness of components or combinations of components of protocols in everyday situations under ordinary circumstances while refining them for more comprehensive evaluation of effectiveness and dissemination.

Step 5: Effectiveness II

Weisz and colleagues (2004) proposed a fifth step to further assess effectiveness of interventions and to prepare those interventions for widespread dissemination. They recommended a series of between-group design clinical trials with random assignment of participants with the intervention protocols implemented by practitioners in community settings after they have been trained on those protocols. Again, they argued that experimental comparisons should be the intervention protocols with "business as usual" (i.e., everyday practices, circumstances, and resources). The goal of this fifth phase is to evaluate "effectiveness and disseminability" of the intervention protocols under representative circumstances. They posit that success for this step will be judged by the affirmative answer to two essential questions: "1) do trained staff practitioners actually adhere to the manual in their treatment sessions, and 2) do clients treated by the manual-trained staff practitioners show greater treatment gains than clients receiving usual care" (Weisz et al., 2004, p. 13).

Step 6: Staying Power

Weisz and colleagues (2004) recommended a final step to function as "goodness of fit" and sustainability assessment. They noted that this phase of investigation should concentrate on the examination of the ongoing implementation of intervention protocols within the community settings. The goal is to carefully evaluate issues that focus on the maintenance of intervention fidelity and positive child outcomes across time after significant levels of programmatic support from researchers have been terminated. Hence, the aim with this step is to determine whether intervention protocols are sufficient to positively affect both children and practitioners across time during real-world circumstances.

Although Weisz and colleagues (2004) delineated a step-wise model, they clearly intended to support an iterative research process, particularly with Steps 4, 5, and 6. For example, they called for the following: determination of necessary and sufficient components of complex intervention protocols; identification of moderators that affect intervention outcomes; evaluation of putative mediators that might influence interventions effectiveness; determination of intervention costs with respect to benefits; research on micro- and macro-organizational variables that might affect intervention implementation; and ongoing evaluation of combinations of intervention procedures, necessary personnel preparation, marketing of intervention protocols, and "goodness-of-fit" with various types of community programs.

The programmatic research model presented by Weisz and colleagues (2004) is daunting, particularly in an age of restricted research and service resources. Nevertheless, their research recommendations are applicable to and relevant for the "state-of-the-art" in peer interaction research. In particular, given restricted resources, continuing single-subject investigations to obtain additional, much-needed efficacy data as well as social validity and intervention fidelity information is critical. As resources become available, however, there is a clear and compelling need to more adequately investigate contemporary peer interaction interventions with better specified populations of children under more diverse and sometimes chaotic community circumstances than has been performed in extant studies (see Guralnick, 1997). Similar to Weisz's Steps 4–6, when the efficacy of interventions is established, studies need to be performed without short-term financial and personnel support from researchers performing the investigations. Especially relevant are issues concerning necessary and sufficient components of intervention protocols and their implementation. Particularly important are questions concerning the nature and composition of peer interaction intervention protocols and the personnel preparation and consultation required to ensure intervention fidelity. Moreover, costs analyses of required programmatic supports and the day-to-day practice and policy issues that might inhibit or promote effective implementation of efficacious peer interaction interventions need to be adequately addressed.

CONCLUSIONS

If we are to better address the gap of research to practice related to preschoolers' peer interaction interventions, we believe that better targeted research and development activities are sorely needed, particularly the development and evaluation of teacher-friendly interventions, which are acceptable and feasible to early childhood educators (see West et al., 2006). Without sustained programmatic research on the implementation of evidence-based peer interaction interventions to improve preschoolers' social interactions and peer relations within early childhood programs, many children may continue to be at risk for less than optimal social competence outcomes. Pending investigators' further development, validation, and widespread dissemination of evidence-based peer interaction interventions that are both acceptable to and feasible for preschool practitioners, the use of existing interventions will probably continue to be underused by many teachers (see Brown et al., 2001). Until the next generation of peer interaction interventions has been better validated, both socially and empirically, by systematic research programs similar to the one proposed by Weisz and colleagues, we believe that a pragmatic position for practitioners will be to employ the hierarchy, described in this chapter, to promote preschoolers' peer interactions with existing evidence-based and promising peer interaction interventions while carefully assessing children's social behavior and social competence.

REFERENCES

Beckman, P.J., & Kohl, F.L. (1984). The effects of social and isolate toys on the interactions and play of integrated and nonintegrated groups of preschoolers. *Education and Training of the Mentally Retarded, 18,* 169–174.

Bredekamp, S., & Copple, C. (1997). *Developmentally appropriate practice in early childhood programs (Rev.).* Washington, DC: National Association for the Education of Young Children (NAEYC).

Bricker, D.D. (1978). A rationale for the integration of handicapped and nonhandicapped preschool children. In M.J. Guralnick (Ed.), *Early intervention and the integration of handicapped and nonhandicapped children* (pp. 3–26). Baltimore: University Park Press.

Brown, W.H., & Conroy, M. (1997). Promoting and supporting peer interactions in inclusive classrooms: Effective strategies for early childhood educators. In W.H. Brown & M. Conroy (Eds.), *Inclusion of preschool children with developmental delays in early childhood programs* (pp. 79–108). Little Rock, AR: Southern Early Childhood Association.

Brown, W.H., & Conroy, M.A. (2001). Promoting peer-related social–communicative competence in preschool children with developmental delays. In H. Goldstein, L. Kaczmarek, & K. English (Eds.), *Promoting social communication in children and youth with developmental disabilities* (pp. 173–210). Baltimore: Paul H. Brookes Publishing Co.

Brown, W.H., McEvoy, M.A., & Bishop, J.N. (1991). Incidental teaching of social behavior: A naturalistic approach to promoting young children's peer interactions. *Teaching Exceptional Children, 24,* 35–58.

Brown, W.H., & Odom, S.L. (1994). Strategies and tactics for promoting generalization and maintenance of young children's social behavior. *Research in Developmental Disabilities, 15,* 99–118.

Brown, W.H., & Odom, S.L. (1995). Naturalistic peer interventions for promoting preschool children's social interactions. *Preventing School Failure, 39,* 38–43.

Brown, W.H., Odom, S.L., & Buysse, V. (2002). Assessment of preschool children's peer-related social competence. *Assessment for Effective Intervention, 27*(4), 61–71.

Brown, W.H., Odom, S.L., & Conroy, M.A. (2001). An intervention hierarchy for promoting preschool children's peer interactions in natural environments. *Topics in Early Childhood Special Education, 21,* 90–134.

Brown, W.H., Odom, S.L., Li, S., & Zercher, C. (1999). Ecobehavioral assessment in early childhood programs: A portrait of preschool inclusion. *The Journal of Special Education 33,* 138–153.

Brown, W.H., Ragland, E.U., & Bishop, J.N. (1989a). A naturalistic teaching strategy to promote young children's peer interactions. *Teaching Exceptional Children, 21,* 8–10.

Brown, W.H., Ragland, E.U., & Bishop, N. (1989b). *A socialization curriculum for preschool programs that integrate children with handicaps.* Nashville, TN: John F. Kennedy Center for Research on Human Development, Vanderbilt University.

Brown, W.H., Ragland, E.U., & Fox, J.J. (1988). Effects of group socialization procedures on the social interactions of preschool children. *Research in Developmental Disabilities, 9,* 359–376.

Campbell, S.B. (2002). *Behavior problems in preschool children: Clinical and developmental issues* (2nd ed.). New York: Guilford Press.

Cavallaro, C.C., Haney, M., & Cabello, B. (1993). Developmentally appropriate strategies for promoting full participation in early childhood settings. *Topics in Early Childhood Special Education, 13,* 293–307.

Chandler, L. (1998). Promoting positive interaction between preschool-age children during free play: The PALS Center. *Young Exceptional Children, 1*(3), 14–20.

Chandler, L.K., Lubeck, R.C., & Fowler, S.A. (1992). Generalization and maintenance of preschool children's social skills: A critical review and analysis. *Journal of Applied Behavior Analysis, 25,* 415–428.

Conroy, M.A., & Brown, W.H. (2004). Early identification, prevention, and early intervention with young children at-risk for emotional or behavioral disorders: Issues, trends, and a call for action. *Behavioral Disorders, 29*(3), 224–237.

Derman-Sparks, L., & Anti-Bias Curriculum Task Force. (1989). *Anti-bias curriculum: Tools for empowering young children.* Washington, DC: National Association for the Education of Young Children.

DeKlyen, M., & Odom, S.L. (1989). Activity structure and social interactions with peers in developmentally integrated play groups. *Journal of Early Intervention, 13,* 342–352.

Diamond, K. (2002). The development of social competence in children with disabilities. In P.K. Smith & C.H. Hart (Eds.), *Blackwell handbook of childhood social development* (pp. 571–587). Malden, MA: Blackwell Publishing.

Domitrovich, C., Cortes, R.C., & Greenberg, M. (2006). *Improving young children's social and emotional competence: A randomized trial of the preschool PATHS curriculum.* University Park: Pennsylvania State University.

English, K., Goldstein, H., Shafer, K., & Kaczmarek, L. (1997). Promoting interactions among preschoolers with and without disabilities: Effects of a buddy skills-training program. *Exceptional Children, 63,* 229–243.

Farran, D.C., Aydogan, C., Kang, S.J., & Lipsey, M.W. (2006). Preschool classroom environments and the quantity and quality of children's literacy and language behaviors. In D.K. Dickinson & S.B. Neuman (Eds.), *Handbook of early literacy research* (Volume 2) (pp. 257–268). New York: Guilford Press.

Favazza, P.C., & Odom, S.L. (1997). Promoting positive attitudes of kindergarten-age children toward people with disabilities. *Exceptional Children, 63,* 405–418.

Favazza, P.C., Roe, J.L., Phillipsen, L., & Kumar, P. (2000). Representing young children with disabilities in classroom environments. *Young Exceptional Children, 3*(3), 2–8.

Frea, W., Craig-Unkefer, L., Odom, S.L., & Johnson, D. (1999). Differential effects of structured social integration and group friendship activities for promoting social interaction with peers. *Journal of Early Intervention, 22,* 230–242.

Goldstein, H., English, K., Shafer, K., & Kaczmarek, L. (1997). Interaction among preschoolers with and without disabilities: Effects of across-the-day peer intervention. *Journal of Speech and Hearing Research, 40,* 33–48.

Greenwood, C., Walker, D., & Bailey, D. (2005, October). Critical issues in measuring outcomes for young children and their families. Presentation at the International Early Childhood Conference on Children with Special Needs of the Council for Exceptional Children's Division for Early Childhood (DEC). Portland, Oregon.

Guralnick, M.J. (1997). Second-generation research in the field of early intervention. In M.J. Guralnick (Ed.), *The effectiveness of early intervention* (pp. 3–22). Baltimore: Paul H. Brookes Publishing Co.

Guralnick, M.J., Connor, R.T., Neville, B., & Hammond, M.A. (2006). Promoting the peer-related social development of young children with mild developmental delays: Effectiveness of a comprehensive intervention. *American Journal of Mental Retardation, 111*(5), 336–356.

Guralnick, M.J., Connor, R.T., Hammond, M.A., Gottman, J.M., & Kinnish, K. (1996). The peer relations of preschool children with communication disorders. *Child Development, 67,* 471–489.

Guralnick, M.J., & Neville, B. (1997). Designing early intervention programs to promote children's social competence. In M.J. Guralnick (Ed.), *The effectiveness of early intervention* (pp. 579–610). Baltimore: Paul H. Brookes Publishing Co.

Han, J., Ostrosky, M.M., & Diamond, K.E. (2006). Children's attitudes toward peers with disabilities: Supporting positive attitude development. *Young Exceptional Children, 10*(1), 2–11.

Hancock, T.B., & Kaiser, A.P. (2005). Enhanced milieu teaching. In R. McCauley & M. Fey (Eds.), *Treatment of language disorders in children* (pp. 203–236). Baltimore: Paul H. Brookes Publishing Co.

Harms, T., Clifford, R.M., & Cryer, D. (1998). *Early Childhood Rating Scale—Revised Edition.* New York: Teachers College Press.

Hartup, W.W., & Stevens, N. (1997). Friendships and adaptations in the life course. *Psychological Bulletin, 121,* 335–370.

Hestenes, L., & Carroll, D.E. (2000). The play interactions of young children with and without disabilities: Individual and environmental influences. *Early Childhood Research Quarterly, 15,* 229–246.

Howes, C., & James, J. (2002). Children's social development within the socialization context of childcare and early childhood education. In P.K. Smith & C.H. Hart (Eds.), *Blackwell handbook of childhood social development* (pp. 137–155). Malden, MA: Blackwell Publishing.

Hymel, S., Vaillancourt, T., McDougall, P., Renshaw, P.D. (2002). Peer acceptance and rejection in childhood. In P.K. Smith & C.H. Hart (Eds.), *Blackwell handbook of childhood social development* (pp. 265–284). Malden, MA: Blackwell Publishing.

Individuals with Disabilities Education Improvement Act (IDEA) of 2004, PL 108–446, 20 U.S.C. §§ 1400 *et seq.*

Jenkins, J.R., Odom, S.L., & Speltz, M.L. (1989). Effects of social integration of preschool children with handicaps. *Exceptional Children, 55,* 420–428.

Kopp, C.B., Baker, B.L., & Brown, K.W. (1992). Social skills and their correlates: Preschoolers with developmental delays. *American Journal of Mental Retardation, 96,* 357–366.

Ladd, G.W., & Coleman, C.C. (1993). Young children's peer relationships: Forms, features, and functions. In B. Spodeck (Ed.), *Handbook of research on the education of young children* (pp. 57–76). New York: Macmillan.

Ladd, G.W., Buhs, E.S., & Troop, W. (2002). Children's interpersonal skills and relationships in school settings: Adaptive significance and implications for school-based prevention and intervention programs. In P.K. Smith & C.H. Hart (Eds.), *Blackwell handbook of childhood social development* (pp. 394–415). Malden, MA: Blackwell Publishing.

McConnell, S.R., McEvoy, M.A., & Odom, S.L. (1992). Implementation of social competence interventions in early childhood special education classes. In S.L. Odom, S.R. McConnell, & M.A. McEvoy, (Eds.), *Social competence of young children with disabilities: Issues and strategies for intervention* (pp. 277–306). Baltimore: Paul H. Brookes Publishing Co.

McEvoy, M.A., Nordquist, V.M., Twardosz, S. Heckaman, K., Wehby, J.H., & Denny, R.K. (1988). Promoting autistic children's peer interaction in an integrated early childhood setting using affection activities. *Journal of Applied Behavior Analysis, 21,* 193–200.

McEvoy, M.A., & Odom, S.L. (1996). Strategies for promoting social interaction and emotional development of infants and young children with disabilities and their families. In S.L. Odom & M.E. McLean (Eds.), *Early intervention/early childhood special education: Recommended practices* (pp. 223–244). Austin, TX: PRO-ED.

McEvoy, M.A., Odom, S.L., & McConnell, S.R. (1992). Peer social competence intervention for young children with disabilities. In S.L. Odom, S.R., McConnell, & M.A. McEvoy, (Eds.), *Social competence of young children with disabilities: Issues and strategies for intervention* (pp. 113–134). Baltimore: Paul H. Brookes Publishing Co.

McGee, G.G., Almeida, C., Sulzer-Azaroff, B., & Feldman, R.S. (1992). Promoting reciprocal interactions via peer incidental teaching. *Journal of Applied Behavior Analysis, 25,* 117–126.

Michnowicz, L.L., McConnell, S.R., Peterson, C.A., & Odom, S.L. (1995). Social goals and objectives of preschool IEPs: A content analysis. *Journal of Early Intervention, 19,* 273–282.

Mize, J., & Ladd, G.W. (1990). A cognitive–social learning approach to social skill training with low-status preschool children. *Developmental Psychology, 26,* 388–397.

Mueller, E., & Silverman, N. (1989). Peer relations in maltreated children. In D. Cicchetti & V. Carlson (Eds.), *Child maltreatment: Theory and research on the causes and consequences of child abuse and neglect* (pp. 529–578). New York: Cambridge University Press.

National Research Council. (2001). *Educating autistic children.* Washington, DC: National Academies Press.

New, R.S., & Mallory, B.L. (1994). Introduction: The ethic of inclusion. In B.L. Mallory & R.S. New (Eds.), *Diversity & developmentally appropriate practices: Challenges for early childhood education* (pp. 1–13). New York: Teachers College Press.

Newcomb, A.F., & Bagwell, C.L. (1995). Children's friendship relations: A meta-analytic review. *Psychological Bulletin, 117,* 306–347.

Odom, S.L., Bender, M.K., Stein, M.L., Doran, L.P., Houden, P.M., McInnes, M., Gilbert, M.M., DeKlyen, M., Speltz, M.L., & Jenkins, J.R. (1988). *The integrated preschool curriculum: Procedures for socially integrating handicapped and nonhandicapped children.* Seattle: University of Washington Press.

Odom, S.L., Brantlinger, E., Gersten, R., Horner, R.H., Thompson, B., & Harris, K.R. (2005). Research in Special Education: Scientific methods and evidence-based practices. *Exceptional Children, 71,* 137–148.

Odom, S.L., & Brown, W.H. (1993). Social interaction skills interventions for children with disabilities in integrated settings. In C.A. Peck, S.L. Odom, & D. Bricker (Eds.), *Integrating young children with disabilities into community programs: Ecological perspectives on research and implementation* (pp. 39–64). Baltimore: Paul H. Brookes Publishing Co.

Odom, S.L., & McLean, M.E. (1996). *Early intervention/early childhood special education: Recommended practices.* Austin, TX: PRO-ED.

Odom, S.L., & McConnell, S.R. (1993). *Play time/social time: Organizing your classroom to build interaction skills.* Tucson, AZ: Communication Skill Builders.

Odom, S.L., McConnell, S.R., & Chandler, L.K. (1994). Acceptability and feasibility of classroom-based social interaction interventions for young children with disabilities. *Exceptional Children, 60,* 226–236.

Odom, S.L., McConnell, S.R., & McEvoy, M.A. (1992). Peer-related social competence and its significance for young children with disabilities. In S.L. Odom, S.R. McConnell, & M.A. McEvoy (Eds.), *Social competence of young children with disabilities: Issues and strategies for intervention* (pp. 3–36). Baltimore: Paul H. Brookes Publishing Co.

Odom, S.L., McConnell, S.R., McEvoy, M.A., Peterson, C., Ostrosky, M., Chandler, L.K., Spicuzza, R.J., Skellenger, A., Creighton, M., & Favazza, P.C. (1999). Relative effects of interventions supporting the social competence of young children with disabilities. *Topics in Early Childhood Special Education, 19,* 75–91.

Odom, S.L., McLean, M.E., Johnson, L.J., & LaMontagne, M.J. (1995). Recommended practice in early childhood special education: Validation and current use. *Journal of Early Intervention, 19,* 1–17.

Odom, S.L., Peck, C.A., Hanson, M., Beckman, P., Kaiser, A., Lieber, J., Brown, W.H., Horn, E., & Schwartz, I.S. (1996). Inclusion at the preschool level: An ecological systems analysis. *Social Policy Report: Society for Research in Child Development, 10* (2, 3), 18–30.

Odom, S.L., Schertz, H., Munson, L., & Brown, W.H. (2004). Assessing social competence. In M. McLean, M. Wolery, & D.B. Bailey (Eds.), *Assessing infants and preschoolers with special needs* (3rd ed., pp. 412–450). Columbus, OH: Merrill.

Odom, S.L., Vitztum, J., Wolery, R., Lieber, J., Sandall, S., Hanson, M.J., Beckman, P., Schwartz, I., & Horn, E.M. (2004). Preschool inclusion in the United States: A review of research from an ecological perspective. *Journal of Research in Special Education Needs, 4*(1), 17–49.

Odom, S.L., Zercher, C., Li, S., Marquart, J.M., Sandall, S., & Brown, W.H. (in press). Social acceptance and social rejection of children with disabilities in inclusive preschool settings. *Journal of Educational Psychology.*

Parke, R.D., Simpkins, S.D., McDowell, D.J., Kim, M., Killian, C., Dennis, J., Flyr, M.L., Wild, M., & Rah, Y. (2002). Relative contributions of families and peers to children's social development. In P.K. Smith & C.H. Hart (Eds.), *Blackwell handbook of childhood social development* (pp. 156–177). Malden, MA: Blackwell Publishing.

Parker, J.G., & Asher, S.R. (1987). Peer relations and later personal adjustment: Are low-accepted children at risk? *Psychological Bulletin, 102,* 357–389.

Petrakos, H., & Howe, N. (1996). The influence of the physical design of the dramatic play center on children's play. *Early Childhood Research Quarterly, 11,* 63–77.

Pretti-Frontczak, K., & Bricker, D. (2004). *An activity-based approach to early intervention* (3rd ed.). Baltimore: Paul H. Brookes Publishing Co.

Richardson, P., & Schwartz, I.S. (1998). Making friends in preschool: Friendship patterns of young children with disabilities. In L. Meyer, H. Park, M. Grenot-Scheyer, I. Schwartz, & B. Harry (Eds.), *Making friends: The influences of culture and development* (pp. 65–80). Baltimore: Paul H. Brookes Publishing Co.

Rogers, S. (1998). Empirically supported comprehensive treatments for young children with autism. *Journal of Clinical Child Psychology, 27*(2), 168–179.

Rubin, K.H., Bukowski, W., & Parker, J.G. (1998). Peer interactions, relationships, and groups. In W. Damon & N. Eisenberg (Eds.), *Handbook of child psychology* (5th ed., Vol. 3, pp. 619–700). New York: Wiley.

Rule, S., Losardo, A., Dinnebeil, L., Kaiser, A., & Rowland, C. (1998). Translating research on naturalistic instruction into practice. *Journal of Early Intervention, 21,* 283–293.

Russell, A., Mize, J. & Bissaker, K. (2002). Parent–child relationships. In P.K. Smith & C.H. Hart (Eds.), *Blackwell handbook of childhood social development* (pp. 205–222). Malden, MA: Blackwell Publishing.

Sandall, S., Hemmeter, M.L., Smith, B.J., & McLean, M.E. (2005). *DEC Recommended practices: A comprehensive guide for practical application in early intervention/early childhood special education.* Longmont, CO: Sopris West.

Sandall, S., McLean, M.E., & Smith, B.J. (2000). *DEC recommended practices in early intervention/early childhood special education.* Longmont, CO: Sopris West.

Schatz, J.N. (2006) Preventing child maltreatment. In J.G. Borkowski & C.M. Weaver (Eds.), *Prevention: The science and art of promoting health child and adolescent development* (pp. 83–112). Baltimore: Paul H. Brookes Publishing Co.

Tattersall, I. (2002). *Monkey in the mirror: Essays on the science of what makes us human.* San Diego, CA: Harcourt, Inc.

Webster-Stratton, C. (1990). *Dina Dinosaur's social, emotional and problem-solving curriculum.* Seattle: University of Washington.

Webster-Stratton, C., & Reid, M.J. (2003). Treating conduct problems and strengthening social emotional competence in young children (ages 4–8 years): The Dina Dinosaur treatment program. *Journal of Emotional and Behavioral Disorders, 11*(3), 130–143.

Weisz, J.R., Jensen, A.L., & McLeod, B.D. (2004). Development and dissemination of child and adolescent psychotherapies: Milestones, methods, and a new deployment-focused model. In E.D. Hibbs & P.S. Jensen (Eds.), *Psychosocial treatments for child and adolescent disorders: Empirically based approaches* (pp. 9–39). (2nd ed.). Washington, DC: American Psychological Association.

West, T.N., Brown, W.H., Grego, J.M., & Johnson, R. (in press). Professionals' judgments of peer interaction interventions: A survey of DEC members.

CHAPTER 8

Promoting Young Children's Social Competence in Early Childhood Programs

KAREN E. DIAMOND, SOO-YOUNG HONG, AND ALISON E. BAROODY

The children I teach are just emerging from life's deep wells of private perspective: babyhood and family....Then, along comes school. It is the first real exposure to the public arena. Children are required to share materials and teachers in a space that belongs to them.... Equal participation is, of course, the cornerstone of most classrooms. This notion usually involves everything except free play, which is generally considered a private matter. Yet, in truth, free acceptance in play, partnerships, and teams is what matters most to any child.

—Paley, 1992, p. 21

The developmental tasks of the preschool period include cognitive, language, and motor skills essential for learning, but also "the ability to get along with other children, to make friends, and become engaged in a social group, as well as the capacity to manage emotions" (Shonkoff & Phillips, 2000, p. 386). This chapter examines young children's development of social and emotional skills as they participate in early childhood programs. We examine teaching practices and curricula that support children's development of social competence and that are used in early childhood classrooms[1] designed for 3- and 4-year-old children who are typically developing. Nevertheless, the practices and curricula we discuss are often applicable to children with developmental delays (Diamond, 2002). Our focus is on "those factors that seem to make a difference in whether the child is equipped to ...make friends and enjoy life" (Shonkoff & Phillips, 2000, p. 92).

---

[1] The term *classroom* is used to refer to any group setting that includes preschool children and is taught or supervised by one or more adults, including child care, preschool, Head Start, and prekindergarten programs.

Preschool children who are socially competent are friendly, cooperative, help-ful, flexible, independent, and less aggressive. They display more positive affect and are generally liked and accepted by their peers (Denham et al., 2003; Hubbard & Coie, 1994; Ladd, Birch, & Buhs, 1999; Mendez, Fantuzzo, & Cicchetti, 2002; Putal-laz & Gottman, 1981). There is substantial evidence that socially competent behav-iors can be learned in child care and preschool group settings (Shonkoff & Phillips, 2000). Yet teachers rate as many as 20% of all children entering kindergarten and 30% of children from low-income families as having poor social skills. This lack of competence interferes with participation in activities with peers and with academic success (Zill & West, 2001).

Ideally, parents and other caregivers should work with preschool programs to teach children those social and emotional competencies that will help them to be successful in their current preschool settings and in the future. Although there is no national consensus about what children should know and be able to do in preschool (Wesley & Buysse, 2003), social-emotional competencies are reflected in many states' preschool standards for early learning (Scott-Little, Kagan, & Frelow, 2003). Social-emotional competence is reflected in these standards and in position state-ments from professional organizations such as the National Association for the Edu-cation of Young Children and the National Association of Early Childhood Specialists in State Departments of Education (NAEYC/NAECS/SDE, 2002).

Given concerns about the importance of preparing preschool children for *academic* success in kindergarten and early elementary grades, one might ask, "Why should social-emotional competence be a component of early childhood curric-ula?" Preschool children's positive peer interactions and social competence are associated with important developmental outcomes and academic achievement (Doctoroff, Greer, & Arnold, 2006; Ialongo, Vaden-Kiernan, & Kellam, 1998). Chil-dren who are socially competent are more likely than less socially competent chil-dren to be included in activities with their peers. Children who enter school with friends tend to have more positive perceptions of school than those who do not have friends, and forming and maintaining friendships during the school year is related to school adjustment and academic gains for children in early elementary grades (Ladd et al., 1999).

Positive relationships between students and teachers can provide the motiva-tion for teachers to spend additional time and energy in promoting children's suc-cess (Hamre & Pianta, 2001). Teachers are likely to spend more time in instructional activities and provide more positive feedback to children who have better social skills (Raver, 2002). Furthermore, social competence is a predictor of later well-being and mental health. Young children who are more aggressive encounter more peer rejection and are likely to experience negative outcomes in the future, including dropping out of school, criminality, delinquency, and psycho-logical disturbances later in life (Dodge et al., 2003; Ialongo et al., 1998).

Social behavior is relatively stable from preschool through the early elementary grades, and it is increasingly difficult for experience alone to alter established developmental trajectories, including those related to social competence (National Institute for Child Health and Human Development Early Childcare Research Net-work, 2003). Children who are well-liked by their peers as preschoolers are likely to continue to be well-liked as they grow older, whereas children who are rejected by peers as preschoolers are likely to be excluded from play as they grow older (Den-ham & Holt, 1993).

The importance of developing social as well as academic competence is reflected in standards for learning in preschool. Just as state standards for kindergarten through Grade 12 provide guidance for what should be taught and what children should be able to do, early learning standards help define what is to be taught and what preschool children will learn (Scott-Little et al., 2003). Moreover, standards provide a common reference point for the development of curricula and materials and for professional development (Committee on the Prevention of Reading Difficulties in Young Children, 1998). In a joint position statement, the National Association for the Education of Young Children and the National Association of Early Childhood Specialists in State Departments of Education (2002) identified social-emotional development as an important component that should be represented in early learning standards, in part because social-emotional competence is associated with positive developmental and academic outcomes, as noted earlier. A content analysis of 46 early learning standards documents from 42 states reveals that while the majority of documents emphasized cognitive (39% of items) and language (30% of items) competencies, 44 of 46 documents also included standards related to social and emotional development (Scott-Little, Kagan, & Frelow, 2006). Overall, social-emotional competencies comprised 11% of items in these early learning standards documents. Clearly, even within a policy framework in which early academic achievement is emphasized, social and emotional development is viewed as important for young children.

From an educational policy perspective, The Head Start Child Outcomes Framework (Administration for Children and Families, 2000) and states' early learning standards documents (Scott-Little et al., 2006) provide the most comprehensive picture of important social-emotional competencies that children are expected to develop during the preschool years. Within early learning standards documents, the majority of social and emotional development items focus on expressing and understanding emotions of oneself and others and on developing relationships and interacting effectively with peers and adults (Scott-Little et al., 2006). These competencies are similar to the elements of social-emotional development in the Head Start Child Outcomes Framework, a guide for curriculum planning in Head Start programs. The Outcomes Framework includes cooperation, social relationships, self-concept, and self-control (including emotion expression and understanding) as important components of social-emotional development. Interestingly, knowledge of families and communities, a component of the Head Start Outcomes Framework, does not appear in most states' standards.

EXPRESSING AND UNDERSTANDING EMOTIONS OF ONESELF AND OTHERS

Recognizing different feelings and regulating negative feelings are important skills that children should acquire during early childhood (Hyson, 2004; Hyson, Copple, & Jones, 2006). Emotion knowledge, or the ability to understand and identify emotion and to respond to others' emotions in an age-appropriate manner, is an important component of children's successful peer interactions (Cassidy, Parke, Butkovsky, & Braungart, 1992; Denham et al., 2003). Knowledge about and understanding of emotions are related to the extent to which children are liked by their classmates and to children's success at entering into group play with peers (Denham, McKinley, Couchoud, & Holt, 1990). In order to enter group play, children not only have to follow social expectations but also they have to accurately read oth- ers' emotions and behave appropriately in response to these emotions. Once chil- dren have entered their peer group play, the ability to accurately read the feelings and emotions of others is essential in coordinating and maintaining mutual play activities. Emotion knowledge may also help in the resolution of conflict: Children who have a better understanding of others' emotional states may respond in more sympathetic ways and choose less-aggressive and more-prosocial methods of conflict resolution (Hyson, 2004).

In addition to emotion knowledge, emotion regulation is important to social competence. Emotion regulation is the ability to adapt and change one's emotions and control emotional displays in a variety of situations, especially those of high social intensity. Children who control their emotions display few overt negative emotions and act in less aggressive ways when compared with other children. They are viewed by peers as more helpful and "nice," and are more popular in the peer group (Eisenberg et al., 1997; Hubbard & Coie, 1994). Positive emotion expression is associated with other prosocial behaviors (Denham et al., 2003). To the extent that children find ways to quickly overcome their negative moods and feelings, they are more likely to have positive interactions with peers.

The ability to regulate emotions, especially in high-intensity situations, may help children to resolve conflicts that interfere with ongoing play. Children are more satisfied with low conflict relationships. Happier classmates seem to make pos- itive impressions on both adults and other children (Denham et al., 2003; Ladd, Kochenderfer, & Coleman, 1996). Children who are able to regulate negative emo- tional responses (e.g., anger, hostility) and respond in socially appropriate ways, even in conflictual situations, are able to mitigate conflicts instead of escalating them (Fabes et al., 1999). Because negative responses may terminate play, children who regulate their own emotions and find ways to resolve conflicts have many opportunities to practice and refine these skills with peers. Both interpersonal and intra-personal negative emotions make "interaction much more difficult across the lifespan; in contrast, more positive individuals" attract others (Denham et al., 2003, p. 252).

Evidence from intervention studies indicates that children can learn skills for understanding and regulating their emotions that are associated with school adjust- ment. McMahon, Washburn, Felix, Yakin, and Childrey (2000) used photographs of children in specific situations, along with puppets and role plays, to promote children's emotion understanding. In this intervention, photographs of children with different facial expressions were used to encourage children to understand emotion cues. Children were encouraged to use self-talk to control their anger and frustration (e.g., "I will take three deep breaths to calm down"). In addition, teach- ing children how to solve social conflicts and how to communicate with others about feelings, modeling, role plays, and group discussions were associated with increased social-emotional competence as well as less peer-directed aggression. Similar outcomes are reported from curriculum intervention studies using *The Incredible Years Parents, Teachers and Children's Training Series* (http://www.incredible years.com; see also Webster-Stratton, 2000; Chapter 9, this volume).

Although no data exist about the long-term influences of these interventions on children's emotional or social development, these classroom-based interven- tions were effective in encouraging children to talk about their emotions rather than using aggression and in helping children understand how to deal successfully with either ambiguous or uncomfortable social situations. These intervention studies clearly demonstrate that professional development may lead to changes in teachers' behaviors that, in turn, are associated with improvement in children's social-emotional competence.

DEVELOPING RELATIONSHIPS AND INTERACTING EFFECTIVELY WITH PEERS AND ADULTS

Peer-related social competence includes preschool children's ability to "initiate and sustain interactions with others, to resolve conflicts, to build friendships, and to achieve related interpersonal goals" (Guralnick & Neville, 1997, p. 579). Developmental abilities, including language, cognitive, and motor skills, and individual characteristics such as temperament are integrated in support of relationships with others. Of particular importance for preschool children are the abilities to join in play with peers and to engage in positive interactions with classmates (Guralnick & Neville, 1997).

Preschool children's interactions with peers are often brief, and young children spend substantial amounts of play time finding new play partners (Corsaro, 1985). The strategies that a child uses to enter a playgroup are strongly related to others' responses and to the likelihood that the child will be included in play. Friendly entry attempts, such as social actions or information questions, are more likely to be met with a positive response from the group than are controlling responses (Ramsey & Lasquade, 1996). In general, children are more successful at entering a group of peers if they understand and are able to share that group's frame of reference instead of trying to divert the group's attention to themselves (Putallaz & Gottman, 1981). In order to share the peer group's perspective, children must understand and balance their own wants and needs with those of their peers in the group that they wish to join. These social tasks require both emotion understanding and emotion regulation. Children also need to understand others' desires and to engage in appropriate exchanges (e.g., synchronous behaviors with group members, information exchanges, utterances connected to group conversation, sharing) that may be mutually rewarding for themselves and their playmates (Dodge, Pettit, McClaskey, & Brown, 1986; Ladd et al., 1999; Putallaz & Gottman, 1981). These social exchanges, along with an understanding of social norms and group expectations, connect children to their peers and make it more likely that children will be successful in entering group play (Dodge et al., 1986; Gagnon & Nagle, 2004).

Children's social behavior that does not consider others' perspectives (e.g., grabbing, rejecting rules, attention seeking, unrelated utterances) undermines peer group goals and can create an adversarial climate (Ladd et al., 1999; Putallaz & Gottman, 1981). Not surprisingly, younger as well as older children who understand and follow social norms and group expectations, instead of being disruptive or disagreeable, tend to be viewed positively and have more positive interactions with their peers (Corsaro, 2005).

Likewise, teachers respond to children's negative emotions and behaviors. Teachers report that it is difficult to teach children who engage in aggressive and antisocial behaviors. Teachers are less likely to provide positive feedback to children who are aggressive (Raver, 2002). When children are aggressive, teachers spend more of their time in interactions that are focused on behavior management and there are fewer adult–child interactions related to learning activities (Doctoroff et al., 2006). Moreover, when teacher–child relationships are characterized by conflict, teachers often respond with attempts to control children's behavior, making it more difficult to provide a positive school environment for them (Hamre & Pianta, 2001). As a consequence, young children who experience rejection from their peers and negative feedback from their teachers tend to dislike school and attend school less often than other children (Raver, 2002). In contrast, children who have secure, positive relationships with their teachers are reported to be less hostile, less withdrawn, and to engage in more prosocial behaviors than their counterparts (Howes, 2000; Howes, Hamilton, & Matheson, 1994).

Specific classroom and program features support the development of positive adult and peer relationships. Howes and Ritchie (2002) suggested that clear, consistent, and predictable classroom routines help children learn that teachers can be trusted. Child care teachers who are with the same group of children for an extended period of time tend to engage in more positive and attentive interactions with those children (Raikes, 1993). Children enrolled in programs in which teacher turnover is frequent have fewer opportunities to develop supportive social relationships with their teachers. Unfortunately for emerging relationships between teachers and children, child care teachers are less likely than elementary school teachers to remain with a group of children for 1 complete school year. Personnel turnover occurs, at least in part, because child care teachers' compensation is relatively low in comparison with that provided in other employment opportunities (Whitebook & Sakai, 2003).

Specific classroom features also support children's social relationships with peers. Substantial evidence from research with older children and adults and some evidence from research with preschool children indicates that teachers' intentional and frequent use of cooperative learning groups is associated with increases in children's peer relationships (Battisch, Schaps, Watson, & Solumon, 1996). It may be that including "the peer group as part of the learning process" (Howes & Ritchie, 2002, p. 100), as occurs in teacher-planned cooperative learning activities, reinforces the importance of positive peer relationships, for both children and adults.

FEATURES OF EARLY CHILDHOOD
CLASSROOMS THAT SUPPORT
CHILDREN'S SOCIAL AND EMOTIONAL DEVELOPMENT

Substantial evidence indicates positive associations between participation in high quality preschool programs and social-emotional development for children who are typically developing and children who are at-risk for school failure, particularly children from low-income families and communities (e.g., Reynolds, Temple, Robertson, & Mann, 2001). Programs that have better adult–child ratios and smaller group sizes,[2] and that focus on the development of positive social relationships between teachers and children, are associated with positive child outcomes, including higher levels of sociability and self-regulation, better peer relations, and lower

---

[2] The National Association for the Education of Young Children's Academy for Early Childhood Program Accreditation (2005) recommends group sizes no larger than 18 children and an adult–child ratio of 1:9 for classrooms of 3-year-olds and group sizes no larger than 20 children and an adult–child ratio of 1:10 for classrooms of 4- and 5-year-olds.

rates of behavior problems (Boyd et al., 2005; Votruba-Drzal, Coley, & Chase-Lansdale, 2004). However, in analyses of data from the NICHD Study of Early Child Care, the number of hours spent in nonmaternal care was associated with teacher ratings of problem behaviors in later grades; namely, children who spent more time in child care over their first 4½ years had slightly higher teacher ratings of problem behavior in kindergarten through sixth grade when compared with ratings of children who attended fewer hours or no preschool (Belsky et al., 2007; NICHD ECCRN, 2003). Nevertheless, the effect sizes were modest and the practical importance of these findings is not yet apparent.

Many characteristics of early childhood classrooms have been associated with children's social competence. These classroom features include 1) overall quality, 2) the balance between child-initiated and teacher-directed activities, 3) teacher educational attainment, 4) teacher–child ratio, 5) teacher compensation, and 6) classroom structure (e.g., Cost, Quality, and Outcomes Study Team, 1995; Lamb, 1998; NICHD ECCRN, 2002). Recent evidence suggests that features such as small group sizes, better teacher–child ratios, and higher levels of teacher educational attainment may be associated with differences in teachers' approaches to instruction, which are then related to higher levels of children's social competence. For example, results from the NICHD Early Child Care Research Network (2002) provided evidence that aspects of classroom environments, including teacher warmth and responsiveness to children, positive regard of children, and cognitive stimulation with children mediate the relationship between measures of child care structural quality such as class size, teacher–child ratio, and teacher education and preschool children's developmental and educational outcomes. These findings, along with others, suggest that the ways in which teachers organize their classrooms and interact with children may be especially important for promoting the development of young children's social competence with peers and adults (see Howes, 2000).

Activities that support creative and pretend play have been associated with higher levels of social play and greater frequency of child–child conversation, for children with and children without disabilities (e.g., Kontos, Burchinal, Howes, Wisseh, & Galinsky, 2002; Odom, Peterson, McConnell, & Ostrosky, 1990; although see Kontos & Keyes, 1999, for different findings). There is not yet sufficient evidence, however, to make claims about the value of specific activities for promoting social development (e.g., block play versus art).

Children's close relationships with their teachers are also associated with positive social and academic outcomes. Children who have a close, positive relationship with their teachers show higher levels of overall school adjustment and may be particularly motivated to succeed in school (Hamre & Pianta, 2001; Pianta, Steinberg, & Rollins, 1995). Conversely, teachers' reports of conflicts in relationships with students are associated with increases in children's problem behaviors and decreases in competent behaviors (Pianta et al., 1995). Hamre and Pianta reported that kindergarten teachers' reports of negativity in their relationships with students "uniquely predicted student grades, standardized test scores, and [student] work habits through lower elementary grades" (2001, p. 634).

The quality of the teacher–child relationship reflects not only teachers' sensitivity to their students but also children's ability to engage with the instructional resources in the classroom environment (Entwisle & Hayduk, 1988). For example, observational studies in kindergarten classrooms suggest that sensitivity to children, including anticipation of students' emotions, timely response to children's needs, and frequency of feedback are important in supporting children's academic and social competence at school (Pianta, LaParo, Payne, Cox, & Bradley, 2002).

Relationships between the intensity and responsiveness of teachers' interactions with children and children's social behaviors have been investigated in a number of studies. Kontos and Wilcox-Herzog (1997) found that teacher involvement was positively associated with children's social behaviors. In most other studies, however, teachers' involvement in children's play is either unrelated or negatively related to children's social behaviors (e.g., Kontos et al., 2002; Kontos, Hsu, & Dunn, 1994; Kontos & Keyes, 1999). Several researchers speculate that the negative relationship between teachers' involvement and children's social behaviors reflects the likely tendency for teachers to be more involved with children who possess less-sophisticated social skills (Kontos & Wilcox-Herzog, 1997). Coplan and Prakash (2003) explored this possibility in a recent study in which they examined the social-emotional characteristics of children who tended to interact frequently with their teachers. The results of their observational study provided evidence that children who frequently initiated interactions with their teachers were also children who engaged in more aggressive behaviors with their peers. Children who frequently elicited teachers' initiations were children who were more shy and anxious than their peers. These findings complement those of Harper and McCluskey (2003), who found that teachers in inclusive preschool classrooms were more likely to initiate interactions when children were alone, whereas teachers were less likely to initiate interactions when children were with peers. Taken together, the results of these studies suggest that teachers may be less likely to interrupt children's positive interactions with peers but more likely to intervene when children are not involved in peer-related social play.

APPROACHES TO SOCIAL-EMOTIONAL COMPETENCE IN TWO PRESCHOOL CURRICULA

The previous discussion suggests that many experiences typically included in early childhood programs support children's social-emotional development. Social-emotional competence is an important component of development that ought to be addressed in early care and education programs (National Research Council, 2001). The authors of many comprehensive preschool curricula (i.e., curricula designed to support development in multiple domains) provide some attention to the ways in which their particular curriculum supports the development of young children's social-emotional competence. Joseph and Strain (2003) reported, however, that all curricula developed to teach young children social-emotional skills have been implemented only with children exhibiting problem behavior or children who are at risk of developing problem behaviors.

In the next section we examine how children might learn important social-emotional competencies in two common, comprehensive curricula: *The Creative Curriculum*® (Dodge, Colker, & Heroman, 2002) and *The High/Scope Curriculum*® (Hohmann & Weikart, 1995). We chose to focus on these two curricula because they are in widespread use in early childhood programs and have been employed more often in Head Start programs than have any other curricula (Shaul et al., 2003).

The Creative Curriculum

The first edition of *The Creative Curriculum*, published in 1978, was based on the idea that "helping teachers to organize their rooms into interest areas" was a critical component of curriculum (Dodge et al., 2002, p. xiii). High-interest areas such as blocks, library, and dramatic play provided much of the developmental content for children's learning, whereas child-initiated, child-directed play was the process through which learning occurred. This approach is similar to that reflected in the first position statement on Developmentally Appropriate Practice (DAP) published by the National Association for the Education of Young Children (Bredekamp, 1987).

The Creative Curriculum: Fourth Edition® (Dodge et al., 2002) maintains the original focus on interest areas as the context for learning while increasing attention to teachers' roles in engaging children in learning activities. Goals and objectives are identified for four developmental areas (social-emotional, physical, cognitive, and language development) and standards are provided for six content areas (literacy, mathematics, science, social studies, the arts, and technology). These goals, objectives, and standards are linked to classroom interest areas. The curriculum then helps teachers identify the competencies that children acquire as they play in each interest area.

Social-emotional development is organized around three goals: 1) sense of self (including emotion understanding and expression), 2) responsibility for self and others (including self-direction), and 3) prosocial behavior (primarily relationships with peers, including problem solving to resolve conflicts). Two of these three goals (*sense of self, prosocial behavior*) are similar to the social-emotional competencies identified in many states' early learning standards and in the Head Start Outcomes Framework (Administration for Children and Families, 2000). The third goal, *responsibility for self and others,* is less directly connected to early learning standards.

Classroom rules, relationships between teachers and individual children, help for children in making friends, and the teaching of problem-solving skills are the contexts within which teachers support children's social-emotional development. Friendship skills, including establishing contact, maintaining a positive relationship, and successfully negotiating conflicts, are identified as important developmental competencies that children learn through participation in a classroom using *The Creative Curriculum.*

Relatively limited attention is devoted to the ways in which teachers may or may not use specific instructional strategies to support children's development of social-emotional competence. Rather, the curriculum provides examples of behaviors that reflect increasing competence for each of the objectives within each developmental goal. For example, the ability to recognize and express one's own feelings and manage them appropriately is one of the objectives under the social-emotional goal, *sense of self.* Examples of children's behaviors that reflect this objective range from forerunners (e.g., crying to express displeasure) to behaviors that reflect competence (e.g., choosing to go to a quiet area to be alone when upset). The curriculum provides examples of the ways in which these competencies might develop as children participate in different classroom interest centers. For example, a child might use a hammer at the woodworking bench when she is angry with a classmate or comment about the way she feels during a music and movement activity; however, no specific instructional strategies are provided.

Teachers are encouraged to make informal and formal observations of children's behavior using the developmental continuum provided for each of the developmental areas. Teachers are to reflect on children's behaviors relative to curriculum objectives and to encourage children's development of more-complex skills. The authors of the curriculum note that direct teaching may be appropriate at times, but no guidance is provided to help teachers decide when or how to use more teacher-directed instruction. There is, as well, no information about effective strategies for teaching either academic or developmental skills, including skills that support children's emotion understanding or peer group participation (Dodge et al., 2002).

The Creative Curriculum is linked to constructivist theories about how young children learn and to early childhood teaching practices supported by national organizations such as the NAEYC. Nevertheless, to date we have been unable to find published research evidence to demonstrate the effectiveness of this curriculum as compared with other curricula used in preschool programs in supporting children's social, developmental, or academic competencies. We note, however, that *The Creative Curriculum* is included in several ongoing preschool curriculum evaluation research projects funded by the Institute of Education Sciences of the U.S. Department of Education. More information about its efficacy in supporting young children's development may be forthcoming as these projects are completed and reported.

The *High/Scope Curriculum*

The *High/Scope Curriculum* is a cognitively oriented curriculum for preschool children developed in the 1970s and based on the constructivist educational theories of Piaget and Dewey (Hohmann & Weikart, 1995). The foundation for the curriculum is the understanding that children's active learning and their creation of new understandings from reflection on their direct, immediate experiences is the "means by which children construct social, emotional, intellectual and physical knowledge" (Hohmann & Weikart, 1995, p. 43). Although the curriculum has been revised from the 1970s to the 2000s, active learning remains its central focus.

Positive adult–child interaction is critical in this curriculum for supporting children's learning, and adults are encouraged to engage in positive interactions with children throughout the school day. The curriculum places a strong emphasis on classroom settings, with classroom layouts and materials organized into high-interest centers. In addition to setting arrangements, the "plan–do–review process" is an important component of children's daily routines. This process is one in which teachers help children plan what they will do and then reflect on their actions, helping children "to consider the meaning of their experiences and ideas…[and to] think about what they have done in the abstract" (Hohmann & Weikart, 1995, p. 226). The curriculum developers suggest that this process helps children become better able to solve problems on their own.

The *High/Scope Curriculum* includes 58 key experiences described as those that "young children encounter repeatedly…," which are "essential for the development of the fundamental abilities that emerge during early childhood" (Hohmann & Weikart, 1995, p. 23). These key experiences, now referred to as key developmental indicators (High/Scope, 2007), are grouped into ten categories: 1) approaches to learning; 2) language, literacy, and communication; 3) social and emotional development, 4) physical development, health and well-being, 5) mathematics, 6) science and technology, 7) social studies, 8) visual art, 9) dramatic art, and 10) music. There is a range of 2 (social studies) to 12 (mathematics, science) indicators within each category. Five key indicators reflect children's social and emotional development. Three of these indicators (*building relationships with children and adults, creating and experiencing collaborative play, dealing with social conflict*) focus on relationships with peers and adults in the context of groups, and one indicator (*expressing feelings in words*) addresses the development of emotional competence. These four indicators reflect skills similar to those identified in many states' early learning standards. An additional key indicator, taking care of one's own needs, does not appear in social-emotional competence components of most early learning standards documents. Emotion regulation, an important contributor to young children's social competence, is not a direct component of any of these key indicators, although it is reflected in expressing feelings and dealing with social conflict (High/Scope Educational Research Foundation, 2007).

A safe and supportive classroom environment and a positive child–teacher relationship are identified as important features of the curriculum that support children's social and emotional development. Specific teaching strategies are provided for key indicators, including the nine key indicators focused on social and emotional development (Graves, 2002). These teaching strategies progress from less- to more-active interventions and include expressing and maintaining interest in children's ideas, giving children time to generate their own solutions, encouraging children's active participation throughout the day, and providing age-appropriate assistance and support (e.g., acknowledging children's feelings, allowing children to hold a familiar adult's hand or letting children sit on the teachers' laps to help them gain control in upsetting situations). Teachers are encouraged to use their observations of children's behavior as a tool for supporting children's developing social relationships (e.g., children who regularly play together are purposely grouped for planning and recall activities or teachers ask children to plan whom they intend to play with that day).

The curriculum provides specific steps, adapted from the conflict-resolution literature, to help children resolve disagreements with peers. In this problem-solving approach, teachers are instructed to 1) approach the situation calmly, 2) recognize children's feelings, 3) restate the problem according to what the children say, 4) ask children for ideas for solutions, 5) restate the suggested solution, 6) encourage children to act on their decisions, and 7) give follow-up support.

This approach to teaching problem-solving skills is similar to that provided in *The Incredible Years Parents, Teachers, and Children's Training Series* (http://www.incredibleyears.com; see also Webster-Stratton, 2000). *The Incredible Years* is a curriculum designed to prevent preschool children's problem behaviors and problem-solving strategies are taught to children on a regular basis outside of the context of a conflict (e.g., daily at circle time). In contrast, the *High/Scope Curriculum* emphasizes the use of these steps to solve an ongoing conflict, reflecting the importance of active learning within the context of key indicators.

Evidence for the effectiveness of *The High/Scope Curriculum* in supporting children's academic and social competence, both during preschool and in subsequent years, has been published in peer-reviewed journals. For example, longitudinal studies of the Perry Preschool Project indicate that children enrolled in the original cognitive curriculum, which was very similar to The *High/Scope Curriculum,* had more positive social and academic outcomes as adults than children in a nonintervention comparison group (Schweinhart & Weikart, 1997). As Golbeck (2002) noted, however, this widely reported and referenced study was performed by the developers of the curriculum with a relatively limited sample of children who were initially recruited in the 1970s. The results must be viewed with caution and not overgeneralized. Indeed, most early childhood curricula, even those with supporting evidence, need to be implemented and evaluated with more diverse samples of children and teachers in more varied circumstances (see Guralnick, 1997).

RECOMMENDATIONS FOR RESEARCH AND PRACTICE RELATED TO EARLY CHILDHOOD CURRICULA

Many researchers suggest that we have a much better understanding of the relationships among peer-related social behaviors, emotional competence, and outcomes for young children than of the ways in which social and emotional competencies are effectively supported or taught in early childhood classrooms (see Howes & James, 2002). The best evidence for the effectiveness of specific social-emotional competence interventions comes from evaluations of well-specified social-emotional curricula that have been evaluated in programs for young children who are at risk for problem behaviors. In a recent evaluation of 10 social-emotional preschool curricula, Joseph and Strain (2003) found that evidence for the effectiveness of the interventions was often less than compelling. In addition, the reviewed social-emotional competence curricula "often compete for teachers' and administrators' attention with other, more 'academic-directed' curricula" (Joseph & Strain, 2003, p. 74). It is not surprising that such focused social-emotional curricula are not common in early childhood programs designed for children who are typically developing. Given recent reports that significant numbers of children are expelled from preschool programs each year, primarily because of behavior problems (Gilliam, 2005), it may be that curricula designed to teach social and emotional competence will become more common in future years. In the final section of this chapter, we make several recommendations for research related to children's social and emotional development in early childhood classroom contexts.

Identifying Features of Early Childhood Programs that Support Children's Social-Emotional Competence

Evidence from observational studies indicates that warm, positive, and supportive relationships between children and their teachers are associated with higher levels of social-emotional competence. The likelihood that children will develop a close relationship with their teachers may be enhanced if children remain in a group with the same adults for at least 1 year (Cryer et al., 2005). This recommendation suggests that program practices that support stability of classroom groups—with attenuated teacher turnover and a consistent group of peers—are likely to be important in supporting young children's social and emotional competence.

The number of children in classrooms may also be an important factor that supports more-positive outcomes for young children. In a study of English infant schools (i.e., 4- to 7-year-old children), smaller group size was associated with increased one-to-one teaching episodes, more active involvement in child–teacher interaction, and more teaching by teachers (Blatchford, Moriarty, Edmonds, &

Martin, 2002). Similar associations between class size and teaching practices were reported for first-grade classrooms in the United States, with positive associations found between children's positive social behaviors and relatively smaller class sizes. Specifically, children in classes with fewer children showed higher levels of social skills, less problem behavior, and more teacher–child closeness (NICHD ECCRN, 2004).

The field of early childhood education needs a better understanding of how structural features of early childhood programs such as group stability, group size, and teacher–child ratio contribute to important developmental and educational outcomes for young children. Whereas randomized trials may be extremely difficult and may not be feasible, quasi-experimental designs that systematically vary group size and ratio in classrooms serving children from similar neighborhoods or communities might be informative about the ways in which structural features of classrooms in combination with child and teacher behaviors are associated with positive social and academic outcomes.

Understanding Relationships Between Social Competence Interventions and Academic Outcomes

Significant associations between social and academic competence have been reported in studies of children in preschool and in the early elementary grades (e.g., Doctoroff et al., 2006); however, relations between social-emotional competence *interventions* and academic achievement (e.g., language, numeracy, literacy) have yet to be examined carefully. One might hypothesize, for instance, that language-based social problem-solving interventions might promote children's language and cognitive as well as social and emotional competence. There may be indirect influences, as when social competence interventions lead to more-positive interactions among children and teachers, resulting in higher levels of instructional interactions with teachers and developmentally enhancing exchanges with peers. This appears to be a particularly fruitful area for research in programs designed for children who are developing typically but who are at elevated risk for school failure and behavioral problems, particularly in publicly funded programs such as Head Start or state prekindergarten programs (Zill & West, 2001).

Emotional Competence Interventions in Early Childhood Classrooms

Researchers have identified how emotional competence characteristics—specifically positive emotion expression, emotion understanding, and emotion regulation—are related to social competence in young children who are mostly from White, middle-income families (Denham et al., 2003). It is as yet unknown whether similar relations might be found for children from different cultural, racial, ethnic, and socioeconomic groups. The ways in which positive emotions foster socially competent behaviors is an emerging area of research (Denham et al., 2003). Information is urgently needed to identify effective adult supports for young children's emotional competence. Children's uncontrolled negativity appears to be particularly salient to peers and teachers and is particularly problematic for younger girls (Crick, Casas, & Mosher, 1997). Basic developmental research that sheds light on precursors of emotional competence as well as systematic evaluations of promising classroom interventions is warranted.

Our review of curricula and of the literature on classroom interventions suggests that, until very recently, scant attention has been given to specific curricula and practices designed to promote children's underlying emotional competencies. Specifically, emotion understanding and emotion regulation are represented to a much more limited degree in comprehensive preschool curricula and in states' standards than are interactions with peers (Scott-Little et al., 2006). We know much less about effective and efficient approaches to helping children acquire these social skills within the context of group settings. Whereas social-emotional competence curricula often include attention to understanding one's own and others' feelings as well as self-regulation (e.g., *The Incredible Years*), evidence about the effectiveness of interventions that promote children's development of emotion understanding and regulation and peer-related social competence is limited for children who are not identified as at risk.

Effective Teaching Strategies

Many suggestions have been offered for ways in which teachers can support young children's social-emotional development. These include reading books that focus on social relationships and friendships, using guidance and problem-solving strategies to resolve conflicts between children, and planning opportunities for cooperative learning (e.g., Kemple, 2004). Nevertheless, we found very limited evidence for the effectiveness of these or any other instructional interventions that support children's social-emotional competence.

Results of observations in preschool settings suggest that teachers may be more likely to interact with young children who are not currently engaged in interactions with peers (Harper & McCluskey, 2003; Kontos & Wilcox-Herzog, 1997). There is considerable evidence from intervention studies in classrooms for young children with developmental delays that specific behavior strategies, including prompting, praising, and direct social skills training interventions, may increase peer interactions for children with disabilities (e.g., Brown, Odom, & Conroy, 2001; Diamond, 2002; Odom, McConnell, & McEvoy, 1999). Nevertheless, comparable research on effective teacher-directed interventions to support engagement in children who are typically developing within their peer groups is lacking. Given the many demands on teachers' time, it is unlikely that they will use intensive interventions in classrooms for preschool children who are typically developing, in which teacher–child ratios are often 1 adult for every 8–10 children. Moreover, recent information indicates that even many early childhood special educators continue to be reluctant to use more intensive and explicit social skills training intervention procedures (West, Brown, Grego, & Johnson, in press). Nonetheless, there are many widely used and well-accepted teaching strategies, including cooperative learning and teacher-planned groupings, that may be effective in promoting children's social and emotional competence and whose use should be evaluated systematically in classrooms for young children.

Classroomwide Interventions

In our experience, most early childhood classrooms include one or two children whose interactions with peers are more negative than those of others, and much of the attention these children receive from teachers focuses on managing problem behaviors. Because peer-related social competence is not only a characteristic of an individual but also is reflected in interactions within the peer group, we suggest that interventions or curricula designed to support social competence should include classroomwide interventions. As others have noted, a high-quality classroom is a necessary condition for implementing developmental interventions for individual children or groups (Brown et al., 2001; Kemple, 2004). General teaching practices that support children's social competence include the development of positive relationships and the provision of a physical environment that supports children's play and exploration individually and within small groups (Hyson et al., 2006; Kemple, 2004).

An example of a novel, classroomwide intervention can be found in a recent study by Harrist and Bradley (2003). In a book about social relationships in a kindergarten classroom, Vivian Paley, the classroom teacher, describes the effects of a new rule, "You can't say you can't play," on children's behaviors. This rule was created in response to her many years of observation that "by kindergarten...certain children have the right to limit the social experiences of their classmates...[they] notify others of their acceptability, and the outsiders learn to anticipate the sting of rejection" (1992, p. 3). In their study, Harrist and Bradley (2003) evaluated the effectiveness of a "You can't say you can't play" rule-based intervention, adapted from Paley's book, for social relationships among children in kindergarten. Partial random assignment was used in assigning classrooms to either the intervention (N=6) or control (N=4) groups. Most children were Euro-American (57%) and Mexican-American (34%). Storytelling and group discussions were used to introduce the "You can't say you can't play" rule in intervention classrooms after the winter break. Banners reminding children of the rule were displayed in each classroom and children were given bookmarks with the rule to take home. Teachers reinforced the rule throughout the day. The results of the intervention were mixed, with children in intervention classrooms significantly more likely than children in control classes to report that they liked to play with classmates at the end of the school year. This finding, which reflected children's reports, was not replicated in analyses of observational or teacher-reported data. It may be that the intervention led to changes in children's attitudes rather than in their behaviors toward peers or that the observational measures were not sensitive to behavior change. There was also some evidence that overall dissatisfaction was higher in intervention classrooms, suggesting, perhaps, that some children believed that playing is not as much fun if anyone can participate. Despite the limitations of this study, we suggest that interventions such as this hold promise, particularly if coupled with approaches designed to help children acquire social skills necessary for successful and satisfying interactions with their peers.

CONCLUSIONS

Characteristics of individual children, including emotion understanding and emotion regulation, support the development of positive interactions with peers and with teachers. There is substantial evidence that children who develop positive relationships with others are more likely to have success both academically and socially. This success in social interactions begins before preschool and extends into the early elementary years.

Qualities of early childhood programs, including structural features such as stability, group size, and teacher–child ratio and process features, including the warmth and closeness of the relationships between teachers and children, contribute to children's developing social and emotional competence. Evidence from interventions in programs for young children who are at risk suggests that children can learn, and teachers can teach, effective, prosocial strategies for solving problems and interacting with peers and adults. Nevertheless, to date, there is negligible evidence of the effectiveness of specific comprehensive preschool curricula in supporting children's development of emotion competence and positive interactions with peers.

A number of challenges and opportunities face early childhood researchers, policy makers, and educators who are concerned about children's social-emotional development. Although the policy emphasis of the early 2000s is focused on supporting preschool children's development of skills in literacy and mathematics, this emphasis does not necessarily conflict directly with concerns about social-emotional development. It is likely that social and emotional competence interventions can have both direct and indirect consequences for children's development in other areas, particularly when interventions are implemented in supportive classroom environments. Identifying these relationships and the ways in which teachers' instructional interactions support children's development and learning in multiple domains is among the most important tasks that face the early childhood field.

REFERENCES

Administration for Children and Families (2000). *The Head Start child outcomes framework.* Retrieved January 26, 2006, from http://www.headstartinfo.org/leaders_guideeng/part2c.htm

Battisch, V., Schaps, E., Watson, M., & Solumon, D. (1996). Preventative effects of the Child Development Project: Early findings from an ongoing multi-site demonstration trial. *Journal of Adolescent Research, 11,* 12–35.

Belsky, J., Vandell, D., Burchinal, M., Clarke-Stewart, K.A., McCartney, K., Tresch-Owen, M., & The NICHD Early Child Care Research Network (2007). Are there long-term effects of early child care? *Child Development, 78,* 681–701.

Blatchford, P., Moriarty, V., Edmonds, S., & Martin, C. (2002). Relationships between class size and teaching: A multimethod analysis of English infant schools. *American Educational Research Journal, 39,* 101–132.

Boyd, J., Barnett, W.S., Bodrova, E., Leong, D.J., Gomby, D., Robin, K.B., & Hustedt, J.T. (2005). *Policy report: Promoting children's social and emotional development through preschool.* National Institute for Early Education Research. Retrieved January 27, 2006, from http://nieer.org/docs/index.php?DocID=125

Bredekamp, S. (1987). *Developmentally appropriate practices in early childhood programs serving children from birth through age 8.* Washington, D.C.: National Association for the Education of Young Children.

Brown, W.H., Odom, S.L., & Conroy, M.A. (2001). An intervention hierarchy for promoting young children's peer interactions in natural environments. *Topics in Early Childhood Special Education, 21,* 162–175.

Cassidy, J., Parke, R.D., Butkovsky, L., & Braungart, J.M. (1992). Family–peer connections: The roles of emotional expressiveness within the family and children's understanding of emotions. *Child Development, 63,* 603–618.

Committee on the Prevention of Reading Difficulties in Young Children (1998). *Preventing reading difficulties in young children.* C.E. Snow, M.S. Burns, & P. Griffin (Eds). Washington, DC: National Academies Press.

Coplan, R.J., & Prakash, K. (2003). Spending time with teacher: Characteristics of preschoolers who frequently elicit versus initiate interactions with teachers. *Early Childhood Research Quarterly, 18,* 143–158.

Corsaro, W. (1985). *Friendship and peer culture in the early years*. Norwood, NJ: Ablex.

Corsaro, W. (2005). *The sociology of childhood* (2nd Ed.). Thousand Oaks, CA: Sage Publications.

Cost, Quality, and Outcomes Study Team. (1995). *Cost, quality, and child outcomes in child care centers: Technical report*. Denver: Economics Department, University of Colorado at Denver.

Crick, N.R., Casas, J.F., & Mosher, M. (1997). Relational and overt aggression in preschool. *Developmental Psychology, 33,* 579–588.

Cryer, D., Wagner-Moore, L., Burchinal, M., Yazejian, N., Hurwitz, S., & Wolery, M. (2005). Effects of transitions to new child care classes on infant/toddler distress and behavior. *Early Childhood Research Quarterly, 20,* 37–56.

Denham, S.A., Blair, K.A., DeMulder, E., Levitas, J., Sawyer, K., Auerbach-Major, S., et al. (2003). Preschool emotional competence: Pathway to social competence? *Child Development, 74,* 238–256.

Denham, S.A., & Holt, R.W. (1993). Preschooler's likability as cause or consequence of their social behavior. *Developmental Psychology, 29,* 271–275.

Denham, S.A., McKinley, M., Couchoud, E.A., & Holt, R. (1990). Emotional and behavioral predictors of preschool peer ratings. *Child Development, 61,* 1145–1152.

Diamond, K. (2002). The development of social competence in children with disabilities. In P.K. Smith & C.H. Hart (Eds.), *Blackwell handbook of childhood social development* (pp. 571–587). Malden, MA: Blackwell Publishing.

Doctoroff, G.L., Greer, J.A., & Arnold, D.H. (2006). Gender differences in the relationship between social behavior and emergent literacy among preschoolers. *Journal of Applied Developmental Psychology, 27,* 1–13.

Dodge, D.T., Colker, L.J., & Heroman, C. (2002). *The Creative Curriculum for Preschool* (4th Ed.) Washington, DC: Teaching Strategies.

Dodge, K.A., Lansford, J.E., Burks, V.S., Bates, J.E., Pettit, G.S., Fontaine, R., et al. (2003). Peer rejection and social information-processing factors in the development of aggressive behavior problems in children. *Child Development, 74,* 374–393.

Dodge, K.A., Pettit, G.S., McClaskey, C.L., & Brown, M.M. (1986). Social competence in children. *Monographs of the Society for Research in Child Development, 51*(2, Serial No. 213).

Eisenberg, N., Guthrie, I.K., Fabes, R.A., Reiser, M., Murphy, B.C., Holgren, R., et al. (1997). The relations of regulation and emotionality to resiliency and competent social functioning in elementary school children. *Child Development, 68,* 295–311.

Entwisle, D.R., & Hayduk, L.A. (1988). Lasting effects of elementary school. *Sociology of Education, 61*(3), 147–159.

Fabes, R.A., Eisenberg, N., Jones, S., Smith, M., Guthrie, I., Poulin, R., et al. (1999). Regulation, emotionality, and preschoolers' socially competent peer interactions. *Child Development, 70,* 432–442.

Gagnon, S.G., & Nagle, R.J. (2004). Relationships between peer interactive play and social competence in at–risk preschool children. *Psychology in the Schools, 41,* 173–189.

Gilliam, W.S. (2005). *Prekindergarteners left behind: Expulsion rates in state prekindergarten systems.* Foundation for Child Development. Retrieved February 1, 2006, from http://www.fcd-us.org/ourwork/f-expulsion.html

Golbeck, S.L. (2002). *Instructional models for early childhood education.* (ERIC Digest. Document Reproduction Service No. ED468565)

Graves, M. (2002). *High/Scope preschool key experiences: Initiative and social relations.* Ypsilanti, MI: High/Scope Press.

Guralnick, M.J. (1997). Second-generation research in the field of early intervention. In M.J. Guralnick (Ed.), *The effectiveness of early intervention* (pp. 3–22). Baltimore: Paul H. Brookes Publishing Co.

Guralnick, M.J., & Neville, B. (1997). Designing early intervention programs to promote children's social competence. In M.J. Guralnick (Ed.), *The effectiveness of early intervention* (pp. 579–610). Baltimore: Paul H. Brookes Publishing Co.

Hamre, B.K., & Pianta, R.C. (2001). Early teacher–child relationships and the trajectory of children's school outcomes through eighth grade. *Child Development, 72,* 625–638.

Harper, L.V., & McCluskey, K.S. (2003). Teacher–child and child–child interactions in inclusive preschool settings: Do adults inhibit peer interactions? *Early Childhood Research Quarterly, 18,* 163–184.

Harrist, A.W., & Bradley, K.D. (2003). "You can't say you can't play": Intervening in the process of social exclusion in the kindergarten classroom. *Early Childhood Research Quarterly, 18,* 185–205.

High/Scope Educational Research Foundation (2007). Alignment of High/Scope key developmental indicators and key experiences. Retrieved May 14, 2007, from http://www.highscope.org/EducationalPrograms/preschoolkeyexp.html

Hohmann, M., & Weikart, D.P. (1995). *Educating young children.* Ypsilanti, MI: High/Scope Educational Research Foundation.

Howes, C. (2000). Social-emotional classroom climate in child care, child–teacher relationships and children's second grade peer relations. *Social Development, 9*(2), 191–204.

Howes, C., Hamilton, C.E., & Matheson, C.C. (1994). Children's relationships with peers: Differential associations with aspects of the teacher–children relationship. *Child Development, 65,* 253–263.

Howes, C., & James, J. (2002). Children's social development within the socialization context of childcare and early childhood education. In P.K. Smith & C.H. Hart (Eds.), *Blackwell handbook of childhood social development* (pp. 137–155). Malden, MA: Blackwell Publishing.

Howes, C., & Ritchie, S. (2002). *A matter of trust: Connecting teachers and learners in the early childhood classroom.* New York: Teachers College Press.

Hubbard, J.A., & Coie, J.D. (1994). Emotional correlates of social competence in children's peer relationships. *Merrill-Palmer Quarterly, 40,* 1–20.

Hyson, M. (2004). *The emotional development of young children.* New York: Teachers College Press.

Hyson, M., Copple, C., & Jones, J. (2006). Early childhood development and education. In W. Damon, R. Lerner, K.A. Renninger, & I. Sigel (Eds.), *Handbook of child development, Vol. 4.* (pp. 3-47). New York: Wiley.

Ialongo, N.S., Vaden-Kiernan, N., & Kellam, S. (1998). Early peer rejection and aggression: Longitudinal relations with adolescent behavior. *Journal of Developmental and Physical Disabilities, 10,* 199–213.

Joseph, G.E., & Strain, P.S. (2003). Comprehensive evidence-based social-emotional curricula for young children: An analysis of efficacious adoption potential. *Topics in Early Childhood Special Education, 23,* 65–76.

Kemple, K.M. (2004). *Let's be friends: Peer competence and social inclusion in early childhood programs.* New York: Teachers College Press.

Kontos, S., Burchinal, M., Howes, C., Wisseh, S., & Galinsky, E. (2002). An eco-behavioral approach to examining the contextual effects of early childhood classrooms. *Early Childhood Research Quarterly, 17,* 239–258.

Kontos, S., Hsu, H-C., & Dunn, L. (1994). Children's cognitive and social competence in child-care centers and family day-care homes. *Journal of Applied Developmental Psychology, 15,* 387–411.

Kontos, S., & Keyes, L. (1999). An ecobehavioral analysis of early childhood classrooms. *Early Childhood Research Quarterly, 14,* 35–50.

Kontos, S., & Wilcox-Herzog, A. (1997). Influences on children's competence in early childhood classrooms. *Early Childhood Research Quarterly, 12,* 247–262.

Ladd, G.W., Birch, S.H., & Buhs, E.S. (1999). Children's social and scholastic lives in kindergarten: Related spheres of influence? *Child Development, 70,* 1373–1400.

Ladd, G.W., Kochenderfer, B.J., & Coleman C.C. (1996). Friendship quality as a predictor of young children's early school adjustment. *Child Development, 67,* 1103–1118.

Lamb, M. (1998). Nonparental child care: Context, quality, correlates, and consequences. In I. Sigel & A. Renninger (Vol. Eds.), W. Damon (Series Ed.), *Handbook of child psychology: Vol. 4: Child psychology in practice* (5th ed., pp. 73–133). New York: Wiley.

McMahon, S.D., Washburn, J., Felix, E.D., Yakin, J., & Childrey, G. (2000). Violence prevention: Program effects on urban preschool and kindergarten children. *Applied and Preventive Psychology, 9,* 271–281.

Mendez, J.L., Fantuzzo, J., & Cicchetti, D. (2002) Profiles of social competence among low-income African American preschool children. *Child Development, 73,* 1085–1100.

National Association for the Education of Young Children. (2005). *NAEYC accreditation criteria.* Retrieved April 18, 2006, from http://naeyc.org/accreditation/criteria/teacher_child_ratios.html

National Association for the Education of Young Children/National Association of Early Childhood Specialists in State Departments of Education. (2002). *Early learning standards: Creating the conditions for success.* Retrieved January 27, 2006, from http://naeyc.org/about/positions/school_readiness.asp

National Institute of Child Health and Human Development Early Child Care Research Network. (2002). Child-care structure —> process —> outcome: Direct and indirect effects of child-care quality on young children's development. *Psychological Science, 13,* 199–206.

National Institute of Child Health and Human Development Early Child Care Research Network. (2003). Does amount of time spent in child care predict socioemotional adjustment during the transition to kindergarten? *Child Development, 74,* 976–1005.

National Institute of Child Health and Human Development Early Child Care Research Network. (2004). Does class size in first grade relate to children's academic and social performance or observed classroom processes? *Developmental Psychology, 40,* 651–664.

National Research Council. (2001). *Eager to learn: Educating our preschoolers.* Committee on Early Childhood Pedagogy. In B.T. Bowman, M.S. Donovan, & M.S. Burns (Eds.), Washington, DC: National Academies Press.

Odom, S.L., McConnell, S.R., & McEvoy, M.A. (1999). Relative effects of interventions supporting the social competence of young children with disabilities. *Topics in Early Childhood Special Education, 19(2),* 75–91.

Odom, S.L., Peterson, C., McConnell, S., & Ostrosky, M. (1990). Ecobehavioral analysis of early education/specialized classroom settings and peer social interaction. *Education and Treatment, 13,* 316–330.

Paley, V.G. (1992). *You can't say you can't play.* Cambridge, MA: Harvard University Press.

Pianta, R.C., La Paro, K.M., Payne, C., Cox, M.J., & Bradley, R. (2002). The relation of kindergarten classroom environment to teacher, family, and school characteristics and child outcomes. *Elementary School Journal, 102,* 225–238.

Pianta, R.C., Steinberg, M.S., & Rollins, L.B. (1995). The first two years of school: Teacher–child relationships and deflections in children's classroom adjustment. *Development and Psychopathology, 7,* 295–312.

Putallaz, M., & Gottman, J.M. (1981). An interactional model of children's entry into peer groups. *Child Development, 52,* 986–994.

Raikes, H. (1993). Relationship duration in infant care: Time with a high ability teacher and infant–teacher attachment. *Early Childhood Research Quarterly, 8,* 309–325.

Ramsey, P.G., & Lasquade, C. (1996). Preschool children's entry attempts. *Journal of Applied Developmental Psychology, 17,* 135–150.

Raver, C.C. (2002). Emotions matter: Making the case for the role of young children's emotional development for early school readiness. *Social Policy Report, 16,* 3–18.

Reynolds, A.J., Temple, J., Robertson, D., & Mann, E. (2001). Long-term effects of an early childhood intervention on educational achievement and juvenile arrest: A 15-year follow-up of low-income children in public schools. *Journal of the American Medical Association, 285,* 2339–2346.

Schweinhart, L.J., & Weikart, D.P. (1997) The High/Scope preschool curriculum comparison study through age 23. *Early Childhood Research Quarterly, 12,* 117–143.

Scott-Little, C., Kagan, S.L., & Frelow, V.S. (2003). Creating the conditions for success with early learning standards: Results from a national study of state-level standards for children's learning prior to kindergarten. *Early Childhood Research and Practice: An Internet Journal on the Development, Care, and Education of Young Children, 5(2).* Retrieved from http://ecrp.uiuc.edu/v5n2/little.html

Scott-Little, C., Kagan, S.L., & Frelow, V.S. (2006). Conceptualization of readiness and the content of early learning standards: The intersection of policy and research? *Early Childhood Research Quarterly, 21,* 153–173.

Shaul, M.S., Ward-Zuckerman, B., Edmondson, S., Moy, L., Moriarty, C., & Picyk, E. (2003). *Head Start: Curriculum use and individual child assessment in cognitive and language development. Report to Congressional requesters.* Retrieved January 17, 2006, from http://www.gao.gov/htext/d031049.html

Shonkoff, J.P., & Phillips. D.A. (Eds.) (2000). *From neurons to neighborhoods: The science of early childhood development.* Washington, DC: National Academies Press.

Votruba-Drzal, E., Coley, R.L., & Chase-Lansdale, P.L. (2004). Child care and low-income children's development: Direct and moderated effects. *Child Development, 75,* 296–312.

Webster-Stratton, C. (2000). *The Incredible Years Training Series. Juvenile Justice Bulletin, June, 2000,* 1–23.

Wesley, P.W., & Buysse, V. (2003). Making meaning of school readiness in schools and communities. *Early Childhood Research Quarterly, 18,* 351–375.

West, T.N., Brown, W.H., Grego, J.M., & Johnson, R. (in press). *Practitioners' judgments of peer interaction interventions: A survey of DEC members.*

Whitebook, M., & Sakai, L. (2003). Turnover begets turnover: An examination of job and occupational instability among child care center staff. *Early Childhood Research Quarterly, 18,* 273–293.

Zill, N., & West, J. (2001). *Entering kindergarten: Findings from the Condition of Education 2000.* National Center for Education Statistics, U.S. Department of Education. Retrieved January 31, 2006, from http://nces.ed.gov/pubsearch/pubsinfo.asp?pubid=2001035

Strengthening Social and Emotional Competence in Young Children Who Are Socioeconomically Disadvantaged

Preschool and Kindergarten School-Based Curricula

CAROLYN WEBSTER-STRATTON AND M. JAMILA REID

The Early Childhood Longitudinal Study (ECLS), a nationally representative sample of more than 22,000 kindergarten children, suggests that exposure to multiple poverty-related risks increases the odds that children who are socioeconomically disadvantaged will demonstrate less social and emotional competence and more behavior problems than more economically advantaged children (West, Denton, & Reaney, 2001). Prevalence of social and emotional problems may be as high as 25% for preschool children who are socioeconomically disadvantaged (Rimm-Kaufman, Pianta, & Cox, 2000; Webster-Stratton & Hammond, 1998). These findings are of concern because research has indicated that children's social, emotional, and behavioral adjustment is as important for school success as cognitive and academic preparedness (Raver & Zigler, 1997). Although exposure to poverty does not necessarily lead to social and emotional problems for all children experiencing it, a significant portion of these children experience negative outcomes (Keenan, Shaw, Walsh, Delliquadri, & Giovannelli, 1997). Offord and col-

This research was supported by the National Institute for Mental Health (NIMH) Grant #1 R01 DA 12881-01A1. The senior author of this paper has disclosed a potential financial conflict of interest because she disseminates the *Incredible Years Parents, Teachers and Children's Series* interventions and stands to gain from a favorable report. Because of this, she has voluntarily agreed to distance herself from certain critical research activities (i.e., recruiting, consenting, primary data handling, and analysis) and the University of Washington has approved these arrangements. Correspondence concerning this article should be sent to Carolyn Webster-Stratton, University of Washington, School of Nursing, Parenting Clinic, 1107 NE 45th St. Suite 305, Seattle, WA 98105.

leagues found low income to be a significant risk factor for the early onset of conduct problems and academic deficits (Offord, Alder, & Boyle, 1986). Moreover, longitudinal data have led investigators to suggest that these early gaps in social competence for children who are socioeconomically disadvantaged persist and even widen over time. Researchers have determined that without intervention, early social, emotional, and behavioral problems (particularly aggression and oppositional behavior) are key risk factors or "red flags" marking the beginning of escalating academic problems, grade retention, school dropout, and antisocial behavior (Snyder, 2001; Tremblay, Mass, Pagani, & Vitaro, 1996; see also Chapter 10).

A number of curricula have been designed for children, teachers, and parents to promote children's social-emotional competence and prevent the development of behavior problems. Unfortunately, few of these have focused on preschool children, and most have not been evaluated for low-income and multicultural families. Early intervention, offered at school entry when behavior is most malleable, would seem to be a beneficial and cost-effective means of reducing the gap between these higher risk children and their more advantaged peers. Effective curricula at this strategic developmental stage can interrupt the progression of early social and emotional problems to poor school achievement and later academic failure. Moreover, strengthening protective factors such as young children's capacity to self-regulate emotions and behaviors, problem solve, and make meaningful friendships may help buffer the negative influences associated with impoverished living situations.

SUPPORTIVE PROTECTIVE FACTORS FOR YOUNG CHILDREN WHO ARE SOCIOECONOMICALLY DISADVANTAGED

How, then, do we assure that young children who are socioeconomically disadvantaged and struggling with a range of emotional and social problems receive the added support they need to develop social competence and self-regulatory skills? Parent training, curricula that address social skills, emotion regulation, problem solving, and teacher training address these issues.

Parent Training

Positive and nurturing parenting is one of the most important protective factors associated with children's resilience (Webster-Stratton & Fjone, 1989). Consequently, interventions that work with parents to strengthen positive parenting, enhance parent–child relationships, and reduce coercive and harsh parenting are the most effective means of promoting children's social competence and reducing behavior problems. In addition, positive parenting approaches have been shown to promote children's emotion-regulation skills, ability to manage conflict, and school readiness (Webster-Stratton & Reid, 2005). Parenting that is emotionally positive and that gives attention to pro-social behaviors is associated with self-regulation and conflict management skills. Conversely, researchers have found that children's lower emotional and social competencies are frequently associated with hostile parenting, high family conflict, and high rates of parental attention to negative behaviors (Cummings, 1994; Webster-Stratton & Hammond, 1999). Poverty and its related aggregation of risk factors can have deleterious effects on parenting (Baydar, Reid, & Webster-Stratton, 2003; Webster-Stratton, 1990c). Depressed, economically stressed, and unsupported parents are less likely to provide the cognitive stimulation and supportive parenting necessary to foster their children's academic performance and social behavior.

Parents, particularly those who are stressed and depressed, can find support in parent group programs designed to teach effective parenting and school collaboration strategies. Indeed, parent training programs have been the single-most successful intervention approach to date for reducing aggressive behavior problems and enhancing social competence (Brestan & Eyberg, 1998). A variety of parenting programs have resulted in clinically significant and sustained reductions in aggressive behavior problems for at least two thirds of young children treated (e.g., for review, see Chapter 14). The intervention goals of these programs are to reduce harsh and inconsistent parenting and promote home–school relationships. Experimental studies provide support for social learning theories that highlight the crucial role that parenting style and discipline effectiveness play in improving children's social competence and reducing behavior problems at home and school (Patterson, DeGarmo, & Knutson, 2000). More recently, efforts have been made to adapt these interventions for use as school-based prevention programs. A review of the literature on school-based parenting programs for early school-age children focusing on preventing poor behaviors indicates that this parent-training approach is very promising (Webster-Stratton & Taylor, 2001). Although there is little research available on school-based parenting programs for preschool children from multiethnic backgrounds, the preliminary studies are quite favorable.

Social Skills, Emotion Regulation, and Problem-Solving Curricula

A second approach for children at high risk of developing social difficulties and behavior problems is for teachers to provide direct instruction in social-emotional regulatory skills. This includes implementing social skills curricula focused on building emotional literacy, self-regulatory skills such as anger management and problem solving, and social skills (e.g., Coie & Dodge, 1998). Teaching these skills to young children who are at risk due to socioeconomic disadvantage can provide them with protective skills to help counteract or cope with various life stressors; however, many teachers acknowledge that they have little training in how to deliver social-emotional curricula. It is therefore necessary to provide teachers with training and materials in order to implement evidence-based social and emotional curricula with fidelity.

Teacher Training

A third approach to the problem of escalating behavior difficulties in preschool and kindergarten is to train teachers in the empirically validated classroom management strategies that are proven to enhance social and emotional competence and reduce aggression. Substantial evidence indicates that the way teachers manage misbehavior in the classroom affects children's social and emotional outcomes. Well-trained and supportive teachers who use high levels of praise and encouragement, proactive teaching strategies, and fair discipline, can play an extremely important role in the development of children's social and emotional skills. In fact, Burchinal, Roberts, Hooper, and Zeisel (2000) demonstrated that children from low-income families in high quality child care or preschool settings are significantly better off, cognitively, socially, and emotionally, than are similar children in low quality settings. Children in preschools with low student–teacher relationships, low levels of problem behaviors, and opportunities for positive social interaction are more socially and academically competent during the first 2 years of school than children from disruptive classrooms. Moreover, having a supportive relationship with at least one teacher has been shown to be one of the most important protective factors influencing the later success of children considered high risk (Pianta & Walsh, 1998; Werner, 1999).

Research by Kellam, Ling, Merisca, Brown, and Ialongo (1998), however, showed that poorly managed classrooms have higher levels of overall aggression and rejection, leading to the development of individual children's aggressive behavior. As early as preschool, children with behavior problems and low social competence are less likely to be accepted by teachers, and they receive less academic instruction, support, and positive feedback for appropriate behavior than their peers who behave more appropriately (Arnold et al., 1999; Phillips, Voran, Kisker, Howes, & Whitebrook, 1994). Moreover, teachers are less likely to recognize cognitive competencies in young children whose behaviors they perceive as negative (Phillips et al., 1994). Low teacher emphasis on academics and social skills, low rates of praise and encouragement, and high teacher–student ratios are shown to be related to oppositional behaviors, low social competence, and poor academic performance. Rejecting responses from teachers further exacerbate the problems of children with social and emotional problems. A 1994 survey found that teachers serving children from predominantly low-income homes used significantly more harsh, detached, and insensitive teaching strategies than teachers serving children from middle income families (Phillips, et al, 1994; Stage & Quiroz, 1997). Providing training in effective classroom management is a part of the support necessary for a learning environment in which children can excel in school socially, emotionally, and academically.

This chapter reviews prevention curricula targeted at training parents, teachers, and children to promote young children's social and emotional competence and to decrease problem behaviors. To be included in this review, programs had to meet the following criteria:

1. The program had to include at least one published, randomized controlled group trial documenting effectiveness compared with an alternate intervention or control condition.

2. The program had to have been evaluated with young children (3–6 years of age).

3. Program outcomes had to have included increases in social competence and reductions in children's aggressive behavior.

4. The program could be replicable by others and was required to provide detailed manuals, training, or other curriculum guidelines.

Originally, we had planned to limit the review to programs that had been tested in a school setting with socioeconomically disadvantaged and multiethnic populations; however, we determined that doing so would limit the scope of the review too dramatically. Consequently, some promising programs that met all the other criteria were included even if they had not been tested in school settings with low-income populations. In addition, several exceptional programs that had been evaluated only with older elementary school children are included because they are strong and comprehensive programs that could be considered for use with younger children. These exceptions are noted.

SPECIFIC TRAINING PROGRAMS

The following are descriptions of specific training programs in each of the three supportive/protective areas.

Parent Training Programs

Parent training programs based on cognitive social learning theory can counteract parent and family risk factors by helping parents develop positive relationships with their children and by teaching them to use nonviolent discipline methods that reduce behavior problems and promote social skills, emotional self-regulatory skills, problem-solving ability, and school readiness. These programs also help parents become actively involved in school.

Historically, parent training has not been delivered in the school setting. However, school-based parent programs have several advantages over traditional mental health settings. First, school-based programs are ideally placed to strengthen the parent–teacher–child links. Second, offering parent interventions in schools eliminates the stigma and some of the practical barriers (e.g., transportation, insurance, child care) that can be associated with traditional mental health services. Third, preventive school programs can be offered in early grades before children's minor behavior problems have escalated into severe symptoms that require referral and extensive clinical treatment. Fourth and finally, school-based interventions can reach a large number of families and children at high risk at comparatively low cost. Mounting evidence from several randomized controlled, longitudinal prevention programs shows that multimodal (parent–teacher–child) interventions delivered in schools can significantly lower behavior problems, promote social competence, and increase positive classroom and school atmosphere.(Webster-Stratton & Reid, 2002).

Positive Parenting Program

The *Positive Parenting Program* (*PPP*) is a system of parent interventions designed as a whole population prevention approach that includes low-income families (Sanders & Dadds, 1993). The program's multilevel framework permits one to offer parenting information universally through brief tip sheets or telephone contact for minor problems (level 1); brief advice (80 minutes or 1 to 2 sessions) for a discrete child problem (level 2); more intensive training (10 hours or 4 sessions) for moderate behavior problems (level 3); or individually tailored, group or self-directed programs (8 to 10 sessions) for families with severe child behavior problems (level 4). In addition, enhanced family interventions are provided when parenting difficulties are complicated by other sources of family problems (e.g., marital conflict). The program targets children from birth to adolescence and is offered in a variety of community settings. The *PPP* program is based on social learning models and teaches child management skills. It recognizes the importance of parental cognitions, expectancies, and beliefs as factors relating to self-efficacy and decision making. Marital conflict and parental distress are also targeted for some levels of intervention.

A number of investigators have compared the various levels of intervention in the *PPP* program and their effectiveness for reducing oppositional behavior in young children (Sanders, 1996; Sanders & Christensen, 1985; Sanders & Dadds, 1993; Sanders, Markie-Dadds, Tully, & Bor, 2000). Investigators across studies indicate that the PPP program results in reductions of parent reports of disruptive child behavior. No studies were found evaluating the delivery of the program in preschools or reporting on its effectiveness in promoting social and emotional competence specifically in children who were economically disadvantaged.

Incredible Years Parents, Teachers, and Children's Training Series

The Incredible Years Parents, Teachers, and Children's Training Series is an overarching term for a number of programs comprising what will be referred to here as the *Incredible Years* (*IY;* http://www.incredibleyears.com). It is delivered in a group format and, like *PPP,* it includes child behavior management training as well as other cognitive behavioral and emotional approaches such as mutual problem-solving strategies, self-management principles, and positive self-talk (Webster-Stratton & Hancock, 1998). The content is embedded in a relational framework based on parent group support and a collaborative relationship with the group leader (Webster-Stratton & Herbert, 1994). There are two versions of the *IY* BASIC parent program, one for preschool children (ages 2–6 years) and one for early school-age children (ages 5–10 years). The content of both versions utilizes videotape examples to foster group discussion about child-directed play skills, social and emotional skills coaching, and problem solving as well as behavior management principles including differential attention, encouragement, praise, effective commands, time-out, consequences, monitoring, and problem solving. The school readiness program adds additional training in interactive reading skills, peer social and academic coaching skills, home–school collaboration, and homework. The BASIC program is 12–14 weeks long (2–2½ hours per week). A supplemental ADVANCED program (Webster-Stratton, 1990d) addresses a number of life stressors (depression, marital discord, lack of support, isolation) in greater depth. This program teaches parents to cope with upsetting thoughts and depression, to give and get support, and to communicate and problem solve with partners and teachers. The additional 10- to 14-week program enhances the effects of BASIC by promoting children's and parents' conflict management skills and self-control techniques (Webster-Stratton, 1994).

The efficacy of the *IY* parent program as an intervention program for children (ages 3–8 years) with conduct problems has been demonstrated in eight randomized trials by the developer (e.g., Webster-Stratton, 1981; Webster-Stratton, 1990b, 1994; Webster-Stratton & Hammond, 1997; Webster-Stratton, Reid, & Hammond, 2004). The program also has been replicated for children with conduct problems by four independent investigators (Mørch, Larsson, Clifford, Drugli, & Fossum, 2004; Scott, Spender, Doolan, Jacobs, & Aspland, 2001; Spaccarelli, Cotler, & Penman, 1992; Taylor, Schmidt, Pepler, & Hodgins, 1998).

The BASIC parent program was adapted as a prevention preschool and school-based program and evaluated by the developer and other investigators with low-income, multiethnic families (Barrera et al., 2002; Baydar et al., 2003; Miller

Brotman et al., 2003; Miller & Rojas-Flores, 1999; Reid, Webster-Stratton, & Hammond, in press; Webster-Stratton, 1998). Results in Head Start (Webster-Stratton, 1998; Webster-Stratton, Reid, & Hammond, 2001a) indicated that, following completion of the parent program, mothers who received intervention were more consistent, more nurturing, and less harsh than control mothers. Children considered aggressive whose mothers attended the parent program showed significant reductions in aggression and increases in prosocial behaviors compared with children in a control group. These results were maintained at 1-year follow up. Mothers with mental health risk factors, such as high depressive symptomatology, experience of physical abuse as children, substance abuse, and high levels of anger were able to engage in the program and benefit from it at levels comparable with mothers without these mental health risk factors (Baydar, Reid, & Webster-Stratton, 2003). Parents from various ethnic groups benefited in similar ways (Reid, Webster-Stratton, & Beauchaine, 2001).

Independent investigators have replicated these results in randomized controlled group studies with socioeconomically disadvantaged populations. One evaluated the program with low-income African-American mothers of toddlers in child care (Gross et al., 2003) and the other with low income Sure Start parents in Wales (Hutchings et al., 2007).

Coping Skills Parenting Program: A Community-Based Parenting Program

Another group-based parenting program for parents of young children is the *Coping Skills Parenting Program* developed by Cunningham, Bremner, and Boyle (1995). The curriculum includes strategies related to problem solving, attending to and rewarding prosocial behavior, transitions, "when–then" (i.e., a strategy that teaches children to anticipate problems and come up with solutions), ignoring, disengaging from coercive interactions, advanced planning for difficult situations, and time-out. Mixed groups of parents of children who are diagnosed with behavior-related problems and who are typically developing meet weekly for 12 sessions. This program uses a coping problem-solving model in which parents view videotaped models of parenting strategies for coping with common child management problems and then generate solutions. Leaders model solutions suggested by participants, and parents role-play the solutions and set homework goals.

This community school-based program was evaluated in a randomized controlled trial, comparing it either with individual parent training (with similar content) or to a no-intervention control. Native English speakers and families whose children exhibited moderate behavior problems were equally likely to participate in the groups or the clinic-based training. However, families for whom English was a second language and families with a child exhibiting severe problems were more likely to participate in the group format. Families who attended the groups reported significantly greater improvement in child behavior at posttest and at a 6-month follow-up. The group training was also substantially less expensive than the clinic-based intervention.

DARE to Be You

DARE to Be You, a 12-week group prevention program for parents of 2- to 5-year-old children who are high risk (Miller-Heyl, MacPhee, & Fritz, 1998), was designed to promote parents' self-efficacy, effective childrearing strategies, understanding of developmental norms, social support, and problem-solving skills. In addition to the parent group, there are 10 parent–child practice sessions. The program was evaluated in a randomized controlled design with low-income and multiethnic populations (Ute Mountain Ute, Hispanic, Anglo-European). Parents reported significant positive changes in self-appraisals, democratic childrearing practices, and children's oppositional behavior (Miller-Heyl et al., 1998).

Summary of Parent-Focused Interventions

Individual, group, and self-administered parent training has been shown to improve parenting practices and reduce behavior problems in children who are socioeconomically disadvantaged. In these highly collaborative, nonprescriptive, and nonjudgmental intervention models, parent factors such as depression, anger, prior experience with abuse, and poverty do not seem to affect parents' engagement in the program as long as logistical barriers such as transportation, dinners, and child care are provided as part of the program (Baydar, Reid, & Webster-Stratton, 2003).

Because of many issues that families living in poverty face, most of the programs described previously have added other components (e.g., curricula on communication, anger management, problem solving). These topics enhance parenting programs by focusing on building more supportive families. Such prevention programs also included meals, transportation, and child care as part of the delivery of their parenting interventions.

Combining Classroom-based Child Training (in Social Competence) with Parent Programs

A substantial number of researchers have provided evidence in the efficacy of preventive child training curriculum for improving elementary-age children and adolescents' social and emotional, behavioral, and cognitive skills (e.g., Greenberg, Domitrovich, & Bumbarger, 1999; Grossman et al., 1977; Weissberg, Barton, & Shriver, 1997; Weissberg & Greenberg, 1998). Effective programs often focus on teaching specific cognitive skills that improve children's social and emotional competence. More recently, similar programs have been developed for preschool and kindergarten that demonstrate a positive impact on children's social competence. A few of those programs have specifically focused on populations of children from low-income families (see descriptions) and have also recognized the importance of including parents in the intervention. The following is a description of classroom-based social and emotional interventions for young children and their families. Some of the programs described below have only been evaluated with elementary school-age children; however, a brief description is included here because of their implications for the preschool population.

First Step to Success

First Step to Success, a school-based selective prevention program (Walker et al., 1998), is designed for kindergarten children who exhibit early signs of antisocial behavior patterns. This program combines the *CLASS* program (a classroom-based intervention) for children who tend to have problems with acting out (Hops et al.,

1978), with a 6-week (1 hour per week) home-based parenting program in which parents are taught to provide adequate monitoring and reinforcement to help children build social competencies. The *CLASS* program (Hops et al., 1978) is a "game" played at school for a month, initially for 20 minutes per day, and gradually expanding to the whole day. During the first 5 days, a consultant sits beside the child with acting out problems to constantly monitor the child's on-task behavior using a card signal. Eventually, the teacher takes over the management of the card system. When the child receives enough points, the entire class wins a prize. Three randomized controlled trials have shown that this program (without the parent component) results in significantly higher levels of appropriate behavior in the classroom, and that benefits are maintained a year later with a new teacher (Hops et al., 1978; Walker, Retana, & Gersten, 1988). In a randomized evaluation of *First Step to Success* (*CLASS* plus the 6-week parent program), 46 kindergartners considered to be high-risk were randomly assigned to the intervention or wait-list control groups. One year later, students in the intervention groups were significantly more adapted, more engaged, and less aggressive than students in control groups. Follow-up results indicated that effects lasted over time (Epstein & Walker, 1999).

The Montreal Longitudinal Experimental Study

The Montreal Longitudinal Experimental Study, a school-based prevention program for boys at high risk, includes classroom social-cognitive skills training and a home-based parent training program. Tremblay and colleagues (Tremblay, Mass, Pagani, & Vitaro, 1996; Tremblay, Pagani, Masse, & Vitaro, 1995; Tremblay et al., 1996) identified 366 6-year-old boys who they determined to be disruptive and randomly assigned them to an intervention or a control condition. The intervention group received a school-based, small-group social skills program based on the work of Shure and Spivak (Shure, 1994; Shure & Spivak, 1982). Coaching, peer modeling, role-playing, and positive reinforcement methods were used to teach anger management and peer problem solving. Parents were offered home-based parent training once every 3 weeks over a 2-year span based on the Oregon Social Learning Center model (Patterson, Reid, Jones, & Conger, 1975). Children in group followed up when they were 12 showed that boys in the intervention condition had higher academic achievement, had committed less burglary and theft, and were less likely to get drunk or be involved in fights than were children from the control groups. These effects increased as the follow-up period lengthened.

Linking the Interests of Families and Teachers

Linking the Interests of Families and Teachers (LIFT) is a school-based, universal prevention program developed by Reid, Eddy, Fetrow, and Stoolmiller, (1999), for elementary school-age children and their families. Two versions of the program are available. The first is tailored to meet the needs of children in Grade 1 and their families; the second is for children making the transition to middle school. The core of the program is parent training over six sessions that promotes consistent and effective parental discipline techniques as well as close and appropriate supervision. This is combined with classroom-based, small-group interpersonal skills training (10 weeks, for a total of 20 hours). During recess, a version of the Good Behavior Game (Kellam et al., 1998) is used to encourage the use of positive skills (children receive credit for good behavior toward class rewards). A controlled study of *LIFT* showed post-intervention reduction of playground aggression, improved classroom behavior, and reductions in maternal criticisms at home (Reid et al., 1999).

Combining Teacher Classroom Management Training with Parent and Child Training

Before successfully delivering a social skills curriculum in the classroom, teachers must be well trained in effective classroom management strategies and be able to manage misbehavior successfully (Webster-Stratton et al., 2001a). In fact, teacher training that focuses on helping teachers develop consistent classroom discipline plans and individualized behavior plans for children with behavior problems has been shown to produce increases in children's social competence even without a specific social skills curriculum (Cotton & Wikelund, 1990; Knoff & Batsche, 1995; Webster-Stratton et al., 2001a). Programs that have evaluated classroom management training for elementary school teachers have consistently demonstrated short-term improvements in disruptive and aggressive behavior in the classroom for approximately 78% of students considered disruptive (Stage & Quiroz, 1997). For example, The Seattle Social Development Project offered a preventive intervention that combined teacher and parent training to all families through the public schools (Hawkins et al., 1992). First-grade teachers were trained in proactive classroom management, interactive teaching, and cooperative learning and then were trained to implement the *I Can Problem Solve* (*ICPS*) curriculum developed by Shure and Spivak (1982). The program evaluation consisted of 643 students (first to fifth graders) from high crime areas in Seattle. Schools were assigned to intervention or control conditions. The 6-year follow-up (Hawkins, Catalano, Kosterman, Abbott, & Hill, 1999) with children who received the full 5-year school-based intervention, including parent training, indicated that students from the intervention group reported fewer violent delinquent acts, lower first drinking age, less sexual activity, and fewer pregnancies by 18 years, and better school achievement and bonding.

Incredible Years Teacher Training Series

The Incredible Years (IY) Teacher Training Series, a videotape-based, group discussion program, is designed to help teachers learn the classroom management strategies that will reduce aggression and behavior problems and promote preschool children's social, emotional, and academic competencies. The *IY Teacher Classroom Management Training Program* is a 6-day workshop (or 42 hours delivered weekly or bimonthly) for preschool, child care, and early school-age teachers that focuses on the following topics: developing positive relationships with difficult students and their parents; proactive teaching strategies; effective use of praise, encouragement, and incentives; development of an effective discipline hierarchy and individual supportive behavior plans for children targeted for services; and strategies to promote social and emotional competence and problem solving. Teachers are also taught techniques to engage children in learning, encourage language and reading development, and become social, emotional, academic, and persistence "coaches" for students. Teachers are encouraged to be sensitive to individual developmental differences (e.g., variation in attention span) and biological deficits in children (e.g., unresponsiveness to aversive stimuli, heightened interest in novelty) and the relevance of these differences for teaching efforts that are positive, accepting and consistent. Physical aggression in unstructured settings (e.g., playground, during choice times) is targeted for close monitoring, teaching, and incentive programs. A theme throughout this training process is to strengthen the teachers' collaboration with parents to promote consistency in responses across settings.

This *IY* teacher-training program was evaluated with teachers who had children (4–8 years old) in their classrooms with diagnosed oppositional defiant disorder or conduct disorder (ODD/CD) (Webster-Stratton et al., 2004). Webster-Stratton and colleagues found that children whose teachers received training were significantly less aggressive and more socially competent in classroom observations than children in intervention conditions without teacher training. At the 2-year follow-up, teacher training added significantly to the parent and child training program outcomes in terms of children's school functioning (Reid, Webster-Stratton, & Hammond, 2003). Two years after intervention, significantly more children from the teacher training conditions were in the typical range, suggesting that intervention across multiple domains (teachers, parents, and children) is beneficial to children with pervasive conduct problems.

In a second randomized controlled study, the effects of the *IY Teacher Classroom Management Training Program* were evaluated with Head Start teachers of children 3–5 years old. The *IY* teacher program and the *IY* parent program were offered together in a randomized controlled group design with 272 families and 61 Head Start teachers (Webster-Stratton et al., 2001a). Results for parent outcomes were described previously in the parenting program section. Teachers in the Head Start intervention program promoted more parent involvement in the classroom, had a more positive classroom atmosphere, and were more positive and less harsh than were teachers in the control group. Children in the intervention classrooms exhibited significantly less noncompliance and physical aggression than did students in control classrooms. Children in the intervention group were more engaged and more socially competent and had higher school readiness skills than did children in the control group. Most of these improvements were maintained 1 year later (Webster-Stratton et al., 2001a). These results highlight the changes that can be made in children's social competence and school readiness by training teachers in proven classroom management strategies.

Social and Emotional Curricula for Young Children

Next, we review three curricula designed to promote social-emotional competence in preschool children, specifically targeting children from low-income families who are ethnically diverse.

Incredible Years Dina Dinosaur Classroom Social, Emotional, and Problem-Solving Curriculum

The *Incredible Years Dina Dinosaur Social, Emotional, and Problem-Solving Curriculum* child training program is based on theory and research indicating the kinds of social, emotional, and cognitive deficits identified in children with behavior problems as well as theory-based behavior change methods (Webster-Stratton, 1990a). It focuses on learning school rules and how to be successful in school; emotional literacy, empathy, or perspective taking; interpersonal problem solving; anger management; and friendship and communication skills. Content is taught in a variety of ways including video vignettes, life-size puppets, dinosaur homework activities, books, cartoons, incentives, and picture cue cards. Parents and teachers are involved in the program through weekly dinosaur letters that explain how they can help reinforce the skills that the children are learning. In addition, homework activities are designed to be done by children with their parents. Comprehensive manuals outline every lesson's content, objectives, videotapes to be shown, and descriptions of small-group activities. More details about this curriculum can be found in an article by Webster-Stratton and Reid (2004), the curriculum manuals (Webster-Stratton, 1990a), and the book, *How to Promote Children's Social and Emotional Competence* (Webster-Stratton, 2000).

Researchers initially evaluated the curriculum as a small-group intervention for young children with diagnosed ODD/CD and established efficacy with that population (Webster-Stratton & Hammond, 1997; Webster-Stratton, Reid, & Hammond, 2001b; Webster-Stratton, Reid, & Hammond, 2004). In two randomized controlled group studies, 4- to 8-year-old children with externalizing behavior problems (ODD/CD) who participated in a weekly, 2-hour, 20- to 22-week intervention program showed reductions in aggressive and disruptive behavior according to independent, observed interactions of these children with teachers and peers. These children also demonstrated increases in pro-social behavior and conflict management skills compared with an untreated control group. These improvements in behavior were maintained 2 years later. Intervention was effective not only for externalizing behavior problems but also for comorbid hyperactivity, impulsivity, and attentional difficulties. Adding the child program to the *IY* parent program enhanced long-term outcomes for children who exhibited pervasive behavior problems across settings (home and school) by reducing behavior problems and improving social functioning in both settings (Webster-Stratton & Hammond, 1997; Webster-Stratton, Reid, & Hammond, 2004). These are the first randomized controlled studies with young children with special needs (ages 4–8 years) that have shown reductions in observed peer aggression.

The favorable impact of the Dina Dinosaur training led to an adaptation of this program for use as a prevention curriculum by preschool through third-grade teachers to promote social, emotional, and academic competencies in the classroom. The classroom version consists of more than 64 lesson plans per year and is delivered 2–3 times a week in a 15- to 20-minute large-group circle time followed by small group practice activities (Webster-Stratton & Reid, 2004). Teachers can choose from more than 300 small group activities that focus on social-emotional skills as well as other school readiness activities, such as pre-reading and pre-writing activities, math and science concepts, fine and gross motor skills, and creative art projects. Problem-solving practice and reinforcement from teachers take place in less structured settings, such as during choice time, in the lunchroom, or on the playground.

The curriculum was evaluated in a randomized study in Head Start and low-income elementary schools in the Seattle area (Webster-Stratton, Reid, & Stoolmiller, in press). Teachers received 4 days of training in this curriculum, which also included some classroom management training. Participants in the study were 1,791 multiethnic students (20% Asian, 18% Hispanic, 18% African American, 8% African, 26% Caucasion). Forty-four percent of students were non-native English speakers. The program was found to be highly effective. Independent observations of children in the classrooms showed significant differences between control and intervention students on variables such as compliance and cooperation, social competence, and aggressive behavior. Intervention classrooms had significantly more positive classroom atmosphere than control classrooms. Moreover, students in intervention classrooms had significantly higher school readiness scores as measured by observed on-task behaviors, compliance during academic time, and cognitive concentration (Webster-Stratton, Reid, & Stoolmiller, & Reid, in press). Recently, this classroom-based intervention was used by two other research teams in combination with the *IY* parent program, and while the independent contribution of the child training program cannot be determined from their research designs, positive outcomes were reported in children's social interactions on the playground and academic variables (Barrera et al., 2002).

Promoting Alternative Thinking Strategies Curriculum

The *Promoting Alternative THinking Strategies* (*PATHS*) prevention curriculum (Kusche & Greenberg, 1994) was developed to promote children's social and emotional competence. It focuses on the skills of emotional literacy, positive peer relations, problem solving, and self-control. Topics include compliments, feelings, a self-control strategy, and problem solving. In addition to lessons, teachers create an environment that promotes social and emotional skills. *PATHS* was originally designed to be taught by elementary school teachers in Grades K–5 and included 131 lessons delivered over a 5-year period. Clinical trials of *PATHS* conducted with children from regular education and children with special needs (Greenberg, Kusche, Cook, & Quamma, 1995) showed that the program successfully improved social cognitions and emotion knowledge and reduced aggression and depression. These improvements were maintained at a 2-year follow-up. The degree of children's behavioral change was shown to be affected by the quality of the teacher's implementation of *PATHS* and quality of the principal's leadership.

The preschool *PATHS* curriculum (Domitrovich, Cortes, & Greenberg, 2006) is a 30-lesson preschool adaptation of *PATHS*. This preschool version of the program was tested with English-speaking children in Head Start programs in 20 classrooms (10 intervention and 10 control). Ten Head Start teachers received a 3-day training and delivered 30 lessons during "circle time." Children in the intervention group had higher emotion knowledge skills and were rated by teachers and parents as more socially competent and less socially withdrawn than children in a control group, although no changes occurred in problem solving or aggression (Domitrovich, Cortes, & Greenberg, 2006).

Al's Pals: Kids Making Healthy Choices

Al's Pals (Wingspan, 1999), designed for children 3 to 8 years old, was developed at the Virginia Institute for Developmental Disabilities. The goal of the program is to promote social-emotional competence in children who are living in stressful life conditions. It consists of 46 lessons implemented by trained teachers in a variety of settings including preschools and child care centers. The lessons are designed to help young children develop skills related to four components, including resiliency–social competence, problem solving, autonomy, and sense of purpose or belief in a bright future (Benard, 1993). The focus of *Al's Pals* is also to infuse resilience-promoting concepts into teaching practices. The curriculum introduces children to topics such as understanding feelings, caring about others, accepting differences, establishing social relationships, managing anger, distinguishing between safe and unsafe situations, and solving problems peacefully. A trained adult leads two lessons a week over 23 weeks. Lessons last 15–20 minutes and include engaging activities, puppets, role-plays, music, books, pictures, and movement. Letters to parents explain what is being taught and offer home activities. A randomized study conducted in Head Start showed that teachers reported increased social independence, pro-social behaviors, and better coping in classrooms in which children received the intervention than in control classrooms (Lynch, Geller, & Schmidt, 2004).

Summary of Child-Focused and Teacher-Focused Interventions

Very few randomized controlled group studies focus on teacher classroom management training by itself as a method of promoting social competence and reducing aggression. However, almost all of the school-based prevention interventions have included some aspect of teacher training as part of their package of services for children of high risk and their parents. Because of this it is difficult to separate the individual contribution of the teacher-training portion of the intervention. Clearly, this would be the most cost-effective way of reaching many young children.

The three social-emotional curricula discussed previously show great promise in their ability to be used by teachers to increase social and emotional skills and reduce aggressive behavior problems in children who are socioeconomically disadvantaged. Each of these curricula focus on content related to emotional literacy, problem solving, anger management, and friendship skills and use child-friendly approaches such as puppets, games, and small group activities. The programs are developmentally appropriate and, as part of their intervention model, can be tailored to meet the needs of children from diverse backgrounds.

CONCLUSION

Several reports, such as the *Surgeon General's 2000 Report on Children's Mental Health* (U.S. Public Health Service, 2000) and *From Neurons to Neighborhoods: The Science of Early Childhood Development* (Shonkoff & Phillips, 2000) have highlighted the need for the adoption of evidence-based practices that support young children's social-emotional competence and prevent and decrease the occurrences of challenging behavior in early childhood. In this chapter, we describe programs for teachers, parents, and children that have evidence for their use in promoting social competence and reducing aggressive behavior problems. The evidence seems to point to the utility of using multiple, interconnecting programs that train parents and teachers to support each other using research-proven behavior management strategies for promoting children's social competence and reducing disruptive behaviors as well as for building strong relationships between parents, teachers, and children and a sense of classroom as family. Once the foundation of good behavior management and strong, nurturing relationships is in place, then classroom curriculum focused on building social skills, emotional literacy, and problem solving can further enhance children's academic competence and future social adjustment.

These programs are most effective when delivered with high fidelity, uphold-ing the integrity of the program's content, process, and methods and using proven behavior management strategies. The good news is that young children's behavior is malleable, and with comprehensive programs we can help children who are socioeconomically disadvantaged to be socially competent and have the skills they need to be successful academically. The warning is that researchers have shown that without these added supports and family interventions, a significant number of these children will continue on a trajectory toward academic failure, violence, and substance abuse.

REFERENCES

Arnold, D.H., Ortiz, C., Curry, J.C., Stowe, R.M., Goldstein, N.E., Fisher, P.H. (1999). Pro-moting academic success and preventing disruptive behavior disorders through commu-nity partnership. *Journal of Community Psychology, 27*, 589–598.

Barrera, M., Biglan, A., Taylor, T.K., Gunn, B., Smolkowski, K., Black, C. (2002). Early ele-mentary school intervention to reduce conduct problems: A randomized trial with His-panic and non-Hispanic children. *Prevention Science, 3*(2), 83–94.

Baydar, N., Reid, M.J., & Webster-Stratton, C. (2003). The role of mental health factors and program engagement in the effectiveness of a preventive parenting program for Head Start mothers. *Child Development, 74*(5), 1433–1453.

Benard, B. (1993). Fostering resiliency in kids. *Educational Leadership, 51*(3), 44–48.

Brestan, E.V., & Eyberg, S.M. (1998). Effective psychosocial treatments of conduct-disordered children and adolescents: 29 years, 82 studies, and 5,272 kids. *Journal of Clini-cal Child Psychology, 27*, 180–189.

Burchinal, M.R., Roberts, J.E., Hooper, S., & Zeisel, S.A. (2000). Cumulative risk and early cognitive development: A comparison of statistical risk models. *Developmental Psychology, 36*, 793–807.

Coie, J.D., & Dodge, K.A. (1998). Aggression and antisocial behavior. In W. Damon & N. Eisenberg (Eds.), *Handbook of child psychology, fifth edition: Social, emotional and personality development* (Vol. 3, pp. 779–862). New York: Wiley.

Cotton, K., & Wikelund, K.R. (Eds.). (1990). *Schoolwide and classroom discipline.* Portland, OR: Northwest Regional Education Laboratory.

Cummings, E.M. (1994). Marital conflict and children's functioning. *Social Development, 3*(1), 16–36.

Cunningham, C.E., Bremner, R., & Boyle, M. (1995). Large group community-based parent-ing programs for families of preschoolers at risk for disruptive behaviour disorders: Uti-lization, cost effectiveness, and outcome. *Journal of Child Psychology and Psychiatry, 36*, 1141–1159.

Domitrovich, C., Cortes, R.C., & Greenberg, M. (2006). *Improving young children's social and emotional competence: A randomized trial of the preschool PATHS curriculum.* University Park, PA: Pennsylvania State University.

Epstein, M.H., & Walker, H.M. (1999). Special education: Best practices and first steps to suc-cess. In B. Burns, K. Hoagwood & M. English (Eds.), *Community-based interventions for youth with serious emotional disorders.* UK: Oxford University Press.

Greenberg, M.T., Domitrovich, C., & Bumbarger, B. (1999). *Preventing mental disorders in school-age children: A review of the effectiveness of prevention programs.* University Park, PA: Pre-vention Research Center, Pennsylvania State University.

Greenberg, M.T., Kusche, C.A., Cook, E.T., & Quamma, J.P. (1995). Promoting emotio-nal competence in school-aged children: The effects of the PATHS curriculum. Special issue: Emotions in developmental psychopathology. *Development and Psychopathology, 7*, 117–136.

Gross, D., Fogg, L., Webster-Stratton, C., Garvey, C.W.J., & Grady, J. (2003). Parent training with families of toddlers in child care in low-income urban communities. *Journal of Con-sulting and Clinical Psychology, 71*, 261–278.

Grossman, D.C., Neckerman, H.J., Koepsell, T.D., Liu, P.Y., Asher, K.N., Beland, K., (1977). Effectiveness of a violence prevention curriculum among children in elementary school. A randomized controlled trial. *Journal of the American Medical Association, 27,* 1605–1611.

Hawkins, J.D., Catalano, R.F., Kosterman, R., Abbott, R., & Hill, K.G. (1999). Preventing adolescent health-risk behaviors by strengthening protection during childhood. *Archives of Pediatrics and Adolescent Medicine, 153,* 226–234.

Hawkins, J.D., Catalano, R.F., Morrison, D.M., O'Donnell, J., Abbott, R.D., & Day, L.E. (1992). The Seattle social development project: Effects of the first four years on protective factors and problem behaviors. In J. McCord & R.E. Tremblay (Eds.), *Preventing antisocial behavior: Intervention from birth through adolescence* (pp. 162–195). New York: Guilford Press.

Hops, H., Walker, H.M., Hernandez, D., Nagoshi, J.T., Omura, R.T., Skindrug, K. (1978). CLASS: A standardized in-class program for acting out children. II Field test evaluations. *Journal of Educational Psychology, 70,* 636–644.

Hutchings, J., Bywater, T., Daley, D., Gardner, F., Whitaker, C., Jones, K., Eames, C., & Edwards, R.T. (2007). Parenting intervention in Sure Start for children at risk of developing conduct disorder: Pragmatic randomized controlled trial. *British Medical Journal,* 2007, pp. 1–7.

Keenan, K., Shaw, D.S., Walsh, B., Delliquadri, E., & Giovannelli, J. (1997). DSM-III-R disorders in preschool children from low-income families. *Journal of American Academy of Child and Adolescent Psychiatry, 36*(5), 620–627.

Kellam, S.G., Ling, X., Merisca, R., Brown, C.H., & Ialongo, N. (1998). The effect of the level of aggression in the first grade classroom on the course and malleability of aggressive behavior into middle school. *Development and Psychopathology, 10,* 165–185.

Knoff, H.M., & Batsche, G.M. (1995). Project ACHIEVE: Analyzing a school reform process for at-risk and underachieving students. *School Psychology Review, 24,* 579–603.

Kusche, C.A., & Greenberg, M.T. (1994). *The PATHS Curriculum.* Seattle, WA: Developmental Research and Programs.

Lynch, K.B., Geller, S.R., & Schmidt, M.G. (2004). Multi-year evaluation of the effectiveness of a resilience-based prevention program for young children. *The Journal of Primary Prevention, 24,* 3353–3353.

Miller Brotman, L., Klein, R.G., Kamboukos, D., Brown, E.J., Coard, S., & Stout Sosinsky, L. (2003). Preventive intervention for urban, low-income preschoolers at familial risk for conduct problems: A randomized pilot study. *Journal of Child Psychology and Psychiatry, 32,* 246–257.

Miller, L.S., & Rojas-Flores, L. (1999). *Preventing conduct problems in urban, Latino preschoolers through parent training: A pilot study.* New York: New York University Child Study Center.

Miller-Heyl, J., MacPhee, D., & Fritz, J.J. (1998). *DARE to Be You:* A family-support, early prevention program. *The Journal of Primary Prevention, 18,* 257–285.

Mørch, W.-T., Larsson, G., Clifford, G., Drugli, M.B., & Fossum, S. (2004). *Treatment of small children with conduct and oppositional defiant disorders.* Unpublished manuscript, University of Tromsø and Norwegian University of Technology and Science, Trondheim, Norway.

Offord, D.R., Alder, R.J., & Boyle, M.H. (1986). Prevalence and sociodemographic correlates of conduct disorder. *The American Journal of Social Psychiatry, 6,* 272–278.

Patterson, G.R., DeGarmo, D.S., & Knutson, N. (2000). Hyperactive and antisocial behaviors: Comorbid or two points in the same process? *Developmental and Psychopathology, 12,* 91–106.

Patterson, G.R., Reid, J.B., Jones, R.R., & Conger, R.W. (1975). *A social learning approach to family intervention* (Vol. 1). Eugene, OR: Castalia.

Phillips, D., Voran, M., Kisker, E., Howes, C., & Whitebrook, M. (1994). Child care for children in poverty: Opportunity or inequity? *Child Development, 65,* 472–492.

Pianta, R.C., & Walsh, D.J. (1998). Applying the construct of resilience in schools: Cautions from a developmental systems perspective. *School Psychology Review, 27,* 407–417.

Raver, C.C., & Zigler, E.F. (1997). Social competence: An untapped dimension in evaluating Head Start's success. *Early Childhood Research Quarterly, 12,* 363–385.

Reid, J.B., Eddy, J.M., Fetrow, R.A., & Stoolmiller, M. (1999). Description and immediate impacts of a preventive intervention for conduct problems. *American Journal of Community Psychology, 27*(4), 483–517.

Reid, M.J., Webster-Stratton, C., & Beauchaine, T.P. (2001). Parent training in Head Start: A comparison of program response among African American, Asian American, Caucasian, and Hispanic mothers. Prevention Science, 2(4), 209–227.

Reid, M.J., Webster-Stratton, C., & Hammond, M. (2003). Follow-up of children who received the Incredible Years Intervention for Oppositional-Defiant Disorder: Maintenance and prediction of 2-year outcome. *Behavior Therapy, 34*, 471–491.

Reid, M.J., Webster-Stratton, C., & Hammond, M. (in press). Preventing aggression and improving social, emotional competence: The Incredible Years Parent Training in high-risk elementary schools. *Journal of Clinical Child and Adolescent Psychology.*

Rimm-Kaufman, S.E., Pianta, R.C., & Cox, M.J. (2000). Teachers' judgments of problems in the transition to kindergarten. *Early Childhood Research Quarterly, 15*, 147–166.

Sanders, M.R. (1996). New directions in behavioral family intervention with children. In T.H. Ollendick & R.J. Prinz (Eds.), *Advances in clinical child psychology* (Vol. 18, pp. 283–320). New York: Plenum Press.

Sanders, M.R., & Christensen, A.P. (1985). A comparison of the effects of child management and planned activities training in five parenting environments. *Journal of Abnormal Child Psychology, 13*(1), 101–117.

Sanders, M.R., & Dadds, M.R. (1993). *Behavioral family intervention.* Needham Heights, MA: Allyn & Bacon.

Sanders, M.R., Markie-Dadds, C., Tully, L.A., & Bor, W. (2000). The Triple P-Positive Parenting Program: A comparison of enhanced, standard and self-directed behavioural family intervention for parents of children with early onset conduct problems. *Journal of Consulting and Clinical Psychology, 68*, 624–640.

Scott, S., Spender, Q., Doolan, M., Jacobs, B., & Aspland, H. (2001). Multicentre controlled trial of parenting groups for child antisocial behaviour in clinical practice. *British Medical Journal, 323*(28), 1–5.

Shonkoff, J.P., & Phillips, D.A. (2000). *From neurons to neighborhoods: The science of early childhood development.* Washington, DC: National Academies Press.

Shure, M. (1994). *I Can Problem Solve (ICPS): An interpersonal cognitive problem-solving program for children.* Champaign, IL: Research Press.

Shure, M.B., & Spivak, G. (1982). Interpersonal problem-solving in young children: A cognitive approach to prevention. *American Journal of Community Psychology, 10*(3), 341–356.

Snyder, H. (2001). Epidemiology of official offending. In R. Loeber & D. Farrington (Eds.), *Child delinquents: Development, intervention and service needs* (pp. 25–46). Thousand Oaks, CA: Sage Publications.

Spaccarelli, S., Cotler, S., & Penman, D. (1992). Problem-solving skills training as a supplement to behavioral parent training. *Cognitive Therapy and Research, 16*, 1–18.

Stage, S.A., & Quiroz, D.R. (1997). A meta-analysis of interventions to decrease disruptive classroom behavior in public education settings. *School Psychology Review, 26*, 333–368.

Taylor, T.K., Schmidt, F., Pepler, D., & Hodgins, H. (1998). A comparison of eclectic treatment with Webster-Stratton's Parents and Children Series in a children's mental health center: A randomized controlled trial. *Behavior Therapy, 29*, 221–240.

Tremblay, R.E., Masse, L.C., Pagani, L., & Vitaro, F. (1996). From childhood physical aggression to adolescent maladjustment: The Montreal prevention experiment. In R.D. Peters & R.J. MacMahon (Eds.), *Preventing childhood disorders, substance abuse and delinquency* (pp. 268–298). Thousand Oaks, CA: Sage Publications.

Tremblay, R.E., Pagani, K.L., Masse, L.C., & Vitaro, F. (1995). A biomodal preventive intervention for disruptive kindergarten boys: Its impact through mid-adolescence. Special Section: Prediction and prevention of child and adolescent antisocial behavior. *Journal of Consulting and Clinical Psychology, 63*, 560–568.

Tremblay, R.E., Vitaro, F., Bertrand, L., LeBlanc, M., Beauchesne, H., Boileau, H. (1996). Parent and child training to prevent early onset of delinquency: The Montreal longitudinal-experimental study. In J. McCord & R.E. Tremblay (Eds.), *Preventing antisocial behavior: Interventions from birth through adolescence* (pp. 117–138). New York: Guilford Press.

U.S. Public Health Service. (2000), *Report of the Surgeon General's Conference on Children's Mental Health: A National Action Agenda.* Retrieved from Washington, DC: Department of Health and Human Services. Retrieved June 15, 2007, from http://www.surgeongeneral.gov/cmh/childreport.htm. Washington, DC: Department of Health and Human Services.

Walker, H.M., Kavanagh, K., Stiller, B., Golly, A., Severson, H.H., & Feil, E.G. (1998). First Step to Success: An Early Intervention Approach for Preventing School Antisocial Behavior. *Journal of Emotional and Behavioral Disorders, 6*, 66-80.

Walker, H.M., Retana, G.F., & Gersten, R. (1988). Replication of the CLASS program in Costa Rica. *Behavior Modification, 12*, 133–154.

Webster-Stratton, C. (1981). Modification of mothers' behaviors and attitudes through video-tape modeling group discussion program. *Behavior Therapy, 12*, 634–642.

Webster-Stratton, C. (1990a). *Dina Dinosaur's Social Skills and Problem-Solving Curriculum*. Seattle, WA: 1411 8th Avenue West.

Webster-Stratton, C. (1990b). Enhancing the effectiveness of self-administered videotape parent training for families with conduct-problem children. *Journal of Abnormal Child Psychology, 18*, 479–492.

Webster-Stratton, C. (1990c). Stress: A potential disruptor of parent perceptions and family interactions. *Journal of Clinical Child Psychology, 19*, 302–312.

Webster-Stratton, C. (1990d). *The Incredible Years Parent Training Program manual: Effective communication, anger management and problem-solving (ADVANCE)*. Seattle, WA: The Incredible Years.

Webster-Stratton, C. (1994). Advancing videotape parent training: A comparison study. *Journal of Consulting and Clinical Psychology, 62*, 583–593.

Webster-Stratton, C. (1998). Preventing conduct problems in Head Start children: Strengthening parenting competencies. *Journal of Consulting and Clinical Psychology, 66*, 715–730.

Webster-Stratton, C. (2000). *How to promote social and academic competence in young children*. London: Sage Publications.

Webster-Stratton, C., & Fjone, A. (1989). Interactions of mothers and fathers with conduct problem children: Comparison with a nonclinic group. *Public Health Nursing, 6*(4), 218–223.

Webster-Stratton, C., & Hammond, M. (1997). Treating children with early-onset conduct problems: A comparison of child and parent training interventions. *Journal of Consulting and Clinical Psychology, 65*, 93–109.

Webster-Stratton, C., & Hammond, M. (1998). Conduct problems and level of social competence in Head Start children: Prevalence, pervasiveness and associated risk factors. *Clinical Child Psychology and Family Psychology Review, 1*(2), 101–124.

Webster-Stratton, C., & Hammond., M. (1999). Marital conflict management skills, parenting style, and early-onset conduct problems: Processes and pathways. *Journal of Child Psychology and Psychiatry, 40*, 917–927.

Webster-Stratton, C., & Hancock, L. (1998). Parent training: Content, methods and processes. In E. Schaefer (Ed.), *Handbook of parent training* (2nd ed., pp. 98–152). New York: Wiley.

Webster-Stratton, C., & Herbert, M. (1994). *Troubled families—problem children: Working with parents: A collaborative process*. New York: Wiley.

Webster-Stratton, C., & Reid, M.J. (2002). An integrated approach to prevention and management of aggressive behavior problems in preschool and elementary students: School-parent collaboration. In K. Lane, F. Gresham & T. O'Shaughnessy (Eds.), *Interventions for students with emotional and behavioral disorders* (pp. 261–272). Needham Heights, MA: Allyn & Bacon.

Webster-Stratton, C., & Reid, M.J. (2003). Treating conduct problems and strengthening social emotional competence in young children (ages 4–8 years): The Dina Dinosaur treatment program. *Journal of Emotional and Behavioral Disorders, 11*(3), 130–143.

Webster-Stratton, C., & Reid, M.J. (2004). Strengthening social and emotional competence in young children—The foundation for early school readiness and success: Incredible Years classroom social skills and problem-solving curriculum. *Infants and Young Children, 17*(2).

Webster-Stratton, C., & Reid, M.J. (2005). Treatment and prevention of conduct problems: Parent training interventions for young children (2–7 years old). In K. McCartney & D.A. Phillips (Eds.), *Blackwell handbook on early childhood development*. Malden, MA: Blackwell.

Webster-Stratton, C., Reid, M.J., & Hammond, M. (2001a). Preventing conduct problems, promoting social competence: A parent and teacher training partnership in Head Start. *Journal of Clinical Child Psychology, 30*(3), 283–302.

Webster-Stratton, C., Reid, M.J., & Hammond, M. (2001b). Social skills and problem solving training for children with early-onset conduct problems: Who benefits? *Journal of Child Psychology and Psychiatry, 42*(7), 943–952.

Webster-Stratton, C., Reid, M.J., & Hammond, M. (2004). Treating children with early-onset conduct problems: Intervention outcomes for parent, child, and teacher training. *Journal of Clinical Child and Adolescent Psychology, 33*(1), 105–124.

Webster-Stratton, C., Reid, M. J., & Stoolmiller, M. (in press). Preventing aggression and improving social, emotional and school readiness: Evaluation of the Incredible Years Dinosaur Classroom Curriculum in high risk schools. Available from http://www.incredibleyears.com

Webster-Stratton, C., & Taylor, T. (2001). Nipping early risk factors in the bud: Preventing substance abuse, delinquency, and violence in adolescence through interventions targeted at young children (ages 0–8 years). *Prevention Science, 2*(3), 165–192.

Weissberg, R.P., Barton, H.A., & Shriver, T.P. (1997). The social competence promotion program for young adolescents. In G.W. Albee & T.P. Gullotta (Eds.), *Primary prevention works.* Thousand Oaks, CA: Sage Publications.

Weissberg, R.P., & Greenberg, M. (1998). School and community competence-enhancement and prevention programs. In I. Siegel & A. Renninger (Eds.), *Handbook of child psychology: Child psychology in practice* (Vol. 4). New York: Wiley.

Werner, E.E. (1999). How children become resilient: Observations and cautions. In N. Henderson, B. Benard & N. Sharp-Light (Eds.), *Resiliency in action: Practical ideas for overcoming risks and building strengths in youth, families, and communities* (pp. 115–134). Gorham, ME: Resiliency in Action.

West, J., Denton, K., & Reaney, L.M. (2001). *The kindergarten year: findings from the early childhood longitudinal study, kindergarten class of 1998–1999 (Publication No. NCES2001-023).* Washington, DC: Department of Education, National Center for Education Statistics.

Wingspan, L.L.C. (1999). *Al's Pals: Kids making healthy choices.* Richmond, VA.

CHAPTER 10

Social Competence Interventions for Young Children with Challenging Behaviors

MAUREEN A. CONROY, WILLIAM H. BROWN, AND MELISSA L. OLIVE

TJ IS A PRESCHOOLER IN Ms. Madison's class at St. Mark's Elementary School. This is Ms. Madison's first year of teaching preschoolers; previously, she taught second graders. In addition to having little experience working with preschoolers, Ms. Madison has had very limited training in working with young children who have severe challenging behaviors. TJ has difficulty meeting Ms. Madison's classroom expectations. He frequently disrupts the class, acts impulsively, and is chronically noncompliant when given directives by Ms. Madison. Often, his noncompliance escalates into full-blown tantrums. She spends much of her time cajoling TJ into complying with her requests. As a result, TJ receives a great deal of her attention. At times, TJ's behavior becomes so disruptive that Ms. Madison stops placing any behavioral demands on him. Unfortunately, Ms. Madison's discipline strategies for TJ's challenging behaviors have the opposite effect of what she intends. Rather than "punishing" TJ's misbehavior, her tendency to give him teacher attention for his challenging behavior and to decrease demands is probably "reinforcing" those behaviors. TJ's challenging behaviors increase to the point that Ms. Madison is unable to manage him and attend to the other classmates. As a result, she refers TJ to the school's child study team.

The child study team completes a functional behavioral assessment (FBA) to determine the environmental variables that may be increasing and maintaining TJ's challenging behaviors. The results of the FBA indicate that TJ lacks the preacademic skills needed to accomplish many of the classroom tasks and the behavioral competence to comply with common adult requests. Moreover, the assessment

Development of this chapter was supported in part with grant funding from the U.S. Department of Education Office of Special Education Programs: 1) Center on Evidence-based Practices: Young Children with Challenging Behavior (#H324Z010001) and 2) Leadership Training in Special Education (#H325D010063A). However, the content and opinions expressed herein do not necessarily reflect the position or policy of the U.S. Department of Education, and no official endorsement should be inferred. Correspondence concerning this chapter should be addressed to Maureen A. Conroy at Virginia Commonwealth University, Richmond, Virginia.

shows that his challenging behaviors have been maintained by Ms. Madison's attention to misbehaviors and his escape from structured, difficult, or less-preferred
classroom activities. Following the FBA, the child study team collaborate with Ms.
Madison to develop an explicit instructional plan that is supportive of TJ's individual
developmental needs and that incorporates function-based behavioral interventions
to address TJ's challenging behaviors.

As discussed by Sainato, Jung, Salmon, and Axe in Chapter 5, developmentally
appropriate classrooms with experienced preschool teachers may provide the physical and social classroom structure needed by children to successfully decrease their
challenging behaviors and increase their appropriate behaviors; however, for children like TJ, this general level of intervention may not be sufficient for ameliorating severe and chronic challenging behaviors. Many children who do not respond
well to general classroom interventions require more intensive, individualized
assessments, interventions, and behavioral supports. Specifically, individualized
assessments of children's physical and social environments and the influences of
those environments on the likelihood of appropriate and challenging behaviors are
warranted.

Since the early 1990s, the use of proactive interventions to prevent and elimi-
nate young children's challenging behaviors has advanced with the development of
a contemporary conceptual framework known as positive behavior support (PBS)
(see Horner, 2000). PBS is a comprehensive approach toward the reduction of challenging behaviors and is based on the principles of applied behavior analysis (e.g.,
Bijou, 1993). The approach includes the careful assessments and manipulations of
environmental events to decrease challenging behaviors and increase appropriate
social and adaptive behaviors (see Horner, 2000). The overall purpose of our chapter is to discuss social competence interventions within a PBS framework for young
children who have severe and chronic challenging behaviors. First, we provide an
overview of young children's challenging behaviors, including a discussion of children's characteristics and needs. Next, we review PBS procedures for young children, including the implementation of scientifically based interventions designed
to develop and support their social and behavioral competence. In particular, we
present a hierarchical approach toward FBA procedures and function-based interventions.

CHARACTERISTICS AND NEEDS OF YOUNG CHILDREN WITH CHALLENGING BEHAVIORS

The number of young children who display severe challenging behaviors continues
to increase at alarming rates (e.g., Campbell, 2002; Serna, Nielsen, Lambros, &
Forness, 2000). Prevalence rates suggest that anywhere from 8% to as much as 25%
of young children engage in challenging behaviors severe enough to impede their
social competence. Clearly, the prevalence of children's challenging behaviors
indicates a growing concern for their teachers and parents (Campbell, 2002).

The expression *challenging behaviors* is a global term used to describe those
behaviors that result in injury to self or others, cause damage to physical environments, interfere with skill acquisition, or isolate children (see Doss & Reichle,
1991). Challenging behaviors are displayed in a variety of forms or topographies

and include both externalizing (noncompliance, disruption, tantrum, aggression, self-injurious behavior, and stereotypy) and internalizing (withdrawal, avoidance) behaviors. Often, these maladaptive behaviors do not occur in isolation; rather, it is common for children's negativistic behaviors to co-occur in a hierarchical manner. For example, many children with repertoires of challenging behaviors may initially be noncompliant with teachers' requests and then become relatively disruptive, with confrontational behaviors that eventually escalate from obstreperous behaviors into prolonged tantrums that completely disrupt classroom activities. Moreover, these behavioral episodes frequently isolate the offending children both within and outside of their classrooms.

Historically, when designing behavioral interventions, the focus has been on describing the *form* or *topography* of challenging behaviors and then implementing behavioral strategies, such as time out from reinforcement or response cost (i.e., loss of privileges), to decrease challenging behaviors. In behavioral research conducted since the 1980s, interventionists have learned that knowing the *outcomes* or *functions* of behaviors can increase the effectiveness of behavioral interventions, particularly for decreasing challenging behaviors (see Carr et al., 1999). Mainly, researchers have frequently demonstrated that the occurrence of challenging behaviors is directly related to the consequences that follow inappropriate behaviors. Hence, children's challenging behaviors may function as a "payoff" for engaging in misbehaviors. Identifying the functions of challenging behaviors and linking behavioral change strategies to those functions often increases the effectiveness of interventions (Carr et al., 1999).

The consensus among researchers is that challenging behaviors serve multiple functions (see Table 10.1). These functions include access to environmental events—including peers' and adults' attention—and preferred foods, materials, and activities. In addition, sensory stimulation is frequently hypothesized as access to "self-reinforcement" for some children. Another fundamental function for many children is *escape from* or *avoidance of* peers' and adults' attention and social interactions as well as nonpreferred materials, activities, foods, and sensory events.

Describing the topographies or forms and identifying the functions or outcomes of children's challenging behaviors are critical components in the FBA process and in planning effective function-based interventions. Determining whether children's challenging behaviors are a result of *performance* or *skill-based*

Table 10.1. Functions of challenging behavior

Functions	External functions		Internal functions
Obtain desirable events	**Attention**	**Tangible**	**Sensory stimulation**
	Adult or peer attention	Objects, materials, or	Sensory feedback
	Affection	activities	Body rocking
	Verbal talk/ social	Food	Visual stimulation
	interaction	Preferred activity or toy	(handflapping)
Escape/avoid	Adult or peer attention	Objects, materials, or	Sensory feedback
Undesirable events	Affection	activities	Pain (body
	Verbal talk/social inter-	Difficult tasks	pressing)
	action	Change in routine	Tactile irritations
		Discontinuation of pre-	(removing clothing)
		ferred activity	Hunger

deficits is also important for developing effective interventions. Children who demonstrate performance deficits have the ability to engage in the desired appropriate behaviors, but environmental circumstances do not always support their adaptive behaviors. Indeed, environmental conditions may accidentally support the occurrence of their challenging behaviors, as illustrated in the following example:

> **BEN WANTS TO OBTAIN HIS MOTHER'S** attention while she is on the phone. Although Ben has the ability to appropriately request his mother's attention, he has learned that his mother often ignores his appropriate requests and continues to talk on the phone. He has learned through coincidence that he is able to quickly obtain his mother's attention whenever he threatens or hits his younger brother. Whenever he is aggressive toward his brother, his mother quickly stops talking on the phone and attends to Ben. Hence, Ben has the ability to perform the socially appropriate behavior to obtain the desired outcome (i.e., asking for his mother's attention); nevertheless, his negative behavior is much more effective and efficient for him when he wants her attention.

Children who demonstrate *skill deficits* do not currently have the ability to perform the desired behaviors and will require systematic instruction to acquire those needed skills. Here is another example to demonstrate this idea:

> **THOMAS HAS SEVERE EXPRESSIVE** and receptive communication deficits and is unable to verbally request preferred items and activities or to communicate his dislikes. Unfortunately, he has learned to communicate his wants with his repertoire of challenging behaviors. When he wants to be left alone, he will cry and physically push others away. If individuals persist in soliciting social contact, Thomas will even become aggressive toward them. When he wants his parents' attention or his favorite toys, he will feign tantrums until one of them determines what he wants and provides them to him. Thomas does not presently know how to request that others leave him alone or how to ask appropriately for his parents' attention or desired toys. He needs to be taught appropriate alternative functional language and communication to replace his challenging behaviors.

In both of these examples, the child's environments should be arranged to better support the use of socially appropriate behaviors to obtain desired outcomes in an efficient and effective manner, thus reducing the child's need for engaging in challenging behaviors and facilitating their emerging social competence.

A number of young children demonstrate challenging behaviors that interfere with their learning and developmental and behavioral competence. Understanding the characteristics, including the topographies and functions of challenging behaviors, is important for designing effective interventions. Until an empirical validation of the function of children's specific challenging behaviors is determined, the development and implemention of interventions that are clearly linked to the putative functions of children's behaviors is a necessary, but not sufficient, component of implementing PBS strategies. In the following section, a PBS model for proactively addressing children's challenging behaviors is discussed.

DESIGNING EFFECTIVE INTERVENTIONS THROUGH POSITIVE BEHAVIOR SUPPORT FOR YOUNG CHILDREN

PBS for young children with challenging behaviors consists of an array of empirical interventions based on antecedent and consequent procedures that are designed to prevent or lower the occurrence of challenging behaviors in schools, homes, and communities (e.g., Dunlap et al., 2003; Lewis & Sugai, 1999). Similar to PBS designed for older children, PBS for preschoolers may be implemented on a schoolwide basis (Fox & Little, 2001), a classroomwide basis (Stormont, Lewis, & Smith, 2005), or on an individual level (Conroy, Davis, Fox, & Brown, 2002; Fox, Dunlap, & Powell, 2002). Conceptually, PBS is composed of a multilevel, hierarchical intervention approach beginning with *universal interventions* that are applicable to all children and progressing to more *individualized interventions* that address the challenging behaviors of only a few children who demonstrate severe and chronic misbehaviors (Conroy et al., 2002; Fox et al., 2002; Fox, Dunlap, Hemmeter, Joseph, & Strain, 2003). In this chapter, we discuss only the critical components of PBS that are applicable to those children such as TJ who demonstrate severe, chronic, challenging behaviors that interfere with their learning and that significantly disrupt their classrooms.

Children whose challenging behaviors have been resistant to universal interventions and whose behaviors have continued to be problematic may need individualized types of behavioral supports to ensure success in their classrooms and homes. Once well-engineered and supportive classrooms are established, skill instruction and antecedent and consequent-based behavioral interventions and supports are needed to decrease specific children's challenging behaviors and increase alternative appropriate social competence behaviors. Horner noted, "The signature feature of positive behavior support has been a committed focus on fixing environments, not people" (2000, p. 97). Therefore, assessments of the physical and social environmental factors that may be contributing to children's challenging behaviors are the initial step in implementing individualized PBS. Within a PBS model, this approach typically includes FBA, and is followed by individualized function-based interventions to meet the needs of the children, families, and teachers. This process is described in the following sections and illustrated in Figure 10.1.

Functional Behavioral Assessment

Many researchers and interventionists recommend an FBA as an initial step for addressing individual children's challenging behaviors that are resistant to other interventions (e.g., Conroy, Dunlap, Clarke, & Alter, 2005; Neilsen & McEvoy, 2003; O'Neill, Horner, Albin, Storey, & Sprague, 1997). FBA may increase the likelihood of successful interventions by providing information about 1) the topography of the challenging behaviors, 2) environmental variables preceding the problem behaviors (i.e., antecedent events), 3) environmental variables following the misbehaviors (i.e., consequent events), and 4) circumstances associated with the absence of inappropriate behaviors. Although no single process for conducting an FBA exists, commonly an FBA is completed by progressing though several information-gathering steps including indirect assessments, direct assessments, and analog assessments (i.e., functional and structural analyses) (Ellingson, Miltenberger,

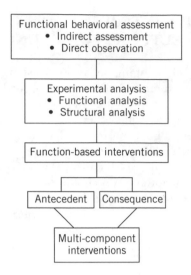

Figure 10.1.   An illustration of the steps involved in positive behavior support (PBS)

& Long, 1999; O'Neill et al., 1997). A brief explanation highlighting the defining features of each of these steps follows.

Indirect Assessments

The primary purpose of indirect assessments is to gather information efficiently from individuals who are familiar with children and who have observed their challenging behaviors and the environmental circumstances surrounding those responses (Fox & Conroy, 1995; O'Neill et al., 1997). Indirect assessments may include several techniques such as reviewing children's educational records, using commercially available functional assessment interviews (e.g., O'Neill et al., 1997), and asking teachers and family members to complete rating scales (e.g., Durand & Crimmins, 1988; Floyd, Phaneuf, & Wilczynski, 2005; Johnston & O'Neill, 2001).

Since the Individuals with Disabilities Education Act Amendments of 1997 (PL 105–17) mandated the use of functional behavioral assessments, many indirect functional behavioral assessments have been developed and can be purchased commercially; however, only limited psychometric information on the reliability or validity of these instruments has been made available. The two more commonly used assessments that have been empirically investigated include the Functional Assessment Interview (FAI; O'Neill et al., 1997) and the Motivation Assessment Scale (MAS; Durand & Crimmins, 1992). Therefore, practitioners may want to consider using one of these two instruments when conducting FBAs.

The FAI, one of the most widely used, indirect functional assessments, examines environmental variables contributing to and maintaining the children's challenging behaviors. Following the completion of the FAI, information about the history of challenging behaviors, antecedent and consequent events surrounding the responses, circumstances in which those behaviors are more or less likely to occur, preferred and nonpreferred materials and activities, and the children's developmental and communicative abilities are revealed (see O'Neill et al., 1997). Typically, teachers or parents who have daily contact with the children of interest and who have observed them engaging in the challenging behaviors complete the FAI. The results of the FAI may provide essential information related to possible outcomes or functions of the challenging behaviors as well as the types of putative reinforcers that may be used during interventions.

The MAS (Durand & Crimmins, 1992) is another rating scale that has been empirically validated and may be useful in the functional assessment process (Floyd et al., 2005; Johnston & O'Neill, 2001). This scale consists of 16 items rated on a 7-point Likert-type scale. The primary focus of the MAS is to identify the functions or outcomes of challenging behaviors rather than particular antecedent events. Similar to the FAI, questions are completed by teachers or parents who are familiar with the children and the challenging behaviors of interest. Four potential functions of children's behaviors are assessed: 1) access to attention, 2) access to tangible items, 3) escape from nonpreferred circumstances, and 4) access to sensory stimulation. Following the completion of the MAS, rank ordering of the four possible functions of challenging behaviors is performed to identify those that are prevalent and relevant to individualized interventions.

One of the strengths of conducting indirect FBAs is that they are relatively easy to complete and may provide general information to guide any subsequent direct observational assessments. However, as with other types of survey or interview instruments, information provided through indirect functional assessments is subject to informant bias, and caution should be exercised when interpreting findings, particularly if they are the sole source of data (e.g., Fox & Conroy, 1995; Floyd et al., 2005). Hence, indirect assessments should be completed as one component of a comprehensive FBA process rather than being used as a single measure of challenging behaviors (e.g., Mace, Lalli, & Pinter-Lalli, 1991; O'Neill et al., 1997; Reichle & Johnston, 1993).

Direct Assessments

Direct assessments (also referred to as *descriptive observations*) are often used to supplement and validate findings from indirect assessments. The primary purpose of direct assessments is to begin to descriptively identify the relationships existing between challenging behaviors and associated antecedent and consequent events. Direct assessments consist of formal observations of the behaviors and the environmental circumstances that surround them. Most often, direct assessments are conducted during times and circumstances in which challenging behaviors are most likely to occur (e.g., Bijou, Peterson, & Ault, 1968; Johnston & O'Neill, 2001). Similar to indirect FBAs, a variety of descriptive direct assessment procedures have been developed to assist with the systematic observation and recording of various antecedent and consequent events. Several common direct assessment procedures include but are not limited to antecedent-behavior-consequence (ABC) recordings (Bijou et al., 1968), Functional Assessment Observation Form (O'Neill et al., 1997), and the ABC Observation Checklist (Miltenberger, 2004).

When performing direct assessments, observers record children's behaviors during identified activities when challenging behaviors are most common, noting occurrences of the misbehaviors and any salient environmental events related to them. Typically, these observations are conducted over several days, and the observers record each instance of challenging behaviors, the antecedent events that precede the behaviors, and any consequent factors that follow the children's responses. Following observations, the frequencies and sequences of behaviors are reviewed and any troublesome patterns in the observed antecedent or consequent circumstances are identified. For instance, in Figure 10.2, the ABC observations for Charmeka show that she engaged in noncompliance and disruptive behavior during antecedent activities such as transitions and outdoor play periods, but not during circle and snack activities. In addition, the ABC analyses revealed that she frequently engaged in misbehaviors following teachers' requests to make a transition from one activity to the next and often gained the teachers' attention in the form of verbal reprimands. At times, Charmeka engaged in aggressive behaviors toward peers to obtain preferred items (e.g., toys, materials) or activities (e.g., line leader, computer access). Following aggressive acts, she often received the teachers' attention in the form of verbal chastisements. Hence, her ABC analysis strongly indicates that antecedent events such as transitions, teachers' demands, and specific classroom activities increase Charmeka's misbehaviors, whereas teachers' attention and obtaining access to preferred items and activities appear to be maintaining her challenging behaviors.

Direct assessments provide valuable information that augments the data obtained through indirect assessments. Similar to indirect methods, direct assessments only provide correlational information; that is, the descriptive assessments do not provide experimental validation of the specific environmental events that contribute to or maintain children's challenging behaviors. Given this limitation, many researchers now employ the use of experimental manipulations such as analog assessments to validate their descriptive analyses (Conroy et al., 2005). Although analog assessments have been used most often for research purposes to experimentally validate environmental events that contribute to and maintain challenging behaviors, these procedures are becoming more common in applied practice settings (for a discussion, see Stichter & Conroy, 2005).

Analog Assessments

Analog assessments differ from descriptive observations because they are experimental in nature and provide validation of the various antecedent and consequent events related to children's challenging behaviors. Two versions of analog assessments may be useful in validating hypotheses developed from the outcomes of descriptive assessments: 1) structural analyses, which evaluate antecedent events, and 2) functional analyses, which evaluate consequent events.

Axelrod (1987) defined *structural analyses* as assessments of antecedent factors that occur prior to or concurrent with children's challenging behaviors and that bring about those misbehaviors (e.g., adult requests followed by child noncompliance). Structural analyses consist of preplanned presentations of analog events that are related to the potential antecedent factors of interest that were identified through the indirect and direct assessments. For instance, if indirect and direct assessments indicated that teachers' demands contributed to children's noncompliance, to validate this hypothesis, analog assessment conditions might include adults making several demands to children over a period of time and, then, systematically recording the children's responses (e.g., noncompliance behaviors, negativistic responses, avoidance behaviors) to those adult initiations. Evaluating the data to determine predictable patterns between teachers' demands and chil-

Child's name: Charmeka

Observer: Carla Murphy

Dates of observation: 1/15/07–1/20/07

Date	Antecedents	Behavior	Consequences	Comments
1/15	**Transition** Teacher requests Charmeka to transition from circle area to center area No teacher demands	Charmeka is noncompliant and runs away	Teacher chases her and says, "No running"	Is transition time difficult? Does Charmeka like the circle activity and not center areas? Does she like the teacher's attention?
1/15	**Snack** Charmeka is seated at the snack table next to peers No teacher demands	Charmeka is eating snack and interacting with her peers No challenging behavior occurs	Teacher praises Charmeka for sitting and talking with her peers	Snack is a preferred activity? Charmeka likes the teacher's and peer's attention?
1/16	**Circle time** Charmeka is seated on the floor and the teacher is singing songs in a group activity	Charmeka is sitting in the circle and singing along with the teacher and peers No challenging behavior occurs	Teacher is attending to all of the children in the circle and several times praises Charmeka for participating in the activity	Charmeka likes circle and singing? Charmeka likes the teacher attention?
1/16	**Outside play** Charmeka is playing on the jungle gym with the other children and one child steps in front of her	Charmeka pushes the child and the child falls down and cries	Teacher reprimands Charmeka and makes her go to "time out" for several minutes	Charmeka may not know how to play with other children? Charmeka wanted to climb on the jungle gym?
1/16	**Transition to handwashing from outside play** After coming in from outside, the teacher asks children to line up for handwashing	Charmeka runs to front of line, pushing several children out of the way	The teacher makes Charmeka go to end of line and reprimands her for pushing	Transitions may be difficult? Charmeka wants the teacher attention?
1/17	**Transition from story to nap** Teacher asks children to move to their mats for naptime	Charmeka is noncompliant and runs around the room stomping on children's mats and blankets	The teacher chases Charmeka and reprimands her saying, "No running, lay down on your mat"	Transitions may be difficult? Charmeka doesn't like to nap? She likes the teacher attention?
1/17	**Snack** Children are seated at the snack table next to her peers	Charmeka is sitting at the table and socially interacting with her peers No challenging behavior	Teacher praises Charmeka for good manners	Charmeka likes snack and the teacher and peer attention?
1/20	**Circle time** Charmeka is seated on the floor in a circle with the other children and teacher is singing a group song	Charmeka is singing and sitting next to her peers on the floor in circle No challenging behavior	Teacher asks Charmeka to pick to lead song	Charmeka likes singing and receiving teacher attention?

Figure 10.2. Sample Antecedent–Behavior–Consequence (ABC) Observation Form for Charmeka.

213

dren's noncompliance should provide direct evidence related to adults' requests as a putative antecedent factor contributing to children's challenging behaviors. Researchers employ structural analyses to evaluate a number of antecedent factors, such as children's preference, instructional activities, and adults' attention (see Conroy et al., 2005).

Axelrod (1987) and Iwata, Dorsey, Slifer, Bauman, and Richman (1994) defined *functional analyses* as assessments of consequent events that maintain or reinforce children's challenging behaviors (e.g., escape from adults' demands, access to preferred activities). During functional analyses, analog assessment conditions are constructed that provide either adults' contingent attention, access to tangible items or activities, or escape from nonpreferred tasks or social demands after children's misbehaviors. In addition, unstructured play periods are commonly employed as control conditions. Children's challenging behaviors are systematically measured across each of these contrived conditions, and behavioral patterns are evaluated in terms of relative changes in the occurrences of problem behaviors. Circumstances in which children's challenging behaviors are most frequent are identified as potential outcomes or functions of those behaviors. If challenging behaviors are undifferentiated across functional analysis conditions, the underlying reason for the occurrence of challenging behaviors is usually thought to be "sensory reinforcement."

A relatively extensive experimental literature provides unambiguous evidence on the effectiveness of structural and functional analyses when identifying environmental variables contributing to the occurrence of children's challenging behaviors (for reviews, see Carr et al., 1999; Conroy et al., 2005). Most often, investigators use analog assessments only in clinical or hospital settings (Derby et al., 1992). Recently, however, researchers have begun to conduct analog assessments in applied practice settings (e.g., classrooms, homes) (e.g., Conroy et al., 2005; Mueller, Sterling-Turner, & Moore, 2005; O'Reilly, Sigafoos, Lancioni, Edrisinha, & Andrews, 2005; Richman & Lindauer, 2005). Although structural and functional analyses establish functional relationships between possible antecedent and consequent events and may be a critical component of children's behavioral assessments, the employment of them by practitioners might be extremely difficult and therefore, is much less common (Stichter, Conroy, & Boyd, 2004). Nevertheless, confirming hypotheses of the putative antecedent and consequent events related to children's challenging behaviors is a fundamental aspect of well-performed FBAs. Therefore, practitioners who are not able to incorporate structural or functional analyses into their assessments may want to consider a triangulation process for the information obtained through FBAs as an alternative method for increasing one's confidence in identification of important environmental and behavioral relationships.

Triangulating Functional Behavioral Assessment Findings

One method for enhancing confidence in the identification of relevant antecedent and consequent events identified through the FBAs is *triangulation* (see Gable, Quinn, Rutherford, Howell, & Hoffman, 1998). Triangulation is a process that assists practitioners in comparing the findings from indirect and direct assessments and developing hypotheses regarding the potential antecedent and consequent events associated with children's challenging behaviors. Hypotheses statements summarize the information obtained through the FBA process and provide "best guesses" about factors related to children's misbehaviors. For example, after completing the FAI (O'Neill et al., 1997), the MAS (Durand & Crimmins, 1992), and ABC observations (Bijou et al., 1968), teachers used triangulation to develop hypothetical statements about the antecedents that are likely to evoke TJ's challenging behaviors and the consequent events that maintain those responses, which they noted on a Data Triangulation Form (see Figure 10.3). Although triangulation does not experimentally validate environmental factors related to behaviors, combining the information obtained from multiple data sources taken at different times provides greater confidence in interpretations of the findings and provides further evidence for developing function-based interventions.

Integrating Functional Behavioral Assessment Information

The results of FBAs may be especially useful in understanding which environmental variables evoke or maintain children's challenging behaviors and may help in determining any deficits in children's behavioral repertoires. Identifying antecedent factors that evoke children's challenging behaviors is important for both the amelioration and prevention of problem behaviors (Stichter et al., 2004). If antecedent conditions are associated with children's adaptive behaviors that are incompatible with challenging behaviors, those circumstances may be used as teaching and learning opportunities when children may practice and become fluent in alternative social and behavioral skills needed in their classrooms, homes, and communities. If, on the other hand, antecedents are linked with occurrences of challenging behaviors, teachers and parents can determine how best to alter those antecedent events and provide effective and efficient behavioral supports to decrease occurrences of inappropriate behaviors. In addition, consequent events may be analyzed to determine which reinforcers are maintaining children's challenging behaviors and which items or activities might be useful in consequating children's appropriate behaviors. Identified reinforcers may then be employed in the development of well-targeted and individualized interventions to ameliorate children's misbehaviors and to teach and practice alternative and appropriate social and adaptive responses (Conroy et al., 2005).

Several effective intervention strategies for children are based on modifying antecedents associated with their challenging behaviors, decreasing the likelihood that children will engage in misbehaviors, teaching appropriate alternative behaviors that match and replace the functions of their problem behaviors, instructing specific adaptive developmental and educational skills, and combining some or all of the three approaches. In fact, Snell, Voorhees, and Chen's (2005) review of function-based interventions showed that 78% of the researchers used consequent-based interventions—which were typically putative positive reinforcement strategies, 65% employed manipulations of antecedent-based interventions, and 49% conducted specific skills training interventions. In additon, Snell and colleagues noted that 78% investigators used two or more of these interventions simultaneously.

FUNCTION-BASED INTERVENTIONS

Function-based interventions are designed and directly linked to the outcomes obtained through the FBA process, and they address the antecedent factors that are likely to contribute to and maintain children's challenging behaviors. Although

Child's name: _____TJ_____   Date: _____1/20/07_____

Challenging behavior: _____Noncompliance, disruption, tantrum behavior_____

Source 1	Source 2	Source 3
Functional Assessment Interview[a]	Motivation Assessment Scale[b]	ABC Observation[c]
Antecedents identified:	**Maintaining consequences:**	**Antecedents identified:**
Teacher demands	Teacher attention (ranked #1)	Teacher request to participate in work related activity
Difficult tasks	Escape (ranked #2)	Nonpreferred activities (manipulative tasks)
Small group work activities		Seated next to specific peers
		Consequences identified:
		Teacher and peer attention
		Escape from tasks
Consequences identified:		
Teacher attention		

Hypotheses statements:

Antecedents: TJ is more likely to engage in challenging behaviors when asked by the teacher to complete structured, nonpreferred tasks.

Consequences: When TJ engages in challenging behaviors, he receives adult attention and escapes nonpreferred tasks.

Possible functions: Obtaining teacher and peer attention, escaping nonpreferred activities

[a]O'Neill, R.E., Horner, R.H., Albin, R.W., Storey, K., & Sprague, J.R. (1997). *Functional assessment and program development for problem behavior: A practical handbook* (2nd ed.). Pacific Grove, CA: Brooks/Cole.

[b]Durand, M., & Crimmins, D. (1992). *Motivation Assessment Scale.* Topeka, KS: Monaco & Associates.

[c]Bijou, S.W., Peterson, R.F., & Ault, M.H. (1968). A method to integrate descriptive and experimental field studies at the level of data and empirical concepts. *Journal of Applied Behavior Analysis, 1,* 175–191.

Figure 10.3. Sample Data Triangulation Form for TJ. (From Gable, R.A., Quinn, M.M., Rutherford, R.B., Howell, K.W., & Hoffman, C.C. [1998]. Addressing student problem behavior–Part II: Conducting a functional behavioral assessment [3rd Ed.] Washington, DC: Center for Effective Collaboration and Practice; adapted by permission.)

antecedent-based procedures and the teaching of specific skills are incorporated into function-based interventions, most often, these procedures involve manipulations of reinforcement through either the systematic delivery of rewards contingent on the absence of challenging behaviors or omission of appropriate behaviors (e.g., Durand & Merges, 2001) or presentation of noncontingent attention (e.g., Vollmer, Marcus, & Ringdahl, 1995).

In the next section, a review of several function-based intervention strategies is provided, beginning with a discussion of antecedent-based interventions that may prevent the occurrence of challenging behaviors followed by a discussion of consequent-based procedures that may be employed to directly decrease children's challenging behaviors. Finally, a review of multi-component intervention strategies is presented.

Antecedent-Based Interventions

Antecedent-based interventions are becoming more common for addressing children's challenging behaviors (for discussion, see Luiselli, 2006; Luiselli & Cameron, 1998). Antecedent-based procedures employ environmental factors identified in FBAs and are implemented prior to occurrences of children's challenging behaviors. Hence, the overall goal of these interventions is to prevent or significantly decrease the likelihood of episodes of problem behaviors. Hypothetically, prevention of children's misbehaviors will afford additional opportunities for children to exhibit appropriate behaviors, receive reinforcement from adults and peers for those adaptive responses, and be meaningfully engaged in developmentally enhancing class, home, and community activities. Researchers have demonstrated frequently that antecedent-based interventions are effective in decreasing children's challenging behaviors (see Conroy & Stichter, 2003; Conroy et al., 2005). Several commonly employed strategies are discussed and highlighted next including making choices, embedding preferred and easy tasks, using high probability requests, determining pre-specified reinforcers, employing curricular modifications, and implementing self-management strategies.

Making Choices

Allowing children to make choices when appropriate is a relatively easy antecedent-based intervention strategy that has been effective in decreasing children's challenging behaviors (e.g., Cole & Levinson, 2002; Dyer, Dunlap, & Winterling, 1990; Jolivette, Stichter, & McCormick, 2002; Kern, Vorndran, Hilt, Ringdahl, Adelman, & Dunlap, 1998). Similar to other function-based procedures, designing choice-making interventions begins with FBAs to identify key circumstances associated with children's challenging behaviors. Following the assessments, teachers and parents determine reasonable options for children to choose from that can be employed just prior to problematic circumstances. For example, if FBA information indicates that children engage in tantrums whenever adults ask them to "clean up the toys," they might rephrase their requests using logical choices. Rather than asking children to "clean up the toys," adults may say, "Do you want to pick up the blocks first or put the trucks away first?" Often, when allowed reasonable choices, children will choose between one of sensible choices rather than engage in challenging behaviors. When implementing choice-making interventions, similar to other effective procedures, adults need to individualize and base them on children's cognitive and language abilities. For example, some children with cognitive and language delays may need three-dimensional objects to represent their preferences, others may require pictures or other symbols to communicate their choices, and some may be able to respond verbally to indicate their selections.

Embedding Preferred Tasks

Similar to choice making, embedding highly preferred or relatively easy tasks into nonpreferred or difficult activities is an antecedent-based intervention that may decrease the probability of challenging behaviors (e.g., Blair, Umbreit, & Bos, 1999; Koegel, Dyer, & Bell, 1987; Umbreit, 1995). Once again, when embedding preferred or easy tasks into nonpreferred or difficult activities, identification of problematic tasks through FBAs is the first essential step. For example, if FBAs indicate that children consistently engage in challenging behaviors when asked to share toys and play with peers, but the children refrain from those misbehaviors and actively interact with peers when the play includes materials related to their favorite themes (e.g., Thomas the Tank Engine, constructing with wooden blocks), teachers should embed children's preferred play materials and themes into the play activities to promote positive peer-related social behaviors. Similarly, if difficult tasks such as teacher-directed, preacademic activities increase children's challenging behaviors, teachers may embed relatively easier tasks into the activity sequence to increase the likelihood of children's compliance and activity engagement. The assumption is that by embedding preferred or easy tasks into nonpreferred or difficult activities, the inherent demands of the tasks are attenuated and more opportunities for children to meaningfully engage in appropriate behaviors are made available. Moreover, practitioners may use these episodes of appropriate behaviors to establish a positive interactive history with children with challenging behaviors.

One of the key features of embedding preferred and easy tasks is to make certain that the activities are identified based on objective observations of children's behaviors. Typically, observing children's engagement during a variety of classroom activities helps to identify preferred tasks. If children spend significant time appropriately engaging with particular activities, then their involvement is evidence that the tasks are preferred. In addition, preferred activities and materials may be identified through functional assessment interviews by asking familiar adults what circumstances children prefer. Likewise, observing the tasks that children engage in independently and frequently and asking familiar adults about children's current developmental and educational abilities may assist in identifying easy tasks for interventions. Tasks should be of only moderate difficulty for children in general and children with misbehaviors in particular. The use of only moderately difficult tasks with easier classroom activities is especially important when initially addressing children's challenging behaviors.

High Probability Request Sequences

High probability request (HPR) sequences, another type of antecedent-based intervention, may be effective in reducing the probability of children's challenging behaviors, particularly children's noncompliance (e.g., Davis, Brady, Hamilton, McEvoy, & Williams, 1994; Davis & Reichle, 1996). HPR sequences are composed of several critical steps. First, through FBAs, a set of requests that children will comply with approximately 80% or more of the time is identified. Next, a set of requests that children typically will not comply with are identified; that is, requests that most often result in noncompliance. Once high and low probability requests are identified, high probability request sequences are implemented by delivering three to five high probability requests during activities in which noncompliance is most likely to occur. Each high probability request is followed with praise and social attention and then, a low probability demand is delivered. For example, if FBAs indicate that children are noncompliant during transitions between classroom activities, teachers may use a high probability request sequence to increase compliance. In this example, teachers ask children to perform four high probability requests (e.g., "Touch your head," "Touch your nose," "Touch your toes," "Stand up"), followed by brief praise for compliance with those requirements and then deliver a low probability request (e.g., "Now, go sit at the table!"). Researchers argue that the "behavioral momentum" of successfully completing a series of high probability demands increases the likelihood that children will comply with the low probability requests (e.g., Davis & Reichle, 1996). In addition, similar to embedding preferred tasks, high probability request sequences may help establish a new and positive behavioral history for children and adults. Specifically, children's compliance may be reinforced at a higher ratio than their noncompliance, breaking a coercive adult-child interaction cycle.

Modifying Curriculum

Another antecedent-based intervention is the implementation of curricular modifications that meet the children's individual needs (e.g., Dunlap, White, & Vera, 1996; Kamps, Ellis, Mancina, Wyble, & Greene, 1995; Kern, Bambara, & Fogt, 2002). Often, challenging behaviors occur, in part, because classroom activities are not appropriate for children's individual developmental and educational needs. For example, if FBAs indicate that children often engage in challenging behaviors to escape activities that require sitting for a long time, one possible reason may be children's inability to attend for those long periods. Therefore, teachers may adjust the length of time children are required to remain in sedentary activities to better match their individual abilities. Several function-based curricular modifications are effective and include 1) lessening the demands or expectations of activities for children, 2) adjusting the time needed to engage in or complete activities, 3) providing higher levels of adult or peer attention and support for children during activities (e.g., Kamps et al., 1995), 4) adapting task-related instructions (e.g., Ellis & Magee, 1999), and 5) substituting an alternative curriculum that is individually appropriate for children's developmental abilities (for a discussion, see Chandler, Dahlquist, Repp, & Feltz, 1999).

Self-Management Strategies

Teaching children to self-manage their behaviors may also be effective in decreasing challenging behaviors (e.g., Connell, Carta, & Baer, 1993; Connell, Carta, Lutz, & Randall, 1993; Kern, Ringdahl, Hilt, & Sterling-Turner, 2001; Reinecke, Newman, & Meinberg, 1999; Sainato, Strain, Lefebvre, & Repp, 1990; Strain, Kohler, Storey, & Danko, 1994). Self-management is an antecedent-based intervention that involves teaching children to systematically observe their behaviors and to better complete activities or engage in positive interactions based on their awareness of those behaviors. Generally, the use of self-management strategies includes processes of self-monitoring and, in some cases, self-assessment; therefore, the majority of research that has investigated the use of self-management has been conducted with kindergarten-age children or with preschoolers who have relatively sophisticated cognitive and language abilities. Self-monitoring requires that children observe and become more aware of their own behaviors, often with adult intercession. For instance, children using self-monitoring may observe whether they followed classroom rules during circle time, whether they played with peers, or whether they made disruptive noises during quiet times. Teaching children to self-monitor is usually accomplished with straightforward teaching techniques including verbal instructions, models, prompts, and reinforcers, which should be faded across time. Children are also taught to become aware of the behaviors of interest in some explicit manner, such as marking a happy face versus a frowning face, checking a picture chart to indicate that a rule was followed, or simply describing their behaviors to adults. A self-assessment component adds a condition in which children specify whether monitored behaviors met a pre-defined performance standard, such as, "I shared three times in the block area!" (e.g., Conroy & Sellers, 2001).

Researchers employ a number of variations of self-management procedures. Most have included adult prompts to initially establish children's independent use of the self-management procedures, and many have combined self-management with teachers' contingent praise. Specific strategies seem to be related to the developmental characteristics of children, the goals of the interventionists, and the preferences of practitioners responsible for implementing the interventions (e.g., Connell et al., 1993; Sainato et al., 1990; Strain et al., 1994).

Overall, when linked to outcomes of FBAs, antecedent-based interventions may be effective in reducing the occurrence of young children's challenging behaviors. In general, they provide children with multiple opportunities that increase the likelihood of engaging in appropriate behaviors and receiving reinforcement for those behaviors. Moreover, collateral decreases in challenging behaviors often occur. Although antecedent-based interventions may be effective, they are often used in combination with consequent-based interventions that are specifically designed to directly decrease the occurrence of the challenging behaviors and increase appropriate, replacement behaviors.

Consequent-Based Interventions

Consequent-based interventions are founded on principles of positive and negative reinforcement that increase appropriate behaviors as well as strategies to decrease or punish the occurrence of challenging behaviors (Miltenberger, 2004). The application of these practices should be directly linked to the functions of children's challenging behaviors that are identified through functional behavioral assessments. Consequent-based interventions systematically address environmental factors identified through the FBA process that maintain children's challenging behaviors—with the overall goal of increasing children's appropriate behaviors and decreasing their challenging behaviors. If children engage frequently in appropriate behaviors and those adaptive responses are reinforced, then they have more opportunities to be involved in meaningful activities in their classrooms, homes, and communities. An important component of consequent-based interventions, however, is also decreasing the occurrence of challenging behaviors. Even with the implementation of antecedent-based interventions that decrease the probability of problem behaviors, many children will continue to demonstrate some misbehaviors. Therefore, consequent-based interventions need to be employed to directly affect any continuing maladaptive behaviors. Historically, researchers have demonstrated a number of effective consequent-based interventions for use with children with challenging behaviors (for a review, see Carr et al., 1999; Conroy et al., 2005). Most of these effective strategies involve teaching children appropriate behaviors that can replace children's problematic behavioral repertoires. One of the most common interventions is the use of functional communication training (FCT). Therefore, the following section begins with an overview of FCT followed by a description of several other consequent-based strategies including the delivery of contingent reinforcement, use of differential reinforcement, and employing extinction.

Functional Communication Training

Functional communication training is an intervention strategy designed for children who engage in challenging behaviors and lack the appropriate communication skills needed to request access to or escape from activities, tangible items, and adults' or peers' attention (e.g., Durand, 1990; Drasgow, Halle, Ostrosky, & Harbers, 1996; Reichle, Drager, & Davis, 2002; Reichle & Wacker, 1993; Vollmer, Marcus, & LeBlanc, 1994). FCT begins by identifying the functions of the challenging behaviors through the FBAs. After the functions of children's behaviors are identified, more desirable and conventional forms of communicative responses are selected to use as *replacements* for children's challenging behaviors. For example, if children engage in challenging behaviors in the form of aggressive and tantrum behaviors, suitable replacement behaviors may be appropriate gestural, speech, or augmentative communications. The functional communicative responses should be skills that children are already capable of using, or behaviors that are easily taught, readily recognized, and immediately reinforced by adults whenever children communicate appropriately. Once new communication forms are selected, FCT intervention involves ignoring children's challenging behaviors, and explicitly and systematically prompting and rewarding use of replacement responses. A critical component of FCT is to implement the procedures when children begin to display their challenging behaviors, to attend to and reinforce their new communicative requests, and to ensure that the problem behaviors do not result in reinforcement. Another key FCT component is that children's response efforts for using the new communicative replacement behaviors should be *less than* the response efforts for engaging in the challenging behaviors (e.g., Richman, Wacker, & Winborn, 2001). That is, when engaging in the appropriate functional communicative responses, children should be able to obtain positive outcomes more easily than when they engage in challenging behaviors. Therefore, the response efficiency for emitting appropriate communicative behaviors learned through FCT should be greatly emphasized (see Horner & Day, 1991). For example, if FBAs indicate that children employ tantrums to obtain preferred tangible items, the FCT for using appropriate behaviors (e.g., gestures, pictures, single word utterances) to request those tangible items should require less effort and be more efficient for them than engaging in tantrums to obtain preferred items. Because of training, children will learn that the appropriate behaviors produce the same outcomes as their challenging behaviors in a more efficient and effective manner (see Carr et al., 1994).

Contingent Reinforcement

The overall goal of function-based interventions is to increase appropriate responses while decreasing challenging behaviors. Although FCT is often used, an additional behavioral intervention that is closely related to FCT is the practice of increasing children's access to contingent reinforcement for appropriate behaviors, regardless of whether the responses are communicative (e.g., Lawry, Storey, & Danko, 1993; Luiselli & Luselli, 1995; Northrup et al., 1995). For example, if the FBAs show that children engage in stereotypic behaviors (e.g., hand flapping, arm waving) during instruction and adults' attention and praise is an effective reinforcer, teachers may want to provide attention contingent upon "quiet hands" (i.e., no stereotypy or those behaviors that are incompatible with self-stimulation). Alternatively, if hand flapping is a reinforcing event, teachers may want to increase children's access to brief self-stimulation contingent on completion of specified adaptive activities (e.g., McGee, Daly, Izeman, Mann, & Risley, 1991; Wolery, Kirk, & Gast, 1985). In both examples, children receive increased access to different forms of contingent reinforcement for engaging in appropriate behaviors.

Given that many children with challenging behaviors have relatively idiosyncratic reinforcers, the forms of and schedules for reinforcement should be based on careful consideration of the information from the FBAs. In particular, teachers may use the FBAs to identify peculiar reinforcers and evaluate the current density of reinforcement that occurs for children's challenging behaviors. During the early stage of interventions, schedules of children's reinforcement for appropriate behaviors may need to be much more frequent than their schedules of reinforcement for challenging behaviors, which should be decreased as soon as possible. For example, if challenging behaviors result in access to reinforcing outcomes following 50% of the behavioral incidents, which is a relatively rich schedule of reinforcement, schedules for appropriate behaviors should be provided at a higher rate of at least 75% of children's appropriate responses. Once children receive predictable and high rates of reinforcement for appropriate behaviors, their adaptive behaviors will become more fluent and a corresponding decrease in the frequency, intensity, or duration of the challenging behaviors may be evident (e.g., Kerr & Nelson, 2002; Miltenberger, 2004). At that time, schedules of reinforcement for appropriate behaviors should be judiciously faded (e.g., Timm, Strain, & Eilers, 1979). Following sufficient behavioral change, children's schedules of reinforcement should be adjusted with a goal of their appropriate behaviors being maintained with forms and schedules of reinforcement similar to their same-age peers in similar circumstances.

Along with examining idiosyncratic forms and schedules of contingent reinforcement, pre-specifying reinforcers may also be useful when implementing contingent rewards. Pre-specifying contingent reinforcers is often referred to as the *Premack Principle* (Premack, 1962), or colloquially as "grandma's rule." When implementing this strategy, FBAs are used to determine activities or events that increase the likelihood of children's challenging behaviors as well as reinforcers that increase the probability of appropriate behaviors. Next, teachers or parents clearly identify for children appropriate behaviors and outcomes for engaging in those adaptive behaviors. For example, parents might state, "If you put your bike away, you can go swing." In this example, the circumstances that increase the likelihood of a child's challenging behaviors is putting his or her bike away, which should be followed by reinforcing events that increase the probability of reinforcement; that is, access to the swing set and preferred swinging. Again, the critical component is systematic application of the reinforcing circumstances contingent on children's appropriate behaviors.

Differential Reinforcement

In addition to increased access to contingent reinforcement, another effective reinforcement strategy for reducing children's challenging behaviors is differential reinforcement (e.g., Conyers, Miltenberger, Romaniuk, Kopp, & Himle, 2003; Matson, Dixon, & Matson, 2005; Repp, Felce, & Barton, 1991). Differential reinforcement of other behaviors (DRO) is the delivery of reinforcers based on the *absence* of specified responses for a predetermined interval of time (e.g., Kerr & Nelson, 2002; Miltenberger, 2004). Similar to increased access to reinforcement, when using DRO, the form of reinforcement and the time interval selected is based on information gathered through FBAs. At the end of the specific time interval, the identified reinforcement is provided only if children's challenging behaviors have not occurred. If no problem behaviors have been emitted and once the reinforcement is delivered, the time interval is reset and the opportunity to earn another reinforcer reoccurs. If challenging behaviors occur during the time interval, however, no reinforcers are provided and the interval is reset and the opportunity to earn future reinforcement begins again. For example, if the FBAs indicate that children engage in challenging behaviors at least once per minute to receive adults' attention during large group activities, teachers might provide adults' attention approximately every minute if the children do not exhibit challenging behaviors during those time periods. In other words, DRO is the delivery of reinforcement (as determined through the FBA) for *not* engaging the challenging behaviors. Careful attention to the forms of the reinforcement and length of the time intervals as determined through the FBAs is important to ensure that the delivery of the reinforcers is effective and the behaviors will be controlled by reinforcement schedules.

Extinction

The function-based interventions described previously provide children with access to reinforcement contingent on appropriate behaviors (e.g., differential reinforcement of alternative behavior, FCT) or in the absence of challenging behaviors (e.g., DRO). Withholding reinforcement, a strategy more commonly referred to as *extinction*, is another function-based intervention that is focused on systematically withholding reinforcers following children's challenging behaviors (e.g., Asmus, Wacker, Harding, Berg, Derby, & Kocis, 1999; Azrin, Hutchinson, & Hake, 1966; Lalli, Zanolli, & Wohn, 1994). For example, when functional behavioral assessment information reveals that children engage in disruptive behaviors to obtain an adults' attention, the use of extinction as a behavioral intervention might require that teachers not attend to children's behavior following disruptions.

As suggested earlier, function-based interventions may be used in combination. Therefore, interventionists may employ extinction as well as differential reinforcement to better address children's challenging behaviors. For example, if FBAs show that reinforcers for challenging behaviors are access to tangible activities, such as computer time, a behavioral intervention strategy may require withholding the reinforcement or access to computers following any display of misbehaviors. Nevertheless, in addition to the withholding of reinforcement, additional function-based interventions may be employed with children's appropriate behaviors. In this example, functional communication training may teach children appropriate behaviors that may be used to replace the challenging behaviors and to gain access to computers. Oftentimes the use of extinction procedures alone may result in increases in the frequency and intensity of children's challenging behaviors, called an *extinction burst.* Pairing extinction with positive reinforcement interventions may reduce the potential for troublesome extinction bursts (e.g., Lerman, Iwata, & Wallace, 1999).

Consequent-based interventions are an important component of designing function-based interventions that directly address children's acquisition and fluent exhibition of appropriate behaviors while decreasing their challenging behaviors. Several different consequent-based procedures that have been effective in increasing children's appropriate behaviors and decreasing their problem behaviors were presented. Most often in the positive behavioral support (PBS) literature, a combination of antecedent and consequent approaches, referred to as multi-component interventions, have been used.

Multi-Component Interventions

Many researchers working in applied settings have employed multi-component interventions to attenuate children's challenging behaviors (for reviews, see Conroy et al., 2005; Snell et al., 2005). For instance, Harding and colleagues (1999) incorporated several environmental variables into a multi-component intervention that included choice making, preferred activities, instructional prompting, contingent social attention, and time out. In addition, Kamps and colleagues (1995) designed multi-component interventions that consist of monitoring by teachers during play, teaching and prompting of social skills, accessing appropriate social behaviors by peers, and increasing reinforcement schedules for appropriate social behaviors. Multi-component interventions typically employ both antecedent- and consequent-based procedures, such as lowering children's activity demands, teaching children to request assistance with difficult or nonpreferred activities, pairing tasks with instructions to explicitly teach children functional communication skills, learning to wait longer periods of time before requesting adults' help, and using contingent reinforcement and extinction. For example, a multi-component intervention may consist of antecedent-based interventions where preferred activities are embedded into nonpreferred activities, and children are provided with contingent adult attention for meaningful engagement while reinforcement is withheld following challenging behaviors. Over time, it may be necessary to assess specific intervention components that are critical to include (e.g., contingent attention for appropriate behaviors) and any components that are less critical (e.g., embedding preferred activities) should be faded first. Ultimately, the goal is for children to participate in their environments successfully with only the minimal behavioral supports necessary to sustain desirable outcomes (e.g., Blair, Umbreit, & Eck, 2000; Carr & Carlson, 1993).

Function-based interventions are becoming more common in the literature. Regardless of whether these procedures employ the use of antecedent- or consequent-based strategies, separately or in some combination, the development and implementation of these interventions are typically linked to the outcomes of the FBAs. Effective interventions may address the functions of children's challenging behaviors (i.e., consequent-based interventions), prevent the occurrence of the challenging behaviors (i.e., antecedent-based interventions), teach specific skills to fluency, and most often, include a combination of those interventions. Frequently, researchers have examined the effectiveness of function-based interventions with children in classrooms. Nevertheless, function-based interventions for ameliorating children's challenging behaviors have also been effectively employed in homes and communities by parents and family members (e.g., Arndorfer, Miltenberger, Woster, Rortvedt, & Gaffaney, 1994; Asmus et al., 1999). Therefore, in the following section, we discuss application of these interventions to other nonschool settings.

Implementing Function-Based Interventions in Homes

Children's challenging behaviors occur across different people, settings, and circumstances and often produce similar problematic outcomes (Asmus, Franzese, Conroy, & Dozier, 2003). Challenging behaviors in homes and communities may negatively influence families' abilities to remain engaged in routine and adaptive activities and may cause stress on the family members (e.g., Emerson, 2003). Hence, function-based interventions for homes and communities may be an essential component of children's interventions. Developing function-based interventions for children's homes may be very similar to development of school plans. Given that homes may be more varied, several specific modifications should be considered.

Because of the potentially sensitive nature of employing interventions in homes, careful consideration should be given to families' routines and activities when developing function-based interventions (e.g., Woods & Goldstein, 2003). For example, if children's challenging behaviors usually occur during families' routines such as meal or bath times, these activities might be especially important circumstances for intervention. Woods and Goldstein (2003) noted that using families' routines as the context for behavioral interventions may provide consistency within familiar routines to better support families, assist family members in predicting when learning opportunities may occur, and make interventions more meaningful and consistent with families' concerns and priorities. In addition, embedding interventions within normally occurring home and community routines and activities may increase positive interactions between children and their parents and siblings. Moreover, the establishment of positive learning histories in families' homes and communities may assist in attenuating "coercive adult–child interaction patterns" (Reid & Patterson, 1991).

CONCLUSIONS

Researchers have repeatedly shown that children's challenging behaviors that are not dealt with effectively early in life are potent predictors of significant—and perhaps for some individuals, relatively intractable—adolescent and adult problems (see Campbell, 2002; Reid & Patterson, 1991). Moreover, many early childhood special educators have argued that prevention and early intervention to ameliorate persistent challenging behaviors is sorely needed for a significant number of young children (e.g., Conroy & Brown, 2004; Olive & McEvoy, 2004; Sigafoos, 2000; Symons, 2000). For many children with developmental delays and disabilities, challenging behaviors are often a primary reason why families request assistance with their children. Timely and effective prevention and early intervention efforts may prevent children's challenging behaviors from evolving into even more serious maladaptive behaviors that greatly restrict educational and social opportunities in their communities (e.g., Carr et al., 1999; Conroy & Brown, 2004). Therefore, effective interventions for children's challenging behaviors are essential to children's future optimal development and educational attainment. Indeed, effective intervention efforts for children with persistent problem behaviors may improve their social and behavioral competence and facilitate their meaningful involvement in less restrictive and more normalized educational and community activities and settings.

REFERENCES

Arndorfer, R.E., Miltenberger, R.G., Woster, S.H., Rortvedt, A.K., & Gaffaney, T. (1994). Home-based descriptive and experimental analysis of problem behaviors in children. *Topics in Early Childhood Special Education, 14*, 64–87.

Asmus, J., Franzese, J.M., Conroy, M.A., & Dozier, C.L. (2003). Clarifying functional analysis outcomes for stereotypy and destructive behaviors via controlling consequence delivery. *School Psychology Review, 32*, 617–623.

Asmus, J.M., Wacker, D.P., Harding, J., Berg, W.K., Derby, M., & Kocis, E. (1999). Evaluation of antecedent stimulus parameters for the treatment of escape-maintained aberrant behavior. *Journal of Applied Behavior Analysis 32*, 495–513.

Azrin, N.H., Hutchinson, R.R., & Hake, D.F. (1966). Extinction produced aggression. *Journal of the Experimental Analysis of Behavior, 9*, 191–204.

Axelrod, S. (1987). Functional and structural analyses of behavior: Approaches leading to reduced use of punishment procedures. *Research in Developmental Disabilities, 8*, 165–178.

Bijou, S.W. (1993). *Behavior analysis of child development* (2nd ed.). Reno, NV: Context Press.

Bijou, S.W., Peterson, R.F., & Ault, M.H. (1968). A method to integrate descriptive and experimental field studies at the level of data and empirical concepts. *Journal of Applied Behavior Analysis, 1*, 175–191.

Blair, K.C., Umbreit, J., & Bos, C.S. (1999). Using functional assessment and children's preferences to improve the behavior of young children with behavioral disorders. *Behavioral Disorders, 24*, 151–166.

Blair, K.C., Umbreit, J., & Eck, S. (2000). Analysis of multiple variables related to a young child's aggressive behavior. *Journal of Positive Behavioral Interventions, 2*, 33–39.

Campbell, S.B. (2002). *Behavior problems in preschool children: Clinical and developmental issues* (2nd ed.). New York: Guilford Press.

Carr, E.G., & Carlson, J.I. (1993). Reduction of severe behavior problems in the community using a multi-component treatment approach. *Journal of Applied Behavior Analysis, 26*, 157–172.

Carr, E.G., Horner, R.H., Turnbull, A.P., Marquis, J.G., McLaughlin, D.M., McAtee, M.L., et al. (1999). Washington, DC: *Positive behavior support for people with developmental disabilities: A research synthesis.* American Association on Mental Retardation.

Carr, E.G., Levin, L., McConnachie, G., Carlson, J.I., Kemp, D.C., & Smith, C.E. (1994). *Communication based intervention for problem behavior: A user's guide for producing positive change.* Baltimore: Paul H. Brookes Publishing Co.

Chandler, L.K., Dahlquist, C.M., Repp, A.C., & Feltz, C. (1999). The effects of team-based functional assessment on the behavior of students in classroom settings. *Exceptional Children, 66,* 101–122.

Cole, C.L., & Levinson, T.R. (2002). Effects of within-activity choices on the challenging behavior of children with severe developmental disabilities. *Journal of Positive Behavior Interventions, 4,* 29–37.

Connell, M.C., Carta, J., & Baer, D.M. (1993). Programming generalization of in-class transition skills: Teaching preschoolers with developmental delays to self-assess and recruit control. *Journal of Applied Behavior Analysis, 26,* 345–352.

Connell, M.C., Carta, J., Lutz, S., & Randall, C. (1993). Building independence during in-class transitions: Teaching in-class transition skills to preschoolers with developmental delays through. *Education and Treatment of Children, 16,* 160–174.

Conroy, M.A., & Brown, W.H. (2004). Early identification, prevention, and early intervention with young children at-risk for emotional or behavioral disorders: Issues, trends, and a call for action. *Behavioral Disorders, 29,* 224–237.

Conroy, M.A., Davis, C.A., Fox, J.J., & Brown, W.H. (2002). Functional assessment of behavior and effective supports for young children with challenging behavior. *Assessment for Effective Instruction, 27,* 35–47.

Conroy, M.A., Dunlap, G., Clarke, S. & Alter, P.J. (2005). A descriptive analysis of positive behavioral intervention research with young children with challenging behavior. *Topics in Early Childhood Special Education, 25,* 157–166.

Conroy, M.A., & Sellers, J. (2001). *Strategies for maintaining positive changes in academic and nonacademic performance.* Reston, VA: CCBD Monograph.

Conroy, M.A., & Stichter, J. (2003). The application of antecedents in the functional assessment process: Existing research, issues, and recommendations. *Journal of Special Education, 37,* 49–87.

Conyers, C., Miltenberger, R., Romaniuk, C., Kopp, B., & Himle, M. (2003). Evaluation of DRO schedules to reduce disruptive behavior in a preschool class. *Child and Behavior Family Therapy, 25,* 1–6.

Davis, C.A., Brady, M.P., Hamilton, R., McEvoy, M.A., & Williams, R.E. (1994). Effects of high-probability requests on the social intention of young children with severe disabilities. *Journal of Applied Behavior Analysis, 27,* 619–637.

Davis, C.A., & Reichle, J. (1996). Variant and invariant high-probability requests: Increasing appropriate behaviors in children with emotional-behavioral disorders. *Journal of Applied Behavior Analysis, 29,* 471–482.

Derby, K.M., Wacker, D.P., Sasso, G., Steege, M., Northup, J., Cigrand, K., & Asmus, J. (1992). Brief functional assessment techniques to evaluate aberrant behavior in an outpatient setting: A summary of 79 cases. *Journal of Applied Behavior Analysis, 25,* 713–721.

Doss, L., & Reichle, J. (1991). Replacing excess behavior with an initial communicative repertoire. In J. Reichle, J. York, & J. Sigafoos (Eds.), *Implementing augmentative and alternative communication: Strategies for learners with severe disabilities* (pp. 215–237). Baltimore: Paul H. Brookes Publishing Co.

Drasgow, E., Halle, J.W., Ostrosky, M.M., & Harbers, H.M. (1996). Using behavioral indication and functional communication training to establish an initial sign repertoire with a young child with severe disabilities. *Topics in Early Childhood Special Education, 16,* 500–521.

Dunlap, G., Conroy, M., Kern, L., DuPaul, G., VanBrakle, J., Strain, P., et al. (2003). *Research synthesis on effective intervention procedures: Executive summary.* Tampa, FL: Center for Evidence-Based Practices.

Dunlap, G., White, R., & Vera, A. (1996). The effects of multi-component, assessment-based curricular modifications on the classroom behavior of children with emotional and behavioral disorders. *Journal of Behavioral Education, 6,* 481–500.

Durand, V.M. (1990). *Severe behavior problems: A functional communication training approach.* New York: Guilford Press.

Durand, V.M., & Crimmins, D.B. (1988). Identifying the variables maintaining self-injurious behavior. *Journal of Autism and Developmental Disabilities, 18,* 99–117.

Durand, M., & Crimmins, D. (1992). *Motivation Assessment Scale.* Topeka, KS: Monaco & Associates.

Durand, V.M., & Merges, E. (2001). Functional communication training: A contemporary behavior analytic intervention for problem behaviors. *Focus on Autism and Other Developmental Disabilities, 16,* 110–119.

Dyer, K., Dunlap, G., & Winterling, V. (1990). Effects of choice making on the serious problem behaviors of students with severe handicaps. *Journal of Applied Behavior Analysis, 23,* 515–524.

Ellingson, S.A., Miltenberger, R.G., & Long, E.S. (1999). A survey of the use of functional assessment procedures in agencies serving individuals with developmental disabilities. *Behavioral Interventions, 14,* 187–198.

Ellis, J., & Magee, S.K. (1999). Determination of environmental correlates of disruptive classroom behavior: Integration of functional analysis into public school assessment process. *Education and Treatment of Children, 22,* 291–316.

Emerson, E. (2003). Mothers of children and adolescents with intellectual disability: Social and economic situation, mental health status, and the self-assessed social and psychological impact of the child's difficulties. *Journal of Intellectual Disabilities Research, 47,* 385–399.

Floyd, R.G., Phaneuf, R.L., & Wilczynski, S.M. (2005). Measurement properties of indirect assessments methods for functional behavioral assessment: A review of research. *School Psychology Review, 34,* 58–73.

Fox, J.J., & Conroy, M.A. (1995). Setting events and behavior problems: An interbehavioral field analysis for research and practice. *Journal of Emotional/Behavioral Disorders, 3,* 130–140.

Fox, L., Dunlap, G., Hemmeter, M.L., Joseph, G., & Strain, P. (2003). The teaching pyramid: A model for supporting social competence and preventing challenging behavior in young children. *Young Children, 58*(4), 48–52.

Fox, L., Dunlap, G., & Powell, D. (2002). Young children with challenging behavior: Issues and considerations for behavior support. *Journal of Positive Behavior Interventions, 4*(4), 208–217.

Fox, L., & Little, N. (2001). Starting early: Developing school-wide behavior support in a community preschool. *Journal of Positive Behavior Interventions, 3*(4), 251–254.

Gable, R.A., Quinn, M.M., Rutherford, R.B., Howell, K.W., & Hoffman, C.C. (1998). *Addressing student problem behavior–Part II: Conducting a functional behavioral assessment* (3rd ed.) Washington, DC: Center for Effective Collaboration and Practice.

Harding, J.W., Wacker, D.P., Berg, W.K., Cooper, L., Asmus, J., Mela, K., & Muller, J. (1999). An analysis of choice making in the assessment of young children with severe behavior problems. *Journal of Applied Behavior Analysis, 32,* 63–82.

Horner, R.H. (2000). Positive behavior supports. *Focus on Autism and Other Developmental Disabilities, 15* (2), 97–105.

Horner, R.H., & Day, H.M. (1991). The effects of response efficiency on functionally equivalent competing behaviors. *Journal of Applied Behavior Analysis, 24,* 719–732.

Individuals with Disabilities Education Act Amendments of 1997, PL 105–17, 20 U.S.C. §§ 1400 *et seq.*

Iwata, B.A., Dorsey, M.F., Slifer, K.J., Bauman, K.E., & Richman, G.S. (1994). Toward a functional analysis of self-injury. *Journal of Applied Behavior Analysis, 27,* 197–209.

Johnston, S.S., & O'Neill, R.E. (2001). Searching for effectiveness and efficiency in conducting functional assessments: A review and proposes process for teachers and other practitioners. *Focus on Autism and Other Developmental Disabilities, 16,* 205–214.

Jolivette, K., Stichter, J.P., & McCormick, K.M. (2002). Making choices, improving behavior, engaging in learning. *Teaching Exceptional Children, 34*(3), 24–29.

Kamps, D.M., Ellis, C., Mancina, C., Wyble, J., & Greene, L. (1995). Case studies using functional analysis for young children with behavior risks. *Education and Treatment of Children, 18,* 243–260.

Kern, L., Bambara, L., & Fogt, J. (2002). Class-wide curricular modification to improve the behavior of students with emotional or behavioral disorders. *Behavioral Disorders, 27,* 317–326.

Kern, L., Ringdahl, J.E., Hilt, A., & Sterling-Turner, H.E. (2001). Linking self-management procedures to functional analysis results. *Behavioral Disorders, 26,* 214–226.

Kern, L., Vorndran, C.M., Hilt, A., Ringdahl, J.E., Adelman, B.E., & Dunlap, G. (1998). Choice as an intervention to improve behavior: A review of the literature. *Journal of Behavioral Education, 8,* 151–170.

Kerr, M.M., & Nelson, C.M. (2002). *Strategies for addressing problem behavior in the classroom* (4th ed.). New York: Merrill.

Koegel, R.L., Dyer, K., & Bell, L.K. (1987). The influence of child-preferred activities on autistic children's social behavior. *Journal of Applied Behavior Analysis, 20,* 243–252.

Lalli, J.S., Zanolli, K., & Wohn, T. (1994). Using extinction to promote response variability in toy play. *Journal of Applied Behavior Analysis, 27,* 735–736.

Lawry, J.R., Storey, K., & Danko, C.D. (1993). Analyzing behavior problems in the classroom: A case study of functional analysis. *Intervention in School and Clinic, 29,* 96–100.

Lerman, D.C., Iwata, B.A., & Wallace, M.D. (1999). Side effects of extinction: Prevalence of bursting and aggression during the treatment of self-injurious behavior. *Journal of Applied Behavior Analysis, 32,* 1–8.

Lewis, T.J., & Sugai, G. (1999). Effective behavior support: A systems approach to proactive schoolwide management. *Focus on Exceptional Children, 31,* 2–24.

Luiselli, J.K. (Ed.) (2006). *Antecedent assessment and intervention: Supporting children and adults with developmental disabilities in community settings.* Baltimore: Paul H. Brookes Publishing Co.

Luiselli, J.K., & Cameron, M.J. (Eds.) (1998). *Antecedent control: Innovative approaches to behavioral support.* Baltimore: Paul H. Brookes Publishing Co.

Luiselli, J.K., & Luiselli, T.E. (1995). A behavior analysis approach toward chronic food refusal in children with gastrostomy-tube dependency. *Topics in Early Childhood Special Education, 15,* 1–18.

Mace, F.C., Lalli, J.S., & Pinter-Lalli, E. (1991). Functional analysis and the treatment of aberrant behavior. *Research in Developmental Disabilities, 12,* 155–180.

Matson, J.L., Dixon, D.R., & Matson, M.L. (2005). Assessing and treating aggression in children and adolescents with developmental disabilities: A 20-year overview. *Educational Psychology, 25,* 151–181.

McGee, G.G., Daly, T., Izeman, S.G., Mann, L.H. & Risley, T.R. (1991). Use of classroom materials to promote preschool engagement. *Teaching Exceptional Children, 23,* 44–47.

Miltenberger, R.G. (2004). *Behavior modification: Principles and procedures.* Belmont: CA: Wadworth/Thompson Learning.

Mueller, M.M., Sterling-Turner, H.E., & Moore, J.W. (2005). Towards developing a classroom-based functional analysis condition to assess escape-to-attention as a variable maintaining problem behavior. *School Psychology Review, 34,* 425–431.

Neilsen, S., & McEvoy, M.A. (2003). Functional behavioral assessment in early education settings. *Journal of Early Intervention, 26,* 115–131.

Northrup, J., Broussard, C., Jones, K., George, T., Vollmer, T.R., & Herring, M. (1995). The differential effects of teacher and peer attention on the disruptive classroom behavior of three children with a diagnosis of attention deficit hyperactivity disorder. *Journal of Applied Behavior Analysis, 28,* 227–228.

Olive, M.L., & McEvoy, M.A. (2004). Issues, trends, and challenges in early intervention. In A. McCray Sorrells, H.J. Rieth, & P.T. Sindelar (Eds.), *Critical issues in special education* (pp. 92–105). Boston: Allyn & Bacon.

O'Neill, R.E., Horner, R.H., Albin, R.W., Storey, K., & Sprague, J.R. (1997). *Functional assessment and program development for problem behavior: A practical handbook* (2nd ed.). Pacific Grove, CA: Brooks/Cole.

O'Reilly, M., Sigafoos, J., Lancioni, G., Edrisinha, C., & Andrews, A. (2005). An examination of the effects of a classroom activity schedule on levels of self-injury and engagement for a child with severe autism. *Journal of Autism & Developmental Disorders, 35,* 305–311.

Premack, D. (1962). Reversibility of the reinforcer relation. *Science, 136,* 255–257.

Reichle, J. Drager, K., & Davis, C. (2002). Using requests for assistance to obtain desired items and to gain release from nonpreferred activities: Implications for assessment and intervention. *Education & Treatment of Children, 25*(1), 47–66.

Reichle, J., & Johnston, S.S. (1993). Replacing challenging behavior: The role of communication intervention. *Topics in Language Disorders, 13,* 61–76.

Reichle, J., & Wacker, D.P. (1993). *Communicative alternatives to challenging behavior: Integrating functional assessment and intervention strategies. In Communication and language intervention series: Vol. 3.* Baltimore: Paul H. Brookes Publishing Co.

Reid, J.B., & Patterson, G.R. (1991). Early prevention and intervention with conduct problems: A social interaction model for the integration of research and practice. In G. Stoner, M.R. Shinn, & H.M. Walker (Eds.), *Interventions for achievement and behavior problems* (pp. 715–739). Silver Spring, MD: National Association of School Psychologists.

Reinecke, D.R., Newman, B., & Meinberg, D.L. (1999). Self-management of sharing in three preschoolers with autism. *Education and Training in Mental Retardation and Developmental Disabilities, 34,* 312–317.

Repp, A.C., Felce, D., & Barton, L.E. (1991). The effects of initial interval size on the efficacy of DRO schedules of reinforcement. *Exceptional Children, 57,* 417–425.

Richman, D.M., & Lindauer, S.E. (2005). Longitudinal assessment of stereotypic, proto-injurious, and self-injurious behavior exhibited by young children with developmental delays. *American Journal on Mental Retardation, 110,* 439–450.

Richman, D.M., Wacker, D.P., & Winborn, L. (2001). Response efficiency during functional communication training: Effects of effort on response allocation. *Journal of Applied Behavior Analysis, 34,* 73–76.

Sainato, D.M., Strain, P.S., Lefebvre, D., & Repp, N. (1990). Effects of self-evaluation on the independent work skills of preschool children with disabilities. *Exceptional Children, 56,* 540–549.

Serna, L., Nielsen, E., Lambros, K., & Forness, S. (2000). Primary prevention with children at risk for emotional or behavioral disorders: Data on a universal intervention for Head Start classrooms. *Behavioral Disorders, 26,* 70–84.

Sigafoos, J. (2000). Communication development and aberrant behaviour in children with developmental disabilities. *Education and Training in Mental Retardation, 35,* 168–176.

Snell, M.E., Voorhees, M.D., & Chen, L.Y. (2005). Team involvement in assessment-based interventions for problem behavior. *Journal of Positive Behavior Interventions, 7,* 140–152.

Stichter, J.P., & Conroy, M. (2005). Structural analysis in natural settings: A responsive functional assessment strategy. *Journal of Behavioral Education, 14*(1), 19–34.

Stichter, J.P., Conroy, M.A., & Boyd, B.A. (2004). The undefined role of the antecedent: Addressing the measurement quagmires in applied research. *Education and Treatment of Children, 27,* 490–508.

Stormont, M., Lewis, T.J., & Smith, S.C. (2005). Behavior support strategies in early childhood settings: Teachers' importance and feasibility ratings. *Journal of Positive Behavior Interventions, 7*(3), 131–139.

Strain, P.S., Kohler, F.W., Storey, K., & Danko, C.D. (1994). Teaching preschoolers with autism to self-monitor their social interactions: An analysis of results in home and school settings. *Journal of Emotional and Behavioral Disorders, 2,* 78–88.

Symons, F.J. (2000). Early intervention for early, aberrant repetitive behavior: Possible, plausible, probable? *Journal of Early Intervention, 23,* 20–21.

Timm, M.A., Strain, P.S., & Eilers, P. (1979). Effects of systematic response-dependent fading and thinning procedure on the maintenance of child-child interaction. *Journal of Applied Behavior Analysis, 12,* 308.

Umbreit, J. (1995). Functional analysis of disruptive behavior in an inclusive classroom. *Journal of Early Intervention, 19,* 18–29.

Vollmer, T.R., & Iwata, B.A. (1993). The role of attention in the treatment of attention-maintained self-injurious behavior: Non-contingent reinforcement and differential reinforcement of other behavior. *Journal of Applied Behavior Analysis, 26,* 9–21.

Vollmer, T.R., Marcus, B.A., & LeBlanc, L.A. (1994). Treatment of self-injury and hand mouthing following inconclusive functional analysis. *Journal of Applied Behavior Analysis, 27,* 331–344.

Vollmer, T.R., Marcus, B.A., & Ringdahl, J.E. (1995). Non-contingent escape as treatment for self-injurious behavior maintained by negative reinforcement. *Journal of Applied Behavior Analysis, 28,* 15–26.

Wolery, M., Kirk, K., & Gast, D.L. (1985). Stereotypic behavior as a reinforcer: Effects and side effects. *Journal of Autism and Developmental Disorders, 15,* 149–161.

Woods, J., & Goldstein, H. (2003). When the toddler takes over: Changing challenging routines into conduits for communication. *Focus on Autism and Other Developmental Disabilities, 18,* 176–181.

CHAPTER 11

Peer-Related Social Competence Interventions for Young Children with Communication and Language Disorders

NAOMI SCHNEIDER AND HOWARD GOLDSTEIN

T his chapter explores the peer-related social competence characteristics of children with communication impairments and language disorders. As we seek to identify social communication needs within this broad population, we begin with an examination of the construct of social competence.

PEER-RELATED SOCIAL COMPETENCE CHARACTERISTICS AND NEEDS OF CHILDREN

Gresham and MacMillan (1997) defined social competence as three interrelated concepts: peer relationship variables (e.g., peer rejection and acceptance, friendship), adaptive behavior, and social skills. McFall (1982) also distinguished between social skills and social competence. According to his definition, *social skills* are behaviors or abilities that an individual displays during a social situation, and *social competence* is based on others' opinions or evaluations of how the individual performed and whether it was adequate. If social skills are behaviors that result in an opinion of social competence about those behaviors, it is especially important to identify social skills that relate to relationship variables and social adaptation.

Social skills are an integral part of child development. From an early age, social skills help children learn, relate, and develop. Refined social skills lead to peer rela-

This research was supported by the U.S. Department of Education Office of Special Education and Rehabilitative Services (Grants #H324B980060, and #H84325D030046) to Florida State University. However, the content and opinions expressed herein do not necessarily reflect the position or policy of the U.S. Department of Education or Florida State University, and no official endorsement should be inferred. Address correspondence to Howard Goldstein, Ph.D., Department of Communication Disorders, 4110 University Center, Building C, The Florida State University, Tallahassee, FL 32306–2651.

tionships and friendships. Different phases of peer relationship development have been proposed (Brenner & Mueller, 1982; Gottman, 1983; Howes, 1983). During early childhood, children use their social skills to interact with peers during play. With the emergence of parallel play and subsequent development of cooperative play, social skills become increasingly necessary (Goldstein & Gallagher, 1992). Parallel play is the least rewarding socially, but has fewer opportunities for conflicts or misunderstandings. Higher levels of play, such as cooperative or fantasy play, place greater social demands on participants but also are more socially rewarding. The latter types of play, however, have increased opportunities for conflict and misunderstandings, which would require negotiation skills.

During middle childhood and into adolescence, the focus turns to peer inclusion, rejection avoidance, and self-definition. From early childhood to adulthood, children's social worlds begin to define who they are. Goldstein and Gallagher (1992) argued that social skills entail clear, appropriate, and polite communication; effective interpersonal perspective-taking; and perceptive code-switching. Social skills, in the broadest sense, highlight the important role of communication in the social commerce of daily life.

According to the *Diagnostic and Statistical Manual of Mental Disorders (4th edition;* American Psychiatric Association [APA], 1994*)*, individuals diagnosed with Expressive Language Disorder or a Mixed Receptive-Expressive Language Disorder show a delay in their production and/or comprehension of language. According to the APA, to receive either diagnosis, children's scores on standardized tests must be "substantially below those obtained from standardized measures of nonverbal intellectual capacity" (p. 56). Children with this diagnosis are delayed in their language development. They are typically referred to as children with specific language impairment (SLI).

When children fall short on the social competence continuum, they are missing not only the skills to communicate but also skills needed for peer friendship, acceptance, and inclusion in social groups. Because children with communication disorders may not have the essential language skills to make peer interactions meaningful and effective, they sacrifice social experiences and opportunities. By missing these experiences, they may lose key opportunities to interact with peers and to observe and learn language structures. When they are not exposed to peer language, they are unable to learn the skills needed to interact meaningfully with others. This becomes a vicious circle; children with SLI or other communication disorders do not have the language necessary to interact; and by not interacting, they are not learning important emerging language skills.

Regardless of the type of disorder, children with speech or language impairments often exhibit deficits in their social competence. For friendships to develop and mature, children need to be accepted by others, particularly peers (Gertner, Rice, & Hadley, 1994). Children with communication disorders may be unable or less able to use their language in effective ways to gain social acceptance. Researchers have found that children who have typically developing speech and language skills are preferred communication partners (e.g., Craig & Gallagher, 1986; Gertner et al., 1994; Goldstein & Gallagher, 1992; Hadley & Rice, 1991; Rice, Sell, & Hadley, 1991). Because children with communication disorders are not chosen as partners as often as children without communication disorders, this limits their chances of interactions and further language learning. Not surprisingly, children with SLI have poorer social skills compared with peers who are typically developing and also have fewer relationships and interactions with peers (Fujiki, Brinton, & Todd, 1996).

Poor social skills can have pervasive effects on children's quality of life. Social skills are necessary for effective peer communication, interaction, and acceptance as well as for psychological adjustment and overall satisfaction (Goldstein & Morgan, 2002). For example, children without friends are lonelier and report higher levels of social dissatisfaction than do children with friends (Parker & Asher, 1993). Moreover, the quality of friendships has been found to relate to children's subsequent school adjustments (Berndt & Keefe, 1995). For instance, Wentzel and Caldwell (1997) determined that group membership and peer relationships predicted classroom achievement.

Only a few researchers have investigated the social interactions of children whose sole problem was a communication disorder. A notable exception is the research program by Rice and her colleagues, who have studied different populations of children with typical intelligence. For example, Rice and colleagues (1991) examined social interactions of 26 children (ages 3:3 to 5:7 years) with different language abilities: SLI, speech impairment (SI), English language learners (ELL), and children with typical language (TL). Social interaction data were collected during play time when children were allowed to choose their own play partners and activities, which included blocks, art, quiet time, and dramatic play. Children were found to adapt their communication styles based on the communication abilities of their peers. The authors concluded that children as young as 3 years are sensitive to differences in communicative competence.

Overall, children with TL initiated more often and were favored partners for peer-initiated interactions. Instead of employing social behaviors that might encourage communication and socialization of children with SLI, SI, and ELL, peers chose to ignore these children and initiate and interact with peers with TL. Children with communication disorders had many opportunities to initiate and interact with peers but chose to interact with adults instead. They also shortened their responses or often relied on nonverbal responses. When they chose to interact with their peers, the members of the SI, SLI, and ELL groups also chose peers with TL. Both adults and children with TL seem to provide more stable interaction opportunities because they are able to maintain the interaction more effectively.

To determine the relationship between linguistic competence and social acceptance among four groups of children (TL, SI, SLI, and ELL), Gertner and colleagues (1994) conducted a follow-up study at the same preschool studied by Rice and colleagues (1991). Social acceptance was based on participants' positive and negative nominations of their classmates. A photograph of each classmate was presented to the child. Positive nominations were obtained by asking each child to choose three children they preferred to play with. Negative nominations were obtained by asking each child to choose three children they did not like to play with. Nomination results placed each child into one of four groups: Liked, Disliked, Low Impact, and Mixed. The Liked group received many positive nominations and few negative nominations. The Disliked group received few positive nominations and many negative nominations. The Low Impact group received few positive and negative nominations, revealing that they were neither readily liked nor disliked. The Mixed group received many high positive and negative nominations, revealing that they were readily liked by some peers and disliked by others. Results revealed that children with TL received significantly more positive nominations than the SI/

SLI group and ELL group. Children with TL were highly represented in the Liked group, whereas SI/SLI and ELL groups fell into the Low Impact or Disliked groups.

The authors also examined other demographic factors that might influence social status such as children's IQs or ages. Results show that children's vocabularies, as measured by the Peabody Picture Vocabulary Test-Revised (PPVT-R; Dunn & Dunn, 1981), was the best predictor of positive nominations by peers. Language ability (PPVT-R and Reynell Developmental Language Scales-Revised, Reynell & Gruber, 1990) uniquely accounted for 41% of the total variance in children's social status, even when IQs and ages were first entered into the regression model. Gertner and colleagues (1994) concluded that children who lack linguistic competence are unable to use their language skills to transform their social interactions into friendships. This seems consistent with the Hadley and Rice (1991) finding that children with language and speech disorders were ignored by peers who were typically developing and did not respond often when dialogues were initiated by peers.

In summary, children with inadequate language abilities are accepted less often by peers in social settings. At a young age, children are able to notice even subtle speech and language disorders. Language, regardless of age or IQ, is a robust predictor of children's peer status. During play routines that are verbally demanding, such as dramatic play, children whose language is limited are not likely to be the most preferred play partners. When compared with children with TL, those with language limitations in early childhood are not as prepared to form and sustain friendships.

Review of Interventions to Promote Peer-Related Social Competence

A number of interventions are available that might facilitate the development of social skills in children with communication impairments and language disorders. Although not developed specifically for use with children with communication impairments, it is useful to consider the array of strategies that have undergone experimental scrutiny, including those developed for children with severe disabilities. Brown, Odom, and Conroy (2001) offered an organization framework to help practitioners distinguish among approaches and make decisions about applications of those strategies (see a recent elaboration in Chapter 8 of this volume). They proposed a hierarchy shown in Chapter 7, Figure 7.1. Within the hierarchy, Brown and colleagues encouraged practitioners to begin with the most typical and least intrusive types of peer interaction interventions prior to implementing more complicated and intensive interventions. At the foundation of the hierarchy, they recommended beginning with two classroomwide interventions: 1) developmentally appropriate practices (DAP) and inclusive environments with socially responsive peers, and 2) affective interventions. In addition, four supplementary types of interventions were suggested on an individualized basis. Specifically, they recommended two naturalistic interventions, *incidental teaching of social behaviors* and *friendships activities*, and two more structured strategies, *social integration activities* and *explicit teaching of social skills*. Working up the hierarchy, when a less intrusive intervention does not produce desired improvements in social competence, then a more intensive intervention may be appropriate.

Brown and colleagues (2001) argued that DAP could facilitate children's peer interactions when combined with programming that includes both children with and without disabilities. By implementing interventions in an inclusive early child-hood program, children are given access to peers without disabilities and provided with multiple opportunities to interact with several peers who are developmentally sophisticated.

Another classroomwide strategy, *affective interventions*, may be incorporated into the curriculum to encourage positive attitudes about children with disabilities. This might be accomplished by encouraging children with and without disabilities to interact, providing direct (e.g., heterogeneous play groups) and indirect (e.g., positive stories about children with disabilities that are read and discussed) experiences. If the two classroomwide interventions are ineffective for some children, a more individualized intervention may be appropriate for these young children.

Incidental teaching of social behaviors involves teachers individualizing appropriate instruction to children in a natural manner and under normal circumstances. During interactions among peers and children with disabilities, teachers may prompt certain responses by modeling important social and linguistic behaviors. By using this strategy, teachers might manipulate or scaffold peer interactions to make them more successful. If the strategy is not effective, other activities in the hierarchy may be more appropriate.

Friendships activities entail teachers modifying preschool activities (e.g., games, songs) to encourage children's social interactions. Teachers use common classroom circumstances to have children frequently model and rehearse appropriate social behaviors while providing systematic encouragements for subsequent interactions. Similar to incidental teaching of social behaviors, this strategy occurs during routine activities. However, the strategy is planned and conducted in groups instead of incidentally, with the intent of providing many more opportunities to participate in and practice peer interactions.

The final two interventions, *social integration activities* and *explicit teaching of social skills*, are more structured and intensive than the previous two and require precise teacher planning. *Social integration activities* require teachers to arrange activities and children with disabilities in ways to provide direct contact with socially sophisticated peers. The children are able to observe peers and participate directly in social interactions. Planning is critical to ensure positive experiences. Developmentally sophisticated peers may be taught tactics for initiating social interactions and encouraged to be responsive to social overtures of children with disabilities during small group and relatively structured activities.

Finally, *explicit teaching of social skills* involves intense direct instruction or training of specific social skills tactics. For example, based on a "peer buddy" research program of Goldstein and colleagues, English, Shafer, Goldstein, and Kaczmarek (2005) provided systematic, step-by-step instructions to train children in a "stay-play-talk" program. Peers without disabilities and children with developmental delays are taught specific social tactics (e.g., eye contact, saying a child's name, persisting proximity and initiating) and are systematically trained to employ those tactics through modeling, practice, discussion, and adult feedback across time.

As reflected in the other chapters in this book, a good deal of attention has focused on investigating social skill interventions with children with developmental disabilities, behavior disorders, autism spectrum disorders, and severe disabilities. Nevertheless, relatively few researchers have focused specifically on children with communication disorders. The review that follows indicates the extent to which extant studies correspond to Brown and colleagues' (2001) hierarchy. The interventions are arranged below from the least intrusive to the most intensive ones.

Redirecting Initiations

Schuele, Rice, and Wilcox (1995) investigated a teacher-implemented program based on *redirects* to increase social interactions between preschoolers with SLI and their peers. A redirect might occur when children direct their interactions to teachers and the adults redirect them to initiate to peers. Schuele and colleagues proposed that this approach takes advantage of motivating situations as children are initiating with individuals and demonstrating clear interests in socially interacting. This intervention is implemented in normal circumstances, and the redirects and their timing are individualized for children. Instead of prompting or directing children to interact with peers when they may not be ready or interested, this strategy allows teachers to wait until children show an interest in interacting. When children initiate with adults, the adults might respond, ignore (no response), or redirect them to peers (see Figure 11.1). If redirected, children may then end their interactions (termination), reinitiate them to continue conversations (conversational override), or direct their interactions to peers (redirect uptake). Peers might reject or ignore, look at but not respond (neutral), or acknowledge and respond to the initiating children. This approach seems most consistent with the strategy of "Incidental Teaching of Social Behaviors" in the Brown and colleagues' (2001) hierarchy.

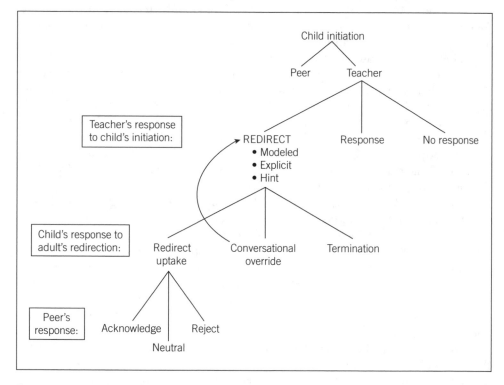

Figure 11.1.   Flowchart for redirecting child initiations. (Reprinted with permission from Schuele, C.M., Rice, M.L., & Wilcox, K.A. [1995]. Redirects: A strategy to increase peer initiations. *Journal of Speech and Hearing Research*. Copyright 1994 by American Speech-Language-Hearing Association. All rights reserved.)

The study by Schuele and colleagues (1995) included four boys (ages 3:11 to 5:4 years) diagnosed with SLI. Teacher training lasted 2 hours, and verbal and written descriptions and video examples of the strategy were provided. Throughout the study, the teacher was provided with explicit feedback on the number of the children's initiations she had redirected. During the first 4 weeks of intervention, the teacher was "blind" as to the status of the participants and implemented the redirects to all children. The results indicated that she was able to implement the intervention classroomwide and, following identification of the four participants, able to increase redirects to those children. During baseline, the teacher rarely implemented redirects, using them on 3% of classwide initiations and on 2% of the participants' initiations. Following training, she redirected 30%–34% of the participants' initiations. Of those redirects, participants responded to 38%–67% (mean = 57%) of the initiations with "redirect uptakes" and children initiated to their peers. On average, 68% of the redirected initiations resulted in an acknowledgment from peers and 26% resulted in a neutral response in which peers looked at initiators but did not respond. Only 7% of the redirected initiations did not result in responses from peers. In addition, "spontaneous initiations to peers" (i.e., social initiations that were not redirected) were examined to assess generalization. Following intervention, the proportion of spontaneous peer initiations increased for three children. Specifically, two of the four children demonstrated large increases in their spontaneous peer initiations; a third child showed improvements, but these improvements appeared to be associated with becoming familiar and comfortable with classmates rather than with the redirection intervention; and the fourth child demonstrated no change in spontaneous peer initiations.

The redirection strategy appears to be a very promising intervention for increasing peer initiations for young children with communication impairments. Teachers can readily learn to redirect children and the strategy may be implemented classroomwide or with a select group. Following training, teachers should be able to redirect children with language disorders who, in turn, should experience considerable success when initiating to peers. Additional strategies and tactics may be needed, however, to promote generalization and maintenance of the learned social behaviors as evidenced by spontaneous initiations to peers (see Brown & Odom, 1994). For example, one might augment the redirection procedure with strategies and tactics further up the hierarchy, such as training peers to initiate or be more responsive or by instituting a peer or group contingency to encourage children's interactions (Kohler et al., 1995). Alternatively, peers might be taught to implement a mand-model procedure for children who rarely initiate. For example, a peer might ask, "What do you want to play with?" If the target child looks at cars, the peer might respond, "You want to play cars. Say 'cars.'"

Peer Models and Play Scripts

Robertson and Weismer (1997) investigated the use of play scripts employed by peer models during sociodramatic play. They contended that play offers children opportunities to interact with peers and experience various aspects of language. The themes, uses of language, and types of information acquired from play routines form the framework of play scripts. Scripts allow children to predict what to say and how to act while providing opportunities to change or elaborate their routines, gain new information, or solve problems. Children with language disorders are at risk for having an inadequate repertoire of scripts because they may be unable to organize information or summarize rules that are essential during particular play routines (Creaghead, 1990; Goldstein, Wickstrom, Hoyson, Jamieson, & Odom, 1988). This approach might be characterized as "Social Integration Activities" in the Brown and colleagues' (2001) hierarchy because of the focus on arranging the environment and involving peers as models.

Robertson and Weismer (1997) enrolled 20 children with SLI (ages 3:8 to 5:1 years) and 10 peers who were typically developing and matched on ages. Children with SLI were randomly assigned to experimental and control groups. The children in the experimental group participated in four 15-minute groups in a play environment specially designed for a "house" theme. The four sessions took place over a 3-week period, and children with SLI were paired with different peer models for each play group. The intervention included playing and interacting with one peer in the house area without adult interactions and directions. Children in the control group were given opportunities to play house in their self-contained classroom with the same toys that the children in the experimental groups had used.

To assess changes in script knowledge, children were asked, "What do you do when you play house?" immediately prior to intervention, immediately after intervention, and 3 weeks after intervention. Despite the apparently nondirective nature of this intervention, significant effects were demonstrated. Following intervention and again at 3 weeks postintervention, the children in the experimental group produced significantly more words, different words, play-theme-related acts, and linguistic markers. These measures reflect social competence and language skills; however, the extent to which changes in these verbal behaviors are associated with changes in peer interaction skills is not known.

In a second study, Roberston and Weismer (1997) included six of the children from the control group from Study 1 as well as two of the peer models. Four dyads were formed: two SLI + SLI pairs and two SLI + peer model pairs. The play sessions were structured to match those in Study 1 except that all dyads played in the specially designed area and a play script was elicited following each session. Using a visual analysis of the data, children in the SLI + peer model pairs replicated the experimental effects produced in Study 1. Children in SLI + SLI pairs demonstrated no improvements. The results of these two studies indicated that pairing a child with SLI with a peer who is typically developing is much more powerful in terms of fostering language and social skills than pairing him or her with another child with SLI or not pairing him or her at all.

Cooperative Work Groups

Johnson and Johnson argued, "Individuals who are part of a cooperative effort learn more social skills and become more socially competent than do persons competing or working individualistically" (1998, p. 21). Brinton, Fujiki, Montague, and Hanton (2000) applied this "Social Integration Activity" perspective as a means to improve peer interaction skills in children with SLI. Three characteristics have been deemed important to implementing cooperative work groups: team rewards, individual accountability, and equal opportunity (Slavin, 1990). For example, everyone in the work group is working toward the same goal or objective. In addition, every member is held accountable for gaining the knowledge and skills necessary to meet the goal. Finally, the input from each member is appreciated and each has equal access to information and supplies. While working in cooperative groups, more sophisticated peers are expected to serve as good language models and provide social interaction opportunities for the less sophisticated participants.

Brinton and colleagues (2000) investigated the social behavior of six children (ages 6:1 to 7:6 years) with LI. Over the course of the study, children participated in four work groups. Each work group consisted of two peers who were typically developing and one child with LI. Roles included a leader, who was responsible for ensuring that the group worked together and remained on-task; a materials manager, who made sure each child had the materials needed; and a checker, who was responsible for keeping track of time so the activity was completed in 20 minutes. Each group was assigned a specific creation to make. Activities included making a collage, creating a tinker toy vehicle, making a milk jug animal, and building a cardboard periscope. Peers, roles, and activities were randomly assigned and children participated in a different activity with two different peers and were assigned a different role for each group. The group was instructed that all members of the group were expected to contribute, and participation was to be evaluated at the end of the task. Equal opportunity was facilitated by having children with LI sit between the peers who were typically developing, and each participant was appointed to a specific role.

Prior to the work group activity, the social profile of children with LI was evaluated and the six participants were fit into three categories: typical social skills, socially withdrawn, and aggressive and withdrawn. The participants with typical social skills fared well in the work groups. They showed interest in their peers' work and were attentive and responsive to peers. Unless the partners were highly encouraging and interactive, the children classified as socially withdrawn often worked alone. The two children characterized as aggressive and withdrawn demonstrated those behaviors in their work groups; they were aggressive to their group partners and either completed parts of projects independently or worked on an unrelated project.

Clearly, implementing cooperative work groups alone does not ensure successful or positive peer interactions. The social profile of participants is an important factor to consider. When structuring groups, children's language, social, and behavioral abilities should be carefully considered. Children's impaired language abilities combined with limited social competencies may exacerbate their ability to cooperate in groups. Hence, the work groups were most successful for children with typical social skills. The group allowed them to participate in social interactions and exposed them to more sophisticated language models. The work groups of children who were withdrawn might be most rewarding if the peers were skilled at including every group member and able to maintain a focus on their overall goal. Developing groups for children who are both aggressive and withdrawn may be the most challenging. They may benefit most from interactions where the peers are trained to deal with aggressive behavior by being assertive and by redirecting aggressive behavior in positive directions. Hence, with groups of children with challenging behaviors, participants may need well-specified instructions and monitoring of group interactions, as well as systematic encouragement and feedback concerning their social behavior.

Early Intervention Language Program

Robertson and Weismer (1999) examined the effects of a 12-week language intervention program for 21 children (ages 21–30 months) with language delays, characterized as late talkers, who had not previously received therapy. They employed an adult-directed intervention approach, but the focus was on linguistic behaviors rather than social skills. Thus, this might be considered an example of "Social Integration Activities." Participants were assigned to experimental or control groups, and children in the experimental group attended biweekly intervention sessions that lasted 75 minutes. The experimental sessions included as many as three other children. Each session was centered on a known routine, and intervention focused on encouraging vocabulary development and expression of two- or three-word combinations. Three intervention techniques were used: parallel talk (i.e., verbally describing children's actions), expansion/expatiation (i.e., repeating and expanding children's utterances while adding grammatical or semantic information), and recasting (i.e., repeating children's utterances while modifying the voice). Because intervention included peers, the sessions provided numerous opportunities for children to interact with other children, share information, and receive putative reinforcement and feedback.

Robertson and Weismer (1999) were interested in the range of short-term effects of early intervention across numerous variables. Children in the intervention group showed improvement in vocabulary growth and other linguistic variables, but also in areas that were not directly addressed by the intervention, such as social skills and intelligibility. Following intervention, large effect sizes were evident in vocabulary, total number of words, number of different words, and percentage of intelligible utterances. A medium effect size was evident in socialization scores on both language and nonlanguage assessments, suggesting that the increase in social skills was not due solely to increases in children's language abilities.

Although the focus of this early intervention program was on linguistic abilities, the grouping of peers along with adult language intervention seemed to promote social skills as well. Interestingly, results on the socialization measure indicated growth in both language-related and nonlanguage-related social skills. Hence, a relatively short communication-based early intervention program, which included language-rich activities with peers, may produce positive short-term gains across a range of developmental dimensions including language and social skills. Given that all of the participating infants and toddlers had developmental delays and most peer intervention studies have included children with and without disabilities, this was a somewhat surprising positive result.

Plan, Play, and Review

Craig-Unkefer and Kaiser (2002) implemented a three-part intervention (i.e., plan, play, review) to increase the social communication skills of preschoolers who were at-risk for problem behaviors and language delays. Six children (ages 3:5 to 3:11 years) were divided into three mixed-gender dyads, and intervention sessions lasted approximately 20 minutes. During the first 5 minutes, interventionists and children planned the play activity. Together, they labeled the toys and the adult asked how the toys might be used. If the children needed additional help, the adult suggested roles. The adult and child dyad role-played play themes and the teacher modeled how children might talk to one another and how to use the toys. This might be characterized as relatively "Explicit Social Skills Training" because all children were targeted with adult help as needing to improve social communication skills.

After planning the play activity, the dyad played for about 10 minutes while the teacher sat away from the children. The adult did not comment or prompt while the dyad was engaged, but verbally redirected (e.g., modeled, provided indirect instruction) or used reflective statements to sustain or maintain the children's interactions. The last 5 minutes of the intervention were devoted to reviewing the play session. The teacher returned to the dyad and asked the children what they played with, how they played, and what they talked about.

Child utterances were coded for descriptive talk (comments, play suggestions, and acknowledgements) and requests (for action, clarification, or answers to yes-no questions). In addition, the type of play behavior was coded to determine whether there were expected improvements in associative and cooperative play. Overall, children used more descriptive talk than requests. Five of the six children exhibited increases in their uses of descriptive talk and requests during intervention. In addition, all children showed an increase in their mean length of utterance and the number of different words used following intervention. All but one child showed an increase in the total number of words used following intervention. Although social interaction skills were not systematically taught, social participation also improved: Associative and cooperative play increased from 6% during baseline to 26% of the time during intervention.

Sociodramatic Play Script Training

Goldstein and colleagues have employed play scripts to improve children's social and language behaviors. For example, Goldstein and colleagues (1988) used socio-dramatic play scripts to increase social and communicative interaction among peers with and without disabilities. In contrast to Robertson and Weismer's (1997) use of play scripts, this approach employed "Explicit Social Skills Training." The first study consisted of two triads of three preschool children in an inclusion program. Two children in each triad were typically developing and the third child was diagnosed with a behavior disorder and language delay. The play scripts included three roles and behaviors centered on common themes. The scripts incorporated both gestural/motor and verbal responses. Scripts were taught to the triad through prompts, demonstrations, and models. Script training alone did not consistently improve children's interactions during free play. When prompted to stay in their role, significant improvements were noted in the social and communicative interactions of children with and without disabilities. The second study involved two triads exclusively comprised of children with disabilities (e.g., Down syndrome, language delay, speech impairment, hearing impairment) and replicated the results of the first study. The play scripts provide both the social expectation and structure needed to enhance interactions with peers and were beneficial for both children with and without disabilities.

Goldstein and Cisar (1992) conducted another follow-up study with children with autism. Goldstein and Cisar extended the prior Goldstein and colleagues (1988) investigation in three important ways. First, they carefully controlled teacher prompting and showed that improvements in social interaction were due to script training and not teacher prompting. Second, they demonstrated how scripts easily may be adapted to accommodate children who were nonverbal or minimally verbal, as well as children with typical language development. Third, they demonstrated that when multiple scripts were taught, each successive one was learned more readily, which may have important implications for maintenance and generalization of newly acquired and practiced peer-related social behavior.

Training Peers to Direct Interactions

The research of Odom, Hoyson, Jamieson, and Strain (1985) has been representative of peer-mediated interventions in which peers who are typically developing learn to initiate to preschoolers with disabilities to facilitate social skills. Odom and colleagues divided their study into five experimental phases: 1) baseline, 2) intervention, 3) withdrawal of reinforcement, 4) reduction in teacher prompts, and 5) reinstatement of prompts. The intervention phase involved pairing a participant with autism spectrum disorder with a trained peer who was developing typically. During five 20-minute peer training sessions, teachers described and demonstrated the target behaviors (e.g., playing, assisting, sharing, complimenting) with a second adult, then instructed peers to demonstrate the behaviors with adults. The peers were taught to continue initiating until adults, who were acting as reticent social partners, responded. During training, teachers introduced a token reinforcement system that was employed during free play time. If peers initiated to the targeted participants and they responded, peers were reinforced and, if a criterion was met, they exchanged tokens for a special reinforcer later in the day.

Prior to sessions during the intervention phase, peers were reminded to interact with the target participants and teachers suggested various initiations. Peers and target children then participated in the activity for 5 minutes. If, during the activity, peers failed to initiate within 15–20 seconds, teachers provided verbal prompts. Following the session, peers were removed from the activity and reinforced. During the subsequent phase, peers were no longer reinforced but were reminded to initiate with the target participants. During the fourth phase, teacher prompts were reduced from 15- to 20-second intervals (i.e., three to four prompts per minute) to no more than one prompt per minute. More frequent prompts were reinstated in the last phase.

Peer initiations were quite low during baseline and increased considerably following peer training. Initiations did not decrease when the reinforcement system was removed. However, initiations decreased substantially when teacher prompting was removed and increased again when teacher prompting was reinstated. Social interactions of the participants were directly linked to the frequency of peer initiations. Interaction levels for participants were low during baseline, increased when the intervention was initiated, remained high when the peer reinforcement system was removed, decreased when teacher prompting was removed, and increased when teacher prompting was reinitiated. Odom and colleagues (1985) suggested that reinforcement systems to motivate peers to initiate may be easy to fade, but some level of teacher prompting may need to be continued. In addition, the study results illustrated the effectiveness of peer initiations with reticent communicators.

This approach to peer-mediated intervention has been extended by a number of investigators. For example, English, Goldstein, Shafer, and Kaczmarek (1997) taught peers to promote social interactions across the school day. Four preschool children with disabilities (e.g., developmental delay, Down syndrome) and six peers who were typically developing participated in the study. Peer training included sensitivity training and strategy use training. The strategies taught were simplified to a "Stay–Play–Talk" strategy (i.e., Stay with your friend, play with your friend, and talk with your friend). Peer strategy training included discussion, modeling, and practice. During the peer strategy-use condition, peers rotated their assignment and served as a buddy to a particular child approximately every third day. In contrast, Goldstein, English, Shafer, and Kaczmarek (1997) had participants maintain a consistent peer buddy relationship throughout the intervention condition. Following the peer strategy-use condition, target children's rate of peer interactions and frequency of communicative acts increased. To build upon these gains, Goldstein and his colleagues also conducted dyadic training with a target children and a buddy to teach specific initiation strategies to the target children. English and colleagues (2005) provide further details on implementing the Stay-Play-Talk intervention.

English and colleagues (1997) and Goldstein and colleagues (1997) produced impressive improvements in children's peer interactions. It appeared that consistent pairing produced greater improvements in sociometric ratings by peers. Teaching peers and children how to initiate and respond to one another increases the likelihood of successful social interactions. Positive social interactions provide rich examples of peer modeling in authentic situations, which provide additional opportunities for children with communication and language disorders to learn more sophisticated language skills.

Teaching Peer Group Entry Skills

Beilinson and Olswang (2003) focused on a skill area that often presents difficulties to children with communication impairments, entry into peer-group activities (Craig & Gallagher, 1986). Their intervention entailed "Explicit Social Skills Training" focused directly on children with these impairments. They implemented an adult-directed intervention to improve peer-group entry with three children in an inclusive kindergarten classroom. The children were diagnosed with Asperger syndrome, autism spectrum disorder, or a global developmental delay. The intervention included teaching entry into a peer group using a prop (i.e., toy) with low-risk entry behaviors (e.g., parallel play, waiting) or high-risk entry behaviors (e.g., making a statement about the group). The children were taught a sequence of steps to facilitate their group entry. The low-risk entry behavioral commands consisted of "Walk," "Watch," "Get a Toy," and "Do the same thing." The high-risk entry behaviors added an additional verbal step, "Tell an idea." The children were taught the sequence through the use of pictures, direct instructions, models, and prompts prior to play sessions. A least-to-most prompting hierarchy was used during play as needed. The number of high-risk entry behaviors the children with disabilities used during peer-group entry increased after intervention and the number of low-risk behaviors did not change. During the high-risk entry behavior condition, the use of props also increased when children entered a group. In addition, the occurrence of cooperative play increased and solitary play decreased during intervention. The use of the prop and the suggested initiation appears to provide the content and contextual support children needed to make successful group entries.

Direct Social Skills Training for Children with Hearing Impairments

Rather than focusing on a single skill area, Rasing and Duker (1992) and Rasing (1993) taught a set of social behaviors to children (ages 7 to 13 years) with severe to profound hearing loss and severe language disabilities. Their approach may be considered another example of "Explicit Social Skills Training." They taught children turn waiting, greeting, initiating interactions, interacting with others, and giving help. The training package involved direct instruction of the children from teachers during nine 30-minute lessons, with teacher or video modeling. The video showed hearing children of the same age demonstrating targeted behaviors appropriately. Under the teachers' directions, the children discussed the video and answered the following four questions about the content of the video: "1) What is the problem? 2) How can I handle it? 3) How should I respond to it? and 4) Did I choose a correct response?" (Rasing & Duker, 1992, p. 727). The children with hearing impairments were also provided with drawings illustrating the four questions. Finally, they role played their responses to Question 3.

During training sessions, teachers provided positive reinforcements for appropriate instances of the target behaviors and corrections for inappropriate instances. Putative reinforcements included verbal praise and tokens that were traded for objects or special activities. Corrections involved prompting children with the drawings or a poster with the four questions. During follow-up, teachers' lessons were discontinued but the reinforcement and correction procedures were continued. Children in both studies demonstrated improvements in appropriate instances of the target behaviors following training. During follow-up, all behaviors (except greetings in Rasing, 1993) remained at previous training levels or above baseline levels.

These two investigations represent the dearth of experimental studies of social skills intervention with children who are deaf or hard of hearing. As an adult-directed social skills intervention, the approach appears to be appropriate for children with other types of communication disorders. Unfortunately, the extent to which the changes in social skills were evident in interactions with peers versus adults was not clear.

Conceptual Framework for Promoting Peer Relationship Development

As reflected by the nine approaches to improving peer interactions and peer-related social competencies, different levels of intervention may be useful for children with communication disorders. The absence of research on "Inclusion in Early Childhood Programs with Socially Responsive Peers" (i.e., the bottom of the Brown et al. [2001] hierarchy) does not mean that this practice is not being employed. It is more likely that this approach is more commonplace, especially for children with mild or no social impairments. Consequently, investigators tend to concentrate their efforts on children who require individualized and intensive interventions. Indeed, one might argue that inclusive programming provides a necessary context for children with communication disorders to develop peer-related social competence. Social psychologists provide a conceptual framework for understanding the role of peers who are typically developing in promoting group dynamics and social relationships. Their research may help us understand conditions that promote not only social acceptance but also friendship development.

Friendships are mutual exchanges that are forever changing. One partner influences and is, in turn, influenced by the other (Berndt & Keefe, 1995). Kelley and Thibaut (1978), in their social interdependence theory, suggested that a history of mutually beneficial experiences is required for relationships to maintain and grow into enduring friendships. Perhaps more relevant to integrating children with disabilities into society is the sociological research on social relationships that has focused on reducing racial prejudice. For example, Allport (1954) sought to identify conditions that support social relationship development. His intergroup contact hypothesis posits that four conditions must exist for optimal group contact: intergroup cooperation, equal status, common goals, and support of authority.

Although research on the intergroup contact hypothesis focused on race relations, the concepts may be applied to individuals with communication disorders. *Intergroup cooperation* means that groups must cooperate without being competitive. In simple play routines or dialogue exchanges, for example, cooperation is present and competitiveness is at a minimum. As exemplified by Brinton and colleagues (2000), cooperative work groups might provide a basic context for improving peer social interaction abilities. Allport (1954) held that each member must have *equal status* within the setting. Researchers have shown that peers who are typically developing discriminate against children with communication disorders in social situations (Gertner et al., 1994; Hadley & Rice, 1991; Rice et al., 1991). To mediate this discriminatory tendency, it is important for teachers to convey to children that they all have equal status. For example, helping students exchange roles, as exemplified in sociodramatic play script training (Goldstein & Cisar, 1992; Goldstein et al., 1988), conveys this value explicitly.

Common goals indicate that team members must work toward the same goal. The goals are likely to change as children mature. Early on, successful playing may involve parallel play. As children develop in early childhood, cooperative play requires sharing and turn taking for them to achieve social success. This development also might be reflected in conversations as children learn to balance being both responsive and assertive during discussions. Group work needed to complete class projects makes the idea of a common goal especially salient for children.

Support from authority demonstrates to peers that acceptance is the expected norm. Support from teachers in the classroom as well as administrators who are willing to implement social skills programs is critical. However, overinvolvement by adults may at times interfere with peer interactions. Teachers need to support peer-mediated interventions in which the children are working with one another, rather than teacher-driven interventions in which adults are the only stable and consistent communication partners.

One should not underestimate the importance of addressing the skills and attitudes of children who are developing typically. For example, Pettigrew (1998) suggested that four interconnected processes make social contacts more effective and change the attitudes of those participating. These practices include *learning about the outgroup, generating affective ties, changing behavior,* and *ingroup reappraisal.* Although he referred to the ingroup as "the majority race" and the outgroup as "the minority race," for our purposes, the ingroup will be defined as children without disabilities and the outgroup will be defined as children with communication disorders or other developmental delays.

Learning about the outgroup is a process through which the ingroup's negative attitudes or beliefs may be changed positively through acquisition of information. As a result, discrimination against the outgroup might be reduced. Specifically, as the ingroup has multiple positive encounters or opportunities to play, interact, and work with members of the outgroup, anxiety may be reduced and affective ties generated. In addition, empathy toward one group member can improve the ingroup's attitudes about an entire outgroup (Batson et al., 1997). With older children, peer support networks (Haring & Breen, 1992) seemed to establish these affective ties. Friendships between the two groups and the associated positive emotions are essential. When affective ties do not occur, a chronic absence of friendships may result. Moreover, investigators have consistently found that the inability to develop friendships has long-term ramifications, putting children at risk for poor social and academic adjustment, antisocial behavior, school dropout, and poor life achievements (Dishion, Patterson, Stoolmiller, & Skinner, 1991; Greenwood, Walker, & Utley, 2002; Parker & Asher, 1987).

Changing behaviors refers to altered attitudes. When ingroups are required to include or accept outgroups, their subsequent behaviors may prompt attitude changes. When requiring ingroups to interact repeatedly with outgroups in varied settings and circumstances, there are more opportunities to change behavior and attitudes. Again, when individuals from ingroups have less contact with one another and more contact with people from outgroups, more opportunities for learning and interactions result. Hence, their views about the outgroup change and prejudice is reduced; that is, the *ingroup is reappraised.* This may be especially relevant when children with communication disorders are making progress in learning new language skills. Peers without opportunities to interact may not have the needed awareness of potential behaviors that might facilitate more successful peer interactions. Additional opportunities for interactions have a tendency to break down social barriers between in- and outgroups and enhance peer relations.

When ingroup children learn about children with communication disorders, their empathy may increase and they have opportunities for their attitudes and behaviors to change. If adults model acceptance, facilitate positive interactions, and celebrate diversity, then any developmental differences are less likely to result in children's isolation. Applying Allport's (1954) and Pettigrew's (1998) conceptual frameworks on racial prejudice to inclusive early childhood programming practices has clear applicability. Given that the effects of intergroup contact are cumulative (Pettigrew), the early social lessons of life may have enduring positive effects for children with and without disabilities. Thus, the earlier the children from the ingroup (i.e., children with normal language) have interactions and experiences with children from the outgroup (i.e., children with communication disorders), the more favorable and likely the social outcomes.

In addition to generalization to different situations and circumstances, practitioners should address generalization from an *individual in the outgroup to the entire outgroup* as well as generalization from the *outgroup to other outgroups* (Pettigrew, 1998). Generalization from the *outgroup individual to the entire outgroup* might involve teaching peers who are typically developing to facilitate interaction with one child with communication disorders initially and then introducing other children with communication disorders into the interactional relationships. Moreover, generalization programming should progress from the *immediate outgroup* (i.e., children with communication disorders) *to other outgroups,* such as having peers in an ingroup interacting with children with behavior disorders, autism spectrum disorders, or other developmental disabilities). Likewise, trained peers who are typically developing who are effective as peer buddies might serve as suitable models when other peers considered typical are being taught to interact with children with developmental delays.

RESEARCH ISSUES AND FUTURE FOCI

By teaching social and language skills to children with communication disorders at a very young age, educators and others increase the opportunities that children with communication and language disorders have for effective peer communications, interactions, and peer relationships, and many future problem behaviors may be prevented (see Conroy & Brown, 2004). These essential skills are needed to improve children's ability to meaningfully participate in less restrictive educational and community settings and to maximize individuals' quality of life. In the future, researchers should focus on refinements of interventions for young children with communication disorders that will expand our knowledge about effective social interaction strategies for children's enhanced social communications, peer interactions, and relationships.

Promising directions for future research include evaluations of interventions that are peer-mediated and performed within common classroom and community circumstances (i.e., "natural environments"). In fact, one might argue that to maximize generalization and maintenance of appropriate behaviors, conducting research in natural environments during common daily circumstances is essential. For example, Stokes and Osnes (1989) proposed that generalization strategies should be programmed into the intervention contexts instead of expecting it to occur automatically. Researchers should focus their efforts on especially important social and language skills that children will need in the future such as social exchange, cooperation, and peer inclusion. Wolf (1978) and Rasing and Duker (1992) recommended that stakeholders who are important to the participants, not a standardized test of socialization or language, should be consulted to choose which skills are most needed and should be taught. Furthermore, these stakeholders should define what constituted appropriate or inappropriate examples of the behaviors of interest. Many of the interventions reviewed sought to establish general classes of behavior (e.g., cooperative play or work skills, group entry skills, sociodramatic scripts, social niceties to social problem solving). An important way to identify especially important social behaviors includes careful observations of children without developmental delays in the everyday situations. Normative comparison data may be a critical facet of social validation for judging peer-related social interactions (Greenwood, Walker, Todd, & Hops, 1981; Paul, 1985).

To increase the possibility of generalization and maintenance of newly learned behaviors, the intervention of social skills should occur in children's day-to-day circumstances (Rasing & Duker, 1992). However, simply pairing children without sufficient training, monitoring, and support by adults is rarely effective. Generally, when investigators paired children with disabilities with other children with and without disabilities, they found the associated intervention to be most promising when they were paired with peers without disabilities (Rice et al., 1991; Robertson & Weismer, 1997).

As mentioned earlier, much of the past research has focused on children with behavioral disorders, autism spectrum disorders, and severe disabilities, but rarely on children with various communication disorders. Interventions used with other populations may likely be effective with children with communication disorders in that many of these disabilities are accompanied with language impairments. In the future, researchers should focus on evaluating the breadth of applicability of promising social skills interventions with children with communication impairments and language disorders.

Children with typically developing language are often aware of the developmental limitations of their peers. However, if peers are well-trained and supported for employing facilitative strategies, then they can be effective teachers of social communication skills (Goldstein & Gallagher, 1992). Not only do peers have the knowledge and skills that need to be conveyed but also they appear to be ideally suited for teaching the social information skills. For example, adults may not have the same sensitivities to what is "cool," the same social status as highly valued peers, or the patience to work at children's developmental levels and share their interests for extended periods. Indeed, children with communication disorders (or other developmental needs) may be more motivated to "fit in" and interact with their peers than with adults. Perhaps because of the clinic-based model of speech-language pathology, speech-language pathologists have been slow to adopt the practice of training peers to serve as intervention agents. In the future, researchers need to continue to carefully examine peer-mediated interventions with children with communication disorders and other language needs. In the past, peer-mediated and explicit social skills intervention approaches have been highly effective with children with relatively severe social impairments, especially with children with mental retardation and autism spectrum disorders. More widespread employment of these strategies with children with communication and language impairments seems long overdue.

REFERENCES

Allport, G.W. (1954). *The nature of prejudice.* Reading, MA: Addison Wesley Longman.

American Psychiatric Association (1994). *Diagnostic and statistical manual of mental disorders* (4th ed.). Washington DC: Author.

Batson, C.D., Polycarpou, M.P., Harmon-Jones, E., Imhoff, H.J., Mitchener, E.C., Badnar, L.L., et al. (1997). Empathy and attitudes: Can feeling for a member of a stigmatized group improve feelings toward the group? *Journal of Personality and Social Psychology, 72*(1), 105–118.

Beilinson, J.S., & Olswang, L.B. (2003). Facilitating peer-group entry in kindergartners with impairments in social communication. *Language, Speech, and Hearing Services in Schools, 34,* 154–166.

Berndt, T.J., & Keefe, K. (1995). Friends' influence on adolescents' adjustment to school. *Child Development, 66,* 1312–1329.

Brenner, J., & Mueller, E. (1982). Shared meaning in boy toddlers' peer relations. *Child Development, 53,* 380–391.

Brinton, B., Fujiki, M., Montague, E.C., & Hanton, J.L. (2000). Children with language impairment in cooperative work groups: A pilot study. *Language, Speech, and Hearing Services in Schools, 31,* 252–264.

Brown, W.H., & Odom, S.L. (1994). Strategies and tactics for promoting generalization and maintenance of young children's social behavior. *Research in Developmental Disabilities, 15,* 99–118.

Brown, W.H., Odom, S.L., & Conroy, M.A. (2001). An intervention hierarchy for promoting young children's peer interactions in natural environments. *Topics in Early Childhood Special Education, 21*(3), 162–175.

Conroy, M.A., & Brown, W.H. (2004). Early identification, prevention, and early intervention with young children at-risk for emotional or behavioral disorders: Issues, trends, and a call for action. *Behavioral Disorders, 29*(3), 224–237.

Craig, H.K., & Gallagher, T.M. (1986). Interactive play: The frequency of related verbal responses. *Journal of Speech and Hearing Research, 29,* 375–383.

Craig-Unkefer, L.A., & Kaiser, A.P. (2002). Improving the social communication skills of at-risk preschool children in a play context. *Topics in Early Childhood Special Education, 22*(1), 3–13.

Creaghead, N. (1990). Mutual empowerment through collaboration: A new script for an old problem. *Best Practices in School Speech-Language Pathology, 1,* 109–116.

Dishion, T.J., Patterson, G.R., Stoolmiller, M., & Skinner, M.L. (1991). Family, school, and behavioral antecedents to early adolescent involvement with antisocial peers. *Developmental Psychology, 27,* 172–180.

Dunn, L.M., & Dunn, L.M. (1981). *Peabody Picture Vocabulary Test-Revised.* Circle Pines, MN: American Guidance Service.

English, K., Goldstein, H., Shafer, K., & Kaczmarek, L. (1997). Promoting interactions among preschoolers with and without disabilities: Effects of a buddy skills-training program. *Exceptional Children, 63,* 229–243.

English, K., Shafer, K., Goldstein, H., & Kaczmarek, L. (2005). Teaching buddy skills to preschoolers. In M.L. Wehmeyer & M. Agran (Eds.), *Mental retardation and intellectual disabilities: Teaching students using innovative and research-based strategies* (pp. 177–195). Annapolis Junction, MD: American Association on Mental Retardation.

Fujiki, M., Brinton, B., & Todd, C.M. (1996). Social skills of children with specific language impairment. *Language, Speech, and Hearing Services in Schools, 27,* 195–202.

Gertner, B.L., Rice, M.L., & Hadley, P.A. (1994). Influence of communicative competence on peer preferences in a preschool classroom. *Journal of Speech and Hearing Research, 37,* 913–923.

Goldstein, H., & Cisar, C.L. (1992). Promoting interaction during sociodramatic play: Teaching scripts to typical preschoolers and classmates with disabilities. *Journal of Applied Behavior Analysis, 25,* 265–280.

Goldstein, H., English, K., Shafer, K., & Kaczmarek, L. (1997). Interaction among preschoolers with and without disabilities: Effects of across-the-day peer intervention. *Journal of Speech, Language, and Hearing Research, 40,* 33–48.

Goldstein, H., & Gallagher, T.M. (1992). Strategies for promoting the social-communicative competence of young children with specific language impairment. In S.L. Odom, S.R. McConnell, & M.A. McEvoy (Eds.), *Social competence of young children with disabilities* (pp. 189–213). Baltimore: Paul H. Brookes Publishing Co.

Goldstein, H., & Morgan, L. (2002). Social interaction and models of friendship development. In H. Goldstein, L.A. Kaczmarek, & K.M. English (Eds.), *Promoting social communication: Children with developmental disabilities from birth to adolescence* (pp. 1–25). Baltimore: Paul H. Brookes Publishing Co.

Goldstein, H., Wickstrom, S., Hoyson, M., Jamieson, B., & Odom, S.L. (1988). Effects of sociodramatic script training on social and communicative interaction. *Education and Treatment of Children, 11,* 97–117.

Gottman, J.M. (1983). How children become friends. *Monographs of the Society for Research in Child Development, 43*(3, Serial No. 201).

Greenwood, C.R., Walker, D., & Utley, C.A. (2002). Relationships between social-communicative skills and life achievements. In H. Goldstein, L.A. Kaczmarek, & K.M. English (Eds.), *Promoting social communication: Children with developmental disabilities from birth to adolescence* (pp. 345–370). Baltimore: Paul H. Brookes Publishing Co.

Greenwood, C.R., Walker, H.M., Todd, N.M., & Hops, H. (1977). Normative and descriptive analysis of preschool free play social interaction rates. *Journal of Pediatric Psychology, 6,* 343–367.

Gresham, F.M., & MacMillan, D.L. (1997). Social competence and affective characteristics with mild disabilities. *Review of Educational Research, 67,* 377–415.

Hadley, P.A., & Rice, M.L. (1991). Conversational responsiveness of speech- and language-impaired preschoolers. *Journal of Speech and Hearing Research, 34,* 1308–1317.

Haring, T., & Breen, C. (1992). A peer-mediated social network intervention to enhance the social integration of persons with moderate and severe disabilities. *Journal of Applied Behavior Analysis, 19,* 319–333.

Howes, C. (1983). Patterns of friendship. *Child Development, 54,* 1041–1053.

Johnson, D.W., & Johnson, R.T. (1998). Cooperative learning and social interdependence theory. In R.S. Tindale, L. Heath, J. Edwards, E.J. Posavac, F.B. Bryant, Y Suarez-Balcazar, E. Henderson-King, & J. Myers (Eds.), *Theory and research on small groups* (pp. 9–35). New York: Kluwer Academic/Plenum Press.

Kelley, H., & Thibaut, J. (1978). *Interpersonal relations: A theory of interdependence.* New York: John Wiley & Sons.

Kohler, F.W., Strain, P.S., Hoyson, M., Davis, L., Donina, W.M., Rapp, N. (1995). Using a group-oriented contingency to increase social interactions between children with autism and their peers: A preliminary analysis of corollary supportive behaviors. *Behavior Modification, 19,* 10–32.

McFall, R.M. (1982). A review and reformulation of the concept of social skills. *Behavioral Assessment, 4,* 1–33.

Odom, S.L., Hoyson, M., Jamieson, B., & Strain, P.S. (1985). Increasing handicapped preschoolers' peer social interactions: Cross-setting and component analysis. *Journal of Applied Behavior Analysis, 18,* 3–16.

Parker, J.G., & Asher, S.R. (1987). Peer relations and later personal adjustment: Are low-accepted children at risk? *Psychological Bulletin, 102,* 357–389.

Parker, J.G., & Asher, S.R. (1993). Friendship and friendship quality in middle childhood: Links with peer group acceptance and feelings of loneliness and social dissatisfaction. *Developmental Psychology, 29,* 611–621.

Paul, L. (1985). Programming peer support for functional language. In S. Warren & A.K. Rogers-Warren (Eds.), *Teaching functional language* (pp. 289–307). Austin, TX: PRO-ED.

Pettigrew, T.F. (1998). Intergroup contact theory. *Annual Review of Psychology, 49,* 65–85.

Rasing, E.J., & Duker, P.C. (1992). Effects of a multifaceted training procedure on the acquisition and generalization of social behaviors in language-disabled deaf children. *Journal of Applied Behavior Analysis, 25,* 723–734.

Rasing, E.J. (1993). Effects of a multifaceted training procedure on the social behaviors of hearing-impaired children with severe language disabilities: A replication. *Journal of Applied Behavior Analysis, 26,* 405–406.

Reynell, J.K., & Gruber, C.P. (1990). *Reynell Developmental Language Scales–U.S. Edition.* Los Angeles, CA: Western Psychological Services.

Rice, M.L., Sell, M.A., & Hadley, P.A. (1991). Social interactions of speech- and language-impaired children. *Journal of Speech and Hearing Research, 34,* 1299–1307.

Robertson, S.B., & Weismer, S.E. (1997). The influence of peer models on the play scripts of children with specific language impairment. *Journal of Speech, Language, and Hearing Research, 40,* 49–61.

Robertson, S.B., & Weismer, S.E. (1999). Effects of treatment on linguistic and social skills in toddlers with delayed language development. *Journal of Speech, Language, and Hearing Research, 42,* 1234–1248.

Schuele, C.M., Rice, M.L., & Wilcox, K.A. (1995). Redirects: A strategy to increase peer initiations. *Journal of Speech and Hearing Research, 38,* 1319–1333.

Slavin, R.E. (1990). Learning together. *The American School Board Journal, 177*(8), 22–23.

Stokes, T.F., & Osnes, P.G. (1989). An operant pursuit of generalization. *Behavior Therapy, 20,* 337–355.

Wentzel, K.R., & Caldwell, K. (1997). Friendships, peer acceptance, and group membership: Relations to academic achievement in middle school. *Child Development, 68,* 1198–1209.

Wolf, M.M. (1978). Social validity: The case for subjective measurement or how applied behavior analysis is finding its heart. *Journal of Applied Behavior Analysis, 11,* 203–214.

CHAPTER 12

Social Competence Interventions for Young Children with Autism

Programmatic Research Findings and Implementation Issues

PHILLIP S. STRAIN, ILENE S. SCHWARTZ, AND EDWARD H. BOVEY II

Autism spectrum disorder (ASD) is a neurodevelopmental disorder that affects 1 in 150 births and 1 to 1.5 million Americans (Autism and Developmental Disabilities Monitoring [ADDM] Network, 2007). It is a disorder characterized by a triad of characteristics: impairments in receptive and expressive communication, impairments in social interaction, and a restricted or repetitive set of interests or activities. Although all children with ASD benefit from early intervention and some children make remarkable progress as a result of early intervention, ASD is a lifelong disability for which there is no known cure. There is, however, a wealth of knowledge about effective intervention strategies for young children with ASD (e.g., Dawson & Osterling, 1997; National Research Council, 2001; Odom, Brown, Frey, Karasu, Smith-Canter, & Strain, 2003). One common characteristic of all successful intervention programs for young children with ASD is explicit and systematic instruction in social interaction.

In this chapter we review the social characteristics of children with ASD and highlight the key areas for intervention. Next, we describe two areas of intervention research (peer-mediated strategies and group-oriented contingencies) in which there is actually a programmatic line of inquiry. That is, a series of studies have been conducted in these areas that tease out the components of intervention, address the question of differential effectiveness across participants, and compare active interventions with one another. Then, using the foundation of the groundbreaking

Support for this chapter was provided, in part by the Institute of Education Sciences Grant # R324E06068 to the University of Colorado at Denver and Health Sciences Center and by the U.S. Department of Education Office of Special Education Grant # H325G02003 to the University of Washington. However, the content and opinions expressed herein do not necessarily reflect the position or policy of the Institute of Education Sciences, the University of Colorado at Denver and Health and Sciences Center, the U.S. Department of Education, and the University of Washington, and no official endorsement should be inferred.

work in peer-mediated intervention, we review the most current research in effective social interventions for children with ASD. Finally, we discuss a number of intervention parameters that we believe are essential to maximizing outcomes for children with ASD.

SOCIAL CHARACTERISTICS OF YOUNG CHILDREN WITH AUTISM SPECTRUM DISORDERS

Deficits in social relationships have always been pivotal determinants of ASD (Kanner, 1943; Rimland, 1964). Currently, widely replicated evidence suggests that young children with ASD often display interaction deficits specific to 1) initiating and responding to social overtures, 2) sophistication of peer play, and 3) use of communicative (verbal and nonverbal) behavior during interaction (National Research Council, 2001).

Whereas most preschoolers are quite reciprocal in their interactions with peers (Guralnick, 2001), young children with ASD seldom initiate social interactions (Strain & Hoyson, 2000) and tend not to respond to the initiations of others (Odom & Ogawa, 1992). Not only does this pattern of behavior tend to isolate children with ASD but it may also discourage peers from interacting with these children in the future.

The lack of sophisticated play skills also inhibits the social relatedness of children with ASD. Because play is the major context in which peer-to-peer interactions occur in early childhood, behavioral deficits in this domain can be particularly debilitating (McEvoy, Shores, Wehby, & Johnson, 1990; Stahmer, 1995). Observational studies (e.g., Charman et al., 1998; Libby, Powell, Messer, & Jordan, 1998) and baseline assessment in intervention research (e.g., Goldstein & Cisar, 1992; Kohler & Strain, 1997; Rogers, Hall, Osaki, Reaven, & Herbison, 2000) have repeatedly shown that the play of young children with ASD tends to be highly repetitive, object oriented, and not imaginative.

Finally, studies have demonstrated that young children with ASD seldom use age-appropriate gestural and verbal behaviors in the context of social interaction (e.g., Corona, Dissanayake, Arbelle, Wellington, & Sigman, 1998; Mundy, Sigman, & Kasari, 1990; Peterson & Haralick, 1977). As a consequence, in interactions with a child with ASD, it is likely that peers may not be able to determine the intent of the child's behavior, whether the child with ASD is having fun, or what kinds of play the child wishes to engage in (Strain & Schwartz, 2001).

PROGRAMMATIC INTERVENTION STRATEGIES

Deficits in social interaction are a defining characteristic of ASD, and developing social relationships and participating in play are primary occupations for all children during the preschool years. Therefore, high quality programs for young children with ASD require staff expertise across a number of areas involved in intervention strategies to improve the quality and quantity of peer interactions. Several of these are described below.

Teaching Peers to be Intervention Agents

Given the limitations associated with adult-mediated intervention (Shores, Hester, & Strain, 1976; Walker, Greenwood, Hops, & Todd, 1979), a systematic series of investigations beginning in the late 1960s began to elicit a better understanding of the potential use of peers as instructional agents. From early naturalistic (e.g., Charlesworth & Hartup, 1967; Guralnick & Paul-Brown, 1986; Kohn, 1966) and intervention (e.g., Bushell, Wrobel, & Michaelis, 1968; Wahler, 1967) research, it is clear that children exert a powerful influence on each other's social behavior. Sometimes this influence yields positive, maturing outcomes and sometimes it does not. If, indeed, peer influence plays a dominant role in the natural development of social and communicative competence, then it seems logical and reasonable to enlist peers in the purposeful development of children's social skills.

Fine-grain analyses of existing normative data on the social interactions of pre-school children by Strain (1984; 1985) revealed that interactions are begun and maintained by specific social overtures that are exchanged on an equitable or recip-rocal basis. Thus, initial intervention efforts were aimed at evaluating the functional effects of an increased level of social overtures or initiations on the social behavior of children with ASD who are severely withdrawn, who by definition rarely were exposed to any positive approach behaviors from peers.

An early study of peer social initiations included eight children, two boys who were typically developing who served as peers and six children with ASD. Four 20-minute training sessions were conducted with each of the two peers (Strain, Shores, & Timm, 1977). In these sessions the two boys learned and rehearsed a number of verbal and motoric behaviors to engage children with ASD in social play. First, the peers learned to initiate play by emitting phrases such as, "Come play," and "Let's play ball." Next, the children were taught to engage in those motor behaviors that would naturally accompany specific verbal play overtures. For exam-ple, the peers would say, "Let's play ball" and then roll a ball to the adult instructor. During the initial baseline period before the training, the six children in the target group with ASD rarely engaged in any positive interaction, and their peers initiated only occasional social behaviors toward them. After the peers were first instructed to play with the children in the target group; however, two things happened. First, the responses of each child in the target group to initiations immediately increased, and second, the positive initiations of all but one child with ASD increased. Inter-vention effects were replicated during subsequent return to baseline (low levels of initiations) and intervention phases.

In order to determine whether the effects produced by this peer-mediated intervention would generalize to another setting and be maintained across a short time-span, a systematic replication with three preschool-age boys with ASD was con-ducted (Strain, 1977). The intervention sessions in the withdrawal of intervention design took place in a small playroom. Generalization was assessed by observing the children in a routine free-play period in their classroom (the peer trainer was absent from this setting). Maintenance of behavior change across time was assessed by conducting generalization, setting observations either immediately or 23 hours after intervention. Strain found both intervention and generalization sessions showed an increase in social responding when intervention was in effect. Mainte-nance effects were obtained with two children, as evidenced by the children's con-sistency in social-responding performance in generalization sessions that occurred immediately after intervention or 23 hours later.

A third experiment in this series examined the interaction between children's problem behaviors and the impact of peer social initiations (Ragland, Kerr, & Strain, 1978). When compared with children participating in earlier studies using peer social initiations, the children with ASD in this investigation engaged in more extensive forms of challenging behavior. The original peer training approach was modified slightly to accommodate the problem behaviors exhibited by the children in the target group. In training sessions, when the experimenter did not respond positively to initiations by the peer trainer, she exhibited some of the self-stimulatory and avoidance behavior typical of the children in the target group. The peer social initiation strategy produced an immediate increase in each child's positive social behavior. In return-to-baseline and subsequent intervention conditions, the intervention effect was replicated. In addition to an increase in positive responding, the social initiation intervention increased two of the children's interactions negatively, especially during the first several days of each intervention phase. The peer trainer often interrupted these children while they were engaged in some self-stimulatory activity. When this happened, the children would often scream and run away. After the first day that this situation occurred, the experimenter made sure to remind the peer after each session that sometimes children would respond this way.

Strain, Kerr, and Ragland (1979) undertook a systematic replication of this study. Four elementary-age children with ASD served as participants. One-half of the peer training was identical to that employed by Ragland, Kerr, and Strain (1978). During the remaining portion, the peer was taught a prompting and reinforcement strategy. Here, the experimenter told the peer that he would be engaging two of the children at a time to play with each other. The peer was instructed to rehearse such prompting statements as "Roll the ball to _____," "Give _____ a block," "Push the truck to _____." Later, the peer began to practice such praise statements as: "Good _____," "That's the way to play," "Very nice _____." Strain and colleagues' (1979) study included four main findings: 1) both intervention procedures resulted in an immediate and substantial increase in the level of positive social behavior by each child; 2) both procedures resulted in brief, slight increases in subjects' negative interactions; 3) a comparable level of positive and negative behavior change was associated with the two procedures; and 4) no generalized behavior change was associated with either procedure.

In several studies using social initiations, a direct relationship between initial baseline performance and the immediate and generalized outcome of intervention was found (Strain, 1977; Strain et al., 1977). Withdrawn children who displayed lower baseline levels of positive social behavior were somewhat less responsive (although differences were slight) than were youngsters with a relatively higher baseline performance. However, when the social initiation intervention was applied to children who engaged in a high level of stereotypic activity, no relationship was noted between subjects' initial baseline performance and immediate or generalized outcomes (e.g., Ragland et al., 1978; Strain et al., 1979). One explanation for these divergent findings is that stereotypic behavior may compete with or mask an existing social repertoire.

In addition to demonstrating the overall efficacy of the peer-mediated strategy, other studies have been conducted to examine the specific components that are responsible for the consistent impact of peer initiation procedures. In one study, Strain and Kohler (1995) investigated the impact of four different variables. Seven preschool staff rated 24 sociodramatic, manipulative, and gross motor activities for their likelihood of facilitating interaction from three children with ASD. Nine different activities rated as high, moderate, and low in terms of sociability were then incorporated into daily play activities involving a child with ASD and two peers who were typically developing. Immediately prior to each session, teachers also predicted each focal child's likely responsiveness or sociability for the upcoming activity (on a Likert Scale from 1–5 points). Teachers were asked to base their prediction on the child's general performance during the preceding 1.5 hours of the day rather than on the type of play materials selected or participating peers. Following an initial baseline, all children in the class participated in social skills training to learn skills involving sharing, offering, and requesting, and how to use play organizers, ask for assistance, and make general comments. Teachers then implemented an individual contingency to reinforce children's use of these skills. All three children in the target group showed considerable variability in their day-to-day interaction with peers. Strain and Kohler (1995) found that the amount/percentage of peer overtures and degree of reciprocity correlated highly with children's levels of social interaction. In contrast, teachers' selection/ratings of play materials and predictions about sociability did not correlate with children's daily interaction levels during either the baseline or intervention phases.

In another investigation, Kohler, Strain, and Shearer (1992) examined the form and function of social overtures that children who were typically developing directed toward three preschoolers with ASD. All children received social skills training with regard to play organizer suggestions, share offers and requests, assistance offers and requests, and general comments. Kohler and colleagues (1992) observed that the four peer behaviors had differential topographical and functional properties. Shares and play organizers occurred an average of 5.5 times per session, whereas assists and general comments averaged less than two occurrences per session. Shares and play organizers also generated the highest percentage of positive responses from all three children with ASD (averages of 73% and 86% respectively). Conversely, assistance and general comments produced positive responses on only 60% of occasions. Yet, the assists that did produce positive responses led to interactions averaging 33.4 seconds in duration, compared with only 15–16 seconds for shares and play organizers.

Odom and Strain (1986) studied the differential effects of adults and peer-mediated intervention in a counterbalanced design. Whereas some differential effects were noted, no clear outcome differences were found across study participants and the magnitude of difference was not considered to be of particular clinical significance.

Self-monitoring has also been studied as a supplemental intervention component. In one investigation, Kohler and colleagues (1996) examined the effects of a self-monitoring procedure that was used to foster engagement and social interaction in three preschoolers with ASD. Each child participated in daily play activities with one peer who was typically developing. Following an initial baseline, two different interventions were implemented in an alternating fashion. A first procedure required an adult to prompt the children to exchange social overtures and move beads to record children's social interactions. Each child also received a small postsession reward if they had completed a certain number of exchanges. On alternating days, children moved their own beads while the adult provided fewer prompts and continued to present the postsession reward. The child-monitoring procedure was then implemented without any adult prompts during a maintenance phase. Kohler and colleagues (1996) indicated that the adult and child-monitoring procedures were equally effective in maintaining children's social engagement and interaction during the alternating intervention phase. In addition, the child-monitoring procedure maintained children's independent exchanges during the maintenance phase.

In a related study, Strain, Kohler, Storey, and Danko (1994) utilized a self-monitoring intervention to increase the social interactions of three preschoolers with ASD. Each child participated in 5-minute play activities with other children within both a home (siblings) and school (peers) setting. Following an initial baseline, teachers and parents conducted an intervention involving adult prompting, edible reinforcement contingent on children's positive exchanges, and self-monitoring of social behaviors. Strain and colleagues found that this intervention increased each child's interactions with his or her peers and siblings. Interestingly, the school and home procedures produced comparable effects on some dimensions of children's social performance, whereas other outcomes were affected differentially. Finally, adult prompts and reinforcement were successfully faded within both the home and school settings.

A complementary line of research has examined different procedures, including self-monitoring, for maintaining peers' rates of social initiations and social interaction with children with ASD. Odom, Chandler, Ostrosky, McConnell, and Reaney (1992) demonstrated that a gradual decline in teachers' prompts to peers could be accomplished without any significant decline in the rates of peers' social initiations or in the overall rate of social interaction for children with ASD. Odom and Watts (1991) showed that peers participating in social interaction interventions could set specific goals for their behavior, and when given feedback about their performance relative to these goals, maintained higher rates of social initiations. Similarly, Sainato, Goldstein, and Strain (1992) added goal setting by peers to a self-recording and self-evaluation procedure; akin to the earlier studies that focused on self-monitoring by children with ASD, this procedure promoted generalization of peer-mediated procedures across settings and play partners with ASD.

Initial peer-mediated procedures were very structured and prescribed with regard to teacher and child involvement. Despite their effectiveness, however, several concerns arose related to the efficiency of these procedures. For one, the high degree of structure restricted the range of classroom activities in which peer-mediated procedures could be incorporated. Indeed, early studies were limited to socio-dramatic, manipulative, gross motor, and other activities that related directly to children's play. Second, the high degree of structure limited the teachers' role in planning and contributing to the development of peer-mediated interventions. Given these issues, subsequent research addressed two questions: 1) Can teachers implement peer-based procedures in a spontaneous fashion? and 2) What are the benefits of this method of implementation?

In an initial pilot study, Strain, Kohler, and Goldstein (1996) asked four preschool teachers to identify naturally occurring opportunities to facilitate children's social interaction during 30-minute gross motor activities (e.g., dancing, climbing, sliding, riding a tricycle). Teachers organized large group games or activities involving all 10–12 children in the inclusive classroom. Throughout the course of these activities, teachers looked for natural or "ideal" opportunities to facilitate peer interaction, such as children holding hands, telling another child to jump, tossing a friend a ball, and so forth. In contrast to earlier interventions, teachers employed methods that appeared natural or suited to children's ongoing actions, such as giving suggestions for new play roles/themes and adding materials to activities that matched children's interest. The four teachers showed considerable variability in their overall success: Children's mean percent of interaction ranged from 15%–45% across teachers. In addition, each teacher also showed a great deal of variability in their individual effectiveness in that children's daily interaction levels ranged from 5%–65%. When interviewed after the study, all four teachers reported that they used the same basic strategies, which appeared to work on some days but not on others. Teachers also thought that this approach generated high quality forms of peer interaction but was difficult to implement successfully on a consistent basis.

In a second investigation, Kohler and colleagues (in press) compared two methods to address preschool children's individualized education program (IEP) objectives. Six teachers conducted their sessions during a variety of different classroom activities. In accordance with the tactics described by Pretti-Frontczak and Bricker (2004), teachers were asked to employ the following three practices: 1) embed antecedents for children's social IEP objectives into the context of ongoing play activities and areas, 2) utilize or follow children's ongoing actions and interests as the impetus for providing instruction, and 3) provide antecedents and consequences that were natural and logically suited to children's actions. Teachers provided all antecedents for addressing children's skills during an initial baseline phase. Conversely, both the teacher and peers (under teacher guidance) provided antecedents in a second phase. Kohler and colleagues' findings revealed that the combined naturalistic and peer-mediated procedure produced high levels of social interaction from 9 of 10 children with ASD. Interestingly, teachers also addressed more IEP objectives with the combined method. The involvement of peers who were typically developing apparently provided teachers with a richer context for facilitating children's social interaction and related developmental skills.

Following a similar peer-mediated training paradigm, Goldstein and colleagues (Goldstein & Cisar, 1992; Goldstein, Kaczmarek, Pennington, & Shafer, 1992; Goldstein & Wickstrom, 1986) demonstrated that preschool peers could be taught to successfully produce the following communication outcomes for children with ASD: 1) on-topic verbal behavior, 2) following roles (e.g., store clerk) associated with common sociodramatic play scripts (e.g., grocery store), and 3) expanded utterances that result in more lengthy and syntactically complex exchanges.

Use of Group-Oriented Contingencies

A second intervention tactic of interest has its historical roots in teacher praise and attention (Barrish, Saunders, & Wolf, 1969; Hart, Reynolds, Baer, Brawley, & Harris, 1968; Milby, 1970; Reynolds & Risley, 1968; Strain & Timm, 1974). From these early studies in which reinforcements were targeted toward individual children, group-oriented procedures that use standardized, dependent, and interdependent contingencies have evolved (Greenwood, Walker, Todd, & Hops, 1981).

Walker and his colleagues (1979) conducted two of the landmark studies on standardized group contingencies. That is, the reinforcement systems were standardized across an entire classroom. Although these initial studies did not include children with ASD, they were directly replicated with children with ASD. In the first experiment, Walker and colleagues (1975) applied social praise and token reinforcement to six children in an experimental class. Increases in rate of interaction and percent of time engaged in positive interaction were observed. After the children were returned to general education classes 3 and 6 months later, the intervention effects were still apparent. In a follow-up study, Walker and colleagues

(1979) found that standardized contingencies applied to "starting interactions," and "responding to peer initiations" did not affect the percent of time spent in interaction. When the contingency was applied to "continuing positive interaction," however, percent of time spent in interaction increased substantially.

When using dependent group contingencies, reinforcement for a group is tied directly to behavioral improvements by some but not all members of that group. Usually, children who have specific social interaction needs must improve if the group is to receive some reward. For example, Walker and Hops (1973) made reinforcement for a student who was considered to be low interacting contingent on her peers' social initiations to her. In addition, these same investigators also made the peer groups' reinforcement contingent on the child's initiations. Although both tactics were eventually effective, the latter resulted in an initial decrease in the child's social behavior, presumably as a result of being overwhelmed by the sudden and massive increases in social initiations directed toward her.

Interdependent contingencies represent conditions in which reinforcement for any one child is partially dependent on the behavior of peers. Based on the successful use of these procedures (Walker, 1979; Walker et al., 1975), several replication studies have been undertaken. In the first study (Lefebvre & Strain, 1989) an interdependent contingency was applied to maintain social interaction gains that had been produced originally by a peer initiation tactic. Here, children with ASD and peers who were typically developing shared in a special activity if each child met a pre-established performance criterion. The interdependent strategy produced a 100% increase in the level of positive interaction over a peer-initiation-only condition. In a follow-up study with three additional children with ASD, the effectiveness of interdependent procedures was replicated (Kohler, Strain, Maretsky, & DeCesare, 1990).

Given the procedural differences that exist between the various group contingency arrangements, it is not surprising that several comparative studies have been conducted (Drabman, 1976; Hayes, 1976; Kazdin, 1977). Greenwood and Hops (1981) pointed out that the evidence is clearly in favor of "no difference." It could hardly be any other way. Consider that for most studies the type of contingency employed for given subjects was a clinical decision based on prior observation and an educated guess about the probable effectiveness of a certain contingency arrangement. Also, none of the prior comparisons have attended to the development of supportive peer behaviors as a side-effect of these contingencies.

What has remained a mystery is why these group procedures have been so effective in terms of maintenance of effects across time and generalization of effects across settings. Most researchers in this area point to the development of "behavioral traps" as the best explanation (Baer & Wolf, 1970). That is, it is often reported anecdotally that children in the contingency arrangements verbally encourage and support one another's behavioral improvements without being instructed or trained directly to do so. Kohler and colleagues (1990) have shown that these peer behavioral traps do, in fact, exist. Also, these traps seem limited to interdependent contingencies. Specifically, Kohler and colleagues (1990) found that individual and group-oriented procedures produced equal increases in the social interactions between two preschoolers with ASD and their peers. However, neither contingency generated consistent levels of supportive behaviors from peers who were typically developing. Given this finding, children were taught to provide supportive prompts to their playmates with ASD and their friends who were typically developing (e.g.,

"Remember to share so that we can earn a happy face"). Following this brief training, children continued to exhibit high levels of social and supportive exchanges with very few teacher prompts during a second group contingency phase.

In a follow-up study, Kohler, Strain, Hoyson, and Davis (1995) once again found that an interdependent group contingency generated few supportive behaviors until children had received explicit training for these responses. Once trained, however, children exhibited an average of 5–10 supportive overtures per 6-minute session during two subsequent group contingency phases with no teacher prompting. According to Kohler and colleagues (1995), peers directed an equal proportion of supportive prompts to their playmates with ASD and children who were typically developing. In addition, these prompts generated positive/compliant responses from their recipients on more than 90% of occasions. Surprisingly, interactions between children with and without ASD occasioned by supportive prompts lasted for more than 20 seconds, compared with 13 seconds for interactions lacking peer support.

Current Status of Social Relationships Interventions for Children with ASD

We often begin training sessions for teachers with the statement, "Children with ASD are children first." That statement underscores the importance of understanding typical development and best practices in early childhood education, as well as being familiar with instructional practices that have been demonstrated to be effective with children with ASD. This idea of "children first" also summarizes what we know about teaching social skills and facilitating the social relationships of young children with ASD (see McConnell, 2002; National Research Council, 2001, for comprehensive reviews). In other words, strategies that are effective in facilitating social relationships in children who are typically developing and children with other developmental disabilities are often effective in facilitating social relationships in children with ASD if done with adequate intensity and presented in an explicit manner. We know that we can create school, community, and home environments that facilitate social interactions of children with ASD, but we also know that being in an inclusive environment is not enough. Placing a child with ASD in an environment with children who are typically developing does not increase social interaction unless we provide support and instruction for the children (e.g., Myles, Simpson, Ormsbee, & Erickson, 1992; Strain, 1983). In other words, if we want to see social interaction, then we need to teach children how to interact across activities, settings, and partners.

We know that children with ASD can learn skills and behaviors that will make them more successful in social interactions. These skills include but are not limited to asking questions, answering questions, giving greetings and compliments, understanding others' perspectives, and imitating peers (e.g., Apple, Billingsley, & Schwartz, 2005; Garfinkle & Schwartz, 2002; LeBlanc, Coates, Daneshvar, Charlop-Christy, Morris, & Lancaster, 2003; Taylor & Levin, 1998; Zanolli, Daggett, & Adams, 1996). When children with ASD are taught these skills so that they can demonstrate them fluently and in generalized settings, they lead to increased social interactions and improved social relationships. We also know that the siblings and peers of young children with ASD can be effective social partners and coaches. These siblings and peers can help children with ASD navigate the social world, form effective friendships, and negotiate the social conflicts that are important learning opportunities for all young children (e.g., Gonzales-Lopez & Kamps, 1997; Kohler et al., 1995; McEvoy et al., 1988). This, however, does not occur spontaneously. Peers and siblings, like teachers and parents, need instruction and support on the most effective and efficient strategies to foster the social development of the young children with ASD in their lives. "Children with ASD are children first" and—like other children—they benefit from consistent, positive relationships with caregivers; they thrive in safe and well-designed environments; they engage in behaviors that are reinforcing; and they learn when they are taught using effective instruction.

Variables Affecting Intervention Efficacy

Establishing the evidence base for an intervention to teach social skills is only the first part of the equation for implementing effective instruction. Knowing what to teach and understanding strategies that are effective for teaching are important; however, a number of variables may affect any intervention for young children. Without understanding and controlling for these variables, the most elegant and well-designed intervention may be rendered ineffective. The variables that we describe next should be considered in determining the overall efficacy of any social skills intervention.

Fidelity of Implementation

The first of these variables refers to the integrity with which the intervention is implemented. Billingsley, White, and Munson (1980) referred to this concept as *procedural reliability*. The issue to be addressed here is whether or not the intervention is implemented correctly and delivered in the way that it is intended. Bellg and colleagues defined treatment fidelity as "the methodological strategies used to monitor and enhance the reliability and validity of behavioral interventions" (2004, p. 443). Let us provide an example of the importance of this issue.

> *TWO TEACHERS IN DIFFERENT CLASSROOMS decided to replicate a video modeling study that was successful in increasing the number of compliments children with ASD provide to their peers (Apple et al., 2005). Each of the teachers developed videos to use with their students. In one classroom, all four participating students learned the target behavior. In the other classroom, only one of the five participating students acquired the skills. What could account for this difference in results? On closer examination it is discovered that the teacher who was more successful made the videos exactly how they were described in the research report. The second teacher could not figure out how to add narration to the tape and, because she thought it probably was not very important, she left it out. What we know from these results and the analysis of implementation is that the teacher who correctly implemented the intervention was successful in changing the behavior of her students. The teacher who did not implement the intervention correctly was unsuccessful.*

At first glance, many implementers may assume that student variables are responsible for differences in teaching outcomes; however, once the fidelity of the intervention is examined, as in this example, it becomes clear that groups did not receive the same intervention. Without careful examination of intervention integrity, implementers and researchers may make incorrect assumptions about the data and elevate irrelevant factors to explain outcomes (Yeaton & Sechrest, 1981).

Although this issue is discussed broadly in the fields of health promotion and clinical psychology, in the field of early childhood special education, there is relatively little discussion of this important topic (Bellg et al., 2004; Peterson, Homer, & Wonderlich, 1982). Attention to the fidelity of interventions could improve the integrity of research on social skills and the quality of services that children receive in schools and in the community. Attention to intervention fidelity could also improve the consistency of social skills interventions for children with ASD and prove to be an important tool in teacher preparation and program evaluation.

Functionality of Behavioral Targets

The quality of the behavioral targets selected for intervention will affect the outcomes of the intervention. Target behaviors that are functional are more likely to be generalized and maintained over time. Functional skills are behaviors that increase a student's independence and enable them to gain access to preferred materials, activities, and routines in normalized environments (Brown et al., 1979). Functional social skills will enable students to improve the breadth of their social networks and the quality of their social relationships. To be functional, objectives should teach students to participate in a variety of social settings, with a variety of social partners, around a variety of topics. For example, functional skills might include interacting with a number of age-appropriate materials that are interesting to others, initiating to and responding to peers and other partners, and joining an ongoing play activity. These skills are pivotal to further progress in social interactions because they increase children's access to other interesting and normalizing activities (Koegel & Koegel, 2006). In other words, some skills and behaviors are keystone behaviors that serve as a bridge to more efficient and effective learning in the future (Wolery, 1991).

Access to Peers Who Are Typically Developing

One of the primary purposes of teaching social skills to young children with ASD is to facilitate their social relationships with other young children, including peers who are typically developing. In order to develop successful and meaningful relationships, children with ASD must have opportunities to interact with peers who are typically developing on a daily basis (Strain, Wolery, & Izeman, 1998). These opportunities need to be planned and supported so that children can be successful. The planning process is an important part of laying the groundwork for success programmatically and for every child. For children with ASD, access to peers who are typically developing is essential, but it is not the only important component of an intervention package to facilitate social relationships. Access needs to be supplemented with systematic instruction about *how* to interact with other children. As students develop more effective interaction skills, adult support can be gradually faded. When facilitating opportunities for children with ASD to interact with peers who are typically developing, one must consider the authenticity of the interaction opportunities (e.g., enrollment of children with and without disabilities in the same class, rather than having children who are typically developing "visit" the special education classroom), the length of the opportunities to interact, the appropriateness of the activities, and preferences of the children with and without ASD (e.g., Ochs, Kremer-Sadlik, Solomon, & Sirota, 2001; Schwartz, Sandall, McBride, & Boulware, 2004; Strain & Hoyson, 2000).

Dosage

Dosage, a multidimensional concept, refers to the intensity (i.e., amount) of intervention that a child receives. Dosage includes the number of intervention sessions, the length of each session, and the percentage of time the child was engaged during the intervention session. Here is a simple example.

> **JONATHAN AND CAMERON ARE PRESCHOOLERS** with ASD who are participating in a peer-mediated intervention program at their preschool. Jonathan's attendance at school is sporadic. Over the course of the 6-week intervention program (30 total days of intervention), he misses 10 days. He has missed 33% of the intervention, or to revert to the medical model for a moment, the intended dose. Not surprisingly, when the teachers review the data they find that although Cameron has made impressive gains in the time he spends interacting with peers who are typically developing, the results for Jonathan are disappointing.
>
> Now let's complicate the example. Let's revisit Jonathan and Cameron and add this factor. During the session, Jonathan is engaged in self-stimulatory behavior for approximately 50% of the intervals, so he is available for intervention about half the time. When Cameron is there, he participates 100% of the time. So, who is receiving a higher dose of the intervention?

The issues surrounding determining and delivering adequate dosage of an intervention, especially an intervention designed to facilitate social relationships, are not always so clear-cut. The potential parameters include amount of intervention, the child's participation in and engagement with the intervention, the frequency of the intervention, and the opportunities to practice the skills targeted in the intervention. In determining dosage we must first consider what the appropriate dosage is for each individual child.

The problem we have when working with young children with ASD is the absence of data. The minimal research and most of the recommendations regarding dosage for young children with ASD involves comprehensive programs only (National Research Council, 2001). In fact, there are no recommendations regarding the amount of specific instruction children with ASD should receive on peer-related social skills and social interaction. A common-sense guideline suggests that children with ASD should receive explicit instruction on social interaction on a daily basis, with appropriate social partners, in conjunction with numerous opportunities to practice appropriate social interaction embedded across all environments in which they spend time. The only way to determine if a child with ASD is receiving the appropriate dose of intervention and support to develop social relationships is to continuously measure outcomes. If the child is making progress, the appropriate dosage is assumed; if not, dosage is one of the change variables to be considered.

Strategies Promoting Generalization and Maintenance

Generalization is the ability to use newly acquired skills across settings, materials, and people. *Maintenance* is the ability to use new skills over time. Some scholars suggest that generalization and maintenance are stages of learning (Wolery, Sugai, & Bailey, 1988), and most would agree that learners must generalize and maintain skills before the target skills can truly be integrated into the learner's repertoire in a way that can improve the quality of their lives. Difficulty with generalization and maintenance is often cited as part of the defining characteristics of ASD. Researchers working in the area of social interaction have produced some of the most important work on strategies to facilitate generalization and maintenance in young children with ASD (see Chandler, Lubeck, & Fowler, 1992; McConnell, 2002, for pertinent reviews).

Stokes and Baer (1977) identified nine strategies that practitioners use to the facilitate generalization and maintenance of newly acquired skills (see Table 12.1). The first, "train and hope," we consider to be a non-strategy in which an interventionist teaches skills in one situation in hopes that the child will generalize the new behavior in a number of different settings and with many different people. For example, conversational skills are taught in a small clinic room in hopes that children with ASD will be able to transfer these skills to the classroom. This approach is the weakest "strategy" identified by Stokes and Baer (1977), although it is still the most likely to be used to facilitate the generalization of social skills for children with ASD (McConnell, 2002). This approach is an example of how interventions are implemented in a manner that does not improve the "real-life" skills and ultimate functional outcomes for children with ASD.

In addition, Stokes and Baer discussed eight "active" strategies that can be used to facilitate generalization. These strategies are grouped into three broad categories: 1) strategies that address what should be taught, 2) strategies that consider how and where behaviors should be taught, and 3) strategies that implement specially designed contingencies.

The ability to generalize and maintain newly acquired skills is essential for optimal outcomes, and for children with ASD, generalization does not occur without specialized intervention. The specialized interventions to facilitate generalization can be implemented in classrooms using the strategies outlined in Table 12.1. The first category of strategies addresses teaching content. In these strategies, skills are

Table 12.1.   Categories of strategies to facilitate generalization

Categories for practitioners	Stokes and Baer (1977) categories
Lack of a strategy or non-strategy (not recommended)	Train and hope
Strategies that address teaching content	Use sequential modification Train sufficient exemplars Program common stimuli
Strategies that address how and where behaviors are taught	Introduce to natural maintaining Use contingencies Train loosely
Strategies that implement specially designed contingencies	Use indiscriminable contingencies Mediate generalization Train "to generalize"

taught repeatedly across settings and people, using different materials. The materials are common items that students come in contact with at school, home, and in the community. For practitioners, this category of strategies implies that instruction on social behaviors must occur across the curriculum, with peer and staff participation and materials such as common toys (viewed as more appropriate than "ASD-specific" social interaction curriculum materials).

Addressing how and where target skills are taught can also facilitate generalization. When new skills increase children's access to preferred activities and materials, these new skills are likely to generalize and maintain because they are being trapped by naturally occurring contingencies (Baer & Wolf, 1970). For example, if a child is taught to request from peers and the peers control a preferred item at snack time, that behavior is likely to generalize because the skill of requesting is providing the child with access to a preferred item. Another example of these strategies would be ensuring that new skills are taught in the environments in which children will need to use them (e.g., classroom, child care, home) rather than the environments that may be more convenient for teaching (e.g., clinic room). Teachers using these strategies may also apply different instructions for the same activity (e.g., alternate between "Do this" and "Do what I do" when teaching imitation is used) and provide children with many different ways to respond. One way of thinking about this strategy is that teachers are systematically instructing children to be flexible in terms of what instructions they respond to, how they respond, and where they respond.

The final category of strategies to facilitate generalization and maintenance includes strategies that implement specially designed contingencies. These include strategies that skillfully embed intermittent reinforcement for the target skill into the ongoing activities and routines (e.g., using indiscriminable contingencies) and that teach children to monitor their own performance (i.e., mediate generalization) as well as those that directly reinforce generalized performance (e.g., train "to generalize"). Examples of these strategies could include providing reinforcement for hand raising by calling on the child for a turn every third time the behavior occurs once hand raising is firmly established, teaching children to count the number of times that they ask their peers questions and then reinforcing them when they reach the target level, or teaching children to ask questions in a clinic room and then providing direct reinforcement when they demonstrate those same skills during small group time in the classroom.

The consistent thread across all of these strategies for promoting generalization is that teachers determine how to facilitate performance of the newly taught skills across time, settings, people, and materials. That is, generalization is never an afterthought; it is an essential component of instructional planning from the time the teaching target is selected. Generalization and maintenance of social behaviors are essential for children with ASD. The question facing teachers, parents, and researchers is not how to teach skills to children with ASD in isolation—we have many validated strategies that are proven effective in doing this. The challenge is how to teach new skills in a manner that promotes their usage in everyday situations when they are most appropriate. When we can teach skills in this manner, we will be closer to teaching skills that will help improve the social lives of children with ASD.

Social Validity

Wolf (1978) introduced social validity in his seminal article in the *Journal of Applied Behavior Analysis*. Social validity (Wolf, 1978) asks consumers of a behavioral or educational intervention to rate the acceptability of the intervention. The purpose of asking people who use the intervention what they think about the intervention is to assess if it is addressing the behaviors that the consumers think are important, acceptable, and sustainable. According to Wolf (1978), social validity should be assessed across three primary components of an intervention: the goals, the procedures, and the outcome.

Social validity is not intended to assess the effectiveness of an intervention. It is intended to determine the *acceptability* of an intervention, once the effectiveness has been determined using validated research methods (Schwartz & Baer, 1991). In fact, helping staff learn how to implement these social validity procedures and continue to use them are among the most important challenges facing researchers in early intervention and early childhood special education. Understanding the social validity of an intervention is an important step in understanding what interventions are more likely to be maintained and implemented with high fidelity by practitioners.

Although the concept of social validity is well accepted, it has not been widely reported in the behavioral literature, and the literature on increasing social interaction with children with ASD is no exception. Even when social validity assessments are reported, they are usually relegated to judging the acceptability of an intervention or behavior change rather than being used to set the agenda of the intervention. Two recent studies are representative examples of how social validity assessments are used in the literature in social interactions for young children with ASD. Thiemann and Goldstein (2001) examined the effectiveness of social stories, written text cues, and video feedback on increasing interaction between students with and without ASD using a panel of 13 raters (7 regular education teachers and 6 graduate students in speech and language) to assess the quality and quantity of behavior change. After watching pre- and post-intervention video segments, all 13 raters reported improvements in the social communication skills of the students with ASD and improvements in the social behavior of the children who were typically developing directed toward the peers with ASD.

Garfinkle and Schwartz (2002) used a more traditional social validity tool—a post-intervention teacher survey. The survey combined open-ended and closed questions asking about the acceptability of the intervention, the likelihood of the intervention being used again, and any other related behavioral changes observed by the teachers. All of the teachers were extremely positive, stated that they would use the intervention again, and in the open-ended questions, described behavior changes that were similar to those demonstrated by the quantitative data (before the teachers saw the data).

FUTURE DIRECTIONS

Acquiring functional social skills that help children with ASD develop and maintain social relationships with their peers may be among the most important behaviors that children with ASD learn during their early schooling. Although we have many validated strategies for teaching social skills to children with ASD (e.g., prompting, reinforcement, modeling) and good programmatic inquiry on peer-mediated techniques and group oriented contingencies, we still have a lot to learn about how to implement these strategies in a manner that will produce generalizable and sustainable skills. As the number of children with ASD continues to increase and more of these children participate in inclusive child care, recreation, and community settings, it is necessary for researchers to develop a better understanding of the characteristics of interventions that contribute to their use with fidelity by teachers, parents, and child care providers in a wide variety of settings. This means that as research moves ahead, we do not need to ask whether children with ASD can acquire social skills (we already know that they can); rather, we need to look at issues such as intervention fidelity, the functionality of behavioral target, dosage, and social validity to determine how the communities of people who support and care about children with ASD can help them use and generalize these important skills every day of their lives.

REFERENCES

Apple, A.L., Billingsley, F., & Schwartz, I.S. (2005). Effects of video modeling alone and with self-management on compliment-giving behaviors or children with high functioning ASD. *Journal of Positive Behavior Interventions, 7,* 33–46.

Autism and Developmental Disabilities Monitoring (ADDM) Network. (2007). *Prevalence of the autism spectrum disorders in multiple areas of the United States, surveillance years 2000 and 2002.* Retrieved July 18, 2008, from http://www.cdc.gov/ncbddd/dd/addmprevalence. htm from the Centers for Disease Control.

Baer, D.M., & Wolf, M.M. (1970). The entry into natural communities of reinforcement. In R. Ulrich, T. Stachnik, & J. Mabry (Eds.), *Control of human behavior. Vol. 2* (pp. 319–324). Glenview, IL: Pearson Scott Foresman.

Barrish, H.H., Saunders, M., & Wolf, M.M. (1969). Good behavior game: Effects of individual contingencies for group consequences on disruptive behavior in a classroom. *Journal of Applied Behavior Analysis, 2,* 119–124.

Bellg, A.J., Borrelli, B., Resnick, B., Hecht, B., Minicucci, J., Sharp, D., et al., (2004). Enhancing treatment fidelity in health behavior change studies: Best practices and recommendations from the NIH Behavior Change Consortium. *Health Psychology, 23,* 443–451.

Billingsley, F., White, O.R., & Munson, R. (1980). Procedural reliability: A rationale and an example. *Behavioral Assessment, 2,* 229–241.

Brown, L. Branston, M.B., Hamre-Nietupski, S., Pumpian, I., Certo, N. & Grunewald, L. (1979). A strategy for developing chronological-age-appropriate and functional curricular content for severely handicapped adolescents and young adults. *Journal of Special Education, 13,* 81–90.

Bushell, D., Wrobel, P.A., & Michaelis, M.L. (1968). Applying "group" contingencies to the classroom study behavior of preschool children. *Journal of Applied Behavior Analysis, 1,* 415–556.

Chandler, L., Lubeck, R., & Fowler, S.A. (1992). Generalization and maintenance of preschool children's social skills: A critical review and analysis. *Journal of Applied Behavior Analysis, 25,* 415–428.

Charlesworth, R., & Hartup, W.W. (1967). Positive social reinforcement in the nursery school peer group. *Child Development, 38,* 993–1002.

Charman, T., Swettenham, J., Baron-Cohen, S., Cox, A., Baird, G., & Drew, A. (1998). An experimental investigation of social-cognitive abilities in infants with autism: Clinical implications. *Infant Mental Health Journal, 19,* 260–275.

Corona, R., Dissanayake, C., Arbelle, S., Wellington, P., & Sigman, M. (1998). Is affect aversive to young children with autism? Behavioral and cardiac responses to experimenter distress. *Child Development, 69,* 1494–1502.

Dawson, G., & Osterling J. (1997). Early intervention in autism. In M.J. Guralnick (Ed.), *The effectiveness of early intervention* (pp. 307–326). Baltimore: Paul H. Brookes Publishing Co.

Drabman, R.S. (1976). Behavior modification in the classroom. In W.E. Craighead, A.E. Kazdin, & M.J. Mahoney (Eds.), *Behavior modification: Principles, issues, and applications.* Boston: Houghton Mifflin.

Garfinkle, A.N., & Schwartz, I.S. (2002). Peer imitation: Increasing social interactions in children with autism and other developmental disabilities in inclusive preschool classrooms. *Topics in Early Childhood Special Education, 22*(1), 26–38.

Goldstein, H., & Cisar, C.L. (1992). Promoting interaction during sociodramatic play: Teaching scripts to typical preschoolers and classmates with handicaps. *Journal of Applied Behavior Analysis, 25,* 265–280.

Goldstein, H., Kaczmarek, L., Pennington, R., & Shafer, K. (1992). Peer-mediated intervention: Attending to, commenting on, and acknowledging the behavior of preschoolers with autism. *Journal of Applied Behavior Analysis, 25,* 289–305.

Goldstein, H., & Wickstrom, S. (1986). Peer intervention effects on communicative interaction among handicapped and nonhandicapped preschoolers. *Journal of Applied Behavior Analysis, 19,* 209–214.

Gonzalez-Lopez, A., & Kamps, D.M. (1997). Social skills training to increase social interactions between children with autism and their typical peers. *Focus on Autism and Other Developmental Disabilities, 12,* 2–14.

Greenwood, C.R., Walker, H.M., Todd, N.M., & Hops, H. (1981). Normative and descriptive analysis of preschool free play social interaction rates. *Journal of Pediatric Psychology, 6*(4), *343–367.*

Guralnick, M.J. (2001). A developmental systems model for early intervention. *Infants and Young Children, 14*(2), 1–18.

Guralnick, M.J., & Paul-Brown, D. (1986). Communicative interactions of mildly delayed and normally developing preschool children: Effects of listener's developmental level. *Journal of Speech and Hearing Research, 29,* 2–10.

Hart, B.M., Reynolds, N.J., Baer, D.M., Brawley, E.R., & Harris, F.R. (1968). Effects of contingent and non-contingent social reinforcement on the cooperative play of a preschool child. *Journal of Applied Behavior Analysis, 1,* 73–76.

Hayes, L.A. (1976). The use of group contingencies for behavioral control: A review. *Psychology Bulletin, 83,* 628–648.

Johnston, J.M. & Johnston, G.T.(1972). Modification of consonant speech-sound articulation in young children. *Journal of Applied Behavior Analysis, 5,* 233–246.

Kanner, L. (1943). Autistic disturbances of affective contact. *Nervous Child, 2,* 217–250.

Kazdin, A.E. (1977). *The token economy: A review and evaluation.* New York: Kluwer Academic/Plenum.

Koegel, R.L. & Koegel, L.K. (with invited contributors). (2006). *Pivotal response treatments for autism: Communication, social, and academic development.* Baltimore: Paul H. Brookes Publishing Co.

Kohler, F.W., & Strain, P.S. (1997). Combining incidental teaching and peer-mediation with young children with autism. *Journal of Autism and Developmental Disorders, 12,* 196–206.

Kohler, F.W., Strain, P.S., & Goldstein, H. (2005). Learning experiences . . . an alternative program for preschoolers and parents: Peer-mediated interventions for young children with autism. In Hibbs, E.D., & Jensen, P.S (Eds), *Psychosocial treatments for child and adolescent disorders: Empirically based strategies for clinical practice* (2nd ed.; pp. 659–687). Washington, DC: American Psychological Association.

Kohler, F.W., Strain, P.S., Hoyson, M., & Davis, L. (1995). Using a group-oriented contingency to increase social interactions between children with autism and their peers: A preliminary analysis of corollary supportive behaviors. *Behavior Modification, 19,* 10–32.

Kohler, F.W., Strain, P.S., Maretsky, S., & DeCesare, L. (1990). Promoting positive and supportive interactions between preschoolers: An analysis of group-oriented contingencies. *Journal of Early Intervention, 14,* 327–341.

Kohler, F.W., Strain, P.S., & Shearer, D.D. (1992). The overtures of preschool social skill intervention agents: Differential rates, forms, and functions. *Behavior Modification, 16,* 525–542.

Kohler, F.W., Strain, P.S., & Shearer, D. (1996). Examining levels of inclusion within an integrated preschool for children with autism. In R.L., Keogel, L.K. Keogel, & R. Horner (Eds.), *Nonaversive intervention for children and youth with severe disabilities.* Baltimore: Paul H. Brookes Publishing Co.

Kohn, M. (1966). The child as a determinant of his peers' approach to him. *The Journal of Genetic Psychology, 109,* 91–100.

Kopstein, F.F., & Seidel, R.J. (1972). Informal education with instructional systems? *Educational Technology, 12*(1), *35–39.*

LeBlanc, L.A., Coates, A.M., Daneshvar, S., Charlop-Christy, M.H., Morris, C., & Lancaster, B.M. (2003). Using video modeling and reinforcement to teach perspective-taking skills to children with autism. *Journal of Applied Behavior Analysis, 36,* 253–257.

Lefebvre, D., & Strain, P.S. (1989). Effects of a group contingency on the frequency of social interactions among autistic and nonhandicapped preschool children: Making LRE efficacious. *Journal of Early Intervention, 13*(4), *329–341.*

Libby, S., Powell, S., Messer, D., & Jordan, R. (1998). Spontaneous play in children with autism. *Journal of Autism and Developmental Disorders, 28,* 487–497.

McConnell, S. (2002). Interventions to facilitate social interaction for young children with autism: Review of available research and recommendations for educational intervention and future research. *Journal of Autism and Developmental Disorders, 32,* 351–372.

McEvoy, M.A., Nordquist, V.M., Twardosz, S., Heckaman, K.A., Wehby, J.H., & Denny, R.K. (1988). Promoting autistic children's peer interaction in an integrated early childhood setting using affection activities. *Journal of Applied Behavior Analysis, 21,* 193–200.

Milby, J.B., Jr. (1970). Modification of extreme social isolation by contingent social reinforcement. *Journal of Applied Behavior Analysis, 3,* 149–152.

Mundy, P., Sigman, M., & Kasari, C. (1990). A longitudinal study of joint attention and language development in autistic children. *Journal of Autism and Developmental Disorders, 20,* 115–128.

Myles, B.S., Simpson, R.L., Ormsbee, C.K., & Erickson, C. (1993). Integrating preschool children with autism with their normally developing peers: Research findings and best practices recommendations. *Focus on Autistic Behavior, 8,* 1–18.

National Research Council. (2001). Educating children with autism. Washington, DC: National Academies Press.

Ochs, E., Kremer-Sadlik, T., Solomon, O., & Sirota, K.G. (2001). Inclusion as social practice: Views of children with autism. *Social Development, 10*(3), 399–419.

Odom, S.L., Brown, W.H., Frey, T., Karasu, N. Smith-Canter, L.L., & Strain, P.S. (2003). Evidence-based practices for young children with autism: Contributions for single-subject design research. *Focus on Autism and Other Developmental Disabilities, 18,* 166–175

Odom, S.L., Chandler, L.K., Ostrosky, M., McConnell, S.R., & Reaney, S.R. (1992). Fading teacher prompts from peer-initiation interventions for young children with disabilities. *Journal of Applied Behavior Analysis, 25,* 307–317.

Odom, S.L., & Ogawa, I. (1992). Direct observation of young children's social interaction with peers: A review of methodology. *Behavioral Assessment, 14,* 443–464.

Odom, S.L., & Strain, P.S. (1986). Combining teacher antecedents and peer responses for promoting reciprocal social interaction of autistic preschoolers. *Journal of Applied Behavior Analysis, 19,* 59–71.

Odom, S.L., & Watts, E. (1991). Reducing teacher prompts in peer-mediated interventions for young children with autism. *Journal of Special Education, 25,* 26–43.

Peterson, N.L., & Haralick, J.G. (1977). Integration of handicapped and nonhandicapped preschoolers: An analysis of play behavior and social interaction. *Education and Training of the Mentally Retarded, 12,* 235–245.

Peterson, L., Homer, A.L., & Wonderlich, S.A. (1982). The integrity of independent variables in behavior analysis. *Journal of Applied Behavior Analysis, 15,* 477–492.

Pretti-Frontczak, K., & Bricker, D. (2004). *An activity-based approach to early intervention* (3rd ed.). Baltimore: Paul H. Brookes Publishing Co.

Ragland, E.U., Kerr, M.M., & Strain, P.S. (1978). Effects of peer social initiations on the behavior of withdrawn autistic children. *Behavior Modification, 2,* 565–578.

Reynolds, N.J., & Risley, T.R. (1968). The role of social and material reinforcers in increasing talking of a disadvantaged preschool child. *Journal of Applied Behavior Analysis, 1,* 253–262.

Rimland, B. (1964). *Infantile autism.* New York: Appleton-Century-Crofts.

Rogers, S.J., Hall, T., Osaki, D., Reaven, J., & Herbison, J. (2000). The Denver model: A comprehensive, integrated educational approach to young children with autism and their families. In J.S. Handleman & S.L. Harris, (Eds.), *Preschool education programs for children with autism* (2nd ed; pp. 95–133). Austin, TX: PRO-ED.

Sainato, D.M., Goldstein, H., & Strain, P.S. (1992). Effects of self-evaluation on preschool children's use of social interaction strategies with their classmates with autism. *Journal of Applied Behavior Analysis, 25,* 127–141.

Schwartz, I.S., & Baer, D.M. (1991). Social-validity assessments: Is current practice state-of-the-art? *Journal of Applied Behavior Analysis, 24,* 189–204.

Schwartz, I.S., Sandall, S.R., McBride, B.J., & Boulware, G.L. (2004). Project DATA: An inclusive, school-based approach to educating children with autism. *Topics in Early Childhood Special Education, 24,* 156–168.

Shores, R.E., Hester, P., & Strain, P.S. (1976). The effects of amount and type of teacher–child interaction on child–child interaction. *Psychology in the Schools, 13,* 171–175.

Stahmer, A.C. (1995). Teaching symbolic play skills to children with autism using pivotal response training. *Journal of Autism and Developmental Disorders, 25(2), 123–141.*

Stokes, T.F., & Baer, D.M. (1977). An implicit technology of generalization. *Journal of Applied Behavior Analysis, 10,* 349–367.

Strain, P.S. (1977). Training and generalization effects of peer social initiations on withdrawn preschool children. *Journal of Abnormal Child Psychology, 5,* 445–455.

Strain, P.S. (1983). Generalization of autistic children's social behavior change: Effects of developmentally integrated and segregated settings. *Analysis & Intervention in Developmental Disabilities, 3,* 23–34.

Strain, P.S. (1984). Social interactions of handicapped preschoolers in developmentally integrated and segregated settings: A study of generalization effects. In T. Field, J.L. Roopnarine, & M. Segal (Eds.), *Friendships in normal and handicapped children* (pp. 187–207). Norwood, NJ: Ablex.

Strain, P.S. (1985). Social and nonsocial determinants of acceptability in handicapped preschool children. *Topics in Early Childhood Special Education, 4(4),* 47–58.

Strain, P.S. (2001). Empirically based social skill intervention. *Behavioral Disorders, 27,* 30–36.

Strain, P.S., & Hoyson, M. (2000). The need for longitudinal, intensive social skill intervention: LEAP follow-up outcomes for children with autism. *Topics in Early Childhood Special Education, 20,* 116–122.

Strain, P.S., Kerr, M.M., & Ragland, E.U. (1979). Effects of peer-mediated social initiations and prompting/reinforcement procedures on the social behavior of autistic children. *Journal of Autism and Developmental Disorders, 9,* 41–54.

Strain, P.S., & Kohler, F.W. (1995). Analyzing predictors of daily social skill performance. *Behavioral Disorders, 21(1), 79–88.*

Strain, P.S., Kohler, F.W., & Goldstein, H. (1996). Peer-mediated interventions for young children with autism. In P. Jensen & T. Hibbs (Eds.), *Psychosocial treatments of child and adolescent disorders.* Bethesda, MD: National Institutes of Health.

Strain, P.S., Kohler, F.W., Storey, K., & Danko, C. (1994). Teaching preschoolers with autism to self-monitor their social interactions: An analysis of results in home and school settings. *Journal of Emotional and Behavioral Disorders, 2,* 78–88.

Strain, P.S., & Schwartz, I.S. (2001). Applied behavior analysis and the development of meaningful social relations for young children with autism. *Focus on Autism and Developmental Disabilities, 16,* 120–128.

Strain, P.S., Shores, R.E., & Timm, M.A. (1977). Effects of peer initiations on the social behavior of withdrawn preschoolers. *Journal of Applied Behavior Analysis, 10,* 289–298.

Strain, P.S., & Timm, M.A. (1974). An experimental analysis of social interaction between a behaviorally disordered preschool child and her classroom peers. *Journal of Applied Behavior Analysis, 7(4),* 583–590.

Strain, P.S., Wolery, M., & Izeman, S. (1998, Winter). Considerations for administrators in the design of service options for young children with autism and their families. *Young Exceptional Children,* 8–18.

Taylor, B.A., & Levin, L. (1998). Teaching a student with autism to make verbal initiations: Effects of a tactile prompt. *Journal of Applied Behavior Analysis, 31,* 651–654.

Thiemann, K.S., & Goldstein, H. (2001). Social stories, written text cues, and video feedback: Effects on social communication of children with autism. *Journal of Applied Behavior Analysis, 34,* 425–446.

Wahler, R.G. (1967). Child–child interactions in free field settings: Some experimental analyses. *Journal of Experimental Child Psychology, 5,* 278–293.

Walker, H.M. (1979). *The acting-out child: Coping with classroom disruption.* Boston: Allyn & Bacon.

Walker, H.M., Greenwood, C.R., Hops, H., & Todd, N.M. (1979). Differential effects of reinforcing topographic components of social interaction: Analysis and direct replication. *Behavior Modification, 3,* 291–321.

Walker, H.M., & Hops, H. (1973). The use of group and individual reinforcement contingencies in the modification of social withdrawal. In L.A. Hamerlynck, L.C. Handy, & E.J. Mash (Eds.), *Behavior change: Methodology, concepts, and practice* (pp. 269–307). Champaign, IL: Research Press.

Walker, H.M., Hops, H., Greenwood, C.R., & Todd, N.M. (1975). *Social interaction: Effects of symbolic modeling and individual and group reinforcement contingencies on the behavior of withdrawn children* (Report No. 15). Center at Oregon for Research in the Behavioral Education of the Handicapped, University of Oregon.

Walker, H.M., Greenwood, C.R., Hops, H., & Todd, N.M. (1979). Differential effects of reinforcing topographic components of social interaction: Analysis and direct replication. *Behavior Modification, 3*(3), *291–321.*

Wolery, M. (1991). Instruction in early childhood special education: Seeing through a glass darkly...knowing in part. *Exceptional Children, 58*(2), 127–135.

Wolery, M., Sugai, G., & Bailey, D.B. (1988). *Effective teaching: Principles and procedures of applied behavior analysis with exceptional students.* Boston: Allyn & Bacon.

Wolf, M.M. (1978). Social validity: The case for subjective measurement, or how applied behavior analysis is finding its heart. *Journal of Applied Behavior Analysis, 11,* 203–214.

Yeaton, W.H., & Sechrest, L. (1981). Critical dimensions in the choice and maintenance of successful treatments: Strength, integrity, and effectiveness. *Journal of Consulting and Clinical Psychology, 49,* 156–167.

Zanolli, K., Daggett, J., & Adams, T. (1996). Teaching preschool-age autistic children to make spontaneous initiations to peers using priming. *Journal of Autism and Developmental Disorders, 26*(4), 407–422.

CHAPTER 13

Social Competence Interventions for Young Children with Severe Disabilities

ERIK DRASGOW, K. ALISA LOWREY, YASEMIN TURAN, JAMES W. HALLE, AND HEDDA MEADAN

This chapter addresses issues related to the social competence of young children with severe disabilities. We begin by describing the characteristics of children with severe disabilities. Next, we define social competence for this population and discuss components associated with social competence. Then we examine ways to assess social competence and review evidence-based interventions that enhance social competence. We conclude by making recommendations for practice and by suggesting future avenues of research that can contribute to improvements in best practices.

CHARACTERISTICS OF CHILDREN WITH SEVERE DISABILITIES

In this chapter, we use the term *severe disability* to refer to children with moderate, severe, or profound cognitive disabilities, with developmental disabilities, or with substantial cognitive disabilities and physical disabilities. Individuals with severe disabilities are characterized by significant challenges in two areas: intellectual functioning and adaptive behavior. Intellectual functioning is a general mental ability (American Association on Mental Retardation [AAMR], 2002; American Psychiatric Association [APA], 1994) and involves problem solving, reasoning, and comprehending abstract or complex ideas. Intellectual functioning usually is measured by standardized intelligence and achievement tests. Adaptive behavior refers to how individuals function in their daily lives and includes practical life skills, levels of personal independence, and coping skills (AAMR, 2002; APA, 1994). Adaptive behavior is usually measured by standardized and informal behavior rating scales.

Correspondence concerning this chapter should be addressed to Erik Drasgow, University of South Carolina, 235-I Wardlaw, 820 Main Street, Columbia, S.C. 29208.

In general, individuals with severe disabilities learn slowly, have deficits in self-help skills, have problems with generalizing behaviors across people, settings, and time, and need long-term supports across multiple environments to enhance their functioning and quality of life. Moreover, many individuals with severe disabilities may have medical conditions (e.g., epilepsy, cerebral palsy) that require intervention (e.g., medication, physical therapy).

Language is a particularly challenging area for individuals with severe disabilities. Language is a symbolic code in which small units of sound (i.e., phonemes) represent meaning (Hoff, 2005). To use language, individuals must learn the code, first, to derive meaning from social partners' language and second, to combine these units of sound to convey meaning to social partners. Children without disabilities acquire language in an effortless manner, but individuals with severe disabilities may struggle to acquire and use conventional language. Furthermore, language occurs in a social context composed of complex rules that include initiating, sustaining, and terminating conversations, responding to nonverbal communicative information (e.g., body posture, facial expressions), and "repairing" misunderstood communications. The severity of problems with communicating in conventional language in large part determine the degree or level of disability (Drasgow & Halle, 1995) and, in turn, influence multiple other domains of daily living.

Several personal characteristics are important to consider for individuals with severe disabilities because there is as much variability in personality among individuals with disabilities as there is among individuals without disabilities (Giangreco, 2006). For example, children with severe disabilities may be introverted or extroverted, energetic or relaxed, and curious or disinterested. Second, individuals labeled with a particular level of disability may have a range of skills and deficits. That is, individuals may have strengths (e.g., self-care skills) existing with deficits (e.g., limited vocabulary, pragmatic skills). These discrepancies exist for all of us because intellectual and adaptive abilities interact with personality, motivation, and learning history. There is great variability in skills within an individual and perhaps even greater variability across individuals labeled with a severe disability. Indeed, individuals with severe disabilities comprise the most heterogeneous group of all students with disabilities (Heward, 2000).

SOCIAL COMPETENCE AND SEVERE DISABILITIES

Guralnick (1992) suggested that social competence is often defined by two features: effectiveness and appropriateness. *Effectiveness* refers to achieving personal outcomes and *appropriateness* refers to achieving those personal outcomes in socially acceptable ways. Other definitions of social competence have emphasized the importance of children initiating and maintaining successful interactions and mutually satisfying relationships with others (Katz & McClellan, 1997). Although these factors may define social competence, their application to children with severe disabilities warrants close examination. Consider the following two children.

JAMES IS 6 YEARS OLD AND HAS MODERATE mental retardation. He wears thick glasses to correct his vision problems and takes medication to control his seizures. He is very soft spoken and has a vocabulary of about 15 words. He is making progress in acquiring spoken language and can communicate his basic needs in single words (e.g., "drink") and in short phrases (e.g., "snack, please"). His parents and teachers describe him as shy but loving. He does not initiate many interactions, and most of his initiations center around gaining access to preferred activities (e.g., listening to his favorite music) or items (e.g., looking at a favorite picture book). He does not enjoy loud voices or group activities, and seems most content in quiet areas with only one person or a few people around. For example, his favorite activity is to sit at the kitchen table and play with his small toy car collection while his parents clean up the area after a meal. He also likes to go for walks in the park with his father and get ice cream cones with either or both parents. At school, he splits his day between a self-contained classroom and a general education kindergarten. He enjoys participating in structured activities and during free time, he rarely seeks out interaction and instead, prefers to interact with toys and materials. When other children approach him and initiate, he often does not respond or walks away. In sum, James has some use of spoken language, is introverted, and is not highly motivated to seek out social interaction. His preferences and interests focus mainly on activities and not on people.

ALICE IS ALSO 6 YEARS OLD. SHE HAS *severe mental retardation and cerebral palsy. She has no spoken language and spends much of her day in a wheelchair. She has limited control over her body but has some voluntary movement in one arm, her neck, and head. She loves people. Alice's face lights up and her body shakes with excitement when adults or other children talk with her. She will cry or scream if she is alone for more than a few minutes. Her parents and teachers are working with her to teach her to use a VOCA (voice output communication aid) to communicate her needs and preferences. She currently communicates though body language and facial expression. Her favorite activities always involve people. She also splits her day between a self-contained classroom and a general education kindergarten. In sum, Alice has no conventional communication skills, is highly extroverted and, thus, is motivated to interact with people. Her preferences and interests focus mainly on people and social activities.*

Although James and Alice both may share the label of *severe disability*, they do, in fact, have different degrees of cognitive impairment, different personalities, different preferences, and different language and communication skills. These differences may affect how social competence is defined or determined for each of them. These differences hold true in general for children with severe disabilities. Because there is so much diversity within the population of young students with disabilities, we next present some factors that affect social competence and discuss their application to children with severe disabilities.

Factors Affecting Social Competence

We begin this section with a discussion of language and its relationship to social competence. Next, we describe the relationship between context and social competence. Then, we provide an analysis of motivation and social competence. We conclude by suggesting that social competence can be viewed along a continuum, with obligatory social responses at one end and optional social responses at the other.

Language

Language marks us as uniquely human; it enables us to express feelings, share ideas, make our desires known, engage in interactions, and form relationships with others (Chadsey-Rusch, Drasgow, Reinoehl, Halle, & Collett-Klingenberg, 1993). Language is the core of many social interactions, providing both the rules of spoken conversation and the rules of nonverbal behavior (i.e., pragmatics) surrounding the conversation. Indeed, language can be viewed as the gateway to social competence because it is the primary mediator of social interaction (Kaczmarek, 2002). Mastering the complex rules of language use, however, can be quite challenging for students with severe disabilities.

The first challenge for students with severe disabilities is to use some form of symbolic representation that various social partners can understand. Researchers have demonstrated that children with severe disabilities communicate in ways other than by using spoken language, and that the form of this communication may be ambiguous, idiosyncratic, or socially undesirable (e.g., Drasgow & Halle, 1995; Keen, Sigafoos, & Woodyatt, 2001). For example, young children may communicate that they want food during a meal by such preverbal behaviors as reaching for the food or by grasping a social partner's hand or wrist and then guiding the partner's hand (i.e., leading) to the desired food. These subtle behaviors may be understood by and acceptable to parents or other caretakers, but may interfere with relationships with peers without disabilities or with other potential social partners (Reichle, Halle, & Drasgow, 1998).

Investigators of children's problem behavior have clearly demonstrated that undesirable behavior serves a communicative function (e.g., Carr & Durand, 1985). Moreover, the function or motivation of children's undesirable behavior is not the issue, but rather, the means by which the function is expressed that becomes the problem. For example, most people agree that it is acceptable for children to want to end interactions with peers, but those same individuals also would agree that it is unacceptable for children to hit or bite peers as a method to terminate interactions. Thus, the first step toward social competence for children with severe disabilities may be to provide them with a portable communication system that enables them to communicate in socially acceptable and effective ways with a variety of social partners.

The second challenge for students with disabilities is to follow the rules of social interaction that involve communication. Social interactions involving language, or conversation, often consist of distinct parts (Owens, 1995). The first step is to initiate the interaction. Initiating may include getting the social partner's attention, making eye contact, orienting the body toward the social partner, and maintaining proximity. Kaczmarek and her colleagues (Kaczmarek, 1990, 2002; Kaczmarek, Evans, & Stever, 1995) refer to these initiation skills as listener preparatory behaviors. The second step is to sustain the interaction and may include taking turns, staying on topic, making eye contact, and nodding or smiling in response to the social partner's communicative turn. The final step in an interaction is to terminate it. Termination may include providing a reason for termination (e.g., "I have to go now") and saying "goodbye" or "see you later." The following scenario is common:

A PARENT OR TEACHER IS WITH A CHILD with a severe disability who has little or no language. Another adult or peer approaches and attempts to engage in an interac-

tion with the child. The child does not have the skills to initiate, sustain, or terminate the conversation with the social partner, so very quickly the parent or teacher often "takes over" the conversation and speaks for the child.

In this situation, the child is not a participant in his or her own conversation. Table 13.1 provides examples of initiating, sustaining, and terminating conversations for James and Alice, two children described previously.

One additional area that is related to language and social competence is *repairing* communicative breakdowns. A breakdown occurs when children initiate communication but do not obtain the desired outcomes; a repair occurs when children continue to communicate in an effort to achieve the desired outcomes (Halle, Brady, & Drasgow, 2004). Golinkoff (1986) examined three preverbal children who were typically developing and reported that only 38% of their initial communication was successfully responded to by their mothers. Wetherby, Alexander, and Prizant (1998) suggested that the rate of initial successful communication for children with severe disabilities may be even lower than what Golinkoff (1986) found. This low success rate means that young children with disabilities will often find themselves in situations in which they must repair failed communicative attempts. Social competence in breakdown situations requires that children successfully negotiate the breakdown to achieve their desired outcomes without terminating interactions or without emitting problem behaviors.

Context

We use *context* to refer to variables that consist of social partners, the physical environment, and events or activities occurring in the physical environment. Social partners may include familiar or unfamiliar family, adults, and peers. Physical environments may include home, school, and community settings. Some examples of events and activities include greetings, conversations, meals, and play. Context interacts with social competence such that the particular behaviors required to meet the social demands of a situation may change as the situation varies. Consider the situations of James and Alice. The forms that socially competent responses may

Table 13.1.   Examples of initiating, sustaining, and terminating conversations

	Initiating communication	Sustaining communication	Terminating communication
James	During snack time, looks at teacher and says, "Cookie, please"	Continues to make eye contact with the teacher and reaches for the cookie container; teacher hands him a cookie	Says, "Thank you" and takes the cookie
	After dinner, points to the cars on the top shelf and says, "Cars"	Approaches his mom and alternates eye gaze between the cars and his mom; she hands him the cars	Smiles and walks away with the cars
Alice	During center time, makes the sound, "ba" and makes eye contact with her teacher	Smiles and shakes her body; the teacher talks to Alice	Turns her head away from the teacher and terminates eye contact
	Reaches toward a doll on the floor and looks at her sister	Her sister hands her the doll	Smiles, looks away, and turns her body away from her sister

Table 13.2.   Examples of social competence skills across different contexts

	Communicative Event	School	Home	Community
James	Greeting	Says "Hello" to teacher; gives "high-5" to peer	Hugs parent; gives "high-5" to sibling	Smiles and waves
	Requesting drink	During snack time, points to juice and says, "More"	Points to refrigerator and says, "Drink, please"	Points to vending machine and says, "Please"
		During recess, leads teacher to door and says, "Drink, please"		
Alice	Requesting social interaction	In the classroom, approaches teacher and makes eye contact	In the playroom, makes eye contact with Dad and smiles	In the grocery store, smiles and nods head up and down
	Rejecting a non-preferred object	In the classroom, makes eye contact with teacher and shakes head, "No"	In the bedroom, pushes away the nonpreferred shirt and reaches for another shirt	On the playground, looks away from ball and alternates gaze between sandbox and mom

assume for James and Alice vary according to whether they are interacting with parents or peers in their homes or schools or in structured or unstructured activities. Table 13.2 provides further examples of social competence skills demonstrated by James and Alice across various contexts, including different places, social partners, and activities.

Context variables present another challenge for young children with severe disabilities. As context changes, so does the corresponding behavior necessary to meet the social competence requirements of that context. Thus, social competence requires that children first identify situations and then behave appropriately in those circumstances. Identifying the context first requires children to discriminate among contexts, and acquiring those discriminations may require substantial instruction (e.g., Carr, Binkoff, Kologinsky, & Eddy, 1978). Second, socially desirable behavior across different contexts involves issues of generalization and maintenance of social behavior, which is a major challenge for children with severe disabilities (e.g., Horner, Dunlap, & Koegel, 1988; Stokes & Baer, 1977). However, generalization and maintenance of social competence skills should be a priority because these processes foster successful and meaningful participation in a variety of situations and settings. We believe that social competence may in fact be a requisite skill for successful inclusion because *social* inclusion involves multiple and sometimes complex human interactions.

Motivation

Earlier we mentioned that there is as much variability in personalities of young children with severe disabilities as there is variability in personalities of children without disabilities. These differences in personalities may affect motivation to engage in interaction. Some children may be highly "social" and seek continual human contact and interaction; other children may have limited or no desire for interaction and prefer to engage in solitary activities. Moreover, children with severe disabilities may possess a broad range of social motivation that varies from high to low, or varies according to which social partners are present. James and Alice represent two young children with severe disabilities who are quite different in personalities and in social motivation.

The differences in personality and social motivation in young children with severe disabilities raise two interesting considerations. First, it is important to define social competence for children according to their individual personal characteristics, preferences, and life situations. Second, careful attention needs to be given to the idea that there is great difficulty discriminating between social motivation arising from personality, and motivation for social interaction that has been shaped by students' previous experiences. For example, if social competence deficits result in a history of failed, frustrating, or aversive interactions, then it is likely that children's social behavior may have been extinguished so that they no longer seek interaction. It may also be that their social attempts have been inadvertently punished so that they have learned to avoid social interactions altogether. Thus, motivation for social interaction by children with severe disabilities is affected by their personality, social behavioral repertoire, and social interaction history.

The Continuum of Social Competence

Young children with disabilities have a range of social competence skills, and this range can be viewed as a continuum with obligatory social competence at one end and optional social competence at the other end. By *obligatory social competence*, we mean skills related to conventional social rules that are basic and necessary in virtually every human interaction. For example, when adults or peers greet children, they are obligated to respond to that greeting. Similarly, when children want access to toys that peers are playing with, they need to request the toy appropriately instead of physically taking it. Optional social competence skills result in extending or expanding social interactions and go beyond meeting the basic expectations of social situations. If optional social competence skills do not occur, they will probably not jeopardize others' perceptions of the individual. For example, if a person bumps into a stranger in the mall, an obligatory social competence reply might be to say, "Excuse me" and an optional social competence response might be make a humorous comment (e.g., "Pardon my big feet") about the situation. Table 13.3 presents more examples of the social competence continuum.

Table 13.3.   Examples of skills demonstrated along the continuum of social competence, from obligatory to optional

	Obligatory social competence	Optional social competence
Children who are typically developing	Stands in line for lunch	Asks peer next in line what he brought for lunch
	Apologizes when hurting another peer	Explains what happened and offers help
James	Requests a car that another peer is playing with	Shows peer a special trick with the car
	Returns greeting to the teacher when entering the classroom	Points to new shoes his parents bought him
Alice	Shakes head "No" to reject a toy	Requests an alternative object by reaching for a different toy
	Waits patiently for her turn in a social game	Smiles at other peers in the group

The social competence continuum provides an avenue for determining skill targets for children with severe disabilities. Obligatory social competence can be viewed as a set of survival social skills that are fundamental in any context, regardless of children's personalities or motivations. Thus, obligatory social competence skills are important and relevant for children with severe disabilities. Optional social competence, on the other hand, enriches social interactions and is related to a child's motivation to sustain and expand social interactions. Optional social competence, especially those behaviors matched to the child's most frequent and routine contexts, is related to his or her personality and social motivation. For example, the emphasis for James should be on obligatory social competence skills that enable him to navigate social contexts within various environments to access and engage in preferred activities (e.g., sharing materials during school activities, waiting in line to get ice cream). The emphasis for Alice should begin with developing obligatory social competence skills in combination with optional social competence skills so that she can initiate and sustain interactions purely because the process is reinforcing for her. However, for Alice, both obligatory and optional social behaviors may likely be easier for her to acquire because the natural consequences will reinforce her performance. In contrast, James may be difficult to teach even obligatory social behavior because the only natural reinforcer may be the termination of the interaction once he has emitted the obligatory responses.

Level of Supports and Partial Participation

Two additional aspects of promoting social competence in young children with severe disabilities are important to discuss. First, we have described children with severe disabilities mostly in terms of their personal characteristics. Another perspective that is relevant to understanding children with severe disabilities is to refocus the emphasis on the environmental supports that promote personal well-being and enhance independent functioning (AAMR, 2002). Young children with severe disabilities are likely to need some level of long-term supports to maximize their social competency. The type of supports that enhance social competence should include systematic instruction of skills and structuring social situations to foster positive peer interaction.

The second aspect of promoting social competence for young children with severe disabilities invokes the principle of *partial participation* (Baumgart et al., 1982). Partial participation refers to the philosophy that children should not be excluded from activities because they may never be able to perform them independently. Moreover, participating to the greatest extent possible in a range of chronologically age-appropriate activities increases individuals' quality of life and positive perceptions of their social partners. Thus, social competence for children with severe disabilities may occur with the use of supports and be consistent with the principle of partial participation. The ultimate goal is to develop critical skills that might reduce the intensity of needed supports and increase meaningful participation in independent and interdependent activities.

Assessment of Social Competence

One of the main purposes of assessment is to collect information that guides the development of high-quality instructional goals (Salvia & Ysseldyke, 2004; Snell &

Brown, 2006). Assessment is particularly important for children with severe disabilities because of the need for precise and specific information that captures their social and behavioral characteristics and life situations. Thus, assessment for children with severe disabilities should consist of an approach that results in the identification of individualized age-appropriate and functional skills. We have yet to find a single assessment that provides a comprehensive evaluation of social competence for children with severe disabilities. Therefore, we recommend the integration of several procedures that have been especially effective in identifying and planning social competence goals for children with severe disabilities. It should be noted that the integrated assessment approach we discuss is also applicable to other developmental and educational areas.

Ecological Inventories

One approach that has been highly effective at generating meaningful instructional content for children with severe disabilities is ecological inventories. Ecological inventories are a type of informal assessment that represents a careful and systematic approach to identifying critical skills that are high priority for individuals (Renzaglia, Karvonen, Drasgow, & Stoxen, 2003). Ecological inventories typically consist of five steps (Brown et al., 1979). We have adapted Brown and colleagues' five steps to focus on the assessment of social competence:

1. Identify social competence as the curricular domain.

2. Identify the child's current and future natural environments.

3. Divide the environments (e.g., school) into sub-environments (e.g., classroom, playground, lunchroom).

4. Inventory the sub-environments to determine the activities that children perform there (e.g., communicating, playing games, engaging in structured group activities).

5. Determine the social competencies required for the performance of the activities (e.g., requesting, rejecting, taking turns, imitating).

Ecological inventories are well matched to the characteristics and needs of children with severe disabilities for several reasons. First, ecological inventories are based on a team approach in which teachers, parents, and others provide essential information for determining current and future environments. Second, the inventory process emphasizes preparing children for the future by focusing on social behaviors and skills that are necessary to be successful in future environments (Snell & Brown, 2006). Third, ecological inventories generate accurate information about real situations that enable teachers to provide explicit instruction on skill sequences that are relevant to the actual situations that children will encounter daily and in the future. Fourth, ecological inventories address generalization and maintenance problems that are especially challenging for children with severe disabilities by identifying materials, times, and places to teach and practice identified skills during routine situations within typical settings. Moreover, given that teaching and learning opportunities are readily available, training functional skills that are well matched to children's environments enhances maintenance (Carr & Lindquist, 1987).

Ecological Inventory			
Natural environment	Sub-environments	Activities	Social competence skills
School	General education classroom	Structured time Group activity Snack time	Greeting Taking turns Requesting
	Self-contained classroom	One-to-one instruction Small group activities Therapies	Imitating Requesting Rejecting Sharing
	Playground	Free play Organized group play	Entering group play Taking turns Playing with others, sharing Organizing

Figure 13.1.   An example of an ecological inventory for James and Alice.

Ecological inventories are derived from an assessment procedure that consists of two main components: interview and direct observation. Interviews are helpful to identify current and future environments, and to identify *general* target areas for intervention. Interviews should also be used to obtain initial information on 1) the range of sub-environments that comprise children's current and future environments, 2) the type of activities that occur in those sub-environments, and 3) the skills that children need to be successful in those activities. The next step should be to observe children in the current and future environments to revise, expand, or validate the necessary skills (see Figure 13.1 for an example of ecological inventory). Ecological inventories are based on an assessment that describes environmental conditions and demands for individual children. Ecological inventories delineate the specific social skills necessary to be active and effective participants in the diverse situations in which children live, play, and learn. The next step is to assess children's current level of performance compared with the results of the ecological inventories.

Assessing Current Levels of Performance

The next step in assessing social competence is to identify children's specific social interaction skills. Social interaction assessment begins with an evaluation of children's social engagement (Kennedy, 2002). Assessing children's preferences is a critical component of this effort. Again, assessment should be accomplished by using both interview and direct observation to evaluate children's current skill levels during social interaction opportunities across multiple environments (e.g., home, school, child care). It is important to obtain information about children's social interactions from several familiar people to provide a better assessment of children's social competence. Using the questions presented next as a guide, individuals performing assessments may interview parents, teachers, and others to collect information about children's social interaction skills and opportunities to interact with others.

1.   When, over the course of the child's day, does the child initiate interaction? What (i.e., what behaviors) does the child use to initiate interaction?

2.   When, over the course of the child's day, does the child respond to another's initiation? How (i.e., what behaviors) does the child use to respond?

3.   With whom does the child most frequently initiate interaction?

4. To whom does the child most frequently respond?

5. How long do interactions last? How many different behaviors does the child use to sustain interactions?

6. What are the purposes for the child's interactions (e.g., access attention or materials from adults or peers, engage in activity with peers or adults)?

7. When do the highest number of interactive attempts or responses and the lowest number of interactive attempts or responses take place (e.g., in which activities, with whom)?

Although interviews often result in useful information, direct observations of routine and typical environments are critical to assessing children's social interaction skills (Kaczmarek, 2002). Observations can be conducted in the natural environment in "real time" or by videotaping. The primary purpose of direct observations is to determine how children behave in their typical social situations. Direct observations may be very specific, such as determining the ways in which children greet others, or they may be more general, such as assessing potential opportunities for social interaction. Direct observations may include narrative recording, A-B-C (antecedent-behavior-consequence) analyses, or structured and formal collection of frequency or interval data. Direct observations can identify the type of topographies (i.e., forms of behavior) that children use to communicate and the frequency and duration of social behaviors. Observational information also can provide objective information to the above questions. Systematic observations may assist in the development of data systems that allow practitioners to collect progress-monitoring information about children (see an example of a data sheet in Figure 13.2).

After assessing children's social interactions, the next step is to assess the social appropriateness of their behaviors within contextual and cultural expectations. We assess social appropriateness or social validity within the context of interactions (see

Data Sheet					
Daily schedule	Social interaction (i.e., initiating, responding, other)	Topography of social behavior (e.g., eye contact, reach)	Primary social contact	Duration of social interaction	Purpose of interaction
Arrival					
7:30–7:45					
Breakfast					
7:45–8:15					
Adapted P.E.					
8:15–8:45					
Structured group activity					
8:45–9:15					
Bathroom break					
9:15–9:30					

Figure 13.2. Data sheet for recording direct observation in the natural environment.

Table 13.4.   Examples of differences between current and appropriate social interaction behavior

	Current social interaction behavior	Appropriate social interaction behavior
James	Grabs desired toy from another peer	Requests toy from peer by pointing to toy and saying, "Please"
	Throws away unwanted object	Says, "All done" and puts toy back in its place
Alice	Cries and screams when social interaction with others is desired	Touches softly or makes eye contact to initiate social interaction
	Terminates eye contact and turns body away from partner to reject a nonpreferred object	Sustains eye contact and shakes head "No" to reject a nonpreferred object

Schwartz & Baer, 1991; Wolf, 1978). Because children's social interactions occur in settings affected by cultural norms, it is necessary to establish which social behaviors are socially valid for corresponding environments. We suggest determining social validity within settings through direct observations of typical child-to-child, child-to-adult, and child-to-family-member interactions. Using the same questions and observation assessment methods that we previously mentioned, teachers and others can then identify behaviors that are socially valid within children's social and culture contexts. Finally, any discrepancies between children's current social repertoire and their level of effective and appropriate social performance guide the identification of social competence instructional content for them (see Table 13.4 for examples from James and Alice).

Preference Assessment

The purpose of a preference assessment is to identify people, items, and activities that are consistently motivating or reinforcing for children (Hughes, Pitkin, & Lorden, 1998). Identifying preferences is important for several reasons. First, children with severe disabilities are often nonverbal and, thus, they may not be able to tell others their needs and desires. Second, by identifying preferences, teachers and parents can systematically strengthen socially desirable behaviors by allowing access to preferred people, items, and activities contingent on the occurrence of those desirable behaviors (Skinner, 1969). Third, structuring activities in ways that reflect children's preferences increases engagement, and meaningful engagement is a good predictor of learning outcomes (Iovannone, Dunlap, Huber, & Kincaid, 2003). Fourth, learning to access preferred people, materials, and activities in effective and socially acceptable ways is a core component of social competence (Guralnick, 1992).

Preference assessments usually consist of direct assessment procedures, interviews, and observations. The direct assessment procedures typically consist of providing children with multiple opportunities to have access to and interact with or choose from several potentially motivating people, items, or events (Brown, Snell, & Lehr, 2006). Interviews alone may prove inadequate to identify children's preferences because the opinions of others may be inaccurate, especially when it comes to evaluating moderate or weak preferences (Green et al., 1988; Reid & Green, 2005). Interview information can, however, guide direct observations by providing important information about when and where preference data should be collected.

There are two main types of direct preference assessment procedures. The first procedure is referred to as *forced choice* (e.g., Fisher, Piazza, Bowman, & Amari, 1996). In forced-choice formats, children are required to select from two or more people, items, or activities. For example, if teachers are assessing food preferences, they may offer children two different foods (e.g., a carrot or a raisin) several times. Children may consistently select raisins, which might lead to the conclusion that raisins are their preferred food. One important consideration to bear in mind is that preferences, or reinforcers, are relative to what is available. That is, in a forced choice situation, the raisin is preferred over the carrot, but the raisin in absolute value may be a food that is not highly preferred when compared with other highly valued options such as candy or pizza, which were not available.

The second preference procedure is *free access* or *free choice* (Reid & Green, 2005). In free choice assessment procedures, children have access to multiple activities and items and they are free to choose any one of them. The items or activities that children consistently select are considered the most preferred. One variant of the free choice assessments is to observe children during routine situations and record the frequency or duration of their interactions with people, activities, and items. In our view, this procedure may be the most accurate because children have access to the largest number of reinforcers that are typically available in their normal settings during daily routines.

Several considerations related to preference assessments are important. First, preferences are variable, and they may fluctuate from moment to moment according to such factors as what is available and when it is available. Although preference assessments may identify preferred people, items, and activities in general, at any given moment the motivating and reinforcing value of those preferences may range from high to nonexistent. Second, some children with severe physical disabilities may not be able to express their preferences in conventional ways (e.g., moving toward the item, grasping the item). Therefore, teachers may need to place items on a table that a child in a wheelchair can have access to, put the items on a wheelchair tray, or look for more subtle behavioral signs of preference such as eye gaze, happy sounds, and changes in affect. Third, children's ability to acquire the social skills needed to obtain access to preferred people, items, and activities in socially acceptable ways is a fundamental aspect of their quality of life because it empowers them to make choices and to have control over their daily lives. Fourth, a challenge for enhancing social competence in young children with severe disabilities arises when interacting with others is a nonpreferred, or even aversive, event.

In summary, our recommended assessment procedures provide comprehensive information that will guide the development of interventions (see Table 13.5). Ecological inventories assess current and future environmental situations and demands. The assessment of children's current performance describes how children communicate in social situations, how well their behavioral repertoire meets relevant social demands, and what they need to learn to be successful in social situations. Preference assessments address motivation by identifying reinforcers and pave the way for teaching socially acceptable methods for children to make choices and increase skills related to self-determination. Although ecological inventories pose potential advantages for maintenance and generalization of social behavior, it is critical to consider children's motivation for initiating or responding to social interaction opportunities. That is, the materials and people, and related social consequences, may be present in everyday settings. Nevertheless, these variables do not guarantee that children will engage in social behavior if the consequences for doing so are not adequately reinforcing to them or if the antecedents do not *inform* them that social acts will likely produce reinforcing outcomes. Motivation is a prerequisite to social behavior (Drasgow & Halle, 1995; Drasgow, Halle, Ostrosky, & Harbers, 1996) and often must be carefully taught to children with severe disabilities. Eco-

Table 13.5.   A summary of the assessment procedures for determining social competence

Ecological inventories

Interview individuals who are familiar with the child.

Use direct observation of the child in natural environments to identify the following:

  Child's current and future natural environments

  Sub-environments within the natural environments

  Activities that children perform in the sub-environments

  Social competencies required for the performance of the activities

Assessment of current levels of performance

Use interviews with individuals who are familiar with the child to collect information about the child's social interaction skills:

  When does the child initiate interaction? Respond to interaction?

  With whom does the child initiate interaction? To whom does the child respond?

  How long do the interactions last?

  What are the purposes of the child's interaction?

Use direct observation in the child's natural environment to identify

  The type of topographies the child uses to communicate or to interact

  The frequency and duration of the topographies

  When does the child initiate interaction? Respond to interaction?

  With whom does the child initiate interaction? To whom does the child respond?

  How long does the interaction last?

  What are the purposes of the child's interaction?

Using the same interviews and direct observation described above, identify behaviors that are socially valid in the child's unique context and culture.

Evaluate gap between the child's current repertoire and level of performance necessary to be successful in socially appropriate interactions.

Preference assessment

Use interviews with individuals who are familiar with the child to identify people, items, and activities that are motivating for the child.

Observe child in natural environment to confirm results found in interviews.

Conduct direct preference assessment procedures (forced choice or free access).

logical inventories, assessments of current levels of performance, and preference assessments should be integrated by embedding preferred people, materials, and activities that function as reinforcers into naturally occurring routines and then beginning social competence instruction with the knowledge of children's social skills and with high-quality functional and individual social competence goals.

EVIDENCE-BASED SOCIAL COMPETENCE INTERVENTIONS FOR CHILDREN WITH SEVERE DISABILITIES

The initial step in designing and implementing effective social skills interventions for children with severe disabilities is to identify functional skills through a comprehensive assessment of social competence. The next step is to develop interventions that are closely linked to the assessment information. We now review intervention strategies for enhancing social competence skills for children with

Table 13.6.   Summary of interventions

Intervention type	Strategy	Other considerations
Interventions to increase motivation	Establish social partners as generalized reinforcers	*Motivation:* Increase motivation for social interaction by developing associations between social partners and positive events (e.g., access to highly preferred objects and activities)
Interventions to increase opportunities for developing social competence skills	Environmental arrangement	*Toys and materials:* Select toys and materials that require engagement with others to produce desired outcome.
		Spatial arrangement: Arrange the physical environment to increase social interaction.
		Activity structure: Structure the activities and assign roles to promote social interaction.
Interventions to increase social competence	Teaching strategies	*Task analysis:* Divide a complex skill into smaller teachable steps.
		Prompts: Help the child by providing additional cues or assistance.
		Reinforcement: Provide motivating consequences for the occurrence of a desired behavior.
		Generalization: Ensure that instruction represents the variability that a child is likely to encounter in natural settings.
		Data collection: Use the numerical information collected on the child's target behavior to guide instructional decisions and monitor progress.

severe disabilities that increase motivation, increase opportunities for social interaction, and develop skills (see Table 13.6 for a summary of these strategies). These strategies should be individualized based on the specific assessment results to develop an intervention package for a particular child.

Interventions to Increase Motivation

Children's motivation for interacting with others influences their social competence and related abilities. Children might not be socially responsive because interactions are not reinforcing for them and thus they avoid social partners. These children may initiate contact only when they want access to a preferred item or activity. Thus, interacting with others is a means to an end and not an end in itself (i.e., others mediate access to preferences). This type of interaction is referred to as *instrumental* or *regulatory* (Wetherby, 1986). Moreover, when others initiate interactions with them, these children may be unresponsive, making future initiations by others less likely. If children lack motivation to socially interact with others, few opportunities for communicating will be available to them, and important skills such as language development, turn taking, and play may be compromised. Therefore, interventions that aim to establish social responsiveness are critical.

We could locate only a few studies on establishing social responsiveness. Some researchers have defined and described social responsiveness or similar phenomena (e.g., Light, Parsons, & Drager, 2002); even more have focused on the development and acquisition of social skills (e.g., Odom & Brown, 1993). Few, however, have focused on establishing social responsiveness in children who lack it. In spite of the limited literature on establishing social responsiveness, Bijou and Baer (1965; see also Bijou, 1993) provided an elegant theoretical description of the earliest forms of socialization from an operant perspective. They view the essential function of mothers as delivering positive reinforcers to infants while removing negative events. Their description offers a functional picture of how mothers behave in response to their infants' behavior. Mothers feed their infants when hungry, maintain warmth with clothing, hold them close for security, offer them toys or play with them to generate novel stimulation, and prepare them for bed when sleepy. By mediating everyday events, mothers become conditioned social reinforcers for their infants.

Similarly, with older children, Carr and colleagues (1994) described a concept they call *building rapport*. They introduce this phrase in the context of developing communication-based interventions for children with severe problem behaviors. Carr and colleagues suggested that communication goals are achieved more easily when caregivers and the children are motivated to interact with each other. Establishing a history of many positive experiences is critical to building rapport. If caregivers and children have shared a variety of enjoyable activities and events in the past, then their mutual presence might be a signal for the other to initiate interaction. Conversely, negative experiences might contribute to the failure of individuals to be responsive partners and might set the occasion for children's avoidance of partner's social initiations or for challenging behavior.

The sources above suggest that social partners might acquire reinforcing properties by association with the presentation of positive reinforcers or by the removal of negative ones. To date, we could locate only two studies that tested this strategy (McLaughlin & Carr, 2005; Turan, 2004). For example, Turan (2004) evaluated the effectiveness of an intervention developed to increase the social responsiveness of two children with moderate and severe disabilities and autism spectrum disorder by attempting to establish peers without disabilities as conditioned social reinforcers. The goal of her intervention was to increase the social responsiveness of the children with disabilities to peers without disabilities by establishing a relationship based solely on positive experiences between them.

To establish a relationship, Turan (2004) conducted dyadic contact sessions between children with disabilities and their peers for 10–15 minutes two to three times a week for a total of 25 sessions for one dyad and 17 sessions for the other. These sessions capitalized on both access to preferred objects and activities and removal of unpreferred objects and activities. An interventionist facilitated the introduction of objects, activities, edibles, and other materials identified through a systematic preference assessment as highly preferred by the children with disabilities. Then, the children with disabilities gained access to these highly preferred items only in the presence of a peer. In fact, often the peer provided the assistance required to get access to the items or was the one who introduced the activities or objects. The researcher attempted to ensure that peers had also identified many of the activities as preferred so that both children would enjoy and benefit from the sessions. Although the researcher established routines, the sessions remained free flowing to the degree that the children's momentary interests often determined the choice of activities. For instance, if a snack had started and the child with disabilities walked to the bookshelf and signaled that she wanted a particular book that was out of reach, the interventionist directed the peer to a stool so that the peer could obtain the book for the target child. Together they looked at the book or, occasionally, the interventionist would sit down with both of them and read the story in an interactive fashion.

In addition to the availability of the highly preferred events during a session, the researcher strategically scheduled sessions to begin with the termination of an unpreferred activity or task. That is, the peer's approach during an unpreferred activity served as a signal to the child with disabilities that she would be leaving the unpreferred activity and would be starting a fun-filled routine. The goal was for peers to acquire reinforcing properties through the continuous association with existing powerful reinforcers (i.e., activities and items identified through preference assessment) and the removal of negative events. The expected outcome of these sessions and routines was to make the peer a conditioned reinforcer so that the child with disabilities would initiate and maintain interaction with the peer.

The results of the investigation were equivocal. That is, the researcher observed small changes in interaction with one of the two dyads during an unstructured play time that occurred immediately prior to the structured sessions. During these probe occasions, the interventionist was present, but was intentionally busy with other tasks and did not interact with the two children. These were the occasions during which the researcher examined the effects of the intervention. The target behaviors monitored included the number of intervals during which interaction between the peers occurred, partner proximity, parallel play, and nonsocial behavior. Although the effects of the intervention were not clear, it is unknown whether the intervention lacked merit or whether its intensity was insufficient. Perhaps 10- to 15-minute sessions two to three times weekly for 8 weeks is not enough exposure to produce the intended effect. How often and how long these dyadic contact sessions would need to continue to produce the meaningful outcomes on children's responsiveness is still untested and unknown.

In summary, some children with severe disabilities may lack the motivation to interact with others. For these children, interventions might enhance social responsiveness by establishing familiar social partners as reinforcers through a rich history of positive social interactions. Although limited research exists that has empirically demonstrated effective procedures to achieve this outcome, it appears to be a fruitful avenue to pursue because motivation is a prerequisite and essential component for social competence skill development.

Interventions to Increase Opportunities for Developing Social Competence Skills

One approach to intervention for building social competence is to identify opportunities in which children can learn and practice social competence skills. For young children with severe disabilities, this approach may be necessary because they need frequent opportunities to acquire and practice skills. Many researchers and practitioners have capitalized on an established set of strategies referred to as *environmental arrangement* (e.g., DeKlyen & Odom, 1989; Ivory & McCollum, 1999; Ostrosky & Kaiser, 1991). We describe examples of these strategies and explain how they may need to be adapted to create functional opportunities for children with severe disabilities to acquire social competence skills.

Selection of Toys and Materials

The selection of high interest toys and materials is critical to increase social exchanges because availability may create multiple opportunities for social interaction (e.g., Ivory & McCollum, 1999; Quilitch & Risley, 1973). Toys and materials can be grouped as social and isolate (Beckman & Kohl, 1984; Ivory & McCollum, 1999). Social toys and materials typically are used cooperatively and may require multiple participants for intended engagement, whereas isolate toys do not require the participation of another to be enjoyed. For example, pretending to purchase items at a store requires the active participation and cooperation of at least two children acting as the shopper and the store cashier, whereas many computer games were designed for only one participant. For children with severe disabilities, however, simply replacing isolate toys with social toys might not promote positive social interactions because these toys may require some level of adult or peer support as well as adaptations to the activity and materials.

Spatial Arrangement

Changes in spatial density (i.e., space available for a group of children in an activity) can affect children's social interactions (Brown, Fox, & Brady, 1987; Spiegel-McGill, Bambara, Shores, & Fox 1984). That is, proximity to peers might set the occasion for social interactions. For example, Speigel-McGill and colleagues (1984) found that peer interaction between children with severe disabilities and their peers without disabilities increased when the children were within 1 to 5 feet of one another compared with when they were within 10 feet of one another. They also found that small groups with two or three children exhibited more peer interaction than larger groups. Classroom environments for children with severe disabilities can easily be arranged and modified to improve proximity with peers without disabilities. This arrangement can be accomplished by restricting open spaces in the classrooms as well as by limiting the number of centers available to children in a given time period. However, it is likely that this strategy alone might not be sufficient to promote improvements in peer interactions for many children with severe disabilities who may not have the necessary social initiation skills, or whose idiosyncratic social behavior may have been ignored by peers in the past. Again, some level of adult or peer support as well as adaptations to the activity and materials may be needed.

Activity Structure

DeKlyen and Odom (1989) found that teacher-structured play activities (i.e., assignment of children to social play activities, assignment of specific social roles) resulted in young children's increased peer interactions. One challenge to implement this intervention strategy might be planning activities that children with diverse abilities enjoy. Often it is difficult to maintain young children's interest in an activity for more than a short time. Maintaining interest is even more challenging when children with severe disabilities are included in the activity because teachers have to select activities that are sufficiently challenging and interesting for all children while allowing peers with disabilities to participate meaningfully. Again, conducting preference assessments to identify peers, materials, and activities that children enjoy is a first step and allows teachers to group children with common interests.

In summary, young children with severe disabilities are likely to require some level of adult and peer support to develop and enhance their social competence skills. One type of support is to identify opportunities or occasions in which children can learn and practice social and play skills and to provide optimal environmental arrangements to promote children's interactions. Initiating, responding, sharing, and turn taking are some examples of social interaction skills that young children can learn and practice during common classroom activities.

Interventions to Increase Social Competence

Because of significant language and cognitive impairments, children with severe disabilities most often do not make adequate progress within traditional academic instructional formats in which teachers "explain" or "demonstrate" how to perform relevant behaviors (Bierne-Smith, Patton, & Kim, 2006). Instead, teachers of children with severe disabilities have much better success with systematic instruction. Systematic instruction refers to teaching that is based on identifying precise learning outcomes, consistently employing specific and focused teaching strategies to achieve those outcomes, and then using frequent progress monitoring information about children's performance to guide daily instructional decisions (e.g., Halle, Chadsey, Lee, & Renzaglia, 2004; Snell & Brown, 2006; Wolery, Ault, & Doyle, 1992). The following three sections provide further explanation of the principles of sytematic instruction.

Identifying Learning Outcomes

The first critical step of intervention is to identify the well-defined outcomes of instruction. These outcomes should be based on the individualized assessment of children's needs and then be operationally defined so that they are clearly observable and measurable for ongoing progress monitoring (Kennedy, 2005; Odom et al., 2003). For example, James's assessment revealed that he did not initiate or respond to the greetings of peers or adults. Thus, the obligatory social competence skill of initiating and responding to the greetings of others is an appropriate learning objective for James. Although greeting behaviors are an important social skill derived from the assessment, that level of definition may be ambiguous, and specification of exactly what social behaviors should be taught, practiced, and generalized is needed. *Greetings* might be operationally defined for James as orienting his body and face toward social partners, raising his hand to wave for approximately 2 seconds, and using his voice to say, "Hi" when he approaches social partners or responds to social partners greeting him. Based on this operational definition, the teacher now knows exactly what social behaviors James should initially learn in order to greet others.

Teaching Strategies

Several systematic teaching strategies are effective for students with severe disabilities (Halle et al., 2004; Snell & Brown, 2006; Westling & Fox, 2004). Typically, these teaching strategies are combined to compose a multicomponent intervention package. An essential teaching strategy is task analysis, which allows practitioners to divide complex skills into meaningful and teachable component skills. For example, if Alice is being taught to play a game with a peer, her task analysis steps may include initiating a request to play, selecting a game to play, following the rules of the game, taking turns, interacting with others during the game, requesting to stop or continue the game, cleaning up, saying thanks, and terminating the activity.

Two features are important to consider when developing a task analysis for children with severe disabilities. Task analyses should regulate the flow of information so that children do not become either bored or overwhelmed. Another critical feature of task analyses is to ensure that they represent meaningful units of behavior that 1) are not unduly limited in scope, 2) do not have an arbitrary beginning and end, and 3) emphasize the qualitative aspects of participation over the motor components of the skill (Brown et al., 2006).

Prompting is another especially important teaching strategy. Prompts are teacher or peer assistance that make children's acquisition, practice, and generalization of behaviors easier. Two fundamental types of prompts are response prompts and stimulus prompts. Response prompts are teacher behaviors that increase the probability of correct responding. Response prompting strategies include verbal (e.g., teachers say, "What do you do next?"), gestural (e.g., teachers motion for the children to orient toward social partners), model (e.g., teachers demonstrate essential aspects of behaviors), or physical (e.g., teachers physically guide children through the critical motor behaviors). All of these prompting strategies have a similar purpose and goal of systematically assisting children to perform essential behaviors independently or to the best of their abilities. Thus, teachers who employ prompting should systematically reduce or fade their assistance over time or children may become overly dependent on others to perform important behaviors. This situation is known as *prompt dependency* and may represent children's "learned helplessness" in social situations. Prompt-fading strategies include most-to-least, least-to-most, constant and progressive time delay, and graduated guidance (for a review, see Wolery et al., 1992).

Stimulus prompts provide environmental cues that assist children in responding correctly. Stimulus prompts may include competent peers performing important behaviors or picture cues depicting critical behaviors. Similar to response prompts, stimulus prompts need to be withdrawn over time so that children are responding to the natural cues in the environment (e.g., routine and common circumstances). Indeed, because both stimulus and response prompts need to be eliminated over time to facilitate children's independent performance, teachers should initially identify natural environmental cues that are relevant to performance of social behaviors.

Another teaching strategy is providing motivating consequences for the occurrence of social behaviors. In other words, teachers need to assess what will reinforce children's social behaviors so that they are likely to repeat those behaviors in the future. We like to think of reinforcement as the most important of three components that compose learning. The first component that children should learn is *when* to engage in social behaviors. They learn this component by attending to the relevant natural cues, and these cues eventually come to signal that reinforcement is available for performing corresponding social behaviors. Second, children have to learn *what* to do. For example, teachers may use a prompting system so that they can systematically teach children the specific motor requirements of social behaviors. The ultimate goal should be that children learn to perform social behaviors because those responses enable them to access reinforcers. Third, children should learn *why* they are performing important behaviors. Children perform behaviors because of the motivation to achieve an outcome. The outcome is the reinforcer. Reinforcers provide motivation and serve as the *why* for performing important behaviors. Technically, this relationship is referred to as Antecedent-Behavior-Consequence and it describes the *when-what-why* of learning. The purpose of many interventions for children with and without severe disabilities is to create meaningful A-B-C chains that enhance social performance.

During the early stages of instruction, reinforcement should be immediate, frequent, and substantial to compensate children for their motor and cognitive efforts to respond correctly (Halle & Drasgow, 2003). As children begin to learn and practice skills, teachers should reduce the frequency and magnitude of reinforcement because there is typically less response effort required by children to produce the correct response. Similar to identifying natural cues, teachers should also determine sources of natural reinforcement that will be readily available to maintain their social behaviors (Carr & Lindquist, 1987). Access to natural reinforcement is likely to result in maintenance of important behavior because motivating consequences for the behavior are easily available.

As mentioned previously, children, particularly children with severe disabilities, may have difficulties in generalizing newly acquired social behaviors to relevant situations. Stokes and Baer (1977) recommended several strategies that have the potential to enhance generalization: 1) using real and relevant materials, people, and environmental circumstances during instruction; 2) employing multiple meaningful examples of these actual circumstances during teaching; and 3) ensuring that instruction reflects the actual and variable conditions children are likely to encounter in their routine and day-to-day circumstances. These effective strategies have been incorporated into a generalization package called *general-case instruction* (e.g., Chadsey-Rusch et al., 1993; Drasgow & Halle, 1995). General-case instruction begins by defining when and where children's newly acquired behaviors ought to occur, then selecting some relevant and clear representative examples as well as nonexamples to employ during teaching, practicing, and monitoring generalization and maintenance of skills. The essential concept of general-case instruction is that systematic teaching and practicing with sufficient representative examples will result in appropriate responding to relevant situations.

Progress Monitoring

A last essential strategy that we recommend is systematic and meaningful data collection and progress monitoring. Data collection consists of clearly defining relevant behaviors and circumstances, and then using ongoing measurement of those factors to guide effective instructional decisions (Miltenberger, 2004). In other words, instructional decisions should be based on children's actual social performance in relevant circumstances. We suggest that teachers should collect three essential types of information: 1) acquisition data for new behaviors in relevant circumstances, 2) generalization information for the newly acquired responses to appropriate situations, and 3) maintenance data across time. Because students with disabilities often acquire skills slowly (Carr et al., 1978; Drasgow et al., 1996), it is important to measure small increments of progress to make instructional decisions about acquisition, generalization, and maintenance of children's social behavior.

CONCLUSIONS

We conclude this chapter by elaborating on three important issues that surfaced in our discussion of enhancing the social competence of young children with severe disabilities. These issues are 1) viewing social motivation as a relatively stable disposition, 2) capitalizing on preference to encourage social engagement, and 3) mapping the continuum of social competence from obligatory to optional social contacts. Our purpose is to highlight relevant practice and research issues.

Social Motivation as a Disposition

Empowerment though socially acceptable communication, independence, and meaningful choices are fundamental goals for individuals with severe disabilities. A question that we rarely ask is this: How should adults encourage interactions of young children who do not interact with others? As adults, we are free to choose to be with others or to spend time alone. Do we have the right to tell children that they should interact with others or should we accept their choice to be alone? Are some children too young or too cognitively unsophisticated to exercise such social control? In response to this dilemma, a reasoned approach may be to investigate *why* children choose to avoid others. At least two possibilities exist: 1) from birth, their motivation to interact with others is limited and they prefer to be alone rather than with others, or 2) they possess the motivation, but lack the necessary social skills to be successful in their interactions with others. If they lack the necessary skills, then their efforts may have failed repeatedly and been unintentionally extinguished, or their efforts may have been inadvertently punished because the behaviors they use to communicate or interact are socially undesirable.

Children's social motivation has important implications for both practice and research. For practice, early childhood educators need to determine where children fall on the continuum of social motivation. If children's social motivation is low, then educators should teach obligatory interaction skills and make efforts to associate adults and peers with highly preferred objects and activities to enhance the value of these potential social partners. If children's social motivation is intact, but their efforts to initiate fail to achieve the desired interactions, then educators should implement well-specified social competence training, knowing that the natural consequences of social interaction may suffice to maintain the newly taught skills (i.e., natural communities of reinforcement, see McConnell, Sisson, Cort, & Strain, 1991).

Motivation for children's social skills (e.g., appropriate communication forms) may be responsible for the limited generalization results often found in research efforts to teach young children with severe disabilities (Drasgow, Halle, & Ostrosky, 1998; Drasgow et al., 1996; Drasgow et al., 1999). Both teacher-directed and peer-directed interventions have typically demonstrated initial acquisition of skills, but maintenance and generalization effects have often been disappointing (see Brown & Odom, 1994; Chandler, Lubeck, & Fowler, 1992). If teachers and peers do not continue to provide external supports for newly acquired social behaviors, responding will probably be extinguished (e.g., Koegel & Rincover, 1977). One interpretation of restricted generalization and maintenance results is that the social consequences for engaging in newly acquired behaviors are not reinforcing and, for some children, they actually may be punishing. Thus, future research should address questions of discriminating between low motivation levels as a function of personality and skill deficits that have resulted in learned helplessness because of a history of extinction, punishment, or both.

Capitalizing on Preference

A potential problem with using an ecological inventory approach to determine *what* to teach young children with severe disabilities is that the results may point to learning targets whose consequences are not reinforcers. In other words, the inventory may reveal that James needs to interact with peers in small group activities because that is the way Mrs. Brown organizes most classroom activities. Without some kind of intervention that clearly links James' preferences with social engagement with peers, his learning targets are probably destined to fail. That is, they will not endure because the social environment offers insufficient support and motivating consequences to sustain peer interactions. A more effective strategy might be for Mrs. Brown to embed James' assessed preferences for activities and materials in small group activities to increase the likelihood that James will participate and interact with others to access these preferred activities and items. The systematic association of preferred events and materials with routine classroom activities should enhance James' participation and engagement, especially if James frequently accesses those items and events only in the context of common classroom activities.

Mapping the Continuum of Social Competence

In this chapter, we alluded only to the two anchoring points on this continuum: obligatory social competence skills and optional social competence skills. Many other levels of social competence skills lie in between those two social extremes. For example, Mrs. Lewis might teach Alice how to respond affirmatively to a peer's invitation to play a board game by first pushing a key on her VOCA that says enthusiastically, "I'd love to play!" and then by pushing another key that says, "What did you do last night?" In this way, Alice has an opportunity not only to interact in the context of the game but also to maintain a conversation. This example demonstrates an optional social competence skill of multiple verbal and nonverbal turntaking. On the opposite end of the continuum, Mrs. Brown might teach James to greet peers by waving to them the first time he sees them each day (i.e., an obligatory social response). Better yet, she might move James further along the continuum by teaching him first to wave hello and then by teaching him to invite a peer to ride the tricycle with a wagon on the back because this is one of James's favorite activities. When employing the continuum of social competence, an array of social behaviors could constitute teaching targets. These targets should consist of obligatory skills and then be expanded to include optional skills that capture children's personalities, motivation, and daily circumstances.

In summary, we believe that the careful consideration of children's social motivations, their preferences, and a continuum of social competence will assist practitioners and researchers in better promoting the social abilities of young children with severe disabilities in meaningful environments.

REFERENCES

American Association on Mental Retardation. (2002). *Mental retardation: Definition, classification, and systems of supports.* Washington, DC: American Association on Mental Retardation.

American Psychiatric Association. (1994). *Diagnostic and statistical manual of mental disorders* (4th ed.). Washington, DC: Author.

Baumgart, D., Brown, L., Pumpian, I., Nisbet, J., Ford, A., Sweet, M., Messina, R., & Schroeder, J. (1982). Principle of partial participation and individualized adaptations in educational programs for severely handicapped students. *Journal for the Association for the Severely Handicapped, 7*(2), 17–27.

Beckman, P.J., & Kohl, F.L. (1984). The effects of social and isolate toys on the interactions and play of integrated and nonintegrated groups of preschoolers. *Education and Training of the Mentally Retarded, 19,* 169–174.

Bierne-Smith, M., Patton, J.R., & Kim, S.H. (2006). *Mental retardation: An introduction to intellectual disabilities* (7th ed.). Upper Saddle River, NJ: Pearson Education.

Bijou, S.W. (1993). *Behavior analysis of child development.* Reno, NV: Context Press.

Bijou, S.W., & Baer, D.M. (1965). *Child development: Universal stage of infancy: Vol. 2.* Englewood Cliffs, NJ: Prentice-Hall.

Brown, L., Branston, M.B., Hamre-Nietupski, S., Pumpian, I., Certo, N., & Gruenwald, L. (1979). A strategy for developing chronologically age appropriate and functional curricular content for severely handicapped adolescents and young adults. *Journal of Special Education, 13,* 81–90.

Brown, W.H., Fox, J.J., & Brady, M.P. (1987). Effects of spatial density on 3- and 4-year-old children's socially directed behavior during freeplay: An investigation of a setting factor. *Education & Treatment of Children, 10*(3), 247–258.

Brown, W.H., & Odom, S.L. (1994). Strategies and tactics for promoting generalization and maintenance of young children's social behavior. *Research in Developmental Disabilities, 15,* 99–118.

Brown, F., Snell, M.E., & Lehr, D. (2006). Meaningful assessment. In M.E. Snell & F. Brown (Eds.), *Instruction of students with severe disabilities* (6th ed., pp. 67–110). Upper Saddle River, NJ: Pearson Education.

Carr, E.G., & Durand, V.M. (1985). Reducing behavior problems through functional communication training. *Journal of Applied Behavior Analysis, 18,* 111–126.

Carr, E.G., Binkoff, J.A., Kologinsky, E., & Eddy, M. (1978). Acquisition of sign language by autistic children. *Journal of Applied Behavior Analysis, 11,* 489–501.

Carr, E.G., & Lindquist, J.C. (1987). Generalization processes in language acquisition. In T.L. Layton (Ed.), *Language and treatment of autistic and developmentally disordered children* (pp. 129–153). Springfield, IL: Charles C. Thomas.

Carr, E.G., Levin, L., McConnachie, G., Carlson, J.I., Kemp, D.C., & Smith, C.E. (1994). *Communication-based intervention for problem behavior: A user's guide for producing positive change.* Baltimore: Paul H. Brookes Publishing Co.

Chadsey-Rusch, J., Drasgow, E., Reinoehl, B., Halle, J.W., & Collet-Klingenberg, L. (1993). Using general-case instruction to teach spontaneous and generalized requests for assistance to learners with severe disabilities. *The Journal of the Association for Persons with Severe Handicaps, 18,* 177–187.

Chandler, L.K., Lubeck, R.C., & Fowler, S.A. (1992). Generalization and maintenance of preschool children's social skills: A critical review and analysis. *Journal of Applied Behavior Analysis, 25,* 415–428.

DeKlyen, M., & Odom, S.L. (1989). Activity structure and social interaction with peers in developmentally integrated play groups. *Journal of Early Intervention, 13,* 342–351.

Drasgow, E., & Halle, J.W. (1995). Teaching social communication to young children with severe disabilities. *Topics in Early Childhood Special Education, 15,* 164–186.

Drasgow, E., Halle, J.W., & Ostrosky, M.M. (1998). Effects of differential reinforcement on the generalization of a replacement mand in three children with severe language delays. *Journal of Applied Behavior Analysis, 31,* 357–374.

Drasgow, E., Halle, J.W., Ostrosky, M.M., & Harbers, H.M. (1996). Using behavioral indication and functional communication training to establish an initial sign repertoire with a young child with severe disabilities. *Topics in Early Childhood Special Education, 16,* 500–521.

Drasgow, E., Halle, J.W., & Sigafoos, J. (1999). Teaching communication to learners with severe disabilities: Motivation, response competition, and generalization. *The Australasian Journal of Special Education, 23,* 47–63.

Fisher, W.W., Piazza, C.C., Bowman, L.G., & Amari, A. (1996). Integrating caregiver report with a systematic choice assessment to enhance reinforcer identification. *American Journal on Mental Retardation, 101,* 15–25.

Giangreco, M.F. (2006). Foundational concepts and practices for educating students with severe disabilities. In M.E. Snell & F. Brown (Eds.), *Instruction of students with severe disabilities* (6th ed., pp. 1–27). Upper Saddle River, NJ: Pearson Education.

Golinkoff, R.M. (1986). "I beg your pardon?" The preverbal negotiation of failed messages. *Journal of Child Language, 13,* 455–476.

Green, C.W., Reid, D.H., White, L.K., Halford, R.C., Brittain, D.P., & Gardner, S.M. (1988). Identifying reinforcers for persons with profound handicaps: Staff opinion versus systematic assessment of preferences. *Journal of Applied Behavior Analysis, 21,* 31–43.

Guralnick, M.J. (1992). A hierarchical model for understanding children's peer-related social competence. In S.L. Odom, S.R. McConnell, & M.A. McEvoy (Eds.), *Social competence of young children with disabilities* (pp. 37–64.) Baltimore: Paul H. Brookes Publishing Co.

Halle, J.W., Brady, N., & Drasgow, E. (2004). Enhancing socially adaptive communicative repairs of beginning communicators with disabilities. *American Journal of Speech-Language Pathology, 13,* 43–54.

Halle, J.W., Chadsey, J., Lee, S., & Renzaglia, A. (2004). Systematic instruction. In C. Kennedy & E. Horn (Eds.), *Including students with severe disabilities* (pp. 54–77). Boston: Pearson.

Halle, J.W., & Drasgow, E. (2003). Response classes: Baer's contribution to understanding their structure and function. In K.S. Budd & T. Stokes (Eds.), *A small matter of proof: The legacy of Donald M. Baer* (pp. 113–124). Las Vegas, NV: Context Press.

Heward, W.L. (2000). *Exceptional children: An introduction to special education* (6th ed.). Upper Saddle River, NJ: Merrill.

Hoff, E. (2005). *Language development* (3rd ed.). Belmont, CA: Thomson Wadsworth.

Horner, R.H., Dunlap, G., & Koegel, R.L. (Eds.). (1988). *Generalization and maintenance: Lifestyle changes in applied settings.* Baltimore: Paul H. Brookes Publishing Co.

Horner, R.H., McDonnell, J.J., & Bellamy, G.T. (1986). Teaching generalized skills: General-case instruction in simulated and community settings. In R.H. Horner, L.H. Meyer, & H.D.B. Fredericks (Eds.), *Education of learners with severe handicaps: Exemplary service strategies* (pp. 289–315). Baltimore: Paul H. Brookes Publishing Co.

Hughes, C., Pitkin, S.E., & Lorden, S.W. (1998). Assessing preferences and choices of persons with severe and profound mental retardation. *Education and Training in Mental Retardation and Developmental Disabilities, 33,* 299–316.

Iovannone, R., Dunlap, G., Huber, H., & Kincaid, D. (2003). Effective educational practices for students with autism spectrum disorders. *Focus on Autism and Other Developmental Disabilities, 18,* 150–165.

Ivory, J.J., & McCollum, J.A. (1999). Effects of social and isolate toys on social play in an inclusive setting. *Journal of Special Education, 32,* 238–243.

Kaczmarek, L.A. (1990). Teaching spontaneous language to individuals with severe handicaps: A matrix model. *Journal of the Association for Persons with Severe Handicaps, 15,* 160–169.

Kaczmarek, L.A. (2002). Assessment of social-communicative competence: An interdisciplinary model. In H. Goldstein, L.A. Kaczmarek, & K.M. English (Eds.), *Promoting social communication: Children with developmental disabilities from birth to adolescence* (pp. 55–115). Baltimore: Paul H. Brookes Publishing Co.

Kaczmarek, L.A., Evans, B.C., & Stever, N.M. (1995). Initiating expressive communication: An analysis of the listener preparatory behaviors of pre-schoolers with developmental disabilities in center-based programs. *Journal of the Association for Persons with Severe Disabilities, 20,* 66–79.

Katz, L.G., & McClellan, D.E. (1997). *Fostering children's social competence: The teacher's role.* Washington, DC: National Association for the Education of Young Children.

Keen, D., Sigafoos, J., & Woodyatt, G. (2001). Replacing prelinguistic behaviors with functional communication. *Journal of Autism and Developmental Disorders, 31,* 385–398.

Kennedy, C.H. (2002). Promoting social-communicative interactions in adolescents. In H. Goldstein, L.A. Kaczmarek, & K.M. English (Eds.), *Promoting social communication: Children with developmental disabilities from birth to adolescence* (pp. 307–329). Baltimore: Paul H. Brookes Publishing Co.

Kennedy, C.H. (2005). *Single case designs for educational research.* Boston: Allyn & Bacon.

Koegel, R.L., & Rincover, A. (1977). Research on the difference between generalization and maintenance in extra-therapy responding. *Journal of Applied Behavior Analysis, 10,* 1–12.

Light, J.C., Parsons, A.R., & Drager, K. (2002). Developing interactions for social closeness with beginning communicators who use ACC. In J. Reichle, D.R. Beukelman, & J.C. Light (Eds.), *Exemplary practices for beginning communicators* (pp. 187–218). Baltimore: Paul H. Brookes Publishing Co.

McConnell, S.R., Sisson, L.A., Cort, C.A., & Strain, P.S. (1991). Effects of social skills training and contingency management on reciprocal interaction of preschool children with behavioral handicaps. *Journal of Special Education, 24,* 473–495.

McLaughlin, D.M., & Carr, E.G. (2005). Quality of rapport as a setting event for problem behavior: Assessment and intervention. *Journal of Positive Behavior Interventions, 7,* 68–91.

Miltenberger, R.G. (2004). *Behavior modification: Principles and procedures* (3rd ed.). Pacific Grove: Brooks/Cole.

Odom, S.L., & Brown, W.H. (1993). Social interaction skills interventions for young children with disabilities in integrated settings. In C.A. Peck, S.L. Odom, & D.D. Bricker (Eds.), *Integrating young children with disabilities into community programs: Ecological perspectives on research and implementation* (pp. 39–64). Baltimore: Paul H. Brookes Publishing Co.

Odom, S.L., Brown, W.H., Frey, T., Karasu, N., Smith-Canter, L.L., & Strain, P.S. (2003) Evidence-based practices for young children with autism: Contributions for single subject design research. *Focus on Autism and Other Developmental Disabilities, 18*(3), 166–175.

Ostrosky, M., & Kaiser, A. (1991). Preschool classroom environments that promote communication. *Teaching Exceptional Children, 23*(4), 6–10.

Owens, R.E., Jr. (1995). *Language development: An introduction* (6th ed.). Boston: Pearson.

Quilitch, H.R., & Risley, T.R. (1973). The effects of play materials on social play. *Journal of Applied Behavior Analysis, 6,* 575–578.

Reichle, J., Halle, J.W., & Drasgow, E. (1998). Implementing augmentative communication systems. In A.M. Wetherby, S.F. Warren, & J. Reichle (Eds.), *Communication and language intervention series: Vol. 7. Transitions in prelinguistic communication* (pp. 417–436). Baltimore: Paul H. Brookes Publishing Co.

Reid, D.H., & Green, C.W. (2005). *Preference-based teaching: Helping people with developmental disabilities enjoy learning without problem behavior.* Morganton, NC: Habilitative Management Consultants, Inc.

Renzaglia, A., Karvonen, M., Drasgow, E., & Stoxen, C.C. (2003). Promoting a lifetime of inclusion. *Focus on Autism and Other Developmental Disabilities, 18,* 140–149.

Salvia, J., & Ysseldyke, J.E. (2004). *Assessment in special and inclusive education* (9th ed.). Boston: Houghton Mifflin.

Schwartz, I.S., & Baer, D.M. (1991). Social validity assessments: Is current practice state of the art? *Journal of Applied Behavior Analysis, 24,* 189–204.

Skinner, B.F. (1969). *Contingencies of reinforcement: A theoretical analysis.* New York: Appleton-Century-Crofts.

Snell, M.E., & Brown, F. (Eds.) (2006). *Instruction of students with severe disabilities* (6th ed.). Upper Saddle River, NJ: Pearson Education.

Spiegel-McGill, P., Bambara, L.M., Shores, R.M., & Fox, J.J. (1984). The effects of proximity on socially directed behaviors of severely multiply handicapped children. *Education & Treatment of Children, 7,* 365–378.

Stokes, T.F., & Baer, D.M. (1977). An implicit technology of generalization. *Journal of Applied Behavior Analysis, 10,* 349–367.

Turan, Y. (2004). *Promoting social responsiveness for young children with disabilities by enhancing the reinforcing value of social interactions.* Unpublished doctoral dissertation, University of Illinois, Urbana-Champaign.

Westling, D.L., & Fox, L. (2004). *Teaching students with severe disabilities* (3rd ed.). Upper Saddle River, NJ: Pearson Education.

Wetherby, A.M. (1986) Ontogeny of communicative functions in autism. *Journal of Autism and Developmental Disorders, 16,* 295–316.

Wetherby, A.M., Alexander, D.G., & Prizant, B.M. (1998). The ontogeny and role of repair strategies. In A.M. Wetherby, S.F. Warren, & J. Reichle (Eds.), *Communication and language intervention series: Vol. 7. Transitions in prelinguistic communication* (pp. 135–167). Baltimore: Paul H. Brookes Publishing Co.

Wolery, M., Ault, M.J., & Doyle, P.M. (1992). *Teaching students with moderate to severe disabilities: Use of response prompting strategies.* Needham Heights, MA: Addison Wesley Longman.

Wolf, M.M. (1978). Social validity: The case for subjective measurement, or how applied behavior analysis found its heart. *Journal of Applied Behavior Analysis, 11,* 203–214.

CHAPTER 14

Competent Families, Competent Children

Family-Based Interventions to Promote Social Competence in Young Children

SUSAN M. SHERIDAN, LISA L. KNOCHE, AND CHRISTINE A. MARVIN

Efforts designed to build and strengthen the abilities of families to confidently and competently nurture the development of their child may be the essential ingredients for success.

—Guralnick, 1989, p. 12.

Children develop skills and competencies as a result of relationships with adults and peers in community and natural contexts (Rogoff, 1991). For young children, families constitute a primary source of influence. Given the considerable impact and influence families have on children's lives, the meaningful participation of family members is an important feature of interventions to promote young children's social competence.

THE IMPORTANCE OF FAMILIES IN THE DEVELOPMENT OF SOCIAL COMPETENCE IN YOUNG CHILDREN

Young children's relationships with peers are affected by foundations established in early relationships with parents and other caring adults. Before participating in any social relationships at school, children experience relationships with family members (e.g., parents, siblings, aunts, uncles, grandparents) as well as members of the neighborhood and community. The earliest environments experienced by children, including the home, community settings, and any naturally occurring learning situations defined and offered by the family significantly affect young children's understanding of relationships and, in turn, how children relate to others (Dunst, 2001; Guralnick & Neville, 1997).

Early relationships and interactions with parents, in particular, guide emerging social competence in young children. Social and emotional competence is enhanced through warm, nurturing, reciprocal relationships with parents. Children in "highly connected" parent–child relationships tend to display positive socioemotional outcomes, such as strong prosocial orientations, numerous and high-quality friendships, and high levels of peer acceptance in kindergarten (Clark & Ladd, 2000; Kerns, Klepac, & Cole, 1996). Through connected interaction with parents, children appear to develop an empathic, socioemotional orientation that serves as a foundation for interpreting social situations and responding prosocially to peers and teachers (Clark & Ladd, 2000). These parent–child experiences are critical to the development of social skills and social competency in the early childhood years.

In families in which parents provide inconsistent guidelines, are harsh or coercive, are disengaged and/or unable to appropriately monitor their children's behavior, children are likely to display difficulties with aggression and antisocial behavior (McFayden-Ketchum, Bates, Dodge, & Pettit, 1996). In studies of child–mother interaction, variation in parenting discipline practices have accounted for between 10%–15% of the variance in behavior problems reported in the early school years (Pianta & Ferguson, 1997). Parents' abilities to provide developmentally sensitive support for autonomous problem solving has been associated with increases in both levels of cognitive competence in young children (Wood, 1980) and communication with peers (Martinez, 1987). Children whose mothers provide support for autonomy tend to display adaptive levels of social assertiveness and self-directedness in social interactions at preschool (Denham, Renwick, & Holt, 1991).

In addition to providing a model and foundation for adult–child relationships, families are important in encouraging the earliest peer relationships of young children. Specifically, the opportunities parents create for play as well as their support of sustained play between peers foster the socioemotional well-being of young children (Guralnick & Neville, 1997; Ladd & Hart, 1992). Parents who provide many opportunities for their children to play with others, support their emerging social competence, and demonstrate warmth and responsivity have children who get along better with other children (Parke & Ladd, 1992; Thompson, 2002). Given parents' influential role in the development of children's social competence, their involvement in social interventions is worthwhile.

THE ROLE OF FAMILIES IN SOCIAL INTERVENTIONS

A substantial proportion of interventions promoting peer-related social competence in young children occur in classroom settings, as has been addressed in this volume. Yet, children spend much of their young lives with adults, in both home and community-based settings. Regardless of children's participation in out-of-home care, they are likely to spend considerable time with a parent or other adult who assumes a parenting role. Implementing social interventions in home and community contexts with these familiar adults facilitates social competence in young children by not only enhancing social learning in children's natural environments and routines but also by promoting continuity of expectations and practices between settings and across adults (Dunst, 2001).

Parents have unique information about their children that is important to children's developmental success. Typically, parents and other familial caregivers possess a particular understanding of their children that pervades time and place. They are able to comment on their children's likes and dislikes; their preferred activities, toys, and playmates; and what they might find motivating or threatening. They have a historical and developmental perspective on their child, and they are typically able to anticipate and describe children's behaviors across contexts. The unique information parents can provide is important in designing interventions that can support children's development in and across contexts.

This ecological view of social learning is based on the reality that much learning occurs in children's natural environments beyond what are considered prescribed "learning times." Parents and family members are often companions of young children in natural learning situations and can take advantage of teachable moments and opportunities that promote social development and social success (Guralnick, 2001). Furthermore, parents generally control the environments within which children function, and in many ways, they control opportunities in these natural contexts for broad-based meaningful social learning to occur. To be maximally effective, interventions aimed at promoting children's social competencies in comprehensive and integrated ways must focus on parents and other caregivers who support this learning in natural environments (Gutkin & Conoley, 1990; Sheridan & Gutkin, 2000).

Young children understand their world through their immediate cultures (e.g., culture of school, culture of home, culture of neighborhood). In addition to the social learning opportunities that family members provide, their unique qualities, beliefs, values, and traditions also influence their children's social learning. Building relationships with parents helps professionals understand how families socialize and share information, as well as ensures the continuity between home traditions and external social expectations for young children. Intervention efforts that incorporate family cultures and needs have been shown to be important in achieving maximum learning outcomes for children (DeGangi, Wietlisbach, & Poisson, 1994; Garcia Coll & Magnuson, 2000). Interventions that are tailored to specific needs of families and children and that address a family's unique cultural beliefs and styles of interacting are also more instrumental in instituting change than are approaches not in accord with family values and practices (Epps & Jackson, 2000).

Partnering with Families

Family involvement in planning, decision making, and intervening on behalf of their child has been shown to be related to a host of positive developmental outcomes, including social competence (Henderson & Berla, 1994; Sheridan, Kratochwill, & Elliott, 1990). Models of service delivery in home and community settings that focus on collaboration between caregivers and professionals provide a unique, strengths-based context for implementing social competence programs for preschool children. Collaborative partnerships emphasize the unique perspectives and expertise offered by participants (e.g., parents, teachers, psychologists) to address mutually determined goals (Friend & Cook, 2006; Welch & Sheridan, 1995). From a partnership perspective, ideas, opinions, values, and priorities are shared among parents and professionals (Dunst, Trivette, & Deal, 1995; Hanft, Rush, & Shelden, 2004). These shared inputs determine the direction of decision making, allowing for the mutual creation of intervention strategies that reflect unique contributions and interacting contexts. Such commitment to the collective process increases participants' ownership and responsibilities in problem solving and implementation of the intervention plan (Duke, Showers, & Imber, 1980; Dunst & Deal, 1994).

Benefits of a Collaborative Approach to Social Interventions

There are many potential benefits to a collaborative approach when working with families. Collaboration allows professionals and family members to pool knowledge and skills related to both process (i.e., how they go about supporting children's social competence) and content (i.e., what they agree are important social skills), resulting in more comprehensive, effective, and efficient interventions. Because multiple perspectives and vantage points on the same issue are shared, an increased understanding of the realities and complexities of children's social competencies and challenges associated with planned interventions can be discerned (Phillips & McCullough, 1990). Collaboration between parents and professionals increases the range and number of possible solutions to shared concerns regarding children (Welch & Sheridan, 1995). Family members are experts on their child's natural environments, preferences, and typical routines and schedules. Parental involvement in creating social learning opportunities for the child is critical, as it encourages greater integrity in the implementation of intervention strategies within natural contexts. Likewise, collaborative problem solving allows for an increased range and diversity of expertise and resources to support the child's social development. Of note, because parents are a constant in the child's life, and because a majority of young children's time is spent with parents and other caregivers, the potential for consistent teaching and learning experiences is greatly enhanced when these individuals are involved in the intervention process.

Although collaborative attitudes are prerequisite to family-based practice (Christenson & Sheridan, 2001), they are not sufficient to ensure the development of effective partnerships. Clear operational procedures for collaborating with families are necessary. We now turn to a structure within which a collaborative ethic (Phillips & McCullough, 1990) is translated into operational, partnership-centered services.

PARTNERSHIP MODELS FOR DELIVERING SOCIAL INTERVENTIONS

Models that focus on partnerships with families in early intervention are based on a family-centered philosophy. Family-centered services aim to provide opportunities for parents and other familial caregivers to demonstrate their competence and confidence in recognizing children's development, needs, and interests; recognizing pertinent learning opportunities in everyday activities; and using or developing their own skills and social networks to support their plans to help their children learn and grow.

At least four elements are essential in effective partnership models. First, social learning opportunities should be provided and available in children's natural environments. Second, structured, data-based problem-solving approaches are useful to guide professional consultation and collaboration with parents. Third, a focus on the parent–child relationship enhances opportunities for the development of social competence. Fourth and finally, partnership models should incorporate evidence-based social competence strategies into the intervention programs that are selected and delivered. Each of these components is discussed next.

Natural Learning Environments

The first element in effective partnership models is natural learning environments. The advantages of using everyday activities (e.g., mealtimes, interactions with siblings, outdoor or indoor play) to promote learning in settings and community locations common to young children of a similar age, culture, and geographic region (Bruder & Dunst, 2000) have been articulated in the literature. Specifically, benefits of using natural learning environments to encourage meaningful socialization is outlined in legislative (e.g., Individuals with Disabilities Education Act Amendments of 1997), empirical (Dunst, Hamby, Trivette, Raab & Bruder, 2000; Santos & Lignugaris-Kraft, 1997), social policy (Bredecamp & Copple, 1997; Sandall, Hemmeter, Smith, & McLean, 2005), and testimonial publications (Bruder, 2000; Mullis, 2002). Also, natural learning environments that engage the interest of children with disabilities have been found to be associated with optimal behavioral changes (Dunst, Bruder, Trivette, Hamby, Raab, & McLean, 2001). Informal support provided to parents (as compared with parent training programs) and teaching and learning in routine classroom, home, or community activities (compared with "pull-out" therapy) can produce positive outcomes (social and otherwise) for children and families (Allen & Petr, 1996).

Although research to date has not always compared intervention outcomes in "natural" versus "unnatural" environments, there appears to be sufficient evidence and call for continued consideration of the use of children's homes and community activities as primary intervention settings. In these settings, interactions with siblings and peers who are typically developing as well as interactions with supportive, competent adults can attract children's interests and facilitate the development of important social skills (McWilliam, 2000). Primary relationships in natural learning environments that are instrumental in facilitating social experiences and opportunities include adult–child and child–child relationships (e.g., fathers, siblings, grandparents, cousins), as well as traditional mother–child or peer–child relationships that typify most clinic or classroom-based interventions (Hanft & Pilkington, 2000). Routine rituals and relationships common in natural environments often provide frequent interactions and opportunities for a child to witness modeling of desired social behaviors by competent children and adults, opportunities for contingent and meaningful support that encourage and reinforce appropriate social behaviors (Cripe & Venn, 1997), and opportunities for incidental teaching and learning. Finally, natural environments often permit a more valid assessment of a child's strengths and interests as well as his or her social, linguistic, cognitive, physical, or social limitations and challenges than non-naturalistic settings allow (Hanft & Pilkington, 2000).

Naturalistic Teaching Strategies

Naturalistic teaching strategies are strategies used within natural learning environments to promote a child's social learning. Naturalistic teaching strategies utilize the child's momentary interest in unstructured and routine activities, materials, and interactions to facilitate learning of appropriate social behaviors (Brown &

Odom, 1995). Sometimes these strategies include prompts for children to engage in a prosocial manner, elaborate on initial attempts to socialize appropriately, and encourage peers/siblings to initiate interactions or model suitable social responses for a child (Brown, McEvoy, & Bishop, 1991). These strategies also may include adult modeling of socially desirable behaviors. Embedded within the activity currently holding the child's interest, naturalistic teaching strategies have the potential to capture children's attention and elicit desired behaviors over time. Parents can be taught to identify natural incidental teaching and learning opportunities within routine activities at parks, restaurants, shopping malls, sporting events, and virtually any home- and community-based setting or function within which the parent and child naturally participate (Dunst et al., 2001). Dunst and colleagues (2001) and Guralnick (2001) have shown that parents' use of contingent responsiveness and incidental teaching are effective at encouraging young children's learning in routine activity settings.

Naturalistic teaching strategies are useful in the context of promoting social competence in young children. Specifically, these strategies reflect the use of guided participation, situated learning and instruction, apprenticeship, and responsiveness in everyday activities (Dunst, 2001):

- *Guided participation* includes actions taken by parents to maximize social learning opportunities in natural settings by engaging with children in child-initiated activities and providing assistance as needed (Rogoff, Mistry, Goncu, & Mosier, 1993; Wertsch, 1985). For example, a mother provides toys or objects for her child and other children to use at a local park sandbox. As other children arrive and observe the parent and child at play, the mother offers to share a shovel with another child and prompts her own child to share the sifter with the children. She also models and prompts the children to take turns playing with the available sand toys, thereby guiding appropriate social interactions.

- In *situated learning,* children observe peers or other competent individuals participating in an activity of interest to the child, thus providing a standard for expected behavior (Clark, 1998; Lancy, 1996).

- *Apprenticeship* engages the parent and child to work in close coordination with one another as the parent supports the child in his or her efforts to use appropriate social behaviors or responses.

- *Parental responsiveness* involves positive physical, social, and verbal attention to the child as he or she demonstrates desirable social behaviors, thereby functioning as a reinforcer to maintain and promote social competence (Mahoney, 1988).

Empirical support is available for the use of natural environments and family members as change agents to advance children's developmental outcomes in the areas of parent–child interactions and secure attachments (van den Boom, 1994), communication/language (Woods, Kashinath, & Goldstein, 2004), motor skills (Tieman, Palisano, Gracely, & Rosenbaum, 2004), and adaptive skills such as eating (Najdowski, Wallace, Doney & Ghezzi, 2003). Social competence outcomes are often inferred or noted inclusively with communication gains in the literature. For example, increased instances of initiated and/or maintained joint attention/activity, social closeness, and redirection or clarification of play scripts and friendships have been noted in preschool children with disabilities following various interventions that focus on targeted communication behaviors (Brown & Conroy, 2002).

Despite the empirical evidence for using natural environments to support child development in these domains, the advantages and methods for using children's natural learning environments to advance specific social competence behaviors deserve attention. Interactions with responsive, competent peers and adults in "natural" settings, however, appear to be associated with important social learning opportunities for young children with disabilities. Natural environments can be instrumental in influencing the incidence of interactions with playmates, reports of friendships, and social skills for young children with disabilities. For example, Dunst and his colleagues (2001) described positive social benefits for a group of infants, toddlers, and preschool-age children with disabilities who were engaged in frequent natural learning activities and responsive parent–child play activities at home or in the community compared with children who had fewer of these opportunities. Furthermore, interaction with siblings appears to be both a focus and by-product of interventions in natural learning environments that can have notable advantages for young children's development of social competence (Baker, 2000; Strain & Danko, 1995). Sibling playmates have been positively correlated with children's later ability to negotiate peer relationships by providing frequent and natural opportunities to socialize, negotiate, and share familiar interests (Downey & Condron, 2004). Finally, preschool children's social competence is influenced by parent-initiated playdates with other children in natural environments (Parke & Bhavnargri, 1989). Children are less anxious, better liked, and have higher levels of social behavior and peer acceptance at preschool if parents arrange more informal, out-of-school contacts. In addition, the degree to which parents engage their children in planning these informal playdates, a social skill in itself, positively affects children's skills in initiating who to invite, when to invite him or her, and what play activity to offer; and in calling and asking a peer to play (Ladd & Hart, 1992).

The value of planning social interventions for young children that focus on natural learning environments and the interactions between parents and children appears clear. Challenges associated with implementing such interventions, however, may explain the limited publication of such efforts. Identifying the natural learning opportunities and following a child's interest in an activity while simultaneously providing guidance and feedback to a caregiver about appropriate supports and guidance to use at the moment with their child can be a tall order for even the most experienced of practitioners, who may have been trained to provide decontextualized, child-focused interventions. Furthermore, knowing how to adjust the supports/strategies for individual caregivers and children while ensuring ample teaching/learning opportunities between professional sessions are additional challenges. The use of structured, data-based collaboration models and integration of evidence-based strategies are explained in the following sections, providing guidance for the design of more successful, systematic social interventions in natural environments with parents.

Structured, Data-Based Collaboration

The second element for aiding the promotion of partnership models of service delivery includes data-based collaboration that focuses on mutually determined goals related to the socioemotional development of children. Decades of research in consultation-based service delivery (see Sheridan, Clarke, & Burt, 2008; Sheridan, Welch, & Orme, 1996) has yielded substantial empirical evidence supporting a structured, data-based model that involves 1) identifying and prioritizing shared goals, 2) analyzing factors that may influence skill development or performance, 3) developing intervention strategies that can address concerns and achieve goals, and 4) evaluating the effectiveness of chosen strategies. These structured service-delivery models have dual goals of promoting positive child outcomes and enhancing skills and competencies of participants (e.g., parents) for future problem solving. The models may be delivered through a professional consultant (e.g., school psychologist, mental health consultant, special education provider) working with teachers and parents (e.g., Sheridan & Kratochwill, 2008; Sheridan, Kratochwill, & Bergan, 1996), or provided by an early childhood professional (e.g., classroom teacher, home visitor) working collaboratively with family members (File & Kontos, 1992).

One such model for achieving data-based collaboration with families is *conjoint behavioral consultation* (CBC; Sheridan et al., 1996; Sheridan & Kratochwill, 2008). CBC is a model of service delivery that attempts to develop effective partnerships among parents, educators, and other service providers. It is defined as "a strength-based, cross-system problem-solving and decision-making model wherein parents, teachers, and other caregivers or service providers work as partners and share responsibility for promoting positive and consistent outcomes related to children's academic, behavioral, and social-emotional development" (Sheridan & Kratochwill, 2008). In CBC, parents and other caregivers engage collaboratively in a structured problem-solving process with a professional consultant to address the needs of children across settings such as home and school. Through a series of structured meetings and frequent unstructured, supportive interactions, parents and teachers work together with consultants to share information in the identification of children's needs and to develop, implement, and evaluate interventions that address those needs. The steps of a collaborative planning process, depicted in Figure 14.1, can occur between an early childhood professional and a parent with or without the aid of a consultant.

Three overarching goals drive collaborative problem solving and decision making:

1. Enhancing positive outcomes for children through mutual planning

2. Promoting parent engagement with children and involvement in interventions within a developmental, culturally sensitive framework

3. Planning collaboratively to strengthen relationships and support networks for parents and children.

This is accomplished by being responsive to the priorities and concerns of families, developing and enhancing competencies and skills of parents and other caregivers, and strengthening social supports and promoting partnerships and collaboration among participants (Sheridan et al., 2008). Thus, the foci of collaborative approaches is to build skills for parents and other caregivers to engage in long-term problem solving and decision making, rather than simply learning a discrete set of intervention steps.

Researchers have consistently demonstrated that CBC is effective in positively enhancing child outcomes across social, behavioral, and academic domains for children in kindergarten through Grade 12 (e.g., Sheridan et al., 2008; Sheridan,

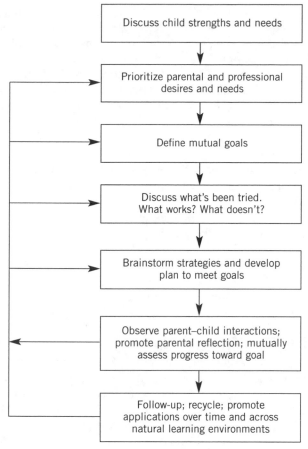

Figure 14.1.   Collaborative planning flowchart.

Eagle, Cowan, & Mickelson, 2001). Its usefulness in promoting social skills has been documented for children in the early elementary grades (Sheridan, Kratochwill, & Elliott, 1990), and children with disabilities (Colton & Sheridan, 1998). The effectiveness of CBC in addressing concerns of families and caregivers in early intervention contexts has also been demonstrated (Sheridan, Clarke, Knoche, & Edwards, 2006). The advantages of this model lie in its focus on parents as competent partners and the use of children's natural social learning opportunities with parents while retaining the data-based decision-making process often found to be successful in classroom-based social programs (Sheridan et al., 2001; Sheridan et al., 1990).

Parent–Child Interaction

The third element in effective partnership models of intervention is a focus on the parent–child relationship. Collaborative partnerships should include efforts to initiate, support, and enhance positive parent–child interactions. The presence of a secure relationship between parent and child (Cohn, Patterson, & Christopoulos, 1991; Guralnick & Neville, 1997) is a universally accepted predictor of healthy child functioning (including social competence). Direct and shared observations of the child and parent–child interactions allow for an assessment of both the child's natural social abilities and tendencies and the parent's prompts and responses concerning the child's social behaviors. In addition, observation of parent–child interactions provides early childhood professionals with opportunities to note and comment on parents' strengths (thereby building their confidence), focus their attention on important child assets and behaviors, provide developmental information (including realistic expectations), model strategies to support a child's learning, and/or provide suggestions to aide the parent in engaging the child successfully, thereby building competence (McCollum & Yates, 1994). Furthermore, in collaboration with parents, professionals can encourage goal-setting related to a child's social competencies (Warnes, Sheridan, & Garbacz, in press).

Parental responsiveness, warmth, sensitivity, and positive affect during parent–child interactions are appropriate targets in collaborative interventions aimed at improving children's social competence. Goals that also focus on the child's responsiveness, exploration, and engagement with others (Lieberman, Weston, & Pawl, 1991; van den Boom, 1994) guide parents to seek opportunities that will increase their child's social networks and chances to model positive affect and emotional regulation. In addition, the focus on parent–child relationships provides opportunities to coach parents on how to provide feedback regarding children's social exchanges, help their child negotiate new social interactions, and teach their child how to read social situations and cues with new and familiar family partners (Hanft et al., 2004).

The degree to which parents view their role regarding their child's development (i.e., their role construct), and their belief in their abilities to support their child's social learning (i.e., their parental efficacy) are also appropriate targets for consultation and collaboration. Consultation efforts that assist parents in constructing an active role for themselves so they can develop a sense of self-efficacy (competence and confidence) in relation to their child's social learning (Sheridan, Warnes, Brown, Schemm, Cowan, & Clarke, 2004) are important for creating a trajectory for future positive parental involvement (Hoover-Dempsey, Walker, & Sandler, 2005).

Use of Evidence-Based Social Competence Strategies and Practices

The fourth component of effective partnership models requires professional consultants to ensure that the strategies and practices used within natural environments are evidence-based, providing empirical support to reach desired social outcomes. We adopt the functional definition of evidence-based practice offered by Dunst and colleagues by conceptualizing these practices as those "that are informed by research, in which the characteristics and consequences of environmental variables are empirically established, and the relationship directly informs what a practitioner can do to produce a desired outcome" (2002, p. 3).

In recent decades, increased attention has been placed on curricula and programs that build or enhance children's social skills. Unfortunately, very few of these programs identify roles and practices for parents and other family members to support social competencies in children in a meaningful way. Likewise, evidence-based social skills curricula and parent-training programs seldom suggest natural learning environments, but rather continue to rely on clinic and classroom locations for delivery of services. Given the strength of practices that coordinate home and school/community influences on learning, and the benefits of a partnership model in home, school, and community settings, we believe many promising social competence programs in existence could be enhanced by including strategies that encourage greater parent involvement, generalization to natural environments, and use of data-based decision making. Adaptation and documentation is needed for the use of some of these promising programs in natural environments with parents, familiar caregivers, or family members as partners.

FAMILY-MEDIATED SOCIAL COMPETENCE PROGRAMS

Of the evidence-based programs and approaches available to build social competence in children (see reviews elsewhere in this volume), five include a specific focus on parents as intervention facilitators. These are *Parent–Child Interaction Therapy* (Hembree-Kigin & McNeil, 1995), *First Step to Success* (Walker, 1998), *The Incredible Years Parents, Teachers, and Children's Training Series* (Webster-Stratton, 1990), *Second Step Program* (Committee for Children, 1989), and *DARE to Be You* (Miller-Heyl, MacPhee, & Fritz, 1998). Each of these is reviewed briefly, with specific attention to the components of partnership-centered models of service delivery.

Parent–Child Interaction Therapy

Parent–Child Interaction Therapy (PCIT; Hembree-Kigin & McNeil, 1995; Herschell, Calzada, Eyberg, & McNeil, 2002), an evidence-based, social skills program, is grounded in attachment theory (i.e., based on the assumption that parents who interact with children in a warm and responsive way will develop an attached relationship with their child; Ainsworth, 1989). The secure attachment results in a positive understanding and model of relationships for children, thereby supporting social competence and development. The key elements of the partnership model focus on the parent–child relationship, taking advantage of the natural interaction between parent and child that occurs during a play session and encouraging parents to extend behavior to settings beyond the clinic. The model does not include collaborative data-based decision making.

PCIT has two phases, child-directed interaction (CDI) and parent-directed interaction (PDI). Both phases are conducted in the context of dyadic (parent–child) play situations. CDI is foundational to PDI. During the CDI phase, parents are taught to allow their child to lead the play activity. Parents learn to use *praise, reflection, imitation, description, and enthusiasm* (PRIDE) with their child, thereby addressing the goal of creating or strengthening positive and mutually rewarding relationships between them. In the PDI phase, parents are taught how to direct their child's activity through the use of clearly stated commands and appropriate consequences for behavior (e.g., praise, time out). The goal of the PDI phase is to decrease problematic behaviors while increasing prosocial behaviors.

Typically, the PCIT intervention lasts for 10–16 weeks, with participants meeting hourly each week in a clinic setting under the guidance of a skilled professional. Researchers have indicated significant improvements in parent–child interaction following PCIT along with measurable declines in behavior problems for children. For example, Eyberg and Robinson (1982) found the PCIT intervention generalized from the clinic to home settings and to untreated siblings. Funderburk and colleagues (1998) noted generalization to school settings, and Newcomb, Eyberg, Funderburk, Eisenstadt, and McNeil (1990) found that the newly learned behaviors were maintained 12 and 18 months later.

First Step to Success Program

The *First Step to Success* program (Walker, 1998) is an evidence-based partnership model with an extensive home component in addition to a kindergarten classroom component (Joseph & Strain, 2003). The program's goal is to divert kindergarten children who show early signs of antisocial behavior patterns from negative developmental pathways. The program comprises three modules, including 1) proactive, universal screening of all kindergartners; 2) school intervention involving teacher, peers, and children in a target group (e.g., the CLASS program); and 3) parent/caregiver training for positive adult support of children's adjustment (e.g., HomeBase).

Following screening, the CLASS component is implemented to teach basic skills to children, such as being prepared for school, getting along with others, and learning to accept limits. After 10 days of participation in the CLASS module, the HomeBase intervention module begins and runs concurrently with the CLASS module. During the HomeBase phase, the consultant meets the student's parents either in their home or another designated meeting space for approximately 45 minutes per week for 6 weeks. Parents are taught skills to enhance their child's adjustment and success in school. Specifically, the home component enlists parents in teaching their children cooperation and friendship building, and children are also taught how to accept limits, problem solve, and share as they develop their self-esteem. A key to the 3-month program is the use of a behavioral coach or consultant who sets up the program, operates it initially, and teaches parents (and teachers in the classroom component) strategies to operate and sustain it.

A study by Walker, Stiller, and Golly (1998) found the *First Step to Success* program to have yielded positive outcomes. Specifically, Walker and colleagues demonstrated that children who participated in the *First Step to Success* program significantly improved on measures of adaptive behavior and significantly reduced aggressive and maladaptive behaviors.

The program follows traditional parent training strategies; therefore, its promotion of a collaborative, data-based partnership approach to working with families is uncertain. Training occurs in the home; thus, opportunities for parents to apply naturalistic teaching strategies are readily available. Whether parents can do this independent of support and guidance is uncertain; however, the program appears well-situated to build in such approaches.

The Incredible Years Parents, Teachers, and Children's Training Series

The Incredible Years (IY) Parents, Teachers, and Children's Training Series (Webster-Stratton, 1990a; see also http://www.incredibleyears.com and Chapter 9, this volume) includes comprehensive, developmentally based curricula for parents delivered in a video mediated or small group training format. Of the various components in the program, the *Dina Dinosaur's Social Skills and Problem-Solving Curriculum* (Webster-Stratton, 1990b) is designed to teach children emotional literacy, friendship skills, empathy, anger management, and other important social skills. This program is child-directed, with classroom teachers or other specialists (and unfortunately, not parents) generally responsible for delivery of the intervention. On the other hand, the *Incredible Years Early Childhood BASIC Parent Training Program* (for children ages 2–7 years) consists of a highly structured, 12-week intervention that teaches parents important precursors to develop children's social competence, including interactive play and reinforcement skills, nonviolent discipline techniques, logical and natural consequences, and problem-solving strategies. The program's content areas are organized into four components: 1) play, 2) praise and rewards, 3) effective limit setting, and 4) means for handling misbehavior. Parent training videotapes, a self-administered manual, comprehensive leader manuals, weekly "refrigerator notes," parent homework assignments, and other support materials are included in the program. A collaborative approach to parent training is encouraged (Webster-Stratton, 1998a; Webster-Stratton & Herbert, 1994).

The *IY program* has been extensively researched to determine its efficacy with children with conduct disorders, oppositional defiant disorders, and attention-deficit/hyperactivity disorders, among other disorders. Researchers investigating the model using rigorous experimental procedures have found that the *IY Program* produces positive attitudinal and behavioral outcomes for both parents and children (e.g., Jones, Daley, Hutchings, Bywater, & Catrin Eames, in press; Webster-Stratton, 1998b).

In terms of key partnership model elements, the *IY Program* is relevant for natural learning environments. The program is not guided by data-based decision making, but collaboration with parents is encouraged. Although the *IY Program* is not focused intentionally on the parent–child interaction, a segment for parents on play strategies and building children's self-esteem is included.

Second Step Program

The *Second Step Program* (Committee for Children, 1989) is an evidence-based, violence prevention program that can be used in preschool through Grade 9 settings to teach empathy, anger management, and impulse control as alternatives to violence. The *Second Step Family Guide* is a 6-session, facilitator-led program designed specifically for families of children attending preschool through elementary school who are participating in the *Second Step Program* in a preschool or youth agency. It includes a "Family Overview" video, three skill-training videos, a facilitator's guide, and problem-solving and anger-management skill magnets for home use. The video-based family guide is designed to develop a positive relationship between home and school, encourage family support of violence prevention efforts, and teach parents the same Second Step skills their children are learning. Skills in empathy, impulse control, problem solving, and anger management are presented to help families practice and reinforce these skills at home.

Grossman and colleagues (1997) conducted research on the *Second Step Program*, finding a decrease in physical and verbal aggression and an increase in prosocial interaction that was maintained over 6 months. No research outcomes on the parent guide have been reported. The *Second Step Program* takes advantage of natural learning environments that children might experience; however, the parent component of the program is very limited. Data-based, collaborative decision-making does not appear to be part of the program's implementation, and no specific focus on parent–child interaction is apparent.

DARE to Be You Program

The DARE to Be You program (Miller-Heyl et al., 1998) is a 12-week (20–30 hours total), multilevel, primary prevention program for children ages 2–5 and their families. The program consists of family, school, and community components. The family component involves parent, youth, and family training activities for teaching decision-making/problem-solving (D), assertiveness/communication skills (A), responsibility/role modeling (R), and empathy and esteem (E). An additional 12-hour parent workshop is offered semiannually to reinforce the concepts. Parent and child activity workbooks are spiral-bound paperbacks filled with activities for parents and their young children that focus on self-concept and self-responsibility and can be integrated into natural environments. The preschool component contains activities for use in preschool settings that focus on increasing self-concept, responsibility, communication, and decision-making skills. The community component focuses on community members who interact with target families including counselors, social service agencies, and others. Miller-Heyl and colleagues (1998) examined the *DARE to Be You* program and reported positive effects for successive cohorts of children randomly assigned to an experimental group on parent and teacher measures.

The *DARE to Be You* program includes a parent training component that encourages extension into natural learning environments. There is no data-based, collaborative decision making incorporated into the program, and enhancement and focus on the parent–child interaction is not emphasized.

CONCLUSIONS AND FUTURE DIRECTIONS

Young children's social competence and relationships with peers are affected by foundational experiences in early connections with parents and other meaningful adults. The community and natural environments experienced by children, including the home setting, play an important role in how young children relate with others (Guralnick & Neville, 1997). Early relationships and interactions with parents, in particular, guide emerging social competence for young children. In addition to providing a model and foundation for relationships, families are important in encouraging the emerging and established peer relationships of young children.

Extending or implementing interventions in home and community contexts facilitates social competence in young children by enhancing learning in natural environments and promoting continuity between settings. Involving parents in a meaningful way in an effort to promote continuity is important in supporting development within and across contexts. Working with families, whether as a specific parent training component of a social skills program or through ongoing communication and collaboration improves the likelihood that parents, professional consultants, and early childhood professionals can work together to mutually meet the social needs of young children.

We believe that collaborative, partnership models of intervention provide a unique, strengths-based context for implementing social competence programs for young children, and support parents' competence and confidence when they incorporate four key characteristics. Specifically, effective partnership models 1) occur in the child's natural environments; 2) employ structured, data-based processes; 3) focus on supporting and enhancing the parent–child interaction; and 4) promote the use of interventions that are research-based. Current intervention programs have certain unique strengths, but are limited in relation to these partnership components. Many of the programs encourage generalization of strategies to natural learning environments, but only one (*First Step to Success*) actually conducts training in home settings. Even with training occurring in home environments, parents may need explicit guidance or coaching in optimal uses of natural settings to encourage skill use. Indeed, many of the programs discussed could be extended to include a more specific use of natural learning environments.

Existing social competence intervention programs that include a family's use of data-based decision making are also limited. One primary goal of early education and intervention is increasing the competencies of caregivers who can continue to provide responsive support to their children after professionals complete their work. Therefore, the development of parents' competencies for immediate and long-term benefit is critical. The programs reviewed here are somewhat generic and not focused on individual children's social needs and goals. An increased focus on individualization and use of data-based, collaborative decision making would strengthen many of the programs currently in use.

Parent–child interactions are not the specific focus of most of the interventions discussed, with the exception of PCIT, which has a clear focus on the parent–child relationship. Increasing parent's awareness of their role in their children's social development and supporting parents' beliefs in their abilities to support their child's social learning is critical to the social success of young children. We recommend that existing and developing programs take this into account and include opportunities for shared observation/discussion of parent–child interactions, such that both the adult's and child's behaviors are considered valued foci for attention by the early childhood professional.

There is a need for future research that considers how the components of partnership models of service delivery can be fully integrated into existing programs, or how new programs could build on these basic components. As of this book's publication we knew of no social competence intervention programs that have been tested that incorporate all of these strategies. In isolation, we know each component is important. The combined effect remains to be understood and is the focus of ongoing research (Sheridan et al., 2003).

The social competence of young children is optimally supported through combined and contiguous classroom, home, and community involvement. Whereas positive gains are seen for children experiencing intervention in a single domain, we advocate for an ecological intervention design and implementation approach to best support and maintain children's developing social competence.

REFERENCES

Ainsworth, M.D.S. (1989). Attachments beyond infancy. *American Psychologist, 44*, 709–716.

Allen, R., & Petr, C. (1996). Toward developing standards and measurements for family-centered practices in family support programs. In G. Singer, L. Powers, & A. Olson (Eds.), *Redefining family support: Innovations in public–private practice* (pp. 57–85). Baltimore: Paul H. Brookes Publishing Co.

Baker, M. (2000). Incorporating thematic ritualistic behaviors of children with autism in games. *Journal of Positive Behavior Interventions, 2*(2), 66–84.

Bredekamp, S., & Copple, C. (Eds.). (1997). *Developmentally appropriate practices in early childhood programs.* Washington, DC: National Association for the Education of Young Children.

Brown, W., & Conroy, M. (2002). Promoting peer-related social-communicative competence in preschool children. In H. Goldstein, L. Kaczmarek, & K. English (Eds.), *Promoting social competence: Children with developmental disabilities from birth to adolescence* (pp. 173–210). Baltimore, MD: Paul H. Brookes Publishing Company.

Brown, W., McEvoy, M., & Bishop, J. (1991). Incidental teaching of social behaviors: A naturalistic approach to promoting young children's peer interactions. *Teaching Exceptional Children, 24,* 35–58.

Brown, W., & Odom, S. (1995). Naturalistic peer interventions for promoting preschool children's social interactions. *Preventing School Failure, 39,* 38–43.

Bruder, M.B. (2000). Renewing the inclusion agenda: Attending to the right variables. *Journal of Early Intervention, 23,* 223–230.

Bruder, M.B., & Dunst, C. (2000). Expanding learning opportunities for infants and toddlers in natural environments. *Zero to Three, 20*(3), 34–36.

Christenson, S.L., & Sheridan, S.M. (2001). *Schools and families: Creating essential connections for learning.* New York: Guilford Press.

Clark, S. (1998). Learning at the public bathhouse. In J. Singleton (Ed.), *Learning in likely places: Varieties of apprenticeship in Japan* (pp. 239–252). New York: Cambridge University Press.

Clark, K.E., & Ladd, G.W. (2000). Connectedness and autonomy support in parent–child relationships: Links to children's socioemotional orientation and peer relationships. *Developmental Psychology, 36,* 485–498.

Cohn, D.A., Patterson, C.J., & Christopoulos, C. (1991). The family and children's peer relations. *Journal of Social and Personal Relationships, 8,* 315–346.

Colton, D., & Sheridan, S.M. (1998). Conjoint behavioral consultation and social skills training: Enhancing the play behavior of boys with attention deficit-hyperactivity disorder. *Journal of Educational and Psychological Consultation, 9,* 3–28.

Committee for Children. (1989). *Second Step violence prevention program.* Seattle, WA: Author.

Cripe, J., & Venn, M. (1997). Family-guided routines for early intervention services. *Young Exceptional Children, 1*(1), 18–26.

DeGangi, G.A., Wietlisbach, S., & Poisson, S. (1994). The impact of culture and socioeconomic status on family-professional collaboration: Challenges and solutions. *Topics in Early Childhood Special Education, 14,* 503–520.

Denham, S.A., Renwick, S.M., & Holt, R.W. (1991). Working and playing together: Prediction of preschool social-emotional competence from mother–child interaction. *Child Development, 62,* 242–249.

Downey, D., & Condron, D. (2004). Playing well with others in kindergarten: The benefit of siblings at home. *Journal of Marriage & Family, 66,* 333–350.

Duke, D.L., Showers, B.K., & Imber, M. (1980). Teachers and shared decision-making: The costs and benefits of involvement. *Educational Administration Quarterly, 16,* 93–106.

Dunst, C. (2001). Participation of young children with disabilities in community learning activities. In M.J. Guralnick (Ed.), *Early childhood inclusion: Focus on change* (pp. 307–333). Baltimore: Paul H. Brookes Publishing Co.

Dunst, C., Bruder, M.B., Trivette, C., Hamby, D., Raab, M., & McLean, M. (2001). Characteristics and consequences of everyday natural learning opportunities. *Topics in Early Childhood Special Education, 21,* 68–92.

Dunst, C., & Deal, A. (1994). A family-centered approach to developing individualized family support plans. In C. Dunst, C. Trivette, & A. Deal (Eds.), *Supporting and strengthening families: Vol. 1: Methods, strategies and practices* (pp.73–89). Cambridge, MA: Brookline Books.

Dunst, C., Hamby, D., Trivette, C., Raab, M., & Bruder, M.B. (2000). Everyday family and community life and children's naturally occurring learning opportunities. *Journal of Early Intervention, 23,* 151–164.

Dunst, C., Trivette, C., & Deal, A. (1995). *Enabling and empowering families: Principles and guidelines for practice.* Cambridge, MA: Brookline Books.

Eyberg, S.M., & Robinson, E.A. (1982). Parent–child interaction training: Effects on family functioning. *Journal of Clinical Child Psychology, 11,* 130–137.

Epps, S., & Jackson, B.J. (2000). *Empowered families, successful children: Early intervention programs that work.* Washington, DC: American Psychological Association.

File, N., & Kontos, S. (1992). Indirect service delivery through consultation: Review and implications for early intervention. *Journal of Early Intervention, 16,* 221–235.

Friend, M., & Cook, L. (2006). *Interactions: Collaboration skills for school professionals.* Boston: Allyn & Bacon.

Funderburk, B.W., Eyberg, S.M., Newcomb, K., McNeil, C.B., Hembree-Kigin, T., & Capage, L. (1998). Parent–child interaction therapy with behavior problem children: Maintenance of treatment effects in the school setting. *Child & Family Behavior Therapy, 20,* 17–38.

Garcia Coll, C., & Magnuson, K. (2000). Cultural differences as sources of developmental vulnerabilities and resources. In J.P. Shonkoff & S.J. Meisels (Eds.), *Handbook of early childhood intervention (2nd ed.)* (pp. 94–114). New York: Cambridge University Press.

Grossman, D.C., Neckerman, H.J., Koepsell, T.D., Liu, P., Asher, K.N., Beland, K., et al. (1997). Effectiveness of a violence prevention curriculum among children in elementary school: A randomized control trial. *Journal of the American Medical Association, 277,* 1605–1611.

Guralnick, M.J. (1989). Recent developments in early intervention efficacy research: Implications for family involvement in PL 99–457. *Topics in Early Childhood Special Education, 9*(3), 1–17.

Guralnick, M.J. (2001). Social competence with peers and early childhood inclusion: Need for alternative approaches. In M.J. Guralnick (Ed.), *Early childhood inclusion: Focus on change* (pp. 481–502). Baltimore: Paul H. Brookes Publishing Co.

Guralnick, M.J., & Neville, B. (1997). Designing early intervention programs to promote children's social competence. In M.J. Guralnick (Ed.), *The effectiveness of early intervention* (pp. 579–610). Baltimore: Paul H. Brookes Publishing Co.

Gutkin, T.B., & Conoley, J.C. (1990). Reconceptualizing school psychology from a service delivery perspective: Implications for practice, training, and research. *Journal of School Psychology, 28,* 203–223.

Hanft, B., & Pilkington, K. (2000). Therapy in natural environments: The means or end goal for early intervention? *Infants & Young Children, 12*(4), 1–13.

Hanft, B.E., Rush, D.D., & Shelden, M.L. (2004). *Coaching families and colleagues in early childhood.* Baltimore: Paul H. Brookes Publishing Co.

Hembree-Kigin, T., & McNeil, C.B. (1995). *Parent–child interaction therapy.* New York: Plenum Publishers.

Henderson, A.T., & Berla, N. (Eds.). (1994). *A new generation of evidence: The family is critical to student achievement.* Columbia, MD: National Committee for Citizens in Education.

Herschell, A.D., Calzada, E., Eyberg, S.M., & McNeil, C.B. (2002). Parent–child interaction therapy: New directions in research. *Cognitive and Behavioral Practice, 9,* 9–16.

Hoover-Dempsey, K.V., Walker, J.M.T., & Sandler, H.M. (2005). Parents' motivations for involvement in their children's education. In E.N. Patrikakou, R.P. Weisberg, S. Redding, & H.J. Walberg (Eds.), *School–family partnerships for children's success* (pp. 40–56). New York: Teachers College Press.

Individuals with Disabilities Education Act Amendments (IDEA) of 1997, PL 105–17, 2U.S.C. §§ 1400 *et seq.*

Jones, K., Daley, D., Hutchings, J., Bywater, T., & Catrin Eames, C. (in press). Efficacy of *The Incredible Years Basic Parent Training Program* as an early intervention for children with conduct problems and ADHD. *Child: Care, Health and Development.*

Joseph, G., & Strain, P. (2003). Comprehensive evidence-based social-emotional curricula for young children. *Topics in Early Childhood Special Education, 23*(2), 65–76.

Kerns, K.A., Klepac, L., & Cole, A. (1996). Peer relationships and preadolescents' perception of security in the child–mother relationship. *Developmental Psychology, 32,* 457–466.

Ladd, G.W., & Hart, C.H. (1992). Creating informal play opportunities: Are parents' and preschoolers' initiations related to children's competence with peers? *Developmental Psychology, 28,* 1179–1187.

Lancy, D.R. (1996). *Playing on the mother ground: Cultural routines for children's development.* New York: Guilford Press.

Lieberman, A.F., Weston, D.R., & Pawl, J.H. (1991). Preventive interventions and outcome with anxiously attached dyads. *Child Development, 62,* 199–209.

Mahoney, G. (1988). Enhancing the developmental competence of handicapped infants. In K. Marfo (Eds.), *Parent–child interaction and developmental disabilities: Theory, research, and intervention* (pp. 203–219). Westport, CT: Praeger Publishers.

Martinez, M. (1987). Dialogues among children and between children and their mothers. *Child Development, 58,* 1035–1043.

McCollum, J.A., & Yates, T.J. (1994). Dyad as focus, triad as means: A family-centered approach to supporting parent–child interactions. *Infants & Young Children, 6,* 54–63.

McFadyen-Ketchum, S.A., Bates, J.E., Dodge, K.A., & Pettit, G.S. (1996). Patterns of change in early childhood aggressive-disruptive behavior: Gender differences in predictions from early coercive and affectionate mother–child interactions. *Child Development, 67,* 2417–2433.

McWilliam, R.A. (2000). It's only natural... To have early intervention in natural environments where it is needed. *Young Exceptional Children, Monograph #2: Natural Environments and Inclusion* (pp. 17–26). Longmont, CO: Sopris West.

Miller-Heyl, J., MacPhee, D., & Fritz, J. (1998). DARE to Be You: A Family Support Early Prevention Program. *Journal of Primary Prevention, 18,* 257–285.

Mullis, L. (2002). Natural environments: A letter from a mother to friends, families and professionals. *Young Exceptional Children, 5,* 21–24.

Najdowski, A., Wallace, M., Doney, J., & Ghezzi, P. (2003). Parental assessment and treatment of food selectivity in natural settings. *Journal of Applied Behavioral Analysis, 36,* 383–386.

Newcomb, K., Eyberg, S., Funderburk, B., Eisenstadt, T., & McNeil, C. (1990). *Parent–child interaction therapy: Maintenance of treatment gains at 8 months and 1 and 1/2 years.* Presented at the annual meeting of the American Psychological Association.

Parke, R., & Bhavnargri, N. (1989). Parents as managers of children's peer relationships. In D. Belle (Ed.), *Children's social networks and social supports* (pp. 241–259). Oxford, UK: John Wiley & Sons.

Parke, R.D., & Ladd, G.W. (Eds.). (1992). *Family–peer relationships: Modes of linkage.* Mahwah, NJ: Lawrence Erlbaum Associates.

Phillips, V., & McCullough, L. (1990). Consultation-based programming: Instituting the collaborative ethic. *Exceptional Children, 56,* 291–304.

Pianta, R.C., & Ferguson, J. (1997). *Prediction of behavior problems in children from mother–child interaction.* Unpublished manuscript, University of Virginia, Charlottesville.

Rogoff, B. (1991). *Apprenticeship in thinking: Cognitive development in social context.* New York: Oxford University Press.

Rogoff, B., Mistry, J., Goncu, A., & Mosier, C. (1993). Guided participation in cultural activities by toddlers and caregivers. *Monographs of the Society for Research in Child Development, 58* (8, Serial No. 236).

Sandall, S., Hemmeter, M.L., Smith, B., & McLean, M. (2005). *DEC recommended practices in early intervention and early childhood special education.* Longmont, CO: Sopris West.

Santos, R., & Lignugaris-Kraft, B. (1997). Integrating research on effective instruction with instruction in the natural environment for young children with disabilities. *Exceptionality, 7*(2), 97–129.

Sheridan, S.M., Clarke, B.L., & Burt, J.D. (2008). Conjoint behavioral consultation: What do we know and what do we need to know? In W.P. Erchul & S.M. Sheridan (Eds.), *Handbook of research in school consultation: Empirical foundations for the field.* Mahwah, NJ: Lawrence Erlbaum Associates.

Sheridan, S.M., Clarke, B.L., Knoche, L.L., & Edwards, C.P. (2006). The effects of conjoint behavioral consultation in early childhood settings. *Early Education and Development 17,* 593–618.

Sheridan, S.M., Eagle, J.W., Cowan, R.J., & Mickelson, W. (2001). The effects of conjoint behavioral consultation: Results of a four-year investigation. *Journal of School Psychology, 39,* 361–385.

Sheridan, S.M., Edwards, C.P., & Knoche, L.L. (2003, November). *Parent engagement and child learning birth to five.* Paper presented at the semi-annual meeting of the Interagency School Readiness Consortium, Washington, D.C.

Sheridan, S.M., & Gutkin, T.B. (2000). The ecology of school psychology: Examining and changing our paradigm for the 21st century. *School Psychology Review, 29,* 485–502.

Sheridan, S.M., & Kratochwill, T.R. (2007). *Conjoint behavioral consultation: Promoting family-school connections and interventions.* New York: Springer.

Sheridan, S.M., Kratochwill, T.R., & Bergan, J.R. (1996). *Conjoint behavioral consultation: A procedural manual.* New York: Plenum.

Sheridan, S.M., Kratochwill, T.R., & Elliott, S.N. (1990). Behavioral consultation with parents and teachers: Delivering treatment for socially withdrawn children at home and school. *School Psychology Review, 19,* 33–52.

Sheridan, S.M., Warnes, E., Brown, M., Schemm, A., Cowan, R.J., & Clarke, B.L. (2004). Family-centered positive psychology: Building on strengths to promote student success. *Psychology in the Schools, 41*, 7–17.

Sheridan, S.M., Welch, M., & Orme, S. (1996). Is consultation effective? A review of outcome research. *Remedial and Special Education, 17*, 341–354.

Strain, P., & Danko, C. (1995). Caregiver's encouragement of positive interactions between preschoolers with autism and their siblings. *Journal of Emotional & Behavioral Disorders, 3*, 2–13.

Thompson, R.A. (2002). The roots of school readiness in social and emotional development. *Set for Success: Building a strong foundation for school readiness based on the social-emotional development of young children* (pp. 8–29). Kansas City, KS: The Ewing Marion Kauffman Foundation.

Tieman, B., Palisano, R., Gracely, E., & Rosenbaum, P. (2004). Gross motor capability and performance of mobility in children with cerebral palsy: A comparison across home, school and outdoors/community settings. *Physical Therapy, 84*, 419–429.

van den Boom, D. (1994). The influence of temperament and mothering on attachment and exploration: An experimental manipulation of sensitive responsiveness among lower-class mothers of irritable infants. *Child Development, 65*, 1457–1477.

Walker, H.M. (1998). *First Step to Success*. Longmont, CO: Sopris West.

Walker, H.M., Stiller, B., & Golly, A. (1998, Winter). *First Step to Success:* A collaborative home-school intervention for preventing antisocial behavior at the point of school entry. *Young Exceptional Children, 1*(2), 2–6.

Warnes, E., Sheridan, S.M., & Garbacz, S.A. (in press). Building social skills in children and adolescents. In S. Goldstein & R. Brooks (Eds.), *Understanding and managing children's classroom behavior* (2nd ed.). New York: Springer.

Webster-Stratton, C. (1990a). *The Incredible Years Parent Training Program manual: Effective communication, anger management and problem-solving (ADVANCE)*. Seattle, WA: The Incredible Years.

Webster-Stratton, C. (1990b). *The teachers and children's videotape series: Dina Dinosaur's Social Skills and Problem-Solving Curriculum*. Seattle: University of Washington Press.

Webster-Stratton, C. (1998a). Parent training with low-income families: Promoting parental engagement through a collaborative approach. In J. Lutzker (Ed.), *Handbook of Child Abuse Research and Treatment* (pp. 183–210). New York: Plenum Press.

Webster-Stratton, C. (1998b). Preventing conduct problems in Head Start Children: Strengthening parent competencies. *Journal of Consulting and Clinical Psychology, 66*, 715–730.

Webster-Stratton, C., & Herbert, M. (1994). *Troubled families—Problem children: Working with parents: A collaborative process*. New York: Wiley.

Welch, M., & Sheridan, S.M. (1995). *Educational partnerships: Serving students at-risk*. San Antonio, TX: Harcourt-Brace Jovanovich.

Wertsch, J.V. (1985). *Vygotsky and the social formation of mind*. Cambridge, MA: Harvard University Press.

Wood, D. (1980). Teaching the young child: Some relationships between social interaction, language and thought. In D.R. Olson (Ed.), *The social function of language and thought* (pp. 87–99). New York: Norton.

Woods, J., Kashinath, S., & Goldstein, H. (2004). Effects of embedding caregiver-implemented teaching strategies in daily routines on children's communication outcomes. *Journal of Early Intervention, 26*, 175–193.

CHAPTER 15

Placing Young Children "At Promise"

Future Directions for Promoting Social Competence

GARY N. SIPERSTEIN AND PADDY C. FAVAZZA

When discussing social competence, a concept offered by Frances Horowitz in the late 1980s stuck in our minds: What if we created programs that placed children "at promise" as opposed to responding to them as "at risk?" (Horowitz, 1989; 2000). That idea shaped our discussion and led us to ask ourselves, "What if?" What if early childhood programs were created from a preventative and proactive stance that maximized children's potential within their own cultural, familial, and individual frame of reference? Doing so would encourage social competence to be viewed from a different perspective, such as through an ecological lens. Would children be seen differently? Would a child's impairments still rise to the forefront or would educators and others be in a better position to understand these impairments and view children at promise? Would the pressing need to place the substantive and comprehensive research that has been conducted in the hands of those most able to make a difference be recognized? Would teacher preparation change? Would the direction of research change if those in a position to do so were to place *all* children at promise?

We recognize that it is difficult to think in terms of the at-promise framework because we are all so accustomed to thinking of children from a deficit perspective. The concept of *at promise* asks us to not only focus on the characteristics of the child but also on the early experiences within the home and school environments that influence the child. Similar to Horowitz (2000), we choose to use the term *experiences* within the environment rather than simply the *environment* because, even within the least optimal environment, for example, what ultimately influences children are their experiences.

With this concept in mind, and after a careful reading of the chapters in this volume, we believe that there are four broad messages to consider if we are to regard children as at promise for success as opposed to at risk for failure. To do so, in this chapter we draw from and highlight the overarching messages so clearly articulated throughout the volume. First, we emphasize the need for an ecological lens to view children's social competence. Second, we advocate that *all* young children be in our sights, including children from culturally and economically diverse backgrounds. Third, we discuss what is critical to facilitating a different view of social competence—translating our valuable research into practice. And fourth, we discuss the need for stronger and sustained partnerships between the school and family.

It is our hope that these four broad messages will provide a roadmap for espousing this perspective, leading to new directions for research and ultimately, to new directions in education. These messages, which are detailed at more length later, point to a need for the following:

1. **Expanding our view of social competence:** There is a need to continue expanding our view of social competence by using an ecological lens to broaden the ways in which we support the development of social competence.

2. **Broadening our scope:** Professionals in the field must broaden their scope to include all children, not just those with disabilities, in programs and instructional strategies designed to promote social competence because the number of children entering early childhood lacking social skills is increasing.

3. **Translating research to practice:** More evidence-based practice must be utilized to ensure that the most effective strategies are used to promote the development of social competence.

4. **Strengthening partnerships:** Stronger partnerships must be built across contexts, most particularly between the school and home, to better nurture social competence.

EXPANDING OUR VIEW OF SOCIAL COMPETENCE

Brofenbrenner's (1979) ecological framework reminded us of the many influences on children's experiences within multiple contexts (e.g., home, school, peer social networks). Using an ecological lens enables individuals to not only see children's deficits in social competence relative to a disability but also to view children's development of social competence, recognizing the influence of their family, school and community values, practices, and social opportunities. As Hanson and SooHoo (Chapter 3) point out, it is important to add a cultural and contextual component when considering social competence. Specifically, by adopting an ecological lens, it is easier to view the child from a multicultural perspective, recognizing that social behaviors are culturally based—that is—each child's social competence is influenced by the values that are deemed important in their culture. For instance, some families place emphasis on individuality and independence, whereas others emphasize interdependence between parents and children. Families also vary in their use of verbal and nonverbal communication and in their interpretation of personal space and appropriateness of physical contact. If professionals in the early childhood field are not sensitive to these variations that ultimately shape a child's social behavior, it would be easy for them to misinterpret what they observe. Consider the following example:

MICHAELA IS A 4-YEAR-OLD GIRL WHOSE family recently emigrated from Romania. In Michaela's family, Romanian is the primary language spoken, leaving her with limited fluency in English. Within her culture, children are often scolded for making eye contact when speaking to adults, as it is viewed as a sign of disrespect. Upon entering an early childhood program, Michaela was scolded by some teachers for lack of eye contact, whereas other teachers thought she exhibited tendencies falling on the autism spectrum (low eye contact, solitary play, low verbal skills). In this instance, use of an ecological lens helped the teachers to recognize Michaela's behaviors as culturally based.

If an ecological perspective had not been employed in Michaela's story, then she could have easily been misunderstood or misdiagnosed. This issue is increasingly relevant because our early childhood programs are progressively becoming more diverse.

Within this ecological perspective, Guralnick (1992) and Brown, Odom, McConnell, and Rathel (Chapter 7) encourage us to define social competence as a social ability that is *both* effective *and* appropriate. Social competence means not just engaging in a set of behaviors that lead to a social interaction but engaging in a set of behaviors that are deemed appropriate for the setting. Consider the following example:

KENDRICK, A YOUNG BOY WITH DEVELOPMENTAL delays, regularly and exuberantly bursts into a social scene. When walking up to his friends, he invades their personal space and uses a tone of voice that is almost always too loud. Kendrick is effective in that he is able to enter into a social interaction; however, his behavior is viewed by his peers as inappropriate. After observations across multiple contexts and discussions with his parents, peers, and teachers, those who worked with and cared for Kendrick were better able to understand that his abrupt entrée into social interactions was a reflection of his enthusiasm on seeing his friends. It was not simply a deficit in his social skills; it was his level of excitement in the setting. Taking an ecological perspective allowed Kendrick's parents, teachers, and peers to better understand the context of his behavior. In doing so, all involved were able to determine that what was effective for Kendrick was not deemed appropriate within the values and norms of the school setting and culture. That is, although Kendrick's behavior was getting the job done (he was able to enter the social situation), it was breaking the rules of acceptability (appropriate use of personal space, tone of voice).

Taken together, the perspectives adopted by Guralnick (1992) and Hanson and SooHoo (Chapter 3) remind us that in today's culturally diverse early childhood classrooms, teachers need to carefully support each child with regard to the child's culture and disability because a child may be struggling to be "culturally and socially savvy" in ways that are both effective and appropriate. The ecological approach implicitly connects schools with the family by taking the culture of the family into consideration when interpreting the social behaviors of the child in the school setting.

Missall and Hojnoski (Chapter 6) also point out that multiple perspectives need to be considered when viewing children's social behaviors in the school setting. The authors present several historical and current perspectives on social competence and suggest that within the early childhood classroom in particular, social competence may be viewed in two ways: having those social skills necessary for learning and those necessary for social interactions. For example, when observing children in the classroom, teachers may consider a child's social behaviors as they relate to learning, such as cooperative participation. However, teachers may also consider these behaviors as they relate to interactions with peers. As pointed out by Buysse, Goldman, West, and Hollingsworth (Chapter 4), peer interactions and friendships play a critical role in our understanding of the development of social competence. It is clear that within the classroom setting there are multiple perspectives by which to view social competence. Adopting an ecological lens allows for better interpretation and understanding of children's social competence in the school setting.

In an early childhood classroom, teachers encounter children with a range of social behaviors that may or may not represent problems in social competence. Simply put, in order to understand how to view children as at promise, observations of children must be interpreted relative to their experiences within their culture, their home environment, and their unique abilities and disabilities. Employing an ecological perspective is a first step in viewing children through an at-promise lens.

BROADENING THE SCOPE

Traditionally, intervention strategies have focused on children who have a high likelihood of experiencing difficulties in social competence, particularly those with specific disabilities (e.g., autism, developmental delays, communication disorders). In this volume, the authors present many examples of such difficulties. For example, children with autism, by definition, have difficulty relating to others socially (Strain, Schwartz, & Bovey, Chapter 12). Children with developmental delays often struggle with cognitive, motor, and communication skills, resulting in challenges with social interactions (Brown et al., Chapter 7), and children with communication disorders often lack the speech and language abilities to engage in meaningful and effective social interactions with peers (Schneider & Goldstein, Chapter 11).

In addition to children with specific disabilities, our attention is drawn to a larger group of children who are lacking in social skills. These children include those who are economically disadvantaged and those from culturally diverse backgrounds (Diamond, Hong, & Baroody, Chapter 8; Webster-Stratton & Reid, Chapter 9). For example, children from impoverished backgrounds may display behavioral problems (aggressive and oppositional behaviors) at a greater rate than children who are less disadvantaged (Webster-Stratton & Reid, Chapter 9), and as many as 25% of preschool children who are socioeconomically disadvantaged are at risk for social and emotional problems (Rimm-Kaufman, Pianta, & Cox, 2000; Webster-Stratton & Hammond, 1998). These findings are underscored by the fact that many of the children growing up in socioeconomically challenged homes are also from culturally diverse backgrounds, as is evidenced by the population in needs-based programs such as Head Start (Hanson & SooHoo, Chapter 3). In fact, in 2003, more that one-fourth of the preschoolers in Head Start were from homes in which Spanish or an East Asian language was the primary language spoken (Italiano-Thomas, 2003). The recognition of this emerging group of children stretches the historical scope or focus to include children without specific diagnoses but who nonetheless are viewed as at risk for developing difficulties in social competence.

With many more children arriving at school with social competence problems, we question whether it is time to get back to basics. Historically, the basic educational skills fell under an umbrella term, the *three Rs*: reading, writing, and arithmetic. But in our more diverse and socially demanding world, in which children are entering early childhood programs at younger ages, with a wider range of abilities and needs, and in which increasing numbers of children lack social skills, perhaps it is time to add to our historical (and almost sacred) educational rubric. That is, adding a fourth "R" to the basics of early education programs: *relationships.*

Across the chapters in this volume, the case has been made for interventions to support specific skill development as well as the need for classwide programs to promote positive social relationships, school adjustment, and academic achievement. Without a comprehensive and intentional focus on the fourth R, relationships, children with disabilities, children from diverse backgrounds, and children who are economically disadvantaged are placed in double jeopardy. That is, in failing the fourth R, they will likely fail the other three Rs as well. Diamond and colleagues (Chapter 8) cited the connection between positive peer relationships and future academic success, making a convincing case for promoting social competence in early childhood programs (Doctoroff, Greer, & Arnold, 2006; Ialongo, Vaden-Kieman, & Kellam, 1998).

There are real challenges to placing greater emphasis on social competence in early childhood programs because more and more schools are incorporating a preacademic or academic curriculum with younger children. Such an intense focus on academics is perhaps edging out adequate instructional space to address the classwide social needs of children. Without expanding educators' scope to respond to the growing number of children who lack social skills, they may inadvertently contribute to placing children at risk as opposed to boosting their at-promise status.

TRANSLATING RESEARCH TO PRACTICE

Those within the research arena understand why children are at risk and recognize that their findings should ultimately inform practices and experiences in the school and in the home. However, evidence suggests that those in the field could be more effective in translating research to practice. Brown and colleagues (Chapter 7) acknowledge the underutilization of evidence-based strategies in early childhood classrooms and point out that most children with disabilities do not have social goals listed on their individualized education program (IEP; Brown & Conroy, 2001). Diamond and colleagues (Chapter 8) concur, citing that teachers are reluctant to use specific social skills training. These findings are discouraging when one considers that even though effective strategies are available to support children who have social competence challenges, children may continually be placed at risk due to underutilization of evidence-based practices.

To better understand why evidence-based practices are not more widely used, one must first look closely at the social validity of the instructional strategies within the contexts of early childhood settings. Although authors of the present volume provide evidence to support the link between social competence and later academic success, the relationship may not be as salient or consistently embraced by teachers. Not all teachers place an equal value on the fourth R (relationships) in comparison with the acquisition of preacademic skills, or view the promotion of social competence as their primary role. However, even when teachers recognize the importance of social competence and its relationship to children's success, they are faced with some very real constraints within the early childhood setting that may work in opposition to promoting social competence. For example, with the increased emphasis placed on high-stakes testing in elementary grades, some early childhood programs may experience greater pressure to succumb to the downward push for more academics, thereby deemphasizing the promotion of social competence. In addition, many early childhood classes are housed within elementary education schools. As a result, early childhood classes are in settings that are more academic in orientation. It may be a struggle to promote the social development of children within the context of play if the school is promoting a more academic focus. Diamond and colleagues (Chapter 8) provide a comprehensive discussion of other school-based challenges to promoting social competence such as teacher turnover, group size, and teacher–child ratio, to name a few.

Another factor that may contribute to the underutilization of evidence-based practices may lie with the protocol. According to Brown and colleagues (Chapter 7), many existing interventions designed to promote social competence do not go beyond general guidelines. In developing strong intervention protocols, professionals in the field of education must first ensure that the protocol serves as an educative tool, providing teachers with information that can lead to greater understanding of the intervention. To do so, the intervention protocols must be theoretically grounded. In addition, it is important that protocols are explicit enough to cover details for effective implementation and yet user friendly for those who are facilitating the implementation. For example, protocols should provide background information and key components of the intervention, such as the materials needed and optimal conditions under which the intervention is effective (Weisz, Jensen, & McLeod, 2004). Simply put, the lack of adequate protocols may be undermining the full utilization of the interventions.

What can be done to address the challenges of the research-to-practice process? One approach is to make salient the value of using existing instructional strategies and programs designed for children with disabilities with *all* children. Perhaps we would see more widespread use if we consider how some of these existing disability-specific strategies are used with other children who may be at risk, such as children who are economically disadvantaged and children from varying linguistic and cultural backgrounds. This is especially relevant as more children without disabilities are demonstrating problems in social competence as they enter kindergarten (Webster-Stratton & Hammond, 1997).

Schneider and Goldstein (Chapter 11) provide several examples of strategies found to be effective with children with communication disorders that may have broader utility with other groups of children. For example, redirection of social and communicative overtures from children to adults holds promise for wider use for increasing spontaneous peer interactions among children with linguistic differences, such as those for whom English is their second language. Similarly, peer modeling, play scripts, and other language-based strategies would be excellent for increasing the linguistic competencies of children during daily social interactions. Environmental arrangement is another strategy developed for children with disabilities that may have excellent utility as a classwide strategy. Environmental arrangement includes carefully structuring the classroom in such a way as to increase the likelihood of social interactions (e.g., the use of high-interest toys, activity structure, spatial density) (Brown et al., Chapter 7; Sainato, Jung, Salmon, & Axe, Chapter 5). This is a strategy that many teachers may already be using in their classrooms, although they may not be aware of its value in promoting the social competence of children. Establishing a portable communication system is another example of a strategy that may have wider utility. Portable communication systems allow children with severe disabilities to communicate successfully within the class and across the school and home environment (Drasgow, Lowrey, Turan, Halle, & Meadan, Chapter 13). It is not too difficult to imagine the utility of such a system for children with communication challenges, such as those with English as their second language. Having a consistent portable communication system serves a highly functional purpose, enabling a child to communicate across various social opportunities during the school day.

In general, classrooms intentionally created to support the success of *all* learners expect teachers to utilize an array of strategies, materials, and adaptations that accommodate the wide range of diverse learners found in early childhood classrooms. Remember the "one-room schoolhouse"? Remember when teachers were required to have knowledge and mastery of a wide range of skills to teach various grade levels and subjects for learners of different ages and developmental levels? Like our earliest school model, today many early childhood classrooms include children with great variation not only in ability but also in developmental level. Perhaps we have come full circle. Perhaps these early childhood classrooms are modern-day versions of the one-room schoolhouse. However, in today's classes we also have the benefit of our increased knowledge of effective strategies that may have wider utility within the diverse inclusive early childhood classes. If we could capitalize on this repertoire of knowledge and strategies (which we know to be effective with children with disabilities), teachers could utilize many of these same strategies in inclusive settings to support the social competence of all children.

Finally, an expanded version of the Hierarchy of Social Interaction (HSI) (Brown, Odom, & Conroy, 2001) would be an excellent tool to help teachers make informed and thoughtful decisions as to the programs and strategies they can use in their classrooms. However, as with any tool, researchers must ensure that it is teacher friendly. In creating this expanded version, an array of evidence-based instructional techniques and programs found in this volume would first need to be organized using the HSI framework: Class-wide Interventions (Level One), Naturalistic Interventions (Level Two), and More Explicit Social Integration and Social Skills Training (Level Three). Some of the authors have already begun to assemble specific strategies within the HSI framework, leveling them from least to most intrusive in the instructional setting (Brown et al., Chapter 7; Buysse et al., Chapter 4; Schneider & Goldstein, Chapter 11). If we continue to place research-based techniques and programs into this framework, the range of options would be more apparent and allow teachers to use HSI as a decision-making tool not only for selecting but also for documenting the effectiveness of the practices.

After organizing evidence-based strategies within the HSI framework, the next step would be for teachers to intentionally use the practices that correspond to each level within the HSI framework when creating their early childhood activities. For example, Level One could include implementation of classwide programs that involve home and school partnerships to promote social competence (e.g., *DARE to Be You* program; *Incredible Years Parents, Teachers, and Children's Training Series* [http://www.incredibleyears.com]; *Promoting Alternative THinking Strategies [PATHS]* program) and classwide affective strategies to support social acceptance of children with differences (i.e., *Special Friends*, Favazza, LaRoe, & Odom, 1999). In addition, other developmentally appropriate strategies could be included such as literacy-based materials and activities to enhance class climate and promote a sense of belonging for all children (Farran, Aydogan, Kang, & Lipsey, 2006; Favazza, LaRoe, Phillipsen, & Kumar, 2000; Han, Ostrosky, & Diamond, 2006).

Next, teachers could intentionally plan to use naturalistic interventions (e.g., incidental teaching of social behaviors and friendship activities from Level Two strategies in the HSI framework) to support social competence. Incidental teaching takes advantage of routines (e.g., snack, lunch, centers, weekly jobs) for promoting the development of social competence (Brown et al., Chapter 7). For example, portable communication or scripts developed for weekly jobs (e.g., office messenger, class weather reporter) may serve to support daily social interactions. Inserting these and other strategies (e.g., social scripts, redirection of initiations) into highly functional routine activities increases the likelihood of their use (Strain et al., Chapter 12; Weisz et al., 2004). It would also be important to recognize that incidental teaching of social behaviors, particularly for children who are at risk, makes deliberate preplanned use of brief, routine teachable moments. It is not a "left-to-chance" opportunity to promote social competence but an intentional and planned use.

One additional step in adapting the HSI framework for use by teachers would be to apply the response to intervention (RTI) approach (Fuchs & Fuchs, 2007). The RTI approach has most often been used as a way to establish the presence of a learning disability. However, it can also be used to ensure that all children receive the supports they need to be successful. In this way, the RTI approach has utility in the instructional and decision-making processes. For example, teachers can systematically select evidence-based strategies that promote social competence from Level One for use with the whole class (e.g., inserting a strategy into morning circle). For those children who are considered nonresponders to this strategy, another strategy might be chosen, perhaps from Level Two. Teachers can select strategies organized within the HSI on a continuum from least to most intrusive, or from Level One to Three, based on their effectiveness with children.

Teachers have selected evidence-based strategies when promoting basic skills such as math and reading. Simply put, it represents good teaching practices. However, what may be new is the notion of organizing specific strategies designed to support social competence within the HSI framework, encouraging teachers to use the HSI framework to create an at-promise classroom with classwide programs, and asking teachers to apply RTI by intentionally selecting strategies to support social competence in children who are considered nonresponders. Increasing the utility of the HSI will allow teachers to more easily determine those strategies that may be effective and those that may be ineffective when working with the whole class and with children who may need more intensive interventions. It may ultimately lead to a greater infusion of research-based strategies related to social competence in our classrooms.

STRENGTHENING PARTNERSHIPS

Although it is most important that teachers understand the essential role that social competence plays in the development of our young children and that they embrace and utilize evidence-based practices to support that development, another factor is of utmost importance: the need for family–school partnerships. This need is most evident when we consider the important role the family plays in the social competence of children (McCollum & Ostrosky, Chapter 2; Schneider & Goldstein, Chapter 11; Webster-Stratton & Reid, Chapter 9). For example, McCollum and Ostrosky clearly, and with great detail, describe three distinct pathways in which social competence is shaped and sculpted within the family: parents as facilitators of positive parent–child interactions, parents as supervisors and advisors in their child's interactions with peers, and parents as providers and links to social opportunities. Children learn how to interact with peers and other adults based on their early interactions with their parents. In later years, building on these first and earliest experiences, the family becomes the launching pad for guiding social interactions with others in which children then try out their skills in various social settings, including the school setting.

The family is not only fundamental to the development of social competence in the early years but they also play a critical role as a partner with the school in carrying out the home component of school interventions. This is particularly important for those children whose development of social competence is delayed or compromised, particularly as we have found with children with disabilities. To be successful, school-based programs must include those individuals that are an integral part of a child's life, those who are most influential in shaping and supporting the child's development of social competence—the family.

As we might expect, very real hurdles make the home–school collaboration difficult to achieve. As this volume stresses, more young children are living in poverty and more children are from multicultural and multilingual families (Hanson & SooHoo, Chapter 3)—the very same family variables that place children at risk. These variables also create challenges when working with families. For example, parents have many obligations (e.g., work, other family members to care for) that may limit the amount of time that they can commit to participating in their child's school. Parents may be limited in English language skills, making it difficult to communicate effectively with teachers. In addition, parents may not place the same level of importance on the development of social competence as the school (Hanson & SooHoo, Chapter 3), or, due to their differing cultural backgrounds, they may not share the same viewpoints regarding social competence. Perhaps the greatest challenge is that not all families share the same views about how involved they should be in their child's schooling or even believe that they *should* be involved (Hanson & SooHoo, Chapter 3). Pragmatically, researchers need to develop and teachers need to employ culturally responsive programs and instructional strategies. However, finding creative and culturally responsive ways to involve family members in promoting social development is difficult. Although the challenges are not insurmountable, they are challenges nonetheless. So, where do we go from here?

First and at a minimum, teachers need to recognize the need for family involvement, understanding that parents are the primary natural socializing agent in promoting social competence. Moreover, this involvement needs to be sustained over time, not just during early childhood but also in the critical years that follow. In the early years children are honing interpersonal skills as well as learning related skills (Missall & Hojnoski, Chapter 6). They are learning how to use skills that are effective and appropriate (Guralnick, 1992) and how to become more socially and culturally savvy in our increasingly multicultural inclusive classes (Hanson & SooHoo, Chapter 3).

Second, we must recognize that in the inclusive multicultural schools of today, all children and their families can benefit from support and training, not just those families of children with disabilities. Webster-Stratton and Reid (Chapter 9) recognize this need and suggest that a multimodal, holistic approach is needed to address the complex, multicultural preschool context. They propose a three-pronged approach that includes a social skills/problem-solving curriculum for children, teacher training to implement the curriculum, and most important, school-based parent training to support and translate the curriculum into the home. Traditionally, programs such as these have been offered in mental health settings, not in schools.

Offering schoolwide programs that provide family support and training to parents of all children (Webster-Stratton & Reid, Chapter 9) is the embodiment of the at-promise perspective. The at-promise perspective begins with the family. Clearly, more sustained, reciprocal partnerships between home and school are needed, recognizing that experiences from one environment affect experiences in the other, and recognizing that implicit within the school environment is the presence of a child's family and the family's culture.

CLOSING THOUGHTS

On the surface, our messages may seem intuitive, and perhaps even naive in some ways. Indeed, we have not added new theories or new definitions of social competence; there is already an abundance of research on the factors that contribute to social competence and many ways to conceptualize and define social competence, all of which have value. We have not added new research directions; the information presented in this volume is rich with research ideas. In addition, we have not added new strategies for addressing deficits in social competence. What we have done is to attempt to synthesize the wealth of information presented and discuss some of the issues related to the promotion of social competence, all in an effort to encourage us to think of all children as at promise.

Although much progress has been made since the first edition of this text (Odom, McConnell, & McEvoy, 1992), many children are still at risk in part because innovations in the classroom lag behind evidence-based practice. This may perhaps be due to the fact that families have changed, or perhaps because the experiences of childhood have changed. Research points clearly to the need to contextualize the instruction in the classroom and the child within that classroom, as well as to contextualize the family environment along with the child within that environment. The relationship between the school and home has been and always will be a dynamic, changing scene. To place children at promise requires us to recognize and respond to that reality.

It is clear that regarding children as at promise is no longer an idealistic or unrealistic dream of researchers, parents, and teachers. Throughout this volume, the authors have metaphorically placed the gauntlet in front of us, asking us to consider the experiences of children in their home and school contexts when understanding what works and what does not work when promoting social competence. The inclusion of more children with disabilities and differences (culturally, economically) in early childhood settings requires the integration of evidence-based practices into the normative routine experiences within the class setting *and* home setting. We must work closely in sustained-over-time-partnership with families of all children, equipped with all of the conceptualizations and strategies we have developed, finding new ways to increase the use of evidence-based practices and recognizing that successful implementation is as important as the intervention itself. To do otherwise may contribute to their at-risk status—not place them at promise.

In conclusion, in gleaning the four messages from this volume, we made a concerted effort to merge the perspective of both the researcher and educator. Throughout the four messages we have tried to emphasize how an at-promise perspective will only become a reality with stronger alliances forged among researchers and practitioners. Similarly, although the relationship between the school and home has been and will always be a dynamic, changing scene, placing children at promise requires us all, researchers and educators alike, to recognize and respond to that reality and find ways to include the family that are culturally responsive.

REFERENCES

Brofenbrenner, U. (1979). *The ecology of human development: Experiments by nature and design.* Cambridge, MA: Harvard University Press.

Brown, W.H., & Conroy, M.A. (2001). Promoting peer-related social-communicative competence in preschool children with developmental delays. In H. Goldstein, L.A. Kaczmarek, & K.M. English (Eds.), *Promoting social communication: Children and youth with developmental disabilities* (pp. 173–210). Baltimore: Paul H. Brookes Publishing Co.

Brown, W.H., Odom, S.L., & Conroy, M.A. (2001). An intervention hierarchy for promoting preschool children's peer interactions in natural environments. *Topics in Early Childhood Special Education, 21,* 90–134.

Doctoroff, G.L., Greer, J.A., & Arnold, D.H. (2006). The relationship between social behavior and emergent literacy among preschool boys and girls. *Journal of Applied Developmental Psychology, 27*(1), 1–13.

Favazza, P.C., LaRoe, J., & Odom, S. (1999). *Special friends: A manual for creating accepting environments, The Strategies for Promoting Social Relationships Between Young Children Project.* Roots & Wings. Boulder, CO.

Favazza, P.C., LaRoe, J.L., Phillipsen, L., & Kumar, P. (2000). Representing young children with disabilities in classroom environments. *Young Exceptional Children, 3*(3), 2–8.

Farran, D.C., Aydogan, C., Kang, S.J., & Lipsey, M.W. (2006). Preschool classroom environments and the quantity and quality of children's literacy and language behaviors. In D.K. Dickinson & S.B Neuman (Eds.), *Handbook of early literacy research, Vol. 2.* (pp. 257–268). New York: Guilford Press.

Fuchs, L.S., & Fuchs, D. (2007). A model for implementing responsiveness to intervention. *Teaching Exceptional Children, 39,* 14–23.

Guralnick, M.J. (1992). A hierarchical model for understanding children's peer-related social competence. In S.L. Odom, S.R. McConnell, & M.A. McEvoy (Eds.), *Social competence of young children with disabilities* (pp. 37–64). Baltimore: Paul H. Brookes Publishing Co.

Han, J., Ostrosky, M.M., & Diamond, K.E. (2006). Children's attitudes toward peers with disabilities: Supporting positive attitude development. *Young Exceptional Children, 10*(1), 2–11.

Horowitz, F.D. (1989). *The concept of risk: A re-evaluation.* Invited address at the Biennial Meeting of the Society for Research in Child Development, Kansas City, MO.

Horowitz, F.D. (2000). Child development and the PITS: Simple questions, complex answers, and developmental theory. *Child Development, 71*(1), 1–10.

Ialongo, N.S., Vaden-Kieman, N., & Kellam, S. (1998). Early peer rejection and aggression: Longitudinal relations with adolescent behavior. *Journal of Developmental and Physical Disabilities, 10,* 199–213.

Italiano-Thomas, G. (2003, July). The national reporting system and English language learners. *Head Start Bulletin, 76,* 18–19.

Odom, S.L., McConnell, S.R., & McEvoy, M.A. (1992). *Social competence of young children with disabilities: Issues and strategies for intervention.* Baltimore: Paul H. Brookes Publishing Co.

Rimm-Kaufman, S.E., Pianta, R.C., & Cox, M.J. (2000). Teachers' judgments of problems in the transition to kindergarten. *Early Childhood Research Quarterly, 15,* 147–166.

Webster-Stratton, C., & Hammond, M. (1998). Conduct problems and level of social competence in Head Start children: Prevalence, pervasiveness and associated risk factors. *Clinical Child Psychology and Family Psychology Review, 1*(2), 101–124.

Weisz, J.R., Jensen, A.L., & McLeod, B.D. (2004). Development and dissemination of child and adolescent psychotherapies: Milestones, methods, and a new deployment-focused model. In E.D. Hibbs & P.S. Jensen (Eds.), *Psychosocial treatments for child and adolescent disorders: Empirically-based approaches* (2nd ed.; pp. 9–39). Washington, DC: American Psychological Association.

Index

Tables, figures, and footnotes are indicated by *t*, *f*, and *n*, respectively.